ELA   LADEZA

PRINCIPLES OF THERAPEUTIC CHANGE THAT WORK

OXFORD SERIES IN CLINICAL PSYCHOLOGY

Principles of Therapeutic Change That Work

Edited by
Louis G. Castonguay
Larry E. Beutler

OXFORD
UNIVERSITY PRESS

2006

OXFORD
UNIVERSITY PRESS

Oxford University Press, Inc., publishes works that further
Oxford University's objective of excellence
in research, scholarship, and education.

Oxford   New York
Auckland   Cape Town   Dar es Salaam   Hong Kong   Karachi
Kuala Lumpur   Madrid   Melbourne   Mexico City   Nairobi
New Delhi   Shanghai   Taipei   Toronto

With offices in
Argentina   Austria   Brazil   Chile   Czech Republic   France   Greece
Guatemala   Hungary   Italy   Japan   Poland   Portugal   Singapore
South Korea   Switzerland   Thailand   Turkey   Ukraine   Vietnam

Published by Oxford University Press, Inc.
198 Madison Avenue, New York, New York 10016

www.oup.com

Library of Congress Cataloging-in-Publication Data
Principles of therapeutic change that work / edited by Louis G. Castonguay, Larry E. Beutler.
p. cm.
ISBN-13 978-0-19-515684-3
ISBN 0-19-515684-6
1. Psychotherapy—Evaluation.   2. Mental illness—Treatment—United States.
I. Castonguay, Louis Georges.   II. Beutler, Larry E.
RC480.5.P66 2005
616.89'14—dc22   2004030356

Preface

BACKGROUND AND ORGANIZATION

This book represents the work of a Task Force jointly sponsored by the Society for Clinical Psychology, which is Division 12 of the American Psychological Association (APA), and the North American Society for Psychotherapy Research (NASPR). This Task Force was initiated at the time that the Editors were beginning their respective terms as Presidents of these two professional groups. The Task Force represented the presidential initiatives of the two sponsoring groups during the year 2002 and extended through the year 2004.

The idea for this book was conceived in a series of discussions between the co-editors, that were initiated at the annual meeting of the international Society for Psychotherapy Research (SPR) and that continued via telephone and e-mail, as well as at a meeting of the American Psychological Association in San Francisco. The discussion brought into high relief the fragmenting effect on the field

of research, which had produced seemingly contradictory evidence about the roles of technical and relationship factors in treatment. Specifically, we were struck by the "either/or" position that many researchers and clinicians seem to take with regard to the variable(s) responsible for change. While some authors seemed to emphasize the importance of relationship above all, others focused on the effects of participant (therapist or patient) factors, and still others drew attention to the salience of certain treatment procedures and models. It struck us that all of these groups of scholars had lost sight of the possibility that relationship, participant factors, *and* treatment procedures were effective and interactive; that the conjunction should be "and" not "or" when describing the things that produce change.

As we were both entering the roles of Presidents of major professional organizations (Division 12 and NASPR), we decided to combine our efforts on behalf of our separate groups, and to initiate a process designed to answer important questions: (1) What is known about the nature of the participants, relationships, *and* procedures within treatment that induce positive effects across theoretical models and methods? (2) How do the factors or variables that are related to participants, relationships, and treatments, work together to enhance change? If we could answer these questions, we reasoned that it may be useful to translate the answers into general statements that identify how therapists might best work to optimize the effectiveness of interventions. That is, we concluded that it might be possible to extract general principles that govern the selection and implementation of therapeutic factors. Both editors had previously argued that such general principles of change might capture a substantial portion of the process of change in psychotherapy (e.g., Beutler, 2002; Castonguay, 2000). In their own way, each of them had also worked on the development of treatment protocols built, more or less extensively, on general principles of change. While Larry Beutler had has some successful experience in constructing a principle driven treatment model (Beutler, Clarkin, & Bongar, 2000; Beutler & Harwood, 2000), Louis Castonguay had been involved in the development of an integrative therapy for generalized anxiety disorder that combines methods from different theoretical approaches based in part on principles of change cutting across these approaches (Castonguay, Newman, Borkovec, Grosse Holtsforth, & Maramba, 2005). Both editors believed that sufficient consensus could be obtained to make the endeavor to find empirically based principles of change worthwhile.

The structure that we selected for this work was in the form of a Presidential Task Force within our respective organizations, and from this Task Force, we set out to produce a written work that would describe what is known and not known about therapeutic change. This book is the product of that decision.

This book is divided into four sections, each one representing a particular disorder or problem area (Dysphoric Disorders, Anxiety Disorders, Personality Disorders, and Substance Abuse Disorders). Within each of these four problem-focused sections are four chapters. Three chapters within each section are focused on a separate domain or group of variables that are thought to influence treatment: participant factors, relationship factors, and technique factors. Each of the domain-specific chapters is aimed at identifying a few salient principles that express the things that clinicians can do to optimize the effectiveness of treatment by attending to specific variables within this domain. The fourth chapter in each section is a summary and integration of the principles that are identified in these latter, three chapters.

While the 12 individual chapters on participant, relationship, and technique factors were independently written, following a general outline and consensus about terminology and scope of work, the integrative chapters, the fourth chapter in each section, arose in part from a delightful and interesting meeting in June 2003. That meeting, which took place at the second Editor's home in Placerville, California, was also devoted to identifying both the "common" principles of change—those that recurred in some form within two or more problem areas, and the "specific principles of change"—those that were found only within one of the problem domains.

IN GRATITUDE

During the course of this work, several people provided support and assistance. First, we wish to thank the Boards/executive committees and members of our respective organizations, NASPR and the Society for Clinical Psychology, Division 12 of APA. While we feel honored that our Task Force was sponsored by these organizations, it is also important to state that its findings and conclusions cannot be viewed as NASPR and/or APA Division 12 official positions with regard to what makes psychotherapy effective.

We also would like to thank Harrianne Mills for helping with the arrangements for our integration meeting, and of course, our families and students whose assistance and support were invaluable.

Of course, we truly appreciate the contributors themselves for working so hard to make this volume possible. Several have made presentations at national and international meetings to let people know what we have been doing, and all have been responsive to our efforts to cajole and encourage their adherence to deadlines. It should be noted that the authors were selected and paired with one another because of their outstanding records of research and theorizing and because they represented somewhat different viewpoints on the topics under discussion. This was done to ensure that many different voices were heard and that the perspectives of relationship therapists, dynamic therapists, experiential therapists, and behavioral and cognitive therapists were heard on most or all issues. The authors applied themselves to this onerous task and stimulated one another's imagination. We believe that the result was a creative and useful way to approach treatment that contrasts with the narrow, theory-bound view that often dictates what is done and what is seen within treatment.

It should also be noted that while the authors ultimately came to share a broad view of treatment as being positively influenced by factors and variables from all three domains (participants, relationships, and techniques), they never came to agree about the relative importance of variables among these classes. This point was best illustrated in a concerted and sometimes heated debate over what to title this book. This volume was planned to be a companion book to the other Task Force Reports published by Oxford University Press, which are respectively titled, *Treatments That Work* (Nathan & Gorman, 1998, 2002) and *Relationships That Work* (Norcross, 2002). We initially tried to define a title that would include all three domains within which we extracted variables, but could not agree on the order that they should be specified. We also felt that *Principles of Effective Treatment* and *Principles of Treatment That Work* seemed, respectively, too mundane and too frenzied. Thus, the current title.

We would also like to thank those who brought us together. While both of us, as Editors, knew each other through our professional writings and shared a common belief and hope for the development of a principle-run treatment, some concerted work by Jim Nagotte from Guilford and Joan Bossert from Oxford University Press got us talking and sharing our ideas. Ultimately, these two publishing houses each offered to publish the work, and our selection of Oxford was a difficult decision. We have appreciated the support and help of Joan Bossert, who has always been on our side to encourage and support. We also thank and acknowledge the catalystic assistance of Jim Nagotte in this process.

We also need to acknowledge that the preparation of this book was supported in part by National Institute of Mental Health Research Grant MH-58593, as well as by a generous grant from Oxford University Press.

This work was supported and authorized by the North American Society for Psychotherapy Research (NASPR) and the Society for Clinical Psychology (Division 12, APA). However, the ideas presented are those of the Editors and contributors. The principles of change are suggestive and should not be interpreted as being "guidelines" in the narrow view of that word.

A few months before we embarked on this ambitious project, Kenneth I. Howard, Ph.D., passed away. So did Sol L. Garfield, Ph.D., just a few weeks before it was completed. Both Ken and Sol had played an important role, as mentors or colleagues, in our respective careers. Each of them had also been pioneer in psychotherapy research, leaving indubitable and long-standing marks on our field. We like to think that they would have appreciated (in their cynical and gruffly kind of ways) the efforts made within this Task Force. During the course of this work, another friend, colleague, and Task Force member, Enrico E. Jones, Ph.D., also succumbed to a long bout with cancer. This was a profound loss at a personal level, as well as a loss to the book. Rico worked to the end and helped bring the chapter that bears his name to fruition. We are sorry that he did not live to see its completion. However, we thank Mary Coombs, a former colleague of Rico's, for stepping in and helping complete the chapter.

We, as Editors and authors, dedicate this volume to the memory of our friends and mentors, Sol L. Garfield, Kenneth I. Howard, and Enrico E. Jones. We'll miss you all.

References

Beutler, L. E. (2002). It isn't the size, but the fit. *Clinical Psychology: Science and Practice, 9,* 434–438.

Beutler, L. E., Clarkin, J. F., & Bongar, B. (2000). *Guidelines for the systematic treatment of the depressed patient.* New York: Oxford University Press.

Beutler, L. E., & Harwood, T. M. (2000). *Prescriptive*

psychotherapy: A practical guide to systematic treatment selection. New York: Oxford University Press.

Castonguay, L. G. (2000). A common factors approach to psychotherapy training. *Journal of Psychotherapy Integration, 10,* 263–282.

Castonguay, L. G., Newman, M. G., Borkovec, T. D., Grosse Holtforth, M., & Maramba, G. G. (2005). Cognitive-behavioral assimilative integration. In J. C. Norcross and M. R. Goldfried (Eds.), *The handbook of psychotherapy*

integration (2nd ed.). New York: Oxford University Press.

Nathan, P. E., & Gorman, J. M. (Eds.). (1998). *A guide to treatments that work.* New York: Oxford University Press.

Nathan, P. E., & Gorman, J. M. (Eds.). (2002). *A guide to treatments that work* (2nd ed.). New York: Oxford University Press.

Norcross, J. C. (Ed.). (2002). *Psychotherapy relationships that work.* New York: Oxford University Press.

Contents

Task Force Members

Chairs
Larry E. Beutler and Louis G. Castonguay

Dysphoric Disorders
Participant Factors
Larry E. Beutler and Sidney J. Blatt

Relationship Factors
Louis G. Castonguay and Enrico E. Jones

Technique Factors
William C. Follette and Leslie S. Greenberg

Anxiety Disorders
Participant Factors
Michelle G. Newman and Paul Crits-Christoph

Relationship Factors
William B. Stiles and Barry E. Wolfe

Technique Factors
Sheila R. Woody and Thomas H. Ollendick

Personality Disorders
Participant Factors
Héctor Fernández-Alvarez, John F. Clarkin, and
Kenneth L. Critchfield

Relationship Factors
Lorna Smith Benjamin and Jacques P. Barber

Technique Factors
Marsha M. Linehan and Gerald C. Davison

Substance Use Disorders
Participant Factors
David A. F. Haaga and Sharon M. Hall

Relationship Factors
Jay Lebow and Rudolf Moos

Technique Factors
Barbara S. McCrady and Peter E. Nathan

Contributors

Shabia Alimohamed
Counseling/Clinical/School Psychology,
University of California, Santa Barbara

Leslie A. Angtuaco
Department of Psychology, The Pennsylvania
State University

Jacques P. Barber
Department of Psychiatry, University of
Pennsylvania School of Medicine

Marna S. Barrett
Department of Psychiatry, University of
Pennsylvania School of Medicine

Rachel A. Beberman
Department of Psychology, The Pennsylvania
State University

Larry E. Beutler
Clinical Psychology Training Program, Pacific
Graduate School of Psychology,
Counseling/Clinical/School Psychology,
University of California, Santa Barbara

Sidney J. Blatt
Departments of Psychiatry and Psychology,
Yale University

James F. Boswell
Department of Psychology, The Pennsylvania
State University

Louis G. Castonguay
Department of Psychology, The Pennsylvania
State University

John F. Clarkin
Department of Psychiatry, Weill Medical
College of Cornell University

Paul Crits-Christoph
Department of Psychiatry, University of
Pennsylvania School of Medicine

Mary Beth Connolly Gibbons
Department of Psychiatry, University of
Pennsylvania School of Medicine

Mary M. Coombs
School of Social Welfare, University of
California, Berkeley

Kenneth L. Critchfield
University of Utah Neuropsychiatric Institute
and Department of Psychology, University of
Utah

Gerald C. Davison
Department of Psychology, University of
Southern California

María del Carmen Salgueiro
Fundación Aiglé, Buenos Aires, Argentina

Thane M. Erickson
Department of Psychology, The Pennsylvania
State University

Héctor Fernández-Alvarez
Fundación Aiglé, Buenos Aires, Argentina

William C. Follette
Department of Psychology, University of
Nevada, Reno

Leslie S. Greenberg
Department of Psychology, York University

Martin Grosse Holtforth
Department of Psychology, The Pennsylvania
State University, and Department of
Psychology, University of Bern

David A. F. Haaga
Department of Psychology, American
University

Amie Haas
Langley Porter Psychiatric Institute, University
of California, San Francisco

Sharon M. Hall
Langley Porter Psychiatric Institute, University
of California, San Francisco

Amy Janeck
Department of Psychology, University of British
Columbia

Enrico E. Jones (deceased)
Department of Psychology, University of
California, Berkeley

Aphrodite A. Kakouros
Department of Psychology, The Pennsylvania
State University

John Kelly
Center for Alcohol and Addiction Studies,
Brown University

Lynne M. Knobloch-Fedders
The Family Institute, Northwestern University

Jay Lebow
The Family Institute, Northwestern University

Kenneth N. Levy
Department of Psychology, The Pennsylvania
State University

Marsha M. Linehan
Department of Psychology, University of
Washington

Thomas R. Lynch
Departments of Psychiatry and Psychology,
Duke University

Barbara S. McCrady
Center of Alcohol Studies and Graduate
School of Applied and Professional Psychology,
Rutgers—The State University of New Jersey

Rudolf Moos
Center for Health Care Evaluation, Department
of Veterans Affairs and Stanford University

Peter E. Nathan
Departments of Psychology and Community
and Behavioral Health, University of Iowa

Michelle G. Newman
Department of Psychology, The Pennsylvania
State University

Thomas H. Ollendick
Department of Psychology, Virginia Polytechnic
Institute and State University

Jay J. Reid, Jr.
Department of Psychology, The Pennsylvania
State University

Cynthia Sanderson (deceased)

Tracey L. Smith
Department of Psychiatry, University of
Washington

Lorna Smith Benjamin
Department of Psychology, University of Utah

William B. Stiles
Department of Psychology, Miami University

Barry E. Wolfe
Rockville, Maryland

Sheila R. Woody
Department of Psychology, University of British
Columbia

Part I

INTRODUCTION

The Task Force on Empirically Based Principles of Therapeutic Change

[handwritten: → comes from experience — based on]

Larry E. Beutler

Louis G. Castonguay

[handwritten left: CBT → form of psychotherapy. It was originally designed to treat depression, but is now used for a number of mental disorders. It works to solve current problems and change unhelpful thinking and behavior.]

[handwritten right: → also focuses on exploring relationships among a person's thoughts, feelings & behaviours.]

Arising from the creative initiative of David Barlow, the Division 12 (American Psychological Association) Task Force on the Promotion and Dissemination of Psychological Procedures (Chambless, Baker, et al., 1998; Chambless, Sanderson, et al., 1996; Task Force, 1995) has been enormously successful in identifying treatments and methods of treatment that are founded on sound scientific research. Through their efforts, first the term "Empirically Validated Treatments" and later "Empirically Supported Treatments" (Chambless & Hollon, 1998) became part of the lexicon of practicing psychologists. This Task Force, and the standing committee of Division 12 that succeeded it, has published the results of several extensive projects that have led to the identification of treatment models that have been shown by controlled research to be reliably more effective than a no-treatment or a placebo treatment control condition. A compendium based on the work of that Task Force (Nathan & Gorman, 1998, 2002) epitomized the identification of treat- *[handwritten: cubes with no affect]* ments that exhibit specific and important influences on peoples' problems and well-being.

The results of that latter Task Force and the associated book, now in its second edition (Nathan & Gorman, 1998, 2002), were highly debated and severely criticized from many quarters. In particular, many of those in the practice and psychotherapy research communities expressed the belief that the Division 12 Task Force authors and report were too closely aligned with cognitive-behavioral treatments to be objective. Those who shared this belief seemed to feel that the search for Empirically Supported Treatments ignored important aspects of relationship-based therapies, notably the role of the therapeutic or working alliance and the role of patient and therapist factors.

The process and criteria used to define empirically supported treatments had taken a page from the procedural manual of the Federal Drug Administration, which seems a logical place to start, but was perhaps not a sufficient method and criteria with which to continue the search. This cri-

[handwritten: Psychotherapy → also known as "talk therapy" is when a person speaks with a trained therapist in a safe and confidential environment to explore and understand feelings and behaviors and gain coping skills.]

ـ.ia identified "proof" of empirical support as the presence of statistically significant findings from two, independently conducted, randomized clinical trials (RCT) in which the targeted treatment was compared with a placebo condition or a no-treatment control group. Unfortunately, RCT designs are not well suited to identifying qualities of the treatment that are either incapable of being randomly assigned or that are nondichotomous and that are embedded both in the treatment relationship and in its participants rather than in the treatment itself.

To address the concern that this criteria ignored participant and relationship factors, a Task Force was constituted by the Division of Psychotherapy (Division 29), under the presidency of John C. Norcross (2002). This latter Task Force was designed to serve as a counterbalance to the original Division 12 Task Force's emphasis on treatment factors. This Division 29 Task Force was aimed at identifying relationship variables that affected treatment outcomes and extended to a consideration of a variety of patient and therapist factors as well. Unfortunately, in doing so, it tended to place all of the emphasis on relationship and participant factors, eschewing the concept of treatment-specific models and manuals. The work of these two Task Forces and the Divisions of APA that sponsored them has frequently come to be viewed as contrasting and contradictory. And, it was in response to this interpretation that we (the Editors) decided to initiate a task force that was specifically designed to serve as a means of integrating the work of the previous two groups.

For Louis Castonguay, this book project was seen as an opportunity to derive from the empirical literature a number of principles of change that are common to a variety of theoretical orientations. Influenced by the work of Goldfried (1980), he believed that many of the procedures assumed to be responsible for the effectiveness of a particular orientation (e.g., challenge of maladaptive thoughts in cognitive therapy and interpretation in psychodynamic therapy) are best viewed as specific manifestations of more global strategies of intervention (e.g., providing a new understanding; Castonguay, 2002, in press). He reasoned that, at the minimum, the delineation of general principles of change would provide clinicians with a set of guidelines (flexible heuristics) that could comple-

ment the lists of procedures (more or less prescribed at specific times in therapy) that one frequently finds in treatment manuals and textbooks. Similar to Beutler's view, he believed that principles of change should not only be concerned with treatment procedure but should also encompass factors related to the relationship (e.g., alliance), and client and therapist characteristics (e.g., expectancies).

For Larry E. Beutler, the idea for this book arose from a prior effort (Beutler, Clarkin, & Bongar, 2000) to develop guidelines for treating depression. Beutler reasoned that a focus on treatment models, and on their respective manuals, frequently overlooked two important research findings: (1) that procedures drawn from many different treatment models were effective, and (2) most treatments produced a variety of effects, ranging from very positive to negative. Together Beutler, Clarkin, and Bongar shared the view that much more would be accomplished if science could identify the ways in which participant, relationship, and treatment factors and qualities interacted and potentiated one another's effects, and did so without assuming the baggage of an entire model or theory of treatment.

In spite of the stellar work of both the Division 12 presidential (David Barlow) initiative that began the process of identifying "Empirically Supported Treatments" (ESTs) and the more recent Division 29 presidential (John C. Norcross) initiative that defined the nature of "Empirically Supported Relationships," the field remains divided on how best to establish the scientific bases of practice. In fact, these two divisional initiatives exaggerate the schism between the relative value of objective and subjective experience that exists in the field, rather than healing it. Reflected in these two presidential initiatives is a division between those who primarily emphasize the roles of techniques and theory, on one hand (those who rely on objective evidence and EST research), and those who mainly emphasize interpersonal processes as ingredients of change (those who rely on subjective experience and research that identifies correlates of change), on the other. Typically, these two positions are represented by different people with very different values and beliefs about psychotherapy. Accordingly, they frequently interpret *the same body of research* in very different ways.

The models and techniques-oriented groups believe that the best method for ensuring the optimization of practice is to identify treatment models that work for patients who are identified by a particular problem (usually conceptualized as the diagnosis), and to encourage practitioners to learn to use these treatments. Treatments to which those who accept this view adhere and espouse are described via manuals. But, most head-to-head scientific comparisons of different treatments, defined in this way, indicate that they all have similar outcomes. With the exception of a small number of clinical problems (e.g., obsessive-compulsive disorder, generalized anxiety disorder), it is hard to find a treatment that works better than another treatment and all seem to be better than doing nothing. Most estimates from such studies reveal that differences among treatments account for no more than 10% of the variability in change (Luborsky, Rosenthal, et al., 2002; Wampold, 2001). Moreover, various groups have identified over 150 different approaches and models to treatment that are effective, each accompanied by a different manual and addressed to a different type of patient (Chambless & Ollendick, 2001). Together, the evidence that there are only minor differences in effectiveness among treatments, and the burgeoning number of treatments that identify themselves as being "empirically supported," has raised doubts for many about whether the benefits of improving practice by developing more manuals is either practical or cost-effective (Beutler, 1998, 2002).

On the other hand, the interpersonal processes-oriented research and practice groups believe that factors that facilitate the development of a therapeutic relationship, rather than the treatment model used, are the most important contributors to effective therapeutic work. These clinicians and scientists think that effective treatments can best be identified in terms of how patients and therapists interact. That is, improvement is best conceptualized as a product of the qualities that patient and therapist bring to the treatment and the relationship that is developed between them.

So far, however, research has indicated that the most robust of the relationship variables, the alliance, accounts for no more of the variation among outcomes than the 10% attributed to specific treatments (Beutler, Malik, et al., 2003; Horvath & Symonds, 1991) and therapist factors may account

for even less of the outcome variance (Beutler, Malik, et al., 2003; Lambert, 1992). Moreover, since research on the therapeutic relationship is invariably correlational in nature, it has been difficult to demonstrate that relationship quality actually *causes* improvement, rather than vice versa, during treatment.

It is time to find a common ground across these perspectives. We must begin to think outside of the narrow view that simply distinguishes between "techniques" and "relationship" qualities, and of one variable versus another, and to begin to look for foundation principles that encompass a variety of therapeutic factors. We think that psychotherapy research has produced enough knowledge to begin to define the basic principles that govern therapeutic change in a way that is not tied to any specific theory, treatment model, or narrowly defined set of concepts.

Principles are general statements that identify participant characteristics, relational conditions, therapist behaviors, and classes of intervention that are likely to lead to change in psychotherapy. Principles are more general than a description of techniques and they are more specific than theoretical formulations. As cogently described by Goldfried and Padawer (1982), these principles of interventions are generally found at a middle level of abstraction, between techniques and the theoretical models that are used to explain the effectiveness of treatments. We believe that stepping outside of the box that is defined by our theories, in this way, may allow us to begin to better understand and help a wider range of patients.

THE TASK FORCE ON EMPIRICALLY BASED PRINCIPLES OF THERAPEUTIC CHANGE

When we formed the Task Force from which this report derives (see preface), we did so with the intent of ensuring that most viable points of view were represented. Thus, the Task Force members (see list following contents page) were initially selected through a process of nomination and discussion. Several criteria were invoked of the Task Force members: (1) they must be established scholars who have achieved visibility in the scientific community for their empirical research in a given problem area and variable domain; (2) they must be willing and interested in working toward integration and synthesis of research findings; (3) they must be willing to work on a chapter with colleagues who do not share their theoretical perspectives; and (4) they must be willing to work hard for little financial compensation.

Interestingly, we had little difficulty finding colleagues who fit these criteria. We first independently constructed lists of potential contributors and debated the pros and cons of each until we were able to agree on a pair of authors within each problem area and variable domain who represented contrasting views from one another about the area of study. These authors were approached and recruited to serve on the Task Force and to work with the identified and contrasting colleague.

Each pair of authors was permitted to recruit additional colleagues to help with the tasks of reviewing literature and extracting principles of change. They also were given several primary sources of readings to reduce the need to revisit already reviewed literature (see below). These readings were identified to coincide with each variable domain, and where possible, each problem area. They then reviewed those selected references in order to abstract the general principles of change. Two definitions aided this process:

1. A *principle* defines the conditions under which a concept (participant, relationship quality, or intervention) will be effective. The concepts to be included should not be too general or theory-specific. Thus, a principle that says "Cognitive Therapy is effective" is too general and adds nothing to the Division 12 list of ESTs. A "principle" might be framed as an "If . . . then" statement or may be more general, such as "Therapists should attempt to create and maintain a strong working alliance that reflects a positive bond and an agreement between the participants in terms of the tasks and goals of therapy."
2. An empirically based principle is one that reflects the role of the participant characteristics, relationship qualities, or components of treatment that are found in the treatments identified by the Division 12 or Division 29 Task Force Reports, or that is supported by a "preponderance of the available evidence" (i.e., 50% or more of the studies on that problem area and domain support the relationship that defines the principle).

This latter definition allowed us to rely on widely accepted secondary sources as the basis for identifying the status of research in the field. For purposes of the current Task Force, several key references served as the means of defining what constructs have been empirically supported. From these constructs, the principles were defined. These principles, and the associated constructs from which they derived, were confined to what has been reported in these references, except in unusual circumstances. That is, the principles were deemed to reflect on qualities, characteristics, and interventions (within and across treatments) that derive directly from these references.

The four groups of authors that wrote the four chapters that focused on participant factors were specifically asked to review what is known about the range of patient and therapist characteristics defined in specific chapters of the Division 29 report (Norcross, 2002). To complement these sources of evidence, they were also asked to consider the relevant reviews of literature offered in the Bergin and Garfield (1994; Lambert, 2003) volumes. Where the literature warranted, some of these authors also included in their respective chapters, a review of research on factors that had been associated with the social context in which the problem occurs or is treated (e.g., family and spousal characteristics). In each case, we asked authors to consider available research on the role of specific variables in predicting treatment outcomes with an eye especially on factors and variables that may serve as moderators of a patient's response to different treatments.

Likewise, the eight Task Force members who were asked to write the four chapters on relationship factors were asked to assess the status of research by carefully reviewing the relevant chapters in the Division 29 report (Norcross, 2002), and by examining the appropriate reviews of literature in the Bergin and Garfield (1994; Lambert, 2003) volumes. Here, the questions addressed related to the type of relationship the therapist should attempt to foster, as well as the interpersonal skills he/she might want to master in order to facilitate client's improvement.

These first two groups of authors were essentially asked to review the general literature, extract the studies that addressed the problem area that they were reviewing, judge whether the current status of the general literature (as defined by the relevant conclusions reached by the Division 29 Task Force) appeared to be valid for the problem area, and then derive the most relevant principles that fit the problem and the domain of participants or relationship variables. If the Task Force members were not able to extract from the general literature a sufficient number of studies from which to derive principles of change directly related to their problem area, we invited them to accept by default (i.e., pending future research) the relevant conclusion reached by the Division 29 Task Force. Although most authors followed our recommendation, some did not elect to accept any conclusion or to derive any principle of change unless they found an adequate number of studies conducted with samples that were representative of their problem area.

Finally, the authors of the four chapters on technique variables were asked to draw from the volumes by Nathan and Gorman (1998, 2002) on effective treatments and on the report by Chambless and Ollendick (2001) on ESTs. These references have focused on treatment models and procedures that are associated with benefit within different diagnostic groupings of patients. While authors were encouraged to take the reports in these relevant volumes as evidence of technique effects, we asked authors to go beyond a simple recounting of what models work for what patient groups and to specify aspects of the treatment procedures used that seem to account for positive changes. Thus, we asked these authors to dismantle the various treatments and to identify the degree to which families, strategies, and characteristics of the intervention, rather than specific techniques, accounted for change. We suggested that, in making these determinations, that they consider qualities along various dimensions, such as the degree to which the treatment focus was on symptomatic and discrete behaviors versus the development of awareness and insight the degree that the therapist assumed a leadership and directive role versus one of facilitating exploration the degree to which interventions focused on intrapersonal versus interpersonal issues, and the degree to which the various models studied worked to enhance and focus emotional experience as opposed to reducing and containing it. As in the case of the other authors, we asked authors of the technique chapters to try to extract general principles that identified the variables that comprised effective treatments, rather than broad models of change.

In the penultimate step to the Task Force's work, we convened a group of 12 authors, representing each chapter. We asked them to bring with them an articulated list of the principles that their work group had distilled from their various reviews, and then we engaged them in a process of distinguishing between principles that were common or virtually the same across multiple problem areas and those that were relatively unique to one or another problem type. Common principles were identified by each of three work groups, representing, respectively, one of the three domains of variables researched (participants, relationship, techniques). Each of these groups was comprised of four authors. Thus, in each of these groups, all four problem areas were represented, but all of the participants had studied the same domain of contributors to outcome. They shared with one another, the principles that they had derived from their separate reviews and subjected these principles to a discussion. This discussion was aimed at identifying and restating, in a common language, the principles that seemed to cut across the four different problem areas. This became the list of "common principles."

Once common principles were identified, the work group was reconfigured in order to identify "specific principles." They were asked to consider the residual principles that had not been duplicated across disorders, and to refine them into a list of principles that were specific to each problem area. The authors within this second set of working groups represented all of the four problem areas, within a particular variable domain. They met together, reviewed the principles that had been defined in their various efforts to define empirically based principles, but that had not been identified as common across patient groups, and extracted from these an articulated list of principles that expressed the conclusions reached from the research reviews and that were simple and communicative. The result was a complementary list of principles that are specific for each problem area and that are relevant to each of the domains of variables (participants, relationships, treatments). The common and specific principles that have been derived from our Task Force are featured (in slightly different ways) in two integrative chapters (Beutler, Castonguay, & Follette, this volume; Critchfield & Benjamin, this volume) as well as in the final chapter of this book.

One word of caution should be expressed with regard to the empirical status of the principles of change, common and specific, identified in this book. It is indeed important to state that very few of them, if any, have been measured directly or found to be causally related to client's improvement in definitive, experimental studies. To our knowledge, none of these principles have been systematically manipulated within experimental studies or sufficiently investigated as potential mediators of change. Thus, rather than referring to them as being "empirically supported," it might be more appropriate to define these principles as "empirically derived" or "empirically grounded." For the same reason, and until they receive more direct support, it would be wise to view these clinical guidelines as hypotheses, rather than as established or factual processes of change.

CONSTRUCTS AND SOURCES

Participant factors, for the purposes of this book, are those characteristics of the patient or therapist that (1) exist solely within the person of the therapist or patient, and (2) represent qualities that are manifest in life beyond psychotherapy. From the Division 29 Task Force report, there were two sets of client or patient variables from which principles should be derived.

Those that represent prognostic factors in outcome include:

Attachment Style
Gender
Ethnicity
Religion and Spirituality
Preferences
Personality Disorders

Those that are identified as moderating variables, that have been found to be demonstrably or probably effective as a means of customizing therapy, include:

Resistance
Functional Impairment
Coping Style
Stages of Change
Anaclitic/Sociotropic and Introjective/Autonomous Styles
Expectations
Assimilation of Problematic Experiences

Relationship factors refer to general qualities of the therapeutic interaction and therapist's interpersonal skills that serve to enhance or impede the process of change and client's improvement. The Division 29 report listed the following factors that we believe are best defined as relationship factors:

Therapeutic Alliance
Cohesion in Group Therapy
Empathy
Goal Consensus and Collaboration
Positive Regard
Congruence/Genuineness
Feedback
Repair of Alliance Ruptures
Self-Disclosure
Management of Countertransference
Quality of Relational Interpretations

Technique factors, as we use this term in this volume, are the specific procedures that comprise the models of psychotherapy that are identified as "probably" and "possibly" efficacious treatments in the Division 12 reports. These lists served as the criteria of what treatments to be inspected to derive principles of change. To determine the nature of the interventions and to extract their underlying principles, authors were asked to inspect the specific manuals listed by the Division 12 reports. Authors were also provided with categories of intervention principles that could be used to regroup techniques from different orientations, based on the presence of similar goals, functions, or demand characteristics. These include: (1) level of therapist directiveness; (2) level of insight versus symptom and behavior change focus; (3) treatment intensity (e.g., length, frequency, multi-modal, etc.);

(4) intrapersonal and/or interpersonal focus of intervention; and (5) interventions that were designed to be emotion enhancing versus supportive.

In all three sections (participants, relationship, technique factors), authors were instructed not to consider findings that pertained exclusively to biological treatments. Thus, the principles of change that have been derived are only relevant to psychosocial therapies. The efforts of the Task Force have also been focused on the adult population and, as such, its conclusions may not be applicable to psychotherapy with children and adolescents, or for that matter, to psychological treatment for adult disorders not covered (e.g., eating disorders, psychotic disorders).

THE PROCESS

As noted, in the foregoing, the various chapters and authors were encouraged to rely, in defining what variables to consider, upon a list of established, secondary sources. But, authors were also encouraged to supplement these references and findings by going to specific studies and studies published after the secondary sources appeared, in order to extract more detail about what was done. Authors were allowed to add factors, qualities, or interventions only if the additions were accompanied by clear and persuasive evidence for efficacy or effectiveness, and only if the authors could convince others that adding some constructs is consistent with the preponderance of available evidence. Thus, while we encouraged authors to introduce new concepts and point to promising directions in research and practice, we did not want this volume to simply be a means for any or all of us to present our own research findings and favorite concepts, no matter how important. We wanted this book to represent the state of the art, while reflecting the creative processes of each group of authors—with the hope that what would result could have an influence on the field for years to come.

ACKNOWLEDGMENTS Preparation of this manuscript was supported in part by National Institute of Mental Health Research Grant MH-58593.

References

Bergin, A. E., & Garfield, S. L. (Eds.). (1994). *Handbook of psychotherapy and behavior change* (4th ed.). New York: John Wiley and Sons.

Beutler, L. E. (1998). Identifying empirically supported treatments: What if we didn't? *Journal of Consulting and Clinical Psychology, 66,* 113–120.

Beutler, L. E. (2002). The dodo bird really is extinct. *Clinical Psychology: Science and Practice, 9,* 30–34.

Beutler, L. E., Clarkin, J., & Bongar, B. (2000). *Guidelines for the systematic treatment of the depressed patient.* New York: Oxford University Press.

Beutler, L. E., Malik, M., Alimohamed, S., Harwood, T. M., Talebi, H., Noble, S., & Wong, E. (2003). Therapist variables. In M. J. Lambert (Ed.), *Handbook of psychotherapy and behavior change* (5th ed., pp. 227–306). New York: John Wiley and Sons.

Castonguay, L. G. (2000). A common factors approach to psychotherapy training. *Journal of Psychotherapy Integration, 10,* 263–282.

Castonguay, L. G. (in press). Personal pathways in psychotherapy integration. *Journal of Psychotherapy Integration.*

Chambless, D. L., Baker, M. J., Baucom, D. H., Beutler, L. E., Calhoun, K. S., Crits-Christoph, P., Daiuto, A., DeRubeis, R., Detweiler, J., Haaga, D. A. F., Johnson, S. B., McCurry, S., Mueser, K. T., Pope, K. S., Sanderson, W. C., Shoham, V., Stickle, T., Williams, D. A., & Woody, S. R. (1998). Update on empirically validated therapies, II. *Clinical Psychologist, 51,* 3–16.

Chambless, D. L., & Hollon, S. D. (1998). Defining empirically supported therapies. *Journal of Consulting and Clinical Psychology, 66,* 7–18.

Chambless, D. L., & Ollendick, T. H. (2001). Empirically supported psychological interventions: Controversies and evidence. *Annual Review of Psychology, 52,* 685–716.

Chambless, D. L., Sanderson, W. C., Shoham, V., Johnson, S. B., Pope, K. S., Crits-Christoph, P., Baker, M., Johnson, B., Woody, S. R., Sue, S., Beutler, L. E., Williams, D. A., & McCurry, S. (1996). An update on empirically validated therapies. *Clinical Psychologist, 49*(2), 5–14.

Goldfried, M. R. (1980). Toward the delineation of therapeutic change principles. *American Psychologist, 35,* 991–999.

Goldfried, M. R., & Padawer, W. (1982). Current status and future directions in psychotherapy. In M. R. Goldfried (Ed.), *Converging themes in psychotherapy* (pp. 3–49). New York: Springer.

Horvath, A. O., & Symonds, B. D. (1991). Relation between working alliance and outcome in psychotherapy: A meta-analysis. *Journal of Counseling Psychology, 38,* 139–149.

Lambert, M. J. (1992). Psychotherapy outcome research: Implications for integrative and eclectic therapists. In J. C. Norcross & M. R. Goldfried (Eds.), *Handbook of psychotherapy integration* (pp. 94–129). New York: Basic Books.

Luborsky, L., Rosenthal, R., Diguer, L., Andrusyna, T. P., Berman, J. S., Levitt, J. T., Seligman, D. A., & Krause, E. D. (2002). The dodo bird verdict is alive and well—mostly. *Clinical Psychology: Science and Practice, 9,* 2–12.

Nathan, P. E., & Gorman, J. M. (Eds.). (1998). *A guide to treatments that work.* New York: Oxford University Press.

Nathan, P. E., & Gorman, J. M. (Eds.). (2002). *A guide to treatments that work* (2nd ed.). New York: Oxford University Press.

Norcross, J. C. (Ed.). (2002). *Psychotherapy relationships that work.* New York: Oxford University Press.

Task Force on Promotion and Dissemination of Psychological Procedures. (1995). Training in and dissemination of empirically validated psychological treatments: Report and recommendations. *The Clinical Psychologist, 48*(1), 3–23.

Wampold, B. E. (2001). *The great psychotherapy debate: Models, methods, and findings.* Hillsdale, NJ: L. Erlbaum Associates.

Part II

DYSPHORIC DISORDERS

2

Participant Factors in Treating Dysphoric Disorders

Larry E. Beutler
Sidney J. Blatt
Shabia Alimohamed
Kenneth N. Levy
Leslie Angtuaco

Separating those factors and qualities that are legitimately characteristic of participants from those that are related to the process of developing a therapeutic relationship, or even those that are characteristic of the treatment being offered is central to the work of the current Task Force. However, it is also a more arbitrary distinction than it would initially seem. For example, in each of the five editions of *The Handbook of Psychotherapy and Behavior Change* (Bergin & Garfield, 1971, 1994; Garfield & Bergin, 1978, 1986; Lambert, 2003), separate chapters are devoted to discussing therapist and patient/client (participant) characteristics, treatment processes (i.e., relationship) variables, and various treatment approaches.[1] Yet, at least 50% of the variables or qualities discussed in any one of these chapters are also discussed in at least one of the other three. Almost any given variable has, at one time or another, been attributed to one of the participants, the treatment relationship or therapeutic alliance, or to an inherent aspect of some treatment model.

To illustrate this complexity, consider whether

you, the reader, consider therapist "warmth," "self-disclosure," and "persuasiveness" to be aspects of the therapeutic relationship, qualities of therapist skillfulness, or ingredients of treatment? They have been included in each of these domains by various authors. Even such supposedly therapist offered conditions as those described by Rogers (1957) have long been known to confound aspects of both the therapist and patient (Gurman, 1977).

Following the guidelines applied to the authors of this volume, we have identified "Participant Factors" as those qualities that (1) exist within the person of the therapist or patient, and (2) that are identifiable outside of what takes place within psychotherapy itself. That is, participant factors are enduring and relatively stable traits that are brought into treatment by the patient or therapist who is involved in the process.

In the current chapter, we have separately considered those variables that are *inferred* to be present by extrapolating from observations made by the patient of the treatment process, and those that are objectively measured or *observed* by other people. This distinction gives order to our presentation and is borrowed from that suggested in previous reviews of this literature (e.g., Beutler, Machado, & Neufeldt, 1994; Beutler, Malik, Alimohamed, Harwood, Talebi, Noble, & Wong, 2003). Thus, drawing from the topics discussed by the Division 29 Task Force on Relationships, sex, ethnicity, resistance to others, coping style, and personality disorder are measurable from behavioral observations of participants, independent of self-reports, while religious belief, expectations, preferences, assimilation of problematic experience, and stages of change, are participant qualities that can only be inferred from some aspect of participant's report.

In a comprehensive meta-analysis of therapist factors, spanning the last decade of the twentieth century, Beutler, Malik, et al. (2003) observed that the independent effects of therapist variables were weak. The strongest effects were observed when either patient and therapist or patient and treatment factors were considered together. That is, participant factors moderate the effects of specific treatment in the same way that treatment procedures sometimes moderate the effects of patient and therapist qualities (Garfield, 1994).

The complex interactions among patient and therapist characteristics were taken into account by the Division 29 Task Force on the "Empirically Supported Therapeutic Relationship" by including patient characteristics that served to moderate treatment effects, leading different types of patients to benefit selectively from various treatment approaches. To ensure that the current chapter retained this perspective, we confined our review of participant variables to the factors that were defined by the Division 29 Task Force. Wherever feasible, we considered the role of shared factors in all dimensions reviewed.

Little research has looked specifically at the effects of patient and therapist variables as predictors of some measurable outcome of treatment. The paucity of this research was noted by the Task Force on the Empirically Supported Relationship (Norcross, 2002), but this latter Task Force, like other scholars in this area, gave little consideration to specific problems and conditions. Our review of participant effects attempted to address this failure to consider the potential impact of different types of patient problem by comparing the conclusions

reached by the Division 29 Task Force with the findings that are revealed when only those studies that employed depressed samples are considered. When inadequate literature was present, we accepted the conclusions of the Division 29 Task Force as likely applicable to depression. However, when literature on depression was present, we sought to confirm or refute validity of the Division 29 conclusions.

To extend, where possible, the body of literature reviewed and considered in testing the generalization of the Division 29 conclusions, we added references and findings from other reviews, especially chapters on participant variables from the most recent edition of the *Handbook of Psychotherapy and Behavior Change* (Lambert, 2003) and other meta-analytic reviews of recent research. In all cases, principles of treatment were only defined as "empirically supported" when (1) a critical mass of literature was available and (2) the "preponderance of evidence" obtained from it favored the identified finding.

OBJECTIVE TRAITS SHARED BY PATIENT AND THERAPIST

Patient and Therapist Sex

General Effects

Sue and Lam (2002), writing for the Division of Psychotherapy (29) Task Force on the Empirically Supported Relationship, examined available research evidence for differences in treatment effects as a function of: (1) women versus men, (2) minority versus nonminority individuals, and (3) bisexuals versus heterosexuals across problem areas. They inspected these comparisons as applied to patient characteristics and then addressed the issue of whether these same qualities when matched with similar qualities in the therapist altered the findings. In most domains, they concluded that research was inadequate to determine whether patient demographic qualities or the similarity of patient and therapist on these dimensions enhanced outcomes of psychotherapy in a meaningful way.

They found a small number of studies ($N = 3$) that suggested the presence of a sex difference among patients. Whenever such differences were observed, women uniformly were more responsive to treatment than men. Similarly, they inspected the effects of same versus different sex matching among patients and therapists. In the three studies in which differences were observed, female–female pairs were associated with more favorable outcomes than were the other dyads.

In a more comprehensive review of 58 studies, Bowman, Scogin, Floyd, and McKendree-Smith (2001) also summarized the effects of therapist sex on treatment outcome using meta-analytic procedures. The authors found a significant but small effect size favoring female therapists (d = .04; $p < .05$), thus, lending support to the observations of Sue and Lam. However, no significant differences were obtained as a function of patient sex.

Similarly, Beutler, Malik, et al. (2003) conducted a meta-analysis of sex effects, based on 10 studies published since 1990. They found a significant but small main effect of therapist sex on outcome ($ES1(r)$ = .12), once again favoring females. Only one study (Sue, Fujino, Hu, Takeuchi, & Zane, 1991) found a significant relationship between patient–therapist sex matching and outcomes. These results favored similar sex pairs in predicting treatment outcome.

Overall, the results from these three reviews are consistent and suggest that a statistically significant but small effect favors female therapists over male therapists in treating a variety of largely mixed outpatient populations. The small number of studies detracts from but does not overshadow the strength of this conclusion. However, the results are less persuasive when applied either to effects associated with patient sex or to those associated with the sex match of patients and therapists. There is no convincing evidence, from these reviews, that sex matching of patients and therapists contributes appreciably to treatment benefit.

Extending the concepts derived from sex matching to more general aspects of gender, Sue and Lam (2002), reporting for the Division 29 Task Force, revisited the findings of Dunkle (1994), who reviewed six studies of patient gay/lesbian/bisexual (GLB) status on therapy change. Unfortunately, only two of the studies measured actual changes in clinical conditions. Sue and Lam identified seven additional outcome studies on this topic, however, and concluded that the preponderance of evidence indicated that GLB patients make significant changes during psychotherapy programs and tend to be reasonably well satisfied with their progress.

Conclusions about patient–therapist match on sexual attitudes are still weak, however. The weak findings may be attributed to design weaknesses in most of the studies. The infrequent use of control groups and a tendency to confound GLB status with such patient characteristics as ethnicity (e.g., Choi et al., 1996; Peterson et al., 1996) reduce the viability of the conclusions. Taking a broader view and employing meta-analytic procedures, Beutler, Malik, et al. (2003) explored the role of therapist–patient matching in the treatment of patients who varied in their gender-related attitudes. They found positive but weak support for the hypothesis that therapists who identify themselves as "feminist" in orientation may be better able to establish a good working relationship than nonfeminist therapists, regardless of the gender preferences of the patient (Cantor, 1991). While outcome is even more weakly affected, whatever the advantage that accrues to therapists who hold nontraditional views of sexual roles, it appears to be most pronounced among female clients, at least when compared to those therapists who hold traditional gender views (e.g., Banikiotes & Merluzzi, 1981; Hart, 1981).

Principles for Treating Depressed Patients

We extracted from the reviews by Sue and Lam (2002) and by Beutler, Malik, et al. (2003) those studies that focused on patient samples that were characterized by clinical depression. A review of these studies (Table 2.1) reveals a pattern that is generally consistent with the overall trend. Unfortunately, the number of studies of depressed samples who were GLB was too small and the effect sizes too weak to reach conclusions about the role of therapist and patient gender-based attitudes. A more substantial and consistent body of studies was available on patient and therapist sex. This sample of studies was comprised of five from the meta-analysis by Beutler, Malik, et al. (2003) and eight from the report by Sue and Lam (2002). Five of the resulting 13 studies found an effect favoring female therapists and five found evidence of pa-

Table 2.1
Sex and Gender

Study	N	Diagnosis	Outcome effects
		Therapist sex	
From Beutler et al., 2003			
Krippner & Hutchinson, 1990	288	Mixed depression/anxiety (clients with homicidal/suicidal ideation excluded)	Significant effect of female therapist gender on State-Trait Anxiety (STAI) scores No significant effect of gender match on STAI scores
Orme & Boswell, 1991	721	Dysphoric	No significant effect of gender on attendance at intake No significant effect of gender match on intake attendance
Sue, Fujino, Hu, Takeuchi, & Zane, 1991	13,439	Dysphoric	Positive effect of gender match on lack of dropout (dropout = failure to return after first session) Positive effect of gender match on length of treatment Positive effect of gender match on Global Assessment Scale (GAS) outcomes
Talley, 1992	72	Dysphoric	No significant effect of gender on multivariate outcome (Beck Depression Inventory, Zung Self-Rating Depression Scale, Zung Self-Rating Anxiety Scale)
Zlotnick, Elkin, & Shea, 1998	203	Major Depressive Disorder	No significant effect of therapist gender on Hamilton Rating Scale for Depression scores (HRSD) No significant effect of gender match on HRSD scores
From Sue & Lam, 2002			
Craig & Huffine, 1976	140 mostly African American	Dysphoric	Non-significant effect of therapist gender on premature termination
Fujino, Okazaki, & Young, 1994	1,132	Dysphoric	Significant effect of gender match on dropout, treatment duration, and functioning level for Asian American women and men, and White American women (match reduced premature termination, increased treatment duration, and predicted higher initial functioning, particularly for Asian American women) No significant effect of gender match on initial diagnosis or posttreatment functioning
Heisler, Beck, Fraps, & McReynolds, 1982	200	Dysphoric (community mental health center)	No significant correlation of client's gender and therapy attendance

Study	N	Diagnosis	Outcome effects
		Therapist sex	
Jones, Krupnick, & Kerig, 1987	60 female	DSM-III PTSD or adjustment disorder, most with anxiety or affective disorders (excluded: those with psychiatric hospitalization, severe character problems, lifestyle of trauma life events)	Effect of therapist gender on symptomatic improvement and client satisfaction (more improvement and satisfaction with female therapists) Significant effect of therapist gender on levels of client intrusive symptomology (lower levels with female therapists) Initial symptomology, client age, and therapist gender account for .22, .13, & .08 of variance in outcome in that order
Jones & Zoppel, 1982	160	Neurotic and personality disorders, depression, and adjustment reactions (psychosis, schizophrenia, and psychotic trends excluded)	Study 1: therapist ratings No effect of client gender on ratings of improvement, but female therapists rate themselves as more successful with female clients, report better alliances, and describe clients in more positive ways than male therapists Study 2: client ratings Significance effect of therapist gender on client ratings of effectiveness of therapeutic alliance (both male and female clients found female therapists more effective in forming therapeutic alliance) No significant effect of gender match on therapy outcome Significant effect of gender match on length of treatment (same sex dyads had longer treatment duration but possible effect of nonrandom assignment of clients to therapists)
Kirshner, Genack, & Hauser, 1978	189; 47% female (university health service; includes faculty)	Dysphoric	Significant effect of therapist gender on patient satisfaction and self-rated improvement (greater satisfaction and improvement with female therapists)
Orlinsky & Howard, 1976	118 women with 78 male & 40 female therapists	Depression, anxiety, and personality disturbance	Significant effect of therapist gender on client therapy experience (clients with male therapists feel more involved, uncomfortable, and self-critical, and less supported) Significant effect of depressive conditions on sensitivity to therapist sex (those with depressive reaction [vs. anxiety reaction and personality disturbance] more sensitive to male therapists) No significant effect of therapist gender on levels of mastery, insight, overall outcome

(continued)

Table 2.1
(continued)

Study	N	Diagnosis	Outcome effects
		Therapist sex	
Weitz, 1982	73 females	Feminist consciousness raising group participation	Significant positive effect of group participation on helplessness and self-esteem Significant positive relationship between self-esteem and helplessness, and depression scores
Bowman, Scogin, Floyd, & McKendree-Smith, 2001	Review of 58 studies	Dysphoric	Modest effect of therapist sex on treatment outcome
		Client sex	

From Sue & Lam, 2002

Study	N	Diagnosis	Outcome effects
Jones & Zoppel, 1982	160	Neurotic and personality disorders, depression, and adjustment reactions (psychosis, schizophrenia, and psychotic trends excluded)	No effect of client gender on ratings of improvement (both male and female clients reported significant improvement) No significant effect of gender match on therapy outcome Significant effect of gender match on length of treatment (same sex dyads had longer treatment duration but possible effect of nonrandom assignment of clients to therapists)
Kirshner, Genack, & Hauser, 1978	189; 47% female (university health service; includes faculty)	Dysphoric	Significant effect of client gender on response to therapy (female patients are more responsive
Talley, Butcher, Maguire, & Pinkerton, 1992	N/A	Dysphoric Disorder	Significant effect of client gender on dysphoria scores (females show greater symptom reduction)
Thase et al., 1994	84	Research Diagnostic Criteria for Major Depression (nonpsychotic, nonbipolar type)	Significant effect of pretreatment depression scores on outcome (higher initial depression scores related to poorer outcomes, particularly for women) No significant interaction effect of gender and time on depression scores
Zlotnick et al., 1996	188	Major Depressive Disorder	No significant main or interaction effects of patient gender (with treatment type, dysfunctional attitudes, life events, or social support) on severity of depressive symptoms

tient–therapist sex similarity as a correlate of positive effects.

While female sex and sexual similarity are relatively consistent correlates of outcome, the percentage of positive findings failed to meet the criteria of a "preponderance of evidence." Thus, we accepted the Division 29 conclusion that:

1. Research on gender effects is insufficient for a clear judgment of effects on the treatment of depressed patients to be made.

This latter conclusion has been reiterated by others with respect to the effects of specific therapies on the treatment of panic disorder (Huppert et al., 2001).

Patient and Therapist Ethnicity and Socioeconomic Status

General Effects of Ethnicity

In the analysis of ethnic status and patient–therapist ethnic similarity, Beutler, Malik, et al. (2003) concluded that there is insufficient research to systematically compare outcomes as a direct effect of therapist race or ethnicity, independently of that of the patient. Most research is relational in nature and assumes that outcome is or may be improved when therapist and patient share certain ethnic experiences and background. These shared perspectives can be assumed to derive from either systematic training to enhance cultural sensitivity (Valdez, 2000) or from the presence of similar cultural backgrounds.

The review of this literature for the Division 29 Task Force shows similarly weak effects of ethnicity on outcome. Reviewing literature on this latter literature, Sue and Lam (2002) separately inspected the effects of treatment that were associated with patient and therapist samples of African Americans, Native Americans, Asian Americans, and Latinos. They noted that among African Americans, a small but proportionately large number of studies (N = 3 of 6) found that African Americans do more poorly in psychotherapy than other ethnic groups. The other three studies obtained nonsignificant findings and no study, to our knowledge, has reported a superior response to

psychotherapy among African-American clients, compared to white or Asian-American samples.

According to Sue and Lam, studies of Native Americans are too sparse to use in any investigation of principles of change (N = 1), and these authors found only two studies conducted on Asian-American samples. These latter studies demonstrated lower satisfaction rates among Asian Americans than among other groups, and both of these studies also demonstrated that patient–therapist ethnic similarity was associated with lower dropout rates. Three studies indicated that directive interventions were preferred and (perhaps) more effective among Asian Americans than among majority groups. These latter conclusions are based upon too little evidence to draw reasonable conclusions at this point, however.

Sue and Lam concluded that improvement among Latinos is comparable to that observed among non-Latino samples. However, they cite three studies that found that matching patient–therapist ethnic similarity enhances the likelihood of improved outcomes. The authors suggest that language commonality may account for these latter findings—sharing a primary language was associated with low dropout rates. They also noted that family involvement in therapy may enhance response to treatment among Latino adolescents.

In their inspection of patient–therapist ethnic similarity, Beutler, Malik, et al. (2003) identified five studies that assessed change over treatment (Hosch et al., 1995; Ricker, Nystul, & Waldo 1999; Snowden, Hu, & Jerrell 1995; Sue et al., 1991; Yeh, Eastman, & Cheung, 1994) and three more that used treatment dropout as an outcome variable (Sterling, Gottheil, Weinstein, & Serota, 1998; Sue et al., 1991; Yeh et al., 1994).

Collectively, the studies cited in these two reviews confirm the hypothesis that, across problem types, patient–therapist ethnic similarity is a factor that contributes to reduced dropout rates. Ethnic match, particularly among Asian Americans (Snowden et al., 1995) and Mexican Americans (Sue et al., 1991), seems to be conducive to improvement, but the effect sizes are small, ranging from 0 to .28. In the Beutler, Malik, et al. (2003) review, the mean (weighted) effect size (r) was only .02 ($p < .05$).

General Effects of Socioeconomic Status

Because socioeconomic status (SES) is often confounded with ethnicity, Sue and Lam (2002) analyzed its potential influence on the foregoing relationships, separately. They conclude that low-income clients are more likely to drop out of treatment prematurely than middle- and high-income clients. They also conclude that there is not a strong or meaningful relationship between social class and direct therapy outcome.

Principles for Treating Depressed Patients

To test the specificity of the foregoing findings to depressed samples, a collected group of 14 studies of samples represented by dysphoria and clinical depression were extracted from the reviews by Beutler, Malik, et al. (2003) and Sue and Lam (2002). Table 2.2 reveals the results of these studies, separately listed by those attending to therapist ethnicity and patient ethnicity. Seven studies (50%) revealed that similar patient–therapist ethnic pairs were associated with better outcomes or lower dropout rates than ethnic-different pairs. Three additional studies reported advantages of adjusting the treatment to the special needs and considerations of ethnic patients, and only one indicated advantages accrued to ethnically mismatched pairs. Another study indicated that language similarity reduced mental health usage of emergency rooms.

The general results of the foregoing studies of depression appear to be somewhat stronger than that noted in the general psychotherapy literature using mixed diagnostic samples of patients. The results confirm the value of ethnic similarity, with a consistent majority of the studies on depressed samples favoring the importance of patient–therapist ethnic similarity in fostering positive response to psychotherapy or reducing dropout. These studies support the following treatment planning principles as applied to the treatment of patients with dysphoria and depression.

1. Patients representing underserved ethnic or racial groups achieve fewer benefits from conventional psychotherapy than patients from Anglo-American groups.
2. If patients and therapists come from the same or similar racial/ethnic backgrounds, dropout rates are positively affected and improvement is enhanced.

We also inspected the conclusions of Sue and Lam (2002) with respect to socioeconomic status (SES) in order to see if these relationships transferred to aspects of social economic status in the treatment of depression. The conclusions of Sue and Lam regarding socioeconomic status were largely based on two prior reviews of empirical literature (Lorion, 1973; Luborsky, Chandler, Auerbach, Cohen, & Bachrach, 1971) and so we inspected these reviews to identify studies that addressed depression. Unfortunately, none of the studies that addressed the role of SES on treatment outcome were conducted on homogeneously diagnosed depressed groups of patients. Three studies, however, used samples that consisted of a mix of depression and other disorders (Brill & Storrow, 1960; Rosenbaum, Friedlander, & Kaplan, 1956; Rosenthal & Frank, 1958), but only one of these (Rosenbaum et al., 1956) found any association between social class and outcome.

Sue and Lam (2002) also inspected social status as a moderator of treatment type. In spite of general claims in the literature, they found only suggestive evidence to support the belief that time-limited and directive therapies are more effective than insight-oriented treatment for low-SES clients. From the studies cited in the Sue and Lam review, only one addressed the role of time-limited therapy as a function of patient SES, using a dominantly depressed sample (Koegler & Brill, 1967). This latter study found no relationship between socioeconomic class and type of treatment.

From among the three studies cited by Sue and Lam (2002) that addressed the question of whether the use of behaviorally oriented, therapist-directed therapy might be better for low-SES clients than more insight-oriented therapy, two employed depressed samples (Organista, Munoz, & Gonzales, 1994; Satterfield, 1998). Unfortunately, neither of these studies employed a comparison group, and the results are ambiguous. In a study of this question that was missed in Sue and Lam's review, however, Sloane, Staples, Cristol, Yorkston, & Whipple (1975) found that "patients with higher incomes and less pathology did better than their opposites in analytically oriented ther-

Table 2.2
Ethnicity/Race

Study	N	Diagnosis	Outcome effects
			Therapist race
From Beutler et al. 2003			
Ricker, Nystul, & Waldo, 1999	51	Dysphoric	Significant effect of ethnic match on SCL-90 Global Severity Index (GSI) scores
Snowden, Hu, & Jerrell, 1995	26,943	Schizophrenia, Adjustment Reaction	Significant effect of ethnic match on decreased use of emergency room Significant effect of language match on decreased use of emergency room
Sue, Fujino, Hu, Takeuchi, & Zane, 1991	13,439	Dysphoric	Effect of ethnic match on Global Assessment Scale (GAS) outcomes Effect of ethnic match on dropout (dropout = failure to return after first session) Significant effect of ethnic match on treatment length
Yeh, Eastman, & Cheung, 1994	4,616	Dysphoric	Effect of ethnic match on GAS outcomes Significant effect of ethnic match on dropout for adolescents (dropout = failure to return after first session) Effect of ethnic match on dropout
From Sue & Lam, 2002			
Brown, Schulberg, Sacco, Perel, & Houck, 1999	160, mostly female	DSM-III R Major Depressive Disorder	No significant effect of race or treatment (interpersonal or pharmacotherapy) on depression outcome scores for intent-to-treat cohorts African Americans more likely to be unemployed, unmarried, and to experience more stressful life events in 6 months pretherapy
Craig & Huffine, 1976	140 mostly African American	Dysphoric	No significant effect of patient or therapist race on continuation in therapy
Flaskerud & Hu, 1994	273 (66% female)	Major Depression	Significant effect of ethnic match and setting on number of sessions but not GAS outcome scores (same sex dyads and treatment in Asian-specific clinic resulted in greater number of sessions) Use of medication positively related to number of sessions and improvement on GAS scores
Fujino, Okazaki, & Young, 1994	1,132	Dysphoric	Ethnic match significantly associated with reduced premature termination increased treatment duration, higher initial functioning No significant effect of ethnic match on initial diagnosis or client functioning at discharge
Gamst, Dana, Der-Karabetian, & Kramer, 2000	4,554	Dysphoric	Significant differential effect of ethnic match on initial and termination GAF scores (matched Latino and Asian clients have higher scores than African American and White clients; African Americans in schizophrenia classification have higher scores, those with mood disorders have lower (scores) Significant differential effect of ethnic match on change in GAF scores (higher for matched Latino and White than for African American clients)

(continued)

Table 2.2
(continued)

Study	N	Diagnosis	Outcome effects
			Therapist race
			Significant differential effects of ethnic match on visits to mental health center (fewer for Latino and African American, higher for White. Higher levels for Asian clients regardless of match)
Rosenheck, Fontana, & Cottrol, 1995	4,726 African American and White male clients and 315 therapists	Dysphoric	Significance effect of unmatched dyads on dropout and number of sessions (African American clients matched with White therapists have higher rates of termination and fewer number of sessions)
Takeuchi, Sue, & Yeh, 1985	4,710 African, Asian, and Mexican Americans	Dysphoric	Better outcomes for clients in ethnic-specific programs and longer stay in treatment (vs. those in mainstream service) No effect of treatment on GAS scores for Mexican Americans (authors suggest GAS is insensitive measure of treatment outcome
			Client race
From Sue & Lam, 2002			
Markowitz, Spielman, Sullivan, & Fishman, 2000	101 African American, Hispanic, & White HIV-positive	Depression	Significant interaction effect of ethnicity and treatment (CBT, interpersonal, supportive, or drug + supportive) on depression scores (African Americans in CBT group had significantly poorer outcomes than other Ss)
In Rosenthal, 2000	Review		
Gomez, Ruiz, & Laval, 1982	12 bilingual Hispanic	Dysthymia and anxiety	Positive effect of treatment (brief psychodynamic therapy) on outcome scores No significant effect of language in therapy on depression, anxiety, or psychoticism scores (no control comparison group)
Szapocznik, Santisteban, Kurtines, Hervis, & Spencer, 1982	100 Cuban Americans elders	Depression	Significant effect of treatment (life enhancement counseling and medication) on depression outcome; no effect of client variables on treatment success
Takeuchi, Sue, & Yeh, 1985	4,710 African, Asian, and Mexican Americans	Dysphoric	Better outcomes for clients in ethnic-specific programs and longer stay in treatment (vs. those in mainstream service) No effect of treatment on GAS scores for Mexican Americans (authors suggest GAS is insensitive measure of treatment outcome)

apy, whereas such differences were not noted in the behavioral group."

As a result of the relative paucity and inconsistency of this research, no conclusions were reached about social class in the Division 29 review (Norcross, 2002). Our own review suggests the following principle:

1. Insufficient research has been conducted on SES to determine if it is a contributor to treatment outcome for depressed patients.

Personality Disorders

General Effects

Research on psychological treatments for patients with personality disorders is still in its infancy. The Division 29 Task Force report (Norcross, 2002) concluded that insufficient research had been done to make a clear judgment about the general role that personality disorders may play in moderating treatment effects. Benjamin and Karpiak (2002) reviewed both the effectiveness of treating those with personality disorders and the role that personality disorders played as moderators of treatment for the Division 29 Task Force on "Relationships that Work." They concluded that "There are effective psychotherapy treatments for personality disorders and they come from a variety of theoretical and practical perspectives" (p. 433). While interesting and important, these data are outside of the scope of the current chapter. Here, our task is to determine if the presence of a co-morbid personality disorder moderates the effectiveness of treating patients with depression. About this latter question, Benjamin and Karpiak are relatively silent. Hence, we reinspected the studies reported in their review with an eye toward discovering principles that may bear on this important question.

Principles for Treating Depressed Patients

In order to inspect the role of personality disorder as a moderator of treatments for depression, we extracted from the chapter by Benjamin and Karpiak (2002) those studies of treatment effectiveness that had been conduced on patients with co-morbid depression and personality disorder. We

added to these studies, several additional studies published in reviews by Reich (2003) and Mulder (2002).

Table 2.3 summarizes the results of 20 studies that inspected the level of treatment effect among patients with co-morbid depression and anxiety. Only five of these studies (Kuyken, Kurzer, De-bubeis, Beck, & Brown, 2001; Shahar, Blatt, Zuroff, & Pilkonis, 2003; Stuart, Simons, Thase, & Pilkonis, 1992; Taylor & McLean, 1993) failed to conclude that the presence of a personality disorder attenuated the effects of psychosocial treatment. Fifteen studies (Table 2.3) found significant or strong evidence that the presence of a personality disorder tends to reduce treatment effects. Thus, this literature tends to support the following principle:

1. Co-morbid personality disorders are negative prognostic indicators in the psychological treatment of depressed patients.

The results of available studies of depressed samples are not strong enough to draw conclusions about differential effectiveness of different treatments. Nor are the findings consistent enough to warrant drawing conclusions about the relative attenuation of effects as a function of different personality or clusters of personality disorders. However, Table 2.3 reveals several studies that suggest that dependent and unstable personality types tend to suffer worse outcomes than other dispositional patterns (e.g., Alnaes & Torgersen, 1997; Hoffart & Martinsen, 1993; Ilardi & Craighead, 1999; Shahar et al., 2003).

Patient Age

General Effects

Among other potential factors on which patient and therapist might contribute to improvement, age effects have been the most frequently studied in general samples. These studies consistently support the conclusion that the age of adult patients is inversely related to the quality of outcome achieved. Indeed, Jones, Krupnick, and Kerig (1987) report that patient age accounted for twice the amount of outcome variance as patient gender, on measures of symptomatic change and satisfac-

Table 2.3
The Role of Personality Disorder in the Treatment of Depression

Study	N	Diagnosis	Treatment used	Outcome effects
Alnaes & Torgersen, 1997	298	Depressed outpatients with co-morbid personality disorder	Naturalistic study	Borderline and dependency traits predicted relapse; avoidant personality disorder and borderline personality disorder predicted new cases
Andreoli et al., 1993	31	Depressed outpatients with co-morbid personality disorder	Naturalistic study; psychotherapy and clomipramine monitored by blood levels (if required)	Worse long-term outcome seen in patients with co-morbid personality disorders
Diguer, Barber, & Luborsky, 1993	25	Depressed outpatients with co-morbid personality disorder	Psychodynamic psychotherapy	Patients with co-morbid personality disorder had worse outcome, although decreased in Beck inventory scores similar
Frank, Kupfer, Jacob, & Jarrett, 1987	68	Depressed outpatients with co-morbid personality disorder	Imipramine; interpersonal psychotherapy	Slow response group (>8 months to recovery) had higher rates of personality disorders
Hardy et al., 1995	114	Depressed outpatients stratified by severity with co-morbid personality disorder	Eight or 16 sessions of cognitive behavior therapy or psychodynamic interpersonal therapy	In PI therapy, PD clients maintained more severe symptomatology than NPD. Among clients in CBT, no significant differences were found between PD and NPD. PD clients with severe depression showed less improvement than both PD and NPD clients with less severe depression
Hoffart & Martinsen, 1993	77	Panic with agoraphobia, major depression, or a combination in impatients	Psychodynamic psychotherapy	Worse outcome at posttreatment seen in patients with dependent and paranoia personality disorders; avoidant personality disorder predicted worse 1 year follow-up
Ilardi & Craighead, 1999	40	Formally depression patients	Cognitive behavior therapy	General personality pathology factor associated with dysfunctional cognitions, though a more specific association between Axis II Cluster C pathology and dysfunctional attitudes was observed
Kuyken et al., 2001	162	Depressed patients with and without a personality disorder	Naturalistic study following cognitive therapy	Maladaptive avoidant and paranoid beliefs, and not personality disorder predicted variance in outcome
Miller, Norman, & Keitner, 1990	69	Depressed outpatients with co-morbid personality disorder impatients	Tricyclic antidepressants; psychotherapy	No difference between "high" and "low" cognitive dysfunction groups

Study	N	Diagnosis	Treatment used	Outcome effects
Patience, McGuire, Scott, & Freeman, 1995	113	Major depression with co-morbid personality disorder	Primary care counseling and amitriptaline as needed	After treatment the personality disorder group had more depression and poorer social functioning, but they caught up with the no-PD group by 18 months
Pilkonis & Frank, 1988	119	Depressed outpatients with co-morbid personality disorder impatients	Imipramine; interpersonal psychotherapy	Those who took more than 8 months to recover had higher rates of personality disorders
Seivewright, Tyrer, & Johnson, 1994	181	Generalized anxiety disorder, panic disorder, or dysthymia	Drug treatment; psychotherapy (cognitive) or self-help	Logistic regression indicated presence of personality disorder was a negative prognostic indicator at 5 years
Shahar et al., 2003	153	Major depression in outpatients with co-morbid personality disorder and perfectionism	Brief treatment for depression	Poor therapeutic outcomes for patients with elevated levels of perfectionism and odd-eccentric and depressive PD features. Patients' contribution to therapeutic alliance was predicted by perfectionism but not by PD
Shea et al., 1990	239	Depressed outpatients with co-morbid personality disorder	Imipramine; cognitive behavior therapy; interpersonal psychotherapy	Patients with any co-morbid personality disorders less likely to recover across all treatment groups and had significantly worse social functioning. Patients with elevated odd-eccentric PD features had elevated depressive symptoms
Stuart et al., 1992	53	Depressed outpatients with co-morbid personality disorder	Cognitive behavior therapy	No difference in response; rates of personality disorder dropped in a limited number of patients
Taylor & McLean, 1993	155	Depressed outpatients with co-morbid personality disorder	Psychotherapy; amitriptyline; behavior therapy; relaxation	High neuroticism scores predicted worse 12-week outcome regardless of treatment
Tyrer, Seivewright, Ferguson, Murphy, & Johnson, 1993	181	Generalized anxiety disorder, panic disorder, or dysthymic outpatients	Dithiepin; diazepam; cognitive behavior therapy	Psychological treatment methods, particularly self-help, were more effective in patients without personality disorder, patients with personality disorders responded better to drug treatment
Viinamaki et al., 2002	117	Major depression with co-morbid personality disorder	Naturalistic follow up	Logistic regression indicated an association between lack of recovery and Cluster C personality disorder
Zuroff & Blatt, 2002	162	Major depressive disorder in outpatients	Interpersonal psychotherapy, CBT, active medication, and placebo	Stress reactivity was predicted by depressive personality at intake

Table 2.4

Age

Study	N	Diagnosis	Outcome effects
		Client age	

From Beutler, Harwood, et al., 2002

Study	N	Diagnosis	Outcome effects
Craig & Huffine, 1976	140 mostly African American	Dysphoric	Significance effect of age and diagnosis on duration in therapy (longer duration for those > age 30 and with psychosis or personality disorders)
Garvey & Schaffer, 1994	177	Depressive illness	Differential effects of age on depressive and anxious symptoms (Ss < 40 years of age more likely to suffer hypersomnia, increased appetite and weight gain, decreased libido, headaches, lower p.m. mood and sad vs. anxious mood. Ss > 40 years of age more likely to have terminal insomnia, lower a.m. mood, endogenous, incapacitated, or agitated mood)
Mazure, Nelson, & Jatlow, 1990	52	DSM III-R nonpsychotic unipolar Major Depression	Inverse relationship between age and likelihood of response to treatment (1 week of hospitalization without antidepressants)

From other sources

Study	N	Diagnosis	Outcome effects
Heisler, Beck, Fraps, & McReynolds, 1982	200	Dysphoric	Significant correlation of client's gender and therapy attendance (early dropouts tend to be younger, less well educated, less likely to be employed, more likely to be diagnosed with personality disorders)
Jones, Krupnick, & Kerig, 1987	60 females	DSM-III PTSD or adjustment disorder. Most with anxiety or affective disorders (excluded: those with psychiatric hospitalization, severe character problems, lifestyle of trauma life events)	2 studies: Study 1: Patient age accounted for twice the outcome variance contributed by gender to symptomatic improvement and patient satisfaction with treatment; both were exceeded by initial symptomology as contributors of variance in outcome. Study 2: 2 female therapists found to arouse less negative affect in female patients, and fewer interpersonal difficulties
Orlinsky & Howard, 1976	118 women with 78 male & 40 female therapists	Depression, anxiety, and personality disturbance	Significant effect of client age on sensitivity to therapist sex (younger single and single women more sensitive to male therapists)
Barber & Muenz, 1996	84	Major Depression with avoidant or obsessive personality	No effect of age or age-similarity on outcome
Beck, 1988	1,500 patients, 250 therapists	Dysphoric	Significant effect of therapist age on treatment outcome (clients whose therapists are > 10 years younger have poorest outcomes)
Dembo, Ikle, & Ciarlo, 1983	2,898	Dysphoric	Significant effect of therapist age on treatment outcome (client–therapist dyads whose age difference is 10 or less years have most positive outcomes for distress and social isolation at posttreatment)

tion. Patient age also appears to moderate the effects of variables such as gender, directly. For example, among males, early dropouts tend to be younger, less well educated, and more likely to be diagnosed with personality disorders (Heisler, Beck, Fraps, & McReynolds, 1982).

Therapist, as compared to patient, age is even a more complex variable, partly because it is confounded by so many other, therapy-relevant factors (e.g., experience). Because of the complexity of moderating effects, however, little can be clearly concluded about the degree to which therapist age or patient–therapist age similarity contributes to outcome. For example, Barber and Muenz (1996) failed to find a significant effect of patient–therapist age similarity on outcome. On the other hand, both Dembo, Ikle, and Ciarlo (1983) and Beck (1988), observed that therapists who are more than 10 years younger than their adult patients tend to produce lower overall outcomes than those who are 10 years or closer to the client's age. Unfortunately, therapist age and experience are confounded in such findings and this precludes strong conclusions.

Principles for Treating Depressed Patients

Nine studies on depressed or largely depressed samples were extracted from the review by Beutler, Malik, et al. (2003) and by Sue and Lam (2002). Table 2.4 summarizes these studies and confirms the conclusion of Sue and Lam as applied to depressed patients. Specifically, older depressed patients experienced fewer gains than younger depressed patients in psychotherapy. The results suggest the validity of the following principle:

1. Age is a negative predictor of a patient's response to general psychotherapy.

INFERRED TRAITS THAT MODERATE TREATMENT EFFECTS

Client Expectations and Preferences

General Effects

Arnkoff, Glass, and Shapiro (2002) have summarized the results of research on client expectancies

and preferences for the Division 29 Task Force, largely restricting their review to the role of patient perceptions. They identified 24 studies that addressed the role of client expectations, 37 that addressed the effects of patient and therapist shared role expectancies, and 13 that addressed patient preferences for either therapy styles (roles) or type of therapy. They found an insufficient number of studies that addressed the effects of either confirming or disconfirming a patient's preferences for a therapist of a given ethnicity or sex. Hence, neither we nor they reviewed these latter studies.

Among the studies of various types of psychopathology, Arnkoff and colleagues found that the preponderance ($N = 12$ of 24) of those that addressed the impact of outcome expectancies revealed a positive relationship between the level of outcome expected by patients and that obtained. Seven studies on this topic found no relationship between outcome expectancy and benefit and seven found a complex relationship in which mediating variables played a role between expectation and outcome.

Likewise, among the 37 studies identified by Arnkoff and colleagues (2002) that addressed the effect of role expectations—the degree to which there is similarity between the actual and expected roles of patient and therapist in a given treatment—on treatment outcome, the majority ($N = 21$) found a positive relationship. The more patients and therapists agreed on the roles to be played by each during psychotherapy, the stronger the benefit achieved. The authors concluded that agreement in expected roles was a contributor to outcome.

Arnkoff and colleagues (2002) undertook a separate analysis of client preferences. They identified 16 studies that addressed either role preferences or preferences for the type of therapy used. Most of these studies failed to demonstrate a significant relationship between either of these types of preference and treatment outcomes.

Principles for Treating Depressed Patients

From the Arnkoff et al. (2002) review, we extracted those that had focused explicitly on patients with depression and reanalyzed the three types of expectancies on which they based their conclusions.

Among the 24 studies of outcome expectations identified by Arnkoff et al., only three were conducted on homogeneous samples of depressed patients. To broaden our review, we compared these three studies to nine that used a general outpatient sample in which depression was expected to be pervasive. Seven of the latter nine samples (Friedman, 1963; Goldstein & Shipman, 1961; Heine, 1962; Lipkin, 1954; Martin, Friedmeyer, Moore, & Claveaux, 1977; Tollinton, 1973; Uhlenhuth & Duncan, 1968) produced a significantly positive relationship between patient expectations of outcome and the level of benefit achieved using a variety of outcome measures. Interestingly, this result was not replicated in the depressed samples. Two of these latter studies (Hardy et al., 1995; Morrison & Shapiro, 1987) obtained indications of the presence of a moderating variable and one (Piper & Wogan, 1970) found nonsignificant results. Collectively, therefore, we were unable to confirm the promising findings of the Division 29 Task Force and conclude that outcome expectations do not consistently contribute to the treatment of clinically depressed patients to the degree that they appear to do so among other dysphoric groups.

To explore the effect of Role Expectations, we identified 13 studies from the original 37 reported by Arnkoff et al. (2002) that assessed the effects of Role Expectations on outcomes among depressed patients. Once again we failed to support the conclusions of Arnkoff et al., and there was no evidence that role expectations meaningfully affected the treatment of depressed samples. Only five of the 13 studies of depression found some positive results (Heine & Trosman, 1960; Kamin & Caughlan, 1963; Heine, 1962; Isard & Sherwood, 1964; Schonfield, Stone, Hoehn-Saric, Imber, & Pande, 1969). Four of the studies found largely nonsignificant findings (Brennan, 1990; Silverberg, 1982; Rosen & Wish, 1980; Volsky, Magoon, Norman, & Hoyt, 1965) and four found a moderating variable that differentially affected the results (Gaston, Marmar, Gallagher, & Thompson, 1989; Heppner & Heesacker, 1983; Martin, Sterne, & Hunter, 1976; Severinsen, 1966).

In a third analysis, we extracted from the 16 papers on preferences reviewed by Arnkoff et al. (2002), four studies that focused on clinically depressed samples. Only two of the latter studies

(Elkin et al., 1999; Chilvers et al., 2001) found that patient preferences contributed to benefit. The other two studies in this series (Addis & Jacobson, 1996; Hardy et al., 1995) found evidence of additional moderators that affected outcome.

Collectively, the foregoing applications to depressed populations failed to support the Division 29 conclusion in the specific case of depression and, instead, indicate that:

1. Principles related to preference and expectance are not sufficiently well defined to be applied to the clinical treatment of depressed patients.

Stages of Change

General Effects

Prochaska and Norcross (2002), reviewing the literature for the Division 29 Task Force, concluded that "different processes of change are differentially effective in certain stages of change" (p. 308). They support this conclusion with a variety of research studies, including a meta-analysis (Rosen, 2000) of 47 of these studies. The samples in these studies range from substance abuse, where the concept of "stages of change" has been used extensively and quite successfully, to "exercise, diet, and psychotherapy" (p. 308). They conclude that effect sizes are relatively large when the construct of stages of change are considered to be differential moderators of treatment effects, and cite a large number of impressive research studies to support this contention.

The Division 29 Task Force, following the lead of Prochaska and Norcross, conclude that consideration of the patient's stage of change in assigning behaviorally or insight-oriented treatments is a promising and probably effective means of enhancing the fit of treatment and patient.

Principles for Treating Depressed Patients

Although a large number of studies are cited by Prochaska and Norcross (2002) in support of patient level or stage of change and the fit of various treatments, this literature has not addressed the role of these factors in treating depression. Only three studies have addressed mental health, non-substance abusing populations, who might be considered to be rather dysphoric and anxious (Brogan, Prochaska, & Prochaska, 1999; Mc-Connaughy, Prochaska, & Velicer, 1983; McConnaughy, DiClemente, Prochaska, & Velicer, 1989), and none of these studies inspected subsamples of depressed patients. The absence of appropriate studies and associated findings render it impossible to adequately evaluate the role of stages of change in treating depression. However, in concert with our default position, in such cases, we find no reason to refute the Division 29 conclusion that a patient's stage of change is a predictor of how well various kinds of psychotherapy might work. Thus, we offer the following working principle:

1. Patient stage of change is a promising (but not proven) variable for fitting patient and treatment and for predicting the level of intervention in which to engage the patient.

Assimilation of Problematic Experiences

General Effects

The assimilation model is a framework to understand change in psychotherapy in terms of particular problematic experiences, instead of changes in a person as a whole. The model suggests that clients will progress through a particular continuum of stages in successful psychotherapy. The eight levels of the model are summarized in the Assimilation of Problematic Experiences Scale (APES; Stiles et al., 1991), labeled 0 to 7: (0) warded off/dissociated; (1) unwanted thoughts/active avoidance; (2) vague awareness/emergence; (3) problem statement/clarification; (4) understanding/insight; (5) application/working through; (6) resourcefulness/problem solution; and (7) integration/mastery. The levels are not considered to be discrete entities, but rather markers along a continuum of change.

Stiles (2002) described a number of studies that have provided support to the assimilation model. As a result, the assimilation of problematic experiences as been retained as a "promising and probably effective" means of customizing therapy by the Division 29 Task Force (Norcross, 2002). As noted by Stiles (2002), the "assimilation model has been most intensively studied with respect to

time-limited (8–20 session) psychotherapy for depression" (p. 360). A first set of empirical investigations (interpretative studies) described by Stiles involves several case studies, which together suggest that the assimilation of problematic experiences follow a pattern that is consistent with the APES.

Principles for Treating Depressed Patients

Of the examples reviewed by Stiles (2002), two reports that describe three case studies involved samples of clinically depressed clients (Field, Barkham, Shapiro, & Stiles, 1994; Honos-Webb, Stiles, Greenberg, & Goldman, 1998) and four case studies (from three reports) involved mixed anxiety and depressed clients (Stiles, Morrison, Haw, Harper, et al., 1991; Stiles, Shapiro, & Harper, 1994; Stiles, Shapiro, Harper, & Morrison, 1995). Based on a second set of studies (hypothesis-testing studies), Stiles (2002) also suggested that clients' APES level of their presenting problem may have an impact on their aptitude for benefiting from one form of treatment as opposed to another (e.g., a client who comes early in therapy with a clear statement of a problem improves more in cognitive behavior therapy than in psychodynamic-interpersonal therapy). The two studies cited in this second set of examples were conducted with purely depressed samples (Stiles, Barkham, Shapiro, & Firth-Cozens, 1992; Stiles, Shankland, Wright, & Field, 1997).

Taken together, the nine empirical studies reviewed above suggest the following principle of change:

1. Benefit may be enhanced when the interventions selected are responsive to and consistent with the patient's level of problem assimilation.

Patient and Therapist Religion and Spirituality

General Effects

The wide interest expressed by scholars in the role of religious and spiritual values and beliefs on the therapy relationship and process has not translated to a large number of research studies applying these concepts to psychotherapy outcome. Most studies of religion have investigated its role in psychopathology and mental health (e.g., Gartner, Larson, & Allen, 1991). Indeed, the Division 29 Task Force on relationships concluded that insufficient research had been conducted on this topic to draw clear conclusions. The review of literature by Worthington and Sandage (2002) for that Task Force provided few additional references over that undertaken nearly a decade earlier (Worthington, Kurusu, McCullough, & Sandage, 1996). Given these conclusions, we will devote the current section of this chapter to a consideration of studies that have addressed religion in various ways, among depressed and dysphoric samples of patients. Specifically, we will concentrate on shared aspects of client–therapist religion and spirituality as related to (a) beliefs and values and (b) efforts to incorporate client religious values in religion accommodative therapy among these dysphoric and depressed samples.

While the terms "religious" and "spiritual" are often used interchangeably, it is useful to distinguish them from one another (Richards & Bergin, 2000). Following the logic of Worthington et al. (1996), "religious" is used in the current context to refer to the degree of commitment or acceptance of a particular faith or organized religious dogma. In contrast, "spiritual" is used to refer to one's subjective sense of personal faith and subjugation to a higher power. Thus, religious people may be said to hold religious beliefs and value religion.

While a significant number of therapists and counselors indicate they are religiously and/or spiritually oriented, and even religiously active (Kelly, 1995), they are often reluctant to examine client presenting issues in spiritual or religious contexts, often considering such themes as inappropriate topics for psychotherapy (Beutler, Machado, & Neufeldt, 1994; Worthington & Sandage, 2002). This viewpoint presents an interesting contrast if not an ethical conundrum in view of the observations that the vast majority (90+%) of Americans consider themselves religious and/or spiritual (Richards & Bergin, 2000). Most of these individuals (79+%), in contrast to their therapists, consider religious values as important topics in therapy (Quackenbos, Privette, & Klentz, 1985).

The methodology of studies examining the impact of religious and spiritual values, value convergence, and client–therapist values similarity on psychotherapy are usually analogue in nature, and infrequently include an assessment of treatment outcomes. They largely examine the influence of client religious values on perceptions of therapists and therapy, and the ramifications of these preferences and expectations for therapy outcome. Only a very small number of studies address client–therapist spirituality and none focus on non-Judeo-Christian values and beliefs.

Principles for Treating Depressed Patients

Our review of studies in the area of values and beliefs that affect treatment outcome is limited to those studies that address (a) value convergence and (b) patient–therapist similarity of religious values. Those studies, as applied to the treatment of depressed samples, are reported in Table 2.5.

Value Convergence

Psychotherapy is far from value free (e.g., Bergin, 1980, 1991; Beutler, Machado, & Neufeldt, 1994; Gibson & Herron, 1990), and patient values tend to converge with those of their therapists in successful treatment (Beutler, Crago, & Arizmendi, 1986; Beutler, Machado, & Neufeldt, 1994; Worthington & Sandage, 2002). However, compared to personal and mental health values, religious values are among the least susceptible to this type of convergence and generally resist change during psychotherapy (Beutler, Machado, & Neufeldt, 1994; Kelly & Strupp, 1992).

Client–Therapist Match

Two studies (see Table 2.5) have examined the effects of client–therapist matching on religious values among depressed samples and have found that a pattern of both similarity and dissimilarity among various values may contribute to improvement (Propst, 1980; Propst et al., 1992). Generally, depressed religious clients receiving religiously congruent cognitive therapy fared better with nonreligious therapists trained to deliver religious therapy than those with therapists who were committed to similar religious beliefs.

Table 2.5
Religion and Spirituality

Study	N	Diagnosis	Outcome effects
		1. Client values: client–therapist match	
Propst, 1980	44	Mild depression	Ss receiving therapy from nonreligious therapists were more improved in religious CBT and religious placebo treatment groups than in standard CBT and wait-list groups
Propst et al., 1992	59	Nonpsychotic, nonbipolar depressive disorder	Religious content CBT and pastoral counseling groups improved in depression and adjustment scores more than those in standard CBT and wait-list conditions; CBT success based on performance of nonreligious therapists with religious Ss
		2. Religious-accommodative studies	
Christian accommodative			
Pecheur & Edwards, 1984	21	Research Diagnostic Criteria for depression	Significant effect of treatment on depression scores at posttreatment and 1-year follow-up (no significant differences between secular and religious versions of CBT; both groups outperform wait-list condition)
Propst, 1980	44	Mild depression	Significant positive effect of treatment on depression scores (religious CBT outperformed self-monitoring and secular CBT treatment groups)
Propst et al., 1992	59	Nonpsychotic, nonbipolar depressive disorder	Significant positive effect of treatment on depression and adjustment scores at posttreatment and follow-up at 3 months and 2 years (religious content CBT and pastoral counseling outperformed standard CBT and wait-list conditions)
Johnson & Ridley, 1992	10	Depression	Significant effect of treatment on depression, automatic negative thought, and depressive irrational beliefs (both religious and secular rational emotive therapy (RET) groups improved on depression and negative thoughts scores, only religious RET group improved on irrational thought measure)
Johnson, DeVries, Ridley, Pettorini & Peterson, 1994	32	Depression	No significant differential effect of treatment on depression and depression-related measures (both religious and secular versions of RET equally improve client depression, automatic negative and irrational thinking, and general pathology)
McCullough, 1999 Meta-analysis of 5 studies noted above	166	Depression	No significant differential effect of treatment on depression and depression-related measures (both standard and religious accommodative versions are equally effective)
Muslim accommodative			
Azhar & Varma, 1995a	30	Major Depressive Disorder (bereavement)	Significant differential effect of treatment on depression scores (patients receiving supportive psychotherapy and medication were less improved than those who also received religious psychotherapy)

(continued)

Table 2.5
(continued)

Study	N	Diagnosis	Outcome effects
		2. Religious-accommodative studies	
Azhar & Varma, 1995b	64	DSM-III R Dysthymic Disorder	Significant differential effect of treatment on depression scores (patients receiving supportive psychotherapy and medication were less improved than those who also received religious psychotherapy. At six months, group differences were nonsignificantly)
Christian group accommodative			
Hawkins, Tan, & Turk, 1999	29	Depression	Significant positive relationship between reduction in depression and spiritual well-being (SWB)
			No significant differential effect of treatment on reduction in depression scores (both Christian and secular CBT performed equally well)
			Significant differential effect of treatment on SWB scores (clients in Christian CBT scored higher than those in secular CBT)
Richards, Owen, & Stein, 1993	15	Perfectionistic and depressed	Significant positive effect of religiously oriented treatment on depression and perfectionistic scores (no control or comparison group)
Rye, 1999	58	Women hurt in romantic relationships	Significant differential effect of treatment on measures of depression, anger, hurt, and avoidance of hope (students in secular forgiveness group improved more in these areas than those in religiously integrated forgiveness group or nontreatment control)

Note. From Worthington & Sandage, 2002.

Religion-Accommodative Approaches

Accommodative therapies insert religious themes into interpretations and directly address religious beliefs and values, frequently offering religion-based solutions for the patient's problems (e.g., recommending prayer). Religiously oriented therapies have compared well to a variety of alternative treatments for various problems (e.g., lay counseling [Toh & Tan, 1997]; pastoral counseling [Propst et al., 1992]; and 12-step approaches to substance abuse [Humphreys, 1999]). However, these accommodative studies often neglect the effects of the therapeutic alliance and several suffer from serious methodological limitations (Worthington & Sandage, 2002).

Christian-accommodative individual therapies. Worthington and Sandage (2002) report the re-sults of a meta-analysis of five treatment outcome studies of cognitive therapy for depression. These studies are cited in Table 2.5. All five studies integrated client religious beliefs into treatment strategies through the use of such procedures as religious imagery, prayer, and religiously based challenges of irrational beliefs. Three of the five studies compared standard and Christian accommodative versions of cognitive-behavioral therapy (CT) and two compared standard and accommodative versions of rational emotive therapy (RET).

Of those studies that adapted CT to accommodate religious beliefs, one (Pecheur & Edwards, 1984) found nonsignificant differences among religious, CT, and wait-list control groups. Two other controlled studies revealed significant advantages favoring both CT and religious placebo conditions over secular therapy. The first of these, using student volunteers and nonreligious therapists found that both religious CT and religious placebo groups outperformed the standard CT and wait-list groups. The second, and later, study found not only that patients in the religious CT and pastoral counseling groups were more improved than the secular counseling groups on depression and social adjustment scores at post-treatment, but that these group differences were attributable to the superior performance of nonreligious therapists in the religious CT group. Additionally, religious counselors had greater success with standard than with religiously constructed CT, and religious subjects in the secular CT/nonreligious therapists group were the least improved. The interaction between therapist religiousness and type of CT indicated that clients improved the most when there was intermediate, rather than low or high levels of similarity to the values of the therapist or correspondence with the orientation of the therapy itself.

Of the two outcome studies reviewed by Worthington and Sandage (2002) in which comparisons were made between standard and Christian-adapted versions of RET, neither found significant differences in outcome among the treatments. However, standard and Christian-modified RET reduced depression and negative thought in both studies. Thus, the weight of evidence fails to confirm the advantages of Christian-modified and adapted treatments over standard interventions. This general conclusion is illustrated by the meta-analysis reported by Worthington and Sandage who found a nonsignificant difference in mean effect size ($d = .18$) between the standard and modified versions.

Muslim-accommodative individual therapies. Worthington and Sandage (2002) found only three studies that compared a religiously based therapy and an alternative treatment among devout Muslim patients. Two studies compared religious therapy with supportive psychotherapy and medication among depressed samples (see Table 2.5). In both studies, clients who received religiously based therapy had significantly better outcomes than those whose therapy did not include a focus on religious beliefs. The significant gains were maintained at follow-up.

Based on only a sample of two studies, we do not believe that conclusions about the efficacy of accommodative therapy among Muslim patients can be reached, though this is a promising area of research.

Christian-accommodative group therapy. Three therapy studies have addressed Christian-accommodative treatments (see Table 2.5). Hawkins, Tan, and Turk (1999) assessed depression as well as spiritual and religious well-being and found significant improvement in depression at post-test, as well as a significant indirect relationship between depression and spiritual well-being. The observed changes in spiritual well-being, favoring those in the religious CT group, may have been a reflection of their high initial preference for religious therapy.

Richards, Owen, and Stein (1993) investigated an integrative Christian therapy based on the CT model, among Mormon undergraduate students who were attending a Mormon institution and who were deemed to be perfectionistic and depressed. Subjects improved significantly on both outcome measures, but the absence of a control group limited the available interpretation.

Finally, Rye (1999) investigated dysphoric college women who were recovering from being hurt in intimate relationships; participants were randomly assigned to a secular or religiously integrated forgiveness group, or a no-treatment control group. Both treatment groups were involved in activities, discussions, and homework assignments designed to foster forgiveness. Neither treatment group demonstrated differential treatment effects: both were equally efficacious on measures of forgiveness, hope, and existential as well as religious well-being and surpassed the control group at post-test and six-week follow-up. Additionally, while the secular forgiveness group improved significantly more on anger, hurt, and avoidance of hope measures, participants in both groups were found to use religiously based forgiveness strategies.

Conclusions

In summary, while the methodology in empirical research has become increasingly more sophisticated in its use of standardized measures, control procedures, and methods of quantitative analyses, there is little quantitative research in the area of religion and spirituality that is not analogue in nature, naturalistic in design, or based on case studies. As currently constituted, nonetheless, the empirical literature on religion and values provides tentative support for two principles:

1. If patients have a preference for religiously oriented psychotherapy, treatment benefit is enhanced if therapists accommodate this preference.
2. If psychotherapists are open, informed, and tolerant of various religious views, treatment effects are likely to be enhanced.

Attachment Style

General Effects

The interpersonal history of patient and therapist has an impact on the therapeutic process and its outcome. Various enduring and persistent ways of attaching to others—secure, anxious-ambivalent, dismissive-avoidant, and disorganized—are all potentially expressed in the therapeutic relationship (Bowlby, 1988). The clinical applications of attachment theory have recently begun to be explored through theory development (Bowlby, 1988; Blatt & Levy, in press; Diamond, Clarkin, Levine, Levy, et al., 1999; Farber, Lippert, & Nevas, 1995; Gunderson, 1996; Holmes, 1996; Levy & Blatt, 1999; Mackie, 1981; Sable, 1992; Shane & Shane, 2001; Slade, 1999; Szajnberg & Crittenden, 1997) and through empirical methods (Dozier, 1990; Dozier, Cue, & Barnett, 1994; Fonagy et al., 1996; Mallinckrodt, Gantt, & Coble, 1995; Tyrell et al., 1999). From this work, authors have begun to delineate how attachment classifications and dimensions contribute to understanding the quality and nature of psychotherapy process as well as psychotherapy outcome (e.g., Blatt, Shahar, & Zuroff, 2002). Research has suggested that patient attachment patterns are both a prognostic indicator of outcome and useful as a vehicle for understanding aspects of the psychotherapeutic process. Complicating the integration of findings to date is that the various studies have used different attachment measures with different patient groups in different types of therapy.

Psychotherapy Outcome as a Function of Attachment Status

From the literature reviewed for the Division 29 Task Force (Meyer & Pilkonis, 2002), there are seven studies that examined psychotherapy outcome as a function of attachment (Cyranowski et al., 2001; Dozier et al., 1994; Fonagy et al., 1996; Kilmann et al., 1999; Meyer et al., 2001; Mosheim et al., 2000; Tyrell et al., 1999). The results converge on four main findings: (a) securely attached patients tend to function better than other patients at both admission and discharge, (b) patients with preoccupied or unresolved attachment status tend to respond more poorly than patients with other attachment patterns and (c) securely attached patients appear to benefit more than other patients from brief treatment whereas dismissively attached, more severely impaired, patients appear to do better in long-term intensive treatment (Fonagy et al., 1996; see also Blatt, 1992; Blatt & Ford, 1994).

Meyer and Pilkonis (2002) speculate that patients with "dismissing attachment may require more concentrated . . . interventions, helping them overcome their characteristic detachment. Once they do connect emotionally with a therapist, however, improvement might be all the more dramatic."

Psychotherapy Process as a Function of Attachment

A series of studies have considered the attachment styles of therapists and their impact on the therapeutic process (Dozier et al., 1994; Hardy et al., 1998; Hardy et al., 2001; Kanninen et al., 2000; Rubino, Barker, Roth, & Fearon, 2000; Tyrell et al., 1999). Generally the findings have suggested that therapists with anxious-attachment styles tended to respond with less empathy, especially to patients with secure and dismissive attachment.

Relatedly, Eames and Roth (2000) found that securely attached patients tended to form an effective alliance whereas fearful avoidant patients tended to rate their alliance as weaker. Interestingly, some evidence also suggested that both preoccupied and dismissive attachment styles were both associated with more positive alliance ratings, but for different reasons. "Patients who yearn for intimacy and fear abandonment might strive with particular persistence to establish a close alliance, given their concerns about a possible rejection. In contrast, patients with dismissive styles might defensively deny problems in the alliance or establish only a superficial relationship while remaining reluctant to connect and self-disclose on a more genuine, personal level" (Eames & Roth, 2000). Consistent with this interpretation, preoccupied attachment was associated with more ruptures and dismissing attachment with fewer ruptures.

Dozier (1990) found that dismissing patients are often resistant to treatment and have difficulty asking for help and retreat from help when it is offered. Dismissing individuals often become more distressed and confused when confronted with emotional issues in therapy (Dozier, Lomax, Tyrell, & Lee, 2001). This observation led Dozier and colleagues to identify patterns of relationship that were likely to occur between patient and therapists with different attachment styles using the Adult Attachment Interview (AAI).

Patients in treatment with therapists who were dissimilar to them on the hyperactivating/deactivating (preoccupied to dismissing) dimension of attachment on the AAI proved to produce better therapeutic outcomes and stronger therapeutic alliances than their counterparts (Dozier et al., 1994; Tyrell et al., 1999). Clinicians classified as secure/autonomous on the AAI tended to challenge the patient's interpersonal style (whether deactivating or hyperactivating), whereas clinicians classified as insecure on the AAI were more likely to compliment the patients' interpersonal style (Dozier et al., 1994; Tyrell et al., 1999). Patients had the best outcome if treated by securely attached clinicians (defined on the AAI) or when the clinician was at the opposite side of the secure/autonomous continuum from the patient's AAI classification (e.g., patient rated preoccupied on AAI and therapist rated at the dismissing end of the autonomous category; Dozier et al., 1994). Consistent with prior research on client–clinician match (e.g., Beutler et al., 1991), the dissimilarities between patients and therapists interpersonal style appears to be advantageous, indicating that patients benefit from interventions that counteract their problematic style of relating to others. Overly emotional patients may require emotion-containing interventions whereas emotionally de-

tached patients may need interventions that facilitate their affective expression and connection (cf. Hardy et al., 1999; Stiles et al., 1998).

Different interpersonal or attachment styles of patients pull for different types of interventions from the therapist. While preoccupied patients pull for emotional-experiential interventions, they appear to benefit from a more cognitive-behavioral strategy that helps them modulate overwhelming feelings (Hardy et al., 1998, 1999). Likewise, avoidant patients pull for rational-cognitive interventions, but appear to benefit from strategies that facilitate emotional engagement (Hardy et al., 1999). Therapists need to recognize how a patient's attachment style influences their response to the patient and their ability to establish a therapeutic alliance.

Diamond and colleagues (Diamond et al., 1999) reported that two patients with borderline personality disorder, treated with Kernberg's Transference Focused Psychotherapy (TFP; Clarkin, Yeomans, & Kernberg, 1999) by the same therapist, progressed from insecure to secure attachment after one year of treatment. Consistent with previous research (e.g., Eames & Roth, 2000; Dolan et al., 1993; Dozier et al., 1994; Mallinckrodt et al., 1995; Tyrell et al., 1999), Diamond et al. noted, however, that each patient interacted with and affected the therapist in a very different way, and that the therapist responds very differently to each patient. The therapist was engaged and active in the treatment of the client initially classified as preoccupied, whereas, the same therapist was much less engaged, often felt dismissed and developed a much weaker therapeutic bond, with the patient initially classified as dismissive on the AAI.

Attachment as a Psychotherapy Outcome Measure

Three studies that employed attachment constructs as an outcome measure (Fonagy et al., 1995; Levy et al., 2004; Travis et al., 2001), Levy and colleagues (Levy, 2002; Levy & Clarkin, 2002; Levy, Clarkin, & Diamond, 2002) used the AAI to assess change in attachment status and reflective function in 25 patients over the course of a one-year long-term randomized clinical trial or in patients diagnosed with borderline personality disorder. Levy and colleagues found that all but two patients were initially rated as insecure with the majority having a primary AAI classification of unresolved for trauma and/or loss. The majority of patients showed a change in attachment after one year of treatment—some patients shifted from unresolved and insecure to secure, others to cannot classify or to a mixed attachment. In addition, they found a significant increase in patients' reflective function. Fonagy and colleagues (Fonagy et al., 1996) reported on changes in attachment status on the AAI for 35 nonpsychotic inpatients following one year of intensive psychodynamic psychotherapy. Although all 35 inpatients were classified as insecure during their initial Adult Attachment Interview, 14 or 40% of the 35 inpatients showed a shift to a secure classification upon discharge. Travis et al. (2001) examined change in attachment patterns over the course of time-limited dynamic psychotherapy in 84 patients and found that a significant number of clients changed from an insecure to a secure attachment pattern. Additionally, significant relationships were also found among changes in attachment, GAS scores, and symptom levels.

Principles for Treating Depressed Patients

From the list of studies on general psychiatric patients, cited in the foregoing, we were able to identify only six studies that employed a dysphoric or clinically depressed sample (see Table 2.6). This

Table 2.6
Attachment Styles

Type of study	N	Treatment	Disorder	Attachment measure	Findings
Outcome					
Cyranowski et al., 2002	162	IPT	Major Depression	RQ	½ women = fearful, no attachment difference in recovery rate, but fearful avoidance was related to delayed remittance
Meyer, Pilkonis, et al., 2001	149	University medical school clinic TAU	Depression, anxiety, substance abuse	Pilkonis prototypes	Security of attachment greater relative improvement
Hardy et al., 2001	24	Time-limited CBT	Depression	IIP	Highly avoidant subjects showed less improvement
Process studies					
Hardy et al., 1998	114	ST PI and ST CB	Depression	IIP	Therapist used more affective and relationship-oriented interventions with overinvolved clients and more cognitive treatments with underinvolved cases
Eames & Roth, 2000	30 of 43	24 CBT, 3 PDT, 1 CAT, 2 ecclectic TAU	General outpatients	RSQ	Fearful with lower alliance, secure with higher alliance, preoccupied & dismissing associated with increased alliance, preoccupied associated with more ruptures and dismissing less (gender differences?)
Attachment as outcome					
Travis et al., 2001	84	Time-limited dynamic therapy	Dysphoric outpatients	Bartholomew Attachment Rating Scale	Significant changes from insecure to attached

was not a sufficiently large sample to address the issue of whether attachment lent itself to do the three tasks described in the foregoing review: (1) predict outcomes, (2) predict process, or (3) serve as an outcome measure.

Three studies (Cyranowski et al., 2002; Hardy et al., 2001; Meyer, Pilkonis, et al., 2001) attempted to predict outcome on the basis of attachment, and all suggested that secure attachments were more predictive of improvement than insecure attachments. Beyond this tentative conclusion, however, little could be determined from the available research on depression.

Two studies (Hardy et al., 2001; Hardy et al., 1998) investigated the use of attachment to predict differential responses or other aspects of therapy process. These studies suggested that attachment may be a moderator of treatment, with affective and relationship-oriented interventions being selected by therapists for overinvolved clients and more cognitively oriented therapies for underinvolved patients. The rate of success, however, was not consistently associated with this selection of treatment strategy.

Another study in this set (Eames & Roth, 2000) found that one's attachment style was predictive of the type and strength of the alliance that developed. Fearful attachment styles were associated with low alliance scores, while secure attachments were associated with the development of higher therapeutic alliances. Preoccupied attachment styles tended to be associated with ruptures in the therapeutic alliance.

Finally, one study (Travis et al., 2001), using a general outpatient sample of dysphoric patients, found that treatment tended to evoke movement toward more stable and secure attachments.

While the preponderance of available studies address aspects of therapy process rather than outcomes, we find sufficient evidence in the foregoing to offer a tentative principle:

1. A secure attachment pattern in both patient and therapist appears to facilitate the treatment process.

Beyond this, the findings do not permit a clear conclusion about the role of attachment as a moderator or contributor to psychotherapy. This remains, as defined by the Division 29 Task Force, a promising variable in the study and prediction of response to psychotherapy.

Resistance

General Effects

Patient resistance, particularly when defined as a trait-like quality of the patient's response to the therapy, has received a good deal of research attention in recent years. Summarizing the results of 11 studies on resistance-like traits on eventual treatment outcome, Beutler, Moleiro, and Talebi (2002) indicate that 82% found clear and negative relationships with various indices of therapeutic output. Similar findings are observed when the sample is restricted to those studies that involved depressed samples.

Principles for Treating Depressed Patients

Table 2.7 presents 18 studies that were originally identified by Beutler, Moleiro, and Talebi (2002) and by Beutler, Malik, et al. (2003), that involved the treatment of depressed samples. The seven studies (Addis & Jacobson, 2000; Beutler, Clarkin, & Bongar, 2000; Beutler, Mohr, Grawe, Engle, & McDonald, 1991; Joyce, Ogrodniczuk, Piper, & McCallum, 2000; Last, Thase, Hersen, Bellack, & Himmelhoch, 1984; Neimeyer & Feixas, 1990; Persons, Burns, & Perloff, 1988) among these that investigated the direct effect of patient resistance-like qualities on treatment outcome all found a negative relationship between resistance and outcome. It should be noted that four of these studies used, as an indicator of resistance, the degree to which patients complied with homework assignments (Addis & Jacobson, 2000; Neimeyer & Feixas, 1990; Last et al., 1984; Persons, Burns, & Perloff, 1988). This narrow view of "resistance" may temper the results, but their consistency with the other studies in this set suggest that there is a relatively robust but negative relationship between level of trait-like resistance and treatment outcome. Since resistance in these studies is represented, frequently, as an ongoing process, the findings also suggest that interventions that avoid inducing resistance are likely to be most effective with most patients.

A related question relates to how one can best

Table 2.7
Resistance and Directiveness

Study	N	Diagnosis	Outcome effects
		. Patient resistance	

From Beutler, Moleiro, & Talebi, 2002

Study	N	Diagnosis	Outcome effects
Addis & Jacobson, 2000	150	Major Depressive Disorder	Positive effect of acceptance of treatment rational and homework compliance on within-treatment change and treatment outcome for depression, with homework compliance contributing to additional change
Beutler, Clarkin, & Bongar, 2000	284	Depression, dysthymia	Patients with high interpersonal resistance respond better with minimal structure, self-directed interventions, nondirective procedures or paradoxical directives; those with low interpersonal resistance, to directive interventions and clinician guidance
Beutler, Engle, Mohr, et al., 1991	63	DSM-III Major Depressive Disorder	Differential effect of patient defensiveness (resistance potential) on depression scores at posttreatment: Low resistance Ss improve more in group cognitive behavior & focused expressive (authoritative) therapies; high resistance Ss in supportive/self-directed therapy
Beutler, Machado, Engle, & Mohr, 1993	49	Major Depressive Disorder	Differential effect of patient resistance potential on depression scores at posttreatment maintained at 1-year-follow-up: greater improvement of high resistance Ss in supportive/self-directed therapy & low-resistance Ss in group cognitive-behavior and focused expressive psychotherapies. Number asymptomatic Ss at follow-up match number at treatment-end
Beutler & Mitchell, 1981	40	Nonpsychotic, nonmedicated, impulsive externalizers and depressive internalizers (MMPI)	Positive effect of treatment on outcome (experiential treatment procedures have positive effect overall; analytic treatments most effective with depressive anxious, and least effective with impulsive externalizing patients)
Beutler, Mohr, Grawe, et al., 1991	60	Moderate & Major Depression (nonpsychotic)	Interactive effects of treatment and level of reactance potential (for cognitive and focused-expressive therapy, high reactance potential negatively related to treatment benefit; for supportive/self-directed therapy nonauthoritative positive relationships are shown)
Greenberg & Watson, 1998	34	Major Depression	No significant differential effect of treatment on depression scores at posttreatment and 6-month follow-up (both process experiential and client-centered groups improve equally). Superior effects of experiential therapy at mid-treatment on depression and at posttreatment on symptoms, self-esteem, and interpersonal problems

Study	N	Diagnosis	Outcome effects
		Patient resistance	
Joyce, Ogrodniczuk, Piper, & McCallum, 2000	144	Axis 1: Major depression (49%), dysthymia (26%), and personality disorders. 47% comorbid	Significant interaction effect of patient qualities and treatment on mid-treatment outcome (for interpretive therapy at mid-treatment high psychologically minded Ss had better outcomes on well-being and current symptoms, high reactance patients had poorer outcomes on current life dysfunction)
Joyce & Piper, 1996	60	Axis 1: adjustment (28%), affective (22%); Axis II: dependent (13%) & 15% are co-morbid with depression	Transference-oriented approach: Significant effect of use of transference interpretation on outcome (for high quality of object-relations [QOR] patients, transference focus + patient work is inversely related to posttherapy outcome for depression and symptom distress) Pretreatment anxiety/symptom distress related to work performance (significant degree of pretherapy anxiety and distress among high QOR Ss can promote work with transference oriented approach)
Last, Thase, Hersen, Bellack, & Himmelhoch, 1984	120	Unipolar depression	No significant differential effect of treatment (skills training, psychotherapy, or drug therapy) on solicited and unsolicited Ss on depression, assertiveness, and social adjustment scores (groups improve equally; no differences in level of attrition)
Neimeyer & Feixas, 1990	63	Research Diagnostic Criteria: unipolar depression	Significant positive effect of homework compliance on positive change in depression symptoms at posttreatment (pretreatment depression scores controlled) Significant positive effect of homework compliance on positive change in depression symptoms at follow-up (pretreatment depression not controlled)
Persons, Burns, & Perloff, 1988	70	Major Depressive, Dysthymic, Bipolar, & Cyclothymic Disorders	Significant effect of initial depression scores, endogenous symptoms, homework compliance on posttreatment depression scores. The effect of homework substantially larger for Ss with high initial depression. Homework compliers improved three times as much as noncompliers Homework compliance: Patients not completing homework more likely to drop out. Dropout possible expression of resistance. Completers average 65.5% reduction in depression scores

(continued)

Table 2.7
(continued)

Study	N	Diagnosis	Outcome effects
		Patient resistance	
Piper, Joyce, McCallum, & Azim, 1998	144	DSM-III-R Major Depressive Disorder, Dysthymic Disorder, & personality disorders; 73% with previous psychiatric treatment	Positive effect of symptom-focused supportive therapy on change in depression scores and global symptomatic distress at posttreatment (supportive vs. interpretive therapy)
Klausner et al., 1998	13	Major Depressive Disorder; residual depressive symptoms	Significant positive effect of directiveness on positive change in depressed mood at post-treatment (Goal Focused group vs. reminiscence therapy)
McLean & Hakstian, 1990	121	Major Depression	Negative effect of directiveness on positive change in depression scores at 2¼ year follow-up (Behavior, Relaxation vs. Nondirective therapy) Significant positive effect of homework compliance on positive change in depression symptoms at follow-up (pretreatment depression not controlled)
Shapiro et al., 1995	104	DSM-III Major Depressive Episode	Positive effect of directiveness on maintenance of gains at 12-month follow-up (cognitive-behavioral vs. psychodynamic-interpersonal)
Shaw et al., 1999	36	Research Diagnostic Criteria: Major Depression	Significant positive effect of directiveness (as session structure in CBT) on positive change in depression scores at posttreatment (pretreatment depression severity and adherence controlled) No effect of therapist directiveness (as session structure) on psychiatric symptom distress scores at posttreatment (pretreatment depression severity and adherence controlled)
Stiles & Shapiro, 1994	39	Present State Examination Index of Definition Category System: depression (77%), anxiety disorders	Positive effect of directiveness on rate of change in depression scores at end-point (cognitive behavioral questions, General Advisement vs. psychodynamic-interpersonal interpretation, exploratory reflections) Positive effect of directiveness on rate of change in global symptom distress scores at end-point (CB questions, General Advisement vs. PI interpretation, exploratory reflections)

deal with resistance when it is present or when the patient embodies a trait-like quality of resistance at the outset of therapy. This question bears on the degree to which patient resistance traits determine what treatments will be effective. In addressing this question, Beutler, Moleiro, and Talebi identified 20 studies that had inspected the differential effects of directive and nondirective treatments as a function of patient resistance traits. Sixteen of these studies (80%) found a significant interaction effect, all of which indicated that (1) high resistant patients did poorly when treated with directive interventions, (2) that low resistant patients did quite well with directive interventions, (3) high resistant patients did best when treated with evocative and nondirective interventions, and (4) low resistant patients did best with highly structured and directed therapies

Of the 20 studies identified by Beutler, Moleiro, and Talebi, 16 were conduced on a depressed sample and are reported in Table 2.7. The results are consistent with the overall finding, with all but two of the studies revealing at least a partial moderating effect of patient resistance traits on the effectiveness of either directive or nondirective treatment, or both. Collectively, the results suggest the validity of the following principles:

1. The most effective treatments are likely to be those that do not induce patient resistance.
2. In dealing with the resistant patient, the therapist's use of directive therapeutic interventions should be planned to inversely correspond with the patient's manifest level of resistant traits and states.

Functional Impairment

General Effects

Beutler, Harwood, Alimohamed, and Malik (2002) reviewed the relationship between the severity of the patient's problems, as expressed in level of social functioning, and the effectiveness of different aspects of psychotherapy procedures. They identified a cluster of variables that seemed to constitute level of functioning. This cluster was comprised of low levels of social support, high levels of social alienation, and multiple areas of reduced functioning, as comprising "Impairment." Collectively, they concluded with Sperry, Brill, Howard, and Grissom (1996), that impairment was best reflected in reduced functioning at work, within intimate and nonintimate relationships, in self-care activities, and in levels of social responsibility assumed. Among these, the level of social support felt by the patient was among the most highly related (inversely) to general estimates of functional impairment levels.

Beutler, Harwood, Alimohamed, and Malik (2002) found a consistent but inverse relationship between initial level of functional impairment and eventual outcome. Seventy-seven percent of the

42 studies reviewed supported this conclusion. Table 2.8 reports the results of the 39 studies from this latter review that addressed the specific problem of depression. These studies demonstrate the consistency of the relationship between level of functioning (or, inversely, functional impairment) and subsequent outcome. High initial levels of impairment were associated with lessened likelihoods and magnitudes of benefit following treatment in nearly 80% of the studies. Notably, however, two studies (Ackerman, Greenland, & Bystritsky, 1994; Lueger, 1996) found that level of impairment actually enhanced the level of improvement achieved and nine of the 11 studies that inspected differential effects found that impairment level moderated the effects of different treatments. High levels of impairment retarded the effects of emotionally focused therapy among inpatients (Beutler, Frank, Scheiber, Calvert, & Gaines, 1984), but low levels of impairment were associated with improved functioning following emotion-focused therapy among outpatients (Beutler, Kim, Davison, Karno, & Fisher, 1996); lengthening treatment or increasing its intensity seemed to overcome some of the negative effects of high impairment levels (Hoglend, 1993; Moos, 1990), an effect that may be especially noted among the interpretive or insight-focused therapies (Joyce, Ogrodniczuk, et al., 2000); and impairment level was positively associated with the likelihood of receiving beneficial effects of pharmacotherapy (Elkin et al., 1995; Ravindran et al., 1999).

Principles for Treating Depressed Patients

Collectively, the available studies on depression (Table 2.8) fail to reveal a single treatment that is better, overall, than others for the treatment of patients with high levels of functional impairment. Two conclusions are warranted, however, and can be extracted as principles of treatment application:

1. Patients who enter treatment with high levels of functional impairment tend to do poorly relative to other patients.
2. Patients with high levels of initial impairment respond better when they are offered long-term, intensive treatment, than when

Table 2.8
Functional Impairment

Study	N	Diagnosis	Outcome effects
From Beutler, Harwood, Alimohamed, & Malik, 2002			
Ackerman, Greenland, & Bystritsky, 1994	520	Obsessive-Compulsive Disorder	Significant relationship between response and baseline depression scores. Higher initial scores more predictive of good response
Andrew, Hawton, Fagg, & Westbrook, 1993	59	Major Depressive Disorder	Negative effect of low self-esteem on depression scores for suicidal women
Barkham, Rees, et al., 1996	212	Most with Major Depressive Disorder	Significant effect of length of treatment on outcome (at treatment end Ss in 8-session group improve more than those at mid-treatment in 16-session group on most measures, i.e., diminished returns from longer treatment) More Ss improve on depression measures than on interpersonal patterns; among depressive symptoms, faster change for those related to acute distress, slower change for those that were characterological
Beutler, Clarkin, & Bongar, 2000	284	Depression, dysthymia	Significant inverse relationship of functional impairment and treatment outcome (high levels indicate poor prognosis, may indicate longer term and intensive treatment)
Beutler, Frank, Scheiber, Calvert, & Gaines, 1984	176	Dysphoric including Major Depressive Disorder	Differential treatment effects on outcome: systematic deterioration among patients in expressive experiential group; best results in interactive process-oriented group which maintained gains at 13-month follow-up
Beutler, Kim, Davison, Karno, & Fisher, 1996	63	Major Depression	Initial distress inversely related to therapy efficacy For low distress patients, clinicians rate cognitive therapy more effective than focused expressive psychotherapy
Burvill, Hall, Stampfer, & Emmerson, 1991	103	Major Depression	No clear effect of chronic physical illness, severity of depression, or severe life events on outcome at 12-month follow-up
Dadds & McHugh, 1992	22	Single parents of conduct problem children	No significant differential effect of treatment (child management training with/without ally support training) on outcome: both groups improve equally on measures of parent depression, social support and behavior, and child deviance Responders more likely than nonresponders to report high levels of social support
Elkin et al., 1995	239	Major Depressive Disorder	Significant interaction effects of initial severity of depression and functional impairment and treatment type on treatment outcome For low initial severity, no effect of treatment type on outcome (all treatments equally effective; CBT = IPT = IMI-CM = PLA-CM)

Study	N	Diagnosis	Outcome effects
			For high initial severity, significant effect of treatment type on outcome (IMI-CM superior to CBT, IPT, and PLA-CM for more severely ill; IPT superior to CBT for more severely depressed) No differences among treatment at 18-month follow-up
Ellicott, Hammen, Gitlin, Brown, & Jamison, 1990	61	Bipolar Disorder	Significant effect of life events and levels of stress on likelihood of relapse: Ss with high stress levels showed greater likelihood of relapse or recurrence; those with low or average stress showed risk of relapse equal to those who stayed well
Fountoulakis, Tsolaki, & Kazis, 2000	50 elderly	DSM-IV Major Depression, Dysthymia	Significant positive effect of pharmacotherapy (fluvoxamine) on depressive thought content and daily functioning at three months
Gitlin, Swendsen, & Heller, 1995	82	Bipolar Disorder	73% risk of relapse into mania or depression after 5 years of maintenance pharmacotherapy; high affective morbidity for those who do not relapse Cumulative affective morbidity stronger correlate of psychosocial functioning than # of relapses Poor psychosocial functioning predicts shorter time to relapse Depression related most strongly to family and social dysfunction
Hardy, Barkham, Shapiro, et al., 1995	114	Depression, Personality Disorders, Non-Personality Disordered	Significant effect of initial symptomology and treatment type on treatment outcome (depression and personality disorder: higher levels initially correlate with higher levels at posttreatment and 1-year follow-up; Ss with severe depression less improved posttreatment than those with less severe depression or non-personality disordered Ss)
Hoencamp, Haffmans, Duivenvoorden Knegtering, & Dijken, 1994	88	Major Depressive Disorder	Differential effects of initial depression, personality disorder, and social functioning: Ss with somatization and passive aggressive personality show poorer response to pharmacotherapy than those with obsessive-compulsive personality and/or high initial level of depression
Hoglend, 1993	45	DSM-III personality disorders, Dysthymia, Major Depression, adjustment, anxiety disorders	Significant positive effect of treatment length on positive dynamic change at 4-year-follow-up ($\geq$ 30 sessions of dynamic psychotherapy show improved problem-solving capacity, self-esteem, interpersonal functioning)
Imber et al., 1990	250	Research Diagnostic Criteria:Major Depression	Positive effect of symptom-focus on improvement in global symptoms at posttreatment (cognitive-behavioral vs. interpersonal therapy) Improved need for social approval CBT>IPT, IMI-CM, placebo

(continued)

Table 2.8
(continued)

Study	N	Diagnosis	Outcome effects
Joyce, Ogrodniczuk, Piper, & McCallum, 2000	144	Axis 1: Major depression (49%), dysthymia (26%), and personality disorders. 47% comorbid.	Significant interaction effect of patient qualities and treatment on mid-treatment outcome (for interpretive therapy at mid-treatment, high psychologically minded Ss had better outcomes on well-being and current symptoms, high reactance patients had poorer outcomes on current life dysfunction)
Keijsers, Hoogduin, & Schaap, 1994	40	Obsessive Compulsive Disorder	Negative effect of depression on treatment outcome. High severity of agoraphobic complaints is strongest predictor
Lueger, 1996	243	Distress, anxiety, depression, anger, problems with romantic partner or spouse, reacting too emotionally to events	Feedback on problem severity, early response to therapy, symptom remediation, and improvement in life functioning predict treatment success Higher severity results in more improvement on average
Maling, Gurtman, & Howard, 1995	307	Axis I or II diagnosis, interpersonal distress	Inverse relationship of salience and distressfulness of interpersonal problems and response to therapy: control issues found more responsive, self-effacing problems more intractable
Mazure, Nelson, & Jatlow, 1990	52	DSM III-R nonpsychotic unipolar Depressive Disorder	Negative association of initial depression severity, melancholia, and panic disorder with response to 1 week of hospitalization without antidepressants. About 50% of non-melancholic and non-panic disordered patients required hospitalization plus medication
McLean & Taylor, 1992	151	Unipolar Depressive Disorder	For severely depressed, nonsignificant effect of treatment on posttreatment depression scores (nondirective psychotherapy, behavior therapy, pharmacotherapy, and relaxation training are not differentially effective)
Mintz, Mintz, Arruda, & Hwang, 1992	Review of 10 studies	Depressive illness	2 studies indicate (a) Significant effect of treatment on work restoration: tricyclic antidepressants restored work more rapidly than psychotherapy (b) Significant effect of treatment duration on work restoration i.e. depressive symptoms improve more rapidly than outcome for work
Moos, 1990	265	Unipolar depression	Negative effect of family conflict and lack of social support on treatment outcome Significant effect of treatment length and level of support on outcome: Ss with high levels of social and family support improve with brief therapy; Ss with low levels of support have better outcome with longer treatment

Study	N	Diagnosis	Outcome effects
Ogles, Sawyer, & Lambert, 1995	162	Major Depressive Disorder.	No differences in clinical significance rates among treatment groups (cognitive-behavioral, interpersonal, pharmacotherapy + clinical management and placebo + clinical management) on measures of depressive symptoms
Prudic, Sackeim, Davanand, & Kiersky, 1993	100	Major Depressive Disorder, double depression	No differential effect of electro-convulsive treatment on depression scores at treatment end for Ss with MDD or double depression Ss with double depression had more residual symptoms posttreatment than Ss with MDD Double depressed also more likely to relapse in year following treatment
Ravindran et al., 1999	97	Primary Dysthymia	Significant differential effect of treatment on functional impairment of depression (improvement with sertraline with/without cognitive behavior therapy exceeded that of CBT alone; effects of CBT equaled those of placebo treatment)
Scogin, Bowman, Jamison, Beutler, & Machado, 1994	133	Mild, moderate, & major depression	Results failed to replicate previous findings of a poorer response to treatment for participants higher in dysfunctional thinking. Cognitive therapy may not be contraindicated for persons evidencing higher levels of dysfunctional thinking
Shapiro, Rees, et al., 1995	104	DSM-III Major Depressive Episode	Positive effect of directiveness on maintenance of gains at 12-month follow-up (CB vs. PI)
Shea et al., 1992	239	Research Diagnostic Criteria: Major Depression	Positive effect of symptom-focus on maintenance of gains (absence of relapse for treatment responders) at 18-month follow-up (cognitive behavioral vs. interpersonal therapy)
Sotsky et al., 1991	239	Major Depressive Disorder	Depression severity, social and cognitive dysfunction, expectation of improvement, endogenous depression, double depression, and current episode duration predicted outcome
Spangler, Simons, Thase, & Monroe, 1997	53	Depression	Significant positive effect of cognitive behavioral treatment on posttreatment depression scores No significant effect of pretreatment cognitive dysfunction or negative stressors on posttreatment outcome
Thase, Simons, Cahalane, McGeary, & Harden, 1991	59	Major Depression with endogenous features	No significant effect of depression severity on depression or global scores posttreatment (more or less severe groups improve equally and at comparable rates), however, more severely depressed tend to remit less completely
Vallejo, Gasto, Catalan, Bulbena, & Menchon, 1991	116	Major Depression with melancholic features	No significant effect of depression severity on pharmacotheraphy outcome. Social support is positively associated with favorable outcome

(continued)

Table 2.8
(continued)

Study	N	Diagnosis	Outcome effects
Veiel, Kuhner, Brill, & Ihle, 1992	190	Discharged depressed patients	No significant effect of stable personality traits on recovery, but for recovered patients severe long-term life difficulties and efforts to seek social support are less likely, while negative outlook and problem avoidance are more likely
Woody et al., 1984	110	Non-psychotic opiate addicts	Low-severity patients made equal progress with drug counseling alone or with psychotherapy Significant effect of added psychotherapy on depression and symptom distress outcome measure for Ss with more severe psychiatric symptoms
Zlotnick et al., 1996	188	Major Depressive Disorder	Correlational 6-month follow-up number of satisfying supports was significant predictor of depressive symptoms. Positive effect of social support on severity of depression posttreatment

they receive nonintensive and brief treatments, regardless of the particular model and type of treatment assigned. Patients with low impairment seem to do equally well in high and low intensive treatments.

Coping Style

General Effects

Coping style subsumes a number of specific concepts and assumptions, ranging from those that are derived from rational logic and theory to those that are descriptive and empirically derived. Rational definitions are extrapolated from observations and assume that patterns of behavior merely reflect the presence of some quality of inner life that characterizes and stabilizes one's behavior. In contrast, empirical definitions rely only on the correlated nature of behaviors to define common qualities or aspects of behavior (Beutler, Malik, et al., 2003). This review will reflect this diversity and will present findings on coping styles ranging from the general to the specific and including both descriptive and theoretical perspectives.

Coping Style as an Empirically Derived Concept

"[C]oping styles" are habitual and enduring patterns of behavior that characterize the individual when confronting new or problematic situations. Thus, coping styles are not discrete behaviors but are a cluster of related behaviors that are distinguished because they are repetitive, enduring, and observable when problems are being addressed. (Beutler, Harwood, et al., 2002, p. 147)

This definition of general coping styles emphasizes that coping styles are defined by the presence of recurring, related behaviors. The recurrence of similar patterns defines these behaviors as being trait-like, and places their measurement squarely within the context of personality variables. Thus, from this general perspective, one's coping style is not merely observed during times of stress, but transcend situational factors and describe one's usual way of being in the world of other people. This view asserts that coping styles are arranged on one or more continua, the most frequently described ranging from "externalizing" patterns in

Table 2.9
Patient Coping Style

Study	N	Diagnosis	Outcome/effects
Beutler, Harwood, et al., 2002			
Barber & Muenz, 1996	250	Major Depressive Disorder	Significant interaction effect of treatment and personality type on depression scores (avoidant patients improve more with cognitive therapy, obsessing clients with interpersonal therapy)
Beutler, Clarkin, & Bongar, 2000	284	Depression, dysthymia	Significant negative effect of functional impairment on likelihood of improvement (prognosis); improvement may be facilitated by high levels of social support. Positive effect of long-term and intensive treatment on functional impairment
Beutler, Engle, Mohr, et al., 1991	63	Major Depressive Disorder	Significant interaction effect of treatment and coping style on depression scores (externalizing patients improve more with group cognitive therapy, internalizing with supportive self-directed therapy)
Beutler, Machado, Engle, & Mohr, 1993	49	Major Depressive Disorder	Significant interaction effect of treatment and coping style on depression scores (externalizing patients improve more with group cognitive therapy, internalizing with supportive self-directed therapy; improvement maintained at 1-year follow up)
Beutler & Mitchell, 1981	40	Dysphoric	Significant interaction effect of treatment and coping style on outcome (impulsive externalizers improve more with experiential therapy, depressive anxious with analytic therapy)
Beutler, Mohr, et al., 1991	131	Moderate depression	Significant effect of coping style and treatment on depression outcome (poorly controlled externalizers improve more with cognitive therapy, more controlled internalizing best with supportive self-directed therapy)
Calvert, Beutler, & Crago, 1988	108	Dysphoric (include Bipolar Affective Disorder, Major Depressive Disorder and Dysthymic Disorder)	Significant interaction of coping style and treatment on outcome (internalizing patients improved more in feelings and behavior with insight-awareness-oriented therapy, while externalizers improved in feelings with behavior-oriented therapy)

which one behaves impulsively, actively, and excessively, to "internalizing" in which one behaves more sedately, distantly, and cognitively. Externalizers deal with the processes of life in active, impulsive, undercontrolled, even gregarious ways. They seek stimulation and are not prone to reason their way through situations as they arise. In contrast, internalizers are prone to use rational and intellectual means for managing their relationships with other people. They are slow to decide, thoughtful, and even self-deprecatory and self-demanding.

In their Division 29 Task Force review, Beutler, Harwood, and colleagues (2002) identified 19 studies that had used some measure of coping style as a potential moderator of treatment efficacy. Fifteen (79%) of these found a clear, differential treatment effect. However, only seven studies have been conducted on groups of homogeneous, depressed patients (see Table 2.9). Nonetheless, all seven found interaction effects in which patients who presented with externalizing coping styles tended to be most receptive to treatments that emphasized skill building, direct behavior change, cognitive management, and symptom reduction procedures. Similarly, those who were classified as internalizers have been prone to benefit the most from models of treatment that emphasized the quality of interpersonal relationships, insight as a method of overcoming problems, and self-understanding.

The consistency of these results suggests that coping style is a moderator of treatment and calls for the differential application of symptom and skill-focused treatments, on one hand, and insight or interpersonal and relationship-focused treatments, on the other. The significance of this finding and conclusion becomes even clearer when it is added to the results of research that addresses theoretical distinctions among coping responses.

Coping Style as a Rational Concept

Blatt and colleagues (e.g., Blatt, 1974, 1995; Blatt & Blass, 1996; Blatt & Shichman, 1983) proposed that personality develops along two fundamental developmental lines—(a) a relatedness (anaclitic) line that involves the development of the capacity to establish mature, mutually satisfying interpersonal relationships, and (b) a self-definitional (introjective) line that involves the development of a consolidated, realistic, essentially positive, differentiated, and integrated self-identity. These two developmental lines evolve throughout life in a dialectic transaction. An increasingly differentiated, integrated, and mature sense of self is contingent on establishing satisfying interpersonal relationships and, conversely, the development of mature and satisfying interpersonal relationships is contingent on the development of a mature self-identity.

Severe and repeated disruptions of this reciprocally balanced, interactive process, at various points in development, can lead to psychopathology. Individuals usually cope with severe developmental disruptions by placing extreme emphasis on one of a small number of fundamental strategies. Females tend to cope with developmental disruptions by becoming preoccupied with interpersonal relatedness while males tend to become preoccupied with issues of self-definition. Thus, various forms of psychopathology can be conceptualized as involving an over-emphasis and exaggeration of one of these developmental lines and the defensive avoidance of the other. This distorted over-emphasis defines two distinct configurations of psychopathology, each containing several types of disorders.

Anaclitic psychopathologies are disorders in which patients are primarily preoccupied with interpersonal issues of trust, caring, intimacy—from more dependent to more mature reciprocal relationships—and use primarily avoidant defenses (e.g., denial and repression). From more to less disturbed, anaclitic disorders include borderline personality disorder, infantile (or dependent) character disorder, anaclitic depression, and the hysterical personality disorder. In contrast, introjective psychopathologies includes disorders that are primarily concerned about establishing and maintaining a viable sense of self, ranging from a basic separateness, through concerns about autonomy and control, to more complex internalized issues of self-worth—and to use counteractive defenses (projection, rationalization, intellectualization, doing and undoing, reaction formation, overcompensation). Introjective patients are more ideational and concerned with establishing, protecting, and maintaining a viable self-concept. Anger and aggression, directed toward the self or others, are usually central to their difficulties. Introjective disorders, ranging from more to less severely disturbed, include the over-ideational borderline, paranoia, and obsessive-compulsive personality disorders; introjective (guilt-ridden) depression, and phallic narcissism (Blatt, 1974, 1995; Blatt & Shichman, 1983).

The distinction between anaclitic and introjective styles of relating has been particularly useful in defining subtypes of depressed patients (e.g., Blatt, 1974, 1998; Blatt, D'Afflitti, & Quinlan, 1976; Blatt et al., 1982). Investigators from different theoretical positions have discussed two major types of depressive experiences: (a) disruptions of gratifying interpersonal relationships (e.g., object loss), and (b) disruptions of an effective and essentially positive sense of self (e.g., guilt, failure). Depressed patients, primarily responsive to one or the other of these two types of experiences, have been characterized by psychoanalytic investigators as anaclitic and introjective (e.g., Blatt, 1974, 1998; Blatt & Shichman, 1983) or dependent and self-critical (Blatt, D'Afflitti, & Quinlan, 1976; Blatt et al., 1982), as dominant other and dominant goal (Arieti & Bemporad, 1980), and anxiously attached and compulsively self-reliant (Bowlby, 1980). In a more recent cognitive-behavioral formulation, Beck (1983), congruent with these psychoanalytic formulations, differentiated between a socially dependent (sociotropic) and an autonomous type of depression. In addition, Blatt (Blatt et al., 1976) and Beck (1983), and their respective colleagues, have developed instruments to assess dependency (sociotopy) and self-criticism (autonomy). Also experienced clinical judges achieved substantial inter-rater agreement about this distinction based on initial case reports (Blatt, 1992; Blatt & Ford, 1994). This anaclitic/introjective distinction was used in three studies of the therapeutic process.

In the *Riggs-Yale Project Research Review* (Blatt & Ford, 1994), therapeutic change was studied in 90 seriously disturbed, treatment-resistant patients who sought long-term, intensive, psychoanalytically oriented, inpatient treatment, including at least four times weekly psychoanalytically-oriented psychotherapy. Introjective patients generally had indications of greater therapeutic progress after, on average, 15 months of treatment, as assessed across a wide range of measures. In addition, systematic differences between anaclitic and introjective patients were found in independent measures of therapeutic change. Introjective patients expressed their change primarily in the intensity of clinical symptoms, as assessed from case reports, and in cognitive functioning, as reliably assessed on psychological tests administered at the beginning and toward the end of treatment (thought disorder on the Rorschach and measures of intelligence). Therapeutic change in anaclitic patients was expressed primarily in changes in their interpersonal relationships, as rated from case reports, and in representations of the human figure on the Rorschach. Thus, anaclitic and introjective patients changed primarily in the modalities of their basic concerns and preoccupations.

The *Menninger Psychotherapy Research Project (MPRP)* undertook analyses of data from the MPRP, comparing the outcome of anaclitic and introjective outpatients treated in psychoanalysis or in long-term supportive-expressive psychotherapy (Blatt, 1992). These analyses indicated that anaclitic and introjective patients were differentially responsive to psychotherapy and psychoanalysis. Based on the evaluation of object representation

(Urist, 1973) on Rorschach protocols at the beginning and end of treatment, anaclitic patients had significantly greater positive change in psychotherapy than in psychoanalysis, while introjective patients had significantly greater positive change in psychoanalysis than in psychotherapy. It seemed consistent that more dependent, interpersonally oriented, anaclitic patients would respond more effectively in a therapeutic context in which there is more direct interaction with the therapist. It also seems consistent that more ideational introjective patients, who stress separation, autonomy, and independence, would respond more effectively in psychoanalysis. This statistically significant ($p <$ .001) patient-by-treatment interaction indicates that a congruence between patients' character style and aspects of the therapeutic situation facilitated treatment outcome.

Depressed patients were the focus in the *Treatment of Depression Collaborative Research Program (TDCRP)*. The NIMH sponsored TDCRP (e.g., Elkin et al., 1989) compared three forms of treatment for depression: interpersonal therapy (IPT), cognitive behavioral therapy (CBT), and imipramine plus clinical management (IMI-CM), with a double-blind placebo plus clinical management (PLA-CM). In the primary analyses of their data, the TDCRP investigators found "no evidence of greater effectiveness of one of the psychotherapies as compared with the other and no evidence that either of the psychotherapies was significantly less effective than . . . imipramine plus clinical management" (Elkin, 1994, p. 971). IPT and IMI-CM, however, were more effective than CBT with severely depressed and functionally impaired patients.

Further analyses of data from the TDCRP, however, indicate the importance of the anaclitic and introjective distinction. These dimensions were introduced into analyses of the TDCRP data by patients' pretreatment scores on the two subscales of the Dysfunctional Attitude Scale (DAS; Weissman & Beck, 1978); Need for Approval (NFA) and Perfectionism (PFT). Previous studies have shown links between these two DAS scales and the anaclitic (dependent) and introjective (self-critical) personality configurations, respectively (e.g., Blaney & Kutcher, 1991).

While NFA tended to facilitate treatment outcome, results failed to reach statistical significance.

Consistent significant effects, however, were found with PFT. Patients' PFT predicted poorer outcome at termination (i.e., after 16 weeks of treatment), as well as at a follow-up 18 months after termination of treatment (Blatt et al., 1995; Blatt et al., 1998). Further analyses revealed that PFT significantly impeded therapeutic progress in two-thirds of the sample, primarily in the latter half of treatment (Blatt et al., 1998) by disrupting patients' interpersonal relations both in treatment and in social relationships outside of treatment (Shahar et al., 2001; Zuroff et al. 2000). Even further, patients with higher pretreatment PFT were more vulnerable to stressful life events during follow-up, leading to increased depression, because they failed at termination to develop a capacity to cope with stressful life events (Zuroff et al., 2001).

Studies of self-critical perfectionism (e.g., Blatt et al., 1979; Mongrain, 1998; Zuroff & Duncan, 1999) suggest that perfectionistic (introjective) individuals have malevolent, harsh, and punitive representations of significant others that interfere with interpersonal relations. In the course of therapy, introjective patients appear to project these negative representations onto the therapist, thus disrupting the therapeutic alliance. Therapists need to be aware of how they are perceived by perfectionist patients early in the course of treatment and how these negative representations limit the capacity of patients to participate in the therapeutic alliance. Thus, treatment with perfectionist patients takes time and patience, and therapists need to be sensitive to the interpersonal processes, within the patient and themselves, that limit the ability of these patients to gain from brief treatment. Data (Blatt, Stayner, Auerbach, & Behrends, 1996) suggest that patients at moderate levels of PFT are able to gain from brief treatment if early in the treatment process they perceive the therapist as empathic, open, and available.

In addition, therapists should be alert to ways in which perfectionistic patients generate a negative social environment outside of treatment. PFT not only interferes with the therapeutic alliance, but it also interferes with patients' establishing and maintaining supportive social relations (Shahar et al., 2001).

Anaclitic and introjective patients come to treatment with different types of problems, different character styles, different needs, and are responsive in different ways to different types of therapeutic intervention. Specifically, perfectionistic patients need to feel early on that the therapeutic relationship is accepting and nonjudgmental—helping them perceive themselves and others in less critical ways—thus facilitating their entering actively into the therapeutic process and understanding more fully how their negative anticipation of self and others impairs their capacity to establish satisfying relationships.

Principles for Treating Depressed Patients

There are obvious similarities between the rational and empirical descriptions of coping styles. For purposes of summary, it is easy to assume that the anaclitic and externalizing descriptions identify the same group of patients and correspondingly, that the introjective and internalizing descriptors apply to similar patterns of behavior. With this consolidation, it is apparent that introjective/internalizing patients and anaclitic/externalizing patients come to treatment with different types of problems, different character styles, different needs, and are responsive in different ways to different types of therapeutic intervention. The identification of patients' personality organization from a theoretical stance can enhance therapists' understanding of their patients' responses to the treatment process and to stressful events that occur in their lives.

Collectively, the current results support the development of two related principles, as follows:

1. Patients whose personalities are characterized by impulsivity, social gregariousness, and external blame for problems benefit more from direct behavioral change and symptom reduction efforts, including building new skills and managing impulses, than they do from procedures that are designed to facilitate insight and self-awareness.
2. Patients whose personalities are characterized by low levels of impulsivity, indecisiveness, self-inspection, and over control tend to benefit more from procedures that foster self-understanding, insight, interpersonal attachments, and self-esteem, than they do from procedures that aim at directly altering symptoms and building new social skills.

DEFINITION AND
CONSOLIDATION OF PRINCIPLES

The current review reveals 18 principles that we believe can be reliably extracted from clinical research literature and applied to treating depressed patients. Four of these principles simply state that evidence is unavailable to support the role of a given variable in the improvement of depressed patients.

1. Research on gender effects is insufficient for a clear judgment of effects on the treatment of depressed patients to be made.
2. Principles related to preference and expectance are not sufficiently well defined to be applied to the clinical treatment of depressed patients.
3. Insufficient research has been conducted on SES to determine if it is a contributor to treatment outcome for depressed patients.
4. Patient stage of change is a promising (but not proven) variable for fitting patient and treatment and for predicting the level of intervention in which to engage the patient.

Thus, effectively 14 principles identify a quality and characteristic of the patient or therapist that can be used in predicting and planning treatment programs. Of these, eight identify variables that relate to patient prognosis and likelihood of change, without regard to the type of treatment employed.

1. Patients representing underserved ethnic or racial groups achieve fewer benefits from conventional psychotherapy than patients from Anglo-American groups.
2. If patients and therapists come from the same or similar racial/ethnic backgrounds, dropout rates are positively affected and improvement is enhanced.
3. If psychotherapists are open, informed, and tolerant of various religious views, treatment effects are likely to be enhanced.
4. Co-morbid personality disorders are negative prognostic indicators in the psychological treatment of depressed patients.
5. Age is a negative predictor of a patient's response to general psychotherapy.

6. Patients who enter treatment with high levels of functional impairment tend to do poorly relative to other patients.
7. A secure attachment pattern in both patient and therapist appears to facilitate the treatment process.
8. The most effective treatments are likely to be those that do not induce patient resistance.

These eight principles can help a therapist determine the degree to which services may be useful and can, therefore, help one set priorities and make referrals.

The remaining six principles relate to ways to fit and match the therapy to particular characteristics of the patient.

1. Benefit may be enhanced when the interventions selected are responsive to and consistent with the patient's level of problem assimilation.
2. If patients have a preference for religiously oriented psychotherapy, treatment benefit is enhanced if therapists accommodate this preference.
3. In dealing with the resistant patient, the therapist's use of directive therapeutic interventions should be planned to inversely correspond with the patient's manifest level of resistant traits and states.
4. Patients with high levels of initial impairment respond better when they are offered long-term, intensive treatment, than when they receive nonintensive and brief treatments, regardless of the particular model and type of treatment assigned. Patients with low impairment seem to do equally well in high and low intensive treatments.
5. Patients whose personalities are characterized by impulsivity, social gregariousness, and external blame for problems benefit more from direct behavioral change and symptom reduction efforts, including building new skills and managing impulses, than they do from procedures that are designed to facilitate insight and self-awareness.
6. Patients whose personalities are characterized by low levels of impulsivity, indecisiveness, self-inspection, and over control tend

to benefit more from procedures that foster self-understanding, insight, interpersonal attachments, and self-esteem, than they do from procedures that aim at directly altering symptoms and building new social skills.

These six principles reflect broadly on both objective traits that can be used for matching with a class of therapists and moderating characteristics that can be used to fit treatments to patient needs. Demographic factors, for example, bear on the advisability of matching patient and therapist background characteristics, while personality and developed attributes bear on the question of fitting and selecting.

These principles collectively bring focus on another, broader issue and associated principle that we believe is important both to advancing research on treatment and advancing the effectiveness of our treatments. In the beginning of this chapter we drew attention to the difficulty of differentiating among factors that are "owned" by the patient, therapist, relationship, and treatment. The magnitude of this difficulty only appears to be greater as we review the foregoing principles of change. Virtually all variables that contribute to outcome involve some interaction among participant, treatment, and relationship factors, to such a degree that distinguishing among them is only possible in an abstract way. The pervasiveness of this interaction suggests that therapists and researchers alike would benefit from reconsidering the unit of analysis in discussing and understanding psychological treatment. Norcross (2002), in summarizing the Division 29 Task Force on the empirically supported therapeutic relationship, concluded that the unit of analysis should be the therapeutic dyad. We would add that even this emphasis may be too simple.

The unit of observation in psychotherapy must encompass the totality of participants, relationships, and treatment events. The balance and priority among these contributors is not entirely known, and at this point, teasing apart of these dimensions in order to assign such priorities and to apportion percentages of variance to attributed constructs is arbitrary and misleading. There can be no treatment without all being involved and they are involved within a pattern of intercorrelations. One can view any treatment as a cloud, comprised of particles and dewdrops, no one of which will give one an understanding of the nature of treatment. This is a true case of the whole being greater than the sum of its parts and we believe that a principle of good conceptualization is one that views the whole as a pattern, not the particles and individual and independent parts.

The latter overarching principle, as well as the 15 specific ones from which it derives, suggests the need for a high level of understanding, flexibility, and skill and for the possession of a wide range of therapeutic skills, on the part of the therapist. Therapists who can appreciate and adapt to patient differences, are aware of cultural factors and beliefs, and who are able to apply insight, behavioral, directive, and nondirective treatments within both a short-term and long-term or intensive format, will likely be maximally or optimally effective in facilitating change among depressed patients.

Editors' Note

1. A. E. Bergin and S. L. Garfield, alternating the senior position, edited the first four editions of this handbook. M. J. Lambert is the Editor of the 5th edition. In the 5th edition, the single process chapter is replaced by several, more specific chapters on aspects of therapeutic processes.

References

Ackerman, D. L., Greenland, S., & Bystritsky, A. (1994). Predictors of treatment response in obsessive-compulsive disorder: Multivariate analyses from a multicenter trial of comipramine. *Journal of Clinical Psychopharmacology, 14*, 247–253.

Addis, M. E., & Jacobson, N. S. (1996). Reasons for depression and the process and outcome of cognitive-behavioral psychotherapies. *Journal of Consulting and Clinical Psychology, 64*, 1417–1424.

Addis, M. E., & Jacobson, N. S. (2000). A closer look at the treatment rationale and homework compliance in cognitive behavioral therapy for depression. *Cognitive Therapy and Research, 24*, 313–326.

Alnaes, R., & Torgersen, S. (1997). Personality and personality disorders predict development and relapses of major depression. *Acta Psychiatrica Scandinavica, 95*, 336–342.

Andreoli, A., Frances, A., Rex-Fabry, M., Aapro, N., Gerin, P., & Dazord, A. (1993). Crisis intervention in depressed patients with and without SDM-III-R disorders. *Journal of Nervous and Mental Disease, 181,* 732–737.

Andrew, B., Hawton, K., Fagg, J., & Westbrook, D. (1993). Do psychosocial factors influence outcome in severely depressed female psychiatric in-patients? *British Journal of Psychiatry, 163,* 747–754.

Arieti, S., & Bemporad, J. R. (1980). The psychological organization of depression. *American Journal of Psychiatry, 137*(11), 1360–1365.

Arnkoff, D. B., Glass, C. R., & Shapiro, S. J. (2002). Expectations and preferences. In J. C. Norcross (Ed.), *Psychotherapy relationships that work* (pp. 335–356). New York: Oxford University Press.

Azhar, M. Z., & Varma, S. L. (1995a). Religious psychotherapy as management of bereavement. *Acta Psychiatrica Scandinavia, 91,* 223–235.

Azhar, M. Z., & Varma, S. L. (1995b). Religious psychotherapy in depressive patients. *Psychotherapy and Psychosomatics, 63,* 165–173.

Banikiotes, P. G., & Merluzzi, T. V. (1981). Impact of counselor gender and counselor sex role orientation on perceived counselor characteristics. *Journal of Counseling Psychology, 28,* 342–348.

Barber, J. P., & Muenz, L. R. (1996). The role of avoidance and obsessiveness in matching patients to cognitive and interpersonal psychotherapy: Empirical findings from the Treatment of Depression Collaborative Research Program. *Journal of Consulting and Clinical Psychology, 64*(5), 951–958.

Barkham, M. R., Rees, A., Stiles, W. B., Shapiro, D. A., Hardy, G. E., & Reynolds, S. (1996). Dose-effect relations in time-limited psychotherapy for depression. *Journal of Consulting and Clinical Psychology, 64*(5), 927–935.

Beck, A. T. (1983). Cognitive therapy of depression: New perspectives. In P. J. Clayton & J. E. Barrett (Eds.), *Treatment of depression: Old controversies and new approaches* (pp. 265–290). New York: Raven.

Beck, D. F. (1988). *Counselor characteristics: How they affect outcomes.* Milwaukee, WI: Family Service of America.

Bergin, A. E. (1980). Behavior therapy and ethical relativism: Time for clarity. *Journal of Consulting and Clinical Psychology, 48*(1), 11–13.

Bergin, A. E. (1991). Values and religious issues in psychotherapy and mental health. *American Psychologist, 46*(4), 394–403.

Bergin, A. E., & Garfield, S. L. (Eds.). (1971). *Handbook of psychotherapy and behavior change* (1st ed.). New York: John Wiley & Sons.

Bergin, A. E., & Garfield, S. L. (Eds.). (1994). *Handbook of psychotherapy and behavior change* (4th ed.). New York: John Wiley & Sons.

Beutler, L. E., Clarkin, J. F., & Bongar, B. (2000). *Guidelines for the systematic treatment of the depressed patient.* New York: Oxford University Press.

Beutler, L. E., Crago, M., & Arizmendi, T. G. (1986). Therapist variables in psychotherapy process and outcome. In S. L. Garfield & A. E. Bergin (Eds.), *Handbook of psychotherapy and behavior change* (3rd ed., pp. 257–310). New York: John Wiley & Sons.

Beutler, L. E., Engle, D., Mohr, D., Daldrup, R. J., Bergan, J., Meredith, K., & Merry, W. (1991). Predictors of differential response to cognitive, experiential, and self-directed psychotherapeutic techniques. *Journal of Consulting and Clinical Psychology, 59,* 333–340.

Beutler, L. E., Frank, M., Scheiber, S. C., Calvert, S., & Gaines, J. (1984). Comparative effects of group psychotherapies in a short-term inpatient setting: An experience with deterioration effects. *Psychiatry, 47,* 66–76.

Beutler, L. E., Harwood, T. M., Alimohamed, S., & Malik, M. (2002). Functional impairment and coping style: Patient moderators of therapeutic relationships. In J. Norcross (Ed.), *Psychotherapy relationships that work: Therapists' relational contributors to effective psychotherapy* (pp. 145–170). New York: Oxford University Press.

Beutler, L. E., Kim, E. J., Davison, E., Karno, M., & Fisher, D. (1996). Research contributions to improving managed health care outcomes. *Psychotherapy, 33,* 197–206.

Beutler, L. E., Machado, P. P., Engle, D., & Mohr, D. (1993). Differential patient X treatment maintenance of treatment effects among cognitive, experiential, and self-directed psychotherapies. *Journal of Psychotherapy Integration, 3,* 15–32.

Beutler, L. E., Machado, P. P. P., & Neufeldt, S. A. (1994). Therapist variables. In A. E. Bergin & S. L. Garfield (Eds.), *Handbook of psychotherapy and behavior change* (4th ed., pp. 229–269). New York: John Wiley & Sons.

Beutler, L. E., Malik, M., Alimohamed, S., Harwood, T. M., Talebi, H., Noble, S., & Wong, E. (2003). Therapist variables. In M. J. Lambert (Ed.), *Handbook of psychotherapy and behavior change* (5th ed., pp. 227–306). New York: John Wiley & Sons.

Beutler, L. E., & Mitchell, R. (1981). Differential psychotherapy outcome among depressed and impulsive patients as a function of analytic and experiential treatment procedures. *Psychiatry: Journal for the Study of Interpersonal Processes, 44*, 297–306.

Beutler, L. E., Mohr, D. C., Grawe, K., Engle, D., & McDonald, R. (1991). Looking for differential effects: Cross-cultural predictors of differential psychotherapy efficacy. *Journal of Psychotherapy Integration, 1*, 121–142.

Beutler, L. E., Moleiro, C., & Talebi, H. (2002). Customizing psychotherapy to patient resistance. In J. Norcross (Ed.), *Psychotherapy relationships that work: Therapists' relational contributors to effective psychotherapy* (pp. 129–143). New York: Oxford University Press.

Blaney, P. H., & Kutcher, G. S. (1991). Measures of depressive dimensions: Are they interchangeable? *Journal of Personality Assessment, 56*(3), 502–512.

Blatt, S. J. (1974). Levels of object representation in anaclitic and introjective depression. *Psychoanalytic Study of the Child, 29*, 107–157.

Blatt, S. J. (1998). Contributions of psychoanalysis to the understanding and treatment of depression. *Journal of the American Psychoanalytic Association, 46*, 723–752.

Blatt, S. J. (1992). The differential effect of psychotherapy and psychoanalysis on anaclitic and introjective patients: The Menninger psychotherapy research project revisited. *Journal of the American Psychoanalytic Association, 40*, 691–724.

Blatt, S. J., & Blass, R. B. (1996). Relatedness and self-definition: A dialectic model of personality development. In *Development and vulnerability in close relationships* (pp. 309–338). England: Lawrence Erlbaum Associates.

Blatt, S. J., D'Afflitti, J. P., Quinlan, D. M. (1976). Experiences of depression in normal young adults. *Journal of Abnormal Psychology, 85*(4), 383–389.

Blatt, S. J., & Ford, R. (1994). *Therapeutic change: An object relations perspective.* New York: Plenum.

Blatt, S. J. & Levy, K. N. (2003). Attachment Theory, Psychoanalysis, Personality Development, and Psychopathology. *Psychoanalytic Inquiry, 23*, 104–152.

Blatt, S. J., Quinlan, D. M., Chevron, E. S., McDonald, C., & Zuroff, D. (1982). Dependency and self-criticism: Psychological dimensions of depression. *Journal of Consulting and Clinical Psychology, 50*, 113–124.

Blatt, S. J., Quinlan, D. M., Pilkonis, P. A. & Shea, T. (1995). Impact of perfectionism and need for approval on the brief treatment of depression: The National Institute of Mental Health Treatment of Depression Collaborative Research Program Revisited. *Journal of Consulting and Clinical Psychology, 63*, 125–132.

Blatt, S. J., Shahar, G., & Zuroff, D. C. (2001). Anaclitic (sociotropic) and introjective (autonomous) dimensions. *Psychotherapy: Theory, Research, Practice, Training, 38*(4), 0033–3204.

Blatt, S. J., Shahar, G., & Zuroff, D. C. (2002). Anaclitic (sociotropic) and introjective (autonomous) dimensions. In J. Norcross (Ed.), *Psychotherapy relationships that work: Therapists' relational contributors to effective psychotherapy* (pp. 315–333). New York: Oxford University Press.

Blatt, S. J., & Shichman, S. (1983). Two primary configurations of psychopathology. *Psychoanalysis & Contemporary Thought, 6*(2). 187–254.

Blatt, S. J., Stayner, D., Auerbach, J., & Behrends, R. S. (1996). Change in object and self-representations in the long-term, intensive, inpatient treatment of seriously disturbed adolescent and young adults. *Psychiatry: Interpersonal and Biological Processes, 59*, 82–107.

Blatt, S. J., Wein, S. J., Chevron, E. S., & Quinlan, D. M. (1979). Parental representations and depression in normal young adults. *Journal of Abnormal Psychology, 88*, 388–397.

Blatt, S. J., Zuroff, D. C., Bondi, C. M., Sanislow, C., & Pilkonis, P. (1998). When and how perfectionism impedes the brief treatment of depression: Further analyses of the NIMH TDCRP. *Journal of Consulting and Clinical Psychology, 66*, 423–428.

Bowlby, J. (1980). *Attachment and loss: Vol. 3. Loss.* New York: Basic Books.

Bowman, D., Scogin, F., Floyd, M., & McKendree-Smith, N. (2001). Psychotherapy length of stay and outcome: A meta-analysis of the effect of therapist sex. *Psychotherapy: Theory, Research & Practice, Training, 38*(2), 142–148.

Brennan, M. J. (1990). Client–counselor role expectations and outcomes of counseling. *Dissertation Abstracts International, 50*(11), 5307B.

Brill, N. Q., & Storrow, H. A. (1960). Social class and psychiatric treatment. *Archives of Psychiatric Treatment, 3*, 340–344.

Brown, C., Schulberg, H. C., Sacco, D., Perel, J. M., & Houck, P. R. (1999). Effectiveness of treatments for major depression in primary medical care practice; A post-hoc analysis of outcomes for African Americans and white patients. *Journal of Affective Disorders*, *53*, 185–192.

Burvill, P. W., Hall, W. D., Stampfer, H. G., & Emmerson, J. P. (1991). The prognosis of depression in old age. *British Journal of Psychiatry*, *158*, 64–71.

Calvert, S. J., Beutler, L. E., & Crago, M. (1988). Psychotherapy outcomes as a function of therapist–patient matching on selected variables. *Journal of Social and Clinical Psychology*, *6*, 104–117.

Cantor, D. W. (1991). Women as therapists: What we already know. In D. W. Cantor (Ed.), *Women as therapists: A multitheoretical casebook* (pp. 3–19). New York: Springer.

Chilvers, C., Dewey, M., Fielding, K., Gretton, V., Miller, P., Palmer, B., Weller, D., Churchill, R., Williams, I., Bedi, N., Duggan, C., Lee, A., & Harrison, G. (2001). Antidepressant drugs and generic counseling for treatment of major depression in primary care: Randomised trial with patient preference arms. *British Medical Journal*, *322*, 772–791.

Choi, J. L., Lew, S., Vittinghoff, E., Catania, J. A., Barrett, D. C., & Coates, T. J. (1996). The efficacy of brief group counseling in HIV risk reduction among homosexual Asian and Pacific Islander men. *AIDS*, *10*, 81–87.

Clarkin, J. F., Yeomans, F. E., & Kernberg, O. F. (1999). *Psychotherapy for borderline personality*. New York: John Wiley & Sons.

Craig, T. J., & Huffine, C. L. (1976). Correlates of patient attendance in an inner-city mental health clinic. *American Journal of Psychiatry*, *133*, 61–65.

Cyranowski, J. M., Bookwala, J., Feske, U., Houck, P., Pilkonis, P., Kostelnik, B., & Frank, E. (2002). Adult attachment profiles, interpersonal difficulties, and response to interpersonal psychotherapy in women with recurrent major depression. *Journal of Social and Clinical Psychology*, *21*, 191–217.

Dadds, M. R., & McHugh, T. A. (1992). Social support and treatment outcome in behavioral family therapy for child conduct problems. *Journal of Consulting and Clinical Psychology*, *60*, 252–259.

Dembo, R., Ikle, D. N., & Ciarlo, J. A. (1983). The influence of client–clinician demographic match on client treatment outcomes. *Journal of Psychiatric Treatment and Evaluation*, *5*, 45–53.

Diamond, D., Clarkin, J., Levine, H., Levy, K.,

Foelsch, P., & Yeomans, F. (1999). Borderline conditions and attachment: A preliminary report. *Psychoanalytic Inquiry*, *19*, 831.

Diguer, L., Barber, J. P., & Luborsky, L. (1993). Three concomitants: Personality disorders, psychiatric severity and outcome of dynamic psychotherapy of major depression. *American Journal of Psychiatry*, *150*, 1246–1248.

Dolan, R. T., Arnkoff, D. B., & Glass, C. R. (1993). Client attachment style and the psychotherapist's interpersonal stance. *Psychotherapy: Theory, Research, Practice, Training*, *30*(3), 408–412

Dozier, M. (1990). Attachment organization and treatment use for adults with serious psychopathological disorders. *Development & Psychopathology*, *2*(1), 47–60.

Dozier, M., Cue, K. L., & Barnett, L. (1994). Clinicians as caregivers: Role of attachment organization in treatment. *Journal of Consulting and Clinical Psychology*, *62*(4), 793–800.

Dozier, M., Lomax, L., & Tyrell, C. L. (2001). The challenge of treatment for clients with dismissing states of mind. *Attachment & Human Development*, *3*(1), 62–76.

Dunkle, J. H. (1994). Counseling gay male clients: A review of treatment efficacy research: 1975–present. *Journal of Gay & Lesbian Psychotherapy*, *2*, 1–19.

Elkin, I., Gibbons, R. D., Shea, M. T., Sotsky, S. M., Watkins, J. T., Pilkonis, P. A., & Hedeker, D. (1995). Initial severity and differential treatment outcome in the National Institute of Mental Health Treatment of Depression Collaborative Research Program. *Journal of Consulting and Clinical Psychology*, *63*(5), 841–847.

Elkin, I., Yamaguchi, J. L., Arnkoff, D. B., Glass, C. R., Sotsky, S. M., & Krupnick, J. L. (1999). "Patient-treatment fit" and early engagement in therapy. *Psychotherapy Research*, *9*, 437–451.

Ellicott, A., Hammen, C., Gitlin, M., Brown, G., & Jamison, K. (1990). Life events and the course of bipolar disorder. *American Journal of Psychiatry*, *147*, 1194–1198.

Farber, B. A., Lippert, R. A., & Nevas, D. B. (1995). The therapist as an attachment figure. *Psychotherapy: Theory, Research, Practice, Training*, *32*(2), 204–212.

Flaskerud, J. H., & Hu, L. (1994). Participation in and outcome of treatment for major depression among low income Asian-Americans. *Psychiatry Research*, *53*, 289–300.

Fonagy, P., Steele, M., & Steele, H. (1995). Attachment, the reflective self, and borderline states:

The predictive specificity of the Adult Attachment Interview and pathological emotional development. In S. Goldberg & R. Muir (Eds.), *Attachment Theory: Social, Developmental, and Clinical Perspectives* (pp. 233–278). Hillsdale, NJ: Analytic.

Fountoulakis, K. N., Tsolaki, M., & Kazis, A. (2000). Target symptoms for fluvoxamine in old age depression. *International Journal of Psychiatry in Clinical Practice, 4*(2), 127–134.

Frank, E., Kupfer, D. J., Jacob, M., & Jarrett, D. (1987). Personality features and response to acute treatment in recurrent depression. *Journal of Personality Disorders, 1*, 14–26.

Friedman, H. J. (1963). Patient-expectancy and symptom reduction. *Archives of General Psychiatry, 8*, 61–67.

Fujino, D. C., Okazaki, S., & Young, K. (1994). Asian-American women in the mental health system: An examination of ethnic and gender match between therapist and client. *Journal of Community Psychology, 22*, 164–176.

Gamst, G., Dana, R. H., Der-Karabetian, A., & Kramer, T. (2000). Ethnic match and client ethnicity effects on global assessment and visitation. *Journal of Community Psychology, 28*, 547–564.

Garfield, S. L. (1994). Research on client variables in psychotherapy. In A. E. Bergin & S. L. Garfield (Eds.), *Handbook of psychotherapy and behavioral change* (4th ed., pp. 190–228). New York: John Wiley & Sons.

Garfield, S. L., & Bergin, A. E. (Eds.). (1978). *Handbook of psychotherapy and behavior change* (2nd ed.). New York: John Wiley & Sons.

Garfield, S. L., & Bergin, A. E. (Eds.). (1986). *Handbook of psychotherapy and behavior change* (3rd ed.). New York: John Wiley & Sons.

Gartner, J., Larson, D. B., & Allen, G. D. (1991). Religious commitment and mental health: A review of the empirical literature. *Journal of Psychology and Theology, 19*(1), 6–25.

Garvey, M. J., & Schaffer, C. B. (1994). Are some symptoms of depression age dependent? *Journal of Affective Disorders, 32*(4), 247–251.

Gaston, L., Marmar, C. R., Gallagher, D., & Thompson, L. W. (1989). Impact of confirming patient expectations of change processes in behavioral, cognitive and brief dynamic psychotherapy. *Psychotherapy, 26*, 296–302.

Gibson, W. C., & Herron, W. G. (1990). Psychotherapists' religious beliefs and their perception of the psychotherapy process. *Psychological Reports, 66*, 3–9.

Gitlin, M. J., Swendsen, J., & Heller, T. L. (1995). Relapse and impairment in bipolar disorder. *American Journal of Psychiatry, 152*, 1635–1640.

Goldstein, A. P., & Shipman, W. G. (1961). Patient expectancies, symptom reduction and aspects of the initial psychotherapeutic interview. *Journal of Clinical Psychology, 17*, 129–133.

Gomez, E. A., Ruiz, P., & Laval, R. (1982). Psychotherapy and bilingualism: Is acculturation important? *Journal of Operational Psychiatry, 13*(1), 13–16.

Greenberg, L. S., & Watson, J. (1998). Experiential therapy of depression: Differential effects of client-centered relationship conditions and process experiential interventions. *Psychotherapy Research, 8*, 210–224.

Gunderson, J. G. (1996). Borderline patient's intolerance of aloneness: Insecure attachments and therapist availability. *American Journal of Psychiatry, 153*(6), 752–758.

Gurman, A. S. (1977). Therapist and patient factors influencing the patient's perception of facilitative therapeutic conditions. *Psychiatry, 40*, 16–24.

Hardy, G. E., Aldridge, J., & Davidson, C. (1999). Therapist responsiveness to client attachment styles and issues observed in client-identified significant events in psychodynamic-interpersonal psychotherapy. *Psychotherapy Research, 9*(1), 36–53.

Hardy, G. E., Barkham, M., Shapiro, D. A., Stiles, W. B., Rees, A., & Reynolds, S. (1995). Impact of Cluster C personality disorders on outcomes of contrasting brief psychotherapies for depression. *Journal of Consulting and Clinical Psychotherapy, 63*, 997–1004.

Hardy, G. E., Cahill, J., Shapiro, D. A., Barkham, M., Rees, A., & Macaskill, N. (2001). Client interpersonal and cognitive styles as predictors of response to time-limited cognitive therapy for depression. *Journal of Consulting and Clinical Psychology, 69*(5), 841–845.

Hardy, G. E., Stiles, W. B., Barkham, M., & Startup, M. (1998). Therapist responsiveness to client interpersonal styles during time-limited treatments for depression. *Journal of Consulting and Clinical Psychology, 66*(2), 304–312.

Hart, L. E. (1981). An investigation of the effect of male therapists' view of women on the process and outcome of therapy with women. *Dissertation Abstracts International, 42*, 2529B.

Hawkins, R. S., Tan, S. Y., & Turk, A. A. (1999). Secular versus Christian inpatient cognitive-behavioral therapy programs: Impact on depression and spiritual well-being. *Journal of Psychology and Theology, 27,* 309–318.

Heine, R. W. (Ed.). (1962). *The student physician as psychotherapist.* Chicago: University of Chicago Press.

Heine, R. W., & Trosman, H. (1960). Initial expectations of the doctor–patient interaction as a factor in continuance in psychotherapy. *Psychiatry, 23,* 275–278.

Heisler, G. H., Beck, N. C., Fraps, C. L., & McReynolds, W. T. (1982). Therapist ratings as predictors of therapy attendance. *Journal of Clinical Psychology, 38,* 754–758.

Heppner, P. P., & Heesacker, M. (1983). Perceived counselor characteristics, client expectations, and client satisfaction with counseling. *Journal of Counseling Psychology, 30,* 31–39.

Hoencamp, E., Haffmans, P. M. J., Duivenvoorden, H., Knegtering, H., & Dijken, A. W. (1994). Predictors of (non)-response in depressed outpatients treated with a three-phase sequential medication strategy. *Journal of Affective Disorders, 31,* 235–246.

Hoffart, A., & Martinsen, E. G. (1993). The effect of personality disorders and anxious-depressive comorbidity on outcome in patients with unipolar depression and with panic disorder and agoraphobia. *Journal of Personality Disorders, 7,* 304–311.

Hoglend, P. (1993). Suitability for brief dynamic psychotherapy: Psychodynamic variables as predictors of outcome. *Acta Psychiatrica Scandinavica, 88*(2), 104–110.

Holmes, J. (1996). *Attachment, intimacy, autonomy: Using attachment theory in adult psychotherapy.* Northvale, NJ: Aronson.

Hosch, H. M., Barrientos, G. A., Fierro, C., Ramirez, J. I., Pelaez, M. P., Cedillos, A. M., Meyer, L. D., & Perez, Y. (1995). Predicting adherence to medications by Hispanics with Schizophrenia. *Hispanic Journal of Behavioral Sciences, 17,* 320–333.

Humphreys, K. (1999). Professional interventions that facilitate 12-step self-help group involvement. *Alcohol Research and Health, 23*(2), 93–98.

Huppert, J. D., Bufka, L. F., Barlow, D. H., Gorman, J. M., Shear, M. K., & Woods, S. W. (2001). Therapists, therapist variables, and cognitive-behaviorial therapy outcome in a multicenter trial for panic disorder. *Journal of Consulting and Clinical Psychology, 69,* 747–755.

Ilardi, S. S., & Craighead, W. E. (1999). The relationship between personality pathology and dysfunctional cognitions in previously depressed adults. *Journal of Abnormal Psychology, 63,* 997–1004.

Imber, S. D., Pilkonis, P. A., Sotsky, S. M., Elkin, I., Watkins, J. T., Collins, J. F., Shea, M. T., Leber, W. R., & Glass, D. R. (1990). Mode-specific effects among three treatments for depression. *Journal of Consulting and Clinical Psychology, 58,* 352–359.

Isard, E. S., & Sherwood, E. J. (1964). Counselor behavior and counselee expectations as related to satisfactions with counseling interview. *Personnel and Guidance Journal, 42,* 920–921.

Johnson, W. B., DeVries, R., Ridley, C. R., Pettorini, D., & Peterson, D. R. (1994). The comparative efficacy of Christian and secular rational-emotive therapy with Christian clients. *Journal of Psychology and Theology, 22,* 130–140.

Johnson, W. B., & Ridley, C. R. (1992). Brief Christian and non-Christian rational-emotive therapy with depressed Christian clients: An exploratory study. *Counseling and Values, 36,* 220–229.

Jones, E. E., Krupnick, J. L., & Kerig, P. K. (1987). Some gender effects in a brief psychotherapy. *Psychotherapy, 24,* 336–352.

Jones, E. E., & Zoppel, C. L. (1982). Impact of client and therapist gender on psychotherapy process and outcome. *Journal of Consulting & Clinical Psychology, 50,* 259–272.

Joyce, A. S., Ogrodniczuk, J., Piper, W. E., & McCallum, M. (2000). *Patient characteristics and mid-treatment outcome in two forms of short-term individual psychotherapy.* Paper presented at the 31st Annual Meeting of the Society for Psychotherapy Research, Chicago, IL.

Joyce, A. S., & Piper, W. E. (1996). Interpretive work in short-term individual psychotherapy: An analysis using hierarchical linear modeling. *Journal of Consulting and Clinical Psychology, 64,* 505–512.

Kamin, I., & Caughlan, J. (1963). Subjective experiences of outpatient psychotherapy. *American Journal of Psychotherapy, 17,* 660–668.

Keijsers, G. P. J., Hoogduin, C. A. L., & Schaap, C. P. D. R. (1994). Predictors of treatment outcome in the behavioral treatment of obsessive-compulsive disorder. *British Journal of Psychiatry, 165,* 781–786.

Kelly, E. W. (1995). Counselor values: A national survey. *Journal of Counseling and Development, 73*(6), 648–653.

Kelly, T. A., & Strupp, H. H. (1992). Patient and therapist values in psychotherapy: Perceived changes, assimilation, similarity and outcome. *Journal of Consulting and Clinical Psychology, 60*(1), 34–40.

Kilmann, P. R., Laughlin, J. E., Carranza, L. V., Downer, J. T., Major, S., & Parnell, M. M. (1999). Effects of an attachment-focused group preventive intervention on insecure women. *Group Dynamics, 3*(2), 138–147

Kirshner, L. A., Genack, A., & Hauser, S. T. (1978). Effects of gender on short-term psychotherapy. *Psychotherapy: Theory, Research & Practice, 15,* 158–167.

Klausner, E. J., Clarkin, J. F., Spielman, L., Pupo, C., Abrams, R., & Alexopoulos, G. S. (1998). Late-life depression and functional disability: The role of goal-focused group psychotherapy. *International Journal of Geriatric Psychiatry, 13,* 707–716.

Koegler, R. R., & Brill, N. Q. (1967). *Treatment of psychiatric outpatients.* Norwalk, CT: Appleton-Century-Crofts.

Krippner, K. M., & Hutchinson, R. L. (1990). Effects of a brief intake interview on clients' anxiety and depression: Follow-up. *International Journal of Short-Term Psychotherapy, 5,* 121–130.

Kuyken, W., Kurzer, N., Debubeis, R. J., Beck, A. T., & Brown, G. K. (2001). Response to cognitive therapy in depression: The role of maladaptive beliefs and personality disorders. *Journal of Consulting and Clinical Psychology, 69,* 560–566.

Lambert, M. J. (Ed.). (2003). *Handbook of Psychotherapy and Behavior Change* (5th ed.). New York: John Wiley & Sons.

Last, C. G., Thase, M. E., Hersen, M., Bellack, A. S., & Himmelhoch, J. M. (1984). Treatment outcome for solicited versus nonsolicited unipolar depressed female outpatients. *Journal of Consulting and Clinical Psychology, 52,* 134.

Levy, K. N., & Blatt, S. J. (1999). Attachment theory and psychoanalysis: Further differentiation within insecure attachment patterns. *Psychoanalytic Inquiry, 19*(4), 541–575.

Levy, K. N., Clarkin, J. F., & Kernberg, O. F. (2004, June). Changes in attachment status during psychotherapy. Symposium paper presented at the 35th Annual Society for Psychotherapy Research, Rome, Italy.

Lipkin, S. (1954). Clients' feelings and attitudes in relation to the outcome of client-centered therapy. *Psychological Monographs, 68*(1, Whole No. 372), 1–30.

Lorion, R. P. (1973). Socioeconomic status and traditional treatment approaches reconsidered. *Psychological Bulletin, 79,* 263–270.

Luborsky, L., Chandler, M., Auerbach, A. H, Cohen, J., & Bachrach, J. M. (1971). Factors influencing the outcome of psychotherapy: A review of quantitative research. *Psychological Bulletin, 75,* 145–185.

Lueger, R. J. (1996). Using feedback on patient progress to predict the outcome of psychotherapy. *Journal of Clinical Psychology, 55,* 1–27.

Mackie, A. J. (1981). Attachment theory: Its relevance to the therapeutic alliance. *British Journal of Medical Psychology, 54*(3), 203–212.

Maling, M. S., Gurtman, M. B., & Howard, K. I. (1995). The response of interpersonal problems to varying doses of psychotherapy. *Psychotherapy Research, 5,* 63–75.

Markowitz, J. C., Spielman, L. A., Sullivan, M., & Fishman, B. (2000). An exploratory study of ethnicity and psychotherapy outcome among HIV-positive patients with depressive symptoms. *Journal of Psychotherapy Practice and Research, 9,* 226–231.

Martin, P. J., Friedmeyer, M. H., Moore, J. E., & Claveaux, R. A. (1977). Patients' expectancies and improvement in treatment: The shape of the link. *Journal of Clinical Psychology, 33,* 827–833.

Martin, P. J., Sterne, A. L., & Hunter, M. L. (1976). Share and share alike: Mutuality of expectations and satisfaction with therapy. *Journal of Clinical Psychology, 32,* 677–683.

Mazure, C. M., Nelson, J. C., & Jatlow, P. I. (1990). Predictors of hospital outcome without antidepressants in major depression. *Psychiatry Research, 33,* 51–58.

McCullough, M. E. (1999). Research on religion-accommodative counseling: Review and meta-analysis. *Journal of Counseling Psychology, 46,* 92–98.

McLean, P. D., & Hakstian, A. R. (1990). Relative endurance of unipolar depression treatment effects: Longitudinal follow-up. *Journal of Consulting and Clinical Psychology, 58,* 482–488.

McLean, P. D., & Taylor, S. (1992). Severity of unipolar depression and choice of treatment. *Behavior Research and Therapy, 30,* 443–451.

Meyer, B., & Pilkonis, P. A. (2001). Attachment style. *Psychotherapy: Theory, Research, Practice, Training, 38,* 466–472.

Meyer, B., & Pilkonis, P. A. (2002). Attachment

style. In John C. Norcross (Ed.), *Psychotherapy relationships that work: Therapist contributions and responsiveness to patients* (pp. 367–382). New York: Oxford University Press.

Miller, I. W., Norman, W. H., & Keitner, G. F. (1990). Treatment response of high cognitive dysfunction depressed inpatients. *Comprehensive Psychiatry, 31*, 62–71.

Mintz, J., Mintz, L. I., Arruda, M. J., & Hwang, S. S. (1992). Treatments of depression and the functional capacity to work. *Archives of General Psychiatry, 49*, 761–768.

Mongrain, M. (1998). Parental representations and support-seeking behaviors related to dependency and self-criticism. *Journal of Personality, 66*(2), 151–173.

Moos, R. H. (1990). Depressed outpatients' life contexts, amount of treatment and treatment outcome. *Journal of Nervous and Mental Diseases, 178*, 105–112.

Morrison, L. A., & Shapiro, D. A. (1987). Expectancy and outcome in prescriptive vs. exploratory psychotherapy. *British Journal of Clinical Psychology, 26*, 59–60.

Mosheim, R., Zachhuber, U., Scharf, L., Hofmann, A., Kemmler, G., Danzl, C., Kinzel, J., Biebl, W., & Richter, R. (2000). Quality of attachment and interpersonal problems as possible predictors of inpatient-therapy outcome. *Psychotherapeut, 45*(4), 223–229.

Mulder, R. T. (2002). Personality pathology and treatment outcome in major depression: A review. *American Journal of Psychiatry, 159*(3), 359–371.

Neimeyer, R. A., & Feixas, G. (1990). The role of homework and skill acquisition in the outcome of group cognitive therapy for depression. *Behavior Therapy, 21*, 281–292.

Norcross, J. (2002). Empirically supported therapy relationships: Summary report of the Division 29 Task Force. *Psychotherapy, 38*, 345–356.

Ogles, B. M., Sawyer, J. D., & Lambert, M. J. (1995). Clinical significance of the National Institute of Mental Health treatment of depression collaborative research program data. *Journal of Consulting and Clinical Psychology, 63*, 321–326.

Organista, K. C., Munoz, R. F., & Gonzales, G. (1994). Cognitive behavioral therapy for depression in low-income and minority medical outpatients: Description of a program and exploratory analyses. *Cognitive Therapy and Research, 18*, 241–259.

Orlinsky, D. E., & Howard, K. I. (1976). The effects of sex of therapist on the therapeutic experiences of women. *Psychotherapy: Theory, Research & Practice, 13*, 82–88.

Orme, D. R., & Boswell, D. (1991). The pre-intake drop-out at a community mental health center. *Community Mental Health Journal, 27*, 375–379.

Patience, D. A., McGuire, R. J., Scott, A. I., & Freeman, C. P. (1995). The Edinburgh primary care depression study: Personality disorder and outcome. *British Journal of Psychiatry, 167*, 324–330.

Pecheur, D. R., & Edwards, K. J. (1984). A comparison of secular and religious versions of cognitive therapy with depressed Christian college students. *Journal of Psychology and Theology, 12*, 45–54.

Persons, J. B., Burns, D. D., & Perloff, J. M. (1988). Predictors of dropout and outcome in cognitive therapy for depression in a private practice setting. *Cognitive Therapy and Research, 12*, 557–575.

Peterson, J. L., Coates, T. J., Catania, J., Hauck, W. W., Acree, M., Daigle, D., Hillard, B., Middelton, L., & Hearst, N. (1996). Evaluation of an HIV risk reduction intervention among African-American homosexual and bisexual men. *AIDS, 10*, 319–325.

Pilkonis, P. A., & Frank, E. (1988). Personality pathology in recurrent depression: Nature, response, and relationship to treatment response. *American Journal of Psychiatry, 145*, 435–441.

Piper, W. E., Joyce, A. S., McCallum, M., & Azim, H. F. (1998). Interpretative and supportive forms of psychotherapy and patient personality variables. *Journal of Consulting and Clinical Psychology, 66*(3), 558–567.

Piper, W. E., & Wogan, M. (1970). Placebo effect in psychotherapy: An extension of earlier findings. *Journal of Consulting and Clinical Psychology, 34*, 447.

Propst, L. R. (1980). The comparative efficacy of religious and nonreligious imagery for the treatment of mild depression in religious individuals. *Cognitive Therapy and Research, 4*, 167–178.

Propst, L. R., Ostrom, R., Watkins, P., Dean, T., & Mashburn, D. (1992). Comparative efficacy of religious and nonreligious cognitive-behavioral therapy for the treatment of clinical depression in religious individuals. *Journal of Consulting and Clinical Psychology, 60*(1), 1–10.

Prudic, J., Sackeim, H. A., Davanand, D. P., & Kiersky, J. E. (1993). The efficacy of ECT in double depression. *Depression, 1,* 38–44.

Quackenbos, S., Privette, G., & Klentz, B, K. (1985). Psychotherapy: Sacred or secular? *Journal of Counseling and Development, 63*(5), 290–293.

Ravindran, A. V., Anisman, H., Merali, Z., Charbonneau, Y., Telner, J., Bialik, R. J., Wiens, A., Ellis, J., & Griggiths, J. (1999). Treatment of primary dysthymia with group cognitive therapy and pharmacotherapy: Clinical symptoms and functional impairment. *American Journal of Psychiatry, 156,* 1608–1617.

Reich, J. (2003). The effects of Axis II disorders on the outcome of treatment of anxiety and unipolar depressive disorders. *Journal of Personality Disorders, 17*(5), 387–405.

Richards, P. S., & Bergin, A. E. (2000). *Toward religious and spiritual competency for mental health professionals* (1st ed.). Washington, DC: American Psychological Association.

Richards, S. P., Owen, L., & Stein, S. (1993). A religiously oriented group counseling intervention for self-defeating perfectionism: A pilot study. *Counseling and Values, 2,* 96–104.

Ricker, M., Nystul, M., & Waldo, M. (1999). Counselors' and clients' ethnic similarity and therapeutic alliance in time-limited outcomes of counseling. *Psychological Reports, 84,* 674–676.

Rogers, C. R. (1957). The necessary and sufficient conditions of therapeutic personality change. *Journal of Consulting Psychology, 21,* 95–103.

Rosen, A., & Wish, E. (1980). Therapist content relevance and patient affect in treatment. *Journal of Clinical Psychology, 36,* 242–246.

Rosenbaum, M., Friedlander, J., & Kaplan, S. M. (1956). Evaluation of results of psychotherapy. *Psychosomatic Medicine, 18,* 113–132.

Rosenheck, R., Fontana, A., & Cottrol, C. (1995). Effect of clinician-veteran racial pairing in the treatment of posttraumatic stress disorder. *American Journal of Psychiatry, 152,* 555–563.

Rosenthal, C. (2000). Latino practice outcome research: A review of the literature. *Smith College Studies in Social Work, 70,* 217–238.

Rosenthal, D., & Frank, J. D. (1958). The fate of psychiatric clinic outpatients assigned to psychotherapy. *Journal of Nervous and Mental Disease, 127,* 330–343.

Rye, M. S. (1999). Evaluation of a secular and a religiously-integrated forgiveness group therapy program for college students who have been wronged by a romantic partner. *Dissertation Abstracts International, 59,* 6495.

Sable, P. (1992). Attachment theory: Application to clinical practice with adults. *Clinical Social Work Journal, 20*(3), 271–283.

Satterfield, J. M. (1998). Cognitive behavioral group therapy for depressed, low-income minority clients: Retention and treatment enhancement. *Cognitive and Behavioral Practice, 25,* 65–80.

Schonfield, J., Stone, A. R., Hoehn-Saric, R., Imber, S. D., & Pande, S. K. (1969). Patient–therapist convergence and measures of improvement in short-term psychotherapy. *Psychotherapy: Theory, Research and Practice, 6,* 267–272.

Scogin, F., Bowman, D., Jamison, C., Beutler, L. E., & Machado, P. P. (1994). Effects of initial severity of dysfunctional thinking on the outcome of cognitive therapy. *Clinical Psychology and Psychotherapy, 1,* 179–184.

Seivewright, H., Tyrer, P., & Johnson, T. (1994). Predication of outcome in neurotic disorder: A 5 year prospective study. *Psychological Medicine, 28,* 1149–1157.

Severinsen, J. (1966). Client expectation and perception of the counselor's role and their relationship to client satisfaction. *Journal of Counseling Psychology, 13,* 109–112.

Shahar, G., Blatt, S. J., Zuroff, D. C., & Pilkonis, P. A. (2003). Role of perfectionism and personality disorder features in response to brief treatment for depression. *Journal of Consulting and Clinical Psychology, 71,* 629–633.

Shane, M. G., & Shane, M. (2001). The attachment motivational system as a guide to an effective therapeutic process. *Psychoanalytic Inquiry, 21*(5), 675–687.

Shapiro, D. A., Rees, A., Barkham, M., Hardy, G., Reynolds, S., & Startup, M. (1995). Effects of treatment duration and severity of depression on the maintenance of gains after cognitive-behavioral and psychodynamic-interpersonal therapy. *Journal of Consulting and Clinical Psychology, 63,* 1–10.

Shaw, B. F., Elkin, I., Yamaguchi, J., Olmsted, M., Vallis, T. M., Dobson, K. S., Lowery, A., Sotsky, S. M., Watkins, J. T., & Imber, S. D. (1999). Therapist competence ratings in relation to clinical outcome in cognitive therapy of depression. *Journal of Consulting and Clinical Psychology, 67*(6), 837–846.

Shea, M. T., Elkin, I., Imber, S. D., Sotsky, S. M., Watkins, J. T., Collins, J. F., Pilkonis, P. A., Beckham, E., Glass, D. R., Dolan, R. T., & Parloff, M. B. (1992). Course of depressive symptoms over followup: Findings from the

National Institute of Mental Health Treatment of Depression Collaborative Research Program. *Archives of General Psychiatry, 49*, 782–787.

Shea, M. T., Pilkonis, P. A., Beckham, E., Collins, J. F., Elkin, I., Sotsky, S. M., & Docherty, J. P. (1990). Personality disorders and treatment outcome in the NIMH Treatment of Depression Collaborative Research Program. *American Journal of Psychiatry, 147*, 711–718.

Silverberg, R. T. (1982). Effects of confirmation or disconfirmation of client role expectations on client satisfaction, length of therapy, and outcome ratings of psychotherapy. *Dissertation Abstracts International, 42*(8), 3442B.

Slade, A. (1999). Attachment theory and research: Implications for the theory and practice of individual psychotherapy with adults. In J. Cassidy & P. R. Shaver (Eds.), *Handbook of attachment: Theory, research, and clinical applications* (pp. 575–594). New York: Guilford.

Sloane, R. B., Staples, F. R., Cristol, A. H., Yorkston, N. J. & Whipple, K. (1975). *Psychotherapy versus behavior therapy.* Cambridge, MA: Harvard University Press.

Snowden, L. R., Hu, T. W., & Jerrell, J. M. (1995). Emergency care avoidance: Ethnic matching and participation in minority-serving programs. *Community Mental Health Journal, 31*, 463–473.

Sotsky, S. M., Glass, D. R., Shea, R. M., Pilkonis, P. A., Collins, J. F., Elkin, I., Watkins, J. T., Imber, S. D., Leber, W. R., Moyer, J., & Oliveri, M. E. (1991). Patient predictors of response to psychotherapy and pharmacotherapy: Findings in the NIMH Treatment of Depression Collaborative Research Program. *American Journal of Psychiatry, 148*, 997–1008.

Spangler, D. L., Simons, A. D., Thase, M. E., & Monroe, S. M. (1997). Response to cognitive-behavioral therapy in depression: Effects of pretreatment cognitive dysfunction and life stress. *Journal of Consulting and Clinical Psychology, 65*, 568–575.

Sperry, L., Brill, P. L., Howard, K. I., & Grissom, G. R. (1996). *Treatment outcomes in psychotherapy and psychiatric interventions.* New York: Brunner/Mazel.

Sterling, R. C., Gottheil, E., Weinstein, S. P., & Serota, R. (1998). Therapist/patient race and sex matching: Treatment retention and 9-month follow-up outcome. *Addiction, 93*, 1043–1050.

Stiles, W. B., & Shapiro, D. A. (1994). Disabuse of the drug metaphor: Psychotherapy process-outcome correlations. *Journal of Consulting and Clinical Psychology, 62*(5), 942–948.

Stuart, S., Simons, A. D., Thase, M. E., & Pilkonis, P. (1992). Are personality assessments valid in acute major depression? *Journal of Affective Disorders, 24*, 281–289.

Sue, S., Fujino, D. C., Hu, L. T., Takeuchi, D. T., & Zane, N. W. S. (1991). Community mental health services for ethnic minority groups: A test of the cultural responsiveness hypothesis. *Journal of Consulting and Clinical Psychology, 59*, 533–540.

Sue, S., & Lam, A. G. (2002). Cultural and demographic diversity. In J. Norcross (Ed.), *Psychotherapy relationships that work: Therapists' relational contributors to effective psychotherapy* (pp. 401–421). New York: Oxford University Press.

Szajnberg, N. M., & Crittenden, P. M. (1997). The transference refracted through the lens of attachment. *Journal of the American Academy of Psychoanalysis & Dynamic Psychiatry, 25*(3), 409–438.

Szapocznik, J., Santisteban, D., Kurtines, W. M., Hervis, O., & Spencer, F. (1982). Life enhancement counseling and the treatment of depressed Cuban American elders. *Hispanic Journal of Behavioral Sciences, 4*(4), 487–502.

Takeuchi, D. T., Sue, S., & Yeh, M. (1995). Return rates and outcomes from ethnicity-specific mental health programs in Los Angeles. *American Journal of Public Health, 85*(5), 638–643.

Talley, J. E. (1992). *The predictors of successful very brief psychotherapy: A study of differences by gender, age, and treatment variables.* Springfield, IL: Charles C. Thomas.

Talley, J. E., Butcher, T., Maguire, M. A., & Pinkerton, R. S. (1992). The effects of very brief of psychotherapy on symptoms of dysphoria. In J. E. Talley (Ed.), *The predictors of successful very brief psychotherapy: A study of differences by gender, age, and treatment variables* (pp. 12–45). Springfield, IL: Charles C. Thomas.

Taylor, S., & McLean, P. (1993). Outcome profiles in the treatment of unipolar depression. *Behavioral Research & Therapy, 31*, 325–330.

Thase, M. E., Reynolds, C. F., Frank, E., Simons, A. D., McGeary, J., Fasiczka, A. L., Garamoni, G. G., Jennings, R., & Kupfer, D. J. (1994). Do depressed men and women respond similarly to cognitive behavior therapy? *American Journal of Psychiatry, 151*, 500–505.

Thase, M. E., Simons, A. D., Cahalane, J., McGeary, J., & Harden, T. (1991). Severity of depression and response to cognitive behavior therapy. *American Journal of Psychiatry, 148,* 784–789.

Toh, Y., & Tan, S. (1997). The effectiveness of church-based lay counselors: A controlled outcome study. *Journal of Psychology and Christianity, 16,* 260–267.

Tollinton, H. J. (1973). Initial expectations and outcome. *British Journal of Medical Psychology, 46,* 251–257.

Travis, L. A., Bliwise, N. G., Binder, J. L., & Horne-Moyer, H. L. (2001). Changes in clients' attachment styles over the course of time-limited dynamic psychotherapy. *Psychotherapy: Theory, Research, Practice, Training, 38,* 149–159.

Tyrer, P., Seivewright, N., Ferguson, B., Murphy, S., & Johnson, L. A. (1993). The Nottingham study of neurotic disorder: Effect of personality status on response to drug treatment, cognitive therapy and self help over two years. *British Journal of Psychiatry, 162,* 219–226.

Uhlenhuth, E. H., & Duncan, D. B. (1968). Subjective change with medical student therapists: II. Some determinants of change in psychoneurotic outpatients. *Archives of General Psychiatry, 18,* 532–540.

Urist, J. (1973). *The Rorschach test as a multidimensional measure of object relations.* Unpublished doctoral dissertation, University of Michigan.

Valdez, J. N. (2000). Psychotherapy with bicultural Hispanic clients. *Psychotherapy, 37,* 240–246.

Vallejo, J., Gasto, C., Catalan, R., Bulbena, A., & Menchon, J. M. (1991). Predictors of antidepressant treatment outcome in melancholia: Psychosocial, clinical and biological indicators. *Journal of Affective Disorders, 21,* 151–162.

Veiel, H. O., Kuhner, C., Brill, G., & Ihle, W. (1992). Psychosocial correlates of clinical depression after psychiatric in-patient treatment: Methodological issue and baseline differences between recovered and non-recovered patients. *Psychological Medicine, 22,* 425–427.

Viinamaki, H., Hintikka, J., Honkalampi, K., Korimaa-Honkanen, H., Kuisma, S., Antikainen, R., Tanskanein, A., & Lehtonen, J. (2002). Cluster C personality disorders impedes alleviation of symptoms in major depression. *Journal of Affective Disorder, 71,* 35–71.

Volsky, T., Jr., Magoon, T. M., Norman, W. T., & Hoyt, D. P. (1965). *The outcomes of counseling and psychotherapy: Theory and research.* Minneapolis: University of Minnesota Press.

Weissman, A. N., & Beck, A. T. (1978, August). *Development and validation of the Dysfunctional Attitudes Scale: A preliminary investigation.* Paper presented at the 86th annual convention of the American Psychological Association, Toronto.

Weitz, R. (1982). Feminist consciousness raising, self-concept, and depression. *Sex Roles, 8,* 231–241.

Woody, G. E., McLellan, A. T., Luborsky, L., O'Brien, C. P., Blaine, J., Fox, S., Herman, I., & Beck, A. T. (1984). Severity of psychiatric symptoms as a predictor of benefits from psychotherapy: The Veterans Administration-Penn Study. *American Journal of Psychiatry, 141,* 1172–1177.

Worthington, E. L., Kurusu, T. A., McCullough, M. E., & Sandage, S. J. (1996). Empirical research on religion and psychotherapeutic processes and outcomes: A 10-year review and research prospectus. *Psychological Bulletin, 119*(3), 448–487.

Worthington, E. L., Jr., & Sandage, S. J. (2002). Religion and spirituality. In J. Norcross (Ed.), *Psychotherapy relationships that work: Therapists' relational contributors to effective psychotherapy* (pp. 383–399). New York: Oxford University Press.

Yeh, M., Eastman, K., & Cheung, M. K. (1994). Children and adolescents in community health centers: Does the ethnicity or the language of the therapist matter? *Journal of Community Psychology, 22,* 153–163.

Zlotnick, C., Elkin, I., & Shea, M. T. (1998). Does the gender of a patient or the gender of a therapist affect the treatment of patients with major depression? *Journal of Consulting and Clinical Psychology, 66,* 655–659.

Zlotnick, C., Shea, M. T., Pilkonis, P., Elkin, I., & Ryan, C. (1996). Gender dysfunctional attitudes, social support, life events, and depressive symptoms over naturalistic follow-up. *American Journal of Psychiatry, 153,* 1021–1027.

Zuroff, D. C., & Blatt, S. J. (2002). Vicissitudes of life after the short-term treatment of depression: roles of stress, social support, and personality. *Journal of Social and Clinical Psychology, 21,* 473–496.

Zuroff, D. C., Blatt, S. J., Krupnick, J. L. & Sotsky, S. M. (2001). Vicissitudes of life after short-term treatment of depression: Stress reactivity and its moderators. Unpublished manuscript.

Zuroff, D. C., Blatt, S. J., Sotsky, S. M., Krupnick, J. L., Martin, D. J., Sanislow, C. A., & Simmens, S. (2000). Relation of therapeutic alliance and perfectionism to outcome in brief outpatient treatment of depression. *Journal of* *Consulting and Clinical Psychology, 68*(1), 0022–006X.

Zuroff, D. C., & Duncan, N. (1999). Self-criticism and conflict resolution in romantic couples. *Canadian Journal of Behavioural Science, 31*(3).

3

Relationship Factors in Treating Dysphoric Disorders

Louis G. Castonguay

Martin Grosse Holtforth

Mary M. Coombs

Rachel A. Beberman

Aphrodite A. Kakouros

James F. Boswell

Jay J. Reid, Jr.

Enrico E. Jones

A substantial number of interpersonal factors have been associated with depression. These factors include parental separation, neglect, rejection and abuse, family discord during childhood, marital discord, lack of social support, and lack of intimate relationships (Klerman & Weissman, 1986). Since evidence suggests that interpersonal factors play a determinant role in depression, it should come as no surprise that variables associated with the interaction between clients and their therapists might have an impact in the *treatment* of depression, as well. The goal of this chapter is to summarize our existing empirical knowledge concerning the role of relationship variables in psychotherapy involving depressed individuals.

In accordance to the guidelines of the Task Force within which this chapter is being written (see Beutler & Castonguay, this volume), our summary is primarily based on the conclusions of the recent Division 29 APA Task Force (Norcross, 2002). When appropriate, these conclusions have been complemented by the findings of other reviews of the empirical literature. Examination of

studies involving depressed individuals led us to determine whether the preponderance of evidence justifies adopting these conclusions for this specific clinical population.[1] Based on such evidence, principles of change were then delineated to guide psychotherapy for depression.

It should be mentioned that, when conducting our review, we divided relevant studies into two categories: (1) studies based on purely or predominantly depressed clients, and (2) studies based on mixed samples, in which a substantial number of clients (and at times all of them) were described as suffering from various forms of dysphoric or depressive disorders (e.g., dysthymic disorder, reactive depression, "anxious-depressed" clients). Included in this second category, are studies in which client samples were described as "neurotic" or "psychoneurotic." As argued by Bohart, Elliott, Greenberg, and Watson (2002), within our current nomenclature, these samples would primarily include affective and anxiety disorders.

Numerous relationship variables have been investigated by Division 29's Task Force. In this chapter, these variables have been organized into three clusters: quality of the therapeutic interaction, therapist interpersonal skills, and therapist clinical skills.

QUALITY OF THE THERAPEUTIC INTERACTION

Three relationship variables covered by Division 29's Task Force refer to the quality of the interaction between the therapist and client: therapeutic alliance, group cohesion, and goal consensus and collaboration.

Therapeutic Alliance

No other ingredient of the process of psychotherapy appears to have received as much empirical attention as the therapeutic alliance. Although many definitions have been provided, two crucial aspects seem to cut across many of them. As pointed out by Constantino, Castonguay, and Schut (2002), it "is generally agreed that the alliance represents interactive, collaborative elements of the relationship (i.e., therapist and client abilities to engage in the tasks of therapy and to agree on the targets of therapy) in the context of an affective bond or positive attachment" (page 86).

The review of research on therapeutic alliance conducted for Division 29's Task Force (Horvath & Bedi, 2002) led to an effect size (ES) of .21 between alliance and outcome; this ES was close to what was found in previous reviews: .22 (Martin, Garske, & Davis, 2000), and .26 (Horvath & Symonds, 1991). Although Horvath and Bedi (2002) recognized that the magnitude of the relationship between alliance and outcome is not excessively high, they nevertheless concluded that "the quality of the alliance is an important element in successful, effective therapy" (p. 61). This conclusion is consistent with Orlinsky, Grawe, & Parks's (1994) authoritative review of process-outcome literature: "The strongest evidence linking process to outcome concerns the *therapeutic bond* or alliance, reflecting more than 1,000 process-outcome findings" (p. 360). Examining Horvath and Bedi's (2002) review of the empirical literature, we were able to find 10 studies involving samples of predominantly or purely depressed individuals (An-

dreoli et al., 1993; Castonguay, Goldfried, Wiser, Raue, & Hayes, 1996; Feeley, 1993; Gaston, Marmar, Thompson, & Gallager, 1991; Gaston, Thompson, Gallager, Cournoyer, & Gagnon, 1998; Krupnick et al., 1994; Krupnick et al., 1996; Marmar, Gaston, Gallager, & Thompson, 1989; Rounsaville et al., 1987; Zuroff et al., 2000). All of them reported at least one significant finding supporting the relationship between good alliance and positive outcome, and none of them reported a significant negative relationship between the quality of the alliance and client improvement. It should be noted, however, that: four of these studies were based on data from the Treatment for Depression Collaborative Research Program (i.e., Krupnick et al., 1994; Krupnick et al., 1996; Rounsaville et al., 1987; Zuroff et al., 2000); three others were based on the same sample of older depressed patients (Gaston et al., 1991, 1998; Marmar et al., 1989); and, finally, two others were based on a data set collected by Hollon et al. (1992) (i.e., Castonguay et al., 1996; Feeley, 1993).

Because of the overlap between these studies with "pure" or predominantly depressed samples, we also considered all of the studies (15) conducted with mixed depressed samples that we could find based on Horvath and Bedi (2002) review (i.e., Clarkin & Crilly, 1987; Crits-Cristoph, Cooper, & Luborsky, 1988; Gomes-Schwartz, 1978; Hatcher & Barends, 1996; Lieberman, von Rehn, Dickie, Elliot, & Egerter, 1992; Marmar, Weiss, & Gaston, 1989; Marziali, 1984; Muran et al., 1995; Ogrodniczuk, Piper, Joyce, & McCallum, 2000; O'Malley, Suh, & Strupp, 1983; Paivio & Bahr, 1998; Piper, Azim, Joyce, McCallum, Nixon, & Segal, 1991; Piper, Boroto, Joyce, McCallum, & Azim, 1995; Safran & Wallner, 1991; Windholz & Silberschatz, 1988). All of these investigations found at least one significant positive relationship between alliance and improvement, and none of them reported a significant negative association.

We also found three studies (based on a purely depressed sample) not included in Horvath and Bedi's (2002) review. While one of them (Stiles, Agnew-Davies, Hardy, Barkham, & Shapiro, 1998) reported significant positive relationships between alliance and outcome, the other two failed to find a significant correlation between alliance and outcome (DeRubeis & Feeley, 1990;

Feeley, DeRubeis, & Gelfand 1999). Despite these inconsistent findings, as well as the overlap between some of the previous studies, it appears that the decision by the Division 29 Task Force to consider the alliance as a "demonstrably effective" element of the therapeutic relationship (Norcross, 2002) is an acceptable conclusion with respect to psychotherapy for depression. This leads us to recommend the following principle of change:

1. When working with clients with dysphoric disorders, therapists should strive to develop and maintain a positive working alliance with their clients.

Cohesion in Group Psychotherapy

In their contribution to the Division 29 Task force, Burlingame, Fuhriman, and Johnson (2002) have argued that the concept of cohesion represents the "essence" of the therapeutic relationship in group psychotherapy. While it involves different categories of interaction than what is found in individual treatment (e.g., member to member, member to leader), cohesion explicitly refers, in the eyes of these authors, to the dimensions of bonding and collaboration. As such, cohesion could be perceived as the group equivalent of the therapeutic alliance in individual psychotherapy. Consistent with this line of reasoning, Orlinsky et al.'s (1994) review of the therapeutic bond or alliance includes studies on group cohesion.

Burlingame et al.'s (2002) consideration of the empirical literature led them to conclude that cohesion is a predictor of outcome. Of the specific studies reported in their chapter, two of them were based on mixed samples involving depressive disorders (e.g., "disturbed neurotic" or "depressed and/or anxious"; Budman et al., 1989; Tschuschke & Dies, 1994). In each of the studies, a significant positive relationship was found between cohesion and improvement, while a significant negative relationship was not found. Similar results were also found in a study that was not included in Burlingame et al.'s (2002) review, but that was conducted with a sample of purely depressed patients (Hoberman, Lewinsohn, & Tilson, 1988). Even though the number of studies is small, the findings of these three studies are consistent with the general conclusion arrived at by Burlingame et al.

(2002), as well as the decision of the Division 29 Task Force to consider cohesion as a "demonstrably effective" element of the therapeutic relationship (Norcross, 2002). As such, it seems appropriate to state the following principle of change:

1. When conducting group therapy with depressed individuals, therapists should foster a strong level of cohesiveness within the group.

Goal Consensus and Collaboration

The Division 29 Task Force drew specific conclusions for goal consensus (i.e., therapist and client agreement on treatment goals) and collaborative involvement (i.e., therapist and client mutual involvement in therapy), even though both elements, and especially goal consensus, seem to be components of the working alliance. In fact, as noted in the Division 29 report, "goal consensus is one aspect of the *working alliance*" (Tryon and Winograd, 2002, p. 109).

Tryon and Winograd (2002) concluded that current research evidence provides a general support for a positive relationship between both goal consensus and collaboration and treatment outcome. This, of course, is hardly surprising considering the findings on alliance presented above. With respect to depressed clients, we found only two studies in Tryon and Winograd's chapter that investigated goal consensus (Gaston et al., 1991; Marmar et al., 1989). Because both of them are already included in our review of alliance studies, we have decided not to derive a conclusion (nor a principle of change) specific to this variable.

With regard to collaborative involvement, five published studies reviewed by Tryon and Winograd (2002) involved predominantly or purely depressive samples. Three of these studies found that involvement (as measured by homework compliance) significantly predicted improvement (Burns & Nolen-Hoeksema, 1991; Burns & Spangler, 2000; Persons, Burns, & Perloff, 1988), whereas the remaining two studies did not find that homework compliance or attendance significantly predicted improvement (Hoberman et al., 1988; Rounsaville, Weissman, & Prusoff, 1981). Five other studies conducted with mixed samples involving depressive or dysphoric disorders (e.g., adjustment disorder with depressed mood, anxiety and affective disorders) found different facets of involvement (e.g., high level of participation, low level of defensiveness or resistance) to be related to outcome (Buckley, Conte, Plutchik, Wild, & Karasu, 1984; Jones, Parke & Pulos, 1992; Kolb, Beutler, Davis, Crago, & Shanfield, 1985; Piper, de Carufel, & Szkrumelak, 1985; Soldz, Budman & Demby, 1992).[2] None of the 10 studies above reported a significant negative relationship between collaborative involvement and client improvement.[3] Taken together, these findings suggest that Tryon and Winograd's (2002) conclusion applies to the treatment of depressive disorders. Accordingly, we endorse the decision of the Division 29 Task Force to identify collaboration as a "demonstrably effective" element of the therapeutic relationship (Norcross, 2002), and recommend the following principle of change:

1. Therapists working with depressed individuals should attempt to facilitate their engagement during and between sessions.

THERAPIST'S SKILLS: ATTUNING TO THE CLIENT

Reflecting the major impact of the client-centered approach on the field, three interpersonal skills have been the focus of considerable amount of research attention: empathy, positive regard, and congruence.

Empathy

Empathy, or the therapist's ability to understand the client's inner experience from the client's frame of reference, has been described in most therapeutic orientations as an essential element of therapy. The Division 29 Task Force has provided empirical support for this theoretical and clinical assumption on the basis of a meta-analysis involving 47 studies (which included, all together, more than 3,000 clients; Bohart et al., 2002). Reflecting a medium effect size, an *r* of .32 was reported as the best summary value of the relationship between empathy and outcome.

The findings of this meta-analysis are consistent with Orlinsky et al.'s (1994) box score review, in which 54% of the reported findings showed a positive significant correlation, and in which no negative correlations were observed.

Forty-seven percent of the study included in Bohart et al.'s (2002) review involved "mixed neurotic" clients. As mentioned above, these authors have argued that such a client population would, in most recent studies, include primarily affective and anxiety disorders. Of the studies reviewed by Bohart et al. (2002) that we examined, however, only one appeared to be either exclusively or predominantly based on a sample of depressed individuals (Burns & Nolen-Hoeksema, 1992). On the basis of a sophisticated structural modeling equation, the finding of this study suggested a causal relationship between the experience of the therapist as being empathic and the client's improvement. We also surveyed 15 studies cited by Bohart and his colleagues (2002) involving less homogeneous samples (e.g., mixed depressed and anxious clients; Bergin & Jasper, 1969; Beutler, Johnson, Neville, & Workman, 1972; Bugge, Hendel, & Moene, 1985; Cooley & Lajoy, 1980; Dormaar, Dijkman, & de Vries, 1989; Kurtz & Grummon, 1972; Lafferty, Beutler, & Crago, 1989; Lorr, 1965; Peake, 1979; Saltzman, Leutgert, Roth, Creaser, & Howard, 1976; Saunders, 2000; Staples, Sloane, Whipple, Cristol, & Yorkston, 1976; Strupp, Fox, & Lessler, 1969; Truax et al., 1966; Truax & Wittmer, 1971). We found that 12 of them reported at least one significant finding supporting a positive relationship between empathy and outcome.[4] We also found three relevant studies with mixed samples (including clients with depressive disorders or described as neurotics) that were not included in Bohart et al.'s (2002) review. While two of them found that empathy correlated significantly with outcome (Conte, Ratto, Clutz, & Karasu, 1995; Truax, 1971), the other did not (Staples & Sloane, 1976). Thus, as a whole 79% of the studies reviewed here reported at least one significant relationship with client's improvement (because two of the studies [Truax et al., 1966, and Truax & Wittmer, 1971] appear to have used the same data set, however, a more conservative ratio of 78% [14 out of 18] might be more appropriate). Furthermore, none of these 19 studies revealed a significant negative link between empathy and improvement. Taken together, these findings suggest that the conclusion of the Division 29 Task Force with regard to the positive role of empathy (as a "demonstrably effective" element of the therapeutic relationship) is likely to be accurate for the treatment of depression. As such, these findings lead us to state the following principle of change:

1. When working with depressed individuals, therapists should relate to their clients in an empathic way.

Positive Regard

In their contribution to the Division 29 Task Force, Farber and Lane (2002) refer to positive regard as a "general constellation of attitudes" that encompasses nonpossessive warmth, acceptance, prizing, and caring. Based on a summary of six previous reviews of the empirical literature, as well as their own review of 16 recent studies, these authors cautioned that it is difficult to draw firm conclusions about positive regard. Nevertheless, they argue that the research suggests there is a positive (although modest) relationship between this component and outcome.

With respect to the magnitude of the relationship between positive regard and improvement, a number of issues appear salient. As observed in Orlinsky et al.'s (1994) review (the most comprehensive one summarized by Farber and Lane [2002]), the effect size varies considerably, which suggests that the relationship may be impacted by different factors. Farber and Lane's (2002) own review showed that the effect sizes appear to be larger with length of stay than with outcome, which, as they cogently note, may indicate that the main helpful impact of positive regard may be to facilitate the client's staying in therapy for a longer period of time. While the authors emphasized that the effect size with regard to outcome appears to be modest, they conclude that it is strongly indicated for the therapist to provide positive regard and that, "at minimum, it sets the stage for other mutative interventions and that, at least in some cases, it may be sufficient itself to effect positive change" (p. 191). Even with these caveats in mind, the authors clearly indicate that there is no evidence to suggest that therapists should avoid being warm, accepting, and caring toward their clients.

Examining the studies reviewed by Farber and Lane (2002), we found seven that involved samples with depressed adults (Bachelor, 1991; Coady, 1991; Conte et al., 1995; Gaston et al., 1991; Hayes & Strauss, 1998; Hynan, 1990; Quintana & Meara, 1990). We also found three other relevant studies not included in this review (Lafferty et al., 1989; Staples & Sloane, 1976; Truax, 1971). Of these 10 studies, six (60%) found at least one significant finding between positive regard and outcome.

It is important to mention, however, that neither of the two studies involving a purely depressed sample found a significant positive relationship between positive regard and outcome (Gaston et al., 1991; Hayes & Strauss, 1998). Such discrepancies in the results obtained with the two types of samples (mixed and pure) should raise caution in our conclusion. Nonetheless, the predominance of the positive findings found in the studies as a whole, and the absence of any negative relationship in all of them, suggest that positive regard can be considered, at least tentatively, as a therapeutic factor in the treatment for depressive or dysphoric disorders. At the minimum, the evidence provides support for the Division 29 Task Force decision to consider positive regard as a "promising and probably effective" element of the therapeutic relationship (Norcross, 2002). This, in turn, leads us to cautiously suggest the following principle of change:

1. When adopted by therapists, an attitude of caring, warmth, and acceptance is likely to be helpful in facilitating therapeutic change in depressed clients.

Congruence

Congruence, the third Rogerian attitude, has been defined in the Division 29 Task Force as "a self-awareness on the part of the therapist, and a willingness to share this awareness in the moment" (Klein, Kolden, Michels, & Chisholm-Stockard, 2002, p. 196). After noting that the consensus emerging from previous reviews (11, completed between 1970 and 1994) pointed to a mixed support for the role of congruence on client's improvement, Klein et al. (2002) conducted their own review of 20 studies. They found that 34% of the reported results were positive, a number similar to the comprehensive reviews of Orlinsky and his colleagues (Orlinsky & Howard, 1986; Orlinsky et al., 1994).

Taking into consideration many of the methodological limitations (e.g., small *N*, restricted variance) that have characterized studies on congruence, the authors concluded that despite the mixed empirical evidence this construct "should be recognized as a key psychotherapy treatment parameter and a potent change process with both interpersonal and intrapersonal dimensions" (p. 210).

We reviewed six studies cited by Klein et al. (2002) that involve clients with depressive disorders (e.g., all of them based on mixed samples; Jones & Zoppel, 1982; Lafferty et al., 1989; Sloane, Staples, Cristol, Yorkson, & Whipple, 1975; Staples & Sloane, 1976; Truax, 1971; Truax et al., 1966). We found that three of these studies (50%) reported a significant positive relationship between congruence and outcome, while none of them reported a significant negative relationship. Because these results meet the criteria proposed and labeled by the current Task Force as "preponderance" of the evidence (i.e., 50% or more; Beutler & Castonguay, this volume), we accept the Division 29 Task Force's categorization of congruence as a promising and potentially effective element of the therapeutic relationship (Norcross, 2002) and recommend the following principle of change:

1. When working with individuals suffering from depressive symptoms, therapists are likely to facilitate change when adopting an attitude of congruence or authenticity.

THERAPIST'S SKILLS: WORKING WITH THE THERAPEUTIC RELATIONSHIP

In addition to investigating the skills involved in the therapist's attunement to the client's experience, researchers have also studied a number of strategies based on the therapist's focus on, attempt to manage, or reaction to aspects of the therapeutic relationship. These strategies include repairing alliance ruptures, feedback, self-disclosure, management of counter-transference, and relational interpretations.

Repairing Alliance

One of the obvious clinical implications of the robust link between the quality of the alliance and outcome is that, when alliance problems emerge (e.g., disagreement about tasks or goals, difficulty in maintaining a strong bond), they should be properly repaired. As noted in the Division 29 report (Safran, Muran, Samstag, & Stevens, 2002), preliminary and/or qualitative studies have begun to suggest that some strategies or processes (e.g., exploring client's negative feelings related to ruptures, therapist's nondefensiveness) are related to the improvement of alliance and outcome, and that the pattern of worsening and repairing of alliance during treatment is positively related to outcome.

None of the studies providing support for such positive relationships specifically involved depressed samples. Following the guideline proposed by the current Task Force (see Beutler & Castonguay, this volume), we thus accept by default (i.e., pending further research) the decision of the Division 29 Task Force to define the repair of alliance rupture as a "promising and probably effective element" of the therapeutic relationship (Norcross, 2002). On this basis, we also tentatively proposed the following principle of change:

1. Repairing alliance ruptures that emerge during treatment is likely to be helpful when working with depressed clients.

It should also be mentioned, however, that three studies conducted with depressed individuals (one based on a purely depressed sample and two based on mixed samples) involved qualitative analyses that suggest that the therapist's persistence in the use of specific interventions (e.g., focus on cognitive model in cognitive therapy, interpretation in psychodynamic therapy) when confronted with alliance problems may foster engagement in a negative interpersonal cycle as opposed to resolving the alliance rupture (Castonguay et al., 1996; Piper, Azim, Joyce, & McCallum, 1991; Piper et al., 1999). While the qualitative nature of these findings calls for caution, we nevertheless believe that they provide at least tentative support for the following principle of change:

2. Therapists working with depressed individuals may find it helpful to adopt an empathic and nondefensive (or nonrigid) attitude when attempting to repair alliance ruptures.

Feedback

Feedback can be considered an essential component of human interactions. In psychology, the term "feedback" has been used to describe "(1) information provided to a person (2) from an external source (3) about the person's behavior or the effects of that behavior" (Claiborn, Goodyear, & Horner, 2002, p. 217). In psychotherapy, two types of feedback seem particularly relevant, that is, feedback in the therapeutic process and feedback about testing results. According to Jacobs (1974; cited in Claiborn et al., 2002), feedback can consist of (1) observation/description of the client's behavior, (2) emotional reaction to the client's behavior, (3) inference about something that is not directly observable in the client, or (4) mirroring (e.g., showing video recordings).

Based on Claiborn et al.'s (2002) review of evidence, feedback was designated as a "promising and probably effective" element of the therapeutic relationship by the Division 29 Task Force (Norcross, 2002). Of the studies reviewed by Claiborn et al. (2002) that investigated the relationship of feedback and outcome, however, none were based on a sample that explicitly included clients with depressive or dysphoric disorders. Thus, in accordance to the guidelines of the present Task Force (see Beutler & Castonguay, this volume), we accept the Division 29 conclusion by default (i.e., pending further research), and tentatively propose the following principle:

1. Depressed clients are likely to benefit from receiving feedback from their therapists.

Therapist Self-Disclosure

Self-disclosure is defined in psychotherapy process research as the therapist act of revealing personal information about oneself to the client. Therapist self-disclosure can be further categorized along dimensions such as its content of disclosure (i.e., simple personal facts, therapist's own life experience, response to the client), type (reassuring or challenging self-disclosures), and level of reciprocity with client or not.

Traditionally therapists were trained to remain neutral, anonymous, and non-self-disclosing. Humanistic and feminist theories of psychotherapy brought this stance into question and encouraged therapist authenticity and mutuality in the therapeutic encounter. Current interest in relational aspects of psychoanalytically and psychodynamically oriented therapies, as well as cognitive-behavioral, experiential, and integrative approaches, may foster further interest in studying the function of therapist self-disclosure in treatment.

In Orlinsky et al.'s (1994) review of process research, the majority of the studies on self-disclosure did not show a significant association with outcome, and where there was a significant relationship, it was negative as often as positive. In the Division 29 Task Force's review, however, self-disclosure appears to receive more credibility as a useful therapeutic intervention. While the studies reviewed by Hill and Knox (2002) revealed mixed findings with regard to post-treatment outcome, they also point to the helpfulness of self-disclosure when the effect of therapy is measured in terms of immediate outcome. As a result, self-disclosure was retained as a "promising and probably effective" element of the therapeutic relationship (Norcross, 2002).

Based on Hill and Knox's (2002) review, we found a relatively small number of studies involving depressed individuals (all of them conducted with mixed samples). In a study comparing the conditions of increased disclosure and limited disclosure, Barrett and Berman (2001) found that heightened therapist disclosure was significantly related to client reports of lower levels of symptom distress and a client's liking of his or her therapist. In another study, self-disclosure was folded into a multivariable therapist dimension (including being more personal, self-disclosing, active, and emphasizing current feelings in their relationship with clients) that correlated positively with good treatment outcome (Beutler & Mitchell, 1981). Using the Structural Analysis of Social Behavior (SASB; Benjamin, 1974), however, Coady (1991) failed to find that the therapist's behavior of disclosing/expressing significantly differentiated between cases of good and poor outcome.

In the first of two studies conducted with the same sample of anxious-depressed clients, Hill et al. (1988) failed to find a significant correlation between self-disclosure and treatment outcome. They did, however, find that self-disclosure received the highest client ratings of helpfulness and experiencing (both defined as immediate outcome) among therapist response modes. Interestingly, therapists tended not to rate self-disclosure as highly as clients, with some of the therapists rating it as the most helpful and others rating it as one of the least helpful response modes. In the second study, Hill, Mahalik, and Thompson (1989) found that reassuring disclosures were rated by clients and therapists as more helpful and related to higher levels of client experiencing than challenging disclosures. However, no support was found for the hypothesis that self-involving disclosures (therapist's personal response to the client) were more helpful than self-disclosing disclosures (past tense statements of therapist's personal experience).

A qualitative study worthy of mention for the light it sheds upon therapist self-disclosure (Knox, Hess, Petersen, & Hill, 1997) examined a predominantly depressed sample of clients' perceptions of the effects of therapist self-disclosure in long-term therapy. Therapists were of varied orientations (behavioral, cognitive-behavioral, psychoanalytic-psychodynamic, humanistic-experiential, and eclectic) and word descriptions were used to evaluate the event of therapist self-disclosure. Clients perceived therapist self-disclosures as important events resulting in positive consequences of insight, a new perspective from which to make changes, a more equalized or improved therapeutic relationship, normalization, and reassurance. Interestingly, all examples were of personal non-immediate information, such as revelations about family, leisure activities, or past similar experiences with those of the client.

As a whole, the evidence reviewed seems to provide support for self-disclosure, at least as a promising and possibly effective relationship factor. However, it should be mentioned that some of the findings reported above were obtained with immediate outcome measures (i.e., clients' perceived helpfulness and level of experiencing), which are distinct from the post-treatment outcome measures that have been used as the primary basis of evaluation in this chapter and the current Task Force. Even when only considering treatment outcome measures, however, 50% of the studies that examined the link between self-disclosure alone or in combination with other variables and improvement found a significant positive relationship. While this meets the criteria proposed for the current Task Force (see Beutler & Castonguay, this volume), one should also keep in mind that the number of the quantitative studies is relatively small (i.e., four, if one counts the two investigations conducted by Hill and her colleagues with the same sample as one study). Taking all of these issues into consideration, it seems indicated to cautiously propose the following principle of change:

1. When working with depressed clients, therapists' use of self-disclosure is likely to be helpful. This may be especially the case for reassuring and supportive self-disclosures, as opposed to challenging self-disclosures.

Management of Countertransference

As Gelso and Hayes (2002) indicate in their review for Division 29's Task Force, the concept of countertransference is associated with a considerable "definitional ambiguity" (p. 267). Following Epstein and Feiner (1988), at least three conceptions of countertransference can be distinguished. In the "classical" view, which we owe to Freud, countertransference is described as "the therapist's unconscious, conflict-based reaction to the client's transference" (Gelso & Hayes, 2002, p. 268). A second perspective, termed "totalistic," defines countertransference as "all of the therapist's emotional reactions to the patient" (Gelso & Hayes, 2002, p. 268). In contrast, the "complementary" view sees countertransference as the "complement to the patient's transference or style of relating" (Gelso & Hayes, 2002, p. 268), that is, the therapist's internal and behavioral responses to the patient's interpersonal "pulls."

Based on Gelso and Hayes's (2002) review of the research evidence, countertransference was retained by the Division 29 Task Force as a "promising and probably effective element" of the therapeutic relationship (Norcross, 2002). However, none of the studies that investigated the link between outcome and the degree of countertransference or the management of countertransference explicitly described their samples as involving clients with depressive or dysphoric disorders. Following the guidelines of the present Task Force (see Beutler & Castonguay, this volume), we thus accept the Division 29 conclusion by default (i.e., pending further research) and tentatively suggest the following principle:

1. When working with depressed clients, therapists are likely to be more effective when they adequately manage their countertransference reactions toward their clients.

Relational Interpretations

As Crits-Christoph and Connolly Gibbons (2002) point out in their review for the Division 29 Task Force, the concept of relational interpretations stands midway between technical and relationship aspects of psychotherapy. Like all techniques, they occur in the context of (and are likely to influence) the therapeutic relationship. In contrast with most other technical procedures, however, they directly focus on client relationship, including the client–therapist interaction.

Crits-Christoph and Connolly Gibbons's (2002) review of the empirical evidence revealed differential findings depending on whether one considers the frequency or the quality of the interpretations. With regard to the relationship between the frequency of relational interpretations and outcome, these authors concluded that the findings have been generally mixed. This conclusion appears to be consistent with Orlinsky et al.'s (1994) review. While they found that interpretation, as an intervention mode, appears to be effective, they also found mixed results with regard to the therapist's direct focus on core personal relationships and transference issues (i.e., "2 of the 27 findings are significantly negative and fewer than 40% indicated significant positive association with outcome," p. 296). Interestingly, Crits-Christoph and Connolly Gibbons (2002) have argued that transference interpretations should be used with care, as recent studies suggest that high rates of this intervention are associated with poor outcome.

An examination of the studies relevant to the frequency of relational interpretation that have been reviewed by Crits-Christoph and Connolly Gibbons (2002) revealed that only one involved a sample of purely depressed individuals (Connolly et al., 1999). For the entire sample, the authors found that the proportion of transference interpretations to total interventions in supportive-expressive therapy did not significantly predict outcome. However, the proportion of transference interpretations predicted worse outcome for clients who specifically demonstrated low quality of interpersonal relations prior to treatment.

When examining Crits-Christoph and Connolly Gibbons's (2002) review, we also found seven studies with mixed samples (including depressed or dysphoric clients) that focused on frequency of relational interpretation (Hill et al., 1988; Høglend, 1993; Malan, 1976, Studies 1 & 2; Piper, Debbane, Bienvenu, de Carufel, & Garant, 1986; Piper, Debbane, de Carufel, & Bienvenu, 1987; Piper, Azim, Joyce, & McCallum, 1991). Four of these studies (Malan, 1976, Studies 1 & 2; Piper et al., 1986, 1987) reported at least one positive significant finding supporting a relationship between the frequency or proportion of relational interpretations and improvement. However, three of these studies (Høglend, 1993; Piper et al., 1986; Piper, Azim, Joyce, & McCallum, 1991) reported at least one negative significant relationship between frequency or proportion of transference interpretations and favorable outcome. In Høglend (1993), however, such negative effect was only significant for clients with a high quality of object relations. Furthermore, when Piper et al. (1986) conducted separate analyses for high versus low quality of object relations, the negative results were significant only for the group with a high quality of object relations.

As a whole, we found that, whereas 50% of the studies with depressed or dysphoric clients reported at least one significant positive finding, 50% of the same group of studies reported at least one significant negative result. Taken together, the evidence lends support to Crits-Christoph and Connolly Gibbons's (2002) conclusion that direct correlations between frequencies of interpretations and outcome yield mixed results. The notable presence of negative results also gives credence to their warning about the potential risk of high rates of relational interpretation and seems to justify the following principle:

1. When working with depressed clients, therapists should avoid high levels of relational interpretations.

With respect to the relationship between the quality of the interpretations and outcome, Crits-Christoph and Connolly Gibbons's (2002) consideration of the empirical literature led them to conclude that "studies of the quality of interpretations have yielded consistent findings suggesting that relatively more favorable treatment outcomes are produced when therapists accurately address central aspects of patients' interpersonal dynamics" (p. 295). All three studies cited by the authors (Crits-Christoph, Cooper, & Luborsky, 1988; Piper, Joyce, McCallum, & Azim, 1993; Norville, Sampson, & Weiss, 1996) were conducted with mixed samples involving clients with dysphoric disorders. All three studies found at least one positive correlation between the quality of interpretations and outcome, and none of them found a negative correlation.

Based on the evidence reviewed above, it appears that the decision of Division 29 to consider the *quality* of relational interpretation as a promising and probably effective element of the therapeutic relationship (see Norcross, 2002, p. 442) is acceptable with regard to psychotherapy for depression. This leads us to recommend the following principle of change:

2. When making relational interpretations, therapists should strive to accurately address client's central interpersonal themes, as a high level of accuracy (or quality) with regard to these interpretations is likely to be beneficial for the client.

CONCLUSION

Summary

From the current state of the literature, largely based on the evidence reviewed within the context of the Division 29 Task Force on therapeutic relationship factors, two sets of principles of change have been derived for psychotherapy with dysphoric clients. The first set is based on the acceptance of conclusions reached by the Division 29 Task Force, even though the evidence supporting these conclusions has not been obtained on samples of clients explicitly identified as having dysphoric or depressive disorders. As such, this first set of principles should be considered tentative.

1. Repairing alliance ruptures that emerge during treatment is likely to be helpful when working with depressed clients.
2. Depressed clients are likely to benefit from receiving feedback from their therapists.
3. When working with depressed clients, therapists are likely to be more effective when they adequately manage their countertransference reactions toward their clients.

The second set of principles is based on some amount of evidence obtained with the dysphoric clients. These principles concern the general quality of the therapeutic relationship, the therapist's interpersonal attitude (deeply anchored in the client-centered tradition), and a number of skills related to the management of the therapeutic relationship.

1. When working with clients with dysphoric disorders, therapists should strive to develop and maintain a positive working alliance with their clients.
2. When conducting group therapy with depressed individuals, therapists should foster a strong level of cohesiveness within the group.
3. Therapists working with depressed individuals should attempt to facilitate their engagement during and between sessions.
4. When working with depressed individuals, therapists should relate to their clients in an empathic way.
5. When adopted by therapists, an attitude of caring, warmth, and acceptance is likely to be helpful in facilitating therapeutic change in depressed clients.
6. When working with individuals suffering from depressive symptoms, therapists are

likely to facilitate change when adopting an attitude of congruence or authenticity.

7. Therapists working with depressed individuals may find it helpful to adopt an empathic and nondefensive (or nonrigid) attitude when attempting to repair alliance ruptures.

8. When working with depressed clients, therapists' use of self-disclosure is likely to be helpful. This may be especially the case for reassuring and supportive self-disclosures, as opposed to challenging self-disclosures.

9. When working with depressed clients, therapists should avoid high levels of relational interpretations.

10. When making relational interpretations, therapists should strive to accurately address client's central interpersonal themes, as a high level of accuracy (or quality) with regard to these interpretations is likely to be beneficial for the client.

Future Directions

Although the majority of these principles have been derived from a considerable amount of process-outcome research, much more needs to be done. To begin with, it is important to recognize that, with the exception of alliance, few studies have been conducted with purely or predominantly depressed samples. This is surprising considering the fact that a substantial number of clinical trials have been conducted specifically on this disorder. Thus, more efforts should be directed toward making use of archival data in order to explore different aspects of the process of change and their links with outcome. Interestingly, more studies investigating alliance with purely depressive samples have recently appeared, providing further evidence for its role in client improvement (Hardy et al., 2001; Klein et al., 2003).

It should also be pointed out that much of the research on relationship variables have been plagued by problems. This could be explained, at least in part, by the fact that, for a number of the relationship constructs, the buck of the empirical investigation was conducted several decades ago— when process-outcome research was still at its infancy. To take the concept of congruence as an ex-

ample, Klein et al. (2002) have noted that most of the process-outcome results came from studies conducted in the 1960s and 1970s, without any such studies conducted after 1989. The authors also concluded that many of the methodological limitations (e.g., small N, low levels of conditions) may have failed to do justice to the relationship between congruence and outcome. It might therefore be appropriate to revisit the status of many relationship variables by conducting new research with better and more powerful designs.

Although the principles listed above recognize the role or potential influence of several relationship variables in the psychological treatment of dysphoric clients, they do not begin to reflect the complexity of the process of change within which these relationship factors are likely to be involved. Not addressed in this chapter are fascinating and, ultimately, crucial questions such as these: Is the contribution of any of the specific relationship variables to client improvement independent of other factors, e.g., does the alliance predict outcome above and beyond the client's pretreatment symptoms and/or the therapist's empathy? Does the quality of relationship factors precede or follow client change, for example, are therapists more effective when they adequately manage their countertransference, or are they less likely to act out their maladaptive internal reactions when clients are experiencing less distress and life difficulties? How are these variables influencing each other, for example, what kind of impact does the therapist's self-disclosure or quality of relational interpretations have on the alliance? Do some of these variables interact among themselves to produce change, for example, is a highly authentic (congruent) therapist more or less effective when clients pull for countertransferential reactions? Can a high level of congruence, low level of countertransference, and moderate level of self-disclosure be an optimal combination of therapeutic components? Is the effect of some relationship variables moderated by client and therapist pretreatment characteristics, for example, are high rates of relational interpretations particularly counter-indicated for some types of clients? Should therapists with relatively poor attachment style refrain from frequent self-disclosure? Do some of these relationship variables serve as mediators of change?

Although some of these specific questions have

begun to receive empirical attention, we believe that researchers should make more use of current sophisticated statistical and qualitative methods to provide contextual, multidimensional, and sequential analyses of the process of change. Rather than restricting ourselves, as we often do, to investigate simple relationships between two variables (e.g., a measure of alliance and a measure of outcome), we should devote more energy to complex effects that are perhaps best expressed by modifications of Paul's (1966) famous question, such as: Under what condition, in combination of which skills and techniques, and with what kind of participants, is a specific relationship component likely to be more beneficial?

Investigation of such complex relationships is likely to provide support for what we believe is a basic principle of change operating in the treatment of depression, as well as all other forms of psychological disorders:

1. Relationship variables are effective when provided in appropriate contexts and in interaction with several other therapeutic factors.

Although the evidence reviewed in this chapter suggests that many relationship variables contribute to client improvement, we do not believe that a few factors (e.g., empathy or alliance) in and of themselves directly lead to good outcome. Accordingly, we hope that future research will attempt to contextualize relationship factors by investigating the interaction of multiple influences operating in the process of change.

Furthermore, while research has made a considerable contribution to our understanding of relationship factors in psychotherapy, it is important to recognize that it has been difficult to operationalize, and therefore formally study, several aspects of the therapeutic relationship that clinicians have long believed to be important. These involve issues such as: the containment function of the relationship; identifications that the client makes concerning the therapist; and the shifts in the therapeutic relationship over time. Future empirical efforts, hopefully conducted in close collaboration between clinicians and researchers, should address these complex issues.

ACKNOWLEDGMENTS   Preparation of this chapter was supported in part by National Institute of Mental Health Research Grant MH-58593. The authors are grateful for the help of Leslie Angtuaco, Shirley Chung, Roger Karlsson, Tai Katzenstein, and Kseniya Moskovskaya in preparing this chapter.

Notes

1. Although we made an effort to conduct a comprehensive review of the relevant studies cited by the Division 29 Task Force, we were not able to find all of them (e.g., conference presentations, unpublished dissertations).

2. In Buckley et al. (1984), the negative relationship between client lack of involvement (i.e., degree of resistance) and outcome was marginally significant ($p < .1$).

3. It should be noted, however, that in one of these studies, the therapeutic participation ("extent and quality of the patient's involvement in the group") interacted with the overall level of activity (as measured by the number of times the patient was the main actor in group therapy) in predicting therapeutic benefit (Soldz et al., 1992). As noted by the authors, "more resistant behavior was connected with better outcome for patients who were the main actor only a few times, whereas the direction of the relationship was reversed for patients who were the main actor more frequently" (p. 60). It should also be mentioned that Soldz et al. (1992) found that the patient's ease of self-expression ("the main actor's spontaneous openness in expressing his/her feelings") negatively correlated with self-esteem improvement. Consistent with Tryon and Winograd's (2002) review, however, we did not consider this process variable to reflect collaborative involvement. Some patients can have difficulty expressing their emotion and still be very much involved in the group, while others may find it difficult to take initiative and work collaboratively and yet be able to easily express their feelings when they talk in the group.

4. In Bugge et al.'s (1985) study, no significance level was provided for "understand your feelings." However, this item was included in the group of process variables that accounted for more than one-third of the variance in either or both of the outcome measures used (i.e., satisfaction with therapy and therapist helpfulness).

References

Andreoli, A., Frances, A., Gex-Mabry, M., Aapro, N., Gerin, P., & Dazord, A. (1993). Crisis intervention in depressed patients with and without DSM-II-R personality disorders. *Journal of Nervous and Mental Disease, 181,* 732–737.

Bachelor, A. (1991). Comparison and relationship to outcome of diverse dimensions of the helping alliance as seen by client and therapist. *Psychotherapy, 28,* 534–549.

Barrett, M., & Berman, J. (2001). Is psychotherapy more effective when therapists disclose information about themselves? *Journal of Consulting and Clinical Psychology, 69,* 597–603.

Benjamin, L. S. (1974). Structural analysis of social behavior. *Psychological Review, 81,* 392–425.

Bergin, A. E., & Jasper, L. G. (1969). Correlates of empathy in psychotherapy: A replication. *Journal of Abnormal Psychology, 74,* 477–481.

Beutler, L. E., Johnson, D. T., Neville, C. W., & Workman, S. N. (1972). "Accurate empathy" and AB dichotomy. *Journal of Consulting and Clinical Psychology, 38,* 372–375.

Beutler, L., & Mitchell, R. (1981). Differential psychotherapy outcome among depressed and impulsive patients as a function of analytic and experiential treatment procedures. *Psychiatry, 44,* 297–306.

Bohart, A. C., Elliott, R., Greenberg, L. S., & Watson, J. C. (2002). Empathy. In J. C. Norcross (Ed.), *Psychotherapy relationships that work* (pp. 89–108). New York: Oxford University Press.

Buckley, P., Conte, H. R., Plutchik, R., Wild, K. V., & Karasu, T. B. (1984). Psychodynamic variables as predictors of psychotherapy outcome. *American Journal of Psychiatry, 141,* 742–748.

Budman, S. H., Soldz, S., Demby, A., Feldstein, M., Springer, T., & Davis, S. (1989). Cohesion, alliance, and outcome in group psychotherapy. *Psychiatry, 52,* 339–350.

Bugge, I., Hendel, D. D., & Moene, R. (1985). Client evaluations of therapeutic processes and outcomes in a university mental health center. *Journal of American College Health, 33,* 141–146.

Burlingame, G. M., Fuhriman, A., & Johnson, J. E. (2002). Cohesion in group psychotherapy. In J. C. Norcross (Ed.), *Psychotherapy relationships that work* (pp. 71–87). New York: Oxford University Press.

Burns, D. D., & Nolen-Hoeksema, S. (1991). Coping styles, homework compliance, and the effectiveness of cognitive-behavioral therapy. *Journal of Consulting and Clinical Psychology, 59,* 305–311.

Burns, D. D., & Nolen-Hoeksema, S. (1992). Therapeutic empathy and recovery from depression in cognitive-behavioral therapy: A structural equation model. *Journal of Consulting and Clinical Psychology, 60,* 441–449.

Burns, D. D., & Spangler, D. L. (2000). Does psychotherapy homework lead to improvements in depression in cognitive-behavioral therapy or does improvement lead to increased homework compliance? *Journal of Consulting and Clinical Psychology, 68,* 46–56.

Castonguay, L. G., Goldfried, M. R., Wiser, S., Raue, P. J., & Hayes, A. M. (1996). Predicting the effect of cognitive therapy for depression: A study of unique and common factors. *Journal of Consulting and Clinical Psychology, 64,* 497–504.

Claiborn, C. D., Goodyear, R. K., & Horner, P. A. (2002). Feedback. In J. C. Norcross (Ed.), *Psychotherapy relationships that work* (pp. 217–233). New York: Oxford University Press.

Clarkin, J. F., & Crilly, J. L. (1987). Therapeutic alliance and hospital treatment outcome. *Hospital and Community Psychiatry, 38,* 871–875.

Coady, N. F. (1991). The association between client and therapist interpersonal processes and outcomes in psychodynamic psychotherapy. *Research on Social Work Practice, 1,* 122–138.

Connolly, M. B., Crits-Christoph, P., Shappell, S., Barber, J. P., Luborsky, L., & Shaffer, C. (1999). Relation of transference interpretations to outcome in the early sessions of brief supportive-expressive psychotherapy. *Psychotherapy Research, 9,* 485–495.

Constantino, M. J., Castonguay, L. G., & Schut, A. J. (2002). The working alliance: A flagship for the scientific-practitioner model in psychotherapy. In G. Shick Tryon (Ed.), *Counseling based on process research* (pp. 81–131). New York: Allyn & Bacon.

Conte, H. R., Ratto, R., Clutz, K., & Karasu, T. B. (1995). Determinants of outpatients' satisfaction with therapists. *Journal of Psychotherapy Practice and Research, 4,* 43–51.

Cooley, E. J., & Lajoy, R. (1980). Therapeutic relationship and improvement as perceived by clients and therapists. *Journal of Clinical Psychology, 36,* 562–570.

Crits-Christoph, P., & Connolly Gibbons, M.-B. (2002). Relational interpretations. In J. C. Norcross (Ed.), *Psychotherapy relationships that* work: Therapist contributions and responsiveness to patients (pp. 285–300). London: Oxford University Press.

Crits-Christoph, P., Cooper, A., & Luborsky, L. (1988). The accuracy of therapists' interpretations and the outcome of dynamic psychotherapy. Journal of Consulting and Clinical Psychology, 56, 490–495.

DeRubeis, R. J., & Feeley, M. (1990). Determinants of change in cognitive therapy for depression. Cognitive Therapy and Research, 14, 469–482.

Dormaar, J. M., Dijkman, C. I., & de Vries, M. W. (1989). Consensus in patient–therapist interactions: A measure of the therapeutic relationship related to outcome. Psychotherapy and Psychosomatics, 51, 69–76.

Epstein, L., & Feiner, A. H. (1988). Countertransference: The therapist's contribution to treatment. In B. Wolstein (Ed.), Essential papers on countertransference (pp. 282–303). New York: New York University Press.

Farber, B. A., & Lane, J. S. (2002). Positive regard. In J. C. Norcross (Ed.), Psychotherapy relationships that work (pp. 175–194). New York: Oxford University Press.

Feeley, M., DeRubeis, R. J., and Gelfand, L. A. (1999). The temporal relation of adherence and alliance to symptom change in cognitive therapy for depression. Journal of Consulting and Clinical Psychology, 67, 578–582.

Feeley, W. M. (1993). Treatment components of cognitive therapy for major depression: The good, the bad, and the inert. Unpublished doctoral dissertation, University of Pennsylvania, Philadelphia.

Gaston, L., Marmar, C. R., Thompson, L. W., & Gallager, D. (1991). Alliance prediction of outcome: Beyond in-treatment symptomatic change as psychotherapy progresses. Psychotherapy Research, 1, 104–112.

Gaston, L., Thompson, L., Gallager, D., Cournoyer, L. G., & Gagnon, R. (1998). Alliance, technique, and their interactions in predicting outcome of behavioral, cognitive, and brief dynamic therapy. Psychotherapy Research, 8, 190–209.

Gelso, C. J., & Hayes, J. A. (2002). The management of countertransference. In J. C. Norcross (Ed.), Psychotherapy relationships that work: Therapist contributions and responsiveness to patients (pp. 285–300). London: Oxford University Press.

Gomes-Schwartz, B. (1978). Effective ingredients in psychotherapy: Prediction of outcome from process variables. Journal of Consulting and Clinical Psychology, 46, 1023–1035.

Hardy, G. E., Cahill, J., Shapiro, D. A., Barkham, M., Rees, A., & Macaskill, N. (2001). Client interpersonal and cognitive styles as predictors of response to time-limited cognitive therapy for depression. Journal of Consulting and Clinical Psychology, 69, 841–845.

Hatcher, R. L., & Barends, A. W. (1996). Patient's view of the alliance in psychotherapy: Exploratory factor analysis of three alliance measures. Journal of Consulting and Clinical Psychology, 64, 1326–1336.

Hayes, A. M., & Strauss, J. L. (1998). Dynamic systems theory as a paradigm for the study of change in psychotherapy: An application to cognitive therapy for depression. Journal of Consulting and Clinical Psychology, 66, 939–947.

Hill, C., & Knox, S. (2002). Self-disclosure. In J. C. Norcross (Ed.), Psychotherapy relationships that work (pp. 255–265). New York: Oxford University Press.

Hill, C., Mahalik, J., Thompson, B. (1989). Therapist self-disclosure. Psychotherapy, 26, 290–295.

Hill, C. E., Helms, J. E., Tichenor, V., Spiegel, S. B., O'Grady, K. E., & Perry, E. S. (1988). Effects of therapist response modes in brief psychotherapy. Journal of Counseling Psychology, 35, 222–233.

Hoberman, H. H., Lewinsohn, P. M., & Tilson, M. (1988). Group treatment of depression: Individual predictors of outcome. Journal of Consulting and Clinical Psychology, 56, 393–398.

Høglend, P. (1993). Transference interpretations and long-term change after dynamic psychotherapy of brief to moderate length. American Journal of Psychotherapy, 47(4), 494–507.

Hollon, S. D., DeRubeis, R. J., Evans, M. D., Wiemer, M., Garvey, M. J., Grove, W. M., & Tuason, V. B. (1992). Cognitive therapy and pharmacotherapy for depression: Singly and in combination. Archives of General Psychiatry, 49, 774–781.

Horvath, A. O., & Bedi, R. P. (2002). The alliance. In J. C. Norcross (Ed.), Psychotherapy relationships that work (pp. 37–69). New York: Oxford University Press.

Horvath, A. O., & Symonds, B. D. (1991). Relation between working alliance and outcome in psychotherapy: A meta-analysis. Journal of Counseling Psychology, 38, 139–149.

Hynan, D. J. (1990). Client reasons and experiences

in treatment that influence termination of psychotherapy. *Journal of Clinical Psychology, 46,* 891–895.

Jacobs, A. (1974). The use of feedback in groups. In A. Jacobs and W. E. Spradlin (Eds.), *The group as an agent of change* (pp. 408–448). New York: Behavioral Publications.

Jones, E. E., Parke, L. A., & Pulos, S. M. (1992). How therapy is conducted in the private consulting room: A multidimensional description of brief psychodynamic treatments. *Psychotherapy Research, 2,* 16–30.

Jones, E. E., & Zoppel, C. L. (1982). Impact and therapist gender on psychotherapy process and outcome. *Journal of Consulting and Clinical Psychology, 50,* 259–272.

Klein, D. K., Schwartz, J. E., Santiago, N. J., Vivian D., Vocisano, C., Castonguay, L. G., Arnow, B., Blalock, J. A, Manber, R., Markowitz, J. C., Riso, L. P, Rothbaum, B., McCullough, J. P., Thase, M. E., Borian, F. E., Miller, I., & Keller, M. B. (2003). The therapeutic alliance in chronic depression: Prediction of treatment response after controlling for prior change and patient characteristics. *Journal of Consulting and Clinical Psychology, 71,* 997–1006.

Klein, M. H., Kolden, G. G., Michels, J. L., & Chisholm-Stockard, S. (2002). Congruence. In J. C. Norcross (Ed.), *Psychotherapy relationships that work* (pp. 195–215). New York: Oxford University Press.

Klerman, G. L., & Weissman, M. M. (1986). The interpersonal approach to understanding depression. In T. Millon and G. L. Klerman (Eds.), *Contemporary directions in psychopathology: Toward the DSM-IV* (pp. 429–456). New York: Guilford.

Knox, S., Hess, S., Petersen, D., & Hill, C. (1997). A qualitative analysis of client perceptions of the effects of helpful therapists self-disclosure in long-term therapy. *Journal of Counseling Psychology, 44,* 274–283.

Kolb, D. L., Beutler, L. E., Davis, C. S., Crago, M., & Shanfield, S. B. (1985). Patient and therapy process variables relating to dropout and change in psychotherapy. *Psychotherapy, 22,* 702–710.

Krupnick, J. L., Elkin, I., Collins, J., Simmens, S., Sotsky, S. M., Pilkonis, A., & Watkings, J. T. (1994). Therapeutic alliance and clinical outcome in the NIMH treatment of depression collaborative research program: Preliminary findings. *Psychotherapy, 31,* 28–35.

Krupnick, J. L., Sotsky, S. M., Simmens, A., Moyer,

J., Elkin, I., Watkins, J., & Pilkonis, P. A. (1996). The role of the alliance in psychotherapy and pharmacotherapy outcome: Findings in the National Institute of Mental Health treatment of depression collaborative research program. *Journal of Consulting and Clinical Psychology, 64,* 532–539.

Kurtz, R. R., & Grummon, D. L. (1972). Different approaches to the measurement of therapist empathy and their relationship to therapy outcomes. *Journal of Consulting and Clinical Psychology, 39,* 106–115.

Lafferty, P., Beutler, L. E., & Crago, M. (1989). Differences between more and less effective psychotherapists: A study of select therapist variables. *Journal of Consulting and Clinical Psychology, 57,* 76–80.

Lieberman, P. B., von Rehn, S., Dickie, E., Elliot, B., & Egerter, E. (1992). Therapeutic effects of brief hospitalization: The role of the therapeutic alliance. *Journal of Psychotherapy Practice and Research, 1,* 56–63.

Lorr, M. (1965). Client perceptions of therapists: A study of therapeutic relation. *Journal of Consulting Psychology, 29,* 146–149.

Malan, D. H. (1976). *Towards the validation of dynamic psychotherapy: Replication.* New York: Plenum.

Marmar, C., Weiss, D. S., & Gaston, L. (1989). Toward the validation of the California Therapeutic Alliance Rating System. *Psychological Assessment, 1,* 46–52.

Marmar, C. R., Gaston, L., Gallager, D., & Thompson, L. W. (1989). Therapeutic alliance and outcome in behavioral, cognitive, and brief dynamic psychotherapy in late-life depression. *Journal of Nervous & Mental Disease, 177,* 464–472.

Martin, D. J., Garske, J. P., & Davis, K. M. (2000). Relation of the therapeutic alliance with outcome and other variables: A meta-analytic review. *Journal of Consulting and Clinical Psychology, 68,* 438–450.

Marziali, E. (1984). Three viewpoints of the therapeutic alliance scales: Similarities, differences, and associations with psychotherapy outcome. *Journal of Nervous and Mental Disease, 172,* 417–423.

Muran, J. C., Gorman, B. S., Safran, J. D., Twining, L., Samstag, I. W., & Winston, A. (1995). Linking in-session change to overall outcome in short term cognitive therapy. *Journal of Consulting and Clinical Psychology, 63,* 651–657.

Norcross, J. C. (2002). *Psychotherapy relationships*

that work: Therapist contributions and respon-siveness to patients. London: Oxford University Press.

Norville, R., Sampson, H., & Weiss, J. (1996). Accurate interpretations and brief psychotherapy outcome. *Psychotherapy Research, 6,* 16–29.

Ogrodniczuk, J. S., Piper, W. E., Joyce, A. S., & McCallum, M. (2000). Different perspectives of the therapeutic alliance and therapist technique in 2 forms of dynamically oriented psychotherapy. *Canadian Journal of Psychiatry, 45,* 452–458.

O'Malley, S. S., Suh, C. S., & Strupp, H. H. (1983). The Vanderbilt Psychotherapy Project Scale: A report on the scale development and a process-outcome study. *Journal of Consulting and Clinical Psychology, 51,* 581–586.

Orlinsky, D. E., Grawe, K., & Parks, B. K. (1994). Process and outcome in psychotherapy: Noch einmal. In S. L. Garfield & A. E. Bergin (Eds.), *Handbook of psychotherapy and behavior change* (4th ed., pp. 270–376). New York: John Wiley & Sons.

Orlinsky, D. E., & Howard, K. I. (1986). The relation of process to outcome in psychotherapy. In S. L. Garfield & A. E. Bergin (Eds.), *Handbook of psychotherapy and behavior change* (2nd ed., pp. 283–329). New York: John Wiley & Sons.

Paivio, S. C., & Bahr, L. B. (1998). Interpersonal problems, working alliance, and outcome in short-term experiential therapy. *Psychotherapy Research, 8,* 392–406.

Paul, G. (1966). *Effects of insight, desensitization, and attention placebo treatment of anxiety.* Stanford, CA: Stanford University Press.

Peake, T. H. (1979). Therapist–patient agreement and outcome in group therapy. *Journal of Clinical Psychology, 35,* 637–646.

Persons, J. B., Burns, D. D., & Perloff, J. M. (1988). Predictors of dropout and outcome in cognitive therapy for depression in a private practice setting. *Cognitive Therapy and Research, 12,* 557–575.

Piper, W. E., Azim, H. F., Joyce, A. S., & McCallum, M. (1991). Transference interpretations, therapeutic alliance, and outcome in short-term individual psychotherapy. *Archives of General Psychiatry, 48,* 946–953.

Piper, W. E., Azim, H. F. A., Joyce, A. S., McCallum, M., Nixon, G. W. H., & Segal, P. S. (1991). Quality of object relations vs. interpersonal functioning as predictor of therapeutic alliance and psychotherapy outcome. *Journal of Nervous and Mental Disease, 179,* 432–438.

Piper, W. E., Boroto, D. R., Joyce, A. S., McCallum, M., & Azim, H. F. A. (1995). Pattern of alliance and outcome in short-term individual psychotherapy. *Psychotherapy, 32,* 639–647.

Piper, W. E., Debbane, E. G., Bienvenu, J. P., de Carufel, F., & Garant, J. (1986). Relationships between the object focus of therapist interpretations and outcome in short-term individual psychotherapy. *British Journal of Medical Psychology, 59,* 1–11.

Piper, W. E., Debbane, E. G., de Carufel, F. L., & Bienvenu, J. P. (1987). A system for differentiating therapist interpretations from other interventions. *Bulletin of the Menninger Clinic, 51,* 532–550.

Piper, W. E., de Carufel, F. L., & Szkrumelak, N. (1985). Patient predictors of process and outcome in short-term individual psychotherapy. *Journal of Nervous and Mental Disease, 173,* 726–733.

Piper, W. E., Joyce, A. S., McCallum, M., & Azim, H. F. A. (1993). Concentration and correspondence of transference interpretations in short-term psychotherapy. *Journal of Consulting and Clinical Psychology, 61,* 586–595.

Piper, W. E., Ogrodniczuk, J. S., Joyce, A. S., McCallum, M., Rosie, J. S., O'Kelly, J. G., & Steinberg, P. I. (1999). Prediction of dropping out in time-limited, interpretive individual psychotherapy. *Psychotherapy, 36,* 114–122.

Quintana, S. M., & Meara, N. M. (1990). Internalization of therapeutic relationships in short-term psychotherapy. *Journal of Counseling Psychology, 2,* 123–130.

Rounsaville, B. J., Chevron, E. S., Prusoff, B. A., Elkin, I., Imber, S., Sotsky, S., & Watkins, J. (1987). The relation between specific and general dimensions of the psychotherapy process in interpersonal psychotherapy of depression. *Journal of Consulting and Clinical Psychology, 55,* 379–384.

Rounsaville, B. J., Weissman, M. M., & Prusoff, B. A. (1981). Psychotherapy with depressed outpatients: Patient process variables as predictors of outcome. *British Journal of Psychiatry, 138,* 67–74.

Safran, J. D., Muran, J. C., Samstag, L. W., & Stevens, C. (2002). Repairing alliance ruptures. In J. C. Norcross (Ed.), *Psychotherapy relationships that work* (pp. 235–254). New York: Oxford University Press.

Safran, J. D., & Wallner, L. K. (1991). The relative predictive validity of two therapeutic alliance measures in cognitive therapy. *Psychological Assessment, 3,* 188–195.

Saltzman, C., Leutgert, M. J., Roth, C. H., Creaser, J., & Howard, L. (1976). Formation of a therapeutic relationship: Experiences during the initial phase of psychotherapy as predictors of treatment duration and outcome. *Journal of Consulting and Clinical Psychology, 44,* 546–555.

Saunders, S. M. (2000). Examining the relationship between the therapeutic bond and the phases of treatment outcome. *Psychotherapy, 37,* 206–218.

Sloane, R. B., Staples, F. R., Cristol, A. H., Yorkson, N. J., & Whipple, K. (1975). *Psychotherapy versus behavior therapy.* Cambridge, MA: Harvard University Press.

Soldz, S., Budman, S., & Demby, A. (1992). The relationship between main actor behaviors and treatment outcome in group psychotherapy. *Psychotherapy Research, 2,* 52–62.

Staples, F. R., & Sloane, R. B. (1976). Truax factors, speech characteristics, and therapeutic outcome. *Journal of Nervous and Mental Disease, 163,* 135–140.

Staples, F. R., Sloane, R. D., Whipple, K., Cristol, A. H., & Yorkston, N. (1976). Process and outcome in psychotherapy and behavior therapy. *Journal of Consulting and Clinical Psychology, 44,* 340–350.

Stiles, W. B., Agnew-Davies, R., Hardy, G. E., Barkham, M., & Shapiro, D. A. (1998). Relations of the alliance with psychotherapy outcome: Findings in the Second Sheffield Psychotherapy Project. *Journal of Consulting and Clinical Psychology, 66,* 791–802.

Strupp, H. H, Fox, R. E., & Lessler, K. (1969). *Patients view their psychotherapy.* Baltimore: Johns Hopkins University Press.

Truax, C. B. (1971). Perceived therapeutic conditions and client outcome. *Comparative Group Studies, 2,* 301–310.

Truax, C. B., Wargo, D. G., Frank, J. D., Imber, S. D., Battle, C. C., Hoehn-Saric, R., Nash, E. H., & Stone, A. R. (1966). Therapist empathy, genuineness, and warmth and patient therapeutic outcome. *Journal of Consulting Psychology, 30,* 395–401.

Truax, C. B. & Wittmer, J. (1971). The effects of therapist focus on patient anxiety source and the interaction with therapist level of accurate empathy. *Journal of Clinical Psychology, 27,* 297–299.

Tryon, G. S., & Winograd, G. (2002). Goal consensus and collaboration. In J. C. Norcross (Ed.), *Psychotherapy relationships that work* (pp. 109–125). New York: Oxford University Press.

Tschuschke, V., & Dies, R. R. (1994). Intensive analysis of therapeutic factors and outcome in long-term inpatient groups. *International Journal of Group Psychotherapy, 44,* 185–208.

Windholz, M. J., & Silberschatz, G. (1988). Vanderbilt psychotherapy process scale: A replication with adult outpatients. *Journal of Consulting and Clinical Psychology, 56,* 56–60.

Zuroff, D. C., Blatt, S. J., Sotsky, S. M., Krupnick, J. L., Martin, D. J., Sanislow, C. A., & Simmens, S. (2000). Relation of therapeutic alliance and perfectionism to outcome in brief outpatient treatment for depression. *Journal of Consulting and Clinical Psychology, 68,* 114–124.

4

Technique Factors in Treating Dysphoric Disorders

William C. Follette

Leslie S. Greenberg

TECHNIQUE FACTORS IN TREATING DYSPHORIC DISORDERS

Since the early 1990s, there has been an increasing emphasis on improving treatment outcomes by selecting interventions that have empirical support for their efficacy. In clinical psychology the movement has not been without controversy (Beutler, 1998; Bohart, 2000; Bohart, O'Hara, & Leitner, 1998; Borkovec & Castonguay, 1998; Chambless & Ollendick, 2001; Elliott, 1998, p. 4; Follette & Beitz, 2003; Henry, 1998; Ingram, Hayes, & Scott, 2000; Lampropoulos, 2000; Messer, 2001; Wilson, 1996). The American Psychological Association has compiled a list of over 100 interventions that occur on the empirically supported treatment (EST) list making it all but impossible to keep current on or even learn all these interventions. As the EST movement began to establish itself, there were suggestions about how programs could be structured to accommodate training of these therapies (e.g., Calhoun, Moras, Pilkonis, & Rehm, 1998; Crits-Christoph, Frank, Chambless, Brody,

& Karp, 1995). There is little research indicating how long it takes an individual therapist to become proficient at a particular EST or how much more quickly, if at all, one learns additional ESTs. Two points are important to note. First, regardless of the efficiency of training full ESTs, it is not probable that practitioners (or even trainers) can learn a significant portion of these interventions using present training methods, let alone keep up with the rapidly expanding list. Second, since the scientific knowledge base that is foundational to empirically supported treatments is shared, there will certainly be common features among the interventions. Thus, there are efficiencies to be gained by identifying common principles of therapeutic change that are present across ESTs.

At this point the virtue of identifying and teaching principles rather than highly specified procedures is particularly appealing because of the lack of definitive research on the efficient dissemination of ESTs, though many researchers are studying this issue (e.g., Addis, Wade, & Hatgis, 1999; Addis & Zamudio, 2001; Barlow, Levitt, &

Bufka, 1999; Schoenwald & Hoagwood, 2001; Tarrier, Barrowclough, Haddock, & McGovern, 1999). While some treatments can be disseminated with success, more complicated interventions often require intensive training and supervision and good adherence or poorer outcomes occur (cf. Henggeler, Melton, Brondino, Scherer, & Hanley, 1997; Petry & Simcic, 2002; Tarrier et al., 1999). In addition to transferring technologies to individuals, other institutional factors have been identified that make it more or less likely that dissemination efforts will be successful (Addis & Zamudio, 2001; Cooke, 2000; Schoenwald & Hoagwood, 2001; Strosahl, 1998; Tarrier et al., 1999).

EMPIRICAL BASIS FOR PRINCIPLES

In trying to identify likely intervention principles, it was useful to examine the components of therapies shown to have evidence of efficacy in clinical trials. The criteria for evaluating the sufficiency of the evidence suggestive of efficacy are well documented in reports on ESTs (Chambless et al., 1998) and proposals for improvements have been offered in additional detail (Chambless & Hollon, 1998). Without repeating those criteria fully, "well-established" treatments require two or more studies demonstrating efficacy by showing superior results to placebo or another treatment or equivalence to already established treatments. "Probably efficacious" treatments show evidence of efficacy, though with less rigor than the well-established treatments. Since the more recent reviews of empirically supported treatments were published (Chambless & Ollendick, 2001; Craighead, Hart, Craighead, & Ilardi, 2002), the updating of the lists await resolution of how the EST program should continue. That does not mean progress has not continued with the addition of new studies that contribute to the empirical knowledge base of what constitutes efficacious treatment. In constructing the principles listed later, the authors identified at least one probably efficacious intervention that seemed based on emerging principles and one intervention we classified as "experimental" based on promising initial results. It remains to be seen whether these principles are as robust as the others.

However, it is not the purpose of this effort to simply recapitulate those reviews (see Chambless & Ollendick, 2001; Nathan & Gorman, 2002) but suggest treatment principles that are common across therapies or are strongly enough grounded in theory or empirical studies to believe they are significantly powerful to consider. Try as one might to avoid imposing theory on these principles, how one phrases and partitions these principles cannot be independent of one's own heuristics for organizing information.

There is considerable literature supporting the overall efficacy of behavior therapy, cognitive therapy, interpersonal therapy, emotion-focused and brief dynamic therapy, problem-solving therapy, self-control therapy, and where appropriate behavioral marital and family therapy in the treatment of dysphoric mood. For geriatric depression, there is evidence that reminiscence therapy is useful. While each therapy may be theoretically relatively distinct, they are often technically eclectic with different therapies sharing elements of one or more of the others. In considering how to organize intervention principles, it was useful to extract principles from therapies that stated causal explanations identifying maintaining factors, interactional patterns and environmental factors that ameliorate or exacerbate dysphoria, or that hypothesized etiologic factors that if properly addressed, could alter the impact of the presumed causes of depression. An abbreviated presentation of the empirically supported treatments used as a foundation for the identification of principles is presented in Table 4.1.

Behavior Therapy

Behavior therapies have generally emphasized the relationship between the loss of or decrease in the rate contingent positive reinforcement. Skinner (1953) suggested that interruptions of established behavioral sequences that previously produced reinforcement could produce depression. Peter Lewinsohn has built on this model and expanded it to include the impact that depressed mood has on the people in the depressed person's environment who provide interest and concern, thus inadvertently reinforcing the depressive behavior. Social skills deficiencies can also contribute to low rates of reinforcement and its maintenance (see Hoberman & Lewinsohn, 1985; Lewinsohn & Gotlib, 1995,

Table 4.1
Empirically Supported Treatments for Depression and Corresponding Principles

Treatment	Well-established	Probably efficacious	Experimental	Contributed to principle
Behavior therapy	A, B			1, 2, 3, 4
Self-control therapy		A, B		2, 3
Social problem-solving therapy		A		2, 3
Behavioral martial therapy	B			4
Cognitive therapy	A, B			1, 2
Interpersonal therapy	A, B			1, 2, 3, 4, 5
Brief dynamic therapy		A		5
Process-experiential therapy		C		5
Mindfulness therapy			C	5

Note. A = As described in Chambless et al., 1998, and Chambless & Ollendick, 2001; *B* = As described in Nathan & Gorman, 2002; C = Treatments based on theory and some empirical evidence still being researched as selected by the authors of this chapter.

for a description of the evolution of behavior therapy for the treatment of depression).

Most behavior therapies focus on increasing the likelihood that depressed patients will be able to identify and attain personally relevant goals. This may be accomplished by use of goal attainment strategies where larger goals are met by setting and meeting smaller, satisfying, relevant goals (Biglan & Dow, 1981). Behavior therapies also address social skills deficits, increase coping skills, and cognitive self-regulation (Lewinsohn & Hoberman, 1982). Skills training strategies frequently make use of didactic sessions, modeling and instruction, behavioral rehearsal, role-playing, and practice in and out of session. Assertion training, communication training, and stress management including relaxation training are staples of many behavioral treatments for depression.

Behavior therapists have long made use of self-monitoring strategies to identify functional relationships between life events and mood with the goal of increasing behaviors that are linked to improved mood and identifying situations that lead to or are associated with depressed mood with the goal of decreasing the number of those situations or improving mastery in high-risk situations. Behavioral deficits that manifest themselves in social situations have received special attention (Mc-Lean, 1981).

Self-control theory produced interventions focusing on increasing self-reinforcement and de-

creasing self-punishment (Fuchs & Rehm, 1977; Rehm, Fuchs, Roth, Kornblith, & Romano, 1979). Research had demonstrated that depressed individuals tended to set unreasonably high standards for themselves leading to low rates of self-delivered reinforcement and high rates of self-punishment. Patients are taught to self-monitor positive activities that are associated with improved mood, develop criteria for specific goals and make use of reward menus when these goals are attained.

Although it would be possible to address behavioral marital therapy (BMT) as a separate intervention, for simplicity one can construe marital as another means to increase access to appropriate interpersonal reinforcers and to reduce the likelihood of inadvertently reinforcing depressive behaviors. Depression and marital satisfaction are inversely related with ambiguity about the direction of causality (Whisman, 2001). Two elements that are common to most forms of BMT are increasing the occurrence of shared positive activities and improving communication (Jacobson & Follette, 1985).

Empirical Support for Behavior Therapy

Empirical findings from four studies were summarized in Nathan and Gorman's review of effective treatments (Craighead et al., 2002, pp. 249–250). Using the BDI or the HRSD evidence suggests that behavior therapies produce approximately a 50% recovery rate. In an older meta-analysis of depression treatment studies, Robinson and colleagues found that behavior therapy produced effect sizes of 1.02 ($p < .05$) compared to wait-list controls and 0.27 compared to general verbal therapies ($p < .05$) excluding cognitive and cognitive behavioral therapies.

Cognitive Therapy

A close paraphrase of the description of cognitive therapy by Hollon, Haman, and Brown (2002, pp. 384–386) emphasizes an interrelationship between behavior and cognition and affect. The therapy begins with an exploration or the patient's dysfunctional beliefs or personal meaning system that includes the well-known negative cognitive triad of negative thoughts about the self, the world, and the future (Beck, Rush, Shaw, & Emery, 1979, p. 11). Treatment then proceeds to a careful examination of that belief system. Evidence speaking for and against the belief system is examined and alternative interpretations are considered. Experimentation by the patient takes place early in the therapy process in the form of activity monitoring to promote symptom relief and, more importantly to the theory, gather empirical data testing the validity of the belief system. Therapy progress is assessed in terms of behavioral outcomes. Testing of negative expectations and interpretations takes place by emitting behavior and assessing whether the behavioral evidence refutes or supports the patient's belief system. In instances where a patient faces significant environmental demands, behavioral strategies including goal attainment strategies and modeling or practicing useful responses to real challenges are utilized. Much of the clinical improvement in cognitive therapy takes place during the initial portions of therapy where therapy focuses on making and testing predictions about how the patient acts in the environment and what the consequences of those actions are.

During cognitive therapy the patient learns to test whether his or her prediction about the outcome of a specific behavior in a particular situation is correct. When it is not, as is frequently the case in depression, the patient has the therapist to help realistically identify the (in)accuracy in their understanding of how the world works. Inaccuracies are often the result of logical error that particular patients display. These include processes such as magnification, minimization, overgeneralization, dichotomous thinking among other examples (Beck et al., 1979). A major component of cognitive therapy is challenging the implicit and explicit rules the patient uses to predict the future and bring their behavior, their cognitions, and ultimately their affective responses back under the more realistic control of actual rather than erroneously assumed contingencies. Results from behavioral and cognitive therapies indicate that affective, cognitive, and behavioral changes go hand-in-hand, though there is spirited debate over what the active component of cognitive therapy actually is (cf. Ilardi & Craighead, 1999; Jacobson et al., 1996; Tang & DeRubeis, 1999a, 1999b).

Empirical Support for Cognitive Therapy

Cognitive therapy has been the subject of a great deal of empirical testing. It has been shown to be effective in clinical populations when compared to minimal treatment controls and at least as effective as other active treatments for depression (Gaffan, Tsaousis, & Kemp-Wheeler, 1995). In the 65 studies reviewed in their meta-analysis, Gaffen and colleagues also demonstrated that allegiance effects accounted for less variability on effect sizes in more recent studies, though advantages of cognitive therapy over other active treatments were decreasing. In older studies the mean effect size compared to wait-list controls was 1.73, while more recent studies produced an effect size of 0.93, still a large effect. Regardless, their meta-analysis clearly supports the effectiveness of cognitive therapy.

Cognitive therapy has been the subject of comparisons with antidepressant medications in several studies. Results from the Treatment of Depression Collaborative Research Program (TDCRP) indicated that cognitive therapy was comparable to other treatment conditions for less severe depression but performed less well than medication (imipramine) for severe depression (Elkin et al., 1995; Elkin et al., 1989; Elkin, Parloff, Hadley, & Autry, 1985). Jacobson and Hollon (1996) reexamined data from the TDCRP and found different treatment responses at different research sites indicating that where cognitive therapy was done more poorly with severely depressed subjects, poorer results were observed. However, at a third site with more experienced therapists, severely depressed subjects responded comparably to other conditions. One interpretation is that psychosocial interventions, or at least cognitive therapy, must be well implemented to be effective. Another analysis that also included data from the TDCRP suggested that adjunctive medication were useful in the treatment of severe depression (Thase et al., 1997). With the exception of studies that include TDCRP data, other studies comparing cognitive therapy with medication in more severely depressed outpatients indicate that cognitive therapy performs comparably to medication treatments if cognitive therapy is well implemented (DeRubeis, Gelfand, Tang, & Simons, 1999). Craighead and colleagues' (2002) summary of treatments that work for depression concluded that 50 to 70% of patients with major depressive disorder (MDD) treated with cognitive behavior therapy (primarily cognitive therapy) no longer met criteria for MDD at the end of treatment.

Interpersonal Psychotherapy

Interpersonal psychotherapy (IPT) is an empirically supported treatment for depression described by Weissman, Markowitz and Klerman (2000). IPT does not identify an etiology to depression, but its intellectual origins are rooted in early interpersonal theory and attachment theory (Klerman, Weissman, Rounsaville, & Chevron, 1984). The treatment itself draws on a variety of techniques and approaches. IPT, although drawing on some basic interpersonal psychoanalytic ideas, focuses on the present and does not include notions of transference nor make use of dream interpretation. At least one study combining elements of IPT and brief psychodynamic indicated similar improvements to those achieved by cognitive therapy (Shapiro et al., 1994). Following research on the importance of links between depression and grief, role disputes, role transitions, and interpersonal deficits, the therapy is conducted in three phases. The first phase lasts approximately four sessions, focuses on assessment and a psychoeducational component wherein the patient is presented with a disease model of depression and an orientation to IPT as a coherent treatment for depression. In the middle 5–12 sessions those areas identified in the assessment phase are actively explored. Symptoms are related to interpersonal events and the patient is encouraged to develop new strategies to deal with these events and then experiment with them. There is less emphasis on homework than with cognitive-behavioral therapies. In addition, IPT focuses less on changing feelings than on identifying and tolerating them. The final phase of therapy occurs in the last three or so sessions and focuses on termination where accomplishments and understandable sadness at the end of treatment are discussed along with encouragement to continue to work on emerging interpersonal themes, the transition from the sick role, and dealing with relapse.

Empirical Support for Interpersonal Psychotherapy

Reports of the efficacy of IPT come primarily from two sources. The first is a study of 81 subjects comparing IPT to amitriptyline to IPT with amitriptyline and to a control condition that was a form of treatment on demand (Weissman et al., 1979). In this study IPT performed as well as the medication condition, and both outperformed the control condition. The combination of IPT and medication performed nonsignificantly better than either treatment alone and both psychotherapies appeared better at preventing relapse compared to the discontinued medication.

The stage where IPT established itself as a particularly promising treatment was the TDCRP (Elkin et al., 1985). In that study, 250 outpatients were randomized into one of four conditions: 16 weeks of IPT, cognitive therapy (CT), medication (imipramine), or placebo plus clinical management (CM). Although the results from the TDCRP are complex and have been repeatedly analyzed for at least 15 years, the initial results indicated that IPT produced similar responses to medication on depression measures and both were superior to placebo. While the medication condition seemed to produce the fastest clinical response, IPT might have been more effective than CT with more severely depressed subjects.

Short-Term Psychodynamic Psychotherapy (STPP)

For the purposes of this chapter, STPP will refer to any therapy that is time-limited and refers to the therapy as psychodynamic, psychodynamic-interpersonal, or emphasizing interpersonal factors (see Blagys & Hilsenroth, 2000, p. 168, for a precedent for this convention). Henry, Strupp, Schacht, and Gaston (1994, p. 468) describe the psychodynamic approach as "an approach to diagnosis and treatment characterized by a way of thinking about both patient and clinician that includes unconscious conflict, deficits and distortions of intrapsychic structures, and internal object relations."

Formal treatment manuals that prescribe and proscribe specific behaviors in particular sessions have not been routinely used in studies of the efficacy of STPP. In the literature on STPP several sources serve as exemplars of how one can conduct STPP, but session by session manuals are rarely used and often seen as not viable ways of defining treatment (see Luborsky, 1984; Luborsky et al., 1995; Malan, 1979; Strupp & Binder, 1984; Wachtel, 1993, as frequently cited sources).

More recently systematic research on the necessary and distinctive techniques that make up STPP has been conducted. In more recent iterations of what techniques contribute to STPP, researchers have considered interpersonal psychotherapy to contain important elements of STPP even though the creators of IPT specifically restrict their use of certain traditional dynamic techniques (e.g., IPT does not focus on transference per se). A study by Blagys and Hilsenroth (2000) identified seven interventions that could distinguish between short-term psychodynamic-interpersonal psychotherapy and cognitive behavioral treatment. These interventions were:

1. a focus on affect and the expression of patients' emotions;
2. an exploration of patients' attempts to avoid topics or engage in activities that hinder the progress of therapy;
3. the identification of patterns in patients' actions, thoughts, feelings, experiences, and relationships;
4. an emphasis on past experiences;
5. a focus on patients' interpersonal experiences;
6. an emphasis on the therapeutic relationship; and
7. an exploration of patients' wishes, dreams, or fantasies. (p. 167)

While some of these differences have been identified by other investigators (e.g., Goldfried, Castonguay, Hayes, Drozd, & Shapiro, 1997), it is not clear how robust these differences in techniques and/or focus of intervention between treatments really are. In a study of master CBT and STPP clinicians, several of the between orientation differences listed above did not emerge. It is not clear how to interpret the observation that master therapists show fewer differences than other therapists.

Empirical Support for Short-Term Psychodynamic Psychotherapy

STPP appears on the list of "probably efficacious" treatment for depression (Chambless et al., 1998, p. 11). Psychodynamic therapy research has not generally embraced randomized clinical trial designs and the strict adherence to treatment manuals that facilitate the development of the type of data that can be easily evaluated for inclusion as an empirically supported treatment. Two possible reasons could account for this fact. First, psychodynamic theorists and therapists tend to make less use of diagnostic category designs where specific patient populations are identified primarily on the basis of symptoms, though that is changing. For psychodynamic theorists, expression of specific symptoms is less important than the common underlying processes behind the symptoms. Second, treatments are tailored for specific individuals making prescribed treatment manuals difficult to adapt to psychodynamic interventions. In any event, STPP has a different sort of empirical basis than other therapies described thus far.

An early meta-analysis by Svartberg and Stiles (1991) suggesting that STPP was inferior to alternate therapies especially in the treatment of depression. One of the interesting aspects of that meta-analysis was that it indicated that the apparent advantage of STPP over no treatment diminished as study designs improved. Subsequently, newer data do provide empirical support for STPP in the treatment of depression.

The study cited in the 1998 update of the then termed "empirically validated therapies" (Chambless et al., 1998) supporting the probable efficacy of STPP was conducted comparing CBT to STPP for depressed family caregivers (Gallagher-Thompson & Steffen, 1994). In that study 66 caregivers of frail, elderly relatives who met the research diagnostic criteria (RDC) (Endicott & Spitzer, 1979) for major, minor, or intermittent depression were randomized to a CBT intervention modified for older adults or an STPP intervention that emphasized themes of independence, activity, self-esteem, or grief. There was no control condition. At the end of 20 sessions 71% of the caregivers were no longer depressed according to Research Diagnostic Criteria and there was no difference between groups. Tapes of the two forms of therapy could be reliably discriminated. This study suffers from the lack of a control condition because it is statistically underpowered to demonstrate equivalence. For example, the STPP condition had a 30% drop-out rate compared to a 14% rate for CBT. This was reported as a nonsignificant difference even though the X^2 test used to evaluate the significance of the observed differential attrition only had a power of approximately .35 to detect a difference of this magnitude in a sample of this size. Many other comparisons in the study also show trends toward CBT producing better results but did not meet statistical significance possibly due to low power. One unexpected and unexplained finding was that depressed caregivers who had been in that role for longer periods of time (> 44 months) were more likely to drop out if assigned to the STPP condition.

A much better designed study with 117 subjects stratified for severity of depression and randomized to a manualized version of CBT or STPP was conducted by Shapiro and colleagues (Shapiro et al., 1994). In that study participants could be assigned to either 8 or 16 weeks of manualized therapy. The study was a treatment method (CBT or STPP) X duration (8 or 16 weeks) X severity factorial design with power of 0.8 to detect an effect size of 0.5. This study, often referred to as the Sheffield II study, found no treatment differences between CBT and STPP, no difference as a function of severity of initial depression, and no difference in rate of improvement between conditions. Across all levels of depression there was no difference between the 8- and 16-week duration protocols though the most severely depressed group improved more after 16 sessions. Prescriptive treatment manuals were used for both conditions and adherence measures assessed.

In 2001 another meta-analysis comparing CBT or behavior therapy (BT) to STPP was conducted using studies in which at least 13 therapy sessions were conducted and each group had at least 20 participants (Leichsenring, 2001). That meta-analysis located only six appropriate studies. The results indicated equivalence between treatments and the author issued a caution about generalizing from the types of STPP studied in this analysis to other forms of STPP. More recently Hilsenroth and colleagues demonstrated that specific STPP techniques were associated with clinically significant improvement in depression using what they termed to be a hybrid effectiveness/efficacy treatment research model (Hilsenroth, Ackerman, Blagys, Baity, & Mooney, 2003). Over time data are accumulating that suggest that STPP may indeed be efficacious. It has taken some time for theorists and therapists to develop research strategies that are convincing to the EST community while at the same time holding to the theory and values foundational to STPP.

Process-Experiential Therapy (PE)

Table 4.1 lists process-experiential psychotherapy of depression as a probably efficacious intervention. PE is defined as an emotion-focused therapy that focuses on helping people regulate their affective functioning by processing their emotional experience (Greenberg & Watson, in press). Emotions are viewed as an adaptive form of information-processing that orients people to their environment, promotes their well-being disposing them to act on their behalf in a given environment, and influences their *mode* of processing (Greenberg & Safran, 1987, 1989; Greenberg & Paivio, 1997; Frijda, 1986).

In an experiential model of depression (Greenberg, Elliott, & Foerster, 1990; Greenberg, Watson, & Goldman, 1998; Greenberg & Watson, in press) psychogenic depression is seen as related to the evocation of a core powerless, weak/bad self, emotion scheme. The "emotion scheme" is seen as the central catalyst of emotion-based self-organizations and at the core of depressive powerlessness. An emotion scheme is viewed as a response producing, internal organization that synthesizes a variety of levels and types of information including sensori-motor, emotional, memorial, and conceptual level information (Greenberg, Rice, & Elliott, 1993). In contrast to a purely representational cognitive schema this is an experiential structure that includes a large component of nonverbal and affective experience. Depression thus is an "emotional disorder of the self" in which the self is organized as helpless or incompetent because of emotion-schematic memories of crucial losses or failures often from prior experience or formative years. These are evoked in response to current losses or failures and cause the self to lose resilience and collapse into powerlessness. These self-organizations both impair people's capacity to process and regulate the intensity of their emotional experiences and influence their mode of processing toward loss, humiliation, and entrapment (Greenberg & Watson, in press).

In the manualized treatment, PE therapists adopt the three client-centered relational attitudes of empathy, positive regard, and congruence. In so doing therapists respond to the person's idiosyncratic experience, encouraging the symbolization of emotion and core meaning to increase awareness of and access to, healthier, more adaptive emotions (Greenberg et al., 1993; Greenberg, 2002). Throughout the therapeutic process, adaptive emotions are accessed to organize the person for adaptive responses and to transform maladaptive emotions. This process of emotion transformation is aided by the use of the specific therapeutic techniques that help stimulate arousal of emotion and its processing. The first three sessions in this approach are spent forming a safe, trusting bond and building a therapeutic alliance. When a safe bond and a strong working alliance has been established, therapists respond to particular markers or verbal indications from clients of various types of processing problems, that suggest the use of interventions appropriate to that state. Interventions include the two-chair dialogue in response to self-critical conflicts, and the empty-chair dialogue in response to unresolved feelings toward a significant other. In addition, focusing is

used in response to an unclear felt sense, and systematic evocative unfolding in response to problematic reactions (Greenberg et al., 1993). Therapists are responsive to clients' momentary states, and do not plan or structure sessions in advance. However, therapists are encouraged, once an alliance had been established, to implement at least one experiential intervention every two to three sessions.

Empirical Support for Process-Experiential Therapy

A manualized form of process-experiential (PE) therapy has been evaluated in the treatment of depression in four studies (Elliott et al., 1990; Goldman, Greenberg, & Angus, 2000, under review; Greenberg & Watson, 1998; Watson, Gordon, Stermac, Kalogerakos, & Steckley, 2003). In addition Beutler, Engle, Mohr, Daldrup, Bergan, Meredith, and Merry (1991) studied the effects of Focused Expressive therapy on depression, which involves the use of one of the PE tasks, empty-chair dialogue. This treatment, which focused mainly on the expression of constricted anger, did not find very promising effects. Elliott et al. (1990), however, found that clients' depressive symptoms were successfully treated with process-experiential therapy, although there was no comparison group. Both client-centered and process-experiential treatments were found to be effective in reducing clients' depressive symptoms with effect sizes comparable to those reported in studies investigating the effectiveness of cognitive-behavioral and behavioral interventions (Goldman et al., 2002, under review; Greenberg & Watson, 1998). In the York I depression study, Greenberg and Watson (1998) compared the effectiveness of PE therapy with one of its components, CC therapy, in the treatment of 34 adults suffering from major depression. Treatments showed no difference in reducing depressive symptoms at termination and six-month follow-up. The process-experiential treatment, however, had superior effects at mid-treatment on depression and at termination on the total level of symptoms, self-esteem, and reduction of interpersonal problems (mean overall comparative effect size for PE vs. CC: +0.33). The addition of specific active interventions at appropriate points in the treatment of depression appeared to hasten and enhance improvement. In the York II depression study, Goldman et al. (2002) replicated the York I study by comparing the effects of CC and PE on 38 clients with major depressive disorder; they obtained a comparative effect size of +0.71 in favor of PE therapy. They then combined the York I and II samples to increase power of detecting differences between treatment groups. Statistically significant differences among treatments were found on all indices of change for the combined sample. This provided evidence that the addition of PE interventions to the basic CC relationship conditions improves outcome.

In another recent study, Watson et al. (2003) carried out a randomized clinical trial comparing PE and CB therapies in the treatment of major depression. Sixty-six clients participated in 16 sessions of psychotherapy once a week. Results indicated that there were no significant differences between groups (comparative ES: +.11). Both treatments were effective in improving clients' level of depression, self-esteem, general symptom distress and dysfunctional attitudes. However, there were significant differences between groups with respect to two subscales of the Inventory of Interpersonal Problems: Clients in PE therapy were significantly more self-assertive and less overly accommodating at the end of treatment than clients in CB therapy. At the end of treatment, clients in both groups developed significantly more emotional reflection for solving distressing problems.

Mestel and Votsmeier-Röhr (2000) reported the results of a 6-week integrative process-experiential inpatient program, involving a large, naturalistic German sample of 412 moderately to severely depressed patients. Using measures of symptoms, interpersonal problems, and quality of self-relationship administered at pretreatment, at discharge, and at 22-month follow-up, they obtained an overall pre-post effect of 1.05.

A set of related studies involving the relational components of PE have also offered evidence of effectiveness. In a large, complex study involving three different substudies, King et al. (2000) compared Cognitive Behavioral and Client Centered therapies to treatment as usual (primarily medication) for depressed clients seen in naturalistic primary care situations in the United Kingdom.

One substudy ($n = 62$) was a three-way randomized clinical trial (RCT) comparing all three conditions; another substudy ($n = 107$) was a two-way RCT comparing CB to CC therapies; while the third substudy ($n = 52$) was a two-way preference trial in which clients were allowed to choose either CB or CC therapy. Measures included self-reports of symptoms and social adjustment measures, as well as estimates of cost, administered pretherapy and at 2 and 10 months later. CC clients received an average of seven sessions. For CC therapy, overall pre-post effects varied from 0.88 (three-way RCT) to 1.17 (two-way RCT). Treatment comparisons found few if any differences between the three treatments: comparative ES for CC therapy vs. treatment as usual: +.10; comparative ESs for CB therapy: −.08 to −.19.

In a meta-analysis of experiential treatments of depression (Elliott, Greenberg, & Lietaer, 2003) 16 comparisons of experiential with nonexperiential therapies supported a conclusion of equivalence (mean comparative ES: −.02; SD: .69; t(.4) = 2.23, $p < .05$). In fact, comparative frequency of substantial positive and negative results were perfectly balanced (positive: 3; negative: 4; neutral: 9). Given the balanced nature of the comparative effects, Chambless and Hollon's (1998) equivalence criterion is most relevant. In fact, both of the studies with large enough samples (> 25 per group; King et al., 2000; Watson et al., 2003) reported no difference in results for clients seen in experiential therapies as compared to CB therapy. In addition, when Greenberg, Goldman, and Angus (2000) combined data from the two York depression studies, they found that clients seen in PE therapy had a significantly better outcome than clients in one of its components (CC therapy), thus adding support from a third study. Finally, the four comparisons between different forms of experiential therapies (three significant differences involving two independent research settings) provide support for process directive experiential therapies as specific and efficacious (Chambless & Hollon, 1998).

In addition, a number of process outcome studies have shown that the alliance, empathy, depth of experiencing and emotional arousal all predict a significant amount of outcome variance and that deeper emotional restructuring around core issues predicts 18 month follow-up and likelihood of nonrelapse (Greenberg & Pedersen, 2001). These studies provide evidence on the proposed mechanisms of change; a type of evidence often lacking in other empirically supported treatments.

Experimental Treatment

Table 4.1 lists mindfulness therapy as an experimental intervention. Although not focused on the treatment of depression but on relapse prevention, mindfulness-based treatments have shown some positive results. At the time this chapter was written the data for including this treatment as possibly efficacious were not available. However, the theoretical and initial clinical work on this intervention sheds light on how aspects of one of the principles of change described below may be instantiated clinically. It also is included because it addresses a different philosophical position on the meaning and experience of depressive symptoms that is more consistent with experiential approaches and has significantly different treatment implications compared to behavior therapy or cognitive therapy strategies and goals.

EXTRACTING INTERVENTION PRINCIPLES

It is difficult to extract intervention principles without imposing one's ontological and epistemic values during the process of organizing information because those assumptions affect how one even defines what could be a principle. Certainly psychotherapy addresses the interplay between public and private behavior, cognition, affect and emotion, environment, biology, and history. Rather than require the reader to agree with a particular causal explanation of how these factors are interrelated, it is useful to presume that for pragmatic purposes, one can effect change in one system by influencing related systems. To make any headway in identifying intervention principles, it is necessary to think of these principles in terms of operational validity rather than construct validity. That is, if a clinician were to implement the principle, it is likely that a useful effect would result. There is no necessary presumption that we agree

on precisely how the operation produces the effect. The notion of causality is not a strict ultimate notion of causality but rather one where there is a temporal order between treatment component implementation and symptom change that reliably suggests a pragmatic causal relationship. Change could occur via a yet to be identified psychological principle that is somehow part of the therapeutic intervention even if not explicitly stated or recognized.

Most of the principles that follow are based on the results of putative or demonstrated mechanisms of actions identified primarily from efficacy studies. To the extent that there are peculiarities in subject selection, experimenter effects, or supervision procedures not captured in the reported protocols, the generalizability of the treatment principles may be imperfect.

The effectiveness studies summarized in Chambless and Ollendick (2001, see pp. 707–708) suggest that transfer of treatment protocols to less selected samples can achieve significantly useful results. For the most part efficacy studies include a range of depressed participants who have met formal screening criteria. One might be inclined to dismiss efficacy studies as being irrelevant to standard clinical practice on the grounds that study patients are not sufficiently similar to less selected patients seen in primary care centers or other practice settings. However, one should also consider that the "less selected" patients in his or her practice setting may include some patients who are more difficult but also some who are less severely depressed or not depressed at all (e.g., adjustment disorder with depressed mood). Such patients may seemingly respond to many treatment elements not listed here, whereas more significantly depressed patients would not. Regardless of the qualifications that may attach from extrapolating from efficacy to effectiveness studies, there is little doubt that such studies represent our best source of data from which to extract principles helpful in the treatment of depression. However, there is certainly a robust debate on the limitations of extrapolating from efficacy to effectiveness studies that will continue for some time (cf. DeRubeis & Stirman, 2001; Lambert, 2001; Nathan, 2001; cf. Stirman, DeRubeis, Crits-Christoph, & Brody, 2003; Westen & Morrison, 2001). In the meantime, patients will continue to present in need of treatment, and therapists must try to responsibly address those needs.

There is another important caution to offer. The principles that are described here are rarely explicitly tested in isolation from other potentially therapeutic activities. The therapy (or therapies) from which a principle is extracted contains many elements. In most instances, it is an article of faith that implementing a principle outside the therapy in which it normally occurs will produce a beneficial effect. In order to be confident that a robust principle existed, one would have to do a number of dismantling studies to determine the smallest discrete intervention responsible for change. In most cases these studies do not exist. That does not negate the potential utility of generating a list of candidates to be called "intervention principles." It simply reminds us that there is still empirical and conceptual work to be done. As clinicians we are asked to help, sometimes with imperfect knowledge. However, imperfect knowledge may turn out to be correct or at least useful. In spite of the fact that there are literally hundreds of diagnoses in the *Diagnostic and Statistical Manual*, there are not hundreds of unique principles of change that have an empirical or theoretical basis.

Clearly, several different types of psychotherapy have received empirical support for the treatment of depression. Reflecting a variety of theoretical assumptions and models, these treatments encompass a large number of therapeutic procedures. However, it is possible to categorize the treatment approaches reviewed above along a number of general dimensions of psychotherapy. This allows a number of commonalities, differences, and potential complementarities to be identified. In line with the guidelines proposed in the current Task Force (see Beutler & Castonguay, this volume), we will categorize the evidence-based treatment for depression according to the following five dimensions: directive, nondirective, and self-directive procedures; thematic/insight-oriented versus symptom/skill building procedures; abreactive versus emotionally supportive procedures; interpersonal/systemic versus intrapersonal/individual procedures; and intensive versus nonintensive/short-term procedures (Malik, Beutler, Gallagher-Thompson, Thompson, & Alimohamed, 2003). Principles of intervention will then be formulated based on these global di-

mensions of psychotherapy, as well as from the more specific description of treatments presented above.

Directive, Nondirective, and Self-Directive Procedures

Most of the treatments that have received empirical support for the treatment of depression are directive, at least in some aspects of their protocol. This is clearly the case in cognitive behavioral therapies, where therapists take an active role in structuring the treatment process. A somewhat directive stance is also adopted when IPT therapists delineate a model of depression and then actively focus on specific types of interpersonal problems, or when PE therapists focus on specific markers of emotional problems and then systematically use prescribed techniques to guide and deepen client's emotional processing. STPP, in contrast, might be best described as a more self-directive approach, as it assigns the primary responsibility of the change process to the client's active exploration of his or her inner experience. A number of variants of this general approach, however, emphasize the importance of identifying and working on specific themes or dynamic foci, which require some level of directiveness in the therapist's stance. PE once it has implemented an intervention at a marker also promotes a fair degree of self-directed exploration.

Thematic/Insight-Oriented Versus Symptom/Skill Building Procedures

As a whole, the empirically based treatments for depression provide support for a broad range of interventions along this general dimension of psychotherapy. While cognitive-behavioral procedures are primarily aimed at the reduction of symptoms and the acquisition of coping skills, the interventions in both STPP and PE are exploratory in nature and are used to increase awareness, facilitate insight, and/or foster the resolution of inner conflict. With its primary focus on the exploration of interpersonal problems, IPT is also best categorized as a "thematic/insight–oriented" treatment. While therapists also encourage clients to find new ways to deal with their interpersonal problems, homework (or behavioral change between sessions) and reduction of depressive symptoms are less emphasized in IPT than in cognitive-behavioral therapy.

Abreactive Versus Emotionally Supportive Procedures

Along the same of line as in the previous dimensions, cognitive-behavioral therapies can be distinguished from "exploratory" type of treatment with respect to how they work with emotions. At the core of PE, IPT, and STPP are procedures aimed at helping clients to explore, express, stay with, an/or deepen their feelings. In contrast, a primary goal in CBT-oriented treatment is to provide a safe environment for the client to acquire the skills necessary to reduce maladaptive emotion.

Interpersonal/Systemic Versus Intrapersonal/Individual Procedures

CT emphasizing as it does cognitive components of functioning (i.e., dysfunctional thoughts, beliefs), focuses its interventions on intrapersonal and interpersonal issues (e.g., skills training). PE focuses on different intrapersonal components of emotion but also focuses on the interpersonal in its emphasis on the therapeutic relationship and the reworking of unfinished business. In contrast, IPT therapists attempt to decrease depression by focusing primarily on interpersonal issues though there is also a significant proportion of treatment that focuses on the experience of depression. Interestingly, while being conceptually and procedurally distinct, both behavior therapy and STPP emphasize intrapersonal (e.g., behavioral change, unconscious conflict) and interpersonal (e.g., impact of depressed symptoms on others, interpersonal patterns) issues.

Intensive Versus Nonintensive/ Short-Term Procedures

Thus far, it seems that only short-term treatments have received sufficient attention in clinical trials. Considering the fact that not all participants benefit from treatment delivered in these time-limited trials, let alone the relapse rate observed in depression, empirical investigations of more intensive or long-term treatment seem indicated (see Jones in Castonguay et al., 1999).

TREATMENT PRINCIPLES

Depression treatment pre-dates the modern classification system (DSM-III and later) and EST movement. There is a vast literature that has contributed to the evolution of treatment intervention principles. In order to keep the list of treatment principles as concise as possible the following list is constructed with broadly stated principles followed by a sampling of examples to give an idea of how one might construe a particular treatment as employing elements of these principles. Again, how a principle's origin is ascribed to a particular therapy is somewhat arbitrary.

1. Challenge cognitive appraisals and behavior with new experience.
2. Increase and diversify the patient's access to contingent positive reinforcement while decreasing reinforcement for depressive and avoidant behaviors.
3. Improve the patient's interpersonal social functioning.
4. Improve the marital, family, and social environment to reduce the establishment, maintenance, or recurrence of depressive behaviors.
5. Improve awareness, acceptance, and regulation of emotion and promote change in maladaptive emotional responses.
6. The treatment process should be structured and an intervention focus should be developed.

Principles 1 and 2 are intended to cover the central themes of contemporary cognitive-behavior therapy with an emphasis on the experimental and clinical work on cognitive theories of depression. They also emphasize the importance of evaluating and altering the social reinforcing properties of the patient's environment. Principle 3 also has a cognitive-behavioral history, but represents a great deal of experimental work on the interpersonal stimulus properties of persons with depression. A large volume of research unquestionably identifies the need to address how depressive behaviors and the depressed individual inadvertently participate in the perpetuation of a depressive episode. While addressing social skills can be understood in the context of other principles, it is listed separately because of the extensive literature that interprets depression as the result of a social skills deficit. Principle 4 recognizes that depressive behaviors can result from social factors or disrupt ongoing social relationships that need to be redressed before maintenance of improvement can occur. In contrast, Principle 5 recognizes the evolution of the confluence of the influences from humanistic, dynamic, mindfulness, acceptance, and emotion-focused therapies, suggesting that cognitive and emotional states including depression when properly explored can lead an individual to understand the origins, functions, and alternatives to depressive emotions and to transform emotional responses. Principle 6 reflects the categorization of the treatments based on the first general dimension of psychotherapy (i.e., directive, nondirective, and self-directive procedures). It should be mentioned that the other principles also reflect many of the features highlighted in the categorization of treatment along general dimensions of psychotherapy. Principles 3 and 4 reflect the interpersonal focus of several empirically based treatments, while Principles 1 and 5 reflect intrapersonal issues important in the treatment of depression. Principle 2 most directly captures the skill building pole of the insight/skill dimension, whereas Principle 5 catches the abreactive pole of the abreaction/support dimension.

Explanation of the Principles

Principle 1: Challenge cognitive appraisals and behavior with new experience. There are several ways one can state this principle, but recent research and the examination of how cognitive therapy is conducted makes this statement seem like a reasonable rapprochement for cognitive and behavior therapists alike. It is simply true that there is an interdependence between cognition, behavior, and affect. Negative thoughts about self, world, and future clearly are related to depressive experience and behavior and core depressogenic beliefs are important sources of dysfunction. Although there are increasing questions regarding exactly how these factors are related, challenging the implicit and explicit beliefs, assumptions, and thoughts by disputation and collection of evidence is a key

form of intervention (see Burns & Spangler, 2001; Jacobson et al., 1996).

Principle 2: Increase and diversify the patient's access to contingent positive reinforcement while decreasing reinforcement for depressive and avoidant behaviors. Some of the earliest behavioral work on the treatment of depression reasoned that depression was either brought about or maintained by a loss of contingent reinforcement related to healthy behavior (Ferster, 1973; Lewinsohn, 1974). Extensions of these earlier positions also identify the importance of how persons in the depressed patient's environment can inadvertently reinforce depressive behavior by supplying sympathy and support at a higher than usual rate or take over the duties of the depressed person thus negatively reinforcing depressive behaviors (Hoberman & Lewinsohn, 1985). Thus, attending to Principle 2 requires the clinician to assess the functional interactions between the patient and other significant people in his or her life. It can be a difficult distinction for people close to the patient to tell when they are being supportive versus when their responses to the patient are inadvertently strengthening behaviors that perpetuate depressive affect and behaviors that lead to avoidance of various kinds of responsibilities. In one of the more thoughtful integrative theories of depression, Lewinsohn and colleagues described how a decrease from normal levels of contingent reinforcement can have cascading effects that include initiating support from the social environment that reinforces depressive behavior. The integrative component of the theory also explicated how disruptions of one's normal behavioral patterns can negatively alter one's usual cognitive appraisals. This disruption of scripts often predisposes one to make negative interpretations of their circumstances which can further adversely affect their activity and personal interactions with others and continue a cycle of depression (Hoberman & Lewinsohn, 1985; Lewinsohn, Hoberman, Teri, & Hautzinger, 1985).

One major component of a behavioral intervention is increasing the rate of behavior leading to contingent positive reinforcement. There has been a resurgence of interest in behavioral activation treatments since the publication of a component analysis of cognitive therapy by Jacobson and colleagues (Jacobson et al., 1996). In that study skilled cognitive therapists delivered a complete version of cognitive therapy, a behavioral activation only component, and a behavioral activation plus attention to automatic thoughts (but not problematic core schema) condition. One set of findings from this study is that each condition produced equivalent results. Perhaps more importantly, the behavioral activation component alone was just as effective as the complete cognitive therapy condition at altering negative thinking and dysfunctional attributional style. Behavioral activation strategies have been manualized (Martell, Addis, & Jacobson, 2001) and made shorter and more purely behavioral (Lejuez, Hopko, & Hopko, 2001, 2002).

While Principles 1 and 2 derive from somewhat different research traditions, there is adequate evidence of mutual influence between cognition and behavior at least as implemented in the treatment programs from which these principles are derived. They are presented as separate principles to remind the clinician that by the end of an intervention both domains should be addressed.

Principle 3: Improve the patient's interpersonal social functioning. In addition to the clear emphasis in IPT on improving social functioning by resolving grief, role disputes, role transitions, and interpersonal deficits, others have taken a more behavioral approach to addressing the interpersonal factors that might contribute to the acquisition and maintenance of depression. In contrast to IPT, these treatments behaviorally examine the antecedents, behaviors, and consequences of interpersonal responses that may contribute to the maintenance of depression. McCullough (2000, 2001) has reported successful results by bringing the tools of a developmental-behavioral analysis to the treatment of interpersonal and situational contributors to chronic depression. McCullough's treatment makes very different assumptions about the development of chronic depression and assigns responsibility for change to the patient. While his general model involves several elements, one primary goal is to have the patient become interpersonally more effective. In this intervention the therapist is very actively involved in treatment and directly attempts to modify the patient's behavior and establish a more empathetic repertoire in the patient with respect to understanding their impact on others.

In a more radical behavioral approach to inter-personal psychotherapy, Kohlenberg and Tsai (1991) described a therapeutic approach (Functional Analytic Psychotherapy [FAP]) that focused on the relationship between the therapist and client and presumed that problematic interpersonal behaviors would occur between the dyad. These behavioral problems are not presumed to be transference issues, but actual problematic behaviors that occur in the natural environment that contribute to patient dysphoria and lack of interpersonal success. Therapy focuses on shaping more useful interpersonal interactions between the client and the therapist by having the therapist contingently respond to clinically relevant behaviors when they occur in session. More recently Kohlenberg and colleagues have been integrating elements of FAP into more traditional cognitive therapy for the treatment of depression with some promising initial results (Bolling, Kohlenberg, & Parker, 2000; Kanter, Parker, & Kohlenberg, 2001; Kohlenberg, Kanter, Bolling, Parker, & Tsai, 2002). FAP sits in contrast to IPT in that IPT discusses interpersonal issues between the patient and others as a topic in therapy, while FAP addresses interpersonal issues as they actually occur between the therapist and patient with the therapist responding, in part, with personal reactions about the impact of the patient's behavior on the therapist.

There is an extensive research literature on the ways in which depressed individuals interact to elicit uncomfortable feelings in others that may serve to maintain or perhaps even contribute to the onset of depression. These experimental studies do not directly map onto specific elements of any ESTs, but are nevertheless obvious to those, including therapists, who interact with persons with depression.

Joiner (2002, p. 295) cites Freud (1917/1951, p. 274) stating "[E]verything derogatory that they say about themselves at the bottom relates to someone else . . . [T]hey give a great deal of trouble, perpetually taking offence [*sic*] and behaving as if they had been treated with great injustice." While the truth of each assertion may be open to question, there is a great deal of modern literature that either describes some problematic aspect of the interpersonal behavior of depressed individuals (e.g., Coyne, 1976) or presents experimental or observational studies demonstrating some undesirable impact of depressive behavior on the depressed person or someone in his or her environment.

Early classic studies focused on the ratings of social skills by depressed and nondepressed subjects (Alloy & Abramson, 1979; Lewinsohn, Mischel, Chaplin, & Barton, 1980) suggesting that depressed individuals gave self-assessments of poor social performance. There was some disagreement about the degree to which these self-assessments were indeed accurate or part of the depressed person's overall tendency toward negative self-evaluation. A 1990 meta-analytic review conducted by Segrin (1990) concluded that there probably were differences in social skills when comparing depressed and nondepressed subjects, but that the actual magnitude of the differences were overestimated by the depressed person assessing his or her own performance. One treatment implication of these findings is that therapy should address how socially skillful one is while interacting with others as well as how accurate the patient is in evaluating how effectively he or she accomplishes desired social goals.

It might seem as if this principle should be "train social skills," but it is not clear exactly how to do this. That is why the principle is stated in terms of improving outcomes without specifying the rules by which this might be achieved. The problem is that one cannot specify exactly how to teach an individual to accomplish this goal. One can train the patient to learn to discriminate his or her social impact and then choose behavioral strategies that work for them (Follette, Dykstra, & Compton, 1992, November; McFall, 1982).

Several specific problematic behaviors have been identified that suggest useful intervention points in order to try to train more effective social functioning. For example, using a lag-sequential analysis, Jacobson and Anderson (1982) found that depressed college students emitted more unsolicited personal, negative self-disclosures than nondepressed subjects and did so earlier in conversations. Another study of this skills deficit suggests the problem occurs to an even greater extent in the context of intimate relationships (Segrin & Flora, 1998).

Joiner (2002) summarizes other micro-behaviors that may help identify targets for

change. He cites works indicating that depressed subjects' facial expressions are more animated while expressing negative affect but otherwise less expressive overall (e.g., Schwartz, Fair, Salt, Mandel, & Klerman, 1976). Depressed subjects also exhibit less eye contact than nondepressed subjects (Segrin, 1992) and give fewer nonverbal social cues during conversations (Troisi & Moles, 1999). While it is tempting to want to design an intervention for these specific behaviors, focusing on them rather than the social function one seeks to achieve can be misleading. There is no logical reason to assume that every patient needs to exhibit the same behaviors in order to achieve a particular successful social outcome. A middle-aged, overweight male may require a very different behavioral repertoire to be socially successful compared to a mid-twenties, normal weight female. The importance of Principle 3 is that therapy addresses establishing successful, healthy social functioning that leads to the creation and maintenance of healthy, socially meaningful relationships that also buffer against stressors.

Principle 4: Improve the marital, family, and social environment to reduce the establishment, maintenance, or recurrence of depressive behaviors. In a classic book based on surveys of women in Camberwell in London, Brown and Harris (1978) strongly implicated social stressors as important factors in the onset of depression. In that study economic stress, relationship distress, the presence of the life events experienced in the previous year were associated with the subsequent onset of depression. Additional vulnerabilities were identified that included the loss of one's mother before the age of 11, an absence of a confiding relationship, having three or more children under age 14 to raise, and not having paid work outside the home. While each of these specific factors has not always been supported in subsequent research, there is consistent evidence that severe life stress, particularly stress involving relationships and occupation, is related to depression and other forms of psychopathology (Dohrenwend, 2000; Mazure, 1998; Monroe & McQuaid, 1994). The research on stress and relationships helps clarify why grief and interpersonal themes are components of IPT and STPP and why the increasing rates of positive behavior may be effective components of some other ESTs. Further these findings suggest that treating depression without assessing antecedent stressors and those which occur concurrently with depression could have an adverse impact on the effectiveness of therapy.

Since interpersonal and social stressors have been shown to be relevant to the onset of depression, it is not surprising that marital and family interventions have been shown to be effective treatment modalities for depression. However, just how the course of therapy for depression might be affected is not clear (Monroe & Hadjiyannakis, 2002, see pp. 319–324). In a meta-analysis examining the relationship between marital satisfaction and depression, Whisman (2001) demonstrated a clear inverse relationship between depression and marital satisfaction. What is not as clear is the directionality of any possible causal relationship (Coyne & Benazon, 2001), though there seems to be an emerging view that the relationship is bidirectional (Beach, 2001). From a treatment perspective married patients frequently experience concomitant depression and marital distress. Several studies have demonstrated that the treatment of relationship distress has a salutary effect on depression. While the research question of cause and effect continues to be studied, the co-occurrence at the time of presentation for treatment is quite common and deserving of intervention.

There is little doubt that depression is much more common for those who have been divorced than those who are still married (Robins & Regier, 1991, p. 64), and there is a reciprocal relationship between marital satisfaction and depression over time (Beach & O'Leary, 1993). There is also evidence that the relationship differs for men compared to women (Fincham, Beach, Harold, & Osborne, 1997). The point is that this treatment principle draws attention to the fact that the marital relationship should be examined as a possible influence on depression or as a possible cause of depression if not properly addressed.

There are many possible interpersonal factors that might be relevant to the onset or maintenance of depression. As an example, Biglan and colleagues (1985) demonstrated that during problem-solving sessions, a wife's depressive behavior functioned to reduce a spouse's aversive behavior. Thus, depression may be maintained by relationship factors that may need to be redressed before the depression would respond to other intervention principles. Thus, depressive behaviors may have an onset for one set of reasons yet be maintained for a different set of functional reasons as people in the environment alter their responses to the patient's depressive behaviors. These alterations may accomplish goals the patient cannot otherwise achieve and subsequent depression may not remit unless these social functions can be accomplished through more appropriate interpersonal and relationship skills.

The application of this principle is particularly important when the patient is a parent. We have already described a relationship between depression and marital functioning and the presence of children. In families with children, depression can adversely impact parent–child interactions and is associated also with increased risk of depression in the children of depressed parents (Goodman & Gotlib, 1999, 2002). The treatment of depression, especially maternal depression, ought to consider the mutual influence of parents and children on the course of depression. Failure to do so may increase the likelihood of depression in children. A cost-effectiveness assessment of family interventions for depression might well be very favorable if one considers not only the effectiveness of the treatment of depression for the identified patient but also considers the fact that additional cases may be prevented if proper family therapy is provided.

Principle 5: Improve awareness, acceptance, and regulation of emotion and promote change in maladaptive emotional responses. Deeper emotional processing, defined as greater depth of experiencing on emotion episodes, has been shown to predict outcome in PE therapy of depression (Pos, Greenberg, Goldman, & Korman, 2003). Greater depth of experience has been shown to predict outcome in CBT as well indicating it is an important change process in alleviating depression. Higher emotional arousal in mid-treatment coupled with reflection on emotion, to make sense of it, has also been found to predict treatment outcome in experiential treatments (Warwar & Greenberg, 2000; Watson & Greenberg, 1996). Resolution of core tasks that involve emotional restructuring also has been found to predict 18-month follow-up and lower likelihood of relapse (Greenberg & Pedersen, 2001).

There is an increasing literature on the importance of emotional processing and on specific neurological characteristics of emotion in depressed populations (Davidson, Pizzagalli, Nitschke, & Putnam, 2002). This principle establishes the importance of addressing the affective bases of behavior and cognition.

Another set of findings bear on the utility of Principle 5. Recently several therapies have investigated the construct of mindfulness. In the depression field attention has focused on the utility of mindfulness in the prevention of relapse in depressed subjects (Ma & Teasdale, 2004; Teasdale et al., 2000). Just as IPT addresses the utility of the patient accepting rather than struggling against depressive feelings, mindfulness interventions try to teach patients to be aware of negative thinking patterns and disengage from the ruminative process. The goal of mindful treatment in the studies cited is to have patients no longer avoid unwanted thoughts or feelings but instead respond to them in an intentional and skillful manner.

Many of the therapeutic procedures discussed in this section are still actively being researched. However, a common theme that gives rise to Principle 5 is that there is something adaptive to be learned from experiencing rather than struggling against feelings and emotions. The consequence of giving up the struggle to avoid these feelings may result in less distressed acceptance of them or the conditioned responses to the feelings may extinguish. In any event, Principle 5 leads one to a very different treatment target than most interventions based on more traditional cognitive or behavior interventions designed to directly improve mood as the primary goal.

Additional experimental psychology research supporting the effects of emotional processing comes from studies that show that acceptance of emotion leads to quicker recovery than its suppression (Levitt, Brown, Orsillo, & Barlow, in press; Hunt, 1998). Pennebaker and colleagues have shown the positive effects of writing about emotional experience on autonomic nervous system activity, immune functioning, and emotional and physical health (e.g., Pennebaker, 1990, 1995). Pennebaker (1995) concludes that through language, individuals are able to organize, structure, and ultimately assimilate both their emotional experiences and the events that may have provoked the emotions. A further related benefit of symbolization in awareness suggested by Rimé, Finkenhauer, Luminet, Zech, and Phillipot (1998) is that it allows for emotional sharing.

Emotion awareness has now been grounded in a measure of levels of emotional awareness (LEAS) (Lane, Quinlan, Schwartz, 1990; Lane & Schwartz, 1992) that move from awareness of physical sensations, to action tendencies, single emotions, blends of emotion, and blends of blends of emotional experience (the capacity to appreciate complexity in the experiences of self and other). Therapists need to work to increase people's awareness of bodily sensations, gain comfort with these sensations, and allow flexibility in responding to these sensations. Body awareness in psychotherapy has taken a number of forms including mindfulness training (Kabat-Zinn, 1990; Linehan, 1993; Orsillo, Roemer, & Barlow, in press; Segal, Williams, & Teasdale, 2002), focusing (Gendlin, 1996), and progressive muscle relaxation (Bernstein, Borkovec, & Hazlett-Stevens, 2000).

LEAS has been found to correlate significantly with self-restraint and impulse control (Barrett, Lane, Sechrest, & Schwartz, 2000). This finding, replicated in independent samples, indicates that greater emotional awareness is associated with greater self-reported impulse control. High LEAS scores have also been associated with better emotion recognition in others no matter whether the task was purely verbal or purely nonverbal (Lane, Sechrest, Reidel, Weldon, & Schwartz, 1996). Salovey, Hsee, & Mayer (1993) also found that individual differences in emotional awareness predicted recovery of positive mood and decrements in ruminative thoughts (Palfia & Salovey, 1993) following a distressing stimulus.

Emotional arousal and the promotion of emotional processing (Foa & Kozak, 1986; Greenberg & Safran, 1984, 1987) are important aspects of the emotion awareness process. Emotional processing has been defined as either increased or decreased emotional responding resulting from exposure to both a fear state, as well as to information inconsistent with the activated cognitive-affective fear structure (Foa & Kozak 1986). By facing dreaded feelings and finding that they survive, people increase their sense of control and become more able to acknowledge painful emotions (Daldrup, Engle,

Holiman, & Beutler, 1994; Greenberg & Bolger, 2001; Williams, Stiles, & Shapiro, 1999). Emotional processing however involves more than exposure alone. It involves a set of steps of cognitive/affective processing that has long been defined in experiential therapy as the deepening of experience (Klein, Mathieu-Coughlan, & Kiesler, 1986). In this process, first clients must *approach* bodily felt feeling by attending to emotional experience. Then clients must *allow* and *tolerate* being in live contact with their emotions. These two stages are somewhat consistent with the more behavioral notions of exposure. Approach, arousal, and tolerance of emotional experience are necessary but possibly not sufficient. Optimum emotional processing involves the integration of cognition and affect (Greenberg, 2002; Greenberg & Pascual-Leone, 1995; Greenberg & Safran, 1987). Once contact with emotional experience is achieved, clients must also cognitively orient to that experience as information, and explore, and make sense of it (Pos, Greenberg, Goldman, & Korman, 2003). Emotional processing thus involves overcoming of avoidance, approach awareness, and tolerance, arousal of emotion, exploration and reflection, and the creation of new meaning. This process has been shown to predict outcome in the psychotherapy of depression (Castonguay, Goldfried, Wiser, Raue, & Hayes, 1996; Goldman & Greenberg, in press; Pos et al., 2003).

Emotional expression also has recently been shown to be a unique aspect of emotional processing that predicts adjustment to breast cancer (Stanton et al., 2000). Women who coped with cancer through expressing emotion had fewer medical appointments, enhanced physical health and vigor, and decreased distress compared to those low in expression.

In a further interesting line of investigation positive emotions have been found to undo lingering negative emotions (Frederickson, 2001; Fredrickson & Levenson, 1998). The basic observation is that key components of positive emotions are incompatible with negative emotions. Davidson (2000) also suggests that the right hemispheric, withdrawal related, negative affect system can be transformed by activation of the approach system in the left prefrontal cortex. He defines resilience as the maintenance of high levels of positive affect and well-being in the face of adversity and high-lights that it is not that resilient people do not feel negative affect but that what characterizes resilience is that the negative affect does not persist. For example in grief, laughter has been found to be a predictor of recovery. Thus being able to remember the happy times and to experience joy helps as an antidote to sadness (Bonanno & Keltner, 1997).

Principle 6: The treatment process should be structured and an intervention focus should be developed. Current empirical literature suggests that treatments that develop a focus and possess some structure appear to be beneficial to depressed clients, especially in brief or time-limited therapies. Following a less directive stance, however, often may be beneficially combined with directive interventions (such as takes place in the first phase of PE and the "self-directive" techniques of STTP). Therapist responsivity (Stiles, Honos-Webb, & Surko, 1998) however is crucial, so directive interventions should not be applied in a rigid way or in a domineering manner but be responsive to different client states and readiness.

Choosing Among Principles

As stated earlier there is a link between affect, cognition, and behavior that suggests altering any one factor is likely to change any other. In the course of treatment planning, the clinician often has to decide whether to identify a salient weakness (e.g., a dysfunctional cognitive style) and try to improve that glaring weakness or build on some other strength. Studies that have systematically matched or mismatched client strengths or deficits are not very common (Shoham & Rohrbaugh, 1995). However, there are some emerging data that would suggest treatment should take advantage of a patient's strengths rather than trying to address the most serious deficit first. This does not mean to ignore patient problems, but rather treatment might proceed more effectively when one builds on those strengths already present in the patient.

Traditional treatment matching approaches would logically argue that a patient with significant amounts of cognitive distortions should be given some kind of cognitive therapy while those who exhibit significant interpersonal difficulties be given something like IPT. Once again, the appeal of this method of treatment planning depends on one's philosophical willingness to tailor one's treatment approach. However, a growing but not yet well summarized body of literature suggests another approach might be more useful.

Turning to outcome studies from which our principles are derived is instructive. In a review of patient responses to treatment conditions in the NIMH Treatment of Depression Collaborative Research Program ([TDCRP] Elkin et al., 1985), it appeared as if patients with more severe cognitive distortions responded less well to cognitive therapy and those with more severe interpersonal difficulties did less well in response to IPT (Sotsky et al., 1991). In a different analysis of TDCRP patients, those who were avoidant and might have been predicted to benefit from IPT and those who were obsessive and might have been predicted to do better in CT actually did better when they received the treatment condition that appeared to be a less good fit for their problem (Rude & Rehm, 1991). The scientific basis for this ordering suggestion is admittedly weak, since the actual research designs that would provide the best information on how robust this recommendation is (patient x treatment studies) are uncommon compared to the less informative prognostic designs (see Hollon & Shelton, 2001, pp. 248–249).

CLOSING RECOMMENDATIONS

The principles outlined in this chapter are extracted from the stated theories that gave rise to the treatment protocols shown to be efficacious in randomized clinical trials. We have offered cautions about the validity of extracting principles from treatments and assuming the principles would produce similar results when applied outside the treatment manuals in which they were imbedded or would directly generalize to populations with significantly different characteristics than were included in the original randomized clinical trials.

This chapter further gives qualified suggestions for ordering the use of principles to build on patient strengths. Separate from applying the principles thoughtfully, it is useful to have an idea of how to plan the course of therapy and fully engage the client. While these points are not derived from the same outcome literature that led to the treatment principles, they do have an empirical basis that may lead to better outcomes at least by virtue of sustaining a strong therapeutic relationship between client and therapist.

As in many outcome studies, the more severe the depression the more guarded the prognosis. Knowledge of this relationship prepares the client and therapist for a course of treatment that anticipates both improvement and the expectation that the change process will not be simple. While treatment matching studies do not allow one to confidently make predictions about outcomes, certain heuristics are useful to consider. Engaging the client's strengths may assist in establishing a collaborative set for change and enhance expectancy for positive change. It may be useful to predicting that there will be a time relatively early in therapy when symptoms lift that may lead the client to wish to terminate because therapy is difficult. Such a prediction can be used to maintain motivation to push forward. Beutler, Clarkin, and Bongar (2000) describe several models for understanding the structure of treatment that includes a rich discussion of factors to consider in planning and implementing the treatment principles we have described.

References

Addis, M. E., Wade, W. A., & Hatgis, C. (1999). Barriers to dissemination of evidence-based practices: Addressing practitioners' concerns about manual-based psychotherapies. *Clinical Psychology: Science & Practice, 6*, 430–441.

Addis, M. E., & Zamudio, A. (2001). Systemic and clinical considerations in psychosocial treatment dissemination: An example of empirically supported treatment for a gay couple. *Behavior Therapist. Special Issue: Research-practice link, 24*, 151–154.

Alloy, L. B., & Abramson, L. Y. (1979). Judgment of contingency in depressed and nondepressed students: Sadder but wiser? *Journal of Experimental Psychology: General, 108*, 441–485.

Barlow, D. H., Levitt, J. T., & Bufka, L. F. (1999). The dissemination of empirically supported treatments: A view to the future. *Behaviour Research & Therapy. Special Issue: Cognitive Behaviour Therapy: Evolution and prospects. A Festschrift in honour of Dr S. Rachman, Editor of Behavior Research and Therapy, 37*, S147–S162.

Barrett, L. F., Lane, R. D., Sechrest, L., & Schwartz, G. E. (2000). Sex differences in emotional awareness. *Personality and Social Psychology Bulletin, 26,* 1027–1035.

Beach, S. R. H. (2001). Marital therapy for co-occurring marital discord and depression. In S. R. H. Beach (Ed.), *Marital and family processes in depression: A scientific foundation for clinical practice* (pp. 205–224). Washington, D.C.: American Psychological Association.

Beach, S. R. H., & O'Leary, K. D. (1993). Dysphoria and marital discord: Are dysphoric individuals at risk for marital maladjustment? *Journal of Marital and Family Therapy, 19,* 355–368.

Beck, A. T., Rush, A. J., Shaw, B. F., & Emery, G. (1979). *Cognitive therapy of depression.* New York: Guilford.

Bernstein, D. A., Borkovec, T. D., & Hazlett-Stevens, H. (2000). *New directions in progressive relaxation training: A guidebook for helping professionals.* Westport, CT: Praeger Publishers.

Beutler, L. E. (1998). Identifying empirically supported treatments: What if we didn't? *Journal of Consulting and Clinical Psychology, 66,* 113–120.

Beutler, L. E., Clarkin, J. F., & Bongar, B. (2000). *Guidelines for the systematic treatment of the depressed patient.* New York: Oxford University Press.

Beutler, L. E., Engle, D., Mohr, D., Daldrup, R. J., Bergan, J., Meredith, K., et al. (1991). Predictors of differential response to cognitive, experiential, and self-directed psychotherapeutic procedures. *Journal of Consulting & Clinical Psychology, 59,* 333–340.

Biglan, A., & Dow, M. G. (1981). Toward a "second generation" model of depression treatment: A problem specific approach. In L. P. Rehm (Ed.), *Behavior therapy for depression: Present status and future directions* (pp. 97–118). New York: Academic Press.

Biglan, A., Hops, H., Sherman, L., Friedman, L. S., Arthur, J., & Osteen, V. (1985). Problem-solving interactions of depressed women and their husbands. *Behavior Therapy, 16,* 431–451.

Blagys, M. D., & Hilsenroth, M. J. (2000). Distinctive features of short-term psychodynamic-interpersonal psychotherapy: A review of the comparative psychotherapy process literature. *Clinic Psychology: Science and Practice, 7,* 167–188.

Bohart, A. C. (2000). Paradigm clash: Empirically supported treatments versus empirically supported psychotherapy practice. *Psychotherapy Research, 10,* 488–493.

Bohart, A. C., O'Hara, M., & Leitner, L. M. (1998). Empirically violated treatments: Disenfranchisement of humanistic and other psychotherapies. *Psychotherapy Research, 8,* 141–157.

Bolling, M. Y., Kohlenberg, R. J., & Parker, C. R. (2000). Behavior analysis and depression. In M. J. Dougher (Ed.), *Clinical behavior analysis* (pp. 127–152). Reno, NV: Context Press.

Bonanno, G. A., & Keltner, D. (1997). Facial expressions of emotion and the course of conjugal bereavement. *Journal of Abnormal Psychology, 106,* 126–137.

Borkovec, T. D., & Castonguay, L. G. (1998). What is the scientific meaning of empirically supported therapy? *Journal of Consulting and Clinical Psychology, 66,* 136–142.

Brown, G. W., & Harris, T. O. (1978). *Social origins of depression: A study of psychiatric disorder in women.* New York: Guilford Press.

Burns, D. D., & Spangler, D. L. (2001). Do changes in dysfunctional attitudes mediate changes in depression and anxiety in cognitive behavioral therapy? *Behavior Therapy, 32,* 337–369.

Calhoun, K. S., Moras, K., Pilkonis, P. A., & Rehm, L. P. (1998). Empirically supported treatments: Implications for training. *Journal of Consulting and Clinical Psychology, 66,* 151–162.

Castonguay, L. G., Arnow, B. A., Blatt, S. J., Jones, E. E., Pilkonis, P. A., & Segal, Z. V. (1999). Psychotherapy for depression: Current and future directions in research, theory, practice, and public policy. *Journal of Clinical Psychology/In Session, 55,* 1347–1370.

Castonguay, L. G., Goldfried, M. R., Wiser, S., Raue, P. J., & Hayes, A. H. (1996). Predicting outcome in cognitive therapy for depression: A comparison of unique and common factors. *Journal of Consulting and Clinical Psychology, 64,* 497–504.

Chambless, D. L., Baker, M., Baucom, D. H., Beutler, L. E., Calhoun, K. S., Crits-Christoph, P., et al. (1998). Update on empirically validated therapies, II. *The Clinical Psychologist, 51,* 3–16.

Chambless, D. L., & Hollon, S. D. (1998). Defining empirically supported therapies. *Journal of Consulting and Clinical Psychology, 66,* 7–18.

Chambless, D. L., & Ollendick, T. H. (2001). Empirically supported psychological interventions: Controversies and evidence. *Annual Review of Psychology, 52,* 685–716.

Cooke, M. (2000). The dissemination of a smoking cessation program: Predictors of program awareness, adoption and maintenance. *Health Promotion International, 15,* 113–124.

Coyne, J. C. (1976). Depression and the response of others. *Journal of Abnormal Psychology, 2,* 186–193.

Coyne, J. C., & Benazon, N. R. (2001). Not agent blue: Effects of marital functioning on depression and implications for treatment. In S. R. H. Beach (Ed.), *Marital and family processes in depression: A scientific foundation for clinical practice* (pp. 25–43). Washington, DC: American Psychological Association.

Craighead, W. E., Hart, A. B., Craighead, L. W., & Ilardi, S. S. (2002). Psychosocial treatments for major depressive disorder. In P. E. Nathan & J. M. Gorman (Eds.), *A guide to treatments that work* (pp. 245–261). London: Oxford University Press.

Crits-Christoph, P., Frank, E., Chambless, D. L., Brody, C., & Karp, J. F. (1995). Training in empirically validated treatments: What are clinical psychology students learning? *Professional Psychology: Research & Practice, 26,* 514–522.

Daldrup, R. J., Engle, D., Holiman, M., & Beutler, L. E. (1994). The intensification and resolution of blocked affect in an experiential psychotherapy. *British Journal of Clinical Psychology, 33,* 129–141.

Davidson, R. (2000). Affective style, psychopathology and resilience: Brain mechanisms and plasticity. *American Psychologist, 5*(11), 1193–1196.

Davidson, R. J., Pizzagalli, D., Nitschke, J. B., & Putnam, K. (2002). Depression: Perspectives from affective neuroscience. *Annual Review of Psychology, 53,* 545–574.

DeRubeis, R. J., Gelfand, L. A., Tang, T. Z., & Simons, A. D. (1999). Medications versus cognitive behavior therapy for severely depressed outpatients: Mega-analysis of four randomized comparisons. *American Journal of Psychiatry, 156,* 1007–1013.

DeRubeis, R. J., & Stirman, S. W. (2001). Determining the pertinence of psychotherapy outcome research findings for clinical practice: Comment on Westen and Morrison (2001). *Journal of Consulting & Clinical Psychology, 69,* 908–909.

Dohrenwend, B. P. (2000). The role of adversity and stress in psychopathology: Some evidence and its implications for theory and research. *Journal of Health and Social Behavior, 41,* 1–19.

Elkin, I., Gibbons, R. D., Shea, M. T., Sotsky, S. M., Watkins, J. T., Pilkonis, P. A., et al. (1995). Initial severity and differential treatment outcomes in the National Institute of Mental Health Treatment of Depression Collaborative Research Program. *Journal of Consulting and Clinical Psychology, 63,* 841–847.

Elkin, I., Shea, M. T., Watkins, J. T., Imber, S. D., Sotsky, S. M., Collins, J. F., et al. (1989). National Institute of Mental Health Treatment of Depression Collaborative Research Program: General effectiveness of treatments. *Archives of General Psychiatry, 46,* 971–982.

Elkin, I. E., Parloff, M. B., Hadley, S. W., & Autry, J. H. (1985). NIMH Treatment of Depression Collaborative Research Program: Background and research plan. *Archives of General Psychiatry, 42,* 305–316.

Elliott, R. (1998). Editor's introduction: A guide to the empirically supported treatments controversy. *Psychotherapy Research, 8,* 115–125.

Elliott, R., Clark, C., Wexler, M., Kemeny, V., Brinkerhoff, J., & Mack, C. (1990). The impact of experiential therapy of depression: Initial results. In G. Lietaer, J. Rombauts, & R. Van Balen (Eds.), *Client-centered and experiential psychotherapy towards the nineties* (pp. 549–577). Leuven, Belgium: Peuven University Press.

Elliott, R., Greenberg, L. S., & Lietaer, G. (2003). Research on experiential psychotherapies. In M. J. Lambert, A. E. Bergin, & S. L. Garfield (Eds.), *Handbook of psychotherapy and behavior change* (5th ed., pp. 493–539). New York: Wiley.

Endicott, J., & Spitzer, R. L. (1979). Use of the Research Diagnostic Criteria and the Schedule for Affective Disorders and Schizophrenia to study affective disorders. *American Journal of Psychiatry, 136,* 52–56.

Ferster, C. B. (1973). A functional analysis of depression. *American Psychologist, 28,* 857–870.

Fincham, F. D., Beach, S. R. H., Harold, G. T., & Osborne, L. N. (1997). Marital satisfaction and depression: Different causal relationships for men and women? *Psychological Science, 8,* 351–357.

Foa, E. B., & Kozak, M. J. (1986). Emotional processing of fear: Exposure to corrective information. *Psychological Bulletin, 99,* 20–35.

Follette, W. C., & Beitz, K. (2003). Adding a more rigorous scientific agenda to the empirically supported treatment movement. *Behavior Modification. Special Issue: Empirically supported treatments, 27,* 369–386.

Follette, W. C., Dykstra, T. A., & Compton, S. N.

(1992, November). *Contingent learning as an alternative to rule governance in teaching complex social behaviors to schizophrenics*. Paper presented at the 26th Annual Meeting of the Association for the Advancement of Behavior Therapy, Boston, MA.

Frederickson, B. (2001). The role of positive emotions in positive psychology: The broaden-and-build theory of positive emotions. *American Psychologist, 56*(3), 218–226.

Fredrickson, B. L., & Levenson, R. W. (1998). Positive emotions speed recovery from the cardiovascular sequelae of negative emotions. *Cognition and Emotion, 12,* 191–220.

Freud, S. (1917/1951). Mourning and melancholia (J. Strachey, Trans.). In J. Strachey (Ed.), *The standard edition of the complete psychological works of Sigmund Freud* (Vol. 14, pp. 237–260). London: Hogarth Press. (Original work published in 1917.)

Frijda, N. H. (1986). *The emotions*. New York: Cambridge University Press.

Fuchs, C. A., & Rehm, L. P. (1977). A self-control behavior therapy program for depression. *Journal of Consulting & Clinical Psychology, 435,* 206–215.

Gaffan, E. A., Tsaousis, J., & Kemp-Wheeler, S. M. (1995). Researcher allegiance and meta-analysis: The case of cognitive therapy for depression. *Journal of Consulting and Clinical Psychology, 63,* 966–980.

Gallagher-Thompson, D., & Steffen, A. M. (1994). Comparative effects of cognitive-behavioral and brief dynamic therapy for depressed family caregivers. *Journal of Consulting & Clinical Psychology, 62,* 543–549.

Gendlin, E. T. (1996). Focusing-oriented psychotherapy: A manual of the experiential method. New York: Guilford Press.

Goldfried, M. R., Castonguay, L. G., Hayes, A. M., Drozd, J. F., & Shapiro, D. A. (1997). A comparative analysis of the therapeutic focus in cognitive-behavioral and psychodynamic-interpersonal sessions. *Journal of Consulting and Clinical Psychology, 65,* 740–748.

Goldman, R. N., & Greenberg, L. S. (in press). Depth of emotional experience and outcome. *Psychotherapy Research.*

Goldman, R. N., Greenberg, L. S., & Angus, L. (2000, June). *Experiential therapy of depression: Comparing the effectiveness of process-experiential and client-centered therapy*. Paper presented at the Society for Psychotherapy Research, Indian Hills, Illinois.

Goldman, R. N., Greenberg, L. S., & Angus, L. (under review). The effects of adding specific emotion-focused interventions to the therapeutic relationship in the treatment of depression. *Psychotherapy Research.*

Goodman, S. H., & Gotlib, I. H. (1999). Risk for psychopathology in the children of depressed mothers: A developmental model for understanding mechanisms of transmission. *Psychological Review, 106,* 458–490.

Goodman, S. H., & Gotlib, I. H. (2002). Transmission of risk to children of depressed parents: Integration and conclusions. In S. H. Goodman & I. H. Gotlib (Eds.), *Children of depressed parents: Mechanisms of risk and implications for treatment* (pp. 307–326). Washington, DC: American Psychological Association.

Greenberg, L. S. (2002). *Emotion-focused therapy: Coaching clients to work through their feelings*. Washington, DC: American Psychological Association.

Greenberg, L. S., & Bolger, L. (2001). An emotion-focused approach to the over-regulation of emotion and emotional pain. *In-Session, 57*(2), 197–212.

Greenberg, L. S., Elliott, R. K., & Foerster, F. S. (1990). Experiential processes in the psychotherapeutic treatment of depression. In C. D. McCann & N. S. Endler (Eds.), *Depression: New direction in theory, research and practice* (pp. 157–185). Toronto: Wall & Emerson, Inc.

Greenberg, L. S., & Paivio, S. C. (1997). *Working with emotions in psychotherapy*. New York: Guilford Press.

Greenberg, L. S., & Pascual-Leone, J. (1995). A dialectical constructivist approach to experiential change. In R. A. Neimeyer & M. J. Mahoney (Eds.), *Constructivism in psychotherapy* (pp. 169–191). Washington, DC: American Psychological Association.

Greenberg, L. S., & Pedersen, R. (2001, June). *Relating the degree of resolution of in-session self criticism and dependence to outcome and follow-up in the treatment of depression*. Paper presented at the North American Chapter of the Society for Psychotherapy Research, Puerto Vallarta, Mexico.

Greenberg, L. S., Rice, L. N., & Elliott, R. (1993). *Facilitating emotional change: The moment-by-moment process*. New York: Guilford Press.

Greenberg, L. S., & Safran, J. D. (1984). Hot cognition—emotion coming in from the cold: A reply to Rachman and Mahoney. *Cognitive Therapy and Research, 8,* 591–598.

Greenberg, L. S., & Safran, J. D. (1987). *Emotion in psychotherapy: Affect, cognition, and the process of change.* New York: Guilford Press.

Greenberg, L. S., & Safran, J. D. (1989). Emotion in psychotherapy. *American Psychologist, 44,* 19–29.

Greenberg, L. S., & Watson, J. (1998). Experiential therapy of depression: Differential effects of client-centered relationship conditions and process experiential interventions. *Psychotherapy Research, 8,* 210–224.

Greenberg, L. S., & Watson, J. (in press). *Emotion-focused therapy of depression.* Washington, DC: American Psychological Association Press.

Greenberg, L. S., Watson, J. C., & Goldman, R. (1998). Process-experiential therapy of depression. In L. S. Greenberg, J. C. Watson, & G. Lietaer (Eds.), *Handbook of experiential psychotherapy* (pp. 227–248). New York: Guilford Press.

Henggeler, S. W., Melton, G. B., Brondino, M. J., Scherer, D. G., & Hanley, J. H. (1997). Multisystemic therapy with violent and chronic juvenile offenders and their families: The role of treatment fidelity in successful dissemination. *Journal of Consulting & Clinical Psychology, 65,* 821–833.

Henry, W. P. (1998). Science, politics, and the politics of science: The use and misuse of empirically validated treatment research. *Psychotherapy Research, 8,* 126–140.

Henry, W. P., Strupp, H. H., Schacht, T. E., & Gaston, L. (1994). Psychodynamic approaches. In A. E. Bergin & S. Garfield (Eds.), *Handbook of psychotherapy and behavior change* (4th ed., pp. 467–508). New York: Wiley.

Hilsenroth, M. J., Ackerman, S. J., Blagys, M. D., Baity, M. R., & Mooney, M. A. (2003). Short-term psychodynamic psychotherapy for depression: An examination of statistical, clinically significant, and technique-specific change. *Journal of Nervous and Mental Disease, 191,* 349–357.

Hoberman, H. M., & Lewinsohn, P. M. (1985). The behavioral treatment of depression. In E. E. Beckham & W. R. Leber (Eds.), *Handbook of depression: Treatment, assessment, and research* (pp. 39–81). Homewood, IL: Dorsey Press.

Hollon, S. D., Haman, K. L., & Brown, L. L. (2002). Cognitive-behavioral treatment of depression. In I. H. Gotlib & C. L. Hammen (Eds.), *Handbook of depression* (pp. 383–403). New York: Guilford Press.

Hollon, S. D., & Shelton, R. C. (2001). Treatment guidelines for major depressive disorder. *Behavior Therapy, 32,* 235–258.

Hunt, M. G. (1998). The only way out is through: Emotional processing and recovery after a depressing life event. *Behaviour Research & Therapy, 36,* 361–384.

Ilardi, S. S., & Craighead, W. E. (1999). Rapid early response, cognitive modification, and nonspecific factors in cognitive behavior therapy for depression: A reply to Tang and DeRubeis. *Clinical Psychology: Science & Practice, 6,* 295–299.

Ingram, R. E., Hayes, A., & Scott, W. (2000). Empirically supported treatments: A critical analysis. In C. R. Snyder & R. E. Ingram (Eds.), *Handbook of psychological change: Psychotherapy processes & practices for the 21st century* (pp. 40–60). New York: John Wiley & Sons, Inc.

Jacobson, N. S., & Anderson, C. A. (1982). Interpersonal skill deficits and depression in college students: A sequential analysis of timing of self-disclosure. *Behavior Therapy, 13,* 271–282.

Jacobson, N. S., Dobson, K. S., Truax, P. A., Addis, M. E., Koerner, K., Gollan, J. K., et al. (1996). A component analysis of cognitive-behavioral treatment for depression. *Journal of Consulting & Clinical Psychology, 64,* 295–304.

Jacobson, N. S., & Follette, W. C. (1985). Clinical significance of improvement resulting from two behavioral marital therapy components. *Behavior Therapy, 16,* 249–262.

Jacobson, N. S., & Hollon, S. D. (1996). Cognitive-behavior therapy versus pharmacotherapy: Now that the jury's returned its verdict, it's time to present the rest of the evidence. *Journal of Consulting and Clinical Psychology, 64,* 74–80.

Joiner, T. E., Jr. (2002). Depression in its interpersonal context. In I. H. Gotlib & C. L. Hammen (Eds.), *Handbook of depression* (pp. 295–313). New York: Guilford Press.

Kabat-Zinn, J. (1990). *Full catastrophe living.* New York: Delta.

Kanter, J. W., Parker, C. R., & Kohlenberg, R. J. (2001). Finding the self: A behavioral measure and its clinical implications. *Psychotherapy: Theory, Research, Practice, Training, 38,* 198–211.

King, M., Sibbald, B., Ward, E., Bower, P., Lloyd, M., Gabbay, M., & Byford, S. (2000). Randomised controlled trial of non-directive counselling, cognitive-behavior therapy and usual general practitioner care in the management of depression as well as mixed anxiety and depression in primary care. *Health Technology Assessment, 4,* 1–83.

Klein, M. H., Mathieu-Coughlan, P., & Kiesler, D. J. (1986). The experiencing scales. In L. S. Greenberg & W. Pisof (Eds.), *The psychotherapeutic process: A research handbook* (pp. 21–71). New York: Guilford Press.

Klerman, G. L., Weissman, M. M., Rounsaville, B. J., & Chevron, E. S. (1984). *Interpersonal psychotherapy of depression.* New York: Basic Books.

Kohlenberg, R. J., Kanter, J. W., Bolling, M. Y., Parker, C., & Tsai, M. (2002). Enhancing cognitive therapy for depression with functional analytic psychotherapy: Treatment guidelines and empirical findings. *Cognitive & Behavioral Practice, 9,* 213–229.

Kohlenberg, R. J., & Tsai, M. (1991). *Functional analytic psychotherapy.* New York: Plenum Press.

Lambert, M. J. (2001). The status of empirically supported therapies: Comment on Westen and Morrison's (2001) multidimensional meta-analysis. *Journal of Consulting & Clinical Psychology, 69,* 910–913.

Lampropoulos, G. K. (2000). A reexamination of the empirically supported treatments critiques. *Psychotherapy Research, 10,* 474–487.

Lane, R. D., Quinlan, D. M., & Schwartz, G. E. (1990). The levels of emotional awareness scale: A cognitive-developmental measure of emotion. *Journal of Personality Assessment, 55,* 124–134.

Lane, R. D., & Schwartz, G. E. (1992). Levels of emotional awareness: Implications for psychotherapeutic integration. *Journal of Psychotherapy Integration, 2,* 1–18.

Lane, R. D., Sechrest, L., Reidel, R., Weldon, V., & Schwartz, G. E. (1996). Impaired verbal and nonverbal emotion recognition in alexithymia. *Psychosomatic Medicine, 58,* 203–210.

Leichsenring, F. (2001). Comparative effects of short-term psychodynamic psychotherapy and cognitive-behavioral therapy in depression: A meta-analytic approach. *Clinical Psychology Review, 21,* 401–419.

Lejuez, C. W., Hopko, D. R., & Hopko, S. D. (2001). A brief behavioral activation treatment for depression: Treatment manual. *Behavior Modification, 25,* 255–286.

Lejuez, C. W., Hopko, D. R., & Hopko, S. D. (2002). *The brief behavioral activation treatment for depression (BATD): A comprehensive patient guide.* Boston: Pearson Custom Publishing.

Levitt, J. T., Brown, T. A., Orsillo, S. M., & Barlow, D. H. (in press). The effects of acceptance versus suppression of emotion on subjective and psychophysiological response to carbon dioxide challenge in patients with panic disorder. *Behavior Therapy.*

Lewinsohn, P. M. (1974). A behavioral approach to depression. In R. M. Friedman & M. M. Katz (Eds.), *The psychology of depression: Contemporary theory and research* (pp. 157–185). New York: Wiley Press.

Lewinsohn, P. M., & Gotlib, I. H. (1995). Behavioral theory and treatment of depression. In E. E. Beckham & W. R. Leber (Eds.), *Handbook of depression* (2nd ed., pp. 352–375). New York: Guilford Press.

Lewinsohn, P. M., & Hoberman, H. M. (1982). Behavioral and cognitive approaches to treatment. In E. S. Paykel (Ed.), *Handbook of affective disorders* (pp. 338–345). Edinburgh: Churchill-Livingston.

Lewinsohn, P. M., Hoberman, H. M., Teri, L., & Hautzinger, M. (1985). An integrative theory of unipolar depression. In S. Reiss & R. R. Bootzin (Eds.), *Theoretical issues in behavioral therapy* (pp. 313–359). New York: Academic Press.

Lewinsohn, P. M., Mischel, W., Chaplin, W., & Barton, R. (1980). Social competence and depression: The role of illusory self-perceptions. *Journal of Abnormal Psychology, 89,* 203–212.

Linehan, M. M. (1993). *Cognitive-behavioral treatment of borderline personality disorder.* New York: Guilford.

Luborsky, L. (1984). *Principles of psychoanalytic psychotherapy: Manual for supportive/expressive treatment.* New York: Basic Books.

Luborsky, L., Mark, D., Hole, A., Popp, C., Goldsmith, B., & Cacciola, J. (1995). Supportive-expressive dynamic psychotherapy of depression: A time-limited version. In J. P. Barber & P. Crits-Christoph (Eds.), *Dynamic psychotherapies for psychiatric disorders (axis I)* (pp. 13–42). New York: Basic Books.

Ma, S. H., & Teasdale, J. D. (2004). Mindfulness-based cognitive therapy for depression: Replication and exploration of differential relapse prevention effects. *Journal of Consulting & Clinical Psychology, 72,* 31–40.

Malan, D. (1979). *Individual psychotherapy and the science of psychodynamics.* London: Butterworths.

Malik, M. L., Beutler, L. E., Gallagher-Thompson, D., Thompson, L., & Alimohamed, S. (2003).

Are all cognitive therapies alike? A comparison of cognitive and non-cognitive therapy process and implications for the application of empirically supported treatments (ESTs). *Journal of Consulting and Clinical Psychology, 71*, 150–158.

Martell, C. R., Addis, M. E., & Jacobson, N. S. (2001). *Depression in context: Strategies for guided action*. New York: Norton & Company.

Mazure, C. M. (1998). Life stressors as risk factors in depression. *Clinical Psychology: Science & Practice, 5*, 291–313.

McCullough, J. P., Jr. (2000). *Treatment for chronic depression: Cognitive behavioral analysis system of psychotherapy (CBASP)*. New York: Guilford Press.

McCullough, J. P., Jr. (2001). *Skills training manual for diagnosing and treating chronic depression: Cognitive behavioral analysis system of psychotherapy*. New York: Guilford Press.

McFall, R. M. (1982). A review and reformulation of the concept of social skills. *Behavioral Assessment, 4*, 1–33.

McLean, P. D. (1981). Remediation of skills and performance deficits in depression: Clinical steps and research findings. In J. Clarkin & H. Glazer (Eds.), *Behavioral and directive strategies* (pp. 172–204). New York: Garland Publishing.

Messer, S. B. (2001). Empirically supported treatments: What's a nonbehaviorist to do? In B. D. Slife, R. N. Williams, et al. (Eds.), *Critical issues in psychotherapy: Translating new ideas into practice* (pp. 3–19). Thousand Oaks, CA: Sage Publications, Inc.

Mestel, R., & Votsmeier-Röhr, A. (2000, June). Long-term follow-up study of depressive patients receiving experiential psychotherapy in an inpatient setting. Paper presented at the Society of Psychotherapy Research, Chicago, IL.

Monroe, S. M., & Hadjiyannakis, K. (2002). The social environment and depression: Focusing on severe life stress. In I. H. Gotlib & C. L. Hammen (Eds.), *Handbook of depression* (pp. 314–340). New York: Guilford Press.

Monroe, S. M., & McQuaid, J. R. (1994). Measuring life stress and assessing its impact on mental health. In W. R. Avison & I. H. Gotlib (Eds.), *Stress and mental health: Contemporary issues and prospects for the future* (pp. 43–73). New York: Plenum Press.

Nathan, P. E. (2001). Deny nothing, doubt everything: A comment on Westen and Morrison (2001). *Journal of Consulting & Clinical Psychology, 69*, 900–903.

Nathan, P. E., & Gorman, J. M. (2002). *A guide to treatments that work* (2nd ed.). New York: Oxford University Press.

Orsillo, S. M., Roemer, L., & Barlow, D. H. (in press). Integrating acceptance and mindfulness into existing cognitive-behavioral treatment for GAD: A case study. *Cognitive and Behavioral Practice*.

Palfia, T. P., & Salovey, P. (1993). The influence of depressed and elated mood on deductive and inductive reasoning. *Imagination, Cognition, and Personality, 13*, 57–71.

Pennebaker, J. W. (1990). *Opening up: The healing power of confiding in others*. New York: William Morrow.

Pennebaker, J. W. (1995). Emotion, disclosure, and health: An overview. In J. W. Pennebaker (Ed.), *Emotion, disclosure, & health* (pp. 3–10). Washington, DC: American Psychological Association.

Petry, N. M., & Simcic, F., Jr. (2002). Recent advances in the dissemination of contingency management techniques: Clinical and research perspectives. *Journal of Substance Abuse Treatment, 23*, 81–86.

Pos, A. E., Greenberg, L. S., Goldman, R. N., & Korman, L. M. (2003). Emotional processing during experiential treatment of depression. *Journal of Consulting & Clinical Psychology, 71*, 1007–1016.

Rehm, L. P., Fuchs, C. Z., Roth, D. M., Kornblith, S. J., & Romano, J. M. (1979). A comparison of self-control and assertion skills treatments of depression. *Behavior Therapy, 10*, 429–442.

Rimé, B., Finkenhauer, C., Luminet, O., Zech, E., & Phillipot, P. (1998). Social sharing of emotion: New evidence and new questions. In W. Stroebe and M. Hewstone (Eds.), *European review of social psychology* (Vol. 9, pp. 225–258). Chichester, England: Wiley.

Robins, L., & Regier, D. A. (1991). *Psychiatric disorders in America: The Epidemiologic Catchment Area Study*. New York: Free Press.

Rude, S. S., & Rehm, L. P. (1991). Response to treatments for depression: The role of initial status on targeted cognitive and behavioral skills. *Clinical Psychology Review, 11*, 493–514.

Salovey, P., Hsee, C., & Mayer, J. C. (1993). Emotional intelligence and the self-regulation of affect. In D. M. Wegner and J. W. Pennebaker (Eds.), *Handbook of mental control* (pp. 125–154). Englewood Cliffs, NJ: Prentice-Hall.

Schoenwald, S. K., & Hoagwood, K. (2001). Effectiveness, transportability, and dissemination of interventions: What matters when? *Psychiatric Services, 52,* 1190–1197.

Schwartz, G. E., Fair, P. L., Salt, P., Mandel, M. R., & Klerman, G. (1976). Facial muscle patterning to affective imagery in depressed and nondepressed subjects. *Science, 192,* 489–491.

Segal, Z. V., Williams, J. M. G., & Teasdale, J. D. (2002). Mindfulness-based cognitive therapy for depression: A new approach to preventing relapse. New York: Guilford Press.

Segrin, C. (1990). A meta-analytic review of social skills deficits in depression. *Communication Monographs, 57,* 292–308.

Segrin, C. (1992). Specifying the nature of social skills deficits associated with depression. *Human Communication Research, 19,* 89–123.

Segrin, C., & Flora, J. (1998). Depression and verbal behavior in conversations with friends and strangers. *Journal of Language and Social Psychology, 17,* 492–503.

Shapiro, D. A., Barkham, M., Rees, A., Hardy, G. E., Reynolds, S., & Startup, M. (1994). Effects of treatment duration and severity of depression on the effectiveness of cognitive-behavioral and psychodynamic-interpersonal psychotherapy. *Journal of Consulting and Clinical Psychology, 62,* 522–534.

Shoham, V., & Rohrbaugh, M. (1995). Aptitude x treatment interaction (ATI) research: Sharpening the focus, widening the lens. In M. Aveline & D. A. Shapiro (Eds.), *Research foundations for psychotherapy practice* (pp. 73–95). Sussex, England: Wiley.

Skinner, B. F. (1953). *Science and human behavior.* New York: Free Press.

Sotsky, S. M., Glass, D. R., Shea, M. T., Pilkonis, P. A., Collins, J. F., Elkin, I., et al. (1991). Patient predictors of response to psychotherapy and pharmacotherapy: Findings in the NIMH treatment of depression collaborative research program. *American Journal of Psychiatry, 148,* 997–1008.

Stanton, A. L., Danoff-Burg, S., Cameron, C. L., Bishop, M., Collins, C. A., Kirk, S. B., Sworowski, L. A., & Twillman, R. (2000). Emotionally expressive coping predicts psychological and physical adjustment to breast cancer. *Journal of Consulting and Clinical Psychology, 68,* 875–882.

Stiles, W. B., Honos-Webb, L., & Surko, M. (1998). Responsiveness in psychotherapy. *Clinical Psychology: Science and Practice, 5,* 439–458.

Stirman, S. W., DeRubeis, R. J., Crits-Christoph, P., & Brody, P. E. (2003). Are samples in randomized controlled trials of psychotherapy representative of community outpatients? A new methodology and initial findings. *Journal of Consulting & Clinical Psychology, 71,* 963–972.

Strosahl, K. (1998). The dissemination of manual-based psychotherapies in managed care: Promises, problems, and prospects. *Clinical Psychology: Science & Practice, 5,* 382–386.

Strupp, H. H., & Binder, J. (1984). *Psychotherapy in a new key.* New York: Basic Books.

Svartberg, M., & Stiles, T. C. (1991). Comparative effects of short-term psychodynamic psychotherapy: A meta-analysis. *Journal of Consulting & Clinical Psychology, 59,* 704–714.

Tang, T. Z., & DeRubeis, R. J. (1999a). Reconsidering rapid early response in cognitive behavioral therapy for depression. *Clinical Psychology: Science & Practice, 6,* 283–288.

Tang, T. Z., & DeRubeis, R. J. (1999b). Sudden gains and critical sessions in cognitive-behavioral therapy for depression. *Journal of Consulting & Clinical Psychology, 67,* 894–904.

Tarrier, N., Barrowclough, C., Haddock, G., & McGovern, J. (1999). The dissemination of innovative cognitive-behavioural psychosocial treatments for schizophrenia. *Journal of Mental Health (UK), 8,* 569–582.

Teasdale, J. D., Segal, Z. V., Williams, J. M. G., Ridgeway, V. A., Soulsby, J. M., & Lau, M. A. (2000). Prevention of relapse/recurrence in major depression by mindfulness-based cognitive therapy. *Journal of Consulting & Clinical Psychology, 68,* 615–623.

Thase, M. E., Greenhouse, J. B., Frank, E., Reynolds, C. F., Pilkonis, P. A., Hurley, K., et al. (1997). Treatment of major depression with psychotherapy-pharmacotherapy combinations. *Archives of General Psychiatry, 54,* 1009–1015.

Troisi, A., & Moles, A. (1999). Gender differences in depression: An ethological study of nonverbal behavior during interviews. *Journal of Psychiatric Research, 33,* 243–250.

Wachtel, P. (1993). *Therapeutic communication: Principles and effective practice.* New York: Guilford.

Warwar, N., & Greenberg, L. S. (2000, June). *Catharsis is not enough: Changes in emotional processing related to psychotherapy outcome.* Paper presented at the International Society for Psychotherapy Research, Indian Hills, Illinois.

Watson, J. C., Gordon, L. B., Stermac, L., Kalogerakos, F., & Steckley, P. (2003). Comparing the effectiveness of process-experiential with cognitive-behavioral psychotherapy in the treatment of depression. *Journal of Consulting & Clinical Psychology, 71*, 773–781.

Watson, J. C., & Greenberg, L. S. (1996). Pathways to change in the psychotherapy of depression: Relating process to session change and outcome. *Psychotherapy: Theory, Research, Practice, Training, 33*, 262–274.

Weissman, M. M., Markowitz, J. C., & Klerman, G. (2000). *Comprehensive guide to interpersonal psychotherapy*. New York: Basic Books.

Weissman, M. M., Prusoff, B. A., DiMascio, A., Neu, C., Goklaney, M., & Klerman, G. L. (1979). The efficacy of drugs and psychotherapy in the treatment of acute depressive episodes. *American Journal of Psychiatry, 136*, 555–558.

Westen, D., & Morrison, K. (2001). A multidimensional meta-analysis of treatments for depression, panic, and generalized anxiety disorder: An empirical examination of the status of empirically supported therapies. *Journal of Consulting & Clinical Psychology, 69*, 875–899.

Whisman, M. A. (2001). The association between depression and marital dissatisfaction. In S. R. H. Beach (Ed.), *Marital and family processes in depression: A scientific foundation for clinical practice* (pp. 3–24). Washington, DC: American Psychological Association.

Williams, J. M, Stiles, W., & Shapiro, D. (1999). Cognitive mechanisms in the avoidance of painful and dangerous thought; elaborating the assimilation model. Cognitive Therapy and Research, *23*(3), 285–306.

Wilson, G. T. (1996). Empirically validated treatments: Reality and resistance. *Clinical Psychology: Science and Practice, 3*, 241–244.

5

Integration of Therapeutic Factors in Dysphoric Disorders

Larry E. Beutler

Louis G. Castonguay

William C. Follette

The goal of this chapter is to integrate the principles of change related to the treatment of depression and dysphoria, those that are shared with the treatment of other disorders, along with those that are unique to psychosocial treatments delivered to these populations. To a large extent, this chapter is based on the conclusions reached by three previous chapters specific to dysphoric disorders (Beutler, Blatt, Alimohamed, Levy, & Angtuaco, this volume; Castonguay et al., this volume; Follette & Greenberg, this volume), as well as on the common and unique principles of change identified in the concluding chapter of this book (Castonguay & Beutler, this volume). The principles delineated in the current chapter, however, are organized and worded in a slightly different way than the one's represented in the chapters mentioned above. As noted in the preface and first chapter of this volume, after the 12 individual chapters on participants, relationships, and technique factors were developed, the Task Force on Principles of Therapeutic Change met to organize the principles into those that were common or similar across

two or more disorders and problems (Common Principles of Change) and those that were relatively unique to different types of problems (Unique Principles). The principles of change identified in the current chapter also reflect the integrative effort that guided this group process.

COMMON PRINCIPLES OF CHANGE

Table 5.1 presents the list of 10 common principles related to participant factors. Because of their extensiveness, these common principles have been subdivided into those that relate to problem severity, therapist characteristics, patient personality factors, and patient demographics. Fundamentally, these principles are of three types. One type of principle identifies contributors to patient prognosis and likelihood that a patient will benefit from treatment. The principles of this type are largely reliant on identifying patient and problem factors that increase or limit the likely benefit one might achieve. There are several principles of this type.

Table 5.1

Common Principles of Therapeutic Change Applied to Participant Factors

Severity

1. The more impaired or severe and disruptive the problem, the fewer benefits are noted for time-limited treatments. It is unclear, across disorder/problems, whether longer-term treatments would be better than time-limited ones for these severe problems. Chronicity appears to be an index of impairment levels and may follow the same parameters as other indices of impairment.
2. If the patient has a co-morbid personality disorder, the gains expected in treatment are weakened.

Therapist characteristics

3. Among patients with personality disorder or who experience depression, therapist flexibility in changing strategies, adapting to patient presentations, tolerance, and creativity are related to improvement. In the treatment of depression, for example, this refers to the importance for the therapist to be open, informed, and tolerant of religious views. There is little data on this cluster of variables among other disorders, but it is logical to suggest that it represents a general phenomenon.
4. The effectiveness of therapy is not substantially benefited by a therapist who has had a personal experience with the same type of problem as the patient. Openness and tolerance on the part of the therapist are more important than shared experience. This has been documented in the treatment of substance use but it is likely that this is a general phenomenon.

Patient psychological factors

5. Among those who have anxiety or who have substance abuse disorders, patient expectations are associated with outcomes. Patient expectations of success are more readily related to outcome than the credibility of treatment. Information is lacking on the effects of patient expectations in the treatment of personality disorder. Interestingly, however, expectations do not appear to be associated with outcome in the treatment of depression.
6. Patient pretreatment readiness for change is a reliable predictor of benefit in substance abuse disorders and likely to be involved in other problem areas, but research is largely absent. However, aside from efforts to address the patient's expectations, there is little evidence to suggest that efforts to alter one's "readiness" contribute substantially to benefit.
7. Among most problems, especially among patients with depression, anxiety, or personality disorders, the patient's attachment/interpersonal style interferes with the process of change and/or outcome. Prognosis is best among those with social approach or nonavoidant styles.

Patient demographics

8. Perceived levels of social support are positive predictors of treatment benefit. Absence of either actual or perceived social support may be indicative of the severity of the problem and the degree of experienced impairment (e.g., co-morbidity and personality disorders). Evidence is inconsistent as to whether efforts to improve social support add benefit to the effects of treatment across problem areas. In depression, improving social support adds some benefit, suggesting that it may be a specific treatment factor.
9. Outcome is not substantially or meaningfully enhanced by variations in patient gender.
10. Among patients who experience either substance abuse or anxiety, low SES is a negative predictor of outcome. The pattern is less clear but still probable among other disorders.

For example, Principles 1 and 2 under problem severity predict that severity and co-morbidity are negatively related to prognosis; Principle 6, under patient psychological factors emphasizes that readiness for change is a prognostic indicator; Principle 7 under the same psychological factors also emphasizes that patient ability to develop a ma-

ture relationship is a predictor of positive change; Principle 10 under patient demographics emphasizes the impeding effect of low SES among many patients who are of this type and emphasizes that severity is negatively associated with the likelihood and magnitude of beneficial change.

A second type of principle is one that, interestingly, identifies factors that do not contribute to change. These principles are included because they run counter to popular myths about how to optimize treatment. Thus, principles such as 6 remind the clinician that efforts to increase patient readiness have not proven their effectiveness and may be ill-advised; Principle 9 reminds the clinician that patient gender is not usually a contributor to outcome. Principle 4 stipulates that the clinician can be effective even if he/she has not had a personal problem that is similar to that of the client.

The remaining principles in Table 5.1 identify the types of procedures and structure to be employed by the therapist as a function of various patient and therapist factors. These principles can guide the therapist to adjust the techniques of treatment to fit certain qualities and to overcome problems related to participant factors that have the capacity to inhibit change. These principles emphasize the importance of staying flexible, especially with patients who present with personality disorders and depression (Principle 3); they indicate patient qualities that raise the need for taking steps to address patient expectations (Principle 5, although, interestingly, this may not be of significant importance in the treatment of depression [see Beutler et al., this volume]); and serve as reminders of the importance of sustaining a positive level of social support (Principle 8).

Table 5.2 provides a similar list of common principles related to the development of the therapeutic relationship. The first six principles emphasize the importance of the quality of the therapist–client interaction, as well as the relationship enhancing attitudes on the part of the therapist. They emphasize the role of a general working alliance and cohesiveness (Principles 1 and 2), the related importance of collaborative engagement (Principle 4), and the influence of Rogerian's interpersonal skills (Principles 3, 5, and 6). The last three principles listed in Table 5.2 provide guidelines to the therapist about ways to work with the therapeutic relationship (i.e., what to do and not to do when providing relational interpretations [Principles 7 and 8], and how to repair alliance ruptures [Principle 9]).

Collectively, the participant and relationship principles set the stage for implementing treatments. The 17 common and basic principles of techniques that cut across problems, treatment approaches, and therapists are outlined in Table 5.3. These principles can guide the therapist's application of techniques and procedures. Fundamental to these common principles is a reminder that all such interventions must be done within the context of a positive working alliance and relationship if they are to be effective (Principle 1). Beyond this, the technique principles are especially important as reminders to the clinician that treatment outcome is enhanced if the interventions focus on the client's most emergent problems (Principle 2), provides an explanation for these problems and a rationale about how to address them (Principle 8), seeks to set and address clearly defined goals (Principle 10), and encourage small and incremental change toward these goals (Principle 9). Treatment is also likely to be beneficial if it includes a clear assessment of the patterns in one's life that cause problems (Principles 4 and 5), and if it helps clients to be aware of the relationship between what they do and feel, on one hand, and the environment, on the other (Principle 6).

Table 5.2
Common Principles Related to the Therapeutic Relationship

1. Effective treatment is enhanced when therapists strive to develop and maintain a positive working alliance with their clients.
2. Group therapy effects are enhanced if therapists successfully foster a strong level of cohesiveness within the group.
3. If the therapist has high levels of empathy, treatment outcomes are improved across a wide range of problem conditions and patient types.
4. Effective treatment is facilitated when therapist and patient share common goals of treatment and are collaborative in seeking to achieve these goals.
5. Therapist positive regard is a probable contributor to patient benefit.
6. Therapist congruence in the expression of feelings or the transmission of knowledge is likely to improve patient outcome.
7. Therapists should be careful not to use relational interpretations excessively.
8. When relational interpretations are used, they are likely to facilitate improvement if they are accurate.
9. Therapists are likely to resolve alliance ruptures when addressing such ruptures in an empathic and flexible way.

Table 5.3

Common Principles of Selecting Techniques and Interventions

1. Principles of technique usage are only of value if carried out within the context of a good therapeutic relationship.
2. Advantageous techniques directly focus on presenting problems and concerns. On the other hand, a laissez-faire approach to therapy, in which the therapist fails to confront the patient, fails to direct the patient's efforts, or avoids raising the patient's distress, has limited effects.
3. Effective treatments directly focus on increasing adaptive way of feeling, behaving, and/or responding (physiologically).
4. Effective treatments are based on an initial assessment to identify patterns of behaving, feeling, and thinking linked to the maintenance of problems.
5. To maximize treatment gains, an ongoing assessment is valuable to determine whether therapy is meeting the goals set by the therapist and patient.
6. Improvement is enhanced when successful efforts are made to facilitate clients' knowledge and awareness of the relationship between their interpersonal (and physical) environment and the way in which they think, feel, and behave.
7. Effective treatment identifies and challenges specific dysfunctional thoughts and negative core beliefs.
8. Helpful treatments educate clients about the nature of the problem and rationale for treatment.
9. If the therapist works to facilitate incremental change, improvement rates are increased.
10. For optimal treatment to occur, the client and therapist should set clear and explicit goals and structure therapy to achieve those goals.
11. Therapists should be able to use skillfully "non-directive" interventions.
12. Facilitating client self-exploration can be useful.
13. Therapeutic change is likely if therapist helps clients accept, tolerate, and at time fully experience their emotion.
14. On the other hand, interventions aimed at controlling emotions can also be helpful.
15. Time-limited therapy can be beneficial (except in the treatment of personality disorders).
16. Therapeutic change may be facilitated by, and may even require, intensive therapy.
17. The use of nonindividual interventions (e.g., group and family therapy) can be beneficial.

Furthermore, therapy is likely to be enhanced if the clinician helps the client to modify his/her maladaptive emotional, behavioral, and/or physiological response patterns (Principle 3), and acquire new ways of perceiving and thinking (Principle 7). In addition, a client is likely to benefit from treatment if the therapist is able to skillfully use "nondirective" (e.g., validating) interventions (Principle 11), facilitate the exploration of his/her experience (Principle 12), and deal appropriately with his/her emotions (Principles 13 and 14). The last three principles (15, 16, and 17) provide guidelines related to the structure of effective therapy (i.e., time frame, intensity, modality).

Collectively, the 36 principles outlined in Tables 5.1 through 5.3 are general principles that seem to apply across a number of problems and are extracted as a distillation of similarities across chapters from the three major domains (participants, relationship, treatment). Thus, they can be viewed as foundation principles for facilitating effective change and should be taken as empirically based guides for helping therapists achieve change. Patients with various presenting problems or major symptoms are likely to get better most of the time when clinicians implement these common principles.[1] However, there appear to be a number of other principles of change that effective therapists are likely to take into consideration when working specifically with patient presenting with depression and unhappiness. This list of unique principles that can be applied to the depressed patient is presented in Table 5.4.

UNIQUE PRINCIPLES OF CHANGE

As a result of our Task Force, 12 principles were judged to be distinctive to the treatment of depression. By identifying some principles as "dis-

Table 5.4
Unique Principles for Treating Depression and Dysphoria

Principles related to the participants

1. Age is a negative predictor of a patient's response to general psychotherapy.
2. Patients representing underserved ethnic or racial groups achieve fewer benefits than Anglo-American groups from conventional psychotherapy.
3. If patients and therapists come from the same or similar racial/ethnic backgrounds, dropout rates are positively affected and improvement is enhanced.
4. If patients have a preference for religiously oriented psychotherapy, treatment benefit is enhanced when therapists accommodate these preferences.
5. Adding treatment components increases the benefits for severely impaired patients. Specifically, adding longer treatment course may improve benefit for severely impaired depressed patients. It should also be noted that while empirical evidence has primarily derived from the treatment of depression, this principle may be also relevant to other forms of disorders. As mentioned by McCrady, Haaga, & Lebow (this volume), "About 50% of those with SUDS [Substance Use Disorders] have another co-morbid Axis I disorder and about one-third have a co-morbid Axis II disorder. Research knowledge about the effective integration of different psychological treatments to manage multiple presenting problems is lacking, but assessment of co-morbid disorders and use of effective treatments for additional presenting problems is appropriate" (p. 348).
6. Benefit may be enhanced when the interventions selected are responsive to and consistent with the patient's level of problem assimilation.
7. Interventions that induce patient's resistance (sometimes measured as collaborative engagement, or lack of thereof) are not likely to enhance outcome. Interventions that activate trait-like resistance include such things as therapist overcontrol, overdirectiveness, and confrontation that exceed the patient's level of tolerance. These interventions tend to reduce patient level of compliance and lead to reduced outcome. Their negative effects have been most documented in the area of depression. Researchers in the substance abuse field, however, have recognized their importance by suggesting that therapist should "roll with the resistance" as a way to neutralize client's reactance (see McCrady, Haaga, & Lebow, this volume). Furthermore, one potential manifestation of resistance (i.e. noncompliance to homework) has been found to predict outcome in anxiety disorders. Findings related to this variable, however, have been considered under the principle of collaborative engagement (see Newman, Stiles, Woody, & Janeck, this volume).
8. The therapist's use of directive therapeutic interventions should be planned to inversely correspond with the patient's manifest level of resistant traits and states.
9. Patients whose personalities are characterized by impulsivity, social gregariousness, and external blame for problems benefit more from direct behavioral change and symptom reduction efforts, including building new skills and managing impulses, than they do from procedures that are designed to facilitate insight and self-awareness.
10. Patients whose personalities are characterized by low levels of impulsivity and high levels of indecisiveness, self-inspection, and overcontrol tend to benefit more from procedures that foster self-understanding, insight, interpersonal attachments, and self-esteem, than they do from procedures that aim at directly altering symptoms and building new social skills.
11. A secure attachment pattern in therapist appears to facilitate the treatment process.

Principles related to the therapeutic relationship

1. When working with depressed clients, therapists' use of self-disclosure is likely to be helpful. This may especially be the case for reassuring and supportive self-disclosures, as opposed to challenging self-disclosures.

tinctive" to the treatment of depression, we do not intend to imply that they are irrelevant to the treatment of other clinical problems and populations. Unique principles are of two types: (a) those that have been validated on depressed samples, but have not been found to be valid in mixed or nondepressed psychiatric samples, and (b) those that have been found to be valid for treating depression but have not been investigated in general psychiatric populations.

Of the 12 principles judged to be unique to the treatment of depression, 11 relate to participants' characteristics, and one pertains to the therapeutic relationship. It should be noted that all of the principles related to interventions and techniques that emerged from our Task Force were judged to be common across two or more disorders.

Three of the unique principles related to participants' characteristics refer to prognostic variables. These principles stipulate that irrespective of therapists or techniques used, client's age (Principle 1), ethnicity (Principle 2), and resistance level (Principle 7) can predict the likelihood of change. The majority of the unique principles, however, refer to the benefit of matching patient with a compatible therapist or intervention. Ethnic matching with the therapist, interestingly, seems to enhance outcomes and reduce dropout rates (Principle 3). Similarly, assigning a therapist who can accommodate to his/her client's religious beliefs appears to provide some benefit (Principle 4). In addition, the outcome of more impaired clients is likely to be enhanced when they receive longer treatment (Principle 5).

Other matching principles emphasize that depressed patients tend to respond positively if the techniques selected are sensitive to certain personality qualities and are adjusted accordingly. Therapists are likely to be more effective when their interventions are responsive to the clients' level of assimilation of problematic experience (Principle 6). Directive interventions are suggested for patients who are not overly resistant, while nondirective and facilitating interventions are recommended for resistant patients (Principle 8). Impulsive and acting out patients are suggested as candidates for behavioral and symptom focused interventions, including those that build new skills (Principle 9), while more insight and awareness interventions are suggested for those who tend to be ruminative and self-blaming (Principle 10).

Interestingly, only one unique principle of change refers to a therapist-related characteristic: The process of change appears to be facilitated when clients work with securely attached therapists (Principle 11).

Similarly, and as mentioned above, only one principle that was related to the therapeutic relationship was identified as being unique to the treatment of depression. Specifically, this principle suggests that the use of self-disclosure, especially if supportive in nature, is likely to enhance therapeutic change.

INTEGRATING PRINCIPLES

In total, 48 principles have been identified (36 common and 12 specific) to guide the clinician in treating patients who present with depression. The relative value of these principles remains unknown, and collectively, they must be considered to be tentative but promising at present. Clearly, however, there are clusters of principles that group together to guide the clinician. One group emphasizes the selection of patients who are most likely to respond to psychotherapy and differentiates them from others who will make slower progress. These prognostic principles may be useful when demand is high and resources are limited and they may be useful for determining what patients might benefit from more intensive interventions or those that rely on pharmacological effects.

A second cluster of principles emphasizes the salience of a working relationship and may guide the therapist in how to develop such a beneficial relationship. Relationship factors, because they form the foundation on which to build effective treatments, may signal adherence to these principles as a high priority in developing treatments. Developing a positive, working relationship should probably be considered the first task of the clinician. Some principles emphasize the role of therapist factors, such as flexibility, empathy, and focus, in developing an effective relationship. Others focus on the fit between the patient's and therapist's background and culture. All of these qualities are clearly part of the evolving therapeutic alliance and help develop and form its nature.

A third cluster of variables are those that are used to tailor the interventions and techniques to the needs of the patient. The discriminative use of directive interventions, procedures that are adjusted to the level of impairment and assimilation, and those that selectively focus on behavioral change versus insight and awareness, are used for the purposes of tailoring the therapy and making it more compatible to a given patient. A focus on these compatibility and matching factors may form a third level of priority in developing a treatment plan for the depressed patient.

Finally, a number of principles emphasize the value of developing a treatment plan, providing help in evaluating progress and change, and reinforcing changes as they occur. These principles also emphasize the importance of acknowledging negative emotions and of developing positive, adaptive responses to replace maladaptive coping patterns. By focusing on these four levels of intervention, treatment of the depressed patient is likely to be enhanced, regardless of the treatment model used.

ACKNOWLEDGMENTS   Preparation of this chapter was supported in part by National Institute of Mental Health Research Grant MH-58593.

Note

1. One should keep in mind, however, that common factors are defined here as variables that are likely to play a role in two or more of the problem areas covered in this book (dysphoric, anxiety, personality, and substance use disorders). This by no mean implies that they are influential in the treatment of all of them, or any other clinical problems.

Part III

ANXIETY DISORDERS

6

Participant Factors in Treating Anxiety Disorders

Michelle G. Newman
Paul Crits-Christoph
Mary Beth Connolly Gibbons
Thane M. Erickson

Despite the relatively robust finding of moderate to large effect sizes for psychosocial treatment of anxiety disorders such as generalized anxiety disorder (GAD; Chambless & Gillis, 1993; Gould, Otto, & Pollack, 1995), social phobia (Gould, Buckminster, Pollack, Otto, & Yap, 1997), and post-traumatic stress disorder (PTSD; Otto, Penava, Pollack, & Smoller, 1996), a sizeable portion of samples receiving treatment fail to demonstrate substantial therapeutic change. For example, gold standard treatments for GAD seem to engender clinically significant change in little more than 50% of those treated (Newman, 2000). Similarly, a substantial minority of persons diagnosed with PTSD fail to recover, regardless of having received treatment or not (e.g., Kessler, Sonnega, Bromet, Hughes, & Nelson, 1995; Zlotnick, Warshaw, Shea, Allsworth, Pearlstein, & Keller, 1999), and chronic PTSD remains challenging to successfully treat (Johnson, Rosenheck, Fontana, Lubin, Southwick, & Charney, 1996; Peterson, Prout, & Schwarz, 1991). Furthermore, although the relative efficacy of treatment for social phobia has been demonstrated, approximately 42% of those treated fail to achieve adequate progress (Heimberg, Liebowitz, Hope, Schneier, Holt, Welkowitz, Juster, Campeas, Bruch, Cloitre, Fallon, & Klein, 1998). Several researchers have documented accounts of treatment resistant obsessive-compulsive disorder (OCD; Jenike, 1990) and specific phobia (Abramowitz & Wieselberg, 1978), as well as relapse in panic disorder (Hofmann & Barlow, 1996). Such observations of limited response to treatment for anxiety disorders lend impetus to the search for predictors and moderators of treatment outcome, particularly because understanding these variables may facilitate tailoring treatments to clients and may thereby increase efficacy. Whereas one valuable body of research attempts to augment treatment efficacy by exploring relational variables (reviewed elsewhere in this volume), the current chapter reviews variables specific to the client and therapist.

Participant factors, defined here as "characteristics of the client or therapist that exist solely within the person of the client or therapist and represent qualities that are manifest in life beyond therapy" (see Beutler & Castonguay, this volume), may predict or moderate therapy outcome. This chapter reviews research findings relevant to participant factors identified by the Division 29 Task Force Report, dwelling exclusively upon results found for anxiety disorders. Additionally, where sufficient empirical research exists, conclusions will be compared with Division 29 Task Force "principles" (conditions under which a treatment will be effective) that have been established when collapsing across disorders. We examine the following participant factors: (a) functional impairment (i.e., severity/distress, duration of symptoms, social support, interpersonal problems, and Axis I co-morbidity), (b) personality pathology and disorders, (c) expectations, (d) attachment, (e) coping style (attributions of control, negative appraisals, personality), (f) stages of change, (g) anaclitic and introjective dimensions, (h) assimilation of problematic experiences, (i) religion/spirituality, (j) resistance, and (k) demographics (age, gender, ethnicity, level of intelligence, socioeconomic status). In addition we will examine therapist experience, ethnic match between client and therapist, and gender match. It should be noted that epidemiological studies are included in this chapter only when all clients were referred for treatment and premature termination is considered an indicator of poor outcome.

CLIENT FACTORS

Functional Impairment

The term "functional impairment" denotes an index of the global severity of clients' presenting psychopathology, as well as the extent of its pervasiveness in various life spheres. Defined in multiple ways, it includes a cluster of variables such as inadequate social support, relational difficulties, distress, co-morbidity, symptom severity and chronicity, and physical health complications (Beutler, Harwood, Alimohamed, & Malik, 2002a). Self-report and assessor ratings of impairment have typically been designated "distress" and "severity," respectively (Beutler et al., 2002a). Ideally, externally observable behavior variables are utilized to

assess functional impairment because self-report indices correlate only modestly with observable behavior and thus appear somewhat suspect (Fisher, Beutler, & Williams, 1999). However, some research suggests that self-report measures may meaningfully relate to more objective measures, especially in anxiety (Eysenck, 1997), and sometimes prove adequate for assessment of treatment efficacy; for example, perceived support predicts outcome more accurately than number of relationships as an objective measure of social support (Coyne & Downey, 1991). The studies reported here include both those with objective indices (assessor ratings) of severity or symptoms and those with clients' self-ratings of distress; the latter were included because they often demonstrated significant relations with outcome, and thus were thought to provide ancillary information.

Baseline Symptom Severity/Distress

Serving as one index of impairment, baseline symptom severity/distress measures were examined as predictors of treatment outcome for anxiety disorders in several studies; clusters of symptoms diagnostically or conceptually relevant to each disorder were reported. It is important to note that it is often difficult to sort out the effects of severity on outcome as studies often use the same measure as a predictor and the outcome. In addition, floor effects and response biases in self-report measures may influence findings. Another important issue is that studies often use different analyses to determine outcome; some analyses examine the extent to which the level of the pretreatment score is correlated with the posttreatment score. In this case, a significant negative correlation may only tell the reader that people who started out with higher pretreatment scores may have demonstrated the same amount of change in response to therapy but simply ended up with higher posttreatment scores than people who began with lower pretreatment scores. On the other hand, some studies examined the extent to which severity was correlated with amount of change in response to therapy. In this case, the analysis provides more specific information. Because these studies provide different levels of information, we are careful to try to discriminate them in our description. Thus, it was only when a study actually analyzed change that we describe the result in these terms (i.e., change, response to therapy, etc.). Unless otherwise noted, predictor variables were assessed pretreatment or at baseline.

In response to anxiety management training or behavior therapy for GAD, clients with higher self-reported anxiety (Butler & Anastasiades, 1988) and higher assessor-rated anxiety (Butler, 1993) at pretreatment also tended to have higher anxiety symptoms at posttreatment compared to people with lower anxiety at pretreatment. These results, though few, remain consistent with the longitudinal data suggesting that greater clinician's ratings of global severity and number of symptoms predicts worse response to medications and/or psychotherapy (Yonkers, Dyck, Warshaw, & Keller, 2000). On the other hand, one study found that higher assessor severity predicted better outcome (Butler & Anastasiades, 1988). Other GAD studies found no significant relationship between assessor rated severity (Barlow, Rapee, & Brown, 1992; Butler, 1993), Hamilton anxiety (Barlow et al., 1992; Biswas & Chattopadhyay, 2001; Durham, Allan, & Hackett, 1997), self-reported anxiety (Barlow et al., 1992; Durham et al., 1997; van den Brink, Ormel, Tiemens, Smit, Jenner, van der Meer, & van Os, 2002) or interference from symptoms (Barlow et al., 1992) and post-therapy severity or degree of change from cognitive behavioral therapy (CBT), CT, self-help, medications, or biofeedback. Severity of self-reported anxiety also failed to predict number of CT sessions attended (Sanderson, Beck, & McGinn, 1994) in a therapy with no predetermined number of sessions. Therefore, severity (1/7 studies) and distress (1/6 studies) appear to be weak predictors of negative therapy outcome for GAD; higher severity predicted better outcome in one study.

Studies of social phobia have found that a decreased response to individual and group CBT was predicted by higher assessor-rated severity of impairment due to social phobia (Scholing & Emmelkamp, 1999). In addition, posttreatment assessor severity was predicted by clinicians' initial severity ratings of anxiety (Safren, Heimberg, & Juster, 1997), and self-reported anxiety (Safran,

Alden, & Davidson, 1980; Van Dam-Baggen & Kraaimaat, 1986). Moreover, being currently hospitalized (versus being an outpatient) increased the probability of dropping out and predicted response to social skills training therapy on measures of social anxiety and internal locus of control (Van Dam-Baggen & Kraaimaat, 1986). Analogously, higher pretreatment assessor-rated severity predicted higher posttreatment distress on multiple self-report measures across cognitive behavioral group therapy (CBGT) and clonazepam conditions (Otto, Pollack, Gould, Worthington, McArdle, Rosenbaum, & Heimberg, 2000). Severity has also been found to predict who agreed to take part in treatment (Turner, Beidel, Wolff, & Spaulding, 1996). In addition, one study found that worse confederate ratings of a social interaction as well as of participants' anxiety predicted greater need for additional treatment (Mersch, Emmelkamp, & Lips, 1991). Ironically, this study also found that lower distress was related to greater likelihood of relapse. Still other studies found no relationship between assessor-rated social impairment or severity and change in response to group CBT (Chambless, Tran, & Glass, 1997), individual anxiety management therapy (Butler, Cullington, Munby, Amies, & Gelder, 1984) or pharmacological treatment (Stein, Stein, Pitts, Kumar, & Hunter, 2002). One study also failed to show that pretreatment distress level predicted posttreatment symptom levels (Reich, Goldenberg, Goisman, Vasile, & Keller, 1994).

Examination of social phobia subtypes may be another way to measure social phobia severity as studies have repeatedly found that participants with generalized social phobia (GSP) score higher on a wide variety of social anxiety measures than do nongeneralized socially phobic persons (e.g., Brown, Heimberg, & Juster, 1995; Hofmann, Newman, Becker, Taylor, & Roth, 1995; Turner, Beidel, & Townsley, 1992). Treatment studies have found that although both subtypes respond to the same treatment with the same amount of change, individuals with GSP remain more impaired after treatment (Brown et al., 1995; Hofmann et al., 1995; Hope, Herbert, & White, 1995; Turner et al., 1996). Thus, whereas a slight majority of findings suggest a positive relation between pretreatment distress (3 out of 5 studies or 60%) and outcome for social phobia, most of the studies examining pretreatment severity (8/10 or 80%) found that it predicted negative outcomes for social phobia. Only one study found greater distress to predict better outcomes.

Baseline severity and distress were reported as predictors of PTSD outcome in a variety of studies. For example, decreased benefit from inpatient treatment was predicted by higher baseline self-reported and assessor-rated PTSD symptoms (Johnson & Lubin, 1997), higher assessor-rated (but not self-reported) PTSD symptoms (Johnson, Lubin, & Corn, 1999), and higher self-rated PTSD symptoms (Ford, Fisher, & Larson, 1997; Hyer, Boudewyns, Harrison, O'Leary, Bruno, Saucer, & Blount, 1988). In addition, negative outcome from partial hospitalization was predicted by higher self-rated (but not assessor-rated) PTSD symptoms at pretreatment (Perconte & Griger, 1991). Moreover, partial remission (versus full remission) from CBT was predicted by assessor-rated impairment (Taylor, Fedoroff, Koch, Thordarson, Fecteau, & Nicki, 2001) and dropping out of CBT was predicted by higher assessor-rated (Marks, Lovell, Noshirvani, Livanou, & Thrasher, 1998) and self-reported (Taylor, Fedoroff, & Koch, 1999) symptoms. Also, inability to benefit from eclectic outpatient treatment was predicted by higher assessor rated PTSD severity (with depression symptoms removed from the diagnosis) (Hyer, Stanger, & Boudewyns, 1999). Interestingly, whereas diminished benefit from exposure treatment was predicted by higher self-reported PTSD symptoms in one study (van Minnen, Arntz, & Keijsers, 2002), it was predicted by lower self-reported PTSD symptoms in another study (Foa, Riggs, Massie, & Yarczower, 1995). Also, in a sample of war trauma veterans on an inpatient PTSD unit, meeting full criteria for PTSD predicted better outcome than meeting subclinical criteria (Ford & Kidd, 1998).

Additional studies have found that individual PTSD symptoms predicted outcome. For example, higher baseline self-reported PSTD reexperiencing symptoms was a significant predictor of both alcohol/drug relapse and PSTD status (remitted/unremitted) in a sample of inpatients with co-morbid substance use (Brown, 2000). In addition, severity of pretreatment numbing symptoms predicted partial response rather than full response

to CBT for road traffic collision PTSD (Taylor et al., 2001).

Contrary to the aforementioned results, baseline severity failed to significantly predict PTSD outcome in clinical trials using imaginal exposure or cognitive therapy (Tarrier, Sommerfield, & Pilgrim, 1999; Tarrier, Sommerfield, Pilgrim, & Faragher, 2000). Similarly, higher assessor-rated symptoms and global pathology did not predict outcome for Vietnam veterans in a partial hospitalization program (Perconte & Griger, 1991) or in response to exposure for rape trauma victims (Jaycox, Foa, & Morral, 1998). Also, higher self-reported PTSD symptoms failed to predict response to CBT (Taylor et al., 1999) and severity failed to predict response to, or dropping out of inpatient treatment for war veterans (Munley, Bains, Frazee, & Schwartz, 1994). Nonetheless, in 42% (5/12) of PTSD studies higher pretreatment severity predicted worse outcome and in 73% (8/11) of the studies worse outcome was predicted by higher pretreatment distress. Distress and severity each inversely predicted outcome in one study.

The findings regarding the relation of diagnostic severity to psychotherapy for panic disorder have been mixed. On the one hand, for cognitive behavioral interventions, greater assessor-rated severity predicted negative two-year outcomes (Brown & Barlow, 1995) and discriminated dropouts from completers (Barlow, Craske, Cerny, & Klosko, 1989). Additional studies found that greater panic attack and/or agoraphobia severity predicted less change at one-year follow-up (Shinoda et al., 1999) or lowered response to exposure versus relaxation combined with medications (Basoglu, Marks, Swinson, et al., 1994). However, a study of combined drug treatment plus supportive psychotherapy found that higher assessor-rated anxiety predicted better social adjustment at 5-year outcome (Scheibe & Albus, 1996). Also, a study comparing cognitive therapy, medications, and placebo found that whereas global assessment of illness did not discriminate responders from nonresponders, panic attack severity did (Black, Wesner, Gabel, Bowers, & Monahan, 1994). On the other hand, severity failed to predict long-term remission from mixed medications and self-help exposure (Fava et al., 2001). In addition, assessor severity did not predict premature termination from couples group therapy (Carter, Turovsky, Sbrocco, Meadows, & Barlow, 1995) or from mixed medication and CBT (Grilo et al., 1998). Additional studies also failed to find a relationship between assessor-rated severity (Basoglu, Marks, Kilic, Brewin, & Swinson, 1994) or assessor-rated impairment (Scheibe & Albus, 1996) and outcome.

Studies of distress as a predictor of outcome in panic disorder have shown that it is a moderately strong predictor. Higher levels of self-reported agoraphobic complaints predicted worse outcome from breathing retraining and exposure (de Beurs, Lange, van Dyck, & Koele, 1995), exposure (Keijsers, Hoogduin, & Schaap, 1994b), medications or supportive therapy (Scheibe & Albus, 1996), medications or CBT (Sharp & Power, 1999), and couples exposure treatment (Hafner & Ross, 1983). In addition, higher self-reported anxiety predicted lower functioning at 4-year follow-up from exposure treatment (Emmelkamp & Kuipers, 1979). In another study, whereas less questionnaire-based anxiety predicted more behavioral and physiological change, more self-rated anxiety during a behavioral avoidance test predicted more change on the behavioral and subjective measures at follow-up from behavior therapy (Jansson, Öst, & Jerremalm, 1987). Additional studies reported that higher self-reported panic attack frequency predicted poor outcome from medication and CBT (Sharp & Power, 1999) and that higher levels of self-reported agoraphobic cognitions predicted poor outcome from behavior therapy (Keijsers et al., 1994b). However, levels of self-reported anxiety and fear were not predictive of outcome from community programs (Bowen, South, Fischer, & Looman, 1994), group CBT (Martinsen, Olsen, Tonset, Nyland, & Aarre, 1998), or five-year outcome from imipramine plus exposure homework (Lelliott, Marks, Monteiro, Tsakiris, & Noshirvani, 1987). In addition, self-reported distress did not predict premature termination from couples group therapy (Carter et al., 1995), mixed medication and CBT (Grilo et al., 1998), or CBT alone (Barlow et al., 1989; Keijsers, Kampman, & Hoogduin, 2001). Also, an investigation of medication and CBT found that across conditions, self-rated intensity of panic attacks was not related to post-

treatment outcome or 6-month follow-up (Sharp & Power, 1999). Thus, 42% (5/12) of panic studies show that greater severity predicts worse outcome, although one study shows that greater severity predicts better outcome. Fifty percent (9/18) of findings show that greater distress predicts worse outcome and one study shows the inverse pattern in predicting outcome.

Several studies have examined whether severity of pretreatment OCD symptoms predicts the outcome of psychosocial treatment for OCD. The psychosocial treatment examined in almost all of these studies was behavior therapy (exposure + response prevention). Although lower severity predicted better outcome in four studies (Abramowitz, Franklin, Zoellner, & DiBernardo, 2002; Basoglu, Lax, Kasvikis, & Marks, 1988; de Haan et al., 1997; Steketee, Eisen, Dyck, Warshaw, & Rasmussen, 1999), and lower distress predicted better outcome in response to therapist or computer-administered ERP (Keijsers, Hoogduin, & Schaap, 1994a; Mataix-Cols, Marks, Greist, Kobak, & Baer, 2002) other studies found that neither OCD severity (De Araujo, Ito, & Marks, 1996; Foa et al., 1983; Steketee, 1993) nor OCD distress (Hoogduin & Duivenvoorden, 1988; O'Sullivan, Noshirvani, Marks, Monteiro, & Lelliott, 1991) predicted outcome. However, one of these studies found that higher assessor-rated severity of anxious mood was predictive of less change in response to treatment (Foa et al., 1983).

Studies have also found that severity of certain OCD symptoms may be predictive. For example studies have found that greater assessor-rated (Basoglu et al., 1988; Foa, 1979; Foa, Abramowitz, Franklin, & Kozak, 1999) or self-reported (Neziroglu, Stevens, McKay, Yaryura, & Jose, 2001; Neziroglu, Stevens, Yaryura, & Jose, 1999) overvalued ideation (the belief that one's fears are realistic) or bizarre and fixed obsessions (Basoglu et al., 1988) predicted worse outcome. On the other hand, Foa and associates (1999) found that participants were more likely to benefit from cognitive behavior therapy if they had greater assessor-rated fear of disastrous consequences.

Additional studies have examined the relation of certain features of the OCD diagnostic syndrome to outcome. OCD symptoms fall primarily into two major categories: washing and checking.

The relation of these aspects of OCD to outcome has been mixed across several studies. No relationship was found in some studies (Foa et al., 1983; Rachman, Marks, & Hodgson, 1973), while one study found that checking was associated with better outcome (Drummond, 1993) and three studies found that washing was associated with better outcome (Basoglu et al., 1988; Boulougouris, 1977; Buchanan, Meng, & Marks, 1996). These findings, though informative, were not included in total counts for severity or distress.

Thus, in OCD greater severity predicted worse outcome in 67% (8/12) of the studies, but predicted better outcome in one study. Similarly, greater distress predicted worse outcome in 71% (5/7) of OCD studies.

Lastly, in mixed anxious-depressive samples, higher baseline self-report state anxiety predicted session attendance in both psychodynamic treatment and CBT (Korobkin, Herron, & Ramirez, 1998), and assessor ratings of global severity have predicted outcome (Hirsch, Jolley, & Williams, 2000).

In conclusion, outcome (level of symptoms) was predicted positively by clients' self-reported symptoms or distress in 26 of 48 studies (54%) and by assessor severity or symptom ratings in 28 of 54 studies (52%). In contrast, higher pretreatment distress predicted better outcomes in 4 of 48 studies (8%) and higher severity predicted better outcomes in 4 of 54 studies (7%). Collapsed across these categories, 54 of 102 findings (53%) provide moderate support for the general principle that relatively lower initial distress and severity indicate better prognosis.

Duration of Morbidity

Duration of morbidity, or chronicity, may also serve as an index of functional impairment. In a trial of biofeedback versus cognitive therapy (CT) for GAD, longer duration of illness predicted a worse therapeutic outcome (Biswas & Chattopadhyay, 2001). Similarly, longer duration of generalized anxiety and history of previous anxious episodes predicted poor course of the disorder in a one-year follow-up of medications and/or psychotherapy (van den Brink et al., 2002). Studies have also found that having received previous psychi-

atric treatment predicted poorer outcome from CT, anxiety management, or analytic therapy (Durham et al., 1997) and from CBT, medications, or anxiety management (Tyrer, Seivewright, Ferguson, Murphy, & Johnson, 1993). The two latter findings are consonant with observations that, for other disorders, past psychiatric treatment is associated with increased functional impairment (Cuijpers & Van Lammeren, 1999; Joyce, Ogrodniczuk, Piper, & McCallum, 2000; Roberts, Kaplan, Shema, & Strawbridge, 1997). In other studies, duration did not predict outcome of biofeedback (Biswas & Chattopadhyay, 2001), or CBT, self-help, or medications (Seivewright, Tyrer, & Johnson, 1998), although in the latter study recurrent bouts of GAD predicted outcome. Age of onset (a variable related to chronicity) and length of illness also did not predict five-year outcome of medication and/or psychotherapy (Yonkers et al., 2000). Nonetheless, the majority of studies preliminarily suggest that duration-related variables have an impact on GAD outcome.

On the other hand, age of onset or duration of illness did not predict recovery as a result of treatment of social phobia (Reich et al., 1994) or response to anxiety management with or without exposure (Butler et al., 1984). Duration also did not predict dropout from CBGT (Heimberg, Dodge, Hope, Kennedy, & Zollo, 1990). Thus, evidence of an effect of duration on social phobia is nonexistent.

Examination of the impact of PTSD duration or chronicity has shown that certain indirect indicators of chronicity predict outcome. For example, presence of assessor-classified "Disorders of Extreme Stress Not Otherwise Specified" (DES-NOS) diagnosis, a constellation of chronic difficulties linked to PTSD and interpersonal trauma in early childhood (Ford & Kidd, 1998) predicted outcome from inpatient hospitalization. In addition, chronicity of psychiatric service utilization predicted outcome from 3-month inpatient treatment (Ford et al., 1997). Likewise, in CBT for PTSD from motor vehicle accidents, number of pain-related bedrest days as well as greater pain severity and interference discriminated partial responders from responders (Taylor et al., 2001). On the other hand, duration of PTSD did not predict outcome from CBT (Marks et al., 1998; Tarrier et al., 2000; Taylor et al., 1999) or imaginal exposure and CT (Tarrier et al., 1999). Similarly, age of onset did not predict outpatient therapy outcome (Kosten, Krystal, Giller, Frank, & Dan, 1992). Further, previous hospitalizations were unrelated to outcome from partial hospitalization (Perconte & Griger, 1991) and psychiatric history was unrelated to outcome from imaginal exposure or CT (Tarrier et al., 1999; Tarrier et al., 2000). Studies have also found no link between outcome and history of prior trauma (Ehlers, Clark, Dunmore, Jaycox, Meadows, & Foa, 1998; Foa, Rothbaum, Riggs, & Murdock, 1991; Ford et al., 1997; Ford & Kidd, 1998; Jaycox et al., 1998; Tarrier et al., 2000). Therefore, although indirect indicators of chronicity such as psychiatric service utilization, pain, and DESNOS may predict PTSD outcome, more direct indicators such as prior trauma, previous hospitalizations, and duration of PTSD may not.

Duration of illness was reported as an outcome predictor in several studies of panic disorder. One investigation of behavioral interventions (de Beurs et al., 1995) and one study of combined medication and supportive therapy (Scheibe & Albus, 1996) found that longer duration of illness significantly predicted the outcome of treatment. Age of onset of panic disorder was examined in one study that found that older onset was associated with better one-year treatment outcomes from a combined drug plus supportive psychotherapy intervention for panic disorder (Shinoda et al., 1999). One study reported that if the individual had met criteria for the disorder in the past it predicted poor treatment outcome at five years (Seivewright et al., 1998). However, four investigations failed to find a relation between duration and treatment outcome (Brown & Barlow, 1995; Clark et al., 1999; Sharp & Power, 1999; Shinoda et al., 1999).

Mixed findings surfaced for duration of illness in OCD. Hoogduin and Duivenvoorden (1988) and Emmelkamp, Hoekstra, and Visser (1985) found no significant relationship between age of onset and outcome of behavior therapy for OCD. However, Foa et al. (1983) found that age of onset predicted outcome such that, somewhat surprisingly, those with an earlier onset of symptoms maintained their treatment gains the best. In con-

trast, Keijsers, Hoogduin, & Schaap (1994a) found longer duration of symptoms to be a poor prognostic sign for behavior therapy for OCD.

Results were reported for other anxiety disorder samples, as well. Age of onset predicted outcome of exposure for a mixed anxiety sample; clients with older age of onset fared worse than those with earlier onset (Cameron, Thyer, Feckner, Nesse, & Curtis, 1986). Also, longer self-reported duration of problem predicted worse outcome for a mixed anxious-depressive sample (Hirsch et al., 2000).

In total, 11 of 22 (50%) findings related to longer duration of illness, 3 of 6 (50%) findings regarding history of receiving psychiatric services, 1 of 9 (11%) findings related to younger age of onset, 2 of 9 (22%) related to older onset age, and 0 of 6 findings concerning prior trauma predicted relatively worse outcome. Thus, if duration is measured based on length of current episode or history of receiving psychiatric services, duration may be considered a negative prognostic indicator for treatment response; however, age of onset and prior trauma may not be negative prognostic indicators.

Social Support

Social support has also been utilized as an indicator of level of functional impairment. Because few treatment studies assessed perceived social support as such, the current review defined this variable loosely, opting to include perceived support as well as the related variable of marital status.

Durham et al. (1997) found that being married was among the strongest predictors of sustained improvement in several treatments for GAD. Furthermore, in an analysis including only married and cohabitating clients, higher reported degree of marital tension significantly diminished the likelihood of sustained therapeutic change. Also, the probability of relapse increased significantly with singlehood and being widowed or divorced. This finding is consistent with longitudinal data for GAD course suggesting that poor spousal relationships are associated with decreased likelihood of remission (Yonkers et al., 2000). On the other hand, marital status did not predict 5-year outcome from CBT, self-help, or medications (Seivewright et al., 1998) and both marital status and social support did not predict 1-year outcome of therapy and/or medication (van den Brink et al., 2002). Therefore, data on the predictability of social support for GAD is mixed.

In contrast, the one social phobia study investigating marital status failed to find differential attrition rates among married and non-married clients in a cognitive behavioral group treatment (Feske, Perry, Chambless, Renneberg, & Goldstein, 1996). Likewise, marital status did not predict outcome for behavior therapy for OCD (Foa et al., 1983; Hoogduin & Duivenvoorden, 1988) or panic disorder (Keijsers et al., 1994b). However, in a study of behavior therapy for panic disorder and OCD, Chambless and Steketee (1999) examined the moderating effects of expressed emotion (EE; criticism, hostility, emotional overinvolvement), which was viewed by the authors of this chapter as being similar to poor quality of social support. Results showed that EE was predictive of negative outcome.

Social support variables are hypothesized to affect treatment outcome for clients with PTSD not only because such variables do so in other disorders, but also because relationship distress has been shown to correlate with symptom severity in such persons (Riggs, Byrne, Weathers, & Litz, 1998). Tarrier, Sommerfield, and Pilgrim (1999) examined the moderating effects of EE in a study comparing CT versus imaginal exposure for PTSD. Clients with a key relative identified via structured interview as high in EE reported significantly more anxiety, depression, and intrusions at posttreatment than those with a key relative low in EE. In fact, EE hostility predicted 19.5% of variance in outcome. Additionally, although also not explicitly a social support variable, residential status, which may be conceived as a proxy variable, significantly predicted outcome at six-month follow-up in an analysis of the parent sample for the previous analysis; living alone predicted worse outcome than living with other people (Tarrier et al., 2000). However, marital status failed to significantly predict outcome in an aforementioned sample (Tarrier et al., 1999) or others undergoing exposure treatment (Ehlers et al., 1998; Foa et al., 1991).

In summary, 5 of 13 studies (38%) testing social support variables as predictors found inverse re-

lationships with outcome symptom levels; no relation was observed in 8 of these studies; however, 3 of 4 studies (75%) found higher scores on social support variables predictive of better outcome when social support was defined based on perceived quality of relationships. Other studies and reviews have reported greater predictive power of social support for treatment outcome (Beutler et al., 2002a; Gonzales, Lewinsohn, & Clarke, 1985; Zlotnick, Shea, Pilkonis, Elkin, & Ryan, 1996); the current review found that less than one half of the studies supported such a relation. This finding may be attributable to the inclusion of imprecise proxy variables for social support (e.g., marital status, when level of conflict is not taken into account).

Interpersonal Problems

Clients' interpersonal behavior itself may also indicate degree of impairment and mitigate treatment effects. In a study comparing behavior therapy (BT; applied relaxation and self-control desensitization), CT, and combined treatments for GAD, self-reported interpersonal problems remaining at posttest correlated negatively with assessor and self-ratings of symptoms at follow-up (Borkovec, Newman, Pincus, & Lytle, 2002). However, client's level of social impairment did not predict degree of improvement in a trial of CBGT for social phobia (Chambless et al., 1997).

Evidence regarding the role of interpersonal problems and social adjustment in panic disorder treatment is mixed. Reports of social maladjustment (Sharp & Power, 1999) have been reported to predict poor treatment response. However, the level of interpersonal problems did not significantly predict treatment outcome elsewhere (Hoffart, 1997).

Findings were also mixed with regard to OCD. Patients with difficulties in interpersonal interactions had relatively poor outcomes in one study (Fals-Stewart & Lucente, 1993), whereas baseline level of psychosocial functioning was not found to be associated with the outcome of BT for OCD (Steketee, 1993).

Similarly, baseline clinical assessment of interpersonal relations in a mixed sample of depressed, anxious, and socially introverted males predicted outcome modestly, as well as participation in the therapeutic relationship (Moras & Strupp, 1982).

Although no studies examined interpersonal problems as predictors of outcome for PTSD treatment, self-report of suspicion and interpersonal sensitivity predicted relatively poor prognosis (Hyer et al., 1988).

Overall, lower interpersonal difficulties were prognostic of better therapeutic outcome in 5 of 8 studies (63%) and failed to predict outcome in 3 studies. Therefore, the presence of interpersonal problems may be considered an aspect of impairment that is prognostic of outcome, although this conclusion may be considered somewhat tentative given the relatively small number of studies included.

Axis I Co-morbidity

A number of studies have investigated the impact of presence versus absence of Axis I co-morbidity on the treatment of anxiety disorders, an important endeavor, considering the high co-morbidity of other disorders with anxiety diagnoses.

Investigation of co-morbidity with GAD seems particularly appropriate given estimates that 90% of those with lifetime GAD have another lifetime psychiatric diagnosis (National Comorbidity Survey: Wittchen, Zhao, Kessler, & Eaton, 1994), most often other anxiety disorders (Goisman, Goldenberg, Vasile, & Keller, 1995). In fact, such high co-morbidity rates may reflect shared mechanisms underlying the constellations of symptoms (Noyes, 2001; Stein, 2001), further supporting the importance of determining the extent to which the breadth of such symptom constellations predict GAD psychotherapy outcome.

For example, the absence of Axis I co-morbidity significantly predicted sustained improvement of clients treated for GAD with cognitive therapy, analytic psychotherapy, or anxiety management training (Durham et al., 1997). Similarly, clients with mixed GAD and dysthymia or GAD, panic disorder, and dysthymia scored higher on a measure of neuroticism (of unreported psychometric properties) at a 12-year follow-up than those with GAD alone, after having received either pill placebo, dothiepin (antidepressant), diazepam, CBT, or self-help (Tyrer, Seivewright, Simmonds, & Johnson, 2001). Regarding continuous measures of depression as predictors of GAD outcome (as opposed to diagnosis), one GAD

treatment study yielded the finding that clients classified as treatment responders reported significantly lower baseline self-report scores of depression symptoms than nonresponders (Barlow et al., 1992). Interestingly, lower baseline self-reported depression, yet higher assessor-rated depressive severity predicted positive outcome in anxiety management for GAD (Butler & Anastasiades, 1988); higher baseline self-rated depressive symptoms predicted positive outcome for CBT or BT (trend) (Butler, 1993). These last results suggest that secondary depressive symptoms may sometimes not interfere with anxiety treatment, although it remains unclear why higher depressive symptoms would predict more favorable outcomes.

Several findings were reported concerning Axis I co-morbidity and social phobia. Clients with co-morbid diagnosis of GAD in primary social phobics reported not only greater self-reported social avoidance, depressed mood, and assessor-rated impairment at baseline (even when other anxiety, mood, and somatoform disorders were statistically controlled), but showed significantly greater levels of impairment in relationships and work productivity at posttest than those without GAD (Mennin, Heimberg, & Jack, 2000). However, the groups responded similarly to treatment and evidenced no differences in attrition rates, suggesting that, although social phobia with co-morbid GAD may be treated as effectively as pure social phobia, co-morbid GAD is associated with heightened severity both before and after treatment. Relatedly, baseline self-report of depressive symptoms predicted symptom levels at outcome in individual and group CBT (Scholing & Emmelkamp, 1999). However, co-morbid depression and anxiety disorders did not predict outcome for group CBT or clonazepam for social phobia (Otto et al., 2000).

With regard to the impact of co-morbidity upon PTSD treatment, few studies were identified; results were mixed. In a trial of cognitive therapy versus imaginal exposure for chronic PTSD, co-morbid diagnosis of GAD was one of nine variables that predicted poor outcome at a six-month follow-up (Tarrier et al., 2000). Likewise, self-rated baseline depressive severity predicted outcome in an inpatient program (Hyer et al., 1988), and partial responders to CBT showed higher self-report depression than responders (Taylor et al., 2001). In contrast, the number of co-morbid disorders at baseline assessment was not a significant outcome predictor in a comparison of CBT (education, applied relaxation, cognitive restructuring, imaginal exposure, in vivo assignments) and a wait-list control group for PTSD from auto accidents (Taylor et al., 1999) or in prolonged exposure treatment for PTSD (Jaycox et al., 1998). Pretest self-reported level of depression similarly failed to predict treatment response to imaginal exposure (van Minnen et al., 2002).

Several studies have examined the relation of co-morbid major depressive disorder (MDD) to treatment outcome for OCD. In 2 of 3 (67%) available studies (Foa, Grayson, & Steketee, 1982; Steketee, Chambless, & Tran, 2001), presence of co-morbid depression was predictive of behavior therapy outcome but in 1 of 3 (33%) it was not (Abramowitz & Foa, 2000). Level of depressive symptoms also predicted outcome in 5 of 18 (28%) studies (Abramowitz, Franklin, Street, Kozak, & Foa, 2000; Foa, 1979; Foa et al., 1983; Keijsers et al., 1994a; Steketee et al., 2001) but failed to predict outcome in 13 of 18 (72%) studies (Basoglu et al., 1988; Cottraux, Mollard, Bouvard, & Marks, 1993; Emmelkamp et al., 1985; Foa, Kozak, Steketee, & McCarthy, 1992; Hoogduin & Duivenvoorden, 1988; Marks, Hodgson, & Rachman, 1975; Mawson, Marks, & Ramm, 1982; O'Sullivan et al., 1991; Riggs, Hiss, & Foa, 1992; Steketee, 1993; Steketee et al., 1999; Steketee & Shapiro, 1995).

The presence of a co-morbid Axis I disorder appears to predict poor treatment response in panic disorder. Four studies demonstrated that comorbid major depression predicts poor treatment outcome (Chambless, Renneberg, Gracely, Goldstein, & Fydrich, 2000; McLean, Woody, Taylor, & Koch, 1998; Scheibe & Albus, 1996; Steketee et al., 2001) and one study demonstrated a positive relationship between co-morbid depression and improvement at one-year follow-up, though not at posttest (Hoffart & Martinsen, 1993). Multiple investigations have further demonstrated that the presence of depressive symptoms and anxiety symptoms significantly predicted poor treatment outcome (Keijsers et al., 1994b; McLean et al., 1998; Scheibe & Albus, 1996; Sharp & Power, 1999). Depressive symptoms similarly predicted outcome of community CBT programs for panic and agoraphobia (Bowen et al., 1994). In contrast

to these findings, two investigations of CBT found that pretreatment depressive symptoms were not associated with treatment outcome (Clark et al., 1999; Martinsen et al., 1998) and one study reported that pretreatment symptoms of hypochondriasis were not related to treatment outcome (Shinoda et al., 1999). Relatedly, though properly included on Axis III instead of Axis I, the role of physical health in the outcome of treatment for panic disorder may also be important. Both high levels of medical co-morbidity and perceived poor health have been found to predict poor treatment outcome (Schmidt & Telch, 1997).

Lastly, self-report scores of co-morbid psychoticism have strongly predicted poor outcome in cognitive therapy (CT), analytic psychotherapy, and anxiety management training for GAD (Durham et al., 1997) and dropout rates in an inpatient program for male Vietnam veterans with PTSD (Boudewyns, Albrecht, Talbert, & Hyer, 1991).

Across various treatments for anxiety disorders, co-morbid Axis I diagnoses and self-reported symptom distress predicted relatively poorer outcomes in 27 of 51 findings (53%), whereas 3/51 (6%) found positive relations between co-morbidity and improvement and 21/51 (41%) yielded no relationship. Largely, these findings buttress the principle that Axis I co-morbidity negatively complicates treatment prognosis.

Although the various variables subsumed under the heading of "functional impairment" for the current review are heterogeneous and yielded variable findings, our conclusions generally reaffirm those of Beutler, Harwood, et al. (2002a): "Patients with good interpersonal contacts, acute problems, and single diagnoses generally are the ones most likely to benefit from treatment and achieve the highest treatment gains" (p. 150). However, no studies were available to compare with the conclusion of Beutler et al. that medication most greatly benefits clients with high functional impairment and low social support. Nonetheless, it remains noteworthy that usage of medications for panic symptoms prior to the psychosocial intervention predicted poor treatment outcome (Brown & Barlow, 1995; de Beurs et al., 1995), while one additional investigation found no relation between medication usage and treatment outcome (McLean et al., 1998). For PTSD treatments, partial responders, compared with responders, were more likely to be taking psychotropic medications (Taylor et al., 2001), although usage of psychotropic medication was unrelated to outcome for PTSD elsewhere (Tarrier et al., 2000).

Personality Pathology and Disorders

Persons with anxiety disorders have frequently been reported to meet criteria for co-morbid personality disorders, most often avoidant, dependent, and sometimes borderline types. In general, Axis II pathology is considered to be a complicating factor that may diminish response to treatment of Axis I disorders (Oldham, Skodol, Kellman, Hyler, Doidge, Rosnick, & Gallaher, 1995). Thus, whether personality disorders (PD) or traits affect outcome for anxiety disorders warrants consideration.

Concerning GAD, few anxiety treatment studies have directly examined relations between PD status and psychotherapy outcome. The available studies provide fairly consistent support for adverse effects on treatment. In a trial of CT for GAD, persons both with (chiefly Avoidant and Dependent) and without personality disorders manifested clinically significant improvement that did not differ between groups. However, those with Axis II diagnoses were significantly more likely to drop out of treatment prematurely than those not receiving such diagnoses (Sanderson et al., 1994). Elsewhere, personality disorder traits were associated with diminished efficacy of CT or self-help treatments for persons with GAD, panic disorder, or dysthymia (Tyrer et al., 1993). Such findings are consistent with longitudinal data suggesting that concurrent cluster B or C PDs decrease the likelihood of GAD remission (Yonkers et al., 2000) and that cluster C PDs have predicted lowered remission likelihood for GAD (Massion, Dyck, Shea, Phillips, Warshaw, & Keller, 2002).

Findings were also mostly consistent for the effect of co-morbid PDs or PD traits on outcome in social phobia than for GAD. Presence or absence of avoidant personality disorder (AVPD) status failed to differentially predict outcome for CBGT in one study (Hope et al., 1995). Several studies of treatments for social phobia found that clients with Axis II disorders benefit similarly to those without such pathology, but that they demonstrate greater symptom severity (e.g., anxiety and/or depression) both before and after treatment. In other words, PDs predict worse absolute outcome, but not relative degree of change. For instance, this pattern of results was evident in studies examining the effects of AVPD on cognitive behavioral group treatments (Brown et al., 1995; Feske et al., 1996; Hofmann et al., 1995). If absolute level of outcome symptoms, but not relative degree of change is considered in these results, they correspond to data in which avoidant personality disorder predicted substantially lower likelihood of remission in social phobia (Massion et al., 2002), as well as the notion that AVPD may represent a severe form of social phobia (rather than a qualitatively different entity) and thereby complicate treatment (van Velzen, Emmelkamp, & Scholing, 2000).

Relatedly, personality disorder traits were investigated as potential predictors of treatment for social phobia. In a group CBT study, clients with avoidant traits improved less in anxious apprehension and speech anxiety than those without such traits, but such traits did not predict overall extent of therapeutic change in group CBT (Chambless et al., 1997). Personality disorder traits were associated with decreased efficacy in a group social skills training program (Turner, 1987). Interestingly, diagnosis and type of traits exerted an interactive effect on outcome in group CT or in vivo exposure. Avoidant traits predicted worse outcome for generalized social phobia, but better outcome for specific social phobia (Scholing & Emmelkamp, 1999). Furthermore, for specific social phobia, histrionic traits were associated with worse outcome, whereas dependent traits predicted positive results at an 18-month follow-up. Overall, PD traits seemed to exert differential effects on treatment for social phobia, depending on which traits were utilized as predictors.

Only four investigations directly assessed the relation of pretreatment Axis II pathology and psychotherapeutic outcomes for panic disorder. These studies reported that the presence of Axis II pathology significantly predicted poor treatment outcome for panic disorder (Chambless et al., 2000; Hoffart & Martinsen, 1993; Keijsers et al., 1994b; Seivewright et al., 1998), inconsistent with data suggesting no decrease in likelihood of panic disorder remission for persons with personality disorders (Massion et al., 2002). A co-morbid Axis II diagnosis, especially schizotypal and borderline, has been associated with relatively poorer outcome in multiple OCD treatment studies (Au-Buchon & Malatesta, 1994; Fals-Stewart & Lucente, 1993; Minichiello, Baer, & Jenike, 1987). Relatedly, Fals-Steward and Lucente (1993) investigated the relation of personality characteristics to the outcome of behavior therapy for OCD and found that patients with no personality pathology and those with dependent traits demonstrated the best overall outcomes; also, histrionic and borderline traits predicted failure to maintain gains at follow-up.

For PTSD, two studies reported Axis II pathology as not predictive of outcome (Jaycox et al., 1998; van Minnen et al., 2002).

Overall, the majority of findings indicated relatively poorer prognosis (including outcome or dropout) for clients with Axis II co-morbidity (22 of 30; 73%). In comparison, 5 findings failed to obtain a relation between personality pathology and indices of outcome, and 3 indicated that the presence of Axis II traits predicted relatively better outcome. Such findings lend considerable support to the principle that the presence of personality disorders signifies relatively greater difficulty in achieving response to treatment, which may potentially necessitate extended treatment duration or heightened treatment intensity in an effort to induce clinically meaningful change.

Expectations

Because hope in amelioration of problems has been considered an integral aspect of successful healing (Frank, 1973), expectations of treatment outcome merit consideration as potential predictors or moderators of outcome. Moreover, the reality of placebo effects argues for the importance of expectations in any modality of therapy (Andrews & Harvey, 1981; Bootzin & Lick, 1979; Kazdin & Wilcoxon, 1976; Rosenthal & Frank, 1956; Shapiro & Shapiro, 1982). Indeed, meta-analytic findings suggest that expectancy may account for as much as half of the efficacy of psychotherapy (Kirsch, 1990). Here we review research investigating the relation between treatment expectancy, typically assessed after the first therapy session, and outcome for treatment of anxiety disorders. Additionally, studies were included that assessed

constructs such as clients' motivation for treatment and perceptions of treatment credibility, which may plausibly be considered as intimately interrelated. Expectations of improvement may even be attributable, to some extent, to perceived treatment credibility (Hardy, Barkham, Shapiro, Reynolds, Rees, & Stiles, 1995).

Expectations regarding positive treatment outcome have predicted substantial portions of outcome variance in several treatment studies for GAD. For instance, expectancy predicted beneficial outcome on a variety of self-report and assessor-rated variables in a study comparing applied relaxation, CBT (applied relaxation, cue detection, CT, self-control desensitization), and nondirective therapy (Borkovec & Costello, 1993), as well as in a study comparing nondirective therapy, cognitive therapy, and coping desensitization for GAD and panic (Borkovec & Mathews, 1988). Relatedly, both expectancy and credibility ratings were higher (trend) for clients later classified as responders versus nonresponders to treatment in a study contrasting relaxation, CT, both treatments combined, and a wait-list control (Barlow et al., 1992). Likewise, clients with recurrent, nonphobic anxiety who were randomly assigned to various relaxation conditions or self-monitoring provided self-ratings of likelihood of practice of learned techniques and expected benefit, which predicted outcome (Lewis, Biglan, & Steinbock, 1978). Additionally, treatment credibility predicted outcome at post, as well as 6- and 12-month follow-up in a study comparing applied relaxation/ self-control desensitization, CT, or combined treatments (Borkovec et al., 2002). In contrast, expectancy in Borkovec et al. failed to predict outcome, and minimal predictive capacity of expectancy or credibility early in treatment were found in a comparisons of progressive muscle relaxation with CT or nondirective therapy for undergraduate clients with GAD (Borkovec, Mathews, Chambers, Ebrahimi, Lytle, & Nelson, 1987) and a randomized trial of CBT versus wait-list control (Ladouceur, Dugas, Freeston, Leger, Gagnon, & Thibodeau, 2000). Lastly, credibility predicted outcome on few or no measures in several aforementioned treatment studies (Borkovec & Costello, 1993; Borkovec & Mathews, 1988; Borkovec et al., 2002).

Results for effects of expectancies for treatment

in social phobia parallel the mixed nature of those for GAD. In studies investigating CBGT for social phobia, initial expectancy has emerged as a significant, though modest, predictor of clinicians' severity ratings and self-report measures after treatment (Safren et al., 1997) and correlated positively with reduction in observer-rated dyad anxiety and skill and improvement in anxious apprehension (Chambless et al., 1997).

Expectancy level also influenced treatment outcome in studies comprised of students that were socially anxious at a subclinical level. Systematic desensitization for students with public speaking anxiety (PSA) conferred the greater client-perceived benefit on those in conditions of high manipulated expectancy than in a neutral condition (Woy & Efran, 1972), whereas students benefited in both high and neutral expectancy conditions in a similar study (Hemme & Boor, 1976). However, expectancy effects showed little predictive ability in a study comparing various exposure and relaxation conditions and manipulating induced expectancy; despite higher initial reaction to and greater decline of heart rate over exposures, as well as subjective effects, expectancy effects were not detected beyond the first session (Borkovec & Sides, 1979).

For OCD, client expectation of improvement was found to relate to positive outcome in one study (Cottraux, Messy, Marks, Mollard, & Bouvard, 1993) but not in another (Lax, Basoglu, & Marks, 1992). A related construct, motivation for treatment, predicted outcome in two studies (Hoogduin & Duivenvoorden, 1988; Keijsers et al., 1994a).

In a study comparing CT and imaginal exposure for PTSD, motivation for treatment predicted outcome (Tarrier et al., 2000). Analogously, neither treatment motivation nor expectations (van Minnen et al., 2002) nor expectations alone (Ehlers et al., 1998) predicted outcome in imaginal exposure interventions.

Only one investigation assessed the relation of pretreatment expectancies and the outcome of treatment for panic disorder. Clark et al. (1999) reported that high positive expectations prior to treatment predicted better outcome to cognitive therapy for panic disorder. Two investigations evaluated motivation for treatment: One investigation found that higher levels of motivation predicted

good outcome to exposure treatment for panic disorder (Keijsers et al., 1994b), while another investigation found no relation between pretreatment motivation and the outcome of a behavioral intervention (de Beurs et al., 1995). Also, perceived treatment suitability was not found to predict treatment outcome (Clark et al., 1999).

Overall, the relation between positive treatment expectancies and outcome was positive in 9 of 17 studies (53%), treatment credibility predicted outcome in 2 of 6 studies (33%), treatment motivation predicted outcome in 4 of 5 (80%) studies, and treatment suitability failed to predict outcome in 1 study. With these categories collapsed, positive views about treatment predicted favorable outcome in 15 of 29 findings (52%). Therefore, although treatment credibility and suitability did not consistently relate to treatment response, the dominant results pertaining to expectancy and motivation for treatment agreed more often than not with the conclusion reported in a recent general review (Arnkoff, Glass, & Shapiro, 2002). Despite the presence of considerable mixed and null findings, the majority of studies support the principle that treatment efficacy increases, in part, as a function of positive expectations.

Attachment

Individuals' attachment styles are considered to reflect their mental representations of self and other, as well as their desires for intimacy or interpersonal distance (Cassidy & Shaver, 1999). Pertinent to this review, clients' attachment styles have been shown to impact treatment outcome (Horowitz, Rosenberg, & Bartholomew, 1993; Meyer & Pilkonis, 2002). No studies were located that directly assessed the impact of attachment style upon outcome of treatment for anxiety disorders. Nonetheless, several pertinent findings emerged for associated constructs.

Several findings applicable to attachment as a predictor for PTSD outcome were located, bearing mixed support for a direct relationship between attachment style and outcome. For instance, in an inpatient multi-treatment for males with PTSD, structured interviews were used to assess clients' object relations, cognitive-affective representations of "self" and important "others" (viz., parent figures)—akin to Bowlby's "internal working models." For clients who completed treatment, quality of object relations strongly inversely predicted PTSD symptoms, anxiety, anger, and domiciliary utilization, and positively predicted psychosocial functioning at post, even with personality disorders statistically controlled (Ford et al., 1997). This finding is consistent with data for inpatient treatment for PTSD combat veterans, in which negative parenting behaviors in childhood (viz., inconsistent love) predicted PTSD symptom severity after treatment (McCranie, Hyer, Boudewyns, & Woods, 1992). However, with regard to more extreme forms of parental mistreatment conceivably related to attachment, neither childhood trauma (Ford & Kidd, 1998) nor childhood abuse (Johnson et al., 1999) predicted treatment response in inpatient treatment programs for chronic PTSD.

Also, a study of group therapy dealing with trauma issues in Palestinian political ex-prisoners (presumably exhibiting some PTSD symptoms) found that self-reported attachment, though failing to predict outcome, predicted alliance quality, which has itself exhibited sizeable predictive power for outcome (Orlinsky, Grawe, & Parks, 1994). Similarly, the sole investigation of the relation between attachment-relevant constructs and the outcome of psychosocial interventions for panic disorder found that perceived parental upbringing was not related to treatment outcome (de Beurs et al., 1995).

Studies have yet to investigate the predictive capacity of attachment style for treatment response in GAD. However, such research is merited given that childhood abuse has predicted negative GAD course (van den Brink et al., 2002), as well as findings that both GAD clients and analogues have reported significantly more troubled attachment patterns (e.g., role-reversal, enmeshment, and anger toward mothers) than controls (Cassidy, 1995).

Similar to studies employing samples of mixed disorders (Meyer, Pilkonis, Proietti, Heape, & Egan, 2001; Mosheim, Zachhuber, Scharf, Hofmann, Kemmler, Danzl, Kinze, Biebl, & Richter, 2000), studies particular to anxiety disorder treatment showed inferior outcomes for individuals with negative perceived parenting/attachment. However, it is important to note that only one study directly assessed attachment style per se.

Heterogeneity of constructs notwithstanding, 4 of 8 studies (50%) reported positive associations between attachment-relevant constructs and outcome and one study found an interaction between attachment style and alliance. As such, half of the studies argue that perceived negative parental upbringing and attachment difficulties predict decreased benefit from treatment of anxiety disorders. However, the paucity of studies warrants further research in this area.

Coping Style

Clients' coping styles are characterized as "descriptive, heritable, relatively stable, trait-like clusters of behaviors" (Beutler et al., 2002a) such styles are often organized along an internalizing-externalizing continuum. According to Beutler and colleagues, an internalizing coping style is characterized by withdrawal, social restraint, self-attribution, self-criticism, and self-blame, whereas an externalizing coping style subsumes impulsiveness, gregariousness, expressivity, blame of others, and external attributions of cause (involving anger, blame, avoidance, etc.) No studies were located that explicitly delineated clients' coping styles or the relationship between such styles and therapy outcome for anxiety disorders. This fact notwithstanding, various findings are reported here that bear upon the foregoing internalizing and externalizing traits and behaviors.

Attributions of Control

Because coping styles have been considered to subsume constructs related to causal attributions, studies bearing upon several cognitive attributional variables are reported here. Locus of control may be conceived as a measure of coping style, with higher internal locus of control resembling the internal attributions of internalizers. Higher internal locus of control predicted positive therapeutic outcome of CT for GAD (Biswas & Chattopadhyay, 2001) and for treatment of recurrent, nonphobic anxiety (Lewis et al., 1978). Similarly, a sense of control and attribution of gains to personal efforts (internal attribution) measured at posttest of treatment for PTSD predicted maintenance of treatment gains at a follow-up (Livanou et al., 2002). Furthermore, in a study of CBT for females with PTSD, segments of clients with poor treatment response were rated as showing significantly greater mental defeat and absence of mental planning for survival (i.e., likely low on internal locus of control) when discussing assault memories than those who responded to treatment (Ehlers et al., 1998).

Heterogeneous results emerged in trials of CBGT for social phobia. In one study, generalized social phobic clients endorsed lower scores of internal locus of control and higher attributions to chance than those with specific social phobia and, in turn, were less likely to manifest clinically significant therapeutic progress (Brown et al., 1995), whereas another study found internal attributions of control to be unrelated to outcome (Leung & Heimberg, 1996). In total, 4 of 5 studies (80%) found a positive relation between internal locus of control and outcome.

Negative Appraisals

Aside from locus of control, several related attributional variables were assessed in relation to outcome, such as self-statements, attributions, and appraisals. In social phobia treatment studies, self-reported frequency of negative self-statements during social interactions correlated positively and highly with self-reported avoidance (outcome criterion) (Scholing & Emmelkamp, 1999), and negative self-statements were higher in clients that eventually dropped out of treatment (Heimberg et al., 1990). In CBT and BT for GAD, the degree to which ambiguous (external) information was interpreted as threatening predicted relatively unfavorable outcomes (Butler, 1993). For PTSD treatment via flooding, clients' negative appraisals of their actions during combat experiences distinguished those who relapsed with depression or alcoholism (Pitman, Altman, Greenwald, Longpre, Macklin, Poire, & Steketee, 1991); relatedly, clients that failed to recover in a prospective study of PTSD were characterized by negative appraisals of others' responses after assault (Dunmore, Clark, & Ehlers, 1997). For panic disorder, more positive pretreatment attributional style was shown to predict better treatment outcomes (Michelson, Bellanti, Testa, & Marchione, 1997). In contrast, baseline beliefs about mistrust, helplessness, meaninglessness, and unjustness of the world were

not predictive of outcome of various cognitive and behavioral treatment conditions for clients with PTSD (Livanou et al., 2002). Thus, 6 of 7 (86%) of the studies showed negative attributions or appraisals to predict relatively poor outcomes.

Personality

Because personality variables resemble coping styles in their cross-situational, enduring nature, they were considered as predictors or moderators of outcome; however, it must be acknowledged that such variables form part of a continuum with more severe manifestations such as personality disorders, and thus grouping them with coping styles is arbitrary, though not unwarranted. Findings regarding personality variables were mixed. Extroversion, a trait typified by persons with externalizing coping style, related positively to treatment outcome for panic disorder (Sharp & Power, 1999). In contrast, poorer prognosis for inpatient PTSD treatment was associated with elevated scores for MCMI Hypomania (Munley et al., 1994), one of the dimensions commonly high in externalizing clients (Beutler et al., 2002a). In contrast, the greatest improvement in social phobia symptoms occurred in a cluster of clients with the most severe MMPI-II scores of Depression-Psychasthenia-Schizophrenia (Levin, Hermesh, & Marom, 2001); this constellation bears similarity with "internalizing" coping styles as defined by Beutler et al. (2002a). Anger, a state related to externalizing when expressed, was associated with decreased treatment benefit for PTSD in a study comparing exposure and wait-list conditions (Foa et al., 1995) and discriminated treatment "responders" from "partial responders" in CBT (Taylor et al., 2001). However, in another study testing imaginal exposure, holding anger in (consistent with internalizing) predicted symptoms at posttest in one sample, but failing to control pent-up anger predicted symptoms in a different sample (van Minnen et al., 2002). Interestingly, one study reported an interaction between coping style and treatment modality: Mixed-diagnosis (depressed and anxious) clients classified via the MMPI as externalizers benefited from experiential more than analytic-based therapy; in contrast, a reverse pattern of response to treatment was found for internalizers (Beutler & Mitchell, 1981).

Other findings relevant to coping style were noted. Level of neuroticism was not associated with treatment outcome for panic disorder (Sharp & Power, 1999) or GAD (Barlow et al., 1992), and better course for GAD (van den Brink et al., 2002). Also pertaining to interventions targeting PTSD, over-reporting on the MMPI (endorsing obvious items at higher rates than other groups) predicted poorer treatment prognosis (Hyer et al., 1988), whereas personality characteristics failed to predict differential treatment response to imaginal exposure (van Minnen et al., 2002). Therefore, personality variables related to the externalizing coping style predicted relatively poorer prognosis in 4 of 5 findings (80%) and 1 of 2 showed variables related to internalizing as predictive of better outcome. Neuroticism and over-reporting were negatively associated with outcome in 2 of 5 (40%) studies and personality characteristics yielded no predictive power in one study. Although one mixed-sample study reported an interesting interaction between coping style and treatment type, no studies examining similar moderator effects for predominantly anxiety-disordered samples were located.

In conclusion, coping styles that are labeled as externalizing predicted relatively poorer prognosis. Similarly, external causal attributions of control were consistently predictive of unfavorable treatment outcomes. On the other hand, internalizing variables such as neuroticism, over-reporting, and negative self and world appraisals also tended to predict negative outcomes. However, it remains difficult to draw firm conclusions from studies employing heterogeneous variables that were not originally intended as measures of the superordinate construct of coping style.

Stages of Change

According to the "stages of change" or transtheoretical model, behavior change occurs over the course of six stages including precontemplation, contemplation, preparation, action, maintenance, and termination. Although no studies examining relations between stages of change and psychotherapy outcome focused exclusively on anxiety disorders, several relevant studies were located. Studies of medication treatment for panic disorder

(Beitman, Beck, Deuser, Carter, Davidson, & Maddock, 1994; Reid, Nair, Mistry, & Beitman, 1996) and GAD (Wilson, Bell Dolan, & Beitman, 1997) found strong correlations between readiness to change and outcome. In addition, in an effectiveness study of therapy for adult survivors of repeated childhood sexual abuse (not directly assessed, but likely exhibiting some trauma symptoms), clients in the action stage scored significantly higher on behavioral change processes than those in the contemplation stage (Koraleski & Larson, 1997), a finding consistent with the general principle that clients in later stages benefit from behavior-change interventions, whereas consciousness-raising interventions apply most aptly to clients in early stages (Prochaska & Norcross, 2002). Although these four studies showed meaningful relations between advanced stages of change and positive outcome, the lack of relevant research with psychosocial interventions precludes conclusions.

Anaclitic and Introjective Dimensions

The paucity of relevant research regarding anaclitic and introjective dimensions and development as they affect therapy outcome for anxiety disorders precludes recommendations for therapists beyond previous reviews (Blatt, Shahar, & Zuroff, 2002). However, the anaclitic and introjective dimensions bear similarity to the dysfunctional attitudes of heightened "need for approval" and "perfectionism," respectively. Meaningful relations between variables interrelated to these dimensions and anxiety have been observed. For example, dysfunctional attitudes have been shown to correlate with scores of anxiety and depression (Burns & Spangler, 2001; Dyck, 1992), as have perfectionism with social phobia (Saboonchi, Lundh, & Öst, 1999) and social and trait anxiety (Juster, Heimberg, Frost, & Holt, 1996), and sociotropy (concern about social disapproval) with OCD (Vogel, Stiles, & Nordahl, 2000) and with social phobia (Brown, Juster, Heimberg, & Winning, 1998). In a treatment study for social phobia, dysfunctional attitudes failed to significantly predict outcome (Otto et al., 2000). Such findings indicate the need for future research in anxiety treatment to examine these variables as predictors/ moderators of outcome.

Assimilation of Problematic Experiences

Previous research, reviewed by Stiles (2002), suggests that clients in therapy often progress through stages of increasing awareness and goal-focused behavior, assimilating painful or threatening memories, wishes, feelings, or behaviors. Levels of assimilation of problematic experiences (APES) have been shown to interact with treatment type for mixed-disorder samples: Clients at the level of problem statement/clarification or higher have responded to CBT over psychodynamic-interpersonal treatment (Stiles, Shankland, Wright, & Field, 1997). The only finding specific to anxiety spectrum disorders for the APES model was from an individual case analysis in which the client responded to treatment as he assimilated angry and resentful feelings from which social anxiety and panic arose (Stiles, Morrison, Haw, Harper, Shapiro, & Firth-Cozens, 1991).

No studies examined interactions between treatment techniques and stages of APES on outcome for anxiety disorders. Because the research specific to APES and anxiety disorders is sparse, it requires further study before it can be supported as a factor in the principles of therapeutic change for anxiety disorders.

Resistance

Only one study of an anxiety treatment directly assessed resistance or reactance. This study showed that low reactance predicted a better response to a restraining or reframing paradoxical intervention for test anxiety (Dowd, Hughs, Brockbank, Halpain, Seibel, & Seibel, 1988). Therefore conclusions with respect to resistance or reactance must remain tentative.

Beutler, Moleiro, and Talebi (2002b) reviewed findings to support the principle that nondirective and paradoxical interventions should be used with resistant clients. Nonetheless we were able to locate only one study that investigated interactions between reactance and treatment type for anxiety (Dowd et al., 1988). This study failed to find an interaction between these two variables and, as

noted earlier, found only a main effect for reactance.

Demographic Variables

Age

Various studies also investigated the predictive potential of clients' current age on outcome and showed mixed results. No significant relationships emerged between age and outcome in treatment studies for PTSD (Ehlers et al., 1998; Foa et al., 1991; Jaycox et al., 1998; Marks et al., 1998; Munley et al., 1994; Perconte & Griger, 1991; Tarrier et al., 1999; Tarrier et al., 2000; Taylor et al., 1999). For OCD treatments, one study found younger age to predict improvement (De Araujo et al., 1996), whereas another did not detect relations between age and outcome (Hoogduin & Duivenvoorden, 1988). Whereas two investigations found no relation between current age and the outcome of panic disorder treatment (de Beurs et al., 1995; Sharp & Power, 1999), one investigation which collapsed across various anxiety disorders found that older patients had poorer treatment outcomes at five-year follow-up (Seivewright et al., 1998). This is similar to findings that older age (over 35) predicted worse course of GAD in a prospective study (van den Brink et al., 2002), although survey data suggest that younger persons are more likely to drop out of treatment (Edlund, Wamg, Berglund, Katz, Lin, & Kessler, 2002). In summary, 12 of 16 (75%) studies suggest no prognostic value for age, whereas three studies found an increasing age to predict worse outcome.

Gender

Few treatment studies that we reviewed examined client gender main effects for clients. In general, gender failed to exert a significant impact on treatment. However, in one study, male gender predicted worse outcome from medications plus exposure homework for OCD (Basoglu et al., 1988). Gender did not differentially predict outcome in treatment studies with samples of clients with GAD, panic disorder, dysthymia (Tyrer et al., 1993), and social phobia (Heimberg et al., 1990; Otto et al., 2000; Reich et al., 1994). Additionally, client gender has not predicted the course of social phobia (Reich et al., 1994), social anxiety and skills deficits (Van Dam-Baggen & Kraaimaat, 1986), OCD (Drummond, 1993; Foa et al., 1983; Hoogduin & Duivenvoorden, 1988), and PTSD (Jaycox et al., 1998; Marks et al., 1998; van Minnen et al., 2002). Also, several studies failed to detect relationships between gender and outcome for psychotherapy versus drug conditions for panic disorder (Sharp & Power, 1999; Shinoda et al., 1999), and for controlled multicenter paroxetine trials for social phobia (Stein et al., 2002). Furthermore, a meta-analysis of 35 controlled studies of cognitive behavioral and pharmacological treatment for GAD yielded a negligible relationship between gender and treatment outcome (Gould, Otto, Pollack, & Yap, 1997).

In contradistinction to these results, gender emerged as a significant contributor to outcome at termination and six-month follow-up for PTSD in one study: Females were more likely to benefit from treatment (Tarrier et al., 2000).

The rate at which client attrition occurs in treatment studies may additionally be interpreted as an index of outcome. The effects of gender upon attrition rates, though largely unreported, were mixed when noted. A marginally significantly higher rate of attrition occurred for men than women in a comparison of behavior therapy and cognitive behavior therapy in the treatment of generalized anxiety disorder (Butler, Fennell, Robson, & Gelder, 1991). Also, another study found that males were more likely than females to drop out of treatment for PTSD (van Minnen et al., 2002). However, differential attrition for gender was not observed in a group form of CBT (exposure, PMR, SD, role-play) for generalized social phobia (Feske et al., 1996).

Our review, though limited by a paucity of anxiety disorder treatment studies testing for client gender as a predictor of outcome, generally matched the general finding (when not limited to anxiety) that gender has regularly failed to predict psychotherapy outcome or premature termination, as noted in a recent review (Sue & Lam, 2002). The majority of the studies (14 of 18; 78%), in addition to meta-analytic findings, complemented this null finding, whereas 4 studies demonstrated greater treatment benefit for females, consistent with some reports elsewhere of superior female response to treatment (e.g., Kirshner, 1978; Mintz, Luborsky, & Auerbach, 1971).

Ethnicity

The predictive or moderating role of client ethnicity or race was not examined in any of the studies on GAD and OCD reviewed, and the only findings regarding social phobia were that client ethnicity did not predict either treatment response or dropout in socially anxious clients receiving group social skills training (Van Dam-Baggen & Kraaimaat, 1986) or dropout from a study comparing CBGT and placebo control (Heimberg et al., 1990).

In contrast, a study of agoraphobia treatment (Chambless & Williams, 1995) found that although in vivo exposure was beneficial to both African American and Caucasian individuals, African American clients were also more severely symptomatic on measures of phobia at both pretreatment and posttreatment. In addition, at follow-up, African Americans had demonstrated less change in frequency of panic attacks.

The majority of relevant findings related to effects for client ethnicity pertained to PTSD treatments. In a four-month inpatient multimodality treatment for Vietnam veterans, trends emerged showing that Caucasian clients reported greater symptomology at discharge and follow-ups than African-American clients, although these subgroups did not differ in their reports of treatment helpfulness (Johnson & Lubin, 1997). A reverse finding emerged from an aforementioned study investigating Disorders of Extreme Stress Not Otherwise Specified (DESNOS) in multimodal treatment for PTSD: American Indian clients were significantly more likely than Caucasian clients to meet the DESNOS diagnosis associated with decreased likelihood of reliable therapeutic change (Ford & Kidd, 1998). Such a result, though isolated, is consistent with a finding from the substance abuse literature that American Indians did not benefit from a treatment program as much as Caucasians (Query, 1985). Also, when a large sample ($N = 4{,}276$) of Caucasian and African-American male Vietnam veterans with PTSD received unspecified treatment at one of 53 sites in the United States, African-American clients showed significantly lower program participation than Caucasian clients on a number of measures

(Rosenheck, Fontana, & Cottrol, 1995). Furthermore, they attended treatment significantly less (regardless of therapist race), seemed less committed to treatment, received more treatment for substance abuse, and showed less improvement in control of violent behavior than Caucasian clients, although the two ethnic groups did not differ in terms of clinicians' improvement ratings.

Nonetheless, ethnicity effects in PTSD treatment failed to emerge in studies testing prolonged imaginal exposure (Ehlers et al., 1998; Jaycox et al., 1998; van Minnen et al., 2002) or contrasting CBT with wait-list control group (Taylor et al., 1999) or exposure, stress inoculation training, supportive counseling, or wait-list control (Foa et al., 1991). In addition, Rosenheck and Fontana (1996, 2002) conducted two follow-up studies. The first study found no outcome differences between 122 African-American clients and 403 Caucasian veterans with PTSD. The second study also failed to find systematic differences in either treatment process or outcome among African-American (N = 2,906), Hispanic (N = 661), and Caucasian patients. Similarly, a review paper on combat-related PTSD also found no evidence that client race predicted outcome (Frueh, Brady, & de Arellano, 1998). In summary, 8 of 12 studies (67%) detected no effect of ethnicity on outcome, congruent with previous studies reporting the absence of ethnicity effects in mixed samples (Jones, 1978, 1982; Lerner, 1972). Nevertheless, the four findings of ethnicity effects suggest the need for further research.

Level of Intelligence

Level of intelligence, another client variable, was unrelated to outcome for GAD (Haaga, DeRubeis, Stewart, & Beck, 1991), OCD (Hoogduin & Duivenvoorden, 1988), PTSD (Munley et al., 1994), and for psychiatric patients reporting social anxiety or skills problems in social situations (Van Dam-Baggen & Kraaimaat, 1986).

Socioeconomic Status

Although often confounded with race effects in research (Acosta, 1980; Vail, 1978), clients' socioeconomic status (SES) often possesses predictive power for impact of treatment. Persons with low SES have been shown as more prone to premature

termination than those with high SES (Baekeland & Lundwall, 1975; Garfield, 1994; Lorion, 1973; Lorion & Fellner, 1986; Reis & Brown, 1999; Wierzbicki & Pekarik, 1993). This relatively robust finding was supported by a comparison of CBT versus counseling for rape victims with PTSD: Clients who dropped out of treatment were significantly more likely than completers to earn annual income under $10,000 and have blue-collar jobs (Foa et al., 1991). Furthermore, relatively higher SES status emerged as one of the best predictors of sustained improvement for GAD treatment (Durham et al., 1997), was associated with lower symptom severity across the duration of treatment for GAD, panic disorder, and dysthymia (Tyrer et al., 1993), and was related to better treatment outcome in OCD (Steketee, 1993) and mixed panic disorder/OCD (Chambless & Steketee, 1999) samples. These results are consonant with survey data not specific to anxiety, in which low income predicted treatment dropout (Edlund et al., 2002). Contrary to these results, SES failed to predict attrition rates for group CBT of generalized social phobia (Feske et al., 1996) or outcome of behavior therapy for OCD (Hoogduin & Duivenvoorden, 1988) and prolonged exposure for PTSD (Jaycox et al., 1998), findings akin to reports of nonsignificant SES effects on psychotherapy outcome elsewhere (Luborsky, Chandler, Auerbach, Cohen, & Bachrach, 1971).

The dearth of studies testing SES effects, as well as heterogeneity of operational definitions and confounding race effects (Lorion & Fellner, 1986), prohibits drawing conclusions with certainty. However, the preponderance of the evidence in available studies (five of eight studies; 63%) suggests that low SES predicts dropout and decreased treatment response. On the other hand, client expectations of treatment length may mediate the relationship between SES and dropout (Pekarik, 1991; Pekarik & Wierzbicki, 1986). Unfortunately, no studies were located that expressly sought to test interactions between level of SES and type of treatment; thus it remains questionable to extend findings from nonanxiety or mixed disorder samples in which low SES clients have benefited from time-limited treatment (Stone & Crowthers, 1972), brief or insight-oriented treatment (Koegler & Brill, 1967), and active, directive treatments (Goin, Yamamoto, & Silvervan, 1965; Organista,

Munoz, & Gonzalez, 1994; Satterfield, 1998) (Azhar, Varma, & Dharap, 1994).

Religion and Spirituality

One treatment study for GAD in a Muslim sample compared supportive psychotherapy and anxiolytic medication with or without "religious psychotherapy" (reading scriptures from, meditating upon, and discussing the Koran). Clients in the religious condition were rated by clinicians as significantly more improved than those in the standard treatment condition at three-month, but not six-month, follow-up (Azhar & Varma, 1995a, 1995b). Despite the fact that this finding stands by itself within the anxiety disorders, it remains consistent with other studies suggesting more favorable outcomes of religiously accommodative than standard treatments for Muslim (Azhar & Varma, 1995a, 1995b) and Christian (Propst, 1980; Propst, Ostrom, Watkins, Dean, & Mashburn, 1992) samples, though several studies suggest modest or absent supplemental benefit of spiritually accommodative treatment beyond standard approaches (Hawkins, Tan, & Turk, 1999; Johnson, Devries, Ridley, Pettorini, & Peterson, 1994; Pecheur & Edwards, 1984).

The dearth of research in the area of anxiety treatments that examine the effect of spirituality/religion of clients on treatment outcome underscores McCullough's (1999) call for research on differential effect of religious treatment for specific problems (e.g., anxiety disorders). The lack of extant research precludes drawing conclusions at the present time. Nonetheless, client's religions orientations and preferences, as part of their framework for meaning, may interact with treatment (e.g., Kelly & Strupp, 1992).

THERAPIST FACTORS

Two studies examined therapist experience as a predictor of outcome of treatment for anxiety disorders. Whereas no correlation was detected between therapists' level of experience and outcome of GAD treatment (Borkovec et al., 1987), therapists' overall experience, but not CBT experience, was related to treatment outcome for panic disorder (Huppert, Bufka, Barlow, Gorman, Shear,

& Woods, 2001). In this study, patients with more experienced therapists showed greater improvement. The latter finding is consistent with a meta-analysis suggesting that differences in experience may partially account for therapist effects (Crits-Christoph, Baranackie, Kurcias, Beck, Carroll, Perry, Luborsky, McLellan, Woody, Thompson, Gallagher, & Zitrin, 1991).

Regrettably, very few studies have attempted to evaluate variables specific to therapists, let alone the effect of such variables on treatment outcome. Apart from therapist experience, the only other relevant findings were reported in the aforementioned outcome study for panic disorder (Huppert et al., 2001): Therapist age and gender were not related to treatment outcome, convergent with meta-analytic results yielding minimal effects for therapist demographic variables (Bowman, Scogin, Floyd, & McKendree Smith, 2001).

FACTORS SHARED BY CLIENT AND THERAPIST

Ethnic Matching

Only one study explicitly addressed the effect of therapist–client racial pairing on outcome in an anxiety disorder. In the aforementioned naturalistic study of veterans with PTSD undergoing treatment, pairing African-American clients with Caucasian therapists was associated with significantly greater premature termination both after one session and before three months of treatment had elapsed than when paired with African-American therapists (Rosenheck et al., 1995). This problematic ethnic match was significantly associated with decreased number of sessions attended, consistent with results elsewhere that ethnic matching is associated with decreased dropout or increased treatment duration (Flaskerud & Hu, 1994; Fujino, Okazaki, & Young, 1994; Gamst, Dana, Der Karabetian, & Kramer, 2001; Lau & Zane, 2000; Sue, Fujino, Hu, Takeuchi, & Zane, 1991; Takeuchi, Sue, & Yeh, 1995). Pairing African-American clients with Caucasian therapists was also associated with decreased clinician's ratings of commitment to treatment and symptom reduction of violent behavior. Yet, many of the other outcome variables did not differ significantly between matched and unmatched pairs. Interestingly, pairing Caucasian clients with African-American therapists did not lead to adverse effects. Additionally, none of the problematic racial pairings continued to be problematic once client treatment involvement and type of treatment were entered into the equation as covariates. Although these results are noteworthy, alone they fail to support conclusions regarding the benefits of ethnic matching.

Gender Matching

The effect of matching client and therapist on gender was investigated in solely one anxiety treatment outcome study; gender match was not a significant predictor in CBT for panic disorder (Huppert et al., 2001), a finding observed outside anxiety disorders (Zlotnick, Elkin, & Shea, 1998).

Clearly, scant research has been conducted concerning the effects of matching client and therapist on specific variables. Whereas past efforts to explore matching have provided negligible predictive utility (Project MATCH Research Group, 1997), future research on the anxiety spectrum must determine the impact of matching within that domain.

CONCLUSION

In review of the foregoing findings, several conclusions have been drawn that apply to client variables in treatment for anxiety disorders.

1. Psychotherapy for anxiety is less likely to be successful if the treated disorder is severe, the client reports a great deal of distress, the client has suffered from the current episode of the disorder for a long period of time or has a history of receiving psychiatric treatment, the client perceives the quality of his/her social support to be highly critical, the client has more interpersonal problems, and the client has Axis I co-morbidity. Thus, functional impairment significantly predicts outcome for anxiety disorders.
2. Psychotherapy for anxiety is less likely to be successful if the client has personality pathology and disorders.
3. Psychotherapy for anxiety is less likely to be

successful if the client has low expectations for the success of the therapy.
4. Psychotherapy for anxiety is less likely to be successful if the client has negative perceived parenting.
5. Psychotherapy for anxiety is less likely to be successful if the client has low internal attributions of control or high negative self-attributions. Thus, rigid externalizing or internalizing coping styles are negative prognostic indicators.
6. Psychotherapy for anxiety is less likely to be successful if the client has a lower socioeconomic status. However, demographic variables of age, gender, ethnicity, and intelligence are not predictive of outcome.

The remaining variables of resistance/reactance, preferences, stages of change, anaclitic and introjective dimensions, assimilation of problematic experiences, and religiosity/spirituality were investigated in an insufficient number of pertinent studies to permit drawing conclusions. Analogously, very few studies incorporated therapist or client–therapist variables. Of course, all of these conclusions must be tempered by an acknowledgment of considerable heterogeneity of study rigor and quality, as well as the fact that some relevant research may have been omitted.

Whereas several relevant principles were extracted regarding the predictive capacity of client variables, almost none of the studies were designed to test interactions between client variables and types of treatment, which might suggest practical intervention strategies for tailoring treatments to clients. Thus, this more interesting issue of "what treatments work for whom," may not be discussed here. Furthermore, therapist factors and the effects of client–therapist matching have seldom been studied in anxiety research, perhaps because most anxiety treatment outcome studies have been conducted from cognitive and behavioral metapsychologies that historically have attributed treatment effects to the potency of the therapeutic techniques, rather than participant factors.

As such, future research from a variety of theoretical orientations must examine the effects of pretreatment therapist factors and matching on anxiety treatment outcome, as well as further studying important client factors. Such research will perhaps augment the efficacy and effectiveness of known interventions, and thereby more fully realize the scientist-practitioner model.

ACKNOWLEDGMENTS   Preparation of this manuscript was supported in part by National Institute of Mental Health Research Grant MH-58593.

References

Abramowitz, J. S., & Foa, E. B. (2000). Does major depressive disorder influence outcome of exposure and response prevention for OCD? *Behavior Therapy, 31*, 795–800.

Abramowitz, J. S., Franklin, M. E., Street, G. P., Kozak, M. J., & Foa, E. B. (2000). Effects of comorbid depression on response to treatment for obsessive-compulsive disorder. *Behavior Therapy, 31*, 517–528.

Abramowitz, J. S., Franklin, M. E., Zoellner, L. A., & DiBernardo, C. L. (2002). Treatment compliance and outcome in obsessive-compulsive disorder. *Behavior Modification, 26*, 447–463.

Abramowitz, S. I., & Wieselberg, N. (1978). Reaction to relaxation and desensitization outcome: Five angry treatment failures. *American Journal of Psychiatry, 135*, 1418–1419.

Acosta, F. X. (1980). Self-described reasons for premature termination of psychotherapy by Mexican American, Black American, and Anglo-American patients. *Psychological Reports, 47*, 435–443.

Andrews, G., & Harvey, R. (1981). Does psychotherapy benefit neurotic patients? A reanalysis of the Smith, Glass, and Miller data. *Archives of General Psychiatry, 38*, 1203–1208.

Arnkoff, D. B., Glass, C. R., & Shapiro, S. J. (2002). Expectations and preferences. In J. C. Norcross (Ed.), *Psychotherapy relationships that work: Therapist contributions and responsiveness to patients* (pp. 335–356). London: Oxford University Press.

AuBuchon, P. G., & Malatesta, V. J. (1994). Obsessive compulsive patients with comorbid personality disorder: Associated problems and response to a comprehensive behavior therapy. *Journal of Clinical Psychiatry, 55*, 448–453.

Azhar, M. Z., & Varma, S. L. (1995a). Religious psychotherapy as management of bereavement. *Acta Psychiatrica Scandinavica, 91*, 233–235.

Azhar, M. Z., & Varma, S. L. (1995b). Religious psychotherapy in depressive patients. *Psychotherapy and Psychosomatics, 63*, 165–173.

Azhar, M. Z., Varma, S. L., & Dharap, A. S. (1994). Religious psychotherapy in anxiety disorder patients. *Acta Psychiatrica Scandinavica, 90*, 1–3.

Baekeland, F., & Lundwall, L. (1975). Dropping out of treatment: A critical review. *Psychological Bulletin, 82*, 738–783.

Barlow, D. H., Craske, M. G., Cerny, J. A., & Klosko, J. S. (1989). Behavioral treatment of panic disorder. *Behavior Therapy, 20*, 261–282.

Barlow, D. H., Rapee, R. M., & Brown, T. A. (1992). Behavioral treatment of generalized anxiety disorder. *Behavior Therapy, 23*, 551–570.

Basoglu, M., Lax, T., Kasvikis, Y., & Marks, I. M. (1988). Predictors of improvement in obsessive-compulsive disorder. *Journal of Anxiety Disorders, 2*, 299–317.

Basoglu, M., Marks, I. M., Kilic, C., Brewin, C. R., & Swinson, R. P. (1994). Alprazolam and exposure for panic disorder with agoraphobia attribution of improvement to medication predicts subsequent relapse. *British Journal of Psychiatry, 164*, 652–659.

Basoglu, M., Marks, I. M., Swinson, R. P., Noshirvani, H., O'Sulllivan, G., & Kuch, K. (1994). Pre-treatment predictors of treatment outcome in panic disorder and agoraphobia treated with alprazolam and exposure. *Journal of Affective Disorders, 30*, 123–132.

Beitman, B. D., Beck, N., Deuser, W., Carter, J., Davidson, R., & Maddock, R. (1994). Patient stage of change predicts outcome in a panic disorder medication trial. *Anxiety, 1*, 64–69.

Beutler, L. E., Harwood, T. M., Alimohamed, S., & Malik, M. (2002a). Functional impairment and coping style. In J. C. Norcross (Ed.), *Psychotherapy relationships that work: Therapist contributions and responsiveness to patients* (pp. 145–170). New York: Oxford University Press.

Beutler, L. E., Moleiro, C. M., & Talebi, H. (2002b). Resistance. In J. C. Norcross (Ed.), *Psychotherapy relationships that work: Therapist contributions and responsiveness to patients* (pp. 129–143). New York: Oxford University Press.

Biswas, A., & Chattopadhyay, P. K. (2001). Predicting psychotherapeutic outcomes in patients with generalised anxiety disorder. *Journal of Personality and Clinical Studies, 17*, 27–32.

Black, D. W., Wesner, R. B., Gabel, J., Bowers, W., & Monahan, P. (1994). Predictors of short-term treatment response in 66 patients with panic disorder. *Journal of Affective Disorders, 30*, 233–241.

Blatt, S. J., Shahar, G., & Zuroff, D. C. (2002). An-aclitic/sociotropic and introjective/autono-mous dimensions. In J. C. Norcross (Ed.), *Psychotherapy relationships that work: Therapist contributions and responsiveness to patients* (pp. 315–333). London: Oxford University Press.

Bootzin, R. R., & Lick, J. R. (1979). Expectancies in therapy research: Interpretive artifact or me-diating mechanism? *Journal of Consulting and Clinical Psychology, 47,* 852–855.

Borkovec, T. D., & Costello, E. (1993). Efficacy of applied relaxation and cognitive-behavioral therapy in the treatment of generalized anxiety disorder. *Journal of Consulting and Clinical Psychology, 61,* 611–619.

Borkovec, T. D., & Mathews, A. M. (1988). Treat-ment of nonphobic anxiety disorders: A com-parison of nondirective, cognitive, and coping desensitization therapy. *Journal of Consulting and Clinical Psychology, 56,* 877–884.

Borkovec, T. D., Mathews, A. M., Chambers, A., Ebrahimi, S., Lytle, R., & Nelson, R. (1987). The effects of relaxation training with cognitive or nondirective therapy and the role of relaxa-tion-induced anxiety in the treatment of gen-eralized anxiety. *Journal of Consulting and Clin-ical Psychology, 55,* 883–888.

Borkovec, T. D., Newman, M. G., Pincus, A. L., & Lytle, R. (2002). A component analysis of cognitive-behavioral therapy for generalized anxiety disorder and the role of interpersonal problems. *Journal of Consulting and Clinical Psychology, 70,* 288–298.

Borkovec, T. D., & Sides, J. K. (1979). The contri-bution of relaxation and expectancy to fear re-duction via graded, imaginal exposure to feared stimuli. *Behaviour Research and Therapy, 17,* 529–540.

Boudewyns, P. A., Albrecht, J. W., Talbert, F. S., & Hyer, L. A. (1991). Comorbidity and treat-ment outcome of inpatients with chronic combat-related PTSD. *Hospital and Commu-nity Psychiatry, 42,* 847–849.

Boulougouris, J. (1977). Variables affecting the be-haviour modification of obsessive-compulsive patients treated by flooding. In J. C. Boulou-gouris & A. D. Rabavilas (Eds.), *The treatment of phobic and obsessive-compulsive disorders* (pp. 73–84). Oxford: Pergamon Press.

Bowen, R., South, M., Fischer, D., & Looman, T. (1994). Depression, mastery and number of group sessions attended predict outcome of pa-tients with panic and agoraphobia in a behav-ioral/medication program. *Canadian Journal of Psychiatry, 39,* 283–288.

Bowman, D., Scogin, F., Floyd, M., & McKendree Smith, N. (2001). Psychotherapy length of stay and outcome: A meta-analysis of the effect of therapist sex. *Psychotherapy: Theory, Research, Practice, Training, 38,* 142–148.

Brown, E. J., Heimberg, R. G., & Juster, H. R. (1995). Social phobia subtype and avoidant personality disorder: Effect on severity of social phobia, impairment, and outcome of cognitive behavioral treatment. *Behavior Therapy, 26,* 467–486.

Brown, E. J., Juster, H. R., Heimberg, R. G., & Win-ning, C. D. (1998). Stressful life events and personality styles: Relation to impairment and treatment outcome in patients with social pho-bia. *Journal of Anxiety Disorders, 12,* 233–251.

Brown, P. J. (2000). Outcome in female patients with both substance use and post-traumatic stress disorders. *Alcoholism Treatment Quar-terly, 18,* 127–135.

Brown, T. A., & Barlow, D. H. (1995). Long-term outcome in cognitive-behavioral treatment of panic disorder: Clinical predictors and alterna-tive strategies for assessment. *Journal of Con-sulting and Clinical Psychology, 63,* 754–765.

Buchanan, A. W., Meng, K. S., & Marks, I. M. (1996). What predicts improvement and com-pliance during the behavioral treatment of ob-sessive compulsive disorder? *Anxiety, 2,* 22–27.

Burns, D. D., & Spangler, D. L. (2001). Do changes in dysfunctional attitudes mediate changes in depression and anxiety in cognitive behavioral therapy? *Behavior Therapy, 32,* 337–369.

Butler, G. (1993). Predicting outcome after treat-ment for generalised anxiety disorder. *Behav-iour Research and Therapy, 31,* 211–213.

Butler, G., & Anastasiades, P. (1988). Predicting re-sponse to anxiety management in patients with generalised anxiety disorders. *Behaviour Re-search and Therapy, 26,* 531–534.

Butler, G., Cullington, A., Munby, M., Amies, P., & Gelder, M. (1984). Exposure and anxiety man-agement in treatment of social phobia. *Journal of Consulting and Clinical Psychology, 52,* 642–650.

Butler, G., Fennell, M., Robson, P., & Gelder, M. (1991). Comparison of behavior therapy and cognitive behavior therapy in the treatment of generalized anxiety disorder. *Journal of Con-sulting and Clinical Psychology, 59,* 167–175.

Cameron, O. G., Thyer, B. A., Feckner, S., Nesse, R., & Curtis, G. C. (1986). Behavior therapy of phobias: Predictors of outcome. *Psychiatry Research, 19,* 245–246.

Carter, M. M., Turovsky, J., Sbrocco, T., Meadows, E. A., & Barlow, D. H. (1995). Patient dropout from a couples' group treatment for panic disorder with agoraphobia. *Professional Psychology: Research and Practice, 26,* 626–628.

Cassidy, J. (1995). Attachment and generalized anxiety disorder. In D. Cicchetti & S. L. Toth (Eds.), *Emotion, cognition, and representation. Rochester symposium on developmental psychopathology* (Vol. 6, pp. 343–370). Rochester, NY: University of Rochester Press.

Cassidy, J., & Shaver, P. R. (Eds.). (1999). *Handbook of attachment: Theory, research, and clinical applications.* New York: Guilford Press.

Chambless, D. L., & Gillis, M. M. (1993). Cognitive therapy of anxiety disorders. *Journal of Consulting and Clinical Psychology, 61,* 248–260.

Chambless, D. L., Renneberg, B., Gracely, E. J., Goldstein, A. J., & Fydrich, T. (2000). Axis I and II comorbidity in agoraphobia: Prediction of psychotherapy outcome in a clinical setting. *Psychotherapy Research, 10,* 279–295.

Chambless, D. L., & Steketee, G. (1999). Expressed emotion and behavior therapy outcome: A prospective study with obsessive-compulsive and agoraphobic outpatients. *Journal of Consulting and Clinical Psychology, 67,* 658–665.

Chambless, D. L., Tran, G. Q., & Glass, C. R. (1997). Predictors of response to cognitive-behavioral group therapy for social phobia. *Journal of Anxiety Disorders, 11,* 221–240.

Chambless, D. L., & Williams, K. E. (1995). A preliminary study of African Americans with agoraphobia: Symptom severity and outcome of treatment with in vivo exposure. *Behavior Therapy, 26,* 501–515.

Clark, D. M., Salkovskis, P. M., Hackmann, A., Wells, A., Ludgate, J., & Gelder, M. (1999). Brief cognitive therapy for panic disorder: A randomized controlled trial. *Journal of Consulting and Clinical Psychology, 67,* 583–589.

Cottraux, J., Messy, P., Marks, I. M., Mollard, E., & Bouvard, M. (1993). Predictive factors in the treatment of obsessive-compulsive disorders with fluvoxamine and/or behaviour therapy. *Behavioural Psychotherapy, 21,* 45–50.

Cottraux, J., Mollard, E., Bouvard, M., & Marks, I. (1993). Exposure therapy, fluvoxamine, or combination treatment in obsessive-compulsive disorder: One-year followup. *Psychiatry Research, 49,* 63–75.

Coyne, J. C., & Downey, G. (1991). Social factors and psychopathology: Stress, social support, and coping processes. *Annual Review of Psychology, 42,* 401–425.

Crits-Christoph, P., Baranackie, K., Kurcias, J. S., Beck, A. T., Carroll, K., Perry, K., Luborsky, L., McLellan, A. T., Woody, G. E., Thompson, L., Gallagher, D., & Zitrin, C. (1991). Meta-analysis of therapist effects in psychotherapy outcome studies. *Psychotherapy Research, 1,* 81–91.

Cuijpers, P., & Van Lammeren, P. (1999). Depressive symptoms in chronically ill elderly people in residential homes. *Aging and Mental Health, 3,* 221–226.

De Araujo, L. A., Ito, L. M., & Marks, I. M. (1996). Early compliance and other factors predicting outcome of exposure for obsessive-compulsive disorder. *British Journal of Psychiatry, 169,* 747–752.

de Beurs, E., Lange, A., van Dyck, R., & Koele, P. (1995). Respiratory training prior to exposure in vivo in the treatment of panic disorder with agoraphobia: Efficacy and predictors of outcome. *Australian and New Zealand Journal of Psychiatry, 29,* 104–113.

de Haan, E., van Oppen, P., van Balkom, A. J. L. M., Spinhoven, P., Hoogduin, K. A. L., & van Dyck, R. (1997). Prediction of outcome and early vs. late improvement in OCD patients treated with cognitive behaviour therapy and pharmacotherapy. *Acta Psychiatrica Scandinavica, 96,* 354–361.

Dowd, E. T., Hughs, S. L., Brockbank, L., Halpain, D., Seibel, C., & Seibel, P. (1988). Compliance-based and defiance-based intervention strategies and psychological reactance in the treatment of free and unfree behavior. *Journal of Counseling Psychology, 35,* 370–376.

Drummond, L. M. (1993). The treatment of severe, chronic, resistant obsessive-compulsive disorder: An evaluation of an in-patient programme using behavioural psychotherapy in combination with other treatments. *British Journal of Psychiatry, 163,* 223–229.

Dunmore, E., Clark, D. M., & Ehlers, A. (1997). Cognitive factors in persistent versus recovered post-traumatic stress disorder after physical or sexual assault: A pilot study. *Behavioural and Cognitive Psychotherapy, 25,* 147–159.

Durham, R. C., Allan, T., & Hackett, C. A. (1997). On predicting improvement and relapse in generalized anxiety disorder following psychotherapy. *British Journal of Clinical Psychology, 36,* 101–119.

Dyck, M. J. (1992). Subscales of the Dysfunctional Attitude Scale. *British Journal of Clinical Psychology, 31,* 333–335.

Edlund, M. J., Wamg, P. S., Berglund, P. A., Katz, S. J., Lin, E., & Kessler, R. C. (2002). Dropping out of mental health treatment: Patterns and predictors among epidemiological survey respondents in the United States and Ontario. *American Journal of Psychiatry, 159,* 845–851.

Ehlers, A., Clark, D. M., Dunmore, E., Jaycox, L., Meadows, E., & Foa, E. B. (1998). Predicting response to exposure treatment in PTSD: The role of mental defeat and alienation. *Journal of Traumatic Stress, 11,* 457–471.

Emmelkamp, P. M., & Kuipers, A. C. (1979). Agoraphobia: A follow-up study four years after treatment. *British Journal of Psychiatry, 134,* 352–355.

Emmelkamp, P. M. G., Hoekstra, R. J., & Visser, A. (1985). The behavioral treatment of obsessive-compulsive disorder: Prediction of outcome at 3.5 years follow-up. In P. Pichot, P. Berner, R. Wolf, & K. Thau (Eds.), *Psychiatry: The state of the art* (pp. 265–270). New York: Plenum.

Eysenck, M. W. (1997). *Anxiety and cognition: A unified theory.* Hove, England: Psychology Press/Erlbaum (UK) Taylor and Francis.

Fals-Stewart, W., & Lucente, S. (1993). An MCMI cluster typology of obsessive-compulsives: A measure of personality characteristics and its relationship to treatment participation, compliance and outcome in behavior therapy. *Journal of Psychiatric Research, 27,* 139–154.

Fava, G. A., Rafanelli, C., Grandi, S., Conti, S., Ruini, C., Mangelli, L., & Belluardo, P. (2001). Long-term outcome of panic disorder with agoraphobia treated by exposure. *Psychological Medicine, 31,* 891–898.

Feske, U., Perry, K. J., Chambless, D. L., Renneberg, B., & Goldstein, A. J. (1996). Avoidant personality disorder as a predictor for treatment outcome among generalized social phobics. *Journal of Personality Disorders, 10,* 174–184.

Fisher, D., Beutler, L. E., & Williams, O. B. (1999). Making assessment relevant to treatment planning: The STS clinician rating form. *Journal of Clinical Psychology, 55,* 825–842.

Flaskerud, J. H., & Hu, L. t. (1994). Participation in and outcome of treatment for major depression among low income Asian-Americans. *Psychiatry Research, 53,* 289–300.

Foa, E. B. (1979). Failure in treating obsessive-compulsives. *Behaviour Research and Therapy, 17,* 169–176.

Foa, E. B., Abramowitz, J. S., Franklin, M. E., & Kozak, M. J. (1999). Feared consequences, fixity of belief, and treatment outcome in patients with obsessive-compulsive disorder. *Behavior Therapy, 30,* 717–724.

Foa, E. B., Grayson, J. B., & Steketee, G. S. (1982). Depression, habituation, and treatment outcome in obsessive-compulsives. In J. Boulougouris (Ed.), *Learning theory approaches to psychiatry* (pp. 129–142). New York: Wiley.

Foa, E. B., Grayson, J. B., Steketee, G. S., Doppelt, H. G., Turner, R. M., & Latimer, P. R. (1983). Success and failure in the behavioral treatment of obsessive-compulsives. *Journal of Consulting and Clinical Psychology, 51,* 287–297.

Foa, E. B., Kozak, M. J., Steketee, G. S., & McCarthy, P. R. (1992). Treatment of depressive and obsessive-compulsive symptoms in OCD by imipramine and behaviour therapy. *British Journal of Clinical Psychology, 31,* 279–292.

Foa, E. B., Riggs, D. S., Massie, E. D., & Yarczower, M. (1995). The impact of fear activation and anger on the efficacy of exposure treatment for posttraumatic stress disorder. *Behavior Therapy, 26,* 487–499.

Foa, E. B., Rothbaum, B. O., Riggs, D. S., & Murdock, T. B. (1991). Treatment of posttraumatic stress disorder in rape victims: A comparison between cognitive-behavioral procedures and counseling. *Journal of Consulting and Clinical Psychology, 59,* 715–723.

Ford, J. D., Fisher, P., & Larson, L. (1997). Object relations as a predictor of treatment outcome with chronic posttraumatic stress disorder. *Journal of Consulting and Clinical Psychology, 65,* 547–559.

Ford, J. D., & Kidd, P. (1998). Early childhood trauma and disorders of extreme stress as predictors of treatment outcome with chronic posttraumatic stress disorder. *Journal of Traumatic Stress, 11,* 743–761.

Frank, J. D. (1973). *Persuasion and healing: A comparative study of psychotherapy* (Rev. ed.). Oxford, England: Schocken.

Frueh, B. C., Brady, K. L., & de Arellano, M. A. (1998). Racial differences in combat-related PTSD: Empirical findings and conceptual issues. *Clinical Psychology Review, 18,* 287–305.

Fujino, D. C., Okazaki, S., & Young, K. (1994). Asian-American women in the mental health system: An examination of ethnic and gender match between therapist and client. *Journal of Community Psychology, 22,* 164–176.

Gamst, G., Dana, R. H., Der Karabetian, A., & Kramer, T. (2001). Asian American mental health clients: Effects of ethnic match and age on global assessment and visitation. *Journal of Mental Health Counseling, 23*, 57–71.

Garfield, S. L. (1994). Research on client variables in psychotherapy. In A. E. Bergin (Ed.), *Handbook of psychotherapy and behavior change* (4th ed., pp. 190–228). Oxford, England: John Wiley & Sons.

Goin, M. K., Yamamoto, J., & Silvervan, J. (1965). Therapy congruent with class-linked expectations. *Archives of General Psychiatry, 13*, 133–137.

Goisman, R. M., Goldenberg, I., Vasile, R. G., & Keller, M. B. (1995). Comorbidity of anxiety disorders in a multicenter anxiety study. *Comprehensive Psychiatry, 36*, 303–311.

Gonzales, L. R., Lewinsohn, P. M., & Clarke, G. N. (1985). Longitudinal follow-up of unipolar depressives: An investigation of predictors of relapse. *Journal of Consulting and Clinical Psychology, 53*, 461–469.

Gould, R. A., Buckminster, S., Pollack, M. H., Otto, M. W., & Yap, L. (1997). Cognitive-behavioral and pharmacological treatment for social phobia: A meta-analysis. *Clinical Psychology: Science and Practice, 4*, 291–306.

Gould, R. A., Otto, M. W., & Pollack, M. H. (1995). A meta-analysis of treatment outcome for panic disorder. *Clinical Psychology Review, 15*, 819–844.

Gould, R. A., Otto, M. W., Pollack, M. H., & Yap, L. (1997). Cognitive behavioral and pharmacological treatment of generalized anxiety disorder: A preliminary meta-analyis. *Behavior Therapy, 28*, 285–305.

Grilo, C. M., Money, R., Barlow, D. H., Goddard, A. W., Gorman, J. M., Hofmann, S. G., Papp, L. A., Shear, M. K., & Woods, S. W. (1998). Pretreatment patient factors predicting attrition from a multicenter randomized controlled treatment study for panic disorder. *Comprehensive Psychiatry, 39*, 323–332.

Haaga, D. A., DeRubeis, R. J., Stewart, B. L., & Beck, A. T. (1991). Relationship of intelligence with cognitive therapy outcome. *Behaviour Research and Therapy, 29*, 277–281.

Hafner, R. J., & Ross, M. W. (1983). Predicting the outcome of behaviour therapy for agoraphobia. *Behaviour Research and Therapy, 21*, 375–382.

Hardy, G. E., Barkham, M., Shapiro, D. A., Reynolds, S., Rees, A., & Stiles, W. B. (1995). Credibility and outcome of cognitive-behavioural and psychodynamic-interpersonal therapy. *British Journal of Clinical Psychology, 34*, 555–569.

Hawkins, R. S., Tan, S. Y., & Turk, A. A. (1999). Secular versus Christian inpatient cognitive-behavioral therapy programs: Impact on depression and spiritual well-being. *Journal of Psychology and Theology, 27*, 309–318.

Heimberg, R. G., Dodge, C. S., Hope, D. A., Kennedy, C. R., & Zollo, L. J. (1990). Cognitive behavioral group treatment for social phobia: Comparison with a credible placebo control. *Cognitive Therapy and Research, 14*, 1–23.

Heimberg, R. G., Liebowitz, M. R., Hope, D. A., Schneier, F. R., Holt, C. S., Welkowitz, L. A., Juster, H. R., Campeas, R., Bruch, M. A., Cloitre, M., Fallon, B., & Klein, D. F. (1998). Cognitive behavioral group therapy vs phenelzine therapy for social phobia: 12-week outcome. *Archives of General Psychiatry, 55*, 1133–1141.

Hemme, R. W., & Boor, M. (1976). Role of expectancy set in the systematic desensitization of speech anxiety: An extension of prior research. *Journal of Clinical Psychology, 32*, 400–404.

Hirsch, C., Jolley, S., & Williams, R. (2000). A study of outcome in a clinical psychology service and preliminary evaluation of cognitive-behavioural therapy in real practice. *Journal of Mental Health UK, 9*, 537–549.

Hoffart, A. (1997). Interpersonal problems among patients suffering from panic disorder with agoraphobia before and after treatment. *British Journal of Medical Psychology, 70*, 149–157.

Hoffart, A., & Martinsen, E. W. (1993). The effect of personality disorders and anxious-depressive comorbidity on outcome in patients with unipolar depression and with panic disorder and agoraphobia. *Journal of Personality Disorders, 7*, 304–311.

Hofmann, S. G., & Barlow, D. H. (1996). Ambulatory psychophysiological monitoring: A potentially useful tool when treating panic relapse. *Cognitive and Behavioral Practice, 3*, 53–61.

Hofmann, S. G., Newman, M. G., Becker, E., Taylor, C. B., & Roth, W. T. (1995). Social phobia with and without avoidant personality disorder: Preliminary behavior therapy outcome findings. *Journal of Anxiety Disorders, 9*, 427–438.

Hoogduin, C. A., & Duivenvoorden, H. J. (1988). A decision model in the treatment of obsessive-compulsive neuroses. *British Journal of Psychiatry, 152*, 516–521.

Hope, D. A., Herbert, J. D., & White, C. (1995). Diagnostic subtype, avoidant personality disorder, and efficacy of cognitive-behavioral group therapy for social phobia. *Cognitive Therapy and Research, 19*, 399–417.

Horowitz, L. M., Rosenberg, S. E., & Bartholomew, K. (1993). Interpersonal problems, attachment styles, and outcome in brief dynamic psychotherapy. *Journal of Consulting and Clinical Psychology, 61*, 549–560.

Huppert, J. D., Bufka, L. F., Barlow, D. H., Gorman, J. M., Shear, M. K., & Woods, S. W. (2001). Therapists, therapist variables, and cognitive-behavioral therapy outcome in a multicenter trial for panic disorder. *Journal of Consulting and Clinical Psychology, 69*, 747–755.

Hyer, L., Boudewyns, P., Harrison, W. R., O'Leary, W. C., Bruno, R. D., Saucer, R. T., & Blount, J. B. (1988). Vietnam veterans: Overreporting versus acceptable reporting of symptoms. *Journal of Personality Assessment, 52*, 475–486.

Hyer, L., Stanger, E., & Boudewyns, P. (1999). The interaction of posttraumatic stress disorder and depression among older combat veterans. *Journal of Clinical Psychology, 55*, 1073–1083.

Jansson, L., Öst, L. G., & Jerremalm, A. (1987). Prognostic factors in the behavioral treatment of agoraphobia. *Behavioural Psychotherapy, 15*, 31–44.

Jaycox, L. H., Foa, E. B., & Morral, A. R. (1998). Influence of emotional engagement and habituation on exposure therapy for PTSD. *Journal of Consulting and Clinical Psychology, 66*, 185–192.

Jenike, M. A. (1990). Approaches to the patient with treatment-refractory obsessive compulsive disorder. *Journal of Clinical Psychiatry, 51*, 15–21.

Johnson, D. R., & Lubin, H. (1997). Treatment preferences of Vietnam veterans with posttraumatic stress disorder. *Journal of Traumatic Stress, 10*, 391–405.

Johnson, D. R., Lubin, H., & Corn, B. (1999). Course of treatment during a cohort-based inpatient program for posttraumatic stress disorder. *Group, 23*, 19–35.

Johnson, D. R., Rosenheck, R., Fontana, A., Lubin, H., Southwick, S., & Charney, D. S. (1996). Outcome of intensive inpatient treatment for combat-related posttraumatic stress disorder. *American Journal of Psychiatry, 153*, 771–777.

Johnson, W. B., Devries, R., Ridley, C. R., Pettorini, D., & Peterson, D. R. (1994). The comparative efficacy of Christian and secular rational-emotive therapy with Christian clients. *Journal of Psychology and Theology, 22*, 130–140.

Jones, E. E. (1978). Effects of race on psychotherapy process and outcome: An exploratory investigation. *Psychotherapy: Theory, Research and Practice, 15*, 226–236.

Jones, E. E. (1982). Psychotherapists' impressions of treatment outcome as a function of race. *Journal of Clinical Psychology, 38*, 722–731.

Joyce, A. S., Ogrodniczuk, J. S., Piper, W. E., & McCallum, M. (2000). *Patient characteristics and mid-treatment outcome in two forms of short-term individual psychotherapy.* Paper presented at the 31st annual meeting of the Society for Psychotherapy Research, Chicago, IL.

Juster, H. R., Heimberg, R. G., Frost, R. O., & Holt, C. S. (1996). Social phobia and perfectionism. *Personality and Individual Differences, 21*, 403–410.

Kazdin, A. E., & Wilcoxon, L. A. (1976). Systematic desensitization and nonspecific treatment effects: A methodological evaluation. *Psychological Bulletin, 83*, 729–758.

Keijsers, G. P. J., Hoogduin, C. A. L., & Schaap, C. P. D. R. (1994a). Predictors of treatment outcome in the behavioural treatment of obsessive-compulsive disorder. *British Journal of Psychiatry, 165*, 781–786.

Keijsers, G. P. J., Hoogduin, C. A. L., & Schaap, C. P. D. R. (1994b). Prognostic factors in the behavioral treatment of panic disorder with and without agoraphobia. *Behavior Therapy, 25*, 689–708.

Keijsers, G. P. J., Kampman, M., & Hoogduin, C. A. L. (2001). Dropout prediction in cognitive behavior therapy for panic disorder. *Behavior Therapy, 32*, 739–749.

Kelly, T. A., & Strupp, H. H. (1992). Patient and therapist values in psychotherapy: Perceived changes, assimilation, similarity, and outcome. *Journal of Consulting and Clinical Psychology, 60*, 34–40.

Kessler, R. C., Sonnega, A., Bromet, E., Hughes, M., & Nelson, C. B. (1995). Posttraumatic stress disorder in the National Comorbidity Survey. *Archives of General Psychiatry, 52*, 1048–1060.

Kirsch, I. (1990). *Changing expectations: A key to effective psychotherapy.* Belmont, CA: Brooks/Cole Publishing Co.

Kirshner, L. A. (1978). Effects of gender on psychotherapy. *Comprehensive Psychiatry, 19*, 79–82.

Koegler, R. R., & Brill, N. Q. (1967). *Treatment of Psychiatric Outpatients.* East Norwalk, CT: Appleton-Century-Crofts.

Koraleski, S. F., & Larson, L. M. (1997). A partial test of the transtheoretical model in therapy with adult survivors of childhood sexual abuse. *Journal of Counseling Psychology, 44,* 302–306.

Korobkin, S. B., Herron, W. G., & Ramirez, S. M. (1998). Severity of symptoms of depression and anxiety as predictors of duration of psychotherapy. *Psychological Reports, 82,* 427–433.

Kosten, T. R., Krystal, J. H., Giller, E. L., Frank, J., & Dan, E. (1992). Alexithymia as a predictor of treatment response in post-traumatic stress disorder. *Journal of Traumatic Stress, 5,* 563–573.

Ladouceur, R., Dugas, M. J., Freeston, M. H., Leger, E., Gagnon, F., & Thibodeau, N. (2000). Efficacy of a cognitive-behavioral treatment for generalized anxiety disorder: Evaluation in a controlled clinical trial. *Journal of Consulting and Clinical Psychology, 68,* 957–964.

Lau, A., & Zane, N. (2000). Examining the effects of ethnic-specific services: An analysis of cost-utilization and treatment outcome for Asian American clients. *Journal of Community Psychology, 28,* 63–77.

Lax, T., Basoglu, M., & Marks, I. M. (1992). Expectancy and compliance as predictors of outcome in obsessive-compulsive disorder. *Behavioural Psychotherapy, 20,* 257–266.

Lelliott, P. T., Marks, I. M., Monteiro, W. O., Tsakiris, F., & Noshirvani, H. (1987). Agoraphobics 5 years after imipramine and exposure: Outcome and predictors. *Journal of Nervous and Mental Disease, 175,* 599–605.

Lerner, B. (1972). *Therapy in the ghetto: Political impotence and personal disintegration.* Baltimore, MD: Johns Hopkins University Press.

Leung, A. W., & Heimberg, R. G. (1996). Homework compliance, perceptions of control, and outcome of cognitive-behavioral treatment of social phobia. *Behaviour Research and Therapy, 34,* 423–432.

Levin, J. B., Hermesh, H., & Marom, S. (2001). Social phobia subtyping with the MMPI-2. *Journal of Clinical Psychology, 57,* 1489–1502.

Lewis, C. E., Biglan, A., & Steinbock, E. (1978). Self-administered relaxation training and money deposits in the treatment of recurrent anxiety. *Journal of Consulting and Clinical Psychology, 46,* 1274–1283.

Livanou, M., Basoglu, M., Marks, I. M., De Silva, P., Noshirvani, H., Lovell, K., & Thrasher, S. (2002). Beliefs, sense of control and treatment outcome in post-traumatic stress disorder. *Psychological Medicine, 32,* 157–165.

Lorion, R. P. (1973). Socioeconomic status and traditional treatment approaches reconsidered. *Psychological Bulletin, 79,* 263–270.

Lorion, R. P., & Fellner, R. D. (1986). Research on psychotherapy with the disadvantaged. In S. L. Garfield & A. E. Bergin (Eds.), *Handbook of psychotherapy and behavior change* (3rd ed., pp. 739–776). New York: Wiley.

Luborsky, L., Chandler, M., Auerbach, A. H., Cohen, J., & Bachrach, J. M. (1971). Factors influencing the outcome of psychotherapy: A review of quantitative research. *Psychological Bulletin, 75,* 145–185.

Marks, I., Lovell, K., Noshirvani, H., Livanou, M., & Thrasher, S. (1998). Treatment of posttraumatic stress disorder by exposure and/or cognitive restructuring: A controlled study. *Archives of General Psychiatry, 55,* 317–325.

Marks, I. M., Hodgson, R., & Rachman, S. (1975). Treatment of chronic obsessive-compulsive neurosis by in-vivo exposure: A two-year follow-up and issues in treatment. *British Journal of Psychiatry, 127,* 349–364.

Martinsen, E. W., Olsen, T., Tonset, E., Nyland, K. E., & Aarre, T. F. (1998). Cognitive-behavioral group therapy for panic disorder in the general clinical setting: a naturalistic study with 1-year follow-up. *Journal of Clinical Psychiatry, 59,* 437–442.

Massion, A. O., Dyck, I. R., Shea, M. T., Phillips, K. A., Warshaw, M. G., & Keller, M. B. (2002). Personality disorders and time to remission in generalized anxiety disorder, social phobia and panic disorder. *Archives of General Psychiatry, 59,* 434–440.

Mataix-Cols, D., Marks, I. M., Greist, J. H., Kobak, K. A., & Baer, L. (2002). Obsessive compulsive symptom dimensions as predictors of compliance with and response to behaviour therapy: Results from a controlled trial. *Psychotherapy and Psychosomatics, 71,* 255–262.

Mawson, D., Marks, I. M., & Ramm, F. (1982). Clomipramine and exposure for chronic obsessive-compulsive rituals: III. Two year follow-up and further findings. *British Journal of Psychiatry, 140,* 584–592.

McCranie, E. W., Hyer, L. A., Boudewyns, P. A., & Woods, M. G. (1992). Negative parenting behavior, combat exposure, and PTSD symptom severity: Test of a person–event interaction model. *Journal of Nervous and Mental Disease, 180,* 431–438.

McCullough, M. E. (1999). Research on religion-accommodative counseling: Review and meta-analysis. *Journal of Counseling Psychology, 46,* 92–98.

McLean, P. D., Woody, S., Taylor, S., & Koch, W. J. (1998). Comorbid panic disorder and major depression: Implications for cognitive-behavioral therapy. *Journal of Consulting and Clinical Psychology, 66,* 240–247.

Mennin, D. S., Heimberg, R. G., & Jack, M. S. (2000). Comorbid generalized anxiety disorder in primary social phobia: Symptom severity, functional impairment, and treatment response. *Journal of Anxiety Disorders, 14,* 325–343.

Mersch, P. P. A., Emmelkamp, P. M. G., & Lips, C. (1991). Social phobia: Individual response patterns and the long-term effects of behavioral and cognitive interventions. A follow-up. *Behaviour Research and Therapy, 29,* 357–362.

Meyer, B., & Pilkonis, P. A. (2002). Attachment style. In J. C. Norcross (Ed.), *Psychotherapy relationships that work: Therapist contributions and responsiveness to patients* (pp. 367–382). London: Oxford University Press.

Meyer, B., Pilkonis, P. A., Proietti, J. M., Heape, C. L., & Egan, M. (2001). Attachment styles and personality disorders as predictors of symptom course. *Journal of Personality Disorders, 15,* 371–389.

Michelson, L. K., Bellanti, C. J., Testa, S. M., & Marchione, N. (1997). The relationship of attributional style to agoraphobia severity, depression, and treatment outcome. *Behaviour Research and Therapy, 35,* 1061–1073.

Minichiello, W. E., Baer, L., & Jenike, M. A. (1987). Schizotypal Personality Disorder: A poor prognostic indicator for behavior therapy in the treatment of Obsessive Compulsive Disorder. *Journal of Anxiety Disorders, 1,* 273–276.

Mintz, J., Luborsky, L., & Auerbach, A. H. (1971). Dimensions of psychotherapy: A factor-analytic study of ratings of psychotherapy sessions. *Journal of Consulting and Clinical Psychology, 36,* 106–120.

Moras, K., & Strupp, H. H. (1982). Pretherapy interpersonal relations, patients' alliance, and outcome in brief therapy. *Archives of General Psychiatry, 39,* 405–409.

Mosheim, R., Zachhuber, U., Scharf, L., Hofmann, A., Kemmler, G., Danzl, C., Kinze, J., Biebl, W., & Richter, R. (2000). Quality of attachment and interpersonal problems as possible predictors of inpatient therapy outcome. *Psychotherapeutics, 45,* 223–229.

Munley, P. H., Bains, D. S., Frazee, J., & Schwartz, L. T. (1994). Inpatient PTSD treatment: A study of pre-treatment measures, treatment dropout, and therapists ratings of response to treatment. *Journal of Traumatic Stress, 7,* 319–325.

Newman, M. G. (2000). Recommendations for a cost-offset model of psychotherapy allocation using generalized anxiety disorder as an example. *Journal of Consulting and Clinical Psychology, 68,* 549–555.

Neziroglu, F., Stevens, K. P., McKay, D., Yaryura, T., & Jose, A. (2001). Predictive validity of the Overvalued Ideals Scale: Outcome in obsessive-compulsive and body dysmorphic disorders. *Behaviour Research and Therapy, 39,* 745–756.

Neziroglu, F. A., Stevens, K. P., Yaryura, T., & Jose, A. (1999). Overvalued ideas and their impact on treatment outcome. *Revista Brasileira de Psiquiatria, 21,* 209–216.

Noyes, R. (2001). Comorbidity in generalized anxiety disorder. *Psychiatric Clinics of North America, 24,* 41–55.

Oldham, J. M., Skodol, A. E., Kellman, H. D., Hyler, S. E., Doidge, N., Rosnick, L., & Gallaher, P. E. (1995). Comorbidity of axis I and axis II disorders. *American Journal of Psychiatry, 152,* 571–578.

Organista, K. C., Munoz, R. F., & Gonzalez, G. (1994). Cognitive behavioral therapy for depression in low-income and minority medical outpatients: Description of a program and exploratory analyses. *Cognitive Therapy and Research, 18,* 241–259.

Orlinsky, D. E., Grawe, K., & Parks, B. K. (1994). Process and outcome in psychotherapy: Noch einmal. In S. L. Garfield & A. E. Bergin (Eds.), *Handbook of psychotherapy and behavior change* (4th ed., pp. 270–376). Oxford, England: John Wiley & Sons.

O'Sullivan, G., Noshirvani, H., Marks, I., Monteiro, W., & Lelliott, P. (1991). Six-year follow-up after exposure and clomipramine therapy for obsessive compulsive disorder. *Journal of Clinical Psychiatry, 52,* 150–155.

Otto, M. W., Penava, S. J., Pollack, R. A., & Smoller, J. W. (1996). Cognitive-behavioral and pharmacologic perspectives on the treatment of posttraumatic stress disorder. In M. H. Pollack, M. W. Otto, & J. F. Rosenbaum (Eds.), *Challenges in clinical practice: Pharmacologic and psychosocial strategies* (pp. 219–260). New York: Guilford Press.

Otto, M. W., Pollack, M. H., Gould, R. A., Worthington, J. J., III, McArdle, E. T., Rosenbaum, J. F., & Heimberg, R. G. (2000). A comparison of the efficacy of clonazepam and cognitive-behavioral group therapy for the treatment of social phobia. *Journal of Anxiety Disorders, 14*, 345–358.

Pecheur, D. R., & Edwards, K. J. (1984). A comparison of secular and religious versions of cognitive therapy with depressed Christian college students. *Journal of Psychology & Theology, 12*, 45–54.

Pekarik, G. (1991). Relationship of expected and actual treatment duration for adult and child clients. *Journal of Clinical Child Psychology, 20*, 121–125.

Pekarik, G., & Wierzbicki, M. (1986). The relationship between clients' expected and actual treatment duration. *Psychotherapy: Theory, Research, Practice, Training, 23*, 532–534.

Perconte, S. T., & Griger, M. L. (1991). Comparison of successful, unsuccessful, and relapsed Vietnam veterans treated for posttraumatic stress disorder. *Journal of Nervous and Mental Disease, 179*, 558–562.

Peterson, K. C., Prout, M. F., & Schwarz, R. A. (1991). *Post-traumatic stress disorder: A clinician's guide*. New York: Plenum Press.

Pitman, R. K., Altman, B., Greenwald, E., Longpre, R. E., Macklin, M. L., Poire, R. E., & Steketee, G. S. (1991). Psychiatric complications during flooding therapy for posttraumatic stress disorder. *Journal of Clinical Psychiatry, 52*, 17–20.

Prochaska, J. O., & Norcross, J. C. (2002). Stages of Change. In J. C. Norcross (Ed.), *Psychotherapy relationships that work: Therapist contributions and responsiveness to patients* (pp. 303–313). London: Oxford University Press.

Project MATCH Research Group. (1997). Matching alcoholism treatments to client heterogeneity: Project MATCH Posttreatment drinking outcomes. *Journal of Studies on Alcohol, 58*, 7–29.

Propst, L. R. (1980). The comparative efficacy of religious and nonreligious imagery for the treatment of mild depression in religious individuals. *Cognitive Therapy and Research, 4*, 167–178.

Propst, L. R., Ostrom, R., Watkins, P., Dean, T., & Mashburn, D. (1992). Comparative efficacy of religious and nonreligious cognitive-behavioral therapy for the treatment of clinical depression in religious individuals. *Journal of Consulting and Clinical Psychology, 60*, 94–103.

Query, J. N. (1985). Comparative admission and follow-up study of American Indians and

Whites in a youth chemical dependency unit on the north central plains. *International Journal of the Addictions, 20*, 489–502.

Rachman, S., Marks, I. M., & Hodgson, R. (1973). The treatment of obsessive-compulsive neurotics by modelling and flooding in vivo. *Behaviour Research and Therapy, 11*, 463–471.

Reich, J., Goldenberg, I., Goisman, R., Vasile, R., & Keller, M. B. (1994). A prospective follow-along study of the course of social phobia: II. Testing for basic predictors of course. *Journal of Nervous and Mental Disease, 182*, 297–301.

Reid, J. C., Nair, S. S., Mistry, S. I., & Beitman, B. D. (1996). Effectiveness of stages of change and adinazolam SR in panic disorder: A neural network analysis. *Journal of Anxiety Disorders, 10*, 331–345.

Reis, B. F., & Brown, L. G. (1999). Reducing psychotherapy dropouts: Maximizing perspective convergence in the psychotherapy dyad. *Psychotherapy: Theory, Research, Practice, Training, 36*, 123–136.

Riggs, D. S., Byrne, C. A., Weathers, F. W., & Litz, B. T. (1998). The quality of the intimate relationships of male Vietnam veterans: Problems associated with posttraumatic stress disorder. *Journal of Traumatic Stress, 11*, 87–101.

Riggs, D. S., Hiss, H., & Foa, E. B. (1992). Marital distress and the treatment of obsessive compulsive disorder. *Behavior Therapy, 23*, 585–597.

Roberts, R. E., Kaplan, G. A., Shema, S. J., & Strawbridge, W. J. (1997). Does growing old increase the risk for depression? *American Journal of Psychiatry, 154*, 1384–1390.

Rosenheck, R., & Fontana, A. (1996). Race and outcome of treatment for veterans suffering from PTSD. *Journal of Traumatic Stress, 9*, 343–351.

Rosenheck, R., & Fontana, A. (2002). Black and Hispanic veterans in intensive VA treatment programs for posttraumatic stress disorder. *Medical Care, 40*, 152–61.

Rosenheck, R., Fontana, A., & Cottrol, C. (1995). Effect of clinician veteran racial pairing in the treatment of posttraumatic stress disorder. *American Journal of Psychiatry, 152*, 555–563.

Rosenthal, D., & Frank, J. D. (1956). Psychotherapy and the placebo effect. *Psychological Bulletin, 53*, 294–302.

Saboonchi, F., Lundh, L. G., & Öst, L. G. (1999). Perfectionism and self-consciousness in social phobia and panic disorder with agoraphobia. *Behaviour Research and Therapy, 37*, 799–808.

Safran, J. D., Alden, L. E., & Davidson, P. O.

(1980). Client anxiety level as a moderator variable in assertion training. *Cognitive Therapy and Research, 4,* 189–200.

Safren, S. A., Heimberg, R. G., & Juster, H. R. (1997). Clients' expectancies and their relationship to pretreatment symptomatology and outcome of cognitive-behavioral group treatment for social phobia. *Journal of Consulting and Clinical Psychology, 65,* 694–698.

Sanderson, W. C., Beck, A. T., & McGinn, L. K. (1994). Cognitive therapy for generalized anxiety disorder: Significance of comorbid personality disorders. *Journal of Cognitive Psychotherapy, 8,* 13–18.

Satterfield, J. M. (1998). Cognitive behavioral group therapy for depressed, low-income minority clients: Retention and treatment enhancement. *Cognitive and Behavioral Practice, 5,* 65–80.

Scheibe, G., & Albus, M. (1996). Predictors of outcome in panic disorder: A 5-year prospective follow-up study. *Journal of Affective Disorders, 41,* 111–116.

Schmidt, N. B., & Telch, M. J. (1997). Nonpsychiatric medical comorbidity, health perceptions, and treatment outcome in patients with panic disorder. *Health Psychology, 16,* 114–122.

Scholing, A., & Emmelkamp, P. M. G. (1999). Prediction of treatment outcome in social phobia: A cross-validation. *Behaviour Research and Therapy, 37,* 659–670.

Seivewright, H., Tyrer, P., & Johnson, T. (1998). Prediction of outcome in neurotic disorder: A 5-year prospective study. *Psychological Medicine, 28,* 1149–1157.

Shapiro, D. A., & Shapiro, D. (1982). Meta-analysis of comparative therapy outcome studies: A replication and refinement. *Psychological Bulletin, 92,* 581–604.

Sharp, D. M., & Power, K. G. (1999). Predicting treatment outcome for panic disorder and agoraphobia in primary care. *Clinical Psychology and Psychotherapy, 6,* 336–348.

Shinoda, N., Kodama, K., Sakamoto, T., Yamanouchi, N., Takahashi, T., Okada, S., Noda, S., Komatsu, N., & Sato, T. (1999). Predictors of 1-year outcome for patients with panic disorder. *Comprehensive Psychiatry, 40,* 39–43.

Stein, D. J. (2001). Comorbidity in generalized anxiety disorder: Impact and implications. *Journal of Clinical Psychiatry, 62,* 29–34.

Stein, D. J., Stein, M. B., Pitts, C. D., Kumar, R., & Hunter, B. (2002). Predictors of response to pharmacotherapy in social anxiety disorder: An analysis of 3 placebo-controlled paroxetine trials. *Journal of Clinical Psychiatry, 63,* 152–155.

Steketee, G. (1993). Social support and treatment outcome of obsessive compulsive disorder at 9-month follow-up. *Behavioural Psychotherapy, 21,* 81–95.

Steketee, G., Chambless, D. L., & Tran, G. Q. (2001). Effects of axis I and II comorbidity on behavior therapy outcome for obsessive-compulsive disorder and agoraphobia. *Comprehensive Psychiatry, 42,* 76–86.

Steketee, G., Eisen, J., Dyck, I., Warshaw, M., & Rasmussen, S. (1999). Predictors of course in obsessive-compulsive disorder. *Psychiatry Research, 89,* 229–238.

Steketee, G., & Shapiro, L. J. (1995). Predicting behavioral treatment outcome for agoraphobia and obsessive compulsive disorder. *Clinical Psychology Review, 15,* 317–346.

Stiles, W. B. (2002). Assimilation of problematic experiences. In J. C. Norcross (Ed.), *Psychotherapy relationships that work: Therapist contributions and responsiveness to patients* (pp. 357–365). London: Oxford University Press.

Stiles, W. B., Morrison, L. A., Haw, S. K., Harper, H., Shapiro, D. A., & Firth-Cozens, J. (1991). Longitudinal study of assimilation in exploratory psychotherapy. *Psychotherapy: Theory, Research, Practice, Training, 28,* 195–206.

Stiles, W. B., Shankland, M. C., Wright, J., & Field, S. D. (1997). Aptitude-treatment interactions based on clients' assimilation of their presenting problems. *Journal of Consulting and Clinical Psychology, 65,* 889–893.

Stone, J. L., & Crowthers, V. (1972). Innovations in program and funding of mental health services for blue-collar families. *American Journal of Psychiatry, 128,* 1375–1380.

Sue, S., Fujino, D. C., Hu, L.-T., Takeuchi, D. T., & Zane, N. W. S. (1991). Community mental health services for ethnic minority groups: A test of the cultural responsiveness hypothesis. *Journal of Consulting and Clinical Psychology, 59,* 533–540.

Sue, S., & Lam, A. G. (2002). Cultural and demographic diversity. In J. C. Norcross (Ed.), *Psychotherapy relationships that work: Therapist contributions and responsiveness to patients* (pp. 401–421). London: Oxford University Press.

Takeuchi, D. T., Sue, S., & Yeh, M. (1995). Return rates and outcomes from ethnicity-specific mental health programs in Los Angeles. *American Journal of Public Health, 85,* 638–643.

Tarrier, N., Sommerfield, C., & Pilgrim, H. (1999). Relatives' expressed emotion (EE) and PTSD treatment outcome. *Psychological Medicine, 29,* 801–811.

Tarrier, N., Sommerfield, C., Pilgrim, H., & Faragher, B. (2000). Factors associated with outcome of cognitive-behavioural treatment of chronic post-traumatic stress disorder. *Behaviour Research and Therapy, 38,* 191–202.

Taylor, S., Fedoroff, I. C., & Koch, W. J. (1999). Posttraumatic stress disorder due to motor vehicle accidents: Patterns and predictors of response to cognitive-behavior therapy. In E. B. Blanchard & E. J. Hickling (Eds.), *The international handbook of road traffic accidents and psychological trauma: Current understanding, treatment and law* (pp. 353–374). New York: Elsevier Science.

Taylor, S., Fedoroff, I. C., Koch, W. J., Thordarson, D. S., Fecteau, G., & Nicki, R. M. (2001). Posttraumatic stress disorder arising after road traffic collisions: Patterns of response to cognitive-behavior therapy. *Journal of Consulting and Clinical Psychology, 69,* 541–551.

Turner, R. M. (1987). The effects of personality disorder diagnosis on the outcome of social anxiety symptom reduction. *Journal of Personality Disorders, 1,* 136–143.

Turner, S. M., Beidel, D. C., & Townsley, R. M. (1992). Social phobia: A comparison of specific and generalized subtypes and avoidant personality disorder. *Journal of Abnormal Psychology, 101,* 326–331.

Turner, S. M., Beidel, D. C., Wolff, P. L., & Spaulding, S. (1996). Clinical features affecting treatment outcome in social phobia. *Behaviour Research and Therapy, 34,* 795–804.

Tyrer, P., Seivewright, H., Simmonds, S., & Johnson, T. (2001). Prospective studies of cothymia (mixed anxiety-depression): How do they inform clinical practice? *European Archives of Psychiatry and Clinical Neuroscience, 251*(Suppl. 2), 53–56.

Tyrer, P., Seivewright, N., Ferguson, B., Murphy, S., & Johnson, A. L. (1993). The Nottingham Study of Neurotic Disorder: Effect of personality status on response to drug treatment, cognitive therapy and self-help over two years. *British Journal of Psychiatry, 162,* 219–226.

Vail, A. (1978). Factors influencing lower-class Black patients remaining in treatment. *Journal of Consulting and Clinical Psychology, 46,* 341.

Van Dam-Baggen, R., & Kraaimaat, F. (1986). A group social skills training program with psychiatric patients: Outcome, drop-out rate and prediction. *Behaviour Research and Therapy, 24,* 161–169.

van den Brink, R. H. S., Ormel, J., Tiemens, B. G., Smit, A., Jenner, J. A., van der Meer, K., & van Os, T. W. D. P. (2002). Predictability of the one-year course of depression and generalized anxiety in primary care. *General Hospital Psychiatry, 24,* 156–163.

van Minnen, ˙A., Arntz, A., & Keijsers, G. P. J. (2002). Prolonged exposure in patients with chronic PTSD: Predictors of treatment outcome and dropout. *Behaviour Research and Therapy, 40,* 439–457.

van Velzen, C. J. M., Emmelkamp, P. M. G., & Scholing, A. (2000). Generalized social phobia versus avoidant personality disorder: Differences in psychopathology, personality traits, and social and occupational functioning. *Journal of Anxiety Disorders, 14,* 395–411.

Vogel, P. A., Stiles, T. C., & Nordahl, H. M. (2000). Cognitive personality styles in OCD outpatients compared to depressed outpatients and healthy controls. *Behavioural and Cognitive Psychotherapy, 28,* 247–258.

Wierzbicki, M., & Pekarik, G. (1993). A meta-analysis of psychotherapy dropout. *Professional Psychology: Research and Practice, 24,* 190–195.

Wilson, M., Bell Dolan, D., & Beitman, B. (1997). Application of the Stages of Change Scale in a clinical drug trial. *Journal of Anxiety Disorders, 11,* 395–408.

Wittchen, H. U., Zhao, S., Kessler, R. C., & Eaton, W. W. (1994). DSM-III—R generalized anxiety disorder in the National Comorbidity Survey. *Archives of General Psychiatry, 51,* 355–364.

Woy, J. R., & Efran, J. S. (1972). Systematic desensitization and expectancy in the treatment of speaking anxiety. *Behaviour Research and Therapy, 10*(1), 43–49.

Yonkers, K. A., Dyck, I. R., Warshaw, M., & Keller, M. B. (2000). Factors predicting the clinical course of generalised anxiety disorder. *British Journal of Psychiatry, 176,* 544–549.

Zlotnick, C., Elkin, I., & Shea, M. T. (1998). Does the gender of a patient or the gender of a therapist affect the treatment of patients with major depression? *Journal of Consulting and Clinical Psychology, 66,* 655–659.

Zlotnick, C., Shea, M. T., Pilkonis, P. A., Elkin, I., & Ryan, C. (1996). Gender, type of treatment, dysfunctional attitudes, social support, life events, and depressive symptoms over naturalistic follow-up. *American Journal of Psychiatry, 153,* 1021–1027.

Zlotnick, C., Warshaw, M., Shea, M. T., Allsworth, J., Pearlstein, T., & Keller, M. B. (1999). Chronicity in posttraumatic stress disorder (PTSD) and predictors of course of comorbid PTSD in patients with anxiety disorders. *Journal of Traumatic Stress, 12,* 89–100.

7

Relationship Factors in Treating Anxiety Disorders

William B. Stiles

Barry E. Wolfe

INTRODUCTION: A SHORTAGE OF SPECIFICALLY TARGETED RESEARCH

Most research on the therapist–client relationship in psychotherapy has not distinguished conceptually among diagnostic categories. Researchers have not seemed to presume—or even to consider—that distinct sorts of relationships might be differentially effective as a function of the client's presenting diagnosis. Many studies focusing on relationship variables have involved mixed or unspecified diagnoses. Others have been conducted in the context of clinical trials in which a diagnosis was specified (most commonly depression; e.g., Krupnick, Sotsky, Simmens, Moyer, Elkin, Watkins, & Pilkonis, 1996; Stiles, Agnew-Davies, Hardy, Barkham, & Shapiro, 1998), but even these have appeared to be samples of convenience rather than chosen expressly for studying the relationship.

Conversely, most of the research that has fo-cused on anxiety disorders has been treatment outcome research rather than process research (see Newman, Crits-Christoph, Gibbons, & Erickson, this volume; Woody & Ollendick, this volume). Anxiety disorders lend themselves to relatively distinct measurement of symptom intensity; phobias can be assessed by closeness of approach to the feared situation, panic attacks can be counted, and so forth. Most of this research has been conducted by investigators associated with cognitive or behavioral approaches, who have not emphasized the therapist–client relationship in their theory or research designs. Reflecting the relative levels of research activity, most of the treatments for anxiety disorders that have achieved "efficacious" or "probably efficacious" status in the list of empirically supported treatments identified by the Division 12 Task Force on Empirically Supported Treatments (EST Task Force) were cognitive and behavioral (Nathan & Gorman, 2002), though many clients presenting with anxiety disorders in clinics and private practices are undoubtedly treated using other approaches. Fortunately for present purposes, such evidence as there is suggests the therapist–client relationship is as important in cognitive and behavioral treatments as in other treatments (Krupnick et al., 1996; Raue & Goldfried, 1994; Stiles et al., 1998). Further, the first conclusion of the Division 29 Task Force on Empirically Supported Therapy Relationships (ESR Task Force) was that "the therapy relationship . . . makes substantial and consistent contributions to psychotherapy outcome independent of the specific type of treatment" (Steering Committee, 2001, p. 495).

Within this pattern of research effort, then, relatively few research reports have specifically targeted relationship factors in the treatment of anxiety disorders. In order to address this topic in this chapter for the Division 12 Task Force on Empirically Supported Principles of Therapeutic Change (ESP Task Force), we must assume, in the absence of compelling contrary evidence and in concert with most other relationship researchers, that relationship factors important in psychotherapy generally are important in the treatment of anxiety disorders in particular. Such evidence as there is, often reported in the context of outcome studies, tends to support this conclusion (Abramowitz, Franklin, Zoellner, & DiBernardo, 2002; Bennun & Schindler, 1988; Constantino, Castonguay, & Schut, 2002; de Araujo, Ito, & Marks, 1996; de Beurs, Lange, van Dyck, & Koele, 1995; Edelman & Chambless, 1995; Hoelscher, Lichstein, & Rosenthal, 1984; Hoffart, Versland, & Sexton, 2002; Hoogduin, de Haan, & Schaap, 1989; Keijsers, Schaap, Hoogduin, & Peters, 1991; Keijsers, Schaap, Hoogduin, & Lammers, 1995; Leung & Heimberg, 1996; Mathews, Johnston, Lancashire, Munby, Shaw, & Gelder, 1976; Michelson, Mavissakalian, Marchione, Dancu, & Greenwald, 1986; Morris & Suckerman, 1974a, 1974b; Park et al., 2001; Rabavilas, Boulougouris, & Perissaki, 1979; Schaap & Hoogduin, 1988; Schmidt & Woolaway-Bickel, 2000; Williams & Chambless, 1990). We know of no directly contradictory findings; however, some studies have failed to find significant relations (Foa, Riggs, Massie, & Yarczower, 1995; Foa, Rothbaum, Riggs, & Murdock, 1991; Gustavson, Jansson, Jerremalm, & Oest, 1985; Keijsers, Hoogduin, & Schaap, 1994; Lax, Basoglu, &

Marks, 1992; Morris & Magrath, 1979; Przeworski, Newman, Castonguay, & Constantino, 2001; Taylor, Fedoroff, Koch, Thordarson, Fecteau, & Nicki, 2001; Woods, Chambless, & Steketee, 2002; Woody & Adessky, 2002). For example, Woody and Adessky (2002) reported that a strong therapeutic alliance and group cohesion were not associated with favorable outcomes in a cognitive-behavioral group treatment of anxiety disordered clients. There is also evidence that, as in many other diagnostic groups, anxiety disordered clients' interpersonal relationships are problematic (e.g., Carter, Turovsky, & Barlow, 1994), so that achieving a positive relationship in the microcosm of therapy may signal or contribute to positive therapeutic results.

The paucity of research specifically targeting the relationship in the treatment of anxiety disorders is even worse when it comes to differentiating among different anxiety disorders. In the DSM-IV (American Psychiatric Association, 1994), *anxiety disorders* is a collection of half a dozen different diagnostic entities (panic disorder; obsessive-compulsive disorder; post-traumatic stress disorder; social phobia; specific phobias; and generalized anxiety disorder). Any logic suggesting that treating anxiety disorders might involve distinctive sorts of relationship–outcome links should also suggest that the half dozen subcategories might each involve distinctive links. For example, in principle, different sorts of relationships might be required to treat GAD effectively than to treat phobias. Again (fortunately for our purposes), we know of no evidence indicating that this is the case.

In the next section, we review the conclusions of the Task Force on ESRs (Steering Committee, 2001, 2002) as they may apply in the treatment of anxiety disorders. In subsequent sections, we comment on some conceptual issues that arise in trying to assess how the therapist–client relationship might contribute to psychotherapy outcome and we speculate about relationship factors that might be important in these disorders on the grounds of theory or clinical lore.

PRINCIPLES FOR THE TREATMENT OF ANXIETY DISORDERS BASED ON CONCLUSIONS OF THE TASK FORCE ON EMPIRICALLY SUPPORTED THERAPY RELATIONSHIPS

Much of this section was drawn from the report of the ESR Task Force (Steering Committee, 2001, 2002). Although the report did not specify the disorders to which its conclusions and recommendations were meant to apply, all indications were that they were meant apply to anxiety disorders as well as other diagnostic categories.

The ESR Task Force's concept of the relationship's effect in therapy was multidimensional: "the therapy relationship acts in concert with discrete interventions, patient characteristics, and clinician qualities in determining treatment effectiveness. A comprehensive understanding of effective (and ineffective) psychotherapy will consider all of these determinants and their optimal combinations" (Steering Committee, 2001, p. 495). The ESR Task Force identified four "general elements of the therapy relationship" that were demonstrably associated with effective treatment. These represented a distillation of the central findings regarding the therapy relationship in general, and hence the relationship with anxiety disordered clients in particular. They were:

1. *The therapeutic alliance*, described as "the quality and strength of the collaborative relationship between client and therapist in therapy" (Horvath, 2001, p. 365; see also Horvath & Bedi, 2002). *The alliance* is a very inclusive concept that encompasses a positive affective bond, consensus about goals and means to achieve the goals, a sense of partnership and shared commitment and engagement, and acceptance of complementary roles and responsibilities.
2. *Cohesion in group therapy*. This is a similarly broad concept that might be described as extending the alliance to all of the therapeutic relationships in the group, including "member-to-leader, member-to-member, and member-to-group relationships" (Burlingame, Fuhriman, & Johnson, 2001, p. 373; see also Burlingame, Fuhriman, & Johnson, 2002).

3. *Empathy*, described as "the therapist's sensitive ability and willingness to understand the client's thoughts, feelings, and struggles from the client's point of view" (Greenberg, Elliott, Watson, & Bohart, 2001, p. 380, after Rogers, 1980, p. 142) as manifested in "the therapist's experience ('empathic resonance'), the observer's view ('expressed empathy'), and the client's experience ('received empathy')" (Greenberg et al., 2001, p. 380; see also Bohart, Greenberg, Elliott, & Watson, 2002).
4. *Goal consensus*, described as "therapist–patient agreement on therapy goals and expectations," and *collaborative involvement*, "the mutual involvement of the patient and therapist in a helping relationship" (Tryon & Winograd, 2001, p. 385; see also Tryon & Winograd, 2002).

Insofar as we may assume that these elements are important in the treatment of anxiety disorders in particular, we may cast them as core treatment principles:

1. Therapeutic change is most likely when therapists strive to achieve and maintain a strong therapeutic alliance with anxiety disordered clients.
2. Therapeutic change is most likely when therapists seek to enhance and maintain cohesion in group therapy for anxiety disorders.
3. Therapeutic change is most likely when therapists strive to be empathic with anxiety disordered clients and to communicate their empathy.
4. Therapeutic change is most likely when therapists seek to negotiate goals and expectations for therapy on which they and their anxiety disordered clients can agree and should monitor and maintain a mutual sense of involvement in the therapeutic enterprise.

In addition to the four demonstrably effective elements, the ESR Task Force identified seven further elements that they judged as promising and probably effective. These included the remaining two (along with empathy) of Carl Rogers's proposed necessary and sufficient conditions of therapeutic personality change (Rogers, 1957), *positive regard* (Farber & Lane, 2001, 2002) and *congruence or genuineness* (Klein, Kolden, Michels, & Chisholm-Stockard, 2001, 2002). They also included two sorts of problem-solving processes, *repair of alliance ruptures* (Safran, Muran, Samstag, & Stevens, 2001, 2002) and *management of countertransference* (Gelso & Hayes, 2001, 2002), two verbal techniques, *therapist self-disclosure* (Hill & Knox, 2001, 2002) and *quality of relational interpretation* (Crits-Christoph & Gibbons, 2001, 2002), and a more general activity, *feedback*, defined as "(a) information provided to a person, (b) from an external source, (c) about the person's behavior or its effects," understood "not as a one-way communication, but rather a reciprocal exchange" (Claiborn, Goodyear, & Horner, 2001, p. 401).

We can cast these promising and probably effective elements as tentative principles for the treatment of anxiety disorders:

1. Therapeutic change is most likely when therapists strive to regard their anxiety disordered clients positively and to be congruent or genuine in their interactions with these clients.

2. Therapeutic change is most likely when therapists master and employ skills of recognizing and repairing alliance ruptures and of recognizing and managing their own countertransference in working with anxiety disordered clients.

3. Therapeutic change is most likely when therapists seek optimum levels of self-disclosure to anxiety disordered clients, strive for moderation and accuracy in offering interpretations dealing with anxiety disordered clients' interpersonal dynamics, and offer feedback to anxiety disordered clients, taking into account the characteristics of the individual client and the context, including the mode and structure of the treatment.

THERAPIST APPROPRIATE RESPONSIVENESS AS A GENERAL TREATMENT PRINCIPLE

Practicing therapists will notice that the foregoing principles do not offer specific step-by-step instructions but instead propose qualities to be optimized or goals to be sought in encounters with anxiety disordered clients. Most of the principles incorporate a substantial evaluative component. In this way, although the principles may be sensible and familiar, they are qualitatively different from the sort of if–then specifications one might find in a pharmacological treatment protocol. They allow much more latitude regarding specific implementing actions, calling on the therapist's skill and judgment. In this section, we offer one way to understand this difference. Our analysis is based on the concept of appropriate responsiveness and a distinction between actions and achievements.

Responsiveness describes behavior being affected by emerging context, including shifting perceptions of others' characteristics and behavior. Psychotherapeutic interaction—and human interaction generally—is intricately responsive on time scales that range from months to milliseconds. Participants answer each other's questions, stay on related topics, take turns speaking, and adjust their behavior moment by moment in response to ever-changing perceptions of each other's state and requirements. Insofar as therapist and client respond to each other, there is a dynamic relationship between variables, involving bi-directional causation and feedback loops. The content and process emerge as the session proceeds, rather than being planned completely in advance. Thus, no two sessions are ever the same (Stiles, Honos-Webb, & Surko, 1998).

The term "responsiveness" is evaluatively neutral. In some contexts, the intent of responsive behavior could be hostile or destructive. Our interest, however, is in *appropriate responsiveness*— doing what is required to produce some positive, beneficial, or desired effect, as judged from the perspective of the treatment approach and the participants' purposes in the encounter. Appropriate responsiveness thus describes therapist behavior that takes emerging client requirements and resources into account. Client requirements and appropriate therapist responsiveness vary with the setting, presenting problem, and the treatment approach's goals, practices, and standards. Viewed in this way, a client's requirements may differ from his or her momentary wishes, and sometimes (e.g., depending on the treatment approach) appropriate responsiveness may involve refusing to comply with a client's requests. The concept of appropriate responsiveness can be used to distinguish two types of therapy elements, which we will call volitional actions and achievements.

Actions are elements that can be classified and counted. They may be used responsively, but their definitions do not require that they be used appropriately. For example, therapist self-disclosure, relational interpretation, or (more broadly and vaguely) feedback could be generally considered as volitional actions. Therapists can decide to do them more or less arbitrarily (though they may sometimes do them inadvertently). Some uses are appropriate and some are not. That is, in principle, the classification of an *action* does not depend on how it is evaluated from a particular perspective.

Achievements are elements that are defined partly by their positive evaluation from some perspective. They require effort and can be understood as the product or goal of actions used with appropriate responsiveness. One cannot tell how a particular action will contribute to an achievement when it is viewed out of context; the same action may contribute positively or negatively depending on whether it is appropriately responsive to this client's requirements and to the context and circumstances, as well as to its timing, delivery, and other response qualities. For example, a particular therapist self-disclosure might strengthen the alliance with one client on one occasion and weaken the alliance with another client or on another occasion. Therapists do not, in general, have complete volitional control over achievements, and their attempts may fail despite their best intentions.

All of the demonstrably effective elements (therapeutic alliance, group cohesion, empathy, goal consensus, and collaboration) and five of the seven promising and probably effective elements (positive regard, congruence or genuineness, repair of ruptures, management of countertransference, and quality of relational interpretations) identified by the ESR Task Force were clearly achievements rather than volitional actions. That is, therapists *strive* for strong alliances, cohesive groups, empathic exchanges, high-quality interpretations, and so forth; they do not just decide that they will do these things. The actual behaviors that contribute to a strong alliance, accurate empathy, high quality interventions, and so forth, differ across cases in response to circumstances of each case. Close reading of the descriptions of the remaining two probably effective elements suggests that they too were understood as achievements—as *appropriate* therapist self-disclosure and *appropriate* feedback, rather than *any* self-disclosure or *any* feedback (Claiborn et al., 2001, 2002; Hill & Knox, 2001, 2002).

Volitional actions, such as therapist self-disclosure, tend to be used if and when they advance the therapeutic process. Consequently, different clients get different amounts, but, because these tend to roughly reflect the amounts they require, the different amounts are not predictive of outcome. (Consider that if all clients got exactly as much of a factor as they needed, their outcomes would be identical insofar as that factor was involved.) Insofar as appropriate responsiveness is characteristic of therapists' use of volitional actions (which, after all, is the whole point of social skill, professional training, and expertise), the correlations of those actions with outcomes tend to be null, or at least unrelated to the actions' therapeutic importance (Stiles, 1988; Stiles & Shapiro, 1994; Stiles et al., 1998). The absence of actions among the relationship elements identified as effective by the ESR Task Force report may thus be a consequence of their being used responsively.

Conversely, when achievements are found to be associated with positive outcomes, the knowledge gain is somewhat illusory. It is less informative to learn that high scores on the alliance, cohesion, empathy, and so forth predict good outcomes because the factors represent poorly specified appropriate responsiveness rather than clear technical actions. The treatment principles that can be derived from such findings are not specific step-by-step instructions but, instead, qualities to be optimized or goals to be sought in encounters with clients, as illustrated in the preceding section. The ESR Task Force acknowledged the role of appropriate responsiveness in their report's subtitle (Norcross, 2002) and in their summary how their findings should be applied: "The preceding conclusions do *not* by themselves constitute a set of practice standards, but represent current scientific knowledge to be understood and applied in the context of all the clinical data available in each case" (Steering Committee, 2002, p. 442).

Perhaps more constructively, appropriate responsiveness can be understood as a general treatment principle. Effective therapy undoubtedly demands that the therapist respond appropriately—as understood within each treatment approach—to the client's emerging requirements. When the therapist is appropriately responsive, it may be expected that the path to positive outcome will tend to be marked by such intermediate achievements as a strong therapeutic alliance, group cohesion, goal consensus and collaboration, empathy, positive regard, genuineness, repair of ruptures, management of countertransference, appropriate self-disclosure, appropriate feedback, and timely, accurate relational interpretations.

CUSTOMIZING: DIFFERENTIAL DIAGNOSIS OR RESPONSIVENESS?

The ESR Task Force suggested that clients who differed in various ways might require different sorts of relationships, concluding that "adapting or tailoring the therapy relationship to specific patient needs and characteristics (in addition to diagnosis) enhances the effectiveness of treatment" (Steering Committee, 2002, p. 441). A substantial portion of their book (Norcross, 2002) was devoted to summarizing empirical evidence regarding a list of elements involved in "customizing the therapy relationship to individual patients."

The report's sections and the Steering Committee conclusions (Steering Committee, 2001, 2002) styled the items on this list as *means* of customizing. The listed items were dimensions or characteristics of clients, however, rather than therapist actions—things that require responsiveness rather than tools with which to respond. Two of them were considered as demonstrably important, including the client's degree of *resistance* (Beutler, Moleiro, & Talebi, 2001, 2002) and of *functional impairment* (Beutler, Harwood, Alimohamed, & Malik, 2001, 2002). "For example, clients presenting with high resistance have been found to respond better to self-control methods and minimal therapist directiveness, whereas patients with low resistance experience improved outcomes with therapist directiveness and explicit guidance" (Steering Committee, 2002, pp. 441–442). Five more were considered as probably im-

portant, including the client's *expectations about the process and outcome treatment* (Arnkoff, Glass, & Shapiro 2002; Glass, Arnkoff, & Shapiro, 2001), *coping style* (Beutler, Harwood, Alimohamed, & Malik, 2001, 2002), *anaclitic/sociotropic or introjective/autonomous style* (Blatt, Shahar, & Zuroff, 2001, 2002), *stage of change* as described in the transtheoretical model (Prochaska & Norcross, 2001, 2002), and *stage of assimilation of problematic experiences* as described in the assimilation model (Stiles, 2001, 2002). Five further client characteristics were studied but found to be supported by insufficient evidence—sadly so, insofar as they were arguably more easily detected characteristics than the demonstrably or probably important ones. They were the client's *gender*, *ethnicity* (Lam & Sue, 2001; Sue & Lam, 2002), *religion and spirituality* (Worthington & Sandage, 2001, 2002), *preferences for particular treatment* (Glass, Arnkoff, & Shapiro, 2001, 2002), *attachment style* (Meyer & Pilkonis, 2001, 2002), and *personality disorder* (Benjamin & Karpiak, 2001, 2002).

At first glance, *customizing* may seem to be an odd term to use in a scientific discussion—something more often applied to consumer goods and services—cars, clothes, interior decoration. However, this term neatly encompasses—or sidesteps—a distinction between *differential diagnosis* and *responsiveness*. Both differential diagnosis and responsiveness suggest that different clients may require different relationships. But whereas differential diagnosis, in the context of adapting treatments, suggests that particular subgroups of clients may require relationships that differ in predictable, and hence prescribable, ways, responsiveness suggests that the requirements are likely to be unpredictable, so that the appropriate response is a matter of therapeutic or social skill and judgment.

The one example of customizing in the brief Steering Committee report, quoted above, sounds like differential diagnosis: Highly resistant clients should receive low levels of therapist directiveness and vice-versa. Our reading of the reports, however, suggests that this sort of if–then protocol recommendation is rare in psychotherapy. Instead, for the most part, the identified elements seem to be offered as dimensions or characteristics that therapists would do well to monitor sensitively and incorporate into their ongoing therapeutic activity.

In other words, they should be appropriately responsive to these client dimensions and characteristics, using means provided by their therapeutic approach. The ESR Task Force's practice recommendations seem consistent with advocating a responsive use of relationship elements: "Practitioners are encouraged to adapt the therapy relationship to specific patient characteristics in the ways shown in this report to enhance therapeutic outcome." "Practitioners are encouraged to routinely monitor patients' responses to the therapy relationship and ongoing treatment. Such monitoring leads to increased opportunities to repair alliance ruptures, to improve the relationship, to modify technical strategies, and to avoid premature termination" (Steering Committee, 2002, p. 442).

SUMMARY

The principles we derived for the contribution of the therapeutic relationship to the treatment of anxiety disorders, listed above, were based directly on the report of the ESR Task Force (Norcross, 2002; Steering Committee, 2001, 2002). That report was meant to apply to anxiety disorders along with other diagnoses, and we found nothing in our investigations to contradict this assumption. The principles were cast as specific achievements to be sought within the therapeutic process rather than as instructions for therapists regarding specified actions to take in specified contingencies. We suggested that each of these achievements can be understood as the product of a responsive process in which therapists integrate emerging information from the client and context, as well as from the treatment approach they are using and act to achieve the specified elements of effective psychotherapy.

We also noted a set of elements found by the ESR Task Force to be important for customizing treatment. We suggested that these can be understood as dimensions and characteristics that therapists can usefully monitor and use to shape appropriately responsive interventions.

ACKNOWLEDGMENTS We thank Michelle G. Newman for alerting us to additional studies not considered in the Division 12 or Division 29 reports.

References

Abramowitz, J. S., Franklin, M. E., Zoellner, L. A., & DiBernardo, C. L. (2002). Treatment compliance and outcome in obsessive-compulsive disorder. *Behavior Modification, 26,* 447–463.

American Psychiatric Association. (1994). *Diagnostic and statistical manual of mental disorders* (4th ed.). Washington, DC: Author.

Arnkoff, D. B., Glass, C. R., & Shapiro, S. J. (2002). Expectations and preferences. In J. C. Norcross (Ed.), *Psychotherapy relationships that work: Therapist contributions and responsiveness to patient needs* (pp. 335–356). New York: Oxford University Press.

Benjamin, L. S., & Karpiak, C. P. (2001). Personality disorders. *Psychotherapy, 38,* 487–491.

Benjamin, L. S., & Karpiak, C. P. (2002). Personality disorders. In J. C. Norcross (Ed.), *Psychotherapy relationships that work: Therapist contributions and responsiveness to patient needs* (pp. 423–438). New York: Oxford University Press.

Bennun, I., & Schindler, L. (1988). Therapist and patient factors in the behavioural treatment of phobic patients. *British Journal of Clinical Psychology, 27,* 145–150.

Beutler, L. E., Harwood, T. M., Alimohamed, S., & Malik, M. (2001). Functional impairment and coping style. *Psychotherapy, 38,* 437–442.

Beutler, L. E., Harwood, T. M., Alimohamed, S., & Malik, M. (2002). Functional impairment and coping style. In J. C. Norcross (Ed.), *Psychotherapy relationships that work: Therapist contributions and responsiveness to patient needs* (pp. 145–170). New York: Oxford University Press.

Beutler, L. E., Moleiro, C. M., & Talebi, H. (2001). Resistance. *Psychotherapy, 38,* 431–436.

Beutler, L. E., Moleiro, C. M., & Talebi, H. (2002). Resistance. In J. C. Norcross (Ed.), *Psychotherapy relationships that work: Therapist contributions and responsiveness to patient needs* (pp. 129–143). New York: Oxford University Press.

Blatt, S. J., Shahar, G., & Zuroff, D. C. (2001). Anaclitic (sociotropic) and introjective (autonomous) dimensions. *Psychotherapy, 38,* 449–454.

Blatt, S. J., Shahar, G., & Zuroff, D. C. (2002). Anaclitic (sociotropic) and introjective (autonomous) dimensions. In J. C. Norcross (Ed.), *Psychotherapy relationships that work: Therapist contributions and responsiveness to patient needs* (pp. 315–333). New York: Oxford University Press.

Bohart, A. C., Elliott, R., Greenberg, L. S., & Watson, J. C. (2002). Empathy. In J. C. Norcross (Ed.), *Psychotherapy relationships that work: Therapist contributions and responsiveness to patient needs* (pp. 89–108). New York: Oxford University Press.

Burlingame, G. M., Fuhriman, A., & Johnson, J. E. (2001). Cohesion in group therapy. *Psychotherapy, 38*, 373–379.

Burlingame, G. M., Fuhriman, A., & Johnson, J. E. (2002). Cohesion in group therapy. In J. C. Norcross (Ed.), *Psychotherapy relationships that work: Therapist contributions and responsiveness to patient needs* (pp. 71–87). New York: Oxford University Press.

Carter, M. M., Turovsky, J., & Barlow, D. H. (1994). Interpersonal relationships in panic disorder with agoraphobia: A review of empirical evidence. *Clinical Psychology: Science & Practice, 1*, 25–34.

Claiborn, C. D., Goodyear, R. K., & Horner, P. A. (2001). Feedback. *Psychotherapy, 38*, 401–405.

Claiborn, C. D., Goodyear, R. K., & Horner, P. A. (2002). Feedback. In J. C. Norcross (Ed.), *Psychotherapy relationships that work: Therapist contributions and responsiveness to patient needs* (pp. 217–233). New York: Oxford University Press.

Constantino, M. J., Castonguay, L. G., & Schut, A. J. (2002). The working alliance: A flagship for the "scientist-practitioner" model in psychotherapy. In G. S. Tryon (Ed.), *Counseling based on process research: Applying what we know* (pp. 81–131). Boston, MA: Allyn & Bacon.

Crits-Christoph, P., & Gibbons, M. B. C. (2001). Relational interpretations. *Psychotherapy, 38*, 423–448.

Crits-Christoph, P., & Gibbons, M. B. C. (2002). Relational interpretations. In J. C. Norcross (Ed.), *Psychotherapy relationships that work: Therapist contributions and responsiveness to patient needs* (pp. 285–300). New York: Oxford University Press.

de Araujo, L. A., Ito, L. M., & Marks, I. M. (1996). Early compliance and other factors predicting outcome of exposure for obsessive-compulsive disorder: results from a controlled study. *British Journal of Psychiatry, 169*, 747–752.

de Beurs, E., Lange, A., van Dyck, R., & Koele, P.

(1995). Respiratory training prior to exposure in vivo in the treatment of panic disorder with agoraphobia: efficacy and predictors of outcome. *Australian and New Zealand Journal of Psychiatry, 29*, 104–13.

Edelman, R. E., & Chambless, D. L. (1995). Adherence during sessions and homework in cognitive-behavioral group treatment of social phobia. *Behaviour Research and Therapy, 33*, 573–577.

Farber, B. A., & Lane, J. S. (2001). Positive regard. *Psychotherapy, 38*, 390–395.

Farber, B. A., & Lane, J. S. (2002). Positive regard. In J. C. Norcross (Ed.), *Psychotherapy relationships that work: Therapist contributions and responsiveness to patient needs* (pp. 175–194). New York: Oxford University Press.

Foa, E. B., Riggs, D. S., Massie, E. D., & Yarczower, M. (1995). The impact of fear activation and anger on the efficacy of exposure treatment for posttraumatic stress disorder. *Behavior Therapy, 26*, 487–499.

Foa, E. B., Rothbaum, B. O., Riggs, D. S., & Murdock, T. B. (1991). Treatment of posttraumatic stress disorder in rape victims: A comparison between cognitive-behavioral procedures and counseling. *Journal of Consulting and Clinical Psychology, 59*, 715–723.

Gelso, C. J., & Hayes, J. A. (2001). Countertransference management. *Psychotherapy, 38*, 418–422.

Gelso, C. J., & Hayes, J. A. (2002). Management of countertransference. In J. C. Norcross (Ed.), *Psychotherapy relationships that work: Therapist contributions and responsiveness to patient needs* (pp. 267–283). New York: Oxford University Press.

Glass, C. R., Arnkoff, D. B., & Shapiro, S. J. (2001). Expectations and preferences. *Psychotherapy, 38*, 455–461.

Greenberg, L. S., Elliott, R., Watson, J. C., & Bohart, A. C. (2001). Empathy. *Psychotherapy, 38*, 380–384.

Gustavson, B., Jansson, L., Jerremalm, A., & Oest, L. G. (1985). Therapist behavior during exposure treatment of agoraphobia. *Behavior Modification, 9*, 491–504.

Hill, C. E., & Knox, S. (2001). Self-disclosure. *Psychotherapy, 38*, 413–417.

Hill, C. E., & Knox, S. (2002). Self-disclosure. In J. C. Norcross (Ed.), *Psychotherapy relationships that work: Therapist contributions and responsiveness to patient needs* (pp. 255–265). New York: Oxford University Press.

Hoelscher, T. J., Lichstein, K. L., & Rosenthal, T. L. (1984). Objective vs subjective assessment of relaxation compliance among anxious individuals. *Behaviour Research and Therapy, 22,* 187–193.

Hoffart, A., Versland, S., & Sexton, H. (2002). Self understanding, empathy, guided discovery, and schema belief in schema focused cognitive therapy of personality problems: A process outcome study. *Cognitive Therapy and Research, 26,* 199–219.

Hoogduin, C. A., de Haan, E., & Schaap, C. (1989). The significance of the patient–therapist relationship in the treatment of obsessive compulsive neurosis. *British Journal of Clinical Psychology, 28,* 185–186.

Horvath, A. O. (2001). The alliance. *Psychotherapy, 38,* 365–372.

Horvath, A. O., & Bedi, R. P. (2002). The alliance. In J. C. Norcross (Ed.), *Psychotherapy relationships that work: Therapist contributions and responsiveness to patient needs* (pp. 37–69). New York: Oxford University Press.

Keijsers, G. P. J., Hoogduin, C. A. L., & Schaap, C. P. D. R. (1994). Prognostic factors in the behavioral treatment of panic disorder with and without agoraphobia. *Behavior Therapy, 25,* 689–708.

Keijsers, G. P. J., Schaap, C. P. D. R., Hoogduin, C. A. L., & Lammers, M. W. (1995). Patient therapist interaction in the behavioral treatment of panic disorder with agoraphobia. *Behavior Modification, 19,* 491–517.

Keijsers, G. P. J., Schaap, C. P. D. R., Hoogduin, C. A. L., & Peters, W. (1991). The therapeutic relationship in the behavioural treatment of anxiety disorders. *Behavioural Psychotherapy, 19,* 359–367.

Klein, M. H., Kolden, G. G., Michels, J. L., & Chisholm-Stockard, S. (2001). Congruence or genuineness. *Psychotherapy, 38,* 396–400.

Klein, M. H., Kolden, G. G., Michels, J. L., & Chisholm-Stockard, S. (2002). Congruence/genuineness. In J. C. Norcross (Ed.), *Psychotherapy relationships that work: Therapist contributions and responsiveness to patient needs* (pp. 195–215). New York: Oxford University Press.

Krupnick, J. L., Sotsky, S. M., Simmens, S., Moyer, J., Elkin, I., Watkins, J., & Pilkonis, P. A. (1996). The role of the therapeutic alliance in psychotherapy and pharmacotherapy outcome: Findings in the National Institute of Mental Health Treatment of Depression Collaborative Research Program. *Journal of Consulting and Clinical Psychology, 64,* 532–539.

Lam, A. G., & Sue, S. (2001). Client diversity. *Psychotherapy, 38,* 479–486.

Lax, T., Basoglu, M., & Marks, I. M. (1992). Expectancy and compliance as predictors of outcome in obsessive-compulsive disorder. *Behavioural Psychotherapy, 20,* 257–266.

Leung, A. W., & Heimberg, R. G. (1996). Homework compliance, perceptions of control, and outcome of cognitive-behavioral treatment of social phobia. *Behaviour Research and Therapy, 34,* 423–432.

Mathews, A. M., Johnston, D. W., Lancashire, M., Munby, M., Shaw, P. M., & Gelder, M. G. (1976). Imaginal flooding and exposure to real phobic situations: Treatment outcome with agoraphobic patients. *British Journal of Psychiatry, 129,* 362–371.

Meyer, B., & Pilkonis, P. A. (2001). Attachment style. *Psychotherapy, 38,* 466–472.

Meyer, B., & Pilkonis, P. A. (2002). Attachment style. In J. C. Norcross (Ed.), *Psychotherapy relationships that work: Therapist contributions and responsiveness to patient needs* (pp. 367–382). New York: Oxford University Press.

Michelson, L., Mavissakalian, M., Marchione, K., Dancu, C. V., & Greenwald, M. (1986). The role of self-directed in vivo exposure in cognitive, behavioral, and psychophysiological treatments of agoraphobia. *Behavior Therapy, 17,* 108.

Morris, R. J., & Magrath, K. H. (1979). Contribution of therapist warmth to the contact desensitization treatment of acrophobia. *Journal of Consulting and Clinical Psychology, 47,* 786–788.

Morris, R. J., & Suckerman, K. R. (1974a). The importance of the therapeutic relationship in systematic desensitization. *Journal of Consulting and Clinical Psychology, 42,* 148.

Morris, R. J., & Suckerman, K. R. (1974b). Therapist warmth as a factor in automated systematic desensitization. *Journal of Consulting and Clinical Psychology, 42,* 244–250.

Nathan, P. E., & Gorman, J. M. (Eds.). (2002). *A guide to treatments that work* (2nd ed.). New York: Oxford University Press.

Norcross, J. C. (Ed.). (2002). *Psychotherapy relationships that work: Therapist contributions and responsiveness to patient needs.* New York: Oxford University Press.

Park, J. M., Mataix-Cols, D., Marks, I. M., Ngamthipwatthana, T., Marks, M., Araya, R., & Al-

Kubaisy, T. (2001). Two-year follow-up after a randomised controlled trial of self- and clinician-accompanied exposure for phobia/panic disorders. *British Journal of Psychiatry, 178,* 543–548.

Prochaska, J. C., & Norcross, J. C. (2001). Stages of change. *Psychotherapy, 38,* 443–448.

Prochaska, J. C., & Norcross, J. C. (2002). Stages of change. In J. C. Norcross (Ed.), *Psychotherapy relationships that work: Therapist contributions and responsiveness to patient needs* (pp. 303–313). New York: Oxford University Press.

Przeworski, A., Newman, M. G., Castonguay, L. G., & Constantino, M. J. (2001, July). *The relationship between therapeutic alliance, compliance with CBT homework, and outcome in GAD.* Paper presented at the World Congress of Behavioral and Cognitive Therapies, Vancouver, British Columbia.

Rabavilas, A. D., Boulougouris, J. C., & Perissaki, C. (1979). Therapist qualities related to outcome with exposure in vivo in neurotic patients. *Journal of Behavior Therapy and Experimental Psychiatry, 10,* 293–294.

Raue, P. J., & Goldfried, M. R. (1994). The therapeutic alliance in cognitive-behavior therapy. In A. O. Horvath and L. S. Greenberg (Eds.), *The working alliance: Theory, research and practice* (pp. 131–152). New York: Wiley.

Rogers, C. R. (1957). The necessary and sufficient conditions of therapeutic personality change. *Journal of Consulting Psychology, 21,* 95–103.

Rogers, C. R. (1980). *A way of being.* Boston: Houghton-Mifflin.

Safran, J. D., Muran, J. C., Samstag, L. W., & Stevens, C. (2001). Repairing alliance ruptures. *Psychotherapy, 38,* 406–412.

Safran, J. D., Muran, J. C., Samstag, L. W., & Stevens, C. (2002). Repairing alliance ruptures. In J. C. Norcross (Ed.), *Psychotherapy relationships that work: Therapist contributions and responsiveness to patient needs* (pp. 235–254). New York: Oxford University Press.

Schaap, C., & Hoogduin, C. A. L. (1988). The therapeutic relationship in behavior therapy: Enhancing the quality of the bond. In P. M. G. Emmelkamp, W. T. A. M. Everaerd, F. Karaaimaat, & M. J. M. van Son (Eds.), *Advances in theory and practice in behaviour therapy* (pp. 71–96). Amsterdam: Swets & Zeitlinger.

Schmidt, N. B., & Woolaway-Bickel, K. (2000). The effects of treatment compliance on outcome in cognitive behavioral therapy for panic disorder:

Quality versus quantity. *Journal of Consulting and Clinical Psychology, 68,* 13–18.

Steering Committee. (2001). Empirically supported therapy relationships: Conclusions and recommendations of the Division 29 Task Force. *Psychotherapy, 38,* 495–497.

Steering Committee. (2002). Conclusions and recommendations for the Task Force on Empirically Supported Therapy Relationships. In J. C. Norcross (Ed.), *Psychotherapy relationships that work: Therapist contributions and responsiveness to patient needs* (pp. 441–443). New York: Oxford University Press.

Stiles, W. B. (1988). Psychotherapy process–outcome correlations may be misleading. *Psychotherapy, 25,* 27–35.

Stiles, W. B. (2001). Assimilation of problematic experiences. *Psychotherapy, 38,* 462–465.

Stiles, W. B. (2002). Assimilation of problematic experiences. In J. C. Norcross (Ed.), *Psychotherapy relationships that work: Therapist contributions and responsiveness to patient needs* (pp. 357–365). New York: Oxford University Press.

Stiles, W. B., Agnew-Davies, R., Hardy, G. E., Barkham, M., & Shapiro, D. A. (1998). Relations of the alliance with psychotherapy outcome: Findings in the Second Sheffield Psychotherapy Project. *Journal of Consulting and Clinical Psychology, 66,* 791–802.

Stiles, W. B., Honos-Webb, L., & Surko, M. (1998). Responsiveness in psychotherapy. *Clinical Psychology: Science and Practice, 5,* 439–458.

Stiles, W. B., & Shapiro, D. A. (1994). Disabuse of the drug metaphor: Psychotherapy process-outcome correlations. *Journal of Consulting and Clinical Psychology, 62,* 942–948.

Sue, S., & Lam, A. G. (2002). Cultural and demographic diversity. In J. C. Norcross (Ed.), *Psychotherapy relationships that work: Therapist contributions and responsiveness to patient needs* (pp. 401–421). New York: Oxford University Press.

Taylor, S., Fedoroff, I. C., Koch, W. J., Thordarson, D. S., Fecteau, G., & Nicki, R. M. (2001). Posttraumatic stress disorder arising after road traffic collisions: Patterns of response to cognitive-behavior therapy. *Journal of Consulting and Clinical Psychology, 69,* 541–551.

Tryon, G. S., & Winograd, G. (2001). Goal consensus and collaboration. *Psychotherapy, 38,* 385–389.

Tryon, G. S., & Winograd, G. (2002). Goal consensus and collaboration. In J. C. Norcross (Ed.),

Psychotherapy relationships that work: Therapist contributions and responsiveness to patient needs (pp. 109–125). New York: Oxford University Press.

Williams, K. E., & Chambless, D. L. (1990). The relationship between therapist characteristics and outcome of in vivo exposure treatment for agoraphobia. *Behavior Therapy, 21,* 111–116.

Woods, C. M., Chambless, D. L., & Steketee, G. (2002). Homework compliance and behavior therapy outcome for panic with agoraphobia and obsessive compulsive disorder. *Cognitive Behaviour Therapy, 31,* 88–95.

Woody, S. R., & Adessky, R. S. (2002). Therapeutic alliance, group cohesion, and homework compliance during cognitive-behavioral group treatment of social phobia. *Behavior Therapy, 33,* 5–27.

Worthington, E. L., Jr., & Sandage, S. J. (2001). Religion and spirituality. *Psychotherapy, 38,* 473–478.

Worthington, E. L., Jr., & Sandage, S. J. (2002). Religion and spirituality. In J. C. Norcross (Ed.), *Psychotherapy relationships that work: Therapist contributions and responsiveness to patient needs* (pp. 383–399). New York: Oxford University Press.

8

Technique Factors in Treating Anxiety Disorders

Sheila R. Woody
Thomas H. Ollendick

The concept of evidence-based medicine, a world-wide movement begun in the United Kingdom (Sackett, Richardson, Rosenberg, & Haynes, 1997, 2000), rests on the premise that quality of patient care is enhanced by the use of empirically supported treatments. According to this view, new developments in research related to effective treatments need to be disseminated to the professional community. Believing this process applies to mental health as much as any other branch of medicine, the Society of Clinical Psychology (Division 12 of the American Psychological Association) formed a Task Force on Promotion and Dissemination of Psychological Procedures to identify treatments with empirical support and promote those treatments through training and dissemination of information to professionals.

The published reports from this Task Force and its successors have provided lists of examples of effective treatments that change and expand as new evidence accumulates. In the initial report, the Task Force (1995) published a preliminary list of 25 treatments that met their criteria for empir-

ical support in treating children, adolescents, and adults. The group continued to review treatments, and by 1998 they had identified 71 empirically supported psychological treatments across the lifespan (Chambless et al., 1996, 1998). Chambless and Ollendick (2001), two members of the Task Force, subsequently reviewed results from this Task Force as well as several other groups working to identify and publicize psychotherapeutic approaches with empirical support. Chambless and Ollendick identified 108 empirically supported treatments for adults and 37 for children and adolescents.

In these reports, several treatments have been listed as empirically supported for the treatment of anxiety and its disorders in adulthood. (Empirically supported strategies for the treatment of anxiety and phobic disorders in childhood and adolescence have also been identified but will not be reviewed here.) Table 8.1 lists interventions identified as empirically supported by various groups, as reviewed by Chambless and Ollendick (2001). Efficacious treatments have been identified for

Table 8.1
Empirically Supported Treatments for Anxiety and Its Disorders

Condition and treatment	Well-established	Probably efficacious	Experimental
Agoraphobia			
Exposure	1, 2, 3?	3?	
Couples communication training as adjunct to exposure		1	
Partner-assisted CBT		2	
Partner-assisted exposure		2	
Partner-assisted exposure with couple communication training		2	
Animal phobia			
Systematic desensitization		1	
Blood/injury phobia			
Applied tension			3
Exposure			3
Coping with stressors			
Stress inoculation training	1		
Generalized Anxiety Disorder			
CBT	1,3?	3?	
CBT (CT + relaxation)	4		
CT	2		
Applied relaxation		1,2	
Obsessive-Compulsive Disorder			
ERP	1,2,3?,4	3?	
CT with rational-emotive therapy + exposure		1,2	3
Family-assisted exposure		2	
Partner-assisted exposure		2	
Relapse prevention		1	
Panic Disorder			
CBT	1,3?	3?	
CT	2		
Education-focused CBT	4		
Exposure	3?	2,3?	
Panic control therapy	3?	3?	
Applied relaxation		1,2	
Panic Disorder with Agoraphobia			
CBT	1,3?	3?	
Exposure	3?,4	3?,4	
Post-Traumatic Stress Disorder			
Exposure	4	1,2	
Stress inoculation training with CT + exposure	3?	3?	
Stress inoculation training		1,2	

Condition and treatment	Well-established	Probably efficacious	Experimental
EMDR		2	
Structured psychodynamic treatment			3
Post-Traumatic Stress Disorder (civilian)			
EMDR		1	
Social anxiety			
Systematic desensitization		1	
Social phobia			
Exposure	3?,4	1,2,3?	
Exposure + CBT	3?	2,3?	
CBT		1	
Multi-component CBT			4
Relaxation techniques			4
Social skills training			4
Specific phobia			
Exposure	1,3?,4	3?	

Note: CBT = cognitive behavior therapy; CT = cognitive therapy; EMDR = eye movement desensitization and reprocessing; ERP = exposure and response prevention.
Work Groups
1. "Update on Empirically Validated Therapies, II," by D. L. Chambless et al., 1998, *The Clinical Psychologist*, 51, 3–16.
2. Special Section of *Journal of Consulting and Clinical Psychology*, 66 (1998).
3. *What Works for Whom?*, by A. Roth and P. Fonagy, 1996, New York: Guilford Press.
4. *A Guide to Treatments That Work* (2nd ed.), by P. E. Nathan and J. M. Gorman, 1998, New York: Oxford University Press.

all of the major anxiety disorders, including generalized anxiety disorder (GAD), obsessive-compulsive disorder (OCD), panic disorder with and without agoraphobia, post-traumatic stress disorder (PTSD), social anxiety disorder or social phobia, and specific phobia.

Treatments demonstrated to be effective have been based largely on behavioral, cognitive, and cognitive-behavioral procedures. Representative treatments include cognitive behavior therapy (CBT) and applied relaxation for GAD, exposure and response prevention (ERP) for OCD, CBT and applied relaxation for panic, stress inoculation and exposure for PTSD, CBT and exposure for social phobia, and systematic desensitization and exposure for specific phobia. Two points should be emphasized. First, the research support for these "empirically supported" interventions is not always robust and is often limited to the acute care of

these disorders. Second, many interventions, including many from other theoretical orientations, have yet to be rigorously tested. It is important to distinguish untested strategies with those that have been tested and found to be not efficacious (Chambless & Ollendick, 2001; Westen & Morrison, 2001).

Many researchers and clinicians have long advocated for research aimed at understanding the psychological principles of change that underlie effective psychosocial interventions (Goldfried & Davison, 1976; Ollendick & Cerny, 1981; Rosen & Davison, 2003). Our goal in this chapter is to contemplate principles of change that might guide empirically supported interventions with the anxiety disorders. Given the large number of behavioral, cognitive, and cognitive-behavioral interventions that have been demonstrated to be effective in the treatment of anxiety disorders, we shall first review the procedures involved so that we might then be in a position to distill or abstract principles that underlie these effective procedures.

ESTS FOR THE ANXIETY DISORDERS: PROCEDURES THAT WORK

In our view, treatment programs should rest on a sound theoretical rationale that addresses both the determinants of the condition or disorder to be changed and the purported mechanisms for bringing about the desired changes. Thus, it is key to begin with an appreciation for the psychopathology of anxiety and its related disorders.

As Barlow (2002, p. 18) observed, "Anxiety kills relatively few people, but many more would welcome death as an alternative to the paralysis and suffering resulting from anxiety in its severe form." Anxiety can be chronic and disabling. Moreover, data from community surveys such as the Epidemiological Catchment Area study (Weissman, 1985) and the more recent National Comorbidity Study (Kessler et al., 1994) indicate that anxiety disorders are highly prevalent and, in fact, are the most prevalent of all psychological disorders. Lifetime prevalence rates for any anxiety disorder in these community surveys are estimated to be about 25%, whereas 12-month prevalence rates are estimated to be 17%. Spitzer et al. (1995) also documented that anxiety disorders are prevalent in primary care settings, where fully 18% of patients reported either panic disorder, GAD, or anxiety symptoms that approximated these disorders. Although these three studies have been conducted in the United States, these figures appear to be representative of prevalence rates found throughout the world.

Anxiety is a complex emotional state (a "felt" experience) that is characterized by behavioral, cognitive, and affective properties. These properties are not always in synchrony and may not be equally balanced within a particular anxious individual (Lang, 1979; Lang, Davis, & Ohman, 2000), but clinicians nevertheless need to recognize these features and address them as a part of the intervention. In fact, we suggest that treatment effectiveness will be directly related to the extent to which the basic psychopathological processes of these disorders are addressed.

Just as effective treatments must consider the underlying psychopathology of the disorders they are intended to treat, they also ideally incorporate the purported mechanisms for bringing about the desired changes in those processes. In recent years, Kraemer and her colleagues suggest researchers might clarify the process of effective change by paying close attention to distinctions between moderators and mediators of treatment change (Kraemer, Stice, Kazdin, Offord, & Kupfer, 2001; Kraemer, Wilson, Fairburn, & Agras, 2002). Moderators can include identifying subgroups of participants for whom treatment was more or less effective (e.g., gender, ethnicity, co-morbid conditions). Moderator analyses can also illuminate which therapist characteristics are associated with differential treatment outcomes. Identifying moderators of treatment response naturally leads to hypotheses as to why the treatment was less effective for some subgroups or some types of therapists. In effect, they specify the important conditions or parameters under which the treatments work or fail to work.

In contrast, mediation analyses directly test the purported mechanisms of change. A mediator helps to explain how and why a treatment exerts its influence. For example, if one believes that cognitive therapy works by altering distorted cognitions, then it would be important to measure such cognitions throughout treatment (not just at the end of treatment) and demonstrate that changes in cognitions precede changes on the outcome variables of interest. Similarly, if one hypothesizes that exposure therapy works because it allows habituation to occur at a physiological level, then it would be important to measure physiological arousal throughout the treatment process and show that changes in such measures (e.g., heart rate, heart rate variability) predict changes on relevant outcome measures.

Empirically supported treatments for anxiety disorders continue to be developed based on emerging research findings and theory related to basic psychopathological processes and mediators of change in psychotherapy. As an example, consider the case of obsessive-compulsive disorder (OCD). The earliest treatment studies examined the effectiveness of exposure to feared stimuli such as contaminants (Meyer, 1966). Exposure as a therapy strategy was based on a conditioning model of the disorder, which essentially focused on the affective or psychophysiological aspects of the problem. Exposure involved bringing the client in contact with frightening stimuli and maintaining that contact until the anxiety habituated or subsided. Subsequent sessions involved presenting increasingly challenging stimuli until the fear was extinguished.

Early on, clinical researchers identified a problem with exposure as a treatment strategy for OCD. This problem was neutralization, or rituals that the client would perform as soon as the therapy session was complete. For some clients, having made a plan to ritualize immediately following exposure significantly reduced their anxiety during the exposure session. Furthermore, research began to show that permitting rituals following exposure was associated with poorer treatment outcome (Foa & Goldstein, 1978; Foa, Steketee, & Milby, 1980). These problems associated with neutralization exposed deficiencies in the theory about mechanisms for change in behavior therapy for OCD; habituation alone could not solve the problem.

Mowrer's (1960) theory on the reinforcing properties of behavioral avoidance also seemed relevant. Rituals were regarded as behavior performed in the service of reducing or managing intense anxiety. Because rituals or neutralization strategies often relieve anxiety, they were seen as interfering with the habituation of exposure, so a second therapeutic strategy was added: ritual prevention (or response prevention). On the strength of randomized controlled trials, exposure and response prevention became the treatment of choice for OCD for clients with at least some overt compulsions (Foa, Steketee, Grayson, Turner, & Latimer, 1984). This treatment strategy was based on understanding of psychopathological processes of behavior and affect involved in OCD as well as a clear theoretical rationale for how to bring about change in those processes.

Over the last decade, theory and treatment research in OCD has increasingly focused on the remaining domain of anxiety: cognition. Cognitive theories for other disorders in anxiety were becoming better articulated, and subsequent improvements in treatment success based on these theories were impressive (Michelson, Marchione, Greenwald, Testa, & Marchione, 1996). Despite the obvious cognitive element in OCD, however, the heterogeneity of the content of OCD concerns slowed the pace of progress until recently. The Obsessive-Compulsive Disorder Cognitions Working Group (1997, 2001) is an international group of researchers who have been working together for nearly 10 years to specify psychopathological cognitive processes in OCD and develop related cognitive measures. They have identified several areas of maladaptive cognition in OCD, including responsibility for harm, the importance of intrusive thoughts, and intolerance of doubt, among others.

Specifying problematic types of OCD-related cognition that could be reliably identified and linked to behavior and affect enabled researchers to develop and test cognitive therapies specifically for OCD (van Oppen et al., 1995). These efforts continue and include ongoing clinical trials in England and Canada of cognitive therapy for clients who have obsessions in the absence of compulsions. (These clients were routinely excluded from participation in earlier studies of exposure and response prevention.) Cognitive therapy for OCD differs from exposure in that the focus is on changing beliefs that maintain anxiety and avoidance or compulsions. Clients learn to examine the evidence in support of their beliefs about the situation (e.g., probability of a house fire) or their symptoms (e.g., thinking something is as bad as doing it) and conduct behavioral experiments to test predicted outcomes (e.g., revealing the content of intrusive thoughts to a trusted friend).

The example of emergent treatments for OCD illustrates how basic research on psychopathological processes and mechanisms of change in psychotherapy can evolve together with clinical trials to gradually establish effective interventions. Within the area of OCD, it is clear that more powerful treatments arose from better understanding and more complete consideration of the psychopathological processes of behavior, cognition, and affect. Less research has focused on mechanisms of change, but this is an important area to examine because current treatments have plenty of room for improvement. Understanding *how* change occurs may help clinicians to target interventions more effectively for individual clients and may illustrate ways therapy can be altered to make it more powerful.

PRINCIPLES OF EMPIRICALLY SUPPORTED TREATMENTS FOR THE ANXIETY DISORDERS

What principles can we identify, and how do we see them at work in the procedures that have been established to be efficacious for anxiety disorders? Although the list of empirically supported treatments for anxiety disorders is fairly lengthy (owing to strong research interest as well as the sheer number of disorders), when one examines the procedures involved in treatments that have been demonstrated to be efficacious, a few principles seem to characterize commonalities across the treatments. Some of these principles are specific to the types of interventions that have been tested in randomized controlled trials; others are derived from the more general dimensions of psychotherapy discussed in this volume. We will first discuss the specific principles, followed later in the chapter by a discussion of the general dimensions.

In comparing various empirically supported treatment protocols for anxiety disorders, we synthesized five technique-oriented principles that appear to cut across most of these protocols. In conducting evidence based treatment for anxiety disorders, therapists should:

1. Challenge misconceptions through discussion and explicitly questioning the evidence.
2. Actively test the validity of erroneous and maladaptive beliefs through behavioral experiments.
3. Use repeated exposure to the feared situation to reduce the intensity of the fear response.
4. Eliminate avoidance of feared situations.
5. Improve skills for handling feared situations.

Within these five principles are strategies to address the three modalities of responding in anxiety disorders: cognition, affect, and behavior. The first two principles are two methods that describe what is commonly referred to as cognitive restructuring. The third principle, that of fear reduction, relates to affect and the physiological arousal that so frequently accompanies it. The last two principles explicitly involve behavior, addressing avoidance and a variety of personal interactive skills. These five principles do not stand in isolation. They each serve to promote the goals of the others, which is one likely explanation for why tested treatments seldom use strategies typifying just one of the principles. For example, eliminating avoidance of feared situations (behavior domain) not only promotes a return to normal and adaptive functioning, but it also promotes exposure to feared situations (affective domain) and probably serves to change maladaptive ideas about bad things that might happen in those situations (cognitive domain).

Cognition

Over the past two decades, researchers have systematically sought to understand cognition in anxiety disorders. Cognitive theories have been specifically formulated around the content of maladaptive beliefs that have been observed to occur in different disorders. Each disorder has its own characteristic set of maladaptive beliefs that is targeted with specific interventions outlined in treatment manuals. Although these manuals look quite different, in terms of what they direct the clinician to do, the differences are largely due to the specificity of the content of misconceptions for each disorder.

As reviewed earlier, cognitive strategies have been well researched for panic disorder, social phobia, GAD, OCD, and PTSD (including acute stress disorder). However, the content of the cognitions that are a part of the problem for these disorders obviously varies. In panic, the primary cognitions involve ideas that the sensations of anxiety are dangerous and indicative of impending physical catastrophe. Social phobia is somewhat more heterogeneous, but the main misconception could be characterized as a belief that social imperfections will lead to negative evaluation from others, which the individual fears will lead to personal ruin. For clients with GAD, worry itself is overvalued as a problem-solving strategy and as a means of controlling negative events. Much of the worry involves inaccurate predictions that catastrophic events are likely to occur. Clients with OCD place great stock in the significance of their thoughts, believing, for example, that having an aggressive thought is just as bad as assaulting someone. Finally, clients who have been traumatized show several characteristic problematic beliefs, including self-blame for the trauma, a belief that others view them as damaged goods, intolerance for the intense affect associated with recollection of the trauma, and an appraisal of the world as an unsafe place.

> Principle 1. Challenge misconceptions by discussing and explicitly questioning the evidence.

Cognitive and cognitive-behavioral interventions for anxiety disorders generally include Principle 1 as an important element. Once the clinician has identified specific automatic thoughts that contribute to the client's maladaptive fear, numerous strategies can be used to help the client question the validity of those thoughts. Some of these strategies include explicitly examining the evidence that supports and refutes a particular idea and developing rational responses to automatic thoughts related to anxiety.

> Principle 2. Actively test the validity of erroneous and maladaptive ideas through behavioral experiments.

Behavioral experiments represent a continuation and intensification of the therapeutic aims outlined for Principle 1. The goal remains to help the client to examine the degree to which maladaptive ideas have merit versus the degree to which they are implausible or improbable. Rather than simply discussing the evidence related to a particular idea, however, behavioral experiments provide a structured way for the client to gather such evidence experientially.

Interoceptive exposure, a strategy used in treatment for panic, provides an instructive example. Interoceptive exposure involves purposely evoking feared bodily sensations such as elevated heart rate or dizziness. This intervention can be used in two different ways, illustrating two different principles of change in anxiety disorders. The first is as a be-

havioral experiment, which will be discussed here. Interoceptive exposure, as its name implies, can also be used in an exposure model, so below we will discuss it again from that perspective. To construct a behavioral experiment, the clinician must first understand the frightening meaning of a particular situation or event. For example, the client may believe that dizziness leads inevitably to fainting (and may have constructed an elaborate fantasy about terrible things that might happen following the fainting episode).

The rationale of a behavioral experiment is to bring about the feared conditions, remove efforts to control the outcome, and determine whether the feared event does occur. In this example, the clinician might lead the client through an episode of hyperventilating, well known to evoke dizziness, and see whether feeling dizzy inevitably leads to fainting if precautions are not taken. Behavioral experiments are rarely single-stage events. Following the first episode of hyperventilating, the client may be intrigued that she did not faint but explain the result by pointing out that she was seated. The clinician would clarify the client's prediction about what would happen if she experienced that same dizziness while standing (e.g., that she would faint this time) and do another behavioral experiment (this time while standing) to test that secondary idea.

Behavioral experiments are powerful because they permit clients to learn something about their maladaptive beliefs in an experiential way. Clients participate in constructing an experiment that they would likely find convincing. These experiments are used in social phobia and OCD as well. For example, in social phobia, clients might be encouraged to purposely commit a perceived social imperfection such as allowing five seconds of silence during a conversation. Clients with OCD might be encouraged to flaunt dangerous thoughts, resisting the urge to respond to a thought about a perceived danger like leaving the water trickling in the bathroom. In each case, it is important to identify the predicted outcome: If the client does not keep the conversation going, the social interaction will end abruptly, or if water is left trickling in the bathroom, the apartment will be flooded.

Affect

Many of the earliest efforts to research effective treatments for anxiety disorders involved focusing on reducing the intensity of the affective response to the feared situation. These approaches continue to be used today, having been demonstrated to be efficacious for reducing fear and avoidance for most anxiety disorders. Exposure to feared situations, the third principle of treatment change for anxiety disorders, has been conducted in different variations: imaginal exposure, *in vivo* exposure, graded exposure, flooding, exposure with response prevention, and systematic desensitization. We will compare and contrast the habituation model, under which most versions of exposure fit, with systematic desensitization, which uses a different approach.

> Principle 3. Use repeated exposure to the feared situation to reduce the intensity of the fear response.

The principle of habituation underlies the therapeutic strategy of exposure, no matter which variation of exposure is used. Moderately high levels of anxiety are evoked by contact with the feared stimulus or situation, and the client continues to engage with the stimulus or remain in the situation until anxiety dissipates. Exposure can be conducted *in vivo*, involving actually touching the object or visiting a situation, or it can be conducted through elaborate imaginal scenarios. If the exposure is *in vivo*, clients are more likely to be successful if they are assisted by a therapist (at least in the early stages) or some other trusted person such as a spouse or friend (Hellstrom & Öst, 1995). If clients are in the habit of taking certain steps to prevent bad things from happening (e.g., rituals), then these responses are prevented (i.e., response prevention).

As with cognitive interventions, the details of situations to be used for exposure vary across the anxiety disorders. These details also vary across clients within the same disorder, depending on the particular stimulus characteristics that evoke fear for the individual client. For example, research has unequivocally shown support for the efficacy of exposure for agoraphobia (Jansson & Öst, 1982; Trull, Nietzel, & Main, 1988). A treatment step in exposure for Client A might involve strolling a shopping mall on a busy Saturday afternoon, while Client B may visit the same shopping mall anytime but focus on being in dressing rooms. Both clients are doing exposure in a shopping mall, and they have the same diagnosis, but Client A specifically fears crowds and Client B fears a sense of being trapped. In these examples, the mall is not the object of exposure; it is the crowd or sense of entrapment.

Exposure is commonly employed as a single strategy only for specific phobias, and the procedure is relatively straightforward. For other disorders, including agoraphobia, exposure is included as one element of a more comprehensive treatment plan that includes strategies like cognitive restructuring. Interoceptive exposure for panic disorder, in which feared sensations are intentionally evoked, can be approached from the perspective of a behavioral experiment as described earlier. However, reducing fear of the sensations can also be approached from a habituation model, in which the client repeatedly practices evoking the sensation until it is no longer frightening. Notice that cognitive change will undoubtedly occur even during a habituation model intervention, as the client observes that feared outcomes (e.g., having a heart attack) do not occur.

Exposure, from a habituation model, is logistically more difficult with the feared situations presented in social phobia. Although a client has control over how long he stays in a shopping mall, for example, social situations involve other people and are often quite brief. Starting a conversation, which is a problem for many people with social phobia, only takes a few seconds, and even a long conversation with a stranger is unlikely to last more than a few minutes. The brevity of these events, and the fact that they cannot easily be repeated, creates a challenge if the goal is to remain in the anxiety-evoking situation until anxiety declines. Accordingly, the most tested treatment protocols for social phobia involve frequent use of role-play simulations of social situations (Heimberg et al., 1990; Heimberg, Salzman, Holt, & Blendell, 1993). Within a role-play, especially in a group therapy setting, the client may initiate conversations repeatedly over several minutes to achieve extinction of the anxiety response.

Exposure alone is not sufficient for OCD. Left

to their own devices, clients will usually engage in some type of neutralizing activity (ritual) to prevent the feared event from occurring. In that case, anxiety does decline, but it is due to the neutralizing behavior rather than the effects of habituation, which simply serves to strengthen the neutralizing behavior (because it works so well to reduce discomfort). Researchers have shown that exposure must be combined with response prevention to optimize the benefits of habituation (Foa et al., 1984).

Trauma theorists have long recognized the need to systematically activate trauma memories in order to bring about recovery, and exposure has been found to be a useful strategy for PTSD following varied forms of trauma (Foa, Rothbaum, Riggs, & Murdock, 1991; Richards, Lovell, & Marks, 1994). Exposure for PTSD is focused on imaginally reliving the trauma "as if it were happening now." As with exposure for other fears, the imaginal exposure for PTSD continues long enough for anxiety and distress to decrease. Imaginal exposure ideally uses as much detail as possible, involving input from all the senses. With PTSD, the client usually describes the scene repeatedly, and it is important to elicit extensive details for the worst part of the trauma. Exposure does evoke intense affect, which can be very upsetting when it involves trauma memories. Accordingly, clinicians go out of their way to establish a collaborative relationship with clients, helping them to feel the exposure is proceeding at a pace within their control. Alternative strategies for imaginal exposure (e.g., eye movement desensitization and reprocessing therapy) have also gained popularity for civilian PTSD.

Like exposure, systematic desensitization also involves repeated exposure to feared stimuli (in imagination), but the idea is for the client to remain as relaxed as possible while imagining the feared situations. Systematic desensitization entails teaching clients to relax deeply and then imagine engagement in the feared situation while remaining in the relaxed state (Wolpe, 1958). Although this approach to treatment was demonstrated to be efficacious for reducing certain types of fears (e.g., animal phobia), it has largely been supplanted by *in vivo* or imaginal exposure, which was demonstrated to be more effective for many problems (Bandura, Blanchard, & Ritter, 1969).

Behavior

Two aspects of behavior are central targets of intervention for anxiety disorders. Avoidance often interferes with the client's life severely enough that it provides the impetus for seeking treatment. In addition to avoidance interfering with normal functioning, clients with anxiety disorders often lack certain skills that are helpful in dealing with feared situations, including social skills, relaxation skills, skills for adaptively coping with fear, problem-solving skills, and, in the case of blood/injury phobia, skills to prevent fainting at the sight of blood. We will discuss eliminating avoidance and bolstering skills as distinct principles of change for treatment of anxiety disorders.

Principle 4. Eliminate avoidance of feared situations.

The primary strategy for eliminating avoidance is exposure. Although exposure within a session facilitates habituation of the fear response, typical treatment protocols that have been empirically tested also involve between session assignments to approach feared situations. Usually, these assignments follow up on work done in the preceding session by having the client return to the situation that was the focus of exposure. Often, these homework assignments build on the previous session by adding realism. For example, following a session in which the client and therapist engaged in role-play simulations of having a conversation while eating food, the client may undertake homework of going out for lunch with a colleague, thereby extending the value of the exposure from habituation to reduction of avoidance. Similarly, interoceptive exposure can be extended beyond strategies specifically designed to evoke feared bodily sensations to include naturally occurring, but previously avoided, situations that evoke the same sensations such as exercise or sex. Naturally, the therapist needs to ascertain that the homework situation is realistically safe.

Principle 5. Improve skills for handling feared situations.

Research on treatment for anxiety disorders has often included strategies that can be grouped loosely under the rubric of skills training. Clients who have been struggling with pervasive fear and avoidance for many years often lack specific skills that would decrease the likelihood of experiencing anxiety and increase the ability to tolerate anxiety when it does occur. These skill-training interventions have typically been investigated as part of a combination of strategies.

Social Skills Training

Researchers have debated for years whether socially phobic clients lack social skills or whether they have intact latent social skills that are difficult for them to demonstrate under conditions of extreme anxiety. Owing to the typically early onset of social phobia and the avoidance that usually accompanies it, many clients with the disorder have not had an opportunity to gain experience with a variety of social situations. Social skills training for social phobia is not usually as basic as is used for clients with schizophrenia, but clients do benefit from training in activities like making small talk, being assertive, or issuing social invitations. Another type of social skill that has been investigated for anxiety disorders is communication training for couples, which has been found to be a useful adjunct to exposure for treating agoraphobia (Arnow, Taylor, Agras, & Telch, 1985; Barlow, O'Brien, & Last, 1984).

Applied Relaxation Skills

Many clients have had some relaxation training before seeking psychotherapy for problems with anxiety, as they have purchased relaxation tapes or enrolled in a meditation class. Applied relaxation is a very specific set of skills demonstrated to be efficacious for panic disorder (Öst, 1987) and for GAD (Borkovec & Costello, 1993). The early steps of applied relaxation are similar to any relaxation program, as the clinician teaches the client to tense and relax muscle groups. Gradually, the practice of relaxation becomes less complicated (dividing the body into fewer muscle groups for practice) and less time-consuming. The unique step in applied relaxation is to systematically apply the relaxation whenever the client notices external or internal cues for anxiety, as well as in anticipation of stressful events.

Applied Tension

Teaching clients to apply tension sounds like a paradoxical strategy, but Öst and his colleagues have demonstrated that exposure for blood/injury phobia is more feasible and successful if clients learn to apply tension selectively to large muscle groups (i.e., quadriceps) in advance of the exposure (Öst, Fellenius, & Sterner, 1991; Öst & Sterner, 1987). The rationale for this strategy is that some clients with blood/injury phobia, unlike those with any other anxiety disorder, do faint upon exposure to the sight of blood or blood-related paraphernalia (e.g., needles). These fainting episodes are characterized by an initial rise in blood pressure and heart rate, followed by a precipitous drop at the point of fainting (Öst, Sterner, & Lindahl, 1984). Applying tension in the large muscle groups boosts blood pressure, thereby preventing the fainting and permitting the exposure to continue safely.

Coping Skills

A variety of different empirically supported strategies for treating anxiety can be considered to boost clients' ability to cope with or tolerate the unpleasantness of anxiety. Tolerating these sensations is important for two reasons. Most obviously, anxiety is an inescapable part of the human experience. In addition, very frightened clients have difficulty engaging in exposure necessary to reduce fear and avoidance, so learning to tolerate anxiety is an important step in helping them to engage in the treatment.

In our observation, skills training for coping with anxiety has been included as a part of tested treatments in two primary ways. The first is to provide structured coping support during exposure. For example, family members or partners have been recruited to serve as supportive assistants with exposure (Arnow et al., 1985; Barlow et al., 1984). Therapists themselves can also serve in this role, as is common in the guided mastery approach in which therapists first perform the exposure themselves and then gradually guide the client toward full engagement with the stimulus. This approach has also been used by videotape (e.g., showing coping dental patients undergoing various procedures).

The second way that coping skills training has

been included in treatment has been more structured. Stress inoculation training, demonstrated to be efficacious for treating PTSD (Foa et al., 1991) is a highly structured approach. The first phase involves education about anxiety as well as development of a trusting and collaborative therapeutic relationship. The second phase involves acquisition of coping skills such as relaxation, awareness of automatic thoughts, gathering relevant information about anxiety-provoking situations, planning for resources in case of an urgent situation, assertiveness, and self-rewards for coping. The third phase of stress inoculation training is to rehearse the skills in role-plays, simulations, and imagery. The idea is to prepare for anxiety-evoking events by rehearsing skills for coping with moderate or overwhelming anxiety. The skills are then actively transferred to the real world during graded exposure and behavioral experiments.

Problem Solving Skills

GAD has been the primary area where problem-solving skills have been applied in anxiety disorders, again as part of a collection of strategies to boost overall anxiety management skills (Dugas et al., 2003). Clients with GAD often inaccurately believe that worry serves a problem-solving function. Good problem-solving skills involve recognizing a given problem and identifying probable causes of the problem, feeling confident in one's ability to manage the problem, making timely decisions in the face of uncertainty, and using time management skills to decrease problem complexity (e.g., delegating tasks, assertively refusing requests, and adhering to agendas).

One particular type of problem—that of how to maintain treatment gains—has received focused psychotherapy research attention. The relapse prevention program for OCD developed by Hiss, Foa, and Kozak (1994) primarily involves problem solving in this dimension. Following a standard course of exposure and response prevention, clients in this program learn to use problem-solving strategies to do self-therapy to manage symptom recurrences early. Clients learn to conduct their own self-directed exposure, set therapeutic goals, recruit social support to promote their goals, anticipate sources of stress, identify maladaptive interpersonal interactions that increase stress, and

set realistic expectations of progress. (In addition to these problem-solving skills, the Hiss et al. relapse prevention program also provided additional cognitive interventions.)

CROSS-CUTTING DIMENSIONS OF EFFECTIVE PSYCHOTHERAPIES

Across various theoretical orientations, psychotherapeutic approaches can be characterized along dimensions such as the degree of directiveness, the role of insight in the therapy, the level of treatment intensity, the use of emotion eliciting strategies, and the emphasis placed upon interpersonal and intrapersonal forces in effecting change. Although research-based treatment protocols for anxiety disorders do not, as a general rule, directly address these more global aspects of the process of change, a careful examination of the protocols nevertheless allows us to draw five principles from the commonalities among them. Empirically supported treatments for anxiety disorders are characterized as:

- Directive, structured, and action-oriented
- Striving for behavior change
- Time-limited and relatively intense
- Emotionally evocative
- Intrapersonal in focus

We will discuss each of these principles in turn.

> Principle 6. Therapists should be directive, and the therapeutic process should be structured and action-oriented.

Most procedures used in empirically supported treatments of anxiety disorders are directive. Note the active language used to describe basic principles that underlie effective change: "*challenge* misconceptions," "*actively test* the validity of maladaptive beliefs," "*use* repeated exposure," "*eliminate* avoidance of the feared situation," and "*improve* skills for handling the feared situation." As is evident in our discussion of the procedures involved in effective interventions as well as the principles that underlie these procedures, the therapist is highly directive and the therapy process itself is structured and action-oriented. This characterization applies whether one is using traditional cognitive therapy, exposure-based therapy, social skills training, applied relaxation, applied tension, or multi-component cognitive behavioral treatments.

Nevertheless, the effective interventions do not just "direct" the client as to what to do, when to do it, where to do it, or how to do it. Rather, a collaborative process is enlisted in which the therapist relies heavily upon the client to help determine the what, when, where, and how of therapy. This collaborative process is evident in determining which behavioral experiments to conduct, what stimuli might comprise a desensitization or exposure hierarchy, and whether to involve partners or other family members in the treatment process. The client and the therapist work collaboratively in an approach that is action-oriented; moreover, the therapist provides the structure and direction necessary to assist the client in making behavior change.

None of the empirically supported interventions for anxiety disorders are "nondirective." In the limited number of studies that have compared these effective interventions to nondirective approaches for anxiety disorders, the overwhelming evidence supports the superiority of the directive, structured approaches. Such support is most evident in work conducted by Borkovec and his colleagues on treatment of GAD (Borkovec et al., 1987; Borkovec & Costello, 1993). In the first of these studies, 30 clients who met criteria for GAD were randomly assigned to progressive muscle relaxation with cognitive therapy (PMR + CT) or to PMR with nondirective therapy (PMR + ND). Although both groups improved at posttreatment and follow-up, the PMR + CT group was superior to the PMR + ND group on almost all of the outcome measures. Borkovec et al. concluded that the addition of CT to PMR was not only more effective than the addition of ND, but also CT contained specific effective components of change that ND did not.

In the second study, 55 clients were assigned to CBT, applied relaxation (AR), and ND interventions. Clients in the ND condition were informed that the goals of treatment were to enhance self-understanding and to help them discover things they might do differently to change how they feel. Standard CBT and AR treatments were implemented and all treatments were identical in length and were reported to be highly credible. At posttreatment and follow-up, the CBT and AR interventions were found to be equally effective and superior to the ND treatment. Moreover, fewer clients in the CBT and AR conditions (approximately 16% in each group) requested and received additional treatment than did those in the ND condition (61%). Based on these studies, as well as others, it appears that interventions that are characterized by active, directive, and structured strategies produce greater change in anxiety disorders than those characterized by nondirective strategies (Barlow, Raffa, & Cohen, 2002).

Principle 7. Treatment strategies should focus on facilitating behavior change.

The effective interventions for treatment of the anxiety disorders are characterized more by behavior change than insight. Of course, as with all of these broad therapeutic dimensions, insight and behavior change are not necessarily incompatible with one another and might more productively be viewed on a continuum. Even on a continuum, however, effective interventions for the anxiety disorders fall on the behavior change side of the fulcrum. For example, although CT relies heavily upon the client being *aware* of the thoughts that characterize the various forms of worry, obsessionality, or fear, behavioral experiments are an indispensable component of effective treatment. Cognitive change may bring a kind of insight, but behavior change is also important for these treatments (Barlow, 2002; McLean & Woody, 2001; Nathan & Gorman, 2002).

Moreover, behavioral change does not depend on insight, at least not the traditional type of insight often discussed in the therapeutic literature. Similarly, interventions such as PMR, AR, social skills training, and others do not rely upon insight to effect change. Rather, they address strategies to effect behavior change. In many instances, insight—if it occurs at all—is said to follow rather than precede behavior change. In the treatment of specific phobias, for example, Öst and his colleagues have repeatedly shown that treatment—even very brief treatment—produces behavior change in the absence of insight (Öst & Sterner, 1987; Öst & Westling, 1995).

It seems safe to conclude that more work needs

to be done on clearly defining and measuring insight, as well as measuring it throughout treatment so more precise conclusions can be drawn as to whether insight precedes or follows change in cognition, behavior, or affect. This is clearly an area in need of further investigation. At this stage, effective interventions for the anxiety disorders appear to rely more on behavioral change than on insight.

Principle 8. Treatment is time-limited and relatively intense.

Many of the empirically supported treatments for anxiety disorders have been tested in both an intense brief format and a lengthier less intense format. This distinction has sometimes been termed "massed versus spaced" treatment. The advantages of massed sessions, typically defined as more than one session per week, include lower attrition rates and lower relapse rates (see Hafner & Marks, 1976; Jansson & Öst, 1982). Disadvantages include the possibility that too frequent sessions may be stressful to the client's interpersonal system (see Barlow, 2002) or that the client will not have an opportunity to generalize treatment gains through between-session homework assignments.

Although the evidence is not robust, on balance the more intense interventions appear to have more support. Franklin and Foa (2002), in a recent review of exposure and response prevention for obsessive-compulsive disorder, address this issue in detail. They define adequate planned systematic exposure as involving confrontation of obsession-evoking stimuli of sufficient duration (typically 90 minutes or longer), frequency (15 to 20 sessions), and spacing (initially at least once a week but typically two or more times per week). They also suggest frequent between-session exposure and response prevention. Franklin and Foa conclude that more frequent and intense sessions of exposure and ritual prevention lead to better outcomes.

Such support, though more mixed, has also been found in the treatment of panic disorder with agoraphobia and specific phobias. Although Chambless (1990) did not find support for the superiority of massed (daily) versus spaced (weekly) exposures, Feigenbaum (1988) found massed *in vivo* exposure to be highly effective. In this study conducted in Germany, massed exposures were conducted in an intense format over 4 to 10 days in which clients engaged in feared situations for several hours every day (e.g., taking an overnight train to a foreign city). Although clients in a less intense treatment approach also improved with treatment and maintained those gains at 8-month follow-up, the intense massed *in vivo* exposure program was more effective at long-term follow-up obtained 5 years later.

Spiegel and Barlow (2000) recently reported a similar finding at their clinic in Boston. Their treatment for clients with panic disorder with moderate to severe agoraphobia is conducted on an outpatient basis over a period of eight days. The emphasis throughout treatment is on the experience of frightening internal sensations. Öst and his colleagues have also shown that intense, massed sessions are highly effective in the treatment of specific phobias. Their pioneering efforts have led to what has been referred to as one-session treatment. Their findings indicate that intense sessions of three hours duration can be highly effective with specific phobias, with recovery rates approaching 85 to 90% (Öst, 1989; Öst, Brandberg, & Alm, 1997).

Overall, support appears to be emerging for the superiority of intense, massed sessions in the treatment of a variety of anxiety disorders. Such findings should not be surprising given the psychopathology and pathophysiology of the anxiety disorders (e.g., avoidance of the feared stimuli, negative reinforcement for avoidance, and the resulting catastrophic cognitions associated with the anxiety response).

Principle 9. Effective treatments for anxiety disorders use emotionally evocative procedures.

A fourth dimension on which effective interventions can be categorized is the degree to which they focus on enhancing or evoking the client's emotional responses versus the extent to which they focus on dampening or quieting emotional responses in an attempt to be emotionally supportive. Without question, the effective interventions for the anxiety disorders use emotionally evocative procedures. Whether the interventions consist of repeated *in vivo* or imaginal exposure, a schedule of massed or spaced sessions, challenging inappropriate and distorted cognitions, or teaching coping and social skills, the purpose of the strategies is to help the client learn more adaptive ways to handle maladaptive emotional responses. Intense emotional responses are often evoked during the implementation of these strategies. Clients' emotional responses are prominent during exposure therapy, as they are confronting what for them are intensely threatening situations.

The primary purpose of these interventions, however, is not solely to evoke emotion; rather, the primary purpose is to challenge cognitions, eliminate behavioral avoidance, or extinguish the anxiety response. Emotion evocation is frequently a byproduct of this process and it is typically enlisted to help the client experience or re-experience the situation and context surrounding the anxiety response so that more adaptive cognitions and behaviors can be learned. As noted by Öst (1989) in his intensive one-session treatment of specific phobias, one of the purposes of this exposure-based treatment is to help the client deal with extreme emotional responses in a *controlled, predictable, graduated,* and *systematic* manner. Outside of treatment, the client's exposure to feared stimuli has often been uncontrolled, unpredictable, intense, and unsystematic. The purpose then is to help the client experience the emotion in a manageable way, not to just experience intense emotion for the sake of experiencing such emotion. This distinction can be subtle at times and is frequently misunderstood by professionals and the public alike.

Of course, the fact that these approaches elicit strong emotions should not be taken to mean that the therapist is not supportive and caring as an integral part of the intervention (Goldfried & Davison, 1976; Ollendick & Cerny, 1981). Oftentimes a supportive approach is explicitly used to help the client experience, challenge, and confront strong emotions. What remains to be determined, however, is the extent to which elicitation of strong emotions in the therapy proper is critical for behavioral and cognitive change to occur. Such studies have simply not been undertaken at this time.

> Principle 10. The focus of empirically supported interventions for anxiety disorders is primarily intrapersonal.

Finally, a fifth general dimension of psychotherapeutic change is the extent to which therapy relies on change within the person versus change facilitated by environmental or interpersonal factors. Clearly, effective interventions for the anxiety disorders have a foot firmly planted at both ends of this dimension. The cognitive and behavioral changes observed in these treatments rely heavily upon intensive individual work: challenging inappropriate and dysfunctional cognitions, exposing oneself to the feared situation repeatedly, and learning new and improved skills for interacting in the previously feared and avoided situation. These tested treatments for anxiety disorders also involve a host of interpersonal factors.

An important issue is whether treatment outcome can be enhanced, or made more efficient, by including environmental and interpersonal factors in treatment. Although it certainly seems intuitive that these factors are important and that attention to them would lead to enhanced outcomes, the evidence is mixed. For example, in the treatment of persons with panic disorder with agoraphobia, it has been hypothesized that the disorder itself is associated with a great deal of interpersonal dependency and that inclusion of spouses or partners might facilitate treatment outcome. Indeed, spousal or partner involvement seems to improve treatment effectiveness for women with agoraphobia (Arnow et al., 1985; Barlow et al., 1984). In the Barlow et al. randomized controlled trial, for example, 86% of the women whose spouses accompanied them to exposure-based treatments improved versus 43% of the women whose spouses did not accompany them. Moreover, the gap in treatment efficacy widened during the first two years following the conclusion of treatment (Cerny, Barlow, Craske, & Himadi, 1987). In contrast to these very promising findings, Cobb, Mathews, Childs-Clarke, and Flowers (1984) reported no additional benefits from including spouses in their exposure-based treatment. Discrepancies in findings such as these are not easily resolved, as few differences were apparent between the trials.

There is also considerable support for the idea that social phobia might best be treated in an interpersonal context rather than an individualistic one. At its core, social phobia is an interpersonal disorder; individuals fear that they will act in a way that is embarrassing or humiliating and that they will manifest visible anxiety symptoms such as sweating, shaking, or blushing. Given the interpersonal nature of the disorder, its treatment in an interpersonal context is intuitive. In fact, all of the studies that have shown exposure-based cognitive therapy to be effective for this disorder have used a group format to provide treatment (Heimberg et al., 1990, 1993, 1998). Still, the specific treatment strategies used in this treatment are intrapersonal, as described earlier in this chapter.

Finally, two studies have also been conducted examining whether exposure and response prevention for OCD is enhanced through partner assistance or family involvement (Emmelkamp, van der Helm, van Zanten, & Ploch, 1980; Mehta, 1990). The Emmelkamp et al. study, conducted in the Netherlands, failed to find an additive effect of partner involvement; the latter, conducted in India, did find an enhanced effect of including family members. Given cultural differences, the latter study used a family-based rather than spouse-based treatment. Although some differences in approach were evident, discrepancies in findings from these two studies are not readily resolved. Franklin and Foa (2002) suggest that these findings may be related to the context of the culture in which the studies were undertaken: family relationships may be more important in India than are spousal relationships in the Netherlands.

Overall, then the jury seems to be out on whether it is advantageous to include partners or families in treatment of OCD or agoraphobia. Moreover, few studies comparing treatment delivered in individual versus group format have been conducted. However, there seems to be strong support for including others in the treatment of social phobia. Future research will need to explore whether interpersonal strategies can be a useful adjunctive approach in the treatment of anxiety disorders.

FUTURE DIRECTIONS FOR RESEARCH AND PRACTICE

Productive future research on effective psychosocial intervention for the anxiety disorders can be undertaken through many different routes, but we will briefly comment on three topics that seem critical: anxiety as an emotional response, comorbidity and its implications for treatment, and the identification of the mechanisms of change for these effective interventions.

Anxiety as an Emotional Response

Barlow (2002) has suggested that our understanding and treatment of the anxiety disorders will be enhanced when we begin to examine them in the broader context of emotions theory. We could not agree more. Clinical researchers are only beginning to tap into the vast and rich tradition associated with emotions theory. As Barlow (2002) said, emotion *is* behavior, it *is* cognition, and it *is* biology. Accordingly, anxiety and fear are behavior, they are cognition, and they too are biology. Above all else, however, anxiety and fear are *felt* and subjective experiences.

Many clients speak of the experience of anxiety and fear: the sense of dread, danger, and drama that leads to flight or fight responses. As clients describe this experience, it is more than cognitions, more than avoidance, and more than physiological arousal. This felt experience seems to be lacking in our current depiction of these core emotions and their treatment. Critical to furthering our knowledge in this domain are recent studies that have begun to examine the subjective experience or meaning of anxiety and fear to the individual client.

Of course, whether attention to such felt experiences and subjective meanings enhance treatment outcome is unknown at this time. Still, one-fourth to one-half of clients treated with empirically supported treatments do not respond favorably (Chambless & Ollendick, 2001; Ollendick & King, 2004), so there is plenty of room for improvement. Achieving a more complete understanding of the phenomena of fear and anxiety, including the aspect of felt experience, may be a window though which to expand our reach.

Co-morbidity: Implications for Treatment

Anxiety is frequently co-morbid with other disorders. In fact, it is more common for anxiety to present with another major psychiatric disorder than to occur alone. Co-morbidity estimates run as high as 75% (Chambless & Renneberg, 1988; Hope & Heimberg, 1993; Reich, Noyes, & Troughton, 1987). As reviewed by Barlow (2002), anxiety disorders frequently co-occur with the depressive disorders and alcohol and substance use disorders, and less frequently but still commonly with major personality disorders. Obvious questions are which of these disorders comes first and what are the implications for treatment of an anxiety disorder when it co-occurs with another disorder.

Several investigators have looked at the question of primacy in co-morbidity, and the answers, so far, are complex and less than satisfactory. Some retrospective studies indicate that anxiety precedes the onset of other disorders, but others indicate the reverse. To date, attempts to ascertain the developmental pathways associated with co-morbidity have been largely unsuccessful. Highly idiographic pathways appear to be the rule. Large-scale prospective studies are needed to ferret out these pathways, and researchers may need to examine anxiety and related disorders from alternative perspectives (i.e., other than the DSM-IV) to get a better handle on the meaning of co-morbidity. Until these pathways are sorted out, the research on implications of co-morbidity in the anxiety disorders focuses primarily on prognosis for treatment response.

Unfortunately, for this question as well, the research literature offers few satisfactory answers. Although co-morbidity rates appear to vary considerably among controlled treatment outcome studies, no consistent treatment outcome patterns associated with co-morbidity have emerged. In many cases, co-morbidity patterns are too idiosyncratic to address this question with much confidence; too few clients present with precisely the same co-morbidity. The limited available information, however, suggests that co-morbidity may lead to poorer treatment outcomes. For example, research on treatment of OCD has shown that clients with co-morbid schizotypal personality disorder (Minichiello, Baer, & Jenike, 1987) or severe depression (Abramowitz, Franklin, Street, Kozak, & Foa, 2000) have poorer outcomes. Still other studies indicate that anxiety disorders and alcohol use disorders may each precipitate the other, and that anxiety contributes to maintenance and re-

lapse in alcohol use disorders and conversely (Kushner, Abrams, & Borchardt, 2000). These findings suggest that co-morbid alcohol disorders might also be associated with poorer outcomes for the anxiety disorders, although this remains to be established empirically.

Thus, considerably more research must be undertaken to determine the extent of co-morbidity in clients with anxiety disorders, the effects of this co-morbidity on treatment outcome, and the nature of co-morbidity itself. See Rachman (1991) for an interesting discussion of this last point. At a minimum, it seems probable that presence of co-morbidity may signal the need for adjunctive therapies designed to address these co-occurring complications (see other chapters in this volume). On the other hand, it may be that certain co-morbid disorders (e.g., personality disorders) moderate the effectiveness of established interventions. Determining the reach and scope of effective interventions will be a task for the next generation of clinical researchers.

Mechanisms of Change

Most of the empirically supported interventions for anxiety disorders are based on a cognitive behavioral model (see Table 8.1), and the principles of change we have distilled from these treatments show that influence. We have, for example, assumed that partner-assisted exposure augments exposure therapy because the partner is instrumental in helping the client achieve more exposure, an intrapersonal process. However, little is known about the mediators of change in these interventions, and it may be that partner-assisted exposure has an interpersonal component that is key to its success.

Considerable study remains to determine the precise mechanisms as to "why" and "how" these interventions work. In our introductory comments we suggested that intervention programs rest on a sound theoretical rationale that ideally incorporates both the determinants of the behavior to be changed (i.e., anxiety and fear in this instance) and the mechanisms for bringing about the desired changes. Inasmuch as most of the empirically supported interventions combine some element of exposure with some form of cognitive restructuring, it will be imperative for future studies to show that both are necessary elements and to elucidate precisely how they lead to treatment changes.

To date, dismantling studies appear to indicate that these two active strategies are associated with significant change over and above other change agents (e.g., relaxation, nondirective support), yet the mechanisms of action are not clear. For example, in a major meta-analytic review, Abramowitz (1996) showed that studies that included strict response prevention instructions in the treatment of OCD yielded greater improvements than those with partial or no response prevention instructions. Although his analysis demonstrates the importance of response prevention, *how* response prevention exerts its influence is still a mystery. Does response prevention result in reduced physiological arousal? Does it change exaggerated negative cognitions? Or is the critical element the additional exposure to feared stimuli afforded by response prevention? Or some combination of all of these mechanisms?

Such research will be very important in understanding the psychopathology of maladaptive fear and identifying the necessary conditions for clinically meaningful change. As noted by Kraemer and colleagues (2002) and by Weersing and Weisz (2002), a major challenge facing researchers hoping to understand psychotherapy is identifying the mechanisms by which interventions mediate change. In psychotherapy research, mediation can be demonstrated by establishing four logical relationships among the treatment, the proposed mediator, and the obtained outcome. Four questions might be posed. First, is the intervention effective? Second, does the intervention affect specific mechanisms? Third, do the altered mechanisms affect the basic psychopathology of the disorder? Finally, are the effects of the intervention accounted for through this causal pathway? Researchers have addressed the first question by developing demonstrably effective interventions for many anxiety disorders. The remaining questions, however, remain largely unanswered.

In short, much has been learned but much remains to be learned. The process does not end with developing, identifying, and promulgating effective interventions. We need also to understand why they work and the conditions under which they work. Coming to this understanding may involve stepping outside the confines of tightly controlled randomized studies of cognitive behavioral interventions of DSM-defined diagnostic categories to develop new paradigms for psychotherapy research in the anxiety disorders.

References

Abramowitz, J. S. (1996). Variants of exposure and response prevention in the treatment of obsessive-compulsive disorder: A meta-analysis. *Behavior Therapy, 27,* 583–600.

Abramowitz, J. S., Franklin, M. E., Street, G. P., Kozak, M. J., & Foa, E. B. (2000). The effects of pre-treatment depression on cognitive-behavioral treatment outcome in OCD clinic outpatients. *Behavior Therapy, 31,* 517–528.

Arnow, B. A., Taylor, C. B., Agras, W. S., & Telch, M. J. (1985). Enhancing agoraphobia treatment outcome by changing couple communication patterns. *Behavior Therapy, 16,* 452–467.

Bandura, A., Blanchard, E. B., & Ritter, B. (1969). Relative efficacy of desensitization and modeling approaches for inducing behavioral, affective, and attitudinal changes. *Journal of Personality and Social Psychology, 13,* 173–199.

Barlow, D. H. (2002). *Anxiety and its disorders* (2nd ed.). New York: Guilford Press.

Barlow, D. H., O'Brien, G. T., & Last, C. G. (1984). Couples treatment of agoraphobia. *Behavior Therapy, 15,* 41–58.

Barlow, D. H., Raffa, S. D., & Cohen, E. M. (2002). Psychosocial treatments for panic disorders, phobias, and generalized anxiety disorder. In P. E. Nathan & J. M. Gorman (Eds.), *A guide to treatments that work* (2nd ed., pp. 301–335). New York: Oxford University Press.

Borkovec, T. D., & Costello, E. (1993). Efficacy of applied relaxation and cognitive-behavioral therapy in the treatment of generalized anxiety disorder. *Journal of Consulting and Clinical Psychology, 61,* 611–619.

Borkovec, T. D., Mathews, A. M., Chambers, A., Ebrahimi, S., Lytle, R., & Nelson, R. (1987). The effects of relaxation training with cognitive or nondirective therapy and the role of relaxation-induced anxiety in the treatment of generalized anxiety. *Journal of Consulting and Clinical Psychology, 55,* 883–933.

Cerny, J. A., Barlow, D. H., Craske, M. G., & Himadi, W. G. (1987). Couples treatment of agoraphobia: A two-year follow-up. *Behavior Therapy, 18,* 401–415.

Chambless, D. L. (1990). Spacing of exposure sessions in treatment of agoraphobia and simple phobia. *Behavior Therapy, 21,* 217–229.

Chambless, D. L., Baker, M. J., Baucom, D. H., Beutler, L. E., Calhoun, K. S., Crits-Christoph, P., Daiuto, A., DeRubeis, R., Detweiler, J., Haaga, D. A. F., Johnson, S. B., McCurry, S., Mueser, K. T., Pope, K. S., Sanderson, W. C., Shoham, V., Stickle, T., Williams, D. A., & Woody, S. R. (1998). Update on empirically validated therapies, II. *The Clinical Psychologist, 51,* 3–16.

Chambless, D. L., & Ollendick, T. H. (2001). Empirically supported psychological interventions: Controversies and evidence. *Annual Review of Psychology, 52,* 685–716.

Chambless, D. L., & Renneberg, B. (1988, September). *Personality disorders of agoraphobics.* Paper presented at the World Congress of Behavior Therapy, Edinburgh, Scotland.

Chambless, D. L., Sanderson, W. C., Shoham, V., Johnson, S. B., Pope, K. S., Crits-Christoph, P., Baker, M., Johnson, B., Woody, S. R., Sue, S., Beutler, L., Williams, D. A., & McCurry, S. (1996). An update on empirically validated therapies. *The Clinical Psychologist, 49,* 5–18.

Cobb, J. P., Mathews, A. M., Childs-Clarke, A., & Flowers, C. M. (1984). The spouse as co-therapist in the treatment of agoraphobia. *British Journal of Psychiatry, 144,* 282–287.

Dugas, M. J., Ladouceur, R., Leger, E., Freeston, M. H., Langlois, F., Provencher, M. D., & Boisvert, J.-M. (2003). Group cognitive behavioral therapy for generalized anxiety disorder: Treatment outcome and long-term follow-up. *Journal of Consulting and Clinical Psychology, 71,* 821–825.

Emmelkamp, P. M. G., van der Helm, M., van Zanten, B. L., & Ploch, I. (1980). Treatment of obsessive-compulsive patients: The contribution of self-instructional training to the effectiveness of exposure. *Behaviour Research and Therapy, 18,* 61–66.

Feigenbaum, W. (1988). Long term efficacy of ungraded exposure versus graded exposure in agoraphobics. In I. Hand & H. Wittchen (Eds.), *Panic and phobias: Treatments and variables affecting course and outcome* (pp. 83–88). Berlin: Springer-Verlag.

Foa, E., & Goldstein, A. (1978). Continuous exposure and complete response prevention in the treatment of obsessive-compulsive neurosis. *Behavior Therapy, 9,* 821–829.

Foa, E. B., Rothbaum, B. O., Riggs, D. S., & Murdock, T. B. (1991). Treatment of posttraumatic stress disorder in rape victims: A comparison between cognitive-behavioral procedures and counseling. *Journal of Consulting and Clinical Psychology, 59,* 715–723.

Foa, E. B., Steketee, G., Grayson, J. B., Turner, R. M., & Latimer, P. (1984). Deliberate exposure and blocking of obsessive-compulsive rituals: Immediate and long-term effects. *Behavior Therapy, 15,* 450–472.

Foa, E. B., Steketee, G. S., & Milby, J. B. (1980). Differential effects of exposure and response prevention in obsessive-compulsive washers. *Journal of Consulting and Clinical Psychology, 48,* 71–79.

Franklin, M. E., & Foa, E. B. (2002). Cognitive behavioral treatments for obsessive compulsive disorder. In P. E. Nathan & J. M. Gorman (Eds.), *A guide to treatments that work* (2nd ed., pp. 367–385). New York: Oxford University Press.

Goldfried, M. R., & Davison, G. C. (1976). *Clinical behavior therapy.* New York: John Wiley.

Hafner, J., & Marks, I. M. (1976). Exposure *in vivo* of agoraphobics: Contributions of diazepam, group exposure, and anxiety evocation. *Psychological Medicine, 6,* 71–88.

Heimberg, R. G., Dodge, C. S., Hope, D. A., Kennedy, C. R., Zallo, L., & Becker, R. E. (1990). Cognitive-behavioral group treatment for social phobia: Comparison to a credible placebo control. *Cognitive Therapy and Research, 14,* 1–23.

Heimberg, R. G., Liebowitz, M. R., Hope, D. A., Schneier, F. R., Holt, C. S., Welkowitz, L. A., Juster, H. R., Campeas, R., Bruch, M. A., Cloitre, M., Fallon, B., & Klein, D. F. (1998). Cognitive-behavior group therapy versus phenelzine therapy for social phobia: 12-week outcome. *Archives of General Psychiatry, 55,* 1133–1141.

Heimberg, R. G., Salzman, D. G., Holt, C. S., & Blendell, K. A. (1993). Cognitive-behavioral group treatment for social phobia: Effectiveness at five-year follow-up. *Cognitive Therapy and Research, 17,* 325–339.

Hellstrom, K., & Öst, L.-G. (1995). One-session therapist directed exposure vs. two forms of manual directed self-exposure in the treatment of spider phobia. *Behaviour Research and Therapy, 33,* 959–965.

Hiss, H., Foa, E. B., & Kozak, M. J. (1994). Relapse prevention program for treatment of obsessive-compulsive disorder. *Journal of Consulting and Clinical Psychology, 62,* 801–808.

Hope, D. A., & Heimberg, R. G. (1993). Social phobia and social anxiety. In D. H. Barlow (Ed.), *Clinical handbook of psychological disorders* (2nd ed., pp. 99–136). New York: Guilford Press.

Jansson, L., & Öst, L.-G. (1982). Behavioral treatments for agoraphobia: An evaluative review. *Clinical Psychology Review, 2,* 311–336.

Kessler, R. C., McGonagle, K. A., Zhao, S., Nelson, C. B., Hughes, M., Eshleman, S., Wiittchen, H.-U., & Kendler, K. S. (1994). Lifetime and 12-month prevalence of DSM-III-R psychiatric disorders in the United States: Results from the National Comorbidity Study. *Archives of General Psychiatry, 51,* 8–19.

Kraemer, H. C., Stice, E., Kazdin, A. E., Offord, D., & Kupfer, D. (2001). How do risk factors work together? Mediators, moderators, and independent, overlapping and proxy risk factors. *American Journal of Psychiatry, 158,* 848–856.

Kraemer, H. C., Wilson, G. T., Fairburn, C. G., & Agras, W. S. (2002). Mediators and moderators of treatment effects in randomized clinical trials. *Archives of General Psychiatry, 59,* 877–884.

Kushner, M. G., Abrams, K., & Borchardt, C. (2000). The relationship between anxiety disorders and alcohol use disorders: A review of major perspectives and findings. *Clinical Psychology Review, 20,* 149–171.

Lang, P. J. (1979). A bio-informational theory of emotional imagery. *Psychophysiology, 16,* 495–512.

Lang, P. J., Davis, M., & Ohman, A. (2000). Fear and anxiety: Animal models and human cognitive psychophysiology. *Journal of Affective Disorders, 61,* 137–159.

McLean, P. D., & Woody, S. R. (2001). *Anxiety disorders in adults: An evidence-based approach to psychological treatments.* New York: Oxford University Press.

Mehta, M. (1990). A comparative study of family-based and patient-based behavioral management in obsessive-compulsive disorder. *British Journal of Psychiatry, 157,* 133–135.

Meyer, V. (1966). Modification of expectations in cases with obsessional rituals. *Behaviour Research and Therapy, 4,* 273–280.

Michelson, L. K., Marchione, K. E., Greenwald, M., Testa, S., & Marchione, N. J. (1996). A comparative outcome and follow-up investigation of panic disorder with agoraphobia: The relative and combined efficacy of cognitive therapy, relaxation training and therapist-assisted exposure. *Journal of Anxiety Disorders, 10,* 297–330.

Minichiello, W. E., Baer, L., & Jenike, M. A. (1987). Schizotypal personality disorder: A poor prognostic indicator for behavior therapy in the treatment of obsessive-compulsive disorder. *Journal of Anxiety Disorders, 1,* 273–276.

Mowrer, O. (1960). *Learning theory and behaviour.* New York: Wiley.

Nathan, P. E., & Gorman, J. M. (Eds.). (1998). *A guide to treatments that work.* New York: Oxford University Press.

Nathan, P. E., & Gorman, J. M. (Eds.). (2002). *A guide to treatments that work* (2nd ed.). New York: Oxford University Press.

Obsessive-Compulsive Disorder Cognitions Working Group. (1997). Cognitive assessment of obsessive-compulsive disorder. *Behaviour Research and Therapy, 35,* 667–681.

Obsessive-Compulsive Disorder Cognitions Working Group. (2001). Development and initial validation of the Obsessive Beliefs Questionnaire and the Interpretation of Intrusions Inventory. *Behaviour Research and Therapy, 39,* 987–1006.

Ollendick, T. H., & Cerny, J. A. (1981). *Clinical behavior therapy with children.* New York: Plenum Press.

Ollendick, T. H., & King, N. J. (2004). Empirically Supported Treatments for children and adolescents: Advances toward evidence-based practice. In P. Barrett & T. H. Ollendick (Eds.), *Handbook of interventions that work with children and adolescents: From prevention to treatment* (pp. 3–25). London: John Wiley & Sons.

Öst, L.-G. (1987). Applied relaxation: Description of a coping technique and review of controlled studies. *Behaviour Research and Therapy, 25,* 397–409.

Öst, L.-G. (1989). One-session treatment for specific phobias. *Behaviour Research and Therapy, 27,* 1–7.

Öst, L.-G., Brandberg, M., & Alm, T. (1997). One versus five sessions of exposure in the treatment of flying phobia. *Behaviour Research and Therapy, 35,* 987–996.

Öst, L.-G., Fellenius, J., & Sterner, U. (1991). Applied tension, exposure in vivo, and tension-only in the treatment of blood phobia. *Behaviour Research and Therapy, 29,* 561–574.

Öst, L.-G., & Sterner, U. (1987). Applied tension: A specific behavioral method for treatment of blood phobia. *Behaviour Research and Therapy, 25,* 25–29.

Öst, L.-G., Sterner, U., & Lindahl, I.-L. (1984). Physiological responses in blood phobics. *Behaviour Research and Therapy, 22,* 109–117.

Öst, L.-G., & Westling, B. E. (1995). Applied relaxation versus cognitive behavior therapy in the treatment of panic disorder. *Behaviour Research and Therapy, 3,* 145–158.

Rachman, S. (1991). A psychological approach to the study of comorbidity. *Clinical Psychology Review, 11,* 461–464.

Reich, J., Noyes, R., & Troughton, E. (1987). Dependent personality disorder associated with phobic avoidance in patients with panic disorder. *American Journal of Psychiatry, 144,* 323–326.

Richards, D. A., Lovell, K., & Marks, I. M. (1994). Post-traumatic stress disorder: Evaluation of a behavioral treatment program. *Journal of Traumatic Stress, 7,* 669–680.

Rosen, G. M., & Davison, G. C. (2003). Psychology should list empirically supported principles of change (ESPs) and not credential trademarked therapies or other treatment packages. *Behavior Modification, 27,* 300–312.

Roth, A., & Fonagy, P. (1996). *What works for whom?* New York: Guilford Press.

Sackett, D., Richardson, W., Rosenberg, W., & Haynes, B. (1997). *Evidence-based medicine.* London: Churchill Livingston.

Sackett, D., Richardson, W., Rosenberg, W., & Haynes, B. (2000). *Evidence-based medicine* (2nd ed.). London: Churchill Livingston.

Spiegel, D. A., & Barlow, D. H. (2000, November). Intensive treatment for panic disorder and agoraphobia. In M. G. Craske (Chair), *Brief cognitive behavioral therapy for anxiety: Interventions and prevention.* Symposium at the 34th annual convention of the Association for the Advancement of Behavior Therapy, New Orleans.

Spitzer, R. L., Kroenke, K., Linzer, M., Hahn, S. R., Williams, J. B. W., deGruy, F. V., III, Brody, D., & Davies, M. (1995). Health related quality of life in primary care patients with mental disorders: Results from the PRIME MD 1000 Study. *Journal of American Medical Association, 274,* 1511–1517.

Task Force on Promotion and Dissemination of Psychological Procedures. (1995). Training in and dissemination of empirically-validated psychological treatments: Report and recommendations. *The Clinical Psychologist, 48,* 3–23.

Trull, T. J., Nietzel, M. T., & Main, A. (1988). The use of meta-analysis to assess the clinical significance of behavior therapy for agoraphobia. *Behavior Therapy, 19,*527–538.

van Oppen, P., de Haan, E., van Balkom, A. J. L. M., Spinhoven, P., Hoogduin, K., & van Dyck, R. (1995). Cognitive therapy and exposure *in vivo* in the treatment of obsessive-compulsive disorder. *Behaviour Research and Therapy, 33,* 379–390.

Weersing, V. R., & Weisz, J. R. (2002). Mechanisms of action in youth psychotherapy. *Journal of Child Psychology and Psychiatry, 43,* 3–29.

Weissman, M. M. (1985). The epidemiology of anxiety disorders: Rates, risks, and familial patterns. In A. H. Tuma & J. D. Maser (Eds.), *Anxiety and the anxiety disorders* (pp. 275–296). Hillsdale, NJ: Erlbaum.

Westen, D., & Morrison, K. (2001). A multidimensional meta-analysis of treatments for depression, panic, and generalized anxiety disorder: An empirical examination of the status of empirically supported therapies. *Journal of Consulting and Clinical Psychology, 69,* 875–899.

Wolpe, J. (1958). *Psychotherapy by reciprocal inhibition.* Stanford, CA: Stanford University Press.

9

Integration of Therapeutic Factors in Anxiety Disorders

Michelle G. Newman
William B. Stiles
Amy Janeck
Sheila R. Woody

In this chapter, we draw on three preceding chapters in an attempt to outline an integrative model for what works in the psychotherapy of anxiety disorders. These chapters sought to summarize current knowledge about the therapeutic techniques (Woody & Ollendick, this volume), participant characteristics (Newman, Crits-Christoph, Gibbons, & Erickson, this volume), and relationship factors (Stiles & Wolfe, this volume) that are related to outcomes. We seek to place these factors and their practice implications within a common framework. Our integration is based on (a) the concept of appropriate responsiveness and (b) a distinction between actions and achievements.

INTEGRATIVE CONCEPTS

Responsiveness refers to behavior being affected by emerging context. Psychotherapeutic interaction is responsive on time scales of months to milliseconds (Stiles, Honos-Webb, & Surko, 1998). Illustrations of responsiveness in psychotherapy include triage, treatment planning, answering questions, staying on related topics, turn-taking, timing of interventions, delivery to facilitate uptake, and adjusting pacing in response to nonverbal reactions. In each of these activities, the therapist's behavior is influenced by the client's characteristics, needs, resources, and ongoing behavior, as well as aspects of the setting and context. Responsiveness is ubiquitous in human interaction generally and in psychotherapy particularly. It is misleading to think of therapy as a protocol planned in advance and merely set into predictable motion at the outset of a treatment, a session, or an intervention.

Technically, responsiveness can refer to any behavior affected by context, but our interest is in *appropriate responsiveness*. In psychotherapy, appropriate responsiveness describes therapists and clients responding to emerging requirements, resources, and opportunities in ways that advance the therapy. Appropriateness must be judged in relation to some goal or principle and may vary across occasions and contexts. Thus, an appropri-

response in pursuit of challenging misconceptions may not be an appropriate response in pursuit of alliance-building. An appropriate response within cognitive therapy may not be an appropriate response within psychoanalytic therapy. An appropriate response in the middle of a long-term treatment may not be an appropriate response in a first session.

Responsiveness involves a person responding (a) with some action (b) to some circumstance. These two aspects of responsiveness link usefully to two of the classes of factors in the preceding chapters. *Responsiveness with* deals with technique factors, whereas *responsiveness to* deals with participant factors. That is, therapists respond *with* interventions *to* characteristics of their clients, their settings, and themselves.

The concept of appropriate responsiveness contributes to a further useful distinction: actions versus achievements (Stiles & Wolfe, this volume). Actions can be classified and counted and can be done more or less arbitrarily. They may or may not be used appropriately. Therapeutic techniques are typically actions. For example, asking a question, challenging a misconception, or exposing a client to the feared stimulus can be considered as actions. Achievements, on the other hand, are products or goals of appropriate action. They cannot be done arbitrarily, and attempts often fail. Typically, achievements carry a positive evaluation. Reduction in symptom intensity is an obvious example of an achievement.

TECHNIQUE FACTORS (INTERVENTIONS)

Woody and Ollendick (this volume) searched intensively through treatment manuals representing empirically supported treatments for anxiety disorders, looking for common techniques. As explained in their chapter, they identified a relatively small number of principles that seemed to occur commonly across these treatments.

Examples of the empirically supported treatments considered by Woody and Ollendick are shown in Table 9.1. As they noted, these treatments do not work for everyone, and many treatments, particularly including those outside cognitive and behavioral theoretical orientations, have

not yet been rigorously tested. Thus, there is no suggestion that the principles they identified are exhaustive. Although most of the anxiety treatments that have been empirically tested are based on cognitive-behavioral theories, the techniques can be applied within the context of other theoretical approaches.

A list of effective interventions that Woody and Ollendick culled from the manuals is shown in Table 9.2. The first two principles describe ways of changing clients' views of self. The next two principles refer to corrective experiences related to the reduction of fear and the ability to cope with anxiety-arousing stimuli. The last principle focuses on facilitating clients' acquisition of new skills.[1]

The basis for selecting the specific techniques/interventions listed in Table 9.2 was their being described in manuals of empirically supported treatments. That is, there was evidence that the therapies of which they were a part had been found to produce improvements. These techniques were tools that practitioners of successful treatments had at their disposal.

The logic of effective techniques is a logic of *responsiveness with*. It is implicit in our understanding, and often explicit in the manuals, that the techniques must be used appropriately, that is,

Table 9.1

Examples of Manualized Empirically Supported Treatments for Anxiety Disorders

Disorder	Manualized treatments
Agoraphobia	Exposure Partner-assisted cognitive-behavior therapy
Panic Disorder	Cognitive-behavior therapy Applied relaxation
Generalized Anxiety Disorder	Cognitive-behavior therapy Applied relaxation
Obsessive-Compulsive Disorder	Exposure and response prevention Cognitive therapy
Post-Traumatic Stress Disorder	Exposure Stress inoculation training
Social phobia	Exposure Cognitive-behavior therapy
Specific phobia	Exposure

Table 9.2
Effective Interventions Culled From Manual by Woody and Ollendick (in press)

Category	Principles
Cognition	1. Challenge misconceptions through discussion and explicitly questioning the evidence.
	2. Actively test the validity of erroneous and maladaptive beliefs through behavioral experiments.
Affect	3. Use repeated exposure to the feared situation to reduce the intensity of the fear response.
Behavior	4. Eliminate avoidance of feared situations.
	5. Improve skills for handling feared situations.

when clinical judgment dictates, and then with proper timing, skillful delivery, and adaptations of all sorts to the client. Even the terms of the principles (e.g., *challenging misconceptions*) refer to broad categories of thought and behavior. Applying them requires a great deal of skillful incorporation of context—what really are the client's misconceptions and which are most relevant or susceptible of change; how can they be successfully challenged? As therapeutic ingredients, these principles' specificity is a far cry from "2 mg clonazepam t.i.d.," though their therapeutic impact may well be greater.

Table 9.2 focuses on common factors—the intersection of lists of techniques used in different treatments for different disorders. In responding to a particular client, any therapist would draw on a far larger repertoire including implicit and explicit clinical skills. Few clients would be treated with strategies selected only from this list. Appropriate responsiveness implies that therapists delivering empirically supported treatments would normally use these strategies as a part of their overall treatment plan when suitable for a given client.

Misconceptions About Manualized Treatments

Although these principles apply to more than one theoretical orientation, the use of empirical research to derive them also creates the possibility that some readers will assume that these principles do not apply to therapy in general practice. In recent times psychotherapy research and manualized therapies haves been criticized for not being applicable to the "real world" of practice. Although some of these critiques are valid, some of them are also based on misconceptions associated with ESTs or manualized therapies. In order to ensure that misconceptions do not prevent people from making use of the principles derived from ESTs to treat anxiety disorders, the authors of this chapter thought it would be important to begin this chapter by attempting to dispel some common misconceptions.

Misconception 1: Psychotherapy manuals are cookbooks to be applied rigidly and with no creativity.

Although there are a plethora of psychotherapy manuals for the treatment of anxiety, researchers neither use them as cookbooks nor do they suggest that therapists use them in this fashion. The optimal way to use a therapy manual is as a means of information regarding underlying principals of change as well as the various techniques that can be used to achieve such change. Once therapists have become expert with a manualized treatment, they understand its underlying principles and strategies and can creatively use the principles to apply techniques tailored to an individual client's needs. Manuals provide an example of how a course of treatment might be structured, but treatment strategies may be applied in a different order or using somewhat different language. Similarly, because therapists frequently encounter issues that are not pre-specified in a manual, it is always up to them to understand the underlying principles of change and to make use of their own creativity in the application of techniques.

Misconception 2: Using an EST means not devoting appropriate or sufficient attention to the therapeutic relationship.

The use of ESTs, or principles derived from them, should not preclude good clinical judgment. As noted by Stiles and Wolfe, good therapists will and do recognize that the client–therapist relationship is important in the treatment of anxiety disorders. All therapists are taught to be responsive to elements of the person and aspects of the relationship and the use of psychotherapy manuals, even manuals that do not specifically address relationship issues, should not prevent therapists from maintaining a responsive posture. In fact, Stiles and Wolfe highlight the importance of customizing responsiveness to the particular client characteristics. It is important to find a balance between being directive, pushing, setting limits and being nondirective and such a balance requires the therapists to follow their clinical intuition.

> Misconception 3: ESTs are only helpful for uncomplicated non-co-morbid clients who meet DSM-IV criteria for a particular anxiety disorder.

Most of the previous psychotherapy trials for anxiety disorders eliminated clients only when they met criteria for co-morbid substance abuse or dependence, psychosis, or when other Axis I disorders were primary. Such studies rarely eliminated people due to other co-morbid Axis I diagnoses. Similarly none of the studies ruled people out for co-morbid Axis II. In fact most of them did not even assess for Axis II. Thus, the principles derived from these trials are likely to generalize to most clients for whom anxiety is the primary presenting problem.

Applying the Technique Factors

As suggested above, the factors listed in Table 9.2 can be clustered within three general categories of intervention: changing view of self, corrective experiences, and skills acquisition. These general (or meta) principles are consistent with a large body of theoretical understanding and clinical lore. This background is brought into play when the technique is applied responsively.

> 1. Therapists help clients become aware of their inaccurate perceptions and help them to think about things more accurately.

Evidence suggests that people with anxiety disorders have a pre-attentive (i.e., outside of conscious awareness) bias to threat cues (Mathews & MacLeod, 1986). In addition, people with anxiety disorders also have an interpretive bias such that they are more likely to interpret ambiguous events as threatening (MacLeod & Cohen, 1993; Mathews, Richards, & Eysenck, 1989) and to overestimate objective personal risk (Butler & Mathews, 1983) than are nonanxious persons. Given this bias, it is *less* likely that anxious individuals will naturally benefit from corrective experiences. In other words, even when they encounter events that objectively disconfirm their fears, people with anxiety disorders are unlikely to experience and interpret these events in ways that convince them that their fears are unfounded. Thus, it is important that psychotherapy for these individuals helps them to become aware of their negative biases, to learn to view encountered situations objectively, to encode new information objectively, and to use this information to reconstruct their worldview.

Whereas cognitive therapy attempts to directly change inaccurate perceptions, cognitive change has been achieved by other therapy approaches, including behavioral strategies. One study also found that a form of brief psychodynamic therapy (short-term anxiety provoking therapy) and a nondirective therapy both led to cognitive changes (Svartberg, Seltzer, Choi, & Stiles, 2001). Thus, it is clearly possible that therapists may use noncognitive therapy techniques to help clients to interpret their experiences more accurately.

> 2. Therapists should engage clients in a corrective emotional experience during which time clients are directly confronted with and face their fear, and can learn that they are able to cope with it and the associated anxiety.

This principle holds true for any client for whom anxiety has led to avoidance of situations, objects, people, imagery, memories, or internal sensations and such avoidance is viewed as maladaptive. In cognitive behavioral therapy, this principle is achieved via repeated exposure with the elimination of avoidance. For this technique clients are often directed to approach a feared object, place themselves in feared situations, focus on feared imagery, recount traumatic memories, or engage in exercises to generate feared internal sensations. In each of these cases clients are asked to remain exposed until their fear has peaked and passed. Among dismantling studies examining single techniques for agoraphobia, in vivo exposure alone was found to be comparable to combined CBT and has been found to be an essential component to treat agoraphobic avoidance. Similarly among combined cognitive-behavioral treatments for agoraphobia, studies that employed cognitive restructuring with in vivo and interoceptive exposure yielded the strongest effect sizes (Clum, Clum, & Surls, 1993; Gould, Otto, & Pollack, 1995). In addition, in cognitive-behavioral treatments for social phobia, exposure-interventions yielded the largest effect size (*ES*) whether alone (*ES* = .89) or combined with cognitive restructuring (*ES* = .80) (Gould, Buckminster, Pollack, Otto, & Yap, 1997).

Avoidance can take many shapes and sizes and is not always obvious. Such avoidance can be subtle as in cases where agoraphobic clients try to remain near the door of any room they might go into, when socially phobic clients avoid voluntarily speaking in a group situation (such as a meeting or class), or when obsessive-compulsive clients use ritualistic thoughts or PTSD clients avoid thinking about a traumatic experience. Therefore, therapists need to conduct a thorough assessment of all possible situations, objects, images, memories, or sensations that clients may fear as well as all possible cognitive or behavioral avoidance strategies clients may be employing. Therapists should also anticipate the possibility that clients may place themselves in a feared situation but at the same time may try to use cognitive strategies to distract themselves from or to otherwise avoid the anxiety associated with exposure. Because anxious clients who avoid objects or situations that generate anxiety are also avoidant of anxious experience, such exposure is only helpful in situations in which the client does not avoid their internal anxious experience. Clients need to learn that they can cope with their anxiety thus making the exposure a corrective experience. Therefore, such clients should be directed to refrain from engaging in avoidance strategies. For example, research on obsessive-compulsive disorder shows that completely preventing ritualistic behaviors or cognitions during exposure was associated with better outcome than partial or no response prevention (Abramowitz, 1996).

Although exposure principles have been empirically tested mainly using CBT techniques, as noted earlier these principles also apply to techniques derived from other theoretical approaches. For example, for some disorders such as GAD (Borkovec & Hu, 1990; Borkovec & Inz, 1990; Turk, Heimberg, Luterek, Mennin, & Fresco, in press) and panic disorder (Williams, Chambless, & Ahrens, 1997) studies have found that in addition to experiencing fear of fear, clients are afraid and avoidant of their emotional experiences in general. Thus, it would follow that emotion-focused therapy techniques (e.g., Greenberg & Safran, 1987) that expose clients to emotional experiencing would be important for these individuals. In the treatment of GAD (for example, Newman, Castonguay, Borkovec, & Molnar, 2004), researchers have begun to test whether experiential techniques are helpful. Similarly, engaging clients in a discussion of traumatic memories in an emotionally immediate way can be beneficial to clients with anxiety disorders, particularly those with PTSD (e.g., Foa, 2000).

3. Therapists help clients develop the skills for handling feared situations.

Some clients' fears are due to an inability to cope with particular situations. For example, clients with social phobia may lack some social skills that would help them interact better with others and those with other anxiety disorders may lack the ability to problem-solve or to relax. Therefore, an important change principle is to help clients to acquire the skills they need to cope with their feared situations as well as with any associated anxiety. In cognitive-behavioral therapy this involves the direct teaching of specific skills whereas within other therapy techniques this may be achieved more indirectly. Future research should examine whether skills training is conducted within non-CBT approaches.

PARTICIPANT FACTORS (CLIENT AND THERAPIST CHARACTERISTICS)

Newman et al. (this volume) used a different strategy to identify common principles in research on participant factors. They searched the literature for evidence that client characteristics, therapist characteristics, or shared characteristics (e.g., ethnic or gender match) were correlated (across cases) with outcome. As they reported, there is little evidence that therapist or shared characteristics consistently predicted outcome. However, a number of client characteristics did predict outcome.

Table 9.3 lists client characteristics that Newman et al. reported as predictive of *poorer* outcome. They are grouped in categories of severity of the presenting anxiety symptom, co-morbidity with other disorders, measured attitudes of the clients and behaviors in treatment, and demographic characteristics. With respect to the last category, it is noteworthy that there was no consistent association of outcome with client age, gender, ethnicity, or intelligence in the literature that Newman et al. reviewed. Strikingly, the empirically supported client factors were all negative characteristics. Clients who entered treatment with greater problems were less likely to be successful. The poor got poorer, or, at least, failed to get richer.

The absence of neutral, descriptive characteristics from Table 9.3, and the consequent dominance of negative client characteristics, can be understood as a manifestation of *responsiveness to*. Briefly, if therapists respond appropriately and adequately to a client characteristic, then clients with and without that characteristic tend to have equivalent outcomes, and that characteristic will not be correlated with outcome. For example, in a study examining psychotherapy for a depressed sample, Hardy, Stiles, Barkham, and Startup (1998) found that therapists delivering manualized treatments tended to use more affective and relationship-oriented interventions with clients who had an over-involved interpersonal style and more cognitive and behavioral interventions with clients who had an under-involved interpersonal style. Yet clients with these different interpersonal styles had approximately equivalent outcomes. One interpretation is that therapists were responsive to these particular needs. The same argument might explain the failure to find correlations between gender and outcome. For example, if women require somewhat different treatment from men (discussion of different topics, different amounts of exposure to feared situations, different styles of challenging misconceptions) and therapists are appropriately responsive to these requirements then both women and men may tend to achieve similar outcomes.

Conversely, then, the client factors that correlated significantly with outcomes are those to which therapists have not—probably could not—respond appropriately and adequately. If therapists were able to respond fully to differences in, for example, severity of the disorder, then clients who presented with different degrees of severity would have similar positive outcomes. The factors in Table 9.3 are predictive precisely because, despite their best efforts, therapists have not fully overcome these negative client characteristics. One implication of this view is that many factors not listed in Table 9.3 are also important in successful therapy process, but that therapists and clients examined in research have generally found ways to appropriately promote therapeutic goals within the context of factors not listed, such as gender, attachment style, therapist background, ethnicity, and so forth.

Thus, client characteristics within the responsive model can be seen as heuristics or markers, which therapists should be alerted to, as not responding to them appropriately is likely to reduce or preclude change. Looked at clinically, the factors listed in Table 9.3 are individual differences to which therapists may need to be especially responsive. A responsive therapist would assess for

Table 9.3
Client Characteristics Associated With Poorer Treatment Outcomes

Category	Poorer outcome associated with
Severity	Greater severity
	Greater chronicity
	Greater self-reported distress
Co-morbidity	Co-morbid depression
	Co-morbid personality disorder
	Co-morbid substance abuse
Client attitudes	Low expectation of success
	Negative perceived parenting
	Low internal attributions
	Negative self-attributions
Client behaviors	Noncompliance with homework
Demographics	Lower socioeconomic status

these predictors and ethically attempt to address them.

The following paragraphs offer suggestions for how therapists might respond to the identified participant factors, keeping in mind that the factors identify clients who are in the greatest need and at the greatest risk.

1. Greater severity, chronicity, and self-reported distress from anxiety tends to predict poorer outcome from treatment of anxiety disorders.

In instances when therapists are attempting to treat persons with greater chronicity, severity, or distress change is likely to occur at a slower rate and these clients may exhibit more symptomatology following successful treatment than clients who begin treatment with lower severity, chronicity, or distress. Most treatment outcome studies provide the same number of sessions to all participants, regardless of severity, which may account for the poorer outcome for those with more severe problems. In clinical practice, it may be important for therapists to lower their expectations with respect to rate of change, to accept smaller changes as progress, and to demonstrate greater flexibility with respect to how they implement an intervention, as well as which interventions they choose to implement, with more effort placed on creatively tailoring interventions to the individual client. The latter point is very important because although there are numerous studies that have shown that severity predicts a negative outcome there is currently no data showing that a particular approach works better for more severely disordered clients than currently tested approaches.

2. For clients who have a primary anxiety disorder, co-morbid depression, personality disorders, and substance abuse, predicts poorer outcome.

It is important to note that co-morbid anxiety disorders do not appear to predict negative outcome. Co-morbidity of depression, personality disorders, and substance abuse can deter effective treatment in several ways. For example, it is possible that depression or substance abuse will prevent clients from becoming more actively involved in the treatment. In addition, substance-abusing clients may be effectively self-medicating and therefore unable to reap the benefits of exposure-based treatment of anxiety without the substance. Further substance use may interfere with anxiety habituation and client attributions for success may be focused on the substance rather than toward their therapeutic work. Moreover, personality disorders may impede therapist's ability to form a strong therapeutic alliance.

In cases where clients have co-morbid depression, it may be optimal for the therapist to address the depression first, to refer the client to a psychiatrist for antidepressant medication, or to directly address the depression and anxiety concurrently. In cases where clients have co-morbid substance abuse, therapists with no expertise in substance abuse intervention should refer the client to a therapist who has such expertise. Therapists who have expertise in substance abuse intervention will want to treat the substance abuse first or concurrently with the anxiety disorder. In cases where clients have a co-morbid personality disorder special attention should be focused on developing and maintaining the therapeutic alliance. In addition, it is likely to be important to address the personality disorder directly.

3. Psychotherapy for anxiety is less likely to be effective if the client perceives his/her social support structure to be high in hostility or criticism.

The quality of clients' social support appears to be an important facet of successful therapy for anxiety. As a result, it may be important to determine whether clients' current levels of social support are high in levels of hostility and criticism. In cases where clients have no close relationships, the therapist may want to work with them to help them build a positive social support network. In addition, in instances where the relationships are strained or highly critical, clients may need referrals for marital therapy or family therapy.

4. Psychotherapy for anxiety is less likely to be effective if the client does not think it will help.

When beginning with a new client it may be helpful to take the time to explain how you work as a therapist, what sort of approach you take to therapy, and what is your theory of change. Sometimes low expectations may arise from a failure to understand why the therapist's approach is as it is. If, after hearing the full rationale, clients have clearly articulated concerns about the therapy really helping them—you may need to reconsider your approach or their goals. Explore—try to understand the reasons behind these concerns. It is probably not wise to continue with the planned intervention under these circumstances but instead it is better to give the client the sense that his or her feelings were being taken into account by trying to work out a course of treatment that seems more in line with what the client was looking for. Also, it may be the case that what the client is looking for does not fit with your theoretical approach. If this is the case, it might be most helpful to refer the client to a therapist whose approach is more consistent with what the client is seeking.

5. Psychotherapy for anxiety is less likely to be successful if the client reports negative perceived parenting behaviors/attachment.

This principle suggests that it may be helpful to routinely assess client attachment and perceptions of parenting behavior. In such cases where clients report negative parenting, it may be helpful to focus more therapy time and attention toward the development of the therapeutic relationship as well as toward helping the clients develop strong interpersonal relationships outside of the therapeutic relationship.

6. Psychotherapy for anxiety is less likely to be successful if the client has low internal attributions of control or high negative self-attributions.

As with the above principle, this is one that should be routinely assessed. These cognitive patterns could be a part of an overall depression. Further, it may be the case that these clients would benefit from interventions directed toward helping them to see that they have more control than they think they do. In addition, the therapy might be directed toward helping clients become aware that they are over-attending to their negative attributes and not sufficiently processing their positive attributes.

7. Psychotherapy for anxiety is less likely to be successful if the client comes from a lower socioeconomic status.

In some cases individuals from lower SES backgrounds may not have the necessary resources (i.e., transportation, baby-sitting) to support the luxury of therapy. Thus the provision of such resources or even the willingness to be more flexible may be helpful to these individuals. It is also possible that this factor may be related to some of the other factors mentioned earlier (e.g., low expectations for the efficacy of therapy), thus, for these individuals, it might also be helpful to devote extra time and attention to helping clients become engaged in the therapeutic relationship. Finally, it may be worthwhile to facilitate lower income clients' access to community resources that may help ease the burden of stressful life circumstances.

RELATIONSHIP FACTORS

In contrast to the plethora of studies on treatment techniques and participant (mostly client) characteristics, there has been relatively little research on relationship factors that is specific to anxiety disorders. Researchers interested in relationship variables typically have not restricted their samples to clients with particular disorders, except when they happened to work on a clinical trial data set (most of which have dealt with depression). Researchers interested in anxiety disorders, on the other hand, have mostly focused on outcome rather than process. Only a limited number of studies have examined process variables in anxiety disorders, and the analyses were often incidental within an outcome study. Nonetheless, most of the available relationship findings in anxiety treatments were consistent with findings in treatments for mixed or unspecified disorders, as summarized in the Norcross (2002) task force report. On this basis, Stiles and Wolfe (this volume) adopted the assumption that relationship factors tend to bear similar relations to the outcome in treatments for anxiety disorders as they do in psychotherapeutic treatments generally.

Table 9.4
Relationship Characteristics Associated With
Positive Treatment Outcomes

Level of evidence	Relationship factor
Empirically supported	Strong therapeutic alliance
	Cohesion in group therapy
	Empathy
	Positive regard
	Collaboration
	Feedback
Accepted by default (as promising and probably effective)	Congruence or genuineness
	Repair of alliance ruptures
	Management of counter-transference
	Therapist self-disclosure
	Quality of relational interpretation

The strategy for identifying the empirically supported relationship factors listed in Table 9.4 was similar to the strategy employed by Newman et al. (this volume) for identifying participant factors. That is, studies had reported statistical associations (usually, correlations across clients) of the relationship factors with indexes of positive outcome. Whereas Stiles and Wolfe (this volume) elected, mainly for conceptual reasons, to adopt by default the relevant conclusions reached by the Division 29 Task Force, in this chapter, we have chosen to cite findings of specific studies that reported such associations. However, to be consistent with Stiles and Wolfe (this volume), we have elected to accept by default the Division 29 conclusions when insufficient findings were available for particular variables (see Table 9.4).

Empirically Supported
Relationship Factors

Similar to what has been found in studies of other disorders, a strong therapeutic alliance (i.e., agreement on task, bond, and goals) predicted a better outcome in the treatment of anxiety disorders in eight studies (Budman, Soldz, Demby, Feldstein, Springer, & Davis, 1989; Cloitre, Koenen, Cohen, & Han, 2002; Hoogduin, de Haan, & Schaap, 1989; Keijsers, Schaap, Hoogduin, & Peters, 1991; Keijsers, Hoogduin, & Schaap, 1994a; Margraf &

Schneider, 1991; Nelson & Borkovec, 1989a; Svartberg, Seltzer, & Stiles, 1998) and in a mixed depression and anxiety sample (Safran & Wallner, 1991) whereas the therapeutic alliance was not significantly predictive of outcome in three studies (de Beurs, Lange, van Dyck, & Koele, 1995; Keijsers, Hoogduin, & Schaap, 1994b; Woody & Adessky, 2002). Alliance increased in strength from middle to later sessions for clients with pre-occupied attachment, but it decreased near the last sessions for those with dismissing styles (Kanninen, Salo, & Punamaeki, 2000). Moreover, in response to group therapy, highly cohesive groups produced better immediate outcome than less cohesive groups in an anxiety sample (Hand, Lamontagne, & Marks, 1974) and in a mixed depression and anxiety sample (Budman et al., 1989). Also, those from highly cohesive groups showed continuous and further improvement during six-month follow-up. (Hand et al., 1974) and another study showed that cohesion was positively related to outcome for cardiac patients treated for exhaustion, anxiety, hostility, and depression (van Andel, Erdman, Karsdorp, Appels, & Trijsburg, 2003). Nonetheless cohesion was not predictive of outcome in two studies (Teasdale, Walsh, Lancashire, & Mathews, 1977; Woody & Adessky, 2002).

There are a number of therapist behaviors that may contribute to client change. For example, therapist warmth predicted positive outcome in four studies (Morris & Suckerman, 1974a, 1974b; Rabavilas, Boulougouris, & Perissaki, 1979; Ryan & Moses, 1979) although therapist warmth was not significantly predictive of outcome in one study (Morris & Magrath, 1979). Also, therapist caring and involvement was predictive of positive outcome in one study (Williams & Chambless, 1990). In addition, another study found that therapist acceptance, respect, interest, and liking were also predictive of positive outcome (Rabavilas et al., 1979). Further, there is some support for the use of empathy (Emmelkamp & Van der Hout, 1983; Rabavilas et al., 1979), positive regard (Bennun, Hahlweg, Schindler, & Langlotz, 1986; Bennun & Schindler, 1988; Emmelkamp & Van der Hout, 1983; Rabavilas et al., 1979), guidance (Bennun & Schindler, 1988), verbal encouragement (Mathews, Johnston, Lancashire, Munby, Shaw, & Gelder, 1976; Rabavilas et al., 1979), helping the client feel understood (Hansen, Hoogduin, Schaap, & de Haan, 1992; Rabavilas et al., 1979) and reinforcement (Wilkins, 1971) in the treatment of anxiety disorders. However, whereas one study found that congruence was significantly related to outcome (Emmelkamp & Van der Hout, 1983) another study found no relationship between congruence and outcome (Staples & Sloane, 1976). Therefore, with regard to relationship variables examined by the Division 29 Task Force (Norcross, 2002), the previous studies support the importance of a strong therapeutic alliance, therapist empathy, positive regard, and cohesion in group therapy.

Examination of therapists' use of feedback has shown that it was significantly related to outcome in two studies (DeVoge, Minor, & Karoly, 1981; Leitenberg, Agras, Allen, & Butz, 1975) and additional studies support the use of video feedback as helpful for socially phobic individuals (Harvey, Clark, Ehlers, & Rapee, 2000; Kim, Lundh, & Harvey, 2002; Rapee & Hayman, 1996).

Several studies also have reported data concerning compliance, which has been considered an element of collaboration in the Division 29 (Norcross, 2002) list of empirically supported relationship factors. One study found that compliance with in-session and homework exposure and response prevention instructions predicted outcome in OCD (Abramowitz, Franklin, Zoellner, & DiBernardo, 2002). Similarly, homework compliance (HWC) predicted improvement from exposure with response prevention for OCD (de Araujo, Ito, & Marks, 1996), decreased social anxiety after CBGT for social phobia (Leung & Heimberg, 1996), outcome at two-year follow-up in self-exposure for phobias (Park, Mataix Cols, Marks, Ngamthipwatthana, Marks, Araya, & Al-Kubaisy, 2001), end-state functioning in self-exposure for agoraphobia (Michelson, Mavissakalian, Marchione, Dancu, & Greenwald, 1986), effectiveness of relaxation for generalized anxiety (Hoelscher, Lichstein, & Rosenthal, 1984), and outcome of CBGT for social phobia at six-month follow-up, but not at post (Edelman & Chambless, 1995). Divergently, HWC failed to predict outcome of CBGT for social phobia (Woody & Adessky, 2002), CBT for PTSD (Taylor, Fedoroff, Koch, Thordarson, Fecteau, & Nicki, 2001), CBT for GAD (Nelson &

Borkovec, 1989b; Przeworski, Newman, Castonguay, & Constantino, 2001), across stress inoculation training, prolonged exposure, supportive counseling, CBT, and wait-list conditions for PTSD (Foa, Riggs, Massie, & Yarczower, 1995; Foa, Rothbaum, Riggs, & Murdock, 1991; Lax, Basoglu, & Marks, 1992; Taylor et al., 2001), couples treatment for agoraphobia (Barlow, O'Brien, & Last, 1984), and *in vivo* exposure for panic with agoraphobia and OCD, taking account of both quantitative and qualitative aspects (Woods, Chambless, & Steketee, 2002). Lastly, therapist or objective ratings, but not client measures, of compliance predicted positive therapeutic change in CBT for panic disorder (Schmidt & Woolaway-Bickel, 2000) and relaxation for GAD (Hoelscher et al., 1984); perhaps this distinction partially explains the mixed findings regarding HWC and outcome. Of the aforementioned findings, 12 of 24 (50%) found a positive relation between HWC and outcome, at least with one type of rating.

Relationship Factors as Achievements

The relationship factors listed in Table 9.4 seem sensible and familiar, but they do not offer step-by-step instructions for how to construct optimal therapeutic relationships or the if–then specifications one might find in a pharmacological treatment protocol. Instead, they indicate goals and qualities to be optimized. They offer a great deal of latitude in implementation, calling, in effect, for exercise or the therapist's skill and judgment. Each of them incorporates a substantial evaluative component.

Thus, as Stiles and Wolfe suggested, the relationship factors that have been identified by the Division 29 Task Force as demonstrating effectiveness (strong alliance, group cohesion, empathy, collaboration) are achievements rather than actions. They may be regarded as the products, rather than the tools, of appropriate responsiveness. That is, they are the products of the right actions at the right time. Even relationship factors that look like actions were, on closer inspection, understood as achievements. For example, it was evidently *appropriate* therapist self-disclosure (not just any self-disclosure) and *appropriate* feedback (not just any feedback) that was found to be associated with positive outcomes.

CONCLUSION

In conclusion, we suggest that the concept of appropriate responsiveness can help integrate the lists of identified technique, participant, and relationship factors (Newman et al., this volume; Stiles & Wolfe, this volume; Woody & Ollendick, this volume). Specifically, the factors include (a) a repertoire of techniques used responsively by successful therapists, (b) client characteristics that predict outcome because they are not adequately responded to, and (c) relationship attributes that are achieved through appropriate responsiveness.

ACKNOWLEDGMENTS Preparation of this manuscript was supported in part by National Institute of Mental Health Research Grant MH-58593.

Note

1. Woody and Ollendick (this volume) identified another set of principles not directly culled from empirically supported manuals, but related to general dimensions of psychotherapy (see Beutler and Castonguay [this volume] for a description of these dimensions). To a large extent, however, these additional principles overlap with those listed in Table 9.2, with the exception of two of them: (1) effective therapy for anxiety disorders is time-limited and relatively intense, and (2) therapists should be directive, data supporting these principles are presented in Woody and Ollendick (this volume). Literature uncovered while preparing the current chapter also provided further support for the second principle. Specifically, three studies found that directiveness was associated with a positive outcome (Bennun et al., 1986; Bennun & Schindler, 1988; Margraf & Schneider, 1991), although one study found support for the use of an empathic and nondirective stance during the first session (Keijsers, Schaap, Hoogduin, & Lammers, 1995).

References

Abramowitz, J. S. (1996). Variants of exposure and response prevention in the treatment of obsessive-compulsive disorder: A meta-analysis. *Behavior Therapy, 27,* 583–600.

Abramowitz, J. S., Franklin, M. E., Zoellner, L. A., & DiBernardo, C. L. (2002). Treatment compliance and outcome in obsessive-compulsive disorder. *Behavior Modification, 26,* 447–463.

Barlow, D. H., O'Brien, G. T., & Last, C. G. (1984). Couples treatment of agoraphobia. *Behavior Therapy, 15,* 41–58.

Bennun, I., Hahlweg, K., Schindler, L., & Langlotz, M. (1986). Therapist's and client's perceptions in behaviour therapy: The development and cross-cultural analysis of an assessment instrument. *British Journal of Clinical Psychology, 25* (Pt. 4), 275–283.

Bennun, I., & Schindler, L. (1988). Therapist and patient factors in the behavioural treatment of phobic patients. *British Journal of Clinical Psychology, 27,* 145–150.

Borkovec, T. D., & Hu, S. (1990). The effect of worry on cardiovascular response to phobic imagery. *Behaviour Research and Therapy, 28,* 69–73.

Borkovec, T. D., & Inz, J. (1990). The nature of worry in generalized anxiety disorder: A predominance of thought activity. *Behaviour Research and Therapy, 28,* 153–158.

Budman, S. H., Soldz, S., Demby, A., Feldstein, M., Springer, T., & Davis, M. S. (1989). Cohesion, alliance and outcome in group psychotherapy. *Psychiatry: Journal for the Study of Interpersonal Processes, 52,* 339–350.

Butler, G., & Mathews, A. (1983). Cognitive processes in anxiety. *Advances in Behaviour Research and Therapy, 5,* 51–62.

Cloitre, M., Koenen, K. C., Cohen, L. R., & Han, H. (2002). Skills training in affective and interpersonal regulation followed by exposure: A phase-based treatment for PTSD related to childhood abuse. *Journal of Consulting and Clinical Psychology, 70,* 1067–1074.

Clum, G. A., Clum, G. A., & Surls, R. (1993). A meta-analysis of treatments for panic disorder. *Journal of Consulting and Clinical Psychology, 61,* 317–326.

de Araujo, L. A., Ito, L. M., & Marks, I. M. (1996). Early compliance and other factors predicting outcome of exposure for obsessive-compulsive disorder: Results from a controlled study. *British Journal of Psychiatry, 169,* 747–752.

de Beurs, E., Lange, A., van Dyck, R., & Koele, P. (1995). Respiratory training prior to exposure in vivo in the treatment of panic disorder with agoraphobia: Efficacy and predictors of outcome. *Australian and New Zealand Journal of Psychiatry, 29,* 104–113.

DeVoge, J. T., Minor, T., & Karoly, P. (1981). Effects of behavioral intervention and interpersonal feedback on fear and avoidance components of severe agoraphobia: A case analysis. *Psychological Reports, 49,* 595–605.

Edelman, R. E., & Chambless, D. L. (1995). Adherence during sessions and homework in cognitive-behavioral group treatment of social phobia. *Behaviour Research and Therapy, 33,* 573–577.

Emmelkamp, P. M. G., & Van der Hout, A. (1983). Failures in treating agoraphobia. In E. B. Foa & P. M. G. Emmelkamp (Eds.), *Failures in behavior therapy.* New York: Wiley.

Foa, E. B. (2000). Psychosocial treatment of posttraumatic stress disorder. *Journal of Clinical Psychiatry, 61,* 43–48; discussion 49–51.

Foa, E. B., Riggs, D. S., Massie, E. D., & Yarczower, M. (1995). The impact of fear activation and anger on the efficacy of exposure treatment for posttraumatic stress disorder. *Behavior Therapy, 26,* 487–499.

Foa, E. B., Rothbaum, B. O., Riggs, D. S., & Murdock, T. B. (1991). Treatment of posttraumatic stress disorder in rape victims: A comparison between cognitive-behavioral procedures and counseling. *Journal of Consulting and Clinical Psychology, 59,* 715–723.

Gould, R. A., Buckminster, S., Pollack, M. H., Otto, M. W., & Yap, L. (1997). Cognitive-behavioral and pharmacological treatment for social phobia: A meta-analysis. *Clinical Psychology: Science and Practice, 4,* 291–306.

Gould, R. A., Otto, M. W., & Pollack, M. H. (1995). A meta-analysis of treatment outcome for panic disorder. *Clinical Psychology Review, 15,* 819–844.

Greenberg, L. S., & Safran, J. D. (1987). *Emotion in psychotherapy: Affect, cognition, and the process of change.* New York: Guilford Press.

Hand, I., Lamontagne, Y., & Marks, I. M. (1974). Group exposure (flooding) in vivo for agoraphobics. *British Journal of Psychiatry, 124,* 588–602.

Hansen, A. M. D., Hoogduin, C. A. L., Schaap, C., & de Haan, E. (1992). Do drop-outs differ from successfully treated obsessive-compulsives? *Behaviour Research and Therapy, 30,* 547–550.

Hardy, G. E., Stiles, W. B., Barkham, M., & Startup, M. (1998). Therapist responsiveness to client interpersonal styles during time-limited treatments for depression. *Journal of Consulting and Clinical Psychology, 66,* 304–312.

Harvey, A. G., Clark, D. M., Ehlers, A., & Rapee, R. M. (2000). Social anxiety and self-impression: Cognitive preparation enhances the beneficial effects of video feedback following a stressful social task. *Behaviour Research and Therapy, 38,* 1183–1192.

Hoelscher, T. J., Lichstein, K. L., & Rosenthal, T. L. (1984). Objective vs subjective assessment of relaxation compliance among anxious individuals. *Behaviour Research and Therapy, 22,* 187–193.

Hoogduin, C. A., de Haan, E., & Schaap, C. (1989). The significance of the patient–therapist relationship in the treatment of obsessive-compulsive neurosis. *British Journal of Clinical Psychology, 28,* 185–186.

Kanninen, K., Salo, J., & Punamaeki, R. L. (2000). Attachment patterns and working alliance in trauma therapy for victims of political violence. *Psychotherapy Research, 10,* 435–449.

Keijsers, G., Schaap, C., Hoogduin, K., & Peters, W. (1991). The therapeutic relationship in the behavioural treatment of anxiety disorders. *Behavioural Psychotherapy, 19,* 359–367.

Keijsers, G. P. J., Hoogduin, C. A. L., & Schaap, C. P. D. R. (1994a). Predictors of treatment outcome in the behavioural treatment of obsessive-compulsive disorder. *British Journal of Psychiatry, 165,* 781–786.

Keijsers, G. P. J., Hoogduin, C. A. L., & Schaap, C. P. D. R. (1994b). Prognostic factors in the behavioral treatment of panic disorder with and without agoraphobia. *Behavior Therapy, 25,* 689–708.

Keijsers, G. P. J., Schaap, C. P. D. R., Hoogduin, C. A. L., & Lammers, M. W. (1995). Patient–therapist interaction in the behavioral treatment of panic disorder with agoraphobia. *Behavior Modification, 19,* 491–517.

Kim, H.-Y., Lundh, L.-G., & Harvey, A. (2002). The enhancement of video feedback by cognitive preparation in the treatment of social anxiety: A single-session experiment. *Journal of Behavior Therapy and Experimental Psychiatry, 33,* 19–37.

Lax, T., Basoglu, M., & Marks, I. M. (1992). Expectancy and compliance as predictors of outcome in obsessive-compulsive disorder. *Behavioural Psychotherapy, 20,* 257–266.

Leitenberg, H., Agras, W. S., Allen, R., & Butz, R. (1975). Feedback and therapist praise during treatment of phobia. *Journal of Consulting and Clinical Psychology, 43,* 396–404.

Leung, A. W., & Heimberg, R. G. (1996). Homework compliance, perceptions of control, and outcome of cognitive-behavioral treatment of social phobia. *Behaviour Research and Therapy, 34,* 423–432.

MacLeod, C., & Cohen, I. L. (1993). Anxiety and the interpretation of ambiguity: A text comprehension study. *Journal of Abnormal Psychology, 102,* 238–247.

Margraf, J., & Schneider, S. (1991, November). *Outcome and active ingredients of cognitive-behavioral treatments for panic disorder.* Paper presented at the Association for the Advancement of Behavior Therapy, New York.

Mathews, A., Richards, A., & Eysenck, M. (1989). Interpretation of homophones related to threat in anxiety states. *Journal of Abnormal Psychology, 98,* 31–34.

Mathews, A. M., Johnston, D. W., Lancashire, M., Munby, M., Shaw, P. M., & Gelder, M. G. (1976). Imaginal flooding and exposure to real phobic situations: Treatment outcome with agoraphobic patients. *British Journal of Psychiatry, 129,* 362–371.

Mathews, A. M., & MacLeod, C. (1986). Discrimination of threat cues without awareness in anxiety states. *Journal of Abnormal Psychology, 95,* 131–138.

Michelson, L., Mavissakalian, M., Marchione, K., Dancu, C. V., & Greenwald, M. (1986). The role of self-directed in vivo exposure in cognitive, behavioral, and psychophysiological treatments of agoraphobia. *Behavior Therapy, 17,* 108.

Morris, R. J., & Magrath, K. H. (1979). Contribution of therapist warmth to the contact desensitization treatment of acrophobia. *Journal of Consulting and Clinical Psychology, 47,* 786–788.

Morris, R. J., & Suckerman, K. R. (1974a). The importance of the therapeutic relationship in systematic desensitization. *Journal of Consulting and Clinical Psychology, 42,* 148.

Morris, R. J., & Suckerman, K. R. (1974b). Therapist warmth as a factor in automated systematic desensitization. *Journal of Consulting and Clinical Psychology, 42,* 244–250.

Nelson, R. A., & Borkovec, T. D. (1989a). Relationship of client participation to psychotherapy. *Journal of Behavior Therapy and Experimental Psychiatry, 20,* 155–162.

Nelson, R. A., & Borkovec, T. D. (1989b). Relation-

ship of client participation to psychotherapy. *Journal of Behavior Therapy and Experimental Psychiatry, 20,* 155–162.

Newman, M. G., Castonguay, L. G., Borkovec, T. D., & Molnar, C. (2004). Integrative Psychotherapy. In R. Heimberg, D. Mennin, & C. Turk (Eds.), *Generalized Anxiety Disorder: Advances in research and practice* (pp. 320–350). New York: Guilford Press.

Norcross, J. C. (Ed.). (2002). *Psychotherapy relationships that work: Therapist contributions and responsiveness to patients*: London: Oxford University Press.

Park, J. M., Mataix Cols, D., Marks, I. M., Ngamthipwatthana, T., Marks, M., Araya, R., & Al-Kubaisy, T. (2001). Two-year follow-up after a randomised controlled trial of self- and clinician-accompanied exposure for phobia/panic disorders. *British Journal of Psychiatry, 178,* 543–548.

Przeworski, A., Newman, M. G., Castonguay, L. G., & Constantino, M. J. (2001, July). *The relationship between therapeutic alliance, compliance with CBT homework, and outcome in GAD.* Paper presented at the the World Congress of Behavioral and Cognitive Therapies, Vancouver, British Columbia.

Rabavilas, A. D., Boulougouris, J. C., & Perissaki, C. (1979). Therapist qualities related to outcome with exposure in vivo in neurotic patients. *Journal of Behavior Therapy and Experimental Psychiatry, 10,* 293–294.

Rapee, R. M., & Hayman, K. (1996). The effects of video feedback on the self-evaluation of performance in socially anxious subjects. *Behaviour Research and Therapy, 34,* 315–322.

Ryan, V. L., & Moses, J. A. (1979). Therapist warmth and status in the systematic desensitization of test anxiety. *Psychotherapy: Theory, Research, Practice, Training, 16,* 178–184.

Safran, J. D., & Wallner, L. K. (1991). The relative predictive validity of two therapeutic alliance measures in cognitive therapy. *Psychological Assessment, 3,* 188–195.

Schmidt, N. B., & Woolaway-Bickel, K. (2000). The effects of treatment compliance on outcome in cognitive behavioral therapy for panic disorder: Quality versus quantity. *Journal of Consulting and Clinical Psychology, 68,* 13–18.

Staples, F. R., & Sloane, R. B. (1976). Truax factors, speech characteristics, and therapeutic outcome. *Journal of Nervous and Mental Disease, 163,* 135–140.

Stiles, W. B., Honos-Webb, L., & Surko, M. (1998).

Responsiveness in psychotherapy. *Clinical Psychology: Science and Practice, 5*, 439–458.

Svartberg, M., Seltzer, M. H., Choi, K., & Stiles, T. C. (2001). Cognitive change before, during, and after short-term dynamic and nondirective psychotherapies: A preliminary growth modeling study. *Psychotherapy Research, 11*, 201–219.

Svartberg, M., Seltzer, M. H., & Stiles, T. C. (1998). The effects of common and specific factors in short-term anxiety-provoking psychotherapy: A pilot process-outcome study. *Journal of Nervous and Mental Disease, 186*, 691–696.

Taylor, S., Fedoroff, I. C., Koch, W. J., Thordarson, D. S., Fecteau, G., & Nicki, R. M. (2001). Posttraumatic stress disorder arising after road traffic collisions: Patterns of response to cognitive-behavior therapy. *Journal of Consulting and Clinical Psychology, 69*, 541–551.

Teasdale, J. D., Walsh, P. A., Lancashire, M., & Mathews, A. M. (1977). Group exposure of agoraphobics: A replication study. *British Journal of Psychiatry, 130*, 186–193.

Turk, C. L., Heimberg, R. G., Luterek, J. A., Mennin, D. S., & Fresco, D. M. (in press). Delineating emotion regulation deficits in generalized anxiety disorder: A comparison with social anxiety. *Cognitive Therapy and Research*.

van Andel, P., Erdman, R. A. M., Karsdorp, P. A., Appels, A., & Trijsburg, R. W. (2003). Group cohesion and working alliance: Prediction of treatment outcome in cardiac patients receiving cognitive behavioral group psychotherapy. *Psychotherapy and Psychosomatics, 72*, 141–149.

Wilkins, W. (1971). Desensitization: Social and cognitive factors underlying the effectiveness of Wolpe's procedure. *Psychological Bulletin, 76*, 311–317.

Williams, K. E., & Chambless, D. L. (1990). The relationship between therapist characteristics and outcome of in vivo exposure treatment for agoraphobia. *Behavior Therapy, 21*, 111–116.

Williams, K. E., Chambless, D. L., & Ahrens, A. (1997). Are emotions frightening? An extension of the fear of fear construct. *Behaviour Research and Therapy, 35*, 239–248.

Woods, C. M., Chambless, D. L., & Steketee, G. (2002). Homework compliance and behavior therapy outcome for panic with agoraphobia and obsessive compulsive disorder. *Cognitive Behaviour Therapy, 31*, 88–95.

Woody, S. R., & Adessky, R. S. (2002). Therapeutic alliance, group cohesion, and homework compliance during cognitive behavioral group treatment of social phobia. *Behavior Therapy, 33*, 5–27.

Part IV

PERSONALITY DISORDERS

10

Participant Factors in Treating Personality Disorders

Héctor Fernández-Alvarez
John F. Clarkin
María del Carmen Salgueiro
Kenneth L. Critchfield

This chapter focuses on patient and therapist characteristics as they influence treatment outcomes for individuals diagnosed with one or more personality disorders (PDs). The treatment goals for personality-disordered individuals can be quite diverse, ranging from amelioration of specific symptoms to change in underlying personality functioning and organization, depending on the therapist's orientation, the treatment setting, and the precise nature of the patient's problems. The patient and therapist factors that contribute to globally conceived "outcome" may thus also be quite diverse and multifaceted. Our aim in this chapter is to review and summarize the empirical literature regarding patient and therapist (i.e., participant) factors in personality disorder treatment in order to distill a set of "principles" that might be used to guide clinical practice and also to help frame an agenda for future research in this area.

Quite frankly, outcome research focused on treatment of personality disorder is only in its infancy and is currently inadequate for us to fulfill our aims with any great confidence. Nevertheless, we believe it is useful to summarize the "early returns" at this point to get a clear picture of current thinking about factors showing promise for predicting outcome in the treatment of PD. Regarding the diversity of possible treatment outcomes, it is important to note at the outset, that where relevant research exists, the focus is often on changes in specific behaviors or symptoms. This departs in many respects from clinical work, where the more common focus of treatment is on complex issues of self-concept, views of others, and related problems encountered in work and intimate relationships. Existing findings may thus be skewed in the direction of symptom change over other changes also valued by clinicians and patients with regard to the Axis II disorders.

In the following sections we briefly discuss the nature of personality pathology and the state of the current empirical literature as it relates to our focus. Following this, we will turn to a presentation and detailed discussion of participant factors that have been addressed in the empirical literature, and conclude with a brief list of principles derived from this discussion.

PERSONALITY PATHOLOGY: A DIVERSE SET OF PERVASIVE AND ENDURING PATTERNS

DSM-IV defines all personality pathology (irrespective of specific category) as pervasive and enduring patterns of cognition, affective experience, interpersonal functioning, and/or impulse control that deviate from the norm and cause significant distress and/or impairment in social and work functions. This definition encompasses a dramatic range and diversity of patterns. However, the global definition allows us to frame personality pathology as involving a few key variables that have received research attention in other settings, for example: (1) functional difficulties that endure across time, (2) difficulties attaching to and bonding with others, and (3) difficulties learning from or collaborating with others (e.g., resistance and reactance).

The advantage of identifying general research variables that speak to PD issues is that it opens up (albeit obliquely) potential sources of data for participant factors predictive of outcome. A problem remains, however, in that the DSM-IV defines 10 commonly occurring constellations of maladaptive personality patterns, with many patients showing complex combinations of these 10 feature sets. Even if only the 10 currently identified DSM disorders are considered, a wide range and diversity of sometimes opposing features are involved. So, while a given empirical finding might seem relevant to treatment of personality pathology in general, it may not apply equally well to all specific Axis II disorders. Interpersonal reactance, for example, has been identified as a predictor of poor outcome in the general treatment literature and is itself implicated in the definition of a number of the personality disorders. However, not all of the Axis II disorders involve high levels of interpersonal reactance, or it serves very different functions for disorders as interpersonally diverse as, for example, dependent PD, antisocial PD, and schizoid PD. General conclusions presented here

must thus be tempered not only by limitations of the empirical database, but also by consideration of the diversity of characteristics and patterns included under the general heading "personality pathology."

PD-SPECIFIC TREATMENT RESEARCH

As was mentioned previously, there is scarce (but accumulating) empirical evidence on the overall effectiveness of psychotherapy for clients with personality disorders. There is still less research that has addressed moderating variables related to treatment outcome. The limited volume of research may be attributed in part to factors inherent to PD that make it a difficult population to study. These factors include marked heterogeneity of defining features, varying degrees (and definitions) of severity relative to these features, extensive comorbidity on both Axis I and Axis II (not to mention ongoing controversies as to precise definitions and taxonomic boundaries).

Given the complex nature of personality pathology, its treatment demands an equally sophisticated and multifaceted treatment approach (Magnavita, 1999; Perris and Skagerlind, 1998). The fact of a more complex treatment poses difficulties for researchers in terms of the logistics of training, ongoing adherence monitoring, and so on. Another important factor potentially contributing to reduced research output is that treatments for PD patients are typically expected to extend over several years in order to achieve positive results, an obstacle that in itself creates large financial and logistical problems for researchers. For some PD subgroups, clinical management risks are also high (e.g., suicide, homicide, assault, or recklessly impulsive behavior are not uncommon) and extensive clinical support infrastructures may be necessary to cover all contingencies. One effective approach to reducing the complexity of the Axis II treatment enterprise has been to develop treatments that focus narrowly on specific target populations. For example, Dialectical Behavior Therapy (DBT; Linehan, 1993) was developed primarily to address the subgroup of borderline PD patients evidencing suicidal and parasuicidal behaviors. However, principles derived from such therapies may or may not prove to generalize to treatment of patients with other PD feature sets.

Sources of data for the present chapter were derived from three main sources: (1) empirical studies of treatment in PD populations or other patient populations in which a high level of comorbid PD was reported and participant factors were also implicated in outcome, (2) simple inspection of existing treatment manuals for PD, and (3) empirical studies of treatment for non-Axis II disorders where identified participant variables had some reasonable relation to the definition of personality disorder itself. In doing this work, we also relied on previous, more general findings and participant factor categories generated by the APA Division 29 Task Force (presented in Norcross, 2002).

With regard to treatment research, Perry, Banon, and Ianni (1999) reviewed 15 studies that reported treatment effects for PD. These studies varied in quality, and included three randomized control trials, three randomized comparisons of active treatments, and nine uncontrolled observational studies. Clients under study had the following disorders: borderline (4 studies), borderline plus schizotypal (1), avoidant (1), antisocial (1), and mixed (8). The treatments varied considerably in terms of their length (from 10 weeks to 25.4 months) and the approach used (psychodynamic-interpersonal, cognitive-behavioral, mixed/eclectic, and supportive approaches were all represented). All 15 studies resulted in an amelioration of the patient complaints under investigation, showing that PD can be successfully treated. In four of the studies, roughly half of treated clients recovered (i.e., no longer met criteria for a PD diagnosis) after treatments that lasted 1.3 years on average. Treatments for the cluster C disorders (i.e., avoidant, dependent, and obsessive-compulsive) tended not to last as long.

The few extant "empirically validated treatments" for PD (Chambless and Ollendick, 2001; Nathan and Gorman, 1998) are limited to two of the DSM-IV categories: avoidant (Alden, 1989) and borderline PD (Linehan, 1993). Some data is available regarding the beneficial effects of brief, group therapies applied to a sample of patients with diverse Axis II diagnoses, mostly from clusters B and C (Winston et al., 1991, 1994). In addition, an uncontrolled study addressed a treatment for avoidant PD (Renneberg, Goldstein, Phillips, & Chambless, 1990), and a case study has been presented for paranoid PD (Williams, 1988).

PARTICIPANT FACTORS EXAMINED IN THIS CHAPTER

Following the Task Force mandate articulated in Beutler & Castonguay (this volume), we review factors related to patients and therapists, which exist outside the process of psychotherapy but may influence outcome. It has repeatedly been observed that the therapeutic alliance is strongly linked to outcome, including for treatments for PD (Smith, Barrett, Benjamin, & Barber, this volume). Bearing this in mind, we also review available evidence regarding participant factors that impact development and maintenance of the therapeutic alliance. We do this under the assumption that such factors will also be important in understanding outcome, especially for a population evidencing chronic relational disturbances that are expected to become manifest in the therapeutic relationship. We will now turn our discussion to the specific factors, divided into the following four major categories:

1. *Patient and therapist socio-demographic factors*, comprising socioeconomic status, education, age, gender, ethnicity, and religion/spirituality.
2. *Patient role-specific factors*, comprising functional impairment and social support, expectations and preferences, coping style and the introversion/extraversion dimension of personality, anaclitic versus introjective personality styles, resistance and reactance, attachment style, interpersonal history, and quality of object relations.
3. *Therapist role-specific factors*, comprising professional training and experience, expectations about therapy, and attachment style.
4. *Participant characteristics impacting the therapeutic alliance*.

SOCIO-DEMOGRAPHIC FACTORS

Patient SES, Education

Very little data is available to speak to these issues in PD treatment per se. However, some findings are available in the general treatment literature regarding the relationship between these two factors and persistence in therapy. Such findings are potentially relevant to PD given the longer expected treatment length. In a recent review, Petry, Tennen, and Affleck (2000) came to the conclusion that there is a positive correlation between social class and persistence in psychotherapy. Specifically, a low socioeconomic status is predictive of premature termination. These authors also observed a positive correlation between education and persistence in treatment. The precise meaning of this latter finding, however, is somewhat unclear given that educational attainment can reflect diverse processes that are themselves related to SES, but are also thought to reflect intelligence, available opportunities and interests, and so on.

Client and Therapist Age

In the empirical literature addressing this issue for non-PD disorders, there is no agreement on whether the relative ages of patient and therapist impact outcome (Beutler, Machado, & Neufeldt, 1994). However, some writers have long maintained that results tend to improve when the therapist is older than his clients (e.g., Beck, 1988). Some researchers have linked the amount of professional experience a therapist has (itself strongly correlated with age) to outcome (see review by Teyber and McClure, 2000). Impact of the level of therapist experience and training per se will be discussed in a later section.

Client and Therapist Gender

No research has addressed this issue in PD treatment. However, some limited evidence exists suggesting that there may be therapist gender and patient–therapist gender matching differences on outcome. Recent reviewers have been reluctant to draw conclusions about this issue due to the limited amount of research as well as the presence of some mixed findings (Huppert et al., 2001; Sue & Lam, 2002; Zlotnick et al., 1998). Individual patients diagnosed with PD often vocalize clear preferences for male versus female therapists, and this preference is often understandable in light of the patient's problem patterns or relational history. General trends for gender preference by Axis II disorder, however, are not readily apparent and have not been the subject of focused research.

Client and Therapist Ethnic Group

It has been suggested that the cultural discrepancy associated with ethnic differences between client and therapist can lead to poor results in psychotherapy (e.g., Teyber & McClure, 2000). This seems to be a reasonable assertion and is consistent with the general push toward acquainting beginning therapists with issues of diversity, as well as encouraging them to have a greater sensitivity to ethnicity, race, and culture when engaging in assessment and treatment activities. Specific outcome research focused on these issues, however, is lacking (for detailed review, see Sue & Lam, 2002), including the degree to which heightened sensitivity to these issues can prevent or ameliorate any related problems.

Client and Therapist Religion and Spirituality

Findings from the general psychotherapy literature suggest that both similarities and differences between the religious values of client and therapist can contribute positively to the progress of therapy. Worthington, McCullough, and Sandage's (1996) extensive review of the influence of religion and spirituality on psychotherapy outcome concludes, among other things, that deeply religious clients prefer a therapist with values similar to their own, even if that therapist is less qualified. In contrast, moderately or nonreligious clients are not concerned about therapists sharing their views. The same review concluded that a therapist's disclosure of his or her religious values contributes positively to the process when both client and therapist share similar beliefs, provided that the treatment process itself does not focus on religious issues (see also Beutler, Machado, & Neufeldt, 1994). Similarly, Propst, Ostrom, Watkins, Dean, and Mashburn (1992) found that religious clients in religion-oriented therapies experience deeper changes in comparison to clients in nonreligious therapies. None of these findings speak directly to the issue of personality disorder. It is plausible, however, that individuals diagnosed with PD would follow the same pattern, with that subset of personality-disordered patients who are also religious being more likely to seek a therapist with similar values. Whether this would in turn contribute to improved outcomes remains to be ascertained.

Patient–Therapist Match on Socio-Demographic and Personality Factors

There are two primary perspectives (other than the null hypothesis) regarding the therapeutic impact of overall demographic similarity between patient and therapist: one favors similarity while the other favors dissimilarity. The early literature in this area proposed that dissimilarity between patient and therapist would be associated with higher dropout rates and premature terminations because patients would be unable to construct an adequate bond with a highly dissimilar therapist (Mendelson & Geller, 1967). In contrast, the perspective favoring dissimilarity holds that therapists who are too similar to their clients will not be as capable of introducing new and different perspectives and thus not be as able to facilitate learning in the therapeutic experience (Fernández-Alvarez, 2001). No research data is available for PD treatments on this issue. However, the issue has been studied to some small degree in the general treatment literature and may provide some guidance.

Dolinsky, Vaughan, Luber, Mellman, and Roose (1998) studied 50 psychodynamic psychotherapy dyads, asking each participant to simply rate the quality of the "match" between them on a 5-point scale ranging from "bad" to "excellent." This study found that in a significant percentage of patient–therapist pairs (33%) there was substantial disagreement regarding whether the match between patient and therapist was generally positive or negative. Positive match ratings, however, were associated with more positive ratings of therapeutic alliance, aspects of the therapeutic process, and outcome. A positive evaluation of the match made by a patient was significantly correlated with a high level of therapist activity. Hersoug, Hoglend, and Monsen (2001) reach a similar conclusion regarding patient preferences for active therapists based on findings that interpersonally warm and dominant therapists tended to have higher patient-rated alliances. In Dolinsky's study, ratings of the match were not associated with a perception of shared personal characteristics. Instead, if a patient was engaged in treatment and the alliance was strong, the match was rated as positive. This suggests that what patients and therapists see as constituting a good "match" between them is not a function of their shared characteristics, but relates strongly to the nature of their relationship together.

Similarity versus dissimilarity between patient and therapist has also been studied with specific reference to behavior, affect, cognitive style, and interpersonal factors. For example, Herman (1998) studied patient/therapist pairs using the Structural Profile Inventory (SPI; Lazarus, 1989). The SPI is a self-report questionnaire that asks persons to rate their functioning in terms of behavior, affect, sensation, imagery, cognition, interpersonal relationships, and biological and physical factors. Earlier work using a similar methodology had shown that therapist theoretical stances are consistent with their profile of "modality structures" (Herman, 1992) and that patient perceptions of their psychological difficulties were predicted by their own SPI scores (Herman, Cave, Kooreman, Miller, et al., 1995). Herman (1998) further found that similarity of modality structures between patient and therapist have a positive effect on the outcome of psychotherapy, further hypothesizing that similarity affected psychotherapeutic process such that techniques were presented more clearly and were more "on target" when patients and therapists shared similar modality structures. While this study was not specifically focused on personality-disordered patients, the conclusions suggest that the match between patient and therapist "personality" (here broadly conceived) impacts outcome and is thus likely to be a promising area for future research with PD populations.

CLIENT FACTORS

Functional Impairment and Social Support

A certain degree of functional impairment is part of the definition of personality disorder in DSM-IV. Typically, individuals with personality disorders manifest this impairment in the interpersonal domain (but not exclusively so), with long-standing functional difficulties in intimate relationships and work settings that are directly related to their problematic personality traits. Functional impairment can be defined and assessed in a number of ways (e.g., through objective rating, self-reported distress, etc.), with varying degrees of tailoring to the specific problems experienced by a given patient. From a broad perspective, a cluster of variables reflecting low levels of social support, disturbances in social and work relationships, chronicity of problems, and co-morbidity of various diagnostic conditions serve to define functional impairment (Beutler, Clarkin, & Bongar, 2000). Domains of central importance to PD are contained in this cluster of variables, most notably problems in social and work relationships. Nevertheless, little direct research has been done to identify the degree to which various forms of functional impairment may be related to treatment outcome for PD.

Stated briefly, there is substantial data suggesting that severity of functional impairment is inversely related to treatment outcome (Beutler, Harwood, Alimohamed, & Malik, 2002). The empirical literature clearly indicates that individuals with positive interpersonal relations, acute (as opposed to chronic) problems, and only a single diagnostic condition benefit the most from treatment. However, these characteristics are not typical of patients with personality disorders. Thus, while these findings also likely apply to PD, researchers have yet to directly address the issue within this population.

Given the central role of disturbed interpersonal relationships in PD, another relevant index of functional impairment is social support. Research on this widely studied construct has produced strong evidence that a patient's subjective sense of the availability of supportive relationships is related to treatment outcome. These results have been surprisingly consistent, with social support being positively related to treatment benefit in 10 of 13 studies reviewed recently (Beutler et al., 2002). Direct research is still needed in PD treatment, but appears to be a promising direction for exploration.

Expectations and Preferences

"Client expectations" is a broad term that usually encompasses the client's ideas about therapeutic gain, the nature of the therapy procedures, the therapist's role, and the duration of treatment (Garfield, 1994). A related concept is the client's preferences, or value judgments, about what is desired in and from the treatment. The empirical literature on these topics is hampered by measurement difficulties and shows mixed and even contradictory results. One difficulty, especially with regard to PD, is that patient expectations and preferences are not simply static, pretreatment conditions. Instead, they evolve in concert with the therapeutic relationship and the treatment itself. This has been noted as an important area for future research (Arnkoff, Glass, & Shapiro, 2002). Maladaptive attitudes, feelings, and beliefs comprising PD may in turn shape this changing and evolving mix between patient and therapist. For example, before the formulation of Axis II in the DSM system in 1980, Tollinton (1973) found that expectations of improvement were not as predictive of actual improvement after neuroticism scores were taken into account. It is quite plausible that those with personality disorders who by definition have chronic difficulties in functioning and relationships will bring to psychotherapy a background of disappointing experience, and not much faith in the help they would receive from another. Any therapy for these individuals will likely be impacted by these issues, but must also in some way address these issues, or at least be alert to their influence early in the treatment. These issues could be addressed, to some degree, under the rubric of the transtheoretical model associated with "stages of change" research (Prochaska & Norcross, 2002). While research addressing a patient's pretreatment readiness for change has not yet been applied in the field of personality disorder treatments, it seems reasonable to assume that such readiness would also be a function of the patient's interpersonal history and impact their expectations for help from mental health professionals.

Coping Style and the Introversion/ Extraversion Dimension of Personality

The manner in which an individual copes with stress and difficulties has been a subject of keen interest to those trying to understand psychopathology and treatment. Beutler and Clarkin (1990) included within the term those styles of coping observed during and following stressful situations. According to their definition, coping styles are habitual and enduring patterns used by the individual when confronting problematic situations. The empirical literature suggests that the importance of a dimension ranging from introverted/introspective styles to extroverted/extratensive styles. This dimension is also prevalent in the general literature on personality disorder and has been used to articulate putative taxonomic relations between PD categories (e.g., Kernberg, 1996). The effect of this dimension in treatment of PD has not been explored. However, in a recent review of the general treatment literature, Beutler et al. (2002) observed that there tends to be a differential effect of type of treatment on coping style. Specifically, symptom-focused and skill-building treatments are most effective with extroverts, while insight-oriented treatments are typically more effective for internalizing patients.

Anaclitic Versus Introjective Personality Styles

Another formulation of clinically relevant personality characteristics, originally developed to capture subtypes of depression, but also relevant here, is the theory reviewed by Blatt, Shahar, and Zuroff (2002), who propose that there are two basic personality configurations called the anaclitic and introjective styles. Briefly, the anaclitic styles are predominantly preoccupied with relatedness and attachments to others, while the introjective styles focus on self-definition and cognitive coping styles. Blatt provides evidence that these two styles respond differentially to different treatment approaches (Blatt, 1992). In addition, these basic personality styles have clear overlap with the personality disorders; the anaclitic dimension seems

primary in disorders such as borderline PD, dependent PD, and histrionic PD, while the introjective dimension is primary for obsessive-compulsive PD and narcissistic PD. Blatt's formulation seems to be a very promising area for future research given initial evidence for differential treatment outcomes, as well as strong conceptual overlap with many PD categories.

Resistance and Reactance

Another major area of clinical concern in treating individuals with personality disorders involves the need to manage and often work to modify the resistance that the patient is likely to manifest during the course of treatment. Resistance/reactance has been framed as general personality dimension, inherent to some degree in all individuals (Beutler, Moleiro, & Talebi, 2002). Relatively high levels of behaviorally expressed resistance are expected from all categories of PD. This is because the disorder is characterized by rigidly held patterns of linked cognition, behavior, and affect related to self-concept, values, and views of others. And, according to Beutler et al., reactance is "differentially responsive to a person's disposition to perceive threat," and would thus be expected of many patients diagnosed with PD. The specific quality and appearance of the behavioral resistance will likely vary depending on the specific personality patterns or DSM-IV categories that characterize a given patient.

High levels of resistance and reactance, conceptualized as manifestations of basic personality traits, have been linked in the general treatment literature to poorer outcome (for review, see Beutler, Moleiro, & Talebi, 2002). No specific study has been done to address this issue for PD treatments. However, an argument may be made to the effect that resistance/reactance serves in part to mark the presence of personality disorder. Future research is needed to address the impact of this issue in PD treatment as well as to tease apart the potential overlap between the reactance trait construct and PD patterns per se.

Attachment Style

There is a small but growing literature on the impact of the patient's attachment style on the process of therapy, the patient's response to treatment, and on the patient's attachment to the therapist (which in turn may elicit complementary attachment-related behaviors from the therapist). Bowlby's (1988) classic work on attachment theory describes the way in which infants attach to caregivers for security and survival. This process is thought to in turn influence close relationships throughout the lifespan, including the therapeutic relationship. As such, the potential impact of patient attachment style seems highly relevant to the treatment of individuals with personality disorders given that the very definition of personality disorder involves the notion of troubled connections to others. Beyond a simple, undifferentiated generalization between non-secure attachment styles and PD, there is also likely to be more specific overlap between individual PD categories and specific non-secure attachment styles. For example, preoccupied attachment has been found to be prevalent in individuals with dependent PD (Brennan, Clark, & Shaver, 1998), as well as borderline PD (Fonagy et. al, 1996).

A recent review (Meyer & Pilkonis, 2002) suggests that the patient's attachment style has an influence on the alliance formed in therapy. In a study of cognitive-behavioral therapy for outpatients, Eames and Roth (2000) found that securely attached patients formed effective therapeutic alliances, contrasting alliance problems experienced by anxious-avoidant patients. Similarly, Mallinckrodt, Gantt, and Coble (1995) found that patients who reported a secure attachment style were also likely to endorse a strong alliance. Attachment style was also observed to affect the treatment alliance as it evolved over time in a study of Palestinian political ex-prisoners (Kanninen, Salo, & Punamäki, 2000). In this study, securely attached patients maintained a stable alliance throughout the treatment. Patients with a preoccupied attachment style progressed from a poor alliance in the middle of treatment to a strong alliance in the later treatment phases. Patients with a dismissive attachment style reported deteriorating alliances toward the end of treatment.

In addition to its impact on the alliance, there is also some data to suggest that patient attachment influences treatment outcome. In a study of patients with mood disorders and severe personality disorders, Fonagy et al. (1996) found that more securely attached patients were at a higher level of functioning both at admission and discharge. However, patients with a dismissive attachment style exhibited the greatest amount of pre-post change in the direction of improvement. However, in contrast to this last result, Meyer, Pilkonis, Proietti, Heape, and Egan (2000) found that secure attachment predicted improvement while non-secure attachment dimensions were unrelated to outcome. Secure attachment has also been associated with benefit from treatment for those suffering from eating disorders, mood disorders, and anxiety disorders (Mosheim, Zachhuber, Scharf, Hofmann, Kemmler et al., 2000).

If patient attachment style in fact influences both treatment alliance and outcome, a next important step would to explore how these effects might occur. It could be the case that effective therapists intuitively sense patient difficulties in relating and thus calibrate their own behavior to accommodate patient needs, but that some styles are more easily accommodated than others (Stiles, Honos-Webb, & Surko 1998). Similarly, "ruptures" in the therapeutic alliance and recovery from them, as articulated by Safran and Muran (2000) may be differentially related to attachment style and differentially responded to by therapists. Some limited evidence exists in support of the idea that therapist interventions are differentially calibrated to patient attachment styles. Hardy et al. (1999) rated session transcripts and found that therapists responded to patient preoccupied styles with more reflection, but to dismissive styles with more interpretation.

Research on interpersonal issues complement findings in the attachment literature and also overlap strongly with features that define personality disorder. A few studies have linked interpersonal difficulties to the outcome of therapy. Most notably, results generated by Hilliard, Henry, and Strupp (2000), using a sample in which 67% of the patients had an Axis II diagnosis, found that (1) a patient's early parental relations had both a direct and an indirect (i.e., mediated through the therapeutic relationship) effect on outcome, and (2) a therapist's early parental relations had a direct effect on the therapy process, which in turn impacted outcome.

Approaching the issue from another framework, Ogrodniczuk, Piper, and Joyce (2001) found that their measure, Quality of Object Relations (QOR), was an important predictor of treatment outcome. Briefly, QOR is operationalized as an individual's ability to establish relationships with others, based in part on their relational history, and ranging along a dimension from primitive to mature. In post-therapy follow-ups, these investigators found that higher QOR was associated with more favorable results for clients in interpretive therapies but not in supportive therapies. In sum, the interpersonal and attachment-based literatures both point to a patient's demonstrated ability to create and maintain positive interpersonal relationships as a predictor of positive treatment outcome. Research in this area is limited, but appears promising not only for predicting outcome, but also for helping therapists attend to the ongoing relational processes of therapy in such a way as to maximize benefit for PD patients who have diverse, but marked problems in this domain.

The interpersonal histories of patients with PD diagnoses frequently contain episodes of severe abuse, neglect, or other trauma of an interpersonal nature that contribute to and/or maintain problematic views of the self and others (Johnson et al., 2000). An emerging framework that may address such issues as they impact the process and outcome of therapy is the Assimilation of Problematic Experiences model developed by Stiles (2002). This model views therapeutic change as being a process involving integration and assimilation of experience into the "community of voices" that represent the self. Problematic/traumatic experiences initially are perceived as threatening and thus often remain split off and unintegrated from the core of experience. This framework has yet to find application in PD treatment, but seems to have great promise to complement existing approaches, especially given its focus on a form of identity development related to trauma. For example, Fonagy et al. (1996) found that borderline PD was associated with lack of resolution of traumatic experiences.

THERAPIST FACTORS

Professional Factors

The impact of training and professional competence on outcome has received considerable attention from clinical researchers, but yielded somewhat mixed results. There are no specific studies dealing with the way these variables impact work with personality-disordered patients. However, it is useful to review existing perspectives and findings to help inform hypotheses for future PD-focused research. Teyber and McClure (2000) maintain that a therapist's level of training interacts with both client age and problem type (specifically, overcontrolled versus undercontrolled) in terms of its impact on outcome. A clear example of this from the child and adolescent treatment literature is the observation that more highly trained professionals perform better with overcontrol problems, but that training level does not differentially predict outcome for undercontrol problems (Weisz, Weisz, Alicke, & Klotz, 1987).

Recasting the issue slightly, Crits-Cristoph et al. (1991) concluded through meta-analysis that a therapist's years of experience working with a targeted group of clients can prove more important than years of overall experience. It remains to be seen whether this finding might be beneficially applied to each category of personality disorder. If so, it may be the case that therapists would do well to specialize in treating one form of personality pathology, rather than seeking more general training. Certainly, treatment manuals and even treatment settings have increasingly focused on single disorders. In the case of PD, however, problems in implementing such an agenda, even if empirically justified, may ensue from the high levels of co-morbidity and overlap between specific DSM-IV categories.

Contrasting the results just cited, Siqueland et al. (2000) studied therapist training effects in a comparative study of psychosocial treatments for cocaine addiction in which 44% of subjects qualified for a PD diagnosis. In this study, general experience as therapists and experience with particular forms of treatment were most associated with outcome. Further complicating the picture, Hersoug et al. (2001) found that level of experience and training did not have a significant impact on patient ratings of the working alliance.

Expectations

Therapist expectations about therapy for a given patient may comprise several elements including the duration of treatment, how the process of therapy will develop over this time, and the probable outcome, among others. It has been suggested that, in light of the inherent difficulties involved in working with clients who have personality disorders, therapist negative expectations may lead to a lack of industriousness and exertion, undermine the therapist's creativity, and thus negatively impact outcomes (Darley & Fazio, 1980). Very little data is available regarding therapist expectations and outcome of treatment for PD. However, Joyce and Piper (1998) examined the issue in a controlled trial of brief, time-limited individual psychotherapy with a sample in which 27% of treated patients had an Axis II diagnosis. They compared patient and therapist expectancies in relation to outcome for the whole sample, concluding (among other things) that (1) expectancies have more direct effects on the establishment of the therapeutic alliance than on the outcome of treatment, and (2) while patient expectancies are strong predictors of therapy outcome, therapist expectancies are not.

Attachment Style

Meyer and Pilkonis (2002) reviewed the literature addressing therapist attachment style and concluded that therapists with a secure attachment style may be better able to cope more easily with alliance ruptures than those with more anxious styles. They cite research (Rubino, Barker, Roth, & Fearon, 2000) in which therapists were asked to watch videotaped segments showing feigned break-ups in therapeutic alliances. The therapists were then asked to respond as if they were working with real clients. Results suggested that anxious therapists more readily interpret alliance ruptures as a sign that clients are trying to give up therapy. It was further suggested that therapist sensitivity to abandonment serves to compromise skills at accurate and empathic listening under these circum-

stances. Limited research is also available suggesting that treatment may be more effective when certain patient and therapist attachment styles are paired. Tyrrell, Dozier, Teague, and Fallot (1999) examined the relationship between patients with severe mental disorders and their case managers by attachment style. They concluded that complementary combinations of attachment were the most productive. For example, more preoccupied patients did better when working with more dismissive therapists. Another perspective also exists that incorporates state- and trait-like perspectives on attachment behavior and suggests for example that an otherwise "securely attached" therapist may behave with a dismissive style in relation to a particular patient (Diamond et al., 1999). While some interesting findings have been generated thus far, more research is clearly needed in this area, especially with regard to Axis II, where problems attaching to and relating with others are often vividly demonstrated.

THERAPEUTIC ALLIANCE

To this point, we have primarily focused on participant factors that impact outcome. One of the primary findings in treatment research, however, has been that the quality of the therapeutic relationship, typically measured as "alliance," strongly predicts treatment outcome. With this in mind, we turn to a brief review of participant factors that impact the therapeutic relationship and may thus indirectly shape outcome in PD treatment. In doing so, we lean heavily on the work of Constantino, Castonguay, and Schut, 2001. According to their review, patient educational level (unlike age or gender) is associated with a stronger alliance. In addition, lower symptom severity is associated with more positive alliances. Other reviewers have disagreed on this point, however (cf. Horvath & Greenberg, 1994). The following patient characteristics have also been found to make establishment of a positive alliance more difficult:

1. A general deficit in social skills
2. Poor object relations
3. A history of poor familial relationships
4. Strong defensive attitudes

5. A hopeless stance
6. Low psychological mindedness
7. High levels of resistance, negativism, and hostility
8. Perfectionism

This list markedly overlaps with descriptions of personality disorder and suggests that a more general statement could be made: that it is more difficult to establish strong alliances with patients exhibiting features consistent with personality disorder. The relationship between alliance and PD, however, will also likely vary depending on the precise nature of their composing features. For example, patients with borderline PD are known clinically as having greater difficulties establishing and maintaining alliances, especially during periods of intense anxiety. The general overlap between alliance and PD features could explain, in part, the treatment-resistant nature of Axis II disorders. It also argues strongly for therapists working with Axis II patients to attend carefully to the therapeutic alliance. These issues are discussed in more detail by other authors in this volume (Smith, Barrett, Benjamin, & Barber, this volume). We concur with these authors in recommending more research to further elucidate these issues, which have clear clinical implications.

Constantino et al. (2001) also conclude that a patient's perception of the therapeutic alliance, both positive and negative, contributes in kind to the alliance. Other researchers have further elaborated the distinction between perceptions of the relationship and the relationship itself, concluding that perceptions of the relationship may be different for clients and therapists, do not necessary converge for both partners, and can evolve differentially over time (Bachelor & Salamé, 2000). These perceptions are themselves likely to be a function of participant expectations and preferences, reviewed in earlier sections. Elkin et al. (1999) have found empirical evidence along these lines, observing that the quality of the alliance was predicted by congruence between a patient's assignment to a specific treatment condition and his or her (pre-assignment) preference for that therapy.

A few factors have also been found suggesting that therapist characteristics (outside of the treatment situation) contribute to their ability to establish and sustain alliances, as well as to avoid and or repair alliance ruptures when they occur. Specifically, stronger alliances are associated with therapists with (1) less self-directed hostility, (2) more perceived social support, and (3) a higher degree of comfort with closeness in interpersonal relationships. Poorer alliances are associated with therapists who have (1) commitments to theoretical or technical aspects of therapy that override interest in their relationship with the patient, (2) high levels of hostility, and (3) negative early object relations. In addition, Henry, Schacht, and Strupp (1990) found a negative association between a therapist's level of self-directed hostility (i.e., a hostile introject) and outcome of treatment.

SUGGESTIONS FOR FUTURE RESEARCH

Work is only just beginning in the area of personality disorder treatment research, and even the most well-established findings reviewed in this chapter would benefit from more attention. Given the intense and demanding nature of treatment with PD patients, we believe that therapist characteristics are an important area for future research, especially characteristics related to the demands of treatment. Given the length of treatments, for instance, therapists must be able to sustain interpersonal links over long periods of time. In addition, therapists will frequently face angry reactions from clients diagnosed with PD. This is due to the fact that personality disorders are normally associated with high levels of resistance and/or difficulties in addressing and expressing negative feelings in moderated ways. Outcomes may thus be improved for therapists high in patience, tolerance, and related qualities (including external supports), that would allow them to cope well, and maintain a therapeutic stance despite the added difficulties. We believe this to be the case, and thus include a number of these factors in our list of principles. Nevertheless, direct and focused research on these issues is sorely needed.

With regard to participant characteristics, we recommend that researchers build into their methods a careful assessment of both patient and therapist qualities that may be explored as moderators of treatment effect. Inclusion of such variables, while not the highest priority for a literature still establishing the presence of treatment main effects, would require only a little forethought and planning as part of basic work in treatment validation and could have great potential to enrich the meager literature in this area. This is especially the case for the diverse and heterogeneous set of features found on Axis II, most of which are thought to have significant impact on treatment processes.

Other promising areas deserving of increased research attention have been articulated by other authors and may profitably be explored in conjunction with awareness of participant characteristics. For example, Benjamin and Karpiak (2002) list a number of empirically inspired and informed principles gleaned from the literature and waiting to be formally tested. These principles all pertain to the kind of relationship formed between patient and therapist as a function of their joint contribution and may thus speak to participant characteristics predictive of outcome (e.g., therapist ability to confront and set limits, patient identity disturbance, specific Axis II disorder, etc.). Bateman and Fonagy (2000) hold that successful treatments of personality disorders tend to be clearly structured, show evidence of collaboration and have a clear focus (e.g., change in a specific behavior; change in a pattern of relating to others), have a long duration, promote a powerful attachment between therapist and client, and are well-articulated with other services available to the client. Similarly, Livesley (2001) proposes that with regard to the client, effective therapies foster admitting problems, self-analysis, acquiring new behaviors, and consolidation and generalization of new learning. With regard to therapists, Livesley recommends that they apply strategies that build and sustain cooperation (i.e., heal ruptures in the therapeutic alliance), validate patients, and foster motivation leading to change. Therapist characteristics that enhance the ability to provide this kind of therapeutic relationship, such as assertiveness (or ability to set and keep limits), patience, the capacity to have and maintain meaningful relationships, the ability to foster change in others, and degree of life experience would be examples of characteristics thus predicted to correlate with outcome.

SUMMARY AND CONCLUSIONS

Following is a list of general principles that we feel can be legitimately derived from our review of the literature on clients and therapist characteristics in the treatment of personality disorders. While the empirical evidence to sustain these general principles can hardly be described as strong, we believe that some of the findings reviewed above point at their direction. The negative influence on the quality of alliance of a rigid level of adherence to a theory or a technique and the finding that it may be more adequate for the therapist to concentrate his experience in a particular type of disorder are examples of such findings. We also need to underline that we did not derive these principles only on the basis of outcome findings. These principles are also in part grounded onto process findings, especially related to alliance research. As stated early in this chapter, we decided to consider participant factors that potentially impact alliance based on the assumption that such factors would also be important in understanding outcome.

The principles of change included in the list below will of necessity overlap with those described in this book's sections on treatment factors and relationship factors. For the most part, however, these principles of change are not directly related to the relationship variables covered by the Division 29 Task Force (Norcross, 2002). In fact, with the exception of the client's attachment, none of these variables received sufficient attention in the treatment of personality disorders. While we have not retained them in our list of general principles, we believe that it is reasonable to suggest that these not-yet-investigated variables are likely to play a role in the treatment for personality disorders. In line with the guidelines of the current Task Force (see Beutler & Castonguay, this volume), we thus accept the conclusions reached by Division 29 and consider, pending future research, the client's resistance and functional impairment as effective variables. Also based on the Division 29 Task Force conclusions, we accept to consider the following as probably effective variables for the treatment of personality disorder: coping style, stages of change, anaclitic and introjective styles, expectations, and assimilation of problematic experiences.

Participant characteristics predictive of outcome

PATIENT CHARACTERISTICS

1. Willingness and ability to engage with treatment
2. Some history of positive attachments/relationships/object-relations

THERAPIST CHARACTERISTICS

1. Open-minded, flexible, and creative in approach (necessitated by the complexity of PD treatments and psychopathology)
2. Comfortable with long-term, emotionally intense relationships
3. Tolerance of own negative feelings regarding the patient and the treatment process
4. Patience
5. Training and experience with a specific Axis II disorder

References

Alden, L. (1989). Short-term structured treatment for avoidant personality disorder. *Journal of Consulting and Clinical Psychology, 57*(6), 756–764.

Arnkoff, D. B., Glass, C. R., & Shapiro, S. J. (2002). Expectations and preferences. In J. C. Norcross (Ed.), *Psychotherapy relationships that work: Therapist contributions and responsiveness to patients* (pp. 335–356). New York: Oxford University Press.

Bachelor, A., & Salamé, R. (2000). Participants' perceptions of dimensions of the therapeutic alliance over the course of therapy. *Journal of Psychotherapy Practice and Research, 9*, 39–53.

Bateman, A. W., & Fonagy, P. (2000). Effectiveness of psychotherapeutic treatment of personality disorder. *British Journal of Psychiatry, 177*, 138–143.

Beck, A. T., Freeman, A., & Associates. (1990). *Cognitive therapy of personality disorders*. New York: Guilford Press.

Beck, D. (1988). *Counselor characteristics: How they affect outcomes*. Milwaukee, WI: Family Service America.

Benjamin, L., & Karpiak, C. (2002). Personality disorders. In J. C. Norcross (Ed.), *Psychotherapy relationships that work: Therapist contributions and responsiveness to patients* (pp. 423–438). New York: Oxford University Press.

Beutler, L. E., & Clarkin, J. F. (1990). *Systematic treatment selection: Toward targeted therapeutic interventions*. New York: Brunner Mazel.

Beutler, L. E., Clarkin, J. F., & Bongar, B. (2000). *Guidelines for the systematic treatment of the depressed patient*. New York: Oxford University Press.

Beutler, L. E., Harwood, T. M., Alimohamed, S., & Malik, M. (2002). Functional impairment and coping style: Patient moderators of therapeutic relationships. In J. C. Norcross (Ed.), *Psychotherapy relationships that work: Therapist contributions and responsiveness to patients* (pp. 145–170). New York: Oxford University Press.

Beutler, L. E., Machado, P. P. P., & Neufeldt, F. A. (1994). Therapist variables. In A. E. Bergin & S. L. Garfield (Eds.), *Handbook of psychotherapy and behavior change* (4th ed., pp. 229–269). New York: John Wiley & Sons.

Beutler, L. E., Moleiro, C. M., & Talebi, H. (2002). Resistance. In J. C. Norcross (Ed.), *Psychotherapy relationships that work: Therapist Contributions and Responsiveness to Patients* (pp. 129–143). New York: Oxford University Press.

Blatt, S. J. (1992). The differential effect of psychotherapy and psychoanalysis on anaclitic and introjective patients: The Menninger Psychotherapy Research Project revisited. *Journal of the American Psychoanalytic Association, 40*, 691–724.

Blatt, S. J., & Shahar, G., & Zuroff, D. C. (2002). Anaclitic (sociotropic) and introjective (autonomous) dimensions. In J. C. Norcross (Ed.), *Psychotherapy relationships that work: Therapist contributions and responsiveness to patients* (pp. 315–333). New York: Oxford University Press.

Bond, M., Banon, E., & Grenier, M. (1998). Differential effects of interventions on the therapeutic alliance with patients with personality disorders. *Journal of Psychotherapy Practice and Research, 7*, 301–318.

Bowlby, J. (1988). *A secure base: Parent–child attachment and healthy human development*. New York: Basic Books.

Brennan, K. A., Clark, C. L., & Shaver, P. R. (1998). Self-report measurement of adult attachment: An integrative overview. In J. A. Simpson & W. S. Rholes (Eds.), *Attachment theory and close relationships* (pp. 46–76). New York: Guilford.

Chambless, D. L., & Ollendick, T. H. (2001). Empirically supported psychological interventions: controversies and evidence. *Annual Review of Psychology, 52*, 685–716.

Clarkin, J. F., Yeomans, F. E., & Kernberg, O. F. (1999). *Psychotherapy for borderline personality*. New York: John Wiley & Sons.

Constantino, M. J., Castonguay, L. G., & Schut, A. J. (2001). The working alliance: A flagship for the scientific-practitioner model in psychotherapy. In G. S. Tyron (Ed.), *Counseling based on process research* (pp. 81–131). New York: Allyn & Bacon.

Crits-Christoph, P., Baranackie, K., Durcias, J. S., Beck, A. T., Carroll, K., Perry, K., Luborsky, L., McLellan, A. T., Woody, G. E., Thompson, L., Gallagher, D., & Zitrin, C. (1991). Meta-analysis of therapist effects in psychotherapy outcome studies. *Psychotherapy Research, 1*(2), 81–91.

Darley, J. M., & Fazio, R. (1980). Expectancy confirmation processes arising in the social interaction sequence. *American Psychologist, 35*, 867–881.

Diamond, D., Clarkin, J. F., Levine, H., Levy, K., Foelsch, P., & Yeomans, F. (1999). Borderline conditions and attachment: A preliminary report. *Psychoanalytic Inquiry, 19*, 831–884.

Dolinsky, A., Vaughan, S. C., Luber, L., Mellman, L., & Roose, S. (1998). A match made in heaven? A pilot study of patient–therapist match. *Journal of Psychotherapy Practice and Research, 7*, 119–125.

Eames, V., & Roth, A. (2000). Patient attachment orientation and the early working alliance: A study of patient and therapist reports of alliance quality and ruptures. *Psychotherapy Research, 10*, 421–434.

Elkin, L., Yamagurlú, J. L., Arnkoff, D. B., Glass, C. R., Sotsky, D. M., & Krupnick, J. L. (1999). "Patient-treatment fit" and early engagement in therapy. *Psychotherapy Research, 9*, 437–451.

Fernández-Alvarez, H. (2001). *Fundamentals of an integrated model of psychotherapy*. Northvale: Jason Aronson.

Fonagy, P., Leigh, T., Steekem, M., Steele, H., Kennedy, R., Mattoon, G., Target, M., & Gerber, A. (1996). The relation of attachment status, psychiatric classification, and response to psychotherapy. *Journal of Consulting and Clinical Psychology, 64*, 22–31.

Garfield, S. L. (1994). Research on client variables in psychotherapy. In A. E. Bergin & S. L. Garfield (Eds.), *Handbook of psychotherapy and behavior change* (4th ed., pp. 190–228). New York: John Wiley & Sons.

Hardy, G. E., Aldridge, J., Davidson, C., Rowe, C., Reilly, S., & Shapiro, D. A. (1999). Therapist responsiveness to patient attachment styles and issues observed in patient-identified significant events in psychodynamic-interpersonal psychotherapy. *Psychotherapy Research, 9*, 36–53.

Henry, W. P., Schacht, T. R., & Strupp, H. H. (1990). Patient and therapist introject, interpersonal process and differential psychotherapy outcome. *Journal of Consulting and Clinical Psychology, 58*, 768–774.

Herman, S. M. (1992). Predicting psychotherapists' treatment theories by multimodal structural profile inventory responses: An exploratory study. *Psychotherapy in Private Practice, 11*(2), 85–100.

Herman, S. M. (1998). The relationship between therapist–client modality similarity and psychotherapy outcome. *Journal of Psychotherapy Practice and Research, 7*, 56–64.

Herman, S. M., Cave, S. K., Kooreman, H. E., Miller, J. S., et al. (1995). Predicting clients' perceptions of their symptomatology by multimodal Structural Profile Inventory responses. *Psychotherapy in Private Practice, 14*(1), 23–33.

Hersoug, A. G., Hoglend, P., & Monsen, J. T. (2001). Quality of working alliance in psychotherapy: Therapist variables and patient/therapist similarity as predictor. *Journal of Psychotherapy Practice and Research, 10*(4), 205–216.

Hilliard, R. B., Henry, W. P., & Strupp, H. H. (2000). An interpersonal model of psychotherapy: Linking patient and therapist developmental history, therapeutic process, and types of outcome. *Journal of Consulting and Clinical Psychology, 68*(1), 125–133.

Horvath, A. O., & Greenberg, L. S. (1994). *The working alliance: Theory, research and practice*. New York: John Wiley & Sons.

Huppert, J. D., Bufka, L. F., Barlow, D. H., Gorman, J. M., Shear, M. K., & Woods, S. W. (2001). Therapists, therapist variables, and cognitive-behavioral therapy outcome in a multicenter trial for panic disorder. *Journal of Consulting and Clinical Psychology, 69*(5), 747–755.

Johnson, J. G., Smailes, E. M., Cohen, P., Brown, J., Bernstein, D. P. (2000). Associations between four types of childhood neglect and personality disorder symptoms during adolescence and early adulthood: Findings of a community-based longitudinal study. *Journal of Personality Disorders, 14*(2), 171–187.

Jones, E. E., & Zoppel, C. L. (1982). Impact of client and therapist gender on psychotherapy process and outcome. *Journal of Consulting and Clinical Psychology, 50,* 259–272.

Joyce, A. S., & Piper, W. E. (1998). Expectancy, the therapeutic alliance, and treatment outcome in short-term individual psychotherapy. *Journal of Psychotherapy Practice and Research, 7,* 236–248.

Kanninen, K., Salo, J., & Punamäki, R. L. (2000). Attachment patterns and working alliance in trauma therapy for victims of political violence. *Psychotherapy Research, 10,* 435–449.

Kernberg, O. F. (1996). A psychoanalytic theory of personality disorders. In J. F. Clarkin & M. F. Lenzenweger (Eds.), *Major theories of personality disorder* (pp. 106–137). New York: Guilford Press.

Lazarus, A. A. (1989). *The practice of multimodal therapy.* Baltimore: Johns Hopkins University Press.

Linehan, M. (1993). *Cognitive-behavioral treatment of borderline personality disorder.* New York: Guilford.

Livesley, W. J. (Ed.). (2001). *Handbook of personality disorders: Theory, research and treatment.* New York: Guilford.

Magnavita, J. (1999). Challenges in treatment of personality disorders: When the disorder demands comprehensive integration. *In session: Psychotherapy in practice, 4*(4), 5–17.

Mallinckrodt, B., Gantt, D. L., & Coble, H. M. (1995). Attachment patterns in the psychotherapy relationship: Development of the patient attachment to therapist scale. *Journal of Counseling Psychology, 42,* 307–317.

Mendelson, G. A., & Geller, M. H. (1967). Similarity, missed sessions, and early termination. *Journal of Counselling Psychology, 14,* 210–215.

Meyer, B., & Pilkonis, P. (2002). Attachment style. In J. C. Norcross (Ed.), *Psychotherapy relationships that work: Therapist contributions and responsiveness to patients* (pp. 367–382). New York: Oxford University Press.

Meyer, B., Pilkonis, P. A., Proietti, J. M., Heape, C. L., & Egan, M. (2000). Influence of adult attachment styles and personality disorders on treatment response. In B. Strauss (Chair), symposium conducted at the 31st annual meeting of the Society for Psychotherapy Research, Chicago, IL.

Mosheim, R., Zachhuber, U., Scharf, L., Hofmann, A., Kemmler, G., Danzl, C., Kinze, J., Biebl, W., & Richter, R. (2000). Bindung und psychotherapie: Bindungsqualität und interpersonale probleme von patienten als mögliche einfluss faktoren auf das ergebrus stationärer psychotherapie. [Quality of attachment and interpersonal problems as possible predictors of inpatient therapy outcome.] *Psychotherapeut, 45,* 223–229.

Nathan, P. E., & Gorman, J. M. (Eds.). (1998). *A guide to treatments that work.* New York: Oxford University Press.

Norcross, J. C. (Ed.). (2002). *Psychotherapy relationships that work: Therapist contributions and responsiveness to patients.* New York: Oxford University Press.

Ogrodniczuk, J. S., Piper, W. E., & Joyce, A. S. (2001). Using DSM Axis II information to predict outcome in short-term individual psychotherapy. *Journal of Personality Disorders, 15*(2), 110–122.

Perris, C., & Skagerlind, L. (1998). An integrated, multilevels, metacognitive approach to the treatment of patients with a schizophrenic disorder or severe personality disorder. In C. Perris & P. D. McGorry (Eds.), *Cognitive psychotherapy of psychotic and personality disorders: Handbook of theory and practice* (pp. 197–211). New York: John Wiley & Sons.

Perry, J. C., Banon, E., & Ianni, F. (1999). Effectiveness of psychotherapy for personality disorders. *American Journal of Psychiatry, 156*(9), 1312–1321.

Petry, N. M., Tennen, H., & Affleck, G. (2000). Stalking the elusive client variable in psychotherapy research. In C. R. Snyder & R. E. Ingram (Eds.), *Handbook of psychological change: Psychotherapy process and practices for the 21st century* (pp. 88–108). New York: John Wiley & Sons.

Prochaska, J. O., & Norcross, J. C. (2002). Stages of change. In J. C. Norcross (Ed.), *Psychotherapy relationships that work: Therapist contributions and responsiveness to patients* (pp. 303–313). New York: Oxford University Press.

Propst, L. R., Ostrom, R., Watkins, P., Dean, T., & Mashburn, F. (1992). Comparative efficacy of religious and nonreligious cognitive-behavioral therapy for the treatment of clinical depression in religious individuals. *Journal of Consulting and Clinical Psychology, 60,* 94–103.

Renneberg, B., Goldstein, A. J., Phillips, D., & Chambless, D. L. (1990). Intensive behavioral group treatment of avoidant personality disorder. *Behavior Therapy, 21,* 363–377.

Rubino, G., Barker, C., Roth, T., & Fearon, P. (2000). Therapist empathy and depth of interpretation in response to potential alliance ruptures: The role of therapist and patient attachment styles. *Psychotherapy Research, 10,* 408–420.

Safran, J. D., & Muran, J. C. (2000). *Negotiating the therapeutic alliance.* New York: Guilford Press.

Siqueland, L., Crits-Christoph, P., Barber, J. P., Butler, S. F., Thase, M., Najavits, L., & Onken, L. S. (2000). The role of therapist characteristics in training effects in cognitive, supportive-expressive, and drug counseling therapies for cocaine dependence. *Journal of Psychotherapy Practice and Research, 9,* 123–130.

Stiles, W. B. (2002). Assimilation of problematic experiences. In J. C. Norcross (Ed.), *A guide to psychotherapy relationships that work.* New York: Oxford University Press.

Stiles, W. B., Honos-Webb, L., & Surko, M. (1998). Responsiveness in psychotherapy. *Clinical Psychology: Science and Practice, 5,* 439–458.

Sue, S., & Lam, A. G. (2002). Cultural and demographic diversity. In J. C. Norcross (Ed.), *Psychotherapy relationships that work: Therapist contributions and responsiveness to patients* (pp. 401–421). New York: Oxford University Press.

Teyber, E., & McClure, F. (2000). Therapist variables. In C. R. Snyder & R. E. Ingram (Eds.), *Handbook of psychological change: Psychotherapy process and practices for the 21st century* (pp. 62–87). New York: John Wiley and Sons.

Tollinton, H. J. (1973). Initial expectations and outcome. *British Journal of Medical Psychology, 46,* 251–257.

Tyrrell, C. L., Dozier, M., Teague, G. B., & Fallot, R. D. (1999). Effective treatment relationships for persons with serious psychiatric disorders: The importance of attachment states of mind. *Journal of Consulting and Clinical Psychology, 67,* 725–733.

Weisz, J., Weisz, R., Alicke, M., & Klotz, M. (1987). Effectiveness of psychotherapy in children and adolescents: A meta-analysis for clinicians. *Journal of Consulting and Clinical Psychology, 55,* 542–549.

Williams, J. G. (1988). Cognitive intervention for a paranoid personality disorder. *Psychotherapy, 25,* 570–575.

Winston, A., Laikin, M., Pollack, J., Samstag, L. W., McCullough, L., & Muran, C. (1994). Short-term psychotherapy of personality disorders. *American Journal of Psychiatry, 151,* 190–194.

Winston, A., Pollack, J., McCullough, L., Flegenheimer, W., Kestenbaum, E., & Trujillo, M. (1991). Brief psychotherapy of personality disorders. *Journal of Nervous and Mental Disease, 179,* 188–193.

Worthington, E. L., McCullough, M. E., & Sandage, S. J. (1996). Empirical research on religion and psychotherapeutic processes and outcomes: A 10-year review and research prospectus. *Psychological Bulletin, 119*(3), 448–487.

Zlotnick, C., Elkin, I., & Shea, M. T. (1998). Does the gender of a patient or the gender of a therapist affect the treatment of patients with major depression? *Journal of Consulting and Clinical Psychology, 66*(4), 655–659.

11

Relationship Factors in Treating Personality Disorders

Tracey L. Smith

Marna S. Barrett

Lorna Smith Benjamin

Jacques P. Barber

INTRODUCTION

The goal of this chapter is to provide a comprehensive picture of the empirical evidence identifying aspects of the therapy relationship that enhance outcome when treating personality disorders. The strictest interpretation of the task argues for a review of treatment studies that assess aspects of the therapy relationship and directly connect them to outcome for samples of personality disordered clients. We selected a more lenient standard because of the paucity of research focused on relationship factors and outcome in personality disorder. We expanded the survey to include studies in which at least half the participants carried (usually co-morbid) personality disorder labels, whether or not any distinct personality disordered groups were identified. Because personality disorder was not the focus, most of these studies reported change in Axis I symptoms, rather than change in personality disorder per se. Therefore, our survey of connections between relationship factors and outcome in personality dis-

order includes many studies of changes in Axis I symptoms when directly studied, or when co-morbid personality disorder had been noted in at least 50% of the sample.

REVIEW OF CURRENT LITERATURE IN CONJUNCTION WITH THE FINDINGS OF THE DIVISION 29 REVIEW

Benjamin and Karpiak (2002) recently completed a closely related survey for the Division 29 Task Force of the American Psychological Association on Empirically Supported Therapy Relationships (Norcross, 2002). We cite and extend findings from this review by expanding the sample as noted above, and by considering additional therapy relationship elements identified in the Division 29 Task Force as "demonstrably effective" or "promising and probably effective" in treatment of general (i.e., not personality disordered) outpatient populations (Norcross, 2002). We also included any more recent relevant studies that met our search criteria. In sum, to be included in our review, a study needed to: (1) link a selected therapy relationship factor from the Division 29 Task Force list to treatment outcome in an eligible sample of personality disordered individuals as described above; (2) or be an effective treatment for personality disorder accompanied by a manual that could be scanned for evidence that the selected relationship factor probably would be present. We indicate variations in credibility of conclusions about what relationship elements might be effective in personality disorder treatment depending upon the characteristics of the study (e.g., directness of the association between relationship factors and personality change, sample size, methodological rigor, or clarity of the representation of diagnoses of personality disorder).

For each relationship factor or element reviewed, we first offer a definition of the factor followed by a summary of the Division 29 Task Force conclusions for the influence of that factor on outcome for the general therapy population. We then discuss whether these general conclusions are consistent with the empirical evidence for associations with change in personality disordered clients. When there was little or no empirical evidence that allowed us to evaluate the applicability of the Division 29 Task Force general conclusions specifically to the personality disorder population, we sometimes speculate on why they might apply to personality disordered individuals, and provisionally accept them pending research specific to personality disorder.

We organize this review into three broad sections, based upon the structure developed by Castonguay, Grosse Holtforth, Coombs, Beberman, Kakouros, Boswell, Reid, and Jones (this volume). The first section of this review consists of factors pertaining to the quality of the therapeutic interaction: alliance, cohesion in group psychotherapy, and goal consensus and collaboration. The second section consists of factors related to therapists' skills of attunement to the client: empathy, congruence, and positive regard. The final section addresses working with the therapeutic relationship: self-disclosure, feedback, relational interpretations, management of countertransference, and repairing alliance ruptures.

QUALITY OF THE THERAPEUTIC INTERACTION

In this section, we examine three aspects of the quality of the therapeutic interaction; each of which the Division 29 review identified as "effective elements" of the therapy relationship in the general therapy population. These factors include alliance, cohesion, and goal consensus and collaboration.

Over the last 20 years, studies have varied considerably in their definition of alliance. Whereas some have viewed the alliance as encompassing the client's belief in the therapist as well as the client's faith and investment in the treatment (e.g., Luborsky, 1976), others have regarded the alliance as a collaboration in which the client and therapist develop a therapeutic bond and agree on goals and tasks (e.g., Bordin, 1994). However, much of the current theoretical and clinical research would agree that the alliance is a collaborative relationship (i.e., affective bond, shared goals, and a mutual commitment to treatment) between client and therapist in therapy (Horvath & Bedi, 2002). Cohesion is a closely related construct to alliance. In fact, one definition of cohesion is the multiple alliances between group members and leaders (Burlingame, Fuhriman, & Johnson, 2002). Although some researchers consider goal consensus and collaboration to be a part of the therapeutic alliance, others suggest these elements have a unique influence on the therapy relationship. Because of this potential to offer a unique contribution to the relationship as well as the decision by the Division 29 Task Force to examine goal consensus and collaboration separately from alliance, we chose to review them separately with a focus on personality disorder.

Alliance

In nearly any population studied, a good therapeutic alliance[1] enhances outcome (Martin, Garske, & Davis, 2000; Horvath, 2001). Whereas some studies of alliance and outcome have had samples that included patients diagnosed with personality disorders (e.g., Barber et al., 1999, 2001; Carroll, Nich, & Rounsaville, 1997; Krupnick et al., 1996), few directly addressed the relation between alliance and outcome for the participants with personality disorders only. Still, with some complications mentioned below,[2] results are taken to indicate that a good therapy alliance is helpful when treating personality disorder.

The Division 29 review of studies of successful individual, group, and milieu treatments of personality disorder (Benjamin & Karpiak, 2002) concluded that effective therapies provide a strong positive relationship (collaboration, alliance) in which the therapist is relatively active, provides clear structure that makes sense to the patient as well as to the therapist, and provides limits on unacceptable behaviors such as parasuicidal events or attacking the therapist. These conclusions were based primarily on exemplary treatment studies (e.g., Koerner & Linehan, 2000; Piper, Rosie, Joyce, & Azim, 1996) and on relevant previous reviews (e.g., Perry, Banon, & Ianni, 1999; Bateman & Fonagy, 2000).

Examination of more recent studies suggests that problems associated with personality disorders can affect alliance formation. For example, Hersoug and colleagues (Hersoug, Monsen, Havik, & Hoglend, 2002) examined factors predictive of early alliance among 270 outpatients, where more than half of the sample (61%) received a diagnosis of personality disorder. Of those patients with a personality disorder diagnosis, the total number of personality disorder criteria was only minimally related to the therapeutic alliance, as measured by the Working Alliance Inventory (Horvath & Greenberg, 1989). However, apart from the personality disorder diagnostic criteria, the quality of current and past relationships, which are often impaired among individuals with personality disorder (e.g., Smith & Benjamin, 2002), was more strongly associated with the development of the working alliance early in treatment (session 3) than later (session 12). Another study (67% personality disorder) found pretreatment hostile-dominant interpersonal problems[3] predicted a poor alliance (Connolly-Gibbons et al., 2003). Given that no separate analyses were done for the participants with personality disorders, we can merely assume that since 67% of the sample had a diagnosed personality disorder that many were included among the subjects who had hostile-dominant interpersonal problems. Other researchers have shown

that these sorts of interpersonal problems are associated with some personality disorders (Soldz, Budman, Demby, & Merry, 1993; Wiggins & Pincus, 1989).

In his recent review of this literature, Horvath (2001) reconfirmed there is a modest (effect size .32) but consistent relation between alliance and outcome, and listed a number of client and therapist factors that may enhance or interfere with alliance. Of special interest to the treatment of personality disorder is Horvath's conclusion that the quality of the alliance is related to the severity of the client's problems, type of impairments, and quality of relationships and attachment styles (ibid., p. 368). More specifically, alliance tends to be poorer when working with clients with more severe problems. Since individuals with a personality disorder are more likely to be functionally impaired (Smith & Benjamin, 2002) and tend to have poor attachment styles (Dickinson & Pincus, 2003; Meyer, Pilkonis, Proietti, Heape, & Egan, 2001), it is not surprising that the few studies which focused on personality disorder in Horvath's survey reported increased difficulty in forming an alliance with individuals with borderline personality disorder (p. 368). In fact, Barber, Morse, Krakauer, Chittams, and Crits-Christoph (1997) presented preliminary data indicating that patient-reported alliance increased across time in a group of patients with avoidant personality disorder, whereas patients with an obsessive-compulsive personality disorder did not have changes in alliance across treatment. Such differences were found between these personality disorder groups despite the fact that researchers found no pretreatment differences in symptom severity.[4] Thus, it is reasonable to conclude that patients with personality disorders are very likely to have problems forming an alliance, which may account for the tendency of individuals with personality disorders to have poorer outcomes (Reich & Vasile, 1993; Shahar, Blatt, Zuroff, & Pilkonis, 2003).

Goal Consensus and Collaboration

Investigators have generally defined goal consensus as an agreement between the therapist and client on therapy goals and expectations. Similarly, researchers view collaboration as the mutual involvement of the therapist and client in developing a therapeutic relationship. Although agreement on goals and collaboration seem to overlap theoretically with the collaborative relationship defined by alliance, many researchers have viewed goal consensus and collaboration as having a unique influence on the therapeutic relationship and therefore have examined them independently from the alliance (Norcross, 2002).

In the Division 29 review of this literature, Tryon & Winograd (2002) examined 17 studies assessing goal consensus and outcome, and another 24 studies examining collaborative involvement and outcome. They concluded that better goal consensus and collaboration are demonstrably effective in improving treatment outcome in general clinical populations. We were unable to find any additional studies conducted since that review that would further inform these conclusions. Nor were we able to find a single pertinent study that directly addressed outcome and these therapy relationship elements within the personality disorder population. Pending further evidence with personality disorder samples, we assume that goal consensus and collaboration operate similarly in this patient group.

Cohesion in Group Psychotherapy

Burlingame, Fuhriman, and Johnson (2002) broadly defined cohesion as the interplay between the multiple alliances in group psychotherapy (member to group, leader to group, member to member, member to leader, and sometimes co-leader to co-leader). Most studies of group psychotherapy examine a subset of these alliances, which limits our ability to compare studies. As with studies of therapeutic alliance, greater cohesion is routinely associated with improved therapeutic outcome across a variety of patient populations. However the picture is complicated by the fact that higher levels of cohesion are also related to: greater self-disclosure; more frequent interpersonal feedback; more listening, verbal interaction, trust, empathy, goal attainment, support, and member responsibility; and greater ability to tolerate in-group conflict during the work stage of group (Burlingame, Fuhriman, & Johnson, 2002).

One study examined the link between cohesion and outcome with personality disorder participants, and reported that cohesion was positively associated with outcome. Marziali, Munroe-Blum, and McCleary (1997) examined the contribution of group cohesion (primarily member-to-member bonds) and group alliance (primarily member-to-therapist bonds) to outcome in a group therapy for patients with borderline personality disorder. Results suggested that the strength of member-to-therapist bonds may be more important to outcome than member-to-member bonds among group members with borderline personality disorder. Due to missing data, only 17 patients contributed to the analyses of alliance and cohesion to outcome so we consider these results as tentative pending further research.

An additional study of group process and outcome did not measure cohesion or process directly but given its implications for the inclusion of personality disorder participants to group treatment, we chose to review it here. Cloitre and Koenen (2001) studied the effect of a 12-week interpersonal process group treatment for 49 women with post-traumatic stress disorder (PTSD) related to childhood sexual abuse. All group members had a PTSD diagnosis and a history of childhood sexual abuse. Eighteen of the treated patients and six control group patients were also diagnosed with co-morbid borderline personality disorder. Researchers compared the (1) groups with at least one member diagnosed with co-morbid borderline personality disorder, (2) groups without any members diagnosed with borderline personality disorder, and (3) the wait-list control group (N = 15). Groups without any co-morbid borderline personality disorder members showed strong to moderate improvement on PTSD, anger, depression, and other symptoms. In contrast, the control group members and members of the treatment groups with at least one member with co-morbid borderline personality disorder either failed to improve on these symptoms or deteriorated by the end of the treatment period. Additionally these group members, regardless of their diagnoses, showed increases in anger problems while the groups without members with co-morbid borderline personality disorders showed moderate improvement in anger problems. The authors conclude that this problematic result came from an "anger contagion effect"[5] in the groups with borderline personality disorder members. The authors note that group treatments that are more structured have better success with borderline personality disorder co-morbidity (Cloitre & Koenen, 2001). Indeed as Benjamin and Karpiak (2002) found in their review, more structure is a feature of treatments that have successfully treated borderline personality disorder patients (Linehan, 1993; Clarkin, Foelsch, Levy, Hull, Delaney, & Kernberg, 2001; Ryle & Golynkina, 2000).

The very limited evidence with personality disorder participants allows us to tentatively suggest that greater group cohesion improves therapeutic outcome for members with personality disorder, which is consistent with the conclusion reached by the Division 29 Task Force for the general therapy population. The study by Marziali and colleagues (1997) suggests that with borderline personality disorder clients, cohesion between member and leader may be more important to predicting outcome than cohesion between group members (Marziali et al., 1997). Additionally, the study by Cloitre & Koenen (2001) suggests that groups that lack sufficient structure to contain the angry externalizing expressions of borderline personality disorder members may negatively affect the therapy outcome of all group members.

Does the Quality of the Therapeutic Interaction Have a Causal Relationship to Outcome?

Studies of outpatients that relate alliance at various stages of therapy to temporal changes in symptoms are beginning to probe the question of whether the alliance has a causal and/or consequent role in symptom change. Barber, Connolly, Crits-Christoph, Gladis, and Siqueland (2000) found that early changes in depressive symptoms facilitated later alliance, but that alliance independently contributed to improvements in depression as well. Focusing strictly on individuals with personality disorders, Westerman, Foote, & Winston (1995) found that rates of change in the alliance had the usual positive association with outcome for one technique (Brief Analytic Therapy), but not for another (Short-Term Dynamic Therapy).

These results suggest that sequence and context (e.g., time of measurement, treatment approach, changes in symptomatology) need to be considered when exploring possible causal connections between alliance and outcome.

The Therapeutic Relationship Is More Than the Alliance

Most studies of the alliance specifically identify features in the relationship that relate to outcome, such as collaboration in the therapy task and bonding. However, the therapy relationship may include more than what is usually considered the alliance and can even be a major component of model-relevant technique. For example, Kernberg's Transference Focused Psychotherapy (TFP; Kernberg, 2001) holds that the therapy relationship is an experiential vehicle for change when treating borderline personality disorder. Similarly, Linehan (1993) specifies that the therapist needs to strike a "dialectical" balance between acceptance of the patient and expectation of change. The dialectical tension is a "relationship" factor that is a basic technique in her Dialectical Behavioral Therapy (DBT) for borderline personality disorder. In other words, the therapeutic relationship, at least in TFP and DBT encompasses more than what is usually studied under the heading, therapy alliance.

In the Division 29 review of relationship factors when treating personality disorder, Shearin and Linehan (1992) were the only identified investigators who measured model-relevant relationship factors[6] and directly connected them to outcome. In our recommendation section, we outline why these model-relevant relationship factors are important in psychotherapy research. Shearin and Linehan (1992) reported there were fewer parasuicidal attempts following sessions during which patients rated therapists higher in the dialectic between acceptance and change (meaning the therapist both accepts the client in her current state as well as simultaneously asks her to change). Unfortunately, that finding failed to replicate on a larger sample over a longer period of time (H. Schmidt, personal communication, 2001).

THERAPIST SKILLS OF ATTUNING TO THE CLIENT

Empathy, Positive Regard, and Congruence

In the early days of psychotherapy research, Rogers (1951) identified empathy, positive regard, and congruence as the necessary and sufficient conditions for therapeutic change. The Division 29 survey concluded that empathy is a "demonstratively effective" element of the therapeutic relationship, while positive regard and congruence are "promising and probably effective elements of the therapy relationship" (Norcross, 2002, p. 441). Although much has been written both theoretically and empirically about these facilitative conditions, there seems to be little agreement in defining these concepts. Empathy is typically defined as an understanding of the client's perspective or way of experiencing the world. Positive regard is usually defined as warmth and acceptance toward one's self or another. Congruence is thought of as the therapist's personal involvement in the relationship through open and honest communication. We review empathy, positive regard, and congruence separately, despite the fact that they are highly intercorrelated, given that they often independently contribute to the strength of the therapeutic alliance (Salvio, Beutler, Wood, & Engle, 1992; see also Horvath & Greenberg, 1989).

Bohart and colleagues (Bohart, Elliott, Greenberg, & Watson, 2002) recently conducted a meta-analytic review of 47 studies and found an effect size of .32 for empathy. Interestingly, the size of effect between empathy and outcome is slightly larger than that found between the therapeutic alliance and outcome ($ES = .25$). This comparison suggests that the interpersonal connection with the client may be as important in determining outcome as other therapy elements such as agreement on tasks or goals.

Researchers have extensively studied the relation between positive regard and therapy outcome. In their recent review of this literature, Farber & Lane (2002) summarized the findings from 92 studies: 67 studies included in Orlinsky's comprehensive review (Orlinsky, Grawe, & Parks, 1994) in addition to 16 studies published between 1990 and 2000. Roughly half of the 202 findings

(54%) showed that positive regard was associated with improved outcome. Moreover, a significant association between positive regard and outcome was much more likely to occur in those studies that had patients rating both positive regard and outcome or patients rating positive regard and therapists rating outcome. Interestingly, positive regard seemed to have its greatest effect on treatment retention rather than symptom reduction (Farber & Lane, 2002) suggesting that clients' perception of warmth and acceptance from the therapist is an important contributor to decisions about continuing treatment and possibly more so than its contribution to outcome. When treating clients with personality disorder, retention may be crucial given that treatments for personality disorder tend to be relatively long (Bateman & Fonagy, 2000; Benjamin, 2003; Linehan, 1993) and these clients may take longer to respond to treatment (e.g., Junkert-Tress, Schnierda, Hartkamp, Schmitz, & Tress, 2001; O'Leary & Costello, 2001; Ruegg & Frances, 1995).

Many clinicians and researchers agree with Rogers (1951) that congruence or genuineness is one of the basic facilitative conditions in therapy. Congruence, sometimes called genuineness, is usually conceptualized as the therapist's personal integration or involvement in the therapy relationship as well as the ability to be open and honest with the client about one's feelings. Thus, in order to be congruent, a therapist must be both self-aware and willing to share this awareness with the client. This openness to personal feelings is not to be confused with indiscriminant disclosure by the therapist. Rather the therapist is to be genuinely himself or herself in ways that are specifically relevant to with the client.

Despite considerable efforts to investigate the possible connection between therapist congruence and outcome (12 reviews over the last 40 years), definitive answers have not been forthcoming. Klein and her colleagues (2002) found that nearly two-thirds of the results failed to demonstrate any relation between congruence and outcome. The remaining third suggested that greater levels of therapist congruence were associated with better therapy outcome (mostly defined as changes in symptoms, well-being, or global adjustment measures). Because of the variability in statistical and methodological rigor among these studies, Klein and colleagues (2002) were unable to ascertain an accurate estimate of the strength of the relation between congruence and outcome.

As was true for goal consensus and collaboration, we did not find a single study that either directly or indirectly addressed the relation between empathy, positive regard, or congruence and outcome within the personality disorder population. Gaining a better understanding of how clients with personality disorders perceive and react to empathy, positive regard, and congruence could be beneficial in designing effective treatments, especially considering that the limited data we have suggests that a therapeutic relationship is harder to develop with patients having a personality disorder. Since we have little evidence to support a link between empathy, positive regard, or congruence and personality disorder outcomes, we accept the general conclusions reached by the Division 29 Task Force that these are either "demonstratively effective" (empathy) or "promising and probably effective" (positive regard and congruence) elements of treatment (Norcross, 2002) and we look forward to studies of the relevance of these relationship components in treatments of personality disorder.

Summary and a Study That Begins to Address Facilitation and Change

Therapist skills of attunement (empathy, positive regard, congruence) to the client have been studied since the early days of psychotherapy research (Rogers, 1951). Rogers believed they were the necessary and sufficient conditions for psychotherapeutic change. Based on the related review by one of the authors (Benjamin & Karpiak, 2002), we have concluded that, in addition to these facilitative conditions, effective personality disorder treatments have relatively active therapists, a clear sensible structure, and limit setting on unacceptable patient behaviors.

A recently conducted study (Linehan, Dimeff, Reynolds, Comtois, et al., 2002) suggests that Rogers's (1951) facilitative conditions (as operationalized in the radical acceptance component of these two treatments) are necessary and sufficient to produce some significant therapy change; nevertheless, this one study also suggests that structure and a change focus are needed for lasting changes (at least in opiate use).

Using a component analysis design, Linehan et al.'s (2002) study compared DBT ($N = 11$) to Comprehensive Validation Therapy plus 12-step (CVT + 12s; $N = 12$) for the treatment of heroin-dependent women with borderline personality disorder. DBT combines behavioral change strategies and limit setting with radical acceptance strategies (which includes empathy, genuineness, self-disclosure, therapeutic warmth, and responsiveness). CVT + 12s used the same radical acceptance strategies. These therapists were nondirective and validated every instance of behavior that was "effective in terms of the client's long term goals, was logically consistent with actual data, or was an instance of normative behavior" (Linehan et al., 2002; p. 17).[7] The difference between the two treatments was that DBT has a change focus and employs limit setting on therapy interfering behaviors.

Both treatments reduced opiate use and levels of psychopathology (symptoms, global and social adjustment, parasuicidal behavior, emergency or inpatient visits) relative to baseline from pre- to post-assessment. However, DBT participants were significantly better in maintaining their reductions in opiate use whereas CVT + 12s participants had significantly increased opiate use in the last third of the trial. The authors suggest that the DBT focus on change and skills development is needed to create lasting behavioral change. Of note, treatment retention was better when change was not a focus of treatment (CVT + 12s retained all participants; DBT retained only 64%). Unfortunately, this differential dropout rate tempers the strength of these conclusions, since it is unclear what differences there were between dropouts and completers. Nevertheless, treatment designs such as these may help to untangle the interactions between relationship factors and model-specific techniques and their relation to various therapy outcomes. We will return to this discussion in our recommendation section.

WORKING WITH THE THERAPEUTIC RELATIONSHIP

The final section of our review examines the ways that therapists relationally contribute to and work with the therapy relationship. Although some might argue that these factors (e.g., self-disclosure, feedback, interpretation, and countertransference) are better conceptualized as therapist techniques or interventions that interact with the therapy relationship and outcomes, we have chosen to view these variables as ways therapists work with the therapeutic relationship. This approach is consistent with that utilized in the Division 29 review. Moreover, the Division 29 committee concluded that the therapy relationship elements in this section were "promising and probably effective elements" in facilitating productive therapeutic relationships (Norcross, 2002, p. 441).

Self-Disclosure

Although self-disclosure may occur as part of some of the relationship components in this review (e.g., genuineness, relational interpretations, countertransference, and feedback), some researchers have studied self-disclosure as a component in itself. For example, Hill and Knox (2002) defined therapist self-disclosure as any statement that reveals something personal about the therapist. Some researchers have defined self-disclosure more narrowly by focusing on specific types of disclosures: those that are made in response to client disclosures; those that are self-involving; or those relating positive or negative experiences outside of therapy (e.g., Hill, Mahalik, & Thompson, 1989). The literature assessing self-disclosure, as with most therapy relationship factors, is largely correlational and raises concerns about differential findings depending on the timing of the assessment. In their recent review of this literature, Hill and Knox (2002) found that in those few studies where the impact of disclosure was assessed immediately after it occurred within a session, disclosure was positively related to outcome. In contrast, six of seven studies assessing the effect of therapist self-disclosure on long-term outcome (end of treatment) failed to find any relation between disclosure and outcome.

Unique amongst the relational factors literature, we found one study that offered an experimental test of self-disclosure on therapy outcome. In this first experimental test of disclosure (Barrett & Berman, 2001), therapists were instructed to increase disclosure with one client and to restrict their use of disclosure with a second client. Self-disclosure was defined as personal information shared in response to a client disclosure. Symptom distress was the main measure of outcome and was assessed at the end of each session. The researchers found that when therapists self-disclosed, clients reported lower levels of distress than when disclosures were limited. Despite the positive findings for a causal effect of disclosure on treatment outcome, the authors caution that disclosures occurred relatively infrequently in both conditions (0–5 per session) and accounted for no more than 61 seconds of a 50-minute session (Barrett & Berman, 2001). Despite these caveats, this initial study provides the first evidence that a small amount of therapist self-disclosure improves the outcome of therapy, although additional research is needed to confirm these findings.

Unfortunately, these interesting and promising new findings have not been explored in samples with identified personality disorders. As with many of the other relationship variables, we failed to identify any study examining the link between outcome and therapist self-disclosure within the personality disorder population. Certainly, this warrants further investigation especially since there is evidence of a causal relationship (albeit one experimental study) between self-disclosure and outcome. However, without any studies including even a subset of patients with personality disorder, we are left to accept the conclusions reached in the Division 29 review that therapist self-disclosure is "probably effective" in improving outcome (Norcross, 2002).

Feedback and Relational Interpretations

Feedback can be defined as descriptive and/or evaluative information shared with a client, about his or her behavior or the effects of those behaviors, for the purpose of influencing the client (Claiborn, Goodyear, & Horner, 2002). Therapists and assessors may use feedback in an attempt to change a client's behavior, perceptions, self-concept, cognitions, and affect. Morran, Robison, and Stockton (1985) differentiate between informational versus motivational aspects of feedback. These different aspects of feedback may produce client change in different ways (Claiborn, Goodyear, & Horner,

2002). In their 2002 review, Claiborn and colleagues found that 8 out of 11 empirical studies demonstrated a positive association between feedback (either quality or quantity) and outcome. However, we were unable to find any studies that addressed the relation between feedback and outcome for personality disorder participants. Because we know that more structure is helpful in treating personality disorder, we would guess that feedback, a form of structure, would be helpful to clients with personality disorders as it is in general outpatient populations studied so far. Thus, we accept the Division 29 Task Force conclusions pending further research.

Relational interpretations (RI) are a form of feedback; however, since relational interpretations have a distinct theoretical history and literature (and following the convention of the Division 29 Task Force), we chose to review this therapy element separately. Interpretation was first described as an analyst's verbal expression aimed at revealing a patient's unconscious thoughts and feelings for the purpose of helping the patient gain insight and eventual relief. Transference interpretations differed from other interpretations in that their content addressed some aspect of an early relationship of the patient's that he or she *transferred* onto the analyst.[8] Relational interpretation is a broader, more inclusive term used to describe therapist interpretations that address a patient's relationship issues in general. Definitions of relational interpretations tend to vary in terms of the degree to which certain elements are emphasized: unconscious process, establishment of links between client statements and events, pointing out patterns, or giving alternative meanings to patient material (Crits-Christoph & Connolly-Gibbons, 2002, p. 287).

In their 2002 review, Crits-Christoph & Connolly-Gibbons examined the relations between frequency of relational interpretations, accuracy of relational interpretations, and outcome. Given that the literature showed a mix of results, the authors selected a subset of studies in the hopes of clarifying the confusing findings. They suggest that the association between RI and outcome is moderated by the quality of object relations (QOR). QOR was defined as a person's internal enduring tendency to establish certain types of relationships,

ranging from primitive to secure (Piper, Azim, Joyce, & McCallum, 1991). Patients with low QOR have good outcomes only when levels of transference interpretations (a special kind of relational interpretations) are low. Patients with high QOR have better outcome when therapists use moderate to low levels of relational interpretations. Of the studies these authors reviewed, five had converging evidence that clients have better outcomes when therapists' RIs maintain a focus on the patient's central interpersonal issues.

Three of the studies from this Division 29 review had samples with at least 50% diagnosed personality disorder. However, two of these studies used the same sample, which converted DSM-II personality disorder diagnoses to DSM-III diagnoses. The third study derived personality disorder diagnoses from the Personality Assessment Form. These diagnostic methods impede their generalizability to DSM-IV personality disorder samples so we mention them only briefly. These three studies are consistent with the review conclusions for the general therapy population that: (1) accuracy of relational interpretations improved patient outcome (Crits-Christoph, Cooper, & Luborsky, 1988); (2) outcomes are improved when relational interpretations are accurate (defined as consistent with the Core Conflict Relational Themes identified at the beginning of therapy) and focused on the patient's central interpersonal issues (Crits-Christoph, Barber, & Kurcias, 1993); and (3) QOR moderate the association between frequency of relational interpretations and outcome (Connolly-Gibbons et al., 1999).

Despite the fact that a few studies had sizable proportions of personality disorder in their samples, their diagnostic methods and lack of separate analyses for those participants with personality disorder allows us to make only provisional suggestions regarding use of relational interpretations with personality disorder clients. Based on this evidence, one could hypothesize that since patients with a personality disorder sometimes have lower QOR (Piper et al., 1996, p. 234) therapists should use low levels of relational interpretations until confident of a client's QOR level. These results are consistent with those from the Division 29 survey (Crits-Christoph & Connolly-Gibbons, 2002), which suggested that when relational interpretations are tailored to certain patient characteristics, they are a promising and probably effective therapy relationship element.

Countertransference

The term "countertransference" was first used to denote the unconscious conflict-based reactions of an analyst invoked by the transference of his patient (see note 7). Gelso and Hayes (2002) define countertransference as the therapist's internal and external reactions to a patient, which are related to the therapist's unresolved conflicts. Internal countertransference (feelings of anxiety or episodes of inaccurate recall of therapy material) is seen as potentially useful whereas overt expression of countertransference (withdrawal, under or over involvement, or avoidance of particular client material) is seen as hindering the therapy process or "acting out on the patient" (Gelso & Hayes, 2002, p. 271). The authors suggest that countertransference phenomena are the result of an interaction between a particular therapist and patient rather than a result of particular "client behaviors or material" (ibid.). Indeed, therapist experience and competence seem to reduce the likelihood that feelings of countertransference will be acted upon in session (Gelso & Hayes, 2002; Singer & Luborsky, 1997).

In their review of this literature, Gelso and Hayes (2002) included only one empirical study demonstrating a direct link between increased countertransference and poorer outcome. The remaining studies suggested that countertransference is related to other psychotherapeutic constructs and therapy events, which are in turn related to outcome. For example, Rosenberger and Hayes (2002) found that frequency of countertransference behavior (operationalized as avoidance of patient material) was associated with a poorer therapeutic alliance. A qualitative study found that therapists endorsed countertransference as one of the most frequent reasons for the development of therapeutic impasses and premature termination (Hill, Nutt-Williams, Heaton, Thompson, & Rhodes, 1996). Therapists in this study indicated that personal conflicts, especially related to family of origin issues, played a strong role in countertransference.

The direct effects of countertransference on outcome are not clear, nevertheless evidence suggests that countertransference is negatively associated with the therapy process, weakens the therapeutic alliance, and thus indirectly influences therapy outcome. As compared with clients not receiving a personality disorder diagnosis, clients with personality disorders are often more interpersonally hostile or withdrawn (Smith, 2002), have a more chronic course, and poorer treatment outcome (e.g. Ruegg & Frances, 1995). Such client behaviors are more likely to rouse strong feelings in their therapists, therefore understanding the relation between countertransference and outcome with this patient population seems important.

As we have done for other variables for which there was little or no evidence related to the treatment of personality disorders, we accept the Division 29 Task Force's conclusion and consider, pending future research, the management of countertransference to be a promising element of the therapeutic relationship.

Repairing Alliance Ruptures

Safran, Muran, Samstag, and Stevens (2002) defined alliance ruptures as the "tension or breakdown in the collaborative relationship between therapist and patient" (p. 236). Ruptures have been classified into three categories: disagreements about tasks, disagreements on goals, or strains in the therapist–client bond.[9] Like countertransference, alliance ruptures are ubiquitous to all therapy sessions (Safran et al., 2002). Since patients with personality disorders are often troubled by interpersonal dysfunction and hostile interpersonal complementarity (e.g., Benjamin, 2003; Benjamin & Karpiak, 2002; Safran et al., 2002; Smith, 2002), one might expect alliance ruptures to be more frequent in the therapies of patients with personality disorders. Additionally, research suggests that training therapists to avoid this hostile process can be challenging[10] (Henry, Schacht, Strupp, Butler, & Binder, 1993; Piper & Ogrodniczuk, 1999).

While the literature clearly links therapy alliance to outcome, there is surprisingly little direct evidence linking repairing alliance ruptures with outcome (Safran et al., 2002). However, there is indirect evidence that some processes (such as a patient's ability and willingness to express negative emotions about therapy and the therapist's ability to respond in a nondefensive manner) can lead to more successful alliance repair and are associated with better outcome. For some patients, a "tear-and-repair" pattern of alliance development was positively associated with outcome (e.g., Foreman & Marmar, 1985; Rhodes, Hill, Thompson, & Elliott, 1994). Safran and colleagues suggest that selecting participants based on their relative abilities to form therapeutic alliances may be a more useful selection method than traditional participant selection criteria (e.g., selection based on DSM diagnosis) in studying this therapeutic phenomenon (and perhaps many others).

At last, we have come to a relationship variable with some good personality disorder studies! Four of the 13 studies reviewed by Safran et al. (2002) regarding the link between alliance ruptures and outcome had samples with appreciable proportions of patients with personality disorders (80% mean prevalence of personality disorder). In addition to these studies, we found a more recent article regarding alliance ruptures (Safran, Muran, Samstag, & Winston, 2003). The related findings from these studies can be briefly summarized as follows: (1) those therapists with hostile self-concepts were more likely to engage in countertransference and rigid adherence to protocol,[11] factors which are likely to lead to further rupture (67% personality disorder; Henry, Schacht, et al., 1993); (2) training helps therapist process most with clients who are "difficult" but well educated (Henry, Strupp, Butler, Schacht, & Binder, 1993); (3) dropout is more likely when patients' perception of therapist friendliness is low, the depth of session is low, and when therapists' rate patients as more hostile and session smoothness[12] as poor (85% personality disorder; Samstag, Batchelder, Muran, Safran, & Winston, 1998); and finally (4) patients with personality disorder may have significantly lower dropout rates and better outcome at termination and follow-up if the therapy model is designed specifically to address alliance ruptures. For instance, recent evidence suggests that Brief Relational Therapy (BRT), which emphasizes process over content, the use of mindfulness, a constructionist perspective (the therapist does not hold a privileged position of knowing), and intensive supervision regarding therapist countertransference, tends to show greater retention rates than

that observed with cognitive behavioral therapy (CBT; Muran and Safran, 2002), and may improve retention over treatments such as short-term dynamic psychotherapy (STDP) as well.

The studies by Muran and colleagues have primarily focused on clinical groups with personality disorders and therefore have directly addressed the link between alliance ruptures and outcome in this patient group. A recent study, offering preliminary results, evaluated the effectiveness of BRT in treating potential treatment failures[13] (Safran et al., 2003). The authors used empirically derived criteria from their previous study of patients' responses to several self-report questionnaires in cases where treatment outcome was known. Then using current patient ratings, the authors statistically identified potential treatment failures ($N = 18$) after Session 8 of their original randomly assigned treatment (CBT or STDP). These patients were offered reassignment to another treatment (control treatment or BRT; 10 accepted reassignment; 8 refused). The treatment assigned in the control condition varied depending upon the initial therapy assignment (Control $N = 5$; BRT $N = 5$). For patients initially assigned to CBT the control treatment was STDP. Likewise, for those patients initially assigned CBT, the control condition was STDP. In the non-control condition, clients who were potential treatment failures (initially assigned to CBT or STDP) were offered BRT as an alternative treatment. Among the 10 patients identified as potential treatment failures and reassigned treatment, dropout was lowest among those reassigned to BRT (3 patients remained in BRT condition; all 5 patients dropped out of the control condition). The three BRT cases showed clinically significant change on 3 of the 4 outcome measures at follow-up. Although stronger conclusions may not be drawn until further studies with more participants are completed, this study employs promising research methods with ecological validity for dismantling the often complex associations among patient characteristics, relationship variables, and therapy outcome.

Summary

In this section, we reviewed five different ways of working with the therapy relationship to facilitate treatment outcome. None of these factors has been definitively linked to outcome in the treatment of patients with personality disorders. In contrast, a few studies, with less than optimal methods of diagnosing personality disorder, suggest that low to moderate levels of relational interpretations, which focus on a client's central interpersonal issues, may improve treatment outcome. Furthermore, although there is limited evidence of a direct link between repairing alliance ruptures and improved outcome, this evidence is based on studies with a high percentage of participants with personality disorders. These studies suggest that alliance rupture is more likely when therapists have hostile self-concepts, engage in overt countertransference, rigidly adhere to protocol, perceive clients as hostile, and sessions as not smooth (see note 12). Ruptures are also more likely to occur when patients perceive their therapists as unfriendly or as failing to focus on issues of depth. Although these findings point to the same general directions, more research is warranted due to the relatively small number of studies.

SUMMARY AND CONCLUSIONS OF PREVIOUS AND PRESENT SURVEY

There are relatively few studies that directly measure the therapy relationship and relate it to outcome for the treatment of personality disorder. The available limited evidence suggests a good alliance can be helpful, depending somewhat on the treatment approach and specific patient qualities. A scan of successful treatments suggests that many individuals with personality disorder respond better to a structured treatment. Setting limits is an example[14] of therapist demands that are likely to accompany successful treatments of personality disorder.

From our review of this literature, there is clearly a great need for research that studies specific aspects of the therapy relationship and outcome for specific treatments of individuals with specific types of personality disorders. Studies of effectiveness of treatment for personality disorder should include assessment of changes in personality pathology as well as the more usual assessment of changes of Axis I symptoms such as depression or anxiety.

Studies of this sort might bring the literature on personality disorder more into line with published psychotherapy research on outpatient populations in general. We would like to go beyond that suggestion and consider changes in research design that could help focus more directly on the question of how therapists can be more effective, whether the mechanism involves relationship or technique or both. Our suggestions for improving studies of personality disorder might be relevant to other populations as well.

RECOMMENDATIONS

Recommendation 1: Relate Outcome to Specific Measures of Relationship Taken at Different Points in Time

Definitions of Relationship Factors

Of course, measures of the alliance should continue to be made and studied in increasing varieties of context. In addition, there should be assessments of other relationship behaviors that according to some therapy models are expected to enhance effectiveness. An example of a *model-specific relationship factor* is: provide a paradoxical injunction that is likely to achieve a specific immediate goal relevant to the case formulation. Consider the practice of "prescribing the symptom," which requires that the therapist become very controlling. When directed toward patients who are compelled to defy control, the hope is that they will be "forced" to get better by the command to get worse.

An example of a *model-specific technique factor* is: relate current crisis behavior to destructive internalized representations. Consider the therapist who says to the desperately suicidal abuse victim: "Oh, I hope you are not going to let him continue to hurt you this way. Given all that we have learned together about your self-destructive behaviors, it seems clear that if you attack yourself, you are, in effect, agreeing with him about how you should be treated. Do you really want to give him so much control even now?"

An example of a *model-specific relationship factor that is part of the technique* is personal disclosure that seeks to block dangerous actions. Consider the therapist who tells the vengeful passive aggressive person threatening suicide "because" she wants to ruin the therapist's reputation: "I would feel very sad in my heart if you were to make that choice, and I hope you do not. It also is possible a few people might wonder if I "dropped the ball" if you go ahead and kill yourself. Yet I know that you are the one with the control over this, and that the most I can do is give you every possible chance to make a better decision." Then, after exploring that idea in greater depth, the therapist might redirect the focus back upon the patient and encourage her to explore possible underlying reasons for her willingness to go to such lengths just to point an accusing finger.

Compare the Interactions of Relationship Factors With Other Variables

Relationship and technique factors should be studied in the context of different populations (e.g., personality disordered, depressed, specific personality disorders), and different treatment approaches (e.g., client centered, cognitive behavioral therapy). In addition, there should be consideration of various definitions of variables (e.g., dimensional and categorical definitions of personality) and outcome (e.g., whether change in symptoms is statistically or clinically significant; Lunnen & Ogles, 1998).

Benjamin (1996) has hypothesized that well-reasoned differential diagnosis is sometimes possible for personality disorder, despite the legendary problem of co-morbidity within Axis II of the DSM (e.g., Morey, 1988). Differential diagnosis can mean that different treatment approaches are needed to optimize effectiveness. For example, Benjamin proposed that offering a structured, sometimes controlling approach for treatment of borderline personality disorder (as in firm therapy rules), probably would be helpful. However, attempts to firmly control a similarly self-destructive person who nonetheless is better described as Passive Aggressive personality disorder, is likely to trigger reactance.[15] Similarly, Barber and Muenz (1996) suggested that a more structured therapy like cognitive therapy would be more effective for depressed avoidant personality patients while a more interpersonally focused therapy such as Interpersonal Therapy (Klerman, Weissman, Roun-

saville, & Chevron, 1984) will be more effective with depressed obsessive-compulsive personality disorder patients.

Make Assessments Often Enough to Permit Sequential Analyses

Assessments of adherence and outcome should be made at regular intervals throughout treatment. Cross lagging, relevant partial correlations, and other sequential analyses could then be used to begin to identify factors that after further study might be considered causal.

Recommendation 2: Perform Direct Tests of Whether and How Technique Adds to or Interacts With the Effectiveness of Clearly Defined Relationship Factors Within Different Populations and Treatment Approaches

We suggest using a Client-Centered Therapy (Rogers, 1951) treatment group as a relationship-only control condition for psychotherapy effectiveness studies. Rogers proposed that the three facilitating conditions: empathy, positive regard, and congruence are necessary *and sufficient*[16] conditions for therapy change. Rogers (1951) was very clear on this point.[17] No other treatment approach has so directly and completely incorporated the therapy relationship into its treatment model, and provided focused (and mostly successful) empirical tests of its central thesis. Unfortunately, we are not aware of any studies that explicitly used Client-Centered Therapy[18] alone for the treatment of personality disorder.[19]

The Rogerian tradition began with and never deviated far from his original book describing Client-Centered Therapy (Rogers, 1951). That tradition now is almost a half century old. One would think that long before the Division 29 Task Force or the present Task Force reports on the power of relationship had appeared, Client-Centered would have been listed as an empirically supported therapy approach. Surely the fact that client-centered studies could not have targeted DSM defined populations[20] should not override the impact of the multiplicity of studies[21] that have provided testimony to the effectiveness of empathy, positive regard, and congruence.

Given the results of current Task Force reviews on the importance of the therapy relationship, treatment manuals should include sections that specifically address the therapy relationship, being clear about how the relationship relates to the purported[22] mechanisms of change.

Outcomes for relationship-only control groups and for treatments advocating techniques should be related to measures of adherence to technique, model-specific relationship factors, and the therapy alliance. Data gathered in studies that clearly define and assess change in personality disorder could provide preliminary answers to questions such as:

1. Is a therapy relationship of a specific sort a necessary but not sufficient condition for treatment change? Is this different for different personality disorders?
2. Is a therapy relationship of a specific sort a sufficient condition for treatment change in all personality disorders?
3. What are the relative contributions of relationship (alliance; model specific relationship factors) and technique to outcome variance in the treatment of personality disorder?
4. How do relationship factors interact with technique and personality disorder diagnosis?
5. How do relationship factors interact with technique and various types of personality disorder?

Treatments that add to outcome variance related to the basic relationship conditions specified by Rogers could attribute differences to model-specific relationship factors[23] and technique. This would be a conservative and harsh test of the question of whether therapy technique adds to relationship components discussed in this review.

PRINCIPLES OF CHANGE

As we described earlier in this chapter, the relative dearth of studies linking relationship factors to outcome in the treatment of personality disorders has led us to accept many of the conclusions of the Division 29 Task Force "by default" or pending future research. However, a number of relationship variables have been the focus of empirical attention, albeit limited, with this patient population. Based on treatment and empirical studies reviewed above, we suggest the following principles of change.

1. As with studies using a general therapy population, a good therapy alliance is likely to enhance outcome when treating individuals with personality disorder.
2. Related to the establishment and maintenance of a good alliance, effective treatments of personality disorder tend to have therapists who are relatively active, provide clear structure, and set limits on behaviors, defined by the treatment model, as unacceptable.
3. Group treatment of personality disorders leads to better therapy outcome when therapists cultivate greater levels of group cohesion.
4. Therapy outcomes for patients with personality disorders are improved when therapists make accurate relational interpretations that are focused on a patient's central interpersonal issues. The frequency of these interpretations should be tailored to certain patient characteristics, such as the quality of their object relations.
5. Therapists of clients with personality disorders are more likely to reduce the frequency of destructive alliance ruptures and improve their resolution if they have benign self-concepts and are perceived as friendly by their clients, are flexible in their adherence to treatment protocols, foster a sense of ease in session interactions, focus on issues of depth in therapy, and skillfully address alliances ruptures by avoiding the overt expression of countertransference.

Notes

1. A recent, highly informative review of the alliance, including definitions, methods of measurement, and research findings is by Constantino, Castonguay, and Schut (2002). Another is by Horvath, 2001.

2. For example, later we will discuss interactions between alliance and patient qualities, such as

quality of object relations, and specific treatment approach, such as Brief Analytic Therapy or Short-Term Dynamic Therapy.

3. As measured by the Interpersonal Problems Inventory (Alden, Wiggins, & Pincus, 1990).

4. Interestingly, obsessive-compulsive personality disorder had better treatment retention, as well as faster loss of and greater chance of losing their personality disorder diagnosis than did those patients with avoidant personality disorder. However, both personality disorder groups showed similar improvements in global functioning, anxiety, and depression. This study points out the importance of examining personality disorder change as an outcome measure as well as the complex interplay between therapy relationship factors, personality pathology, and treatment response. We will return to this point in our recommendation section.

5. Based on clinical observation, group members with borderline personality disorder were more reactive to group process and more likely to get angry as a result of group interactions. The authors hypothesize that this resulted in hostile complementarity on the part of other members in the group who were not co-morbidly diagnosed. There were no measures of group process so this hypothesis is tentative.

6. Other than the generic therapy alliance.

7. Importantly, CVT + 12s did not prescribe indiscriminate validation, which may increase symptomatic outcome (Karpiak & Benjamin, 2004). By indiscriminant validation we mean validating the patient's expressions without regard to whether those expressions are adaptive or maladaptive in terms of the patient's interpersonal process with others.

8. Freud said transference occurs when the patient's "feelings do not arise from the present situation and do not apply to the person of the doctor, but . . . are repeating something that happened to [the patient] earlier." *Introductory Lectures on Psychoanalysis—Transference* given at the University of Vienna, 1916–1917. Manuscript Division, Library of Congress (51B).

9. A content analysis (Jilton et al., 1994) by independent raters of patients' reports of rupture events yielded eight clusters of rupture: "feeling judged and incompetent; feeling attacked and defensive; being assertive and challenging toward the therapist; feeling frustrated and angry; feeling misunderstood; difficulty trusting and being open; feeling confused about how to respond and express feelings; and feeling pressured to accept the therapist's task or agenda" (Muran, 2002, p. 126).

10. Some effective treatments for personality disorder actually prescribe the use of complex humor, which may contain hostile elements, paradoxical interventions, or control when used to block patients' maladaptive behavior (e.g., Benjamin, 2003; Linehan, 1993). However, these are not aimed at the patient's self-definition or sense of reality, for instance.

11. Compared to therapists with more benign self-concepts.

12. Feelings of comfort, safety, and ease of interacting (Stiles, Shapiro, & Firth-Cozens, 1990, p. 13).

13. Using post-session ratings from patients and therapists in a previous sample, the authors examined reliable change indices to determine good outcome and poor outcome cases. They next examined which ratings could distinguish between these cases and dropouts. Finally, these ratings were used to create an algorithm for identifying potential treatment failures.

14. Based on clinical experience and theory, we develop the argument later in this chapter that successful procedures with one disorder (e.g., limit setting for borderline personality disorder) may not enhance outcome with another (e.g., passive-aggressive personality disorder, PAG).

15. This conclusion is based on clinical observation, not on formal research protocol. It is predicted that if effective differentials between borderline personality disorder and passive-aggressive personality disorder were made, results for DBT for borderline personality would be improved.

16. Some of the Division 29 Task Force reviewers just cited did not indicate that Roger's model is confirmed by the observed correlations of conditions with outcome. Instead, they focused on hypotheses about how these Rogerian conditions might interact with various treatment approaches.

17. "In this safe relationship he can perceive for the first time the hostile meaning and purpose of certain aspects of his behavior. The therapist perceives the client's self as the client has known it, and accepts it; he perceives the contradictory aspects which have been denied to awareness and accepts those too as being a part of the client; and both of these acceptances have in them the same warmth and respect. Thus it is that the client, experiencing in another an acceptance of both these aspects of himself, can take toward himself the same attitude. He finds that he too can accept himself even with the additions and alterations that are necessitated by these new perceptions of himself as hostile. . . . He has been enabled to do this (if our theory is correct) because another person has been able to adopt his

frame of reference, to perceive with him, yet to perceive with acceptance and respect" (p. 41). "The process of therapy is, by these hypotheses, being seen as synonymous with the experiential relationship between client and therapist" (p. 172).

18. We do not classify "supportive therapy," which has been used as a contrast condition in several studies of treatment for personality disorder, as client-centered.

19. However, we reviewed one study (Linehan et al., 2002) that seemed to come close to creating such a control condition based on its description alone. However, without further detail on the specific relationship factors in and adherence to the control condition manual, we cannot tell how close this control condition was to that described by Rogers.

20. One of the required features that define an Empirically Supported Therapy (Chambless & Ollendick, 2000).

21. And other treatment approaches that have incorporated the Rogerian conditions.

22. We recognize that some behavioral therapists are not interested in mechanisms of change. Their manuals should, if standards like these were adopted, nonetheless recognize that relationship is a part of therapy, whether there is a related theory or not. This group of therapists might consider at a minimum, how relationship variables might affect acceptance of behavioral instructions.

23. Such a conclusion would have to be fine-tuned by adherence data.

References

Alden, L. E., Wiggins, J. S., & Pincus, A. L. (1990). Construction of circumplex scales for the inventory of interpersonal problems. *Journal of Personality Assessment, 55*, 521–536.

Barber, J. P., Connolly, M. D., Crits-Christoph, P., Gladis, L., & Siqueland, L. (2000). Alliance predicts patients' outcome beyond in-treatment change in symptoms. *Journal of Consulting and Clinical Psychology, 68*, 1027–1032.

Barber, J. P., Luborsky, L., Crits-Christoph, P., Thase, M. E., Weiss, R., Frank, A., Onken, L., & Gallop, R. (1999). Therapeutic alliance as a predictor of outcome in treatment of cocaine dependence. *Psychotherapy Research, 9*, 54–73.

Barber, J. P., Luborsky, L., Gallop, R., Crits-Christoph, P., Frank, A., Weiss, R. D., Thase, M. E., Connolly, M. B., Gladis, M., Foltz, C., & Siqueland, L. (2001). Therapeutic alliances as a predictor of outcome and retention in the National Institute on Drug Abuse Collaborative Cocaine Treatment Study. *Journal of Consulting and Clinical Psychology, 69*, 119–124.

Barber, J. P., Morse, J. Q., Krakauer, I., Chittams, J., & Crits-Christoph, P. (1997). Change in obsessive-compulsive and avoidant personality disorders following time-limited supportive-expressive therapy. *Psychotherapy, 34*, 133–143.

Barber, J. P., & Muenz, L. R. (1996). The role of avoidance and obsessiveness in matching patients to cognitive and interpersonal psychotherapy: Empirical findings from the Treatment for Depression Collaborative Research Program. *Journal of Consulting and Clinical Psychology, 64*, 951–958.

Barrett, M. S., & Berman, J. S. (2001). Is psychotherapy more effective when therapists disclose information about themselves? *Journal of Consulting and Clinical Psychology, 69*, 597–603.

Bateman, A. W., & Fonagy, P. (2000). Effectiveness of psychotherapeutic treatment of personality disorder. *British Journal of Psychiatry, 177*, 138–143.

Benjamin, L. S. (1996). *Interpersonal diagnosis and treatment of personality disorders* (2nd ed.). New York: Guilford.

Benjamin, L. S. (2003). *Interpersonal Reconstructive Therapy (IRT)*. New York: Guilford Press.

Benjamin, L. S., & Karpiak, C. (2002). Personality disorders. In J. C. Norcross (Ed.), *Psychotherapy relationships that work: Therapist contributions and responsiveness to patients* (pp. 423–438). New York: Oxford University Press.

Bohart, A. C., Elliott, R., Greenberg, L. S., & Watson, J. C. (2002). Empathy. In J. C. Norcross (Ed.), *Psychotherapy relationships that work: Therapist contributions and responsiveness to patients* (pp. 89–108). New York: Oxford University Press.

Bordin, E. S. (1994). Theory and research on the therapeutic working alliance: New directions. In A. O. Horvath & L. S. Greenberg (Eds.), *The working alliance: Theory, research and practice* (pp. 13–37). New York: Wiley.

Burlingame, G. M., Fuhriman, A., and Johnson, J. E. (2002). Cohesion in group psychotherapy. In J. C. Norcross (Ed.), *Psychotherapy relationships that work: Therapist contributions and responsiveness to patients* (pp. 71–88). New York: Oxford University Press.

Carroll, K. M., Nich, C., & Rounsaville, B. J. (1997). Contribution of the therapeutic alliance to outcome in active versus control psychotherapies. *Journal of Consulting and Clinical Psychology*, 65, 510–514.

Chambless, D. L. & Ollendick, T. H. (2000). Empirically supported psychological interventions: Controversies and evidence. *Annual Review of Psychology*, 52, 685–716.

Claiborn, C. D., Goodyear, R. K., & Horner, P. A. (2002). Feedback. In J. C. Norcross (Ed.), *Psychotherapy relationships that work: Therapist contributions and responsiveness to patients* (pp. 217–233). New York: Oxford University Press.

Clarkin, J. F., Foelsch, P. A., Levy, K. N., Hull, J. W., Delaney, J. C., & Kernberg, O. F. (2001). The development of a psychodynamic treatment for patients with borderline personality disorder: A preliminary study of behavioral change. *Journal of Personality Disorders*, 15, 487–495.

Cloitre, M., & Koenen, K. C. (2001). The impact of borderline personality disorder on process group outcome among women with posttraumatic stress disorder related to childhood abuse. *International Journal of Group Psychotherapy*, 51, 379–398.

Connolly-Gibbons, M. B., Crits-Christoph, P., de la Cruz, C., Barber, J. P., Siqueland, L., & Gladis, M. (2003). Pretreatment expectations, interpersonal functioning, and symptoms in the prediction of the therapeutic alliance across supportive-expressive psychotherapy and cognitive therapy. *Psychotherapy Research*, 13, 59–76.

Connolly-Gibbons, M. B., Crits-Christoph, P., Shappell, S., Barber, J. P., Luborsky, L., & Shaffer, C. (1999). Relation of transference interpretations to outcome in the early sessions of brief supportive-expressive psychotherapy. *Psychotherapy Research*, 9, 485–495.

Constantino, M. J., Castonguay, L. G., & Schut, A. J. (2002). The working alliance: A flagship for the "scientist-practitioner" model in psychotherapy. In G. S. Tryon (Ed.), *Counseling based on process research: Applying what we know* (pp. 81–131). Boston: Allyn & Bacon.

Crits-Christoph, P., Barber, J. P., & Kurcias, J. (1993). The accuracy of therapists' interpretations and the development of the therapeutic alliance. *Psychotherapy Research*, 3, 25–35.

Crits-Christoph, P., & Connolly-Gibbons, M. B. (2002). Relational interpretations. In J. C. Norcross (Ed.), *Psychotherapy relationships that work: Therapist contributions and responsiveness to patients* (pp. 285–300). New York: Oxford University Press.

Crits-Christoph, P., Cooper, A., & Luborsky, L. (1988). The accuracy of therapists' interpretations and the outcome of dynamic psychotherapy. *Journal of Consulting and Clinical Psychology*, 56, 490–495.

Dickinson, K. A., & Pincus, A. L. (2003). Interpersonal analysis of grandiose and vulnerable narcissism. *Journal of Personality Disorders*, 17, 188–207.

Farber, B. A., & Lane, J. S. (2002). Positive regard. In J. C. Norcross (Ed.), *Psychotherapy relationships that work: Therapist contributions and responsiveness to patients* (pp. 175–194). New York: Oxford University Press.

Gelso, C. J., & Hayes, J. A. (2002) The management of countertransference. In J. C. Norcross (Ed.), *Psychotherapy relationships that work: Therapist contributions and responsiveness to patients* (pp. 267–283). New York: Oxford University Press.

Foreman, S. A., & Marmar, C. R. (1985). Therapist actions that address initially poor therapeutic alliances in psychotherapy. *American Journal of Psychiatry*, 142, 922–926.

Henry, W. P., Schacht, T. E., Strupp, H. H., Butler, S. F., & Binder, J. L. (1993). Effects of training in time-limited dynamic psychotherapy: Mediators of therapists' responses to training. *Journal of Consulting and Clinical Psychology*, 61, 441–447.

Henry, W. P., Strupp, H. H., Butler, S. F., Schacht, T. E., & Binder, J. L. (1993). Effects of training in time-limited dynamic psychotherapy: Changes in therapist behavior. *Journal of Consulting and Clinical Psychology*, 61, 434–440.

Hersoug, A. G., Monsen, J. T., Havik, O. E., & Hoglend, P. (2002). Quality of early working alliance in psychotherapy: Diagnoses, relationship, and intrapsychic variables as predictors. *Psychotherapy and Psychosomatics*, 71, 18–27.

Hill, C. E., & Knox, S. (2002). Self-disclosure. In J. C. Norcross (Ed.), *Psychotherapy relationships that work: Therapist contributions and responsiveness to patients* (pp. 255–265). New York: Oxford University Press.

Hill, C. E., Mahalik, J. R., & Thompson, B. J. (1989). Therapist self-disclosure. *Psychotherapy*, 26, 290–295.

Hill, C. E., Nutt-Williams, E., Heaton, K. J., Thompson, B. J., & Rhodes, R. H. (1996). Therapist retrospective recall impasses in long-term psychotherapy: A qualitative analysis. *Journal of Counseling Psychology*, 43, 207–217.

Horvath, A. O. (2001). The alliance. *Psychotherapy*, *38*, 365–372.

Horvath, A. O., & Bedi, R. P. (2002). The alliance. In J. C. Norcross (Ed.), *Psychotherapy relationships that work: Therapist contributions and responsiveness to patients* (pp. 37–70). New York: Oxford University Press.

Horvath, A. O., & Greenberg, L. S. (1989). Development and validation of the Working Alliance Inventory. *Journal of Counseling Psychology*, *36*, 223–233.

Jilton, R., Batchelder, S., Muran, J. C., Gorman, B. S., Safran, J. D., Samstag, L. W., Winston, A. (1994, June). *Content analysis of therapeutic alliance rupture events*. Paper presented at the annual conference of the Society for Psychotherapy Research, York, UK.

Junkert-Tress, B., Schnierda, U., Hartkamp, N., Schmitz, N., & Tress, W. (2001). Effects of short-term dynamic psychotherapy for neurotic, somatoform, and personality disorders: A prospective 1-year follow-up study. *Psychotherapy Research*, *11*, 187–200.

Karpiak, C. P., & Benjamin, L. S. (2004). Therapist affirmation and the process and outcome of psychotherapy: Two sequential analytic studies. *Journal of Clinical Psychology*, *60*, 659–676.

Kernberg, O. F. (2001). The suicidal risk in severe personality disorders: Differential diagnosis and treatment. *Journal of Personality Disorders*, *15*, 195–208.

Klein, M. H., Kolden, G. G., Michels, J. L., & Chisholm-Stockard, S. (2002). Congruence or genuineness. *Psychotherapy: Theory, Research, Practice, Training*, *38*, 396–400.

Klerman, G. L., Weissman, M. M., Rounsaville, B. J., & Chevron, E. S. (1984). *Interpersonal psychotherapy of depression*. New York: Basic Books.

Koerner, K., & Linehan, M. M. (2000). Research on dialectical behavior therapy for patients with borderline personality disorder. *Psychiatric Clinics of North America*, *23*, 151–167.

Krupnick, J. L., Sotsky, S. M., Simmens, S., Moyer, J., Elkin, I., Watkins, J., & Pilkonis, P. A. (1996). The role of the therapeutic alliance in psychotherapy and pharmacotherapy outcome: Findings in the NIMH TDCRP. *Journal of Consulting and Clinical Psychology*, *64*, 532–539.

Linehan, M. M. (1993). *Cognitive-behavioral treatment of borderline personality disorder*. New York: Guilford.

Linehan, M. M., Dimeff, L. A., Reynolds, S. K., Comtois, K. A., Welch, S. S., Heagerty, P., & Kivlahan, D. R. (2002). Dialectical behavior therapy versus comprehensive validation therapy plus 12-step for the treatment of opioid-dependent women meeting criteria for borderline personality disorder. *Drug and Alcohol Dependence*, *67*, 13–26.

Luborsky, L. (1976). Helping alliances in psychotherapy. In J. L. Cleghorn (Ed.), *Successful psychotherapy* (pp. 92–116). New York: Brunner/Mazel.

Lunnen, K. M., & Ogles, B. M. (1998). A multiperspective, multivariable evaluation of reliable change. *Journal of Consulting and Clinical Psychology*, *66*, 400–410.

Martin, D. J., Garske, J. P., & Davis, K. M. (2000). Relation of the therapeutic alliance with outcome and other variables: A meta-analytic review. *Journal of Consulting and Clinical Psychology*, *68*, 438–450.

Marziali, E., Munroe-Blum, H., & McCleary, L. (1997). The effects of the therapeutic alliance on the outcomes of individual and group psychotherapy with borderline personality disorder. *Psychotherapy Research*, *9*, 452–467.

Meyer, B., Pilkonis, P. A., Proietti, J. M., Heape, C. L., & Egan, M. (2001). Attachment styles and personality disorders as predictors of symptom course. *Journal of Personality Disorders*, *15*, 371–389.

Morey, L. C. (1988). The categorical representation of personality disorder: A cluster analysis of DSM-III-R features. *Journal of Abnormal Psychology*, *97*, 314–321.

Morran, D. K., Robison, F., & Stockton, R. (1985). Feedback exchange in counseling groups: An analysis of message content and receiver acceptance as a function of leader versus member delivery, session, and valence. *Journal of Counseling Psychology*, *32*, 57–67.

Muran, J. C. (2002). A relational approach to understanding change: Plurality and contextualism in a psychotherapy research program. *Psychotherapy Research*, *12*, 113–138.

Muran, J. C., & Safran, J. D. (2002). *A comparative treatment study of personality disorders*. Paper presented at the international meeting of the Society of Psychotherapy Research, Santa Barbara, CA.

Norcross, J. C. (2002). *Psychotherapy relationships that work: Therapist contributions and responsiveness to patients*. New York: Oxford University Press.

O'Leary, D. O., & Costello, F. (2001). Personality and outcome in depression: An 18-month prospective follow-up. *Journal of Affective Disorders, 63*, 67–78.

Orlinsky, D. E., Grawe, K., & Parks, B. K. (1994). Process and outcome in psychotherapy—Noch einmal. In A. E. Bergin & S. L. Garfield (Eds.), *Handbook of psychotherapy and behavior change* (4th ed., pp. 270–376). New York: Wiley.

Perry, J. C., Banon, E., & Ianni, F. (1999). Effectiveness of psychotherapy for personality disorders. *American Journal of Psychiatry, 156*, 1312–1321.

Piper, W. E., Azim, H. F. A., Joyce, A. S., & McCallum, M. (1991). Transference interpretations, therapeutic alliance, and outcome in short-term individual psychotherapy. *Archives of General Psychiatry, 48*, 946–953.

Piper, W. E., & Ogrodniczuk, J. S. (1999). Therapy manuals and the dilemma of the dynamically oriented therapists and researchers. *American Journal of Psychotherapy, 53*, 467–482.

Piper, W. E., Rosie, J. S., Joyce, A. S., & Azim, H. F. A. (1996). *Time-limited day treatment for personality disorders: Integration of research and practice in a group program*. Washington, DC: American Psychological Association.

Reich, J. H., & Vasile, R. G. (1993). Effect of personality-disorders on the treatment outcome of Axis-I conditions—An update. *Journal of Nervous and Mental Disease, 181*, 475–484.

Ruegg, R., & Frances, A. (1995). New research in personality disorders. *Journal of Personality Disorders, 9*, 1–48.

Rhodes, R. H., Hill, C. E., Thompson, B. J., & Elliott, R. (1994). Client retrospective recall of resolved and unresolved misunderstanding events. *Journal of Counseling Psychology, 41*, 473–483.

Rogers, C. R. (1951). *Client-centered therapy*. Cambridge, MA: Riverside Press.

Rosenberger, E. W., & Hayes, J. A. (2002). Origins, consequences, and management of countertransference: A case study. *Journal of Counseling Psychology, 49*, 221–232.

Ryle, A., & Golynkina, K. (2000). Effectiveness of time-limited cognitive analytic therapy of borderline personality disorder: Factors associated with outcome. *British Journal of Medical Psychology, 73*, 197–210.

Safran, J. D., Muran, J. C., Samstag, L. W., & Stevens, C. (2002). Repairing alliance ruptures. In J. C. Norcross (Ed.), *Psychotherapy relationships that work: Therapist contributions and responsiveness to patients* (pp. 235–254). New York: Oxford University Press.

Safran, J. D., Muran, J. C., Samstag, L. W., & Winston, A. (2003). *Evaluating the efficacy of an alliance-focused intervention for potential treatment failures*. Manuscript submitted for publication.

Salvio, M. A., Beutler, L. E., Wood, J. M., & Engle, D. (1992). The strength of the therapeutic alliance in three treatments for depression. *Psychotherapy Research, 2*, 31–36.

Samstag, L. W., Batchelder, S., Muran, J. C., Safran, J. D., & Winston, A. (1998). Predicting treatment failure from in-session interpersonal variables. *Journal of Psychotherapy Practice and Research, 5*, 126–143.

Shahar, G., Blatt, S. J., Zuroff, D. C., & Pilkonis, P. A. (2003). Role of perfectionism and personality disorder features in response to brief treatment for depression. *Journal of Consulting & Clinical Psychology, 71*, 629–633.

Shearin, E., & Linehan, M. M. (1992). Patient therapist ratings and relationship to progress in Dialectical Behavior Therapy for borderline personality disorder. *Behavior Therapy, 23*, 730–736.

Singer, B. A., & Luborsky, L. (1997). Countertransference: The status of clinical versus quantitative research. In A. S. Gurman & A. M. Razin (Eds.), *Effective psychotherapy: A handbook of research* (pp. 433–451). New York: Pergamon.

Smith, T. L. (2002). *Specific psychosocial perceptions and specific symptoms of personality and other psychiatric disorders*. Unpublished dissertation, University of Utah.

Smith, T. L., & Benjamin, L. S. (2002). The functional impairment associated with personality disorders. *Current Opinion in Psychiatry, 15*, 135–141.

Soldz, S., Budman, S., Demby, A., & Merry, J. (1993). Representation of personality disorders in circumplex and five-factor space: Explorations with a clinical sample. *Psychological Assessment, 5*, 41–52.

Stiles, W. B., Shapiro, D. A., & Firth-Cozens, J. A. (1990). Correlations of session evaluations with treatment outcome. *British Journal of Clinical Psychology, 29*, 13–21.

Tryon, G. S., & Winograd, G. (2002). Goal consensus and collaboration. In J. C. Norcross (Ed.), *Psychotherapy relationships that work: Therapist contributions and responsiveness to patients* (pp. 109–125). New York: Oxford University Press.

Westerman, M. A., Foote, J. P., & Winston, A. (1995). Change in coordination across phases of psychotherapy and outcome: Two mechanisms for the role played by patients' contribution to the alliance. *Journal of Consulting & Clinical Psychology, 63*, 672–675.

Wiggins, J. S., & Pincus, A. L. (1989). Conceptions of personality disorders and dimensions of personality. *Psychological Assessment, 1*, 305–316.

12

Technique Factors in Treating Personality Disorders

Marsha M. Linehan
Gerald C. Davison
Thomas R. Lynch
Cynthia Sanderson

While the title of this chapter suggests that it will focus primarily on technical factors, it is important to mention that establishing a working relationship, increasing the client's expectations of positive outcome, and other similar strategies are well described, operationalized, and essential techniques in empirically supported treatments. It is important to note that relationship factors cannot and should not be divorced from technical factors when treating personality disorders (especially so for the treatment of BPD). Consequently, our chapter integrates a discussion of relationship factors and related strategies throughout the text and covers a broader area than purely "technical" factors.

For personality disorders there is only one treatment with one disorder that meets criteria for being efficacious, specific, and demonstrated by at least two independent research teams, making a chapter focusing on the integration of therapeutic change across treatments and personality disorder diagnosis difficult to actualize. Thus, to guide our review of the literature we used a tripartite ap-

proach developed by Chambless and Hollon (1998) to categorize treatments in which "possibly efficacious" ones are those that are not yet replicated, "efficacious" treatments are defined as those better than no treatment in at least two independent studies, and "efficacious and specific" are those better than an alternative treatment or placebo. This strategy allowed us to include a greater number of differing theoretical perspectives and diagnostic groups in our review yet remain within established guidelines.

Overall, the chapter is organized in four overlapping ways. First, we briefly articulate the importance of basing recommendations regarding treatment interventions on results from randomized clinical trials (RCTs). Second, we briefly examine findings regarding RCTs for personality disorders that demonstrated only within-group treatment effects (changes over time) but not between-group advantages for the experimental treatment over an alternative treatment or placebo control. Third, we review RCTs that demonstrated between-group advantages for a treatment. These interventions meet criteria for being possibly efficacious or efficacious, but do not meet criteria as defined by Chambless and Hollon for being efficacious and specific and/or have not been demonstrated by two or more independent research labs. At the end of each reviewed treatment we summarize relevant clinical observations made by the study investigators based on treatment manuals (if available), comments made in the original published RCT, and/or discussion with the authors. Fourth, we end the chapter by focusing on borderline personality disorder (BPD), the only disorder to date that has been studied sufficiently such that one particular treatment (Dialectical Behavior Therapy) meets the American Psychological Association's Division 12 (Society of Clinical Psychology) criteria of "well-established" and is both efficacious, specific, and has been demonstrated to be effective by three independent research teams. This section ends with general treatment guidelines based on published treatment manuals and discussions with investigators. Essentially, recommendations based on the broader review of the literature should be considered very tentative and suggestions based on Dialectical Behavior Therapy for borderline personality disorder can be considered less tentative.

THE IMPORTANCE OF RANDOMIZED CONTROLLED TRIALS (RCTS)

In making the commitment to science, a field acknowledges that objectivity and replicability play central roles in structuring tests of its theories. In clinical settings randomized controlled trials or rigorously controlled single subject designs, particularly multiple baseline designs, may be the only definitive method to test outcomes. At a minimum, a researcher should control for eight factors listed by Campbell (1957) that jeopardize internal validity: history, maturation of participants, testing, instrumentation, statistical regression, selection, experimental mortality, and selection history and selection maturation. Translated within a well-designed treatment study these features typically include a control group, random assignment of subjects to the control or treatment condition, prospective observation across time, appropriate

diagnostic interviews, blind raters of treatment outcome and controls for assessment bias, therapist expertise and experience, expectancy of improvement, and provision of a non-contingent warm and caring therapeutic relationship (Linehan, 1999; Seligman, 1998). However, it is also important to note that the absence of controlled research for a particular therapy does not necessarily invalidate the therapy. Indeed, naturalistic, noncontrolled, or nonrandomized studies have utility early in treatment development (e.g., to determine effect sizes, develop treatment manuals). However, treatment recommendations are best based only on carefully controlled studies in order to minimize potential harm for patients and maximize treatment benefits. Without controlled between-group comparisons or multiple baseline controlled studies, treatment recommendations are relegated to the realm of professional judgment, a useful but limited basis for decision making.

There have been several recent reviews of the psychotherapy treatment literature for personality disorders, one qualitative (Crits-Christoph, 1998) and two meta-analytic (Leichsenring & Leibing, 2003; Perry, Banon, & Ianni, 1999). However, we believe that drawing treatment recommendations from these reviews is premature. For example, 40% to 57% of the studies included in Leichsenring and Leibing's (2003) and Perry et al.'s (1999) meta-analytic reviews reported results from therapy studies that did not include a control group and did not entail the basic elements of experimental design like random assignment of patients to contrasting treatment conditions. In addition, some treatment orientations were incorrectly identified (e.g., Springer, Buchtel, & Silk, 1996), relevant RCTs were excluded (Koons et al., 2001), and/or the limitations of some study designs were minimized. For example, Woody, McLellan, Luborsky, and O'Brien's (1985) study was listed as an RCT comparing psychodynamic and cognitive-behavioral interventions. However, findings from this study are based on one treatment intervention that was created by collapsing two interventions into one and compared psychotherapy treatment outcomes across different DSM-III personality disorders diagnoses without a control group for the intervention within each diagnostic category (Woody et al., 1985). As another example, Liberman and Eckman's (1981) study that was in-cluded in both meta-analyses focused on suicidal behavior and did not include a diagnostic assessment of personality disorder. Although results indicated the superiority of a behavioral therapy package, without diagnostic assessment it is impossible to conclude that the treatment targeted personality disorders per se.

RCTS DEMONSTRATING WITHIN-GROUP CHANGES

Hardy et al. (1995) studied the effects of Psychodynamic-Interpersonal (PI) and Cognitive Behavioral Therapy (CBT) interventions for treatment of patients meeting DSM-III-R criteria for a cluster C personality disorder (Obsessive-Compulsive, Avoidant, and Dependent Personality Disorders) and mild to moderate depression compared to patients not personality disordered (NPD) with mild to moderate depression. Both treatments used in this study were originally designed to treat depression and were not specifically adapted for treatment of personality disorders. Participants were assigned to either 8 or 16 weeks of PI or CBT treatment. At initial assessment, 27 participants received a PD diagnosis, and 87 participants received an NPD diagnosis. Within group analyses showed that CBT therapies significantly improved depression scores for both the NPD and PD groups, while PI treatment was effective in treating depression only in the NPD diagnostic group. There were no between-group differences, no intent-to-treat analyses, and no therapist adherence ratings. The authors concluded that personality disorders respond better to more structured directive interventions.

Springer et al. (1996) evaluated the effectiveness of a Creative Coping (CC) group compared to a discussion control group for treatment of 31 inpatients meeting criteria for one or more personality disorders using the Millon Clinical Multiaxial Inventory, Version II (MCMI-II; Millon & Green, 1989). Thirteen met criteria for borderline personality disorder (BPD). The authors contended that the CC group was a modified version of Dialectical Behavior Therapy (DBT). However, it is important to note that there are a number of important differences between CC and DBT. First, the length of treatment in CC (10 weeks) is substantially shorter than the six months typically required to complete all modules in standard DBT skills training. Second, not all DBT treatment modalities were present (e.g., individual therapy, consultation team). Third, mindfulness skills training, which is a core feature of DBT, was not included in CC. Fourth and most importantly, CC allowed free discussion of parasuicidal acts by group participants, which is antithetical to DBT skills training approaches. The CC group was compared to a Wellness and Lifestyles (W&L) group developed by the researchers. The W&L group was designed to discuss issues relevant to the clients' lives, but was specifically designed to broach these issues without the goals of increasing introspection and self-understanding. Results failed to show between group differences on any outcome measure and reaction to treatment did not differ substantially from diagnosis to diagnosis across PDs. Notably, participants "acted out" more in the CC group than did participants in the W&L group. The authors concluded that focusing on parasuicidality within a short-term hospitalization may be iatrogenic, confirming contentions by Linehan (1993b) that group skill interventions for suicidal BPD patients not include free-flowing discussion of parasuicidal acts (e.g., "self-injury war stories").

Evans et al. (1999) compared a manual-assisted cognitive therapy (MACT) to treatment as usual (TAU) for treatment of 34 recently parasuicidal patients with histrionic, antisocial, or borderline personality disorder. PD diagnoses at baseline were obtained with the ICD-10 version of the Personality Assessment Schedule (Merson, Tyrer, Duke, & Henderson, 1994) and a second assessment was done six months later. MACT consisted of two to six treatment sessions covering problem solving, basic cognitive techniques to manage emotions and negative thinking, and relapse prevention strategies. TAU included standard care of inpatient, outpatient, day-hospital care, and/or community treatment. There were no significant between-group findings. However, the MACT group showed a significant reduction in depressive symptoms over time.

Munroe-Blum and Marziali (1995) studied a short-term interpersonal group psychotherapy (IGP) compared to individual dynamic psychotherapy (IDP; Kernberg, 1975) for treatment of 48 borderline personality disorder (BPD) patients diagnosed with the Diagnostic Interview for Borderlines (Gunderson, Kolb, & Austin, 1981). IGP consisted of 30 weekly manualized group sessions that focused on BPD problems of excessive dependence "upon here and now interpersonal transactions for self-definition" (Munroe-Blum & Marziali, 1995). IDP functioned as a control condition and included one to two individual psychodynamic sessions per week for an open-ended period of time. No significant between-condition differences in outcome were found. Within-group analyses revealed that both treatment conditions showed significant improvements over time on behavioral indicators (e.g., hospitalizations), social adjustment, global symptoms, and depression at the 12- and 24-month follow-up points of assessment.

POSSIBLY EFFICACIOUS TREATMENTS SHOWING TENTATIVE PROMISE

Avoidant Personality Disorder

There have been two studies examining treatment of avoidant personality disorder, each demonstrating the benefits of social skills training and general cognitive-behavioral approaches. However, neither study included an alternative treatment or placebo condition controlling for attention and expectancy. Thus, although the data are compelling, further research is required in order to consider these treatments as "well-established" according to APA Division 12 guidelines. The first of these studies was conducted by Stravynski, Marks, and Yule (1982). The authors used a multiple-baseline within-subject design to examine differences in treatment for outpatients with diffuse social phobia and avoidant personality disorder. Participants were randomly assigned to Social Skills Training (SST, $n = 11$) or SST + Cognitive Modification ($n = 11$). Treatment was provided by one therapist and varied from either small group or individual. Ratings by a blind assessor verified via audiotaped sessions that the treatments adhered to the treatment manuals. Patients improved equally with regard to social activity, social anxiety, isolation, relations with co-workers, depression, and irrational social beliefs. Outcomes did not differ between treatment groups, suggesting that cognitive modification did not enhance outcome. However, diagnostic interviews were not used for subject inclusion, there were no intent to treat analyses, and it is not possible to know whether SST would be effective alone since there was no control group. The authors conclude that in order to minimize fears of ridicule and rejection, clinicians should aim at improving social skills (e.g., teach how to have a conversation, how to ask open-ended questions, skills on how not to change the subject of conversation, etc.). Patients were also prompted to give supportive feedback to each other after social skills role plays.

The second study was conducted by Alden (1989), who randomized 76 patients diagnosed with avoidant personality disorder to three active treatments (graduated exposure [GE], GE + interpersonal skill training [ST], or GE + ST + intimacy focus) or a wait-list control. Treatment consisted of 10 weeks of group intervention. Compared to the no treatment wait-list group, all treated subjects showed significantly improved outcome on social reticence, anxiety, satisfaction with social activities, social interference, work interference, individualized social targets, and objective ratings of social performance. However, the three active treatments were all equally effective and a wait-list control does not control for nonspecific factors associated with attention. Findings also did not include intent-to-treat analyses and there were no clinically significant differences found between the active treatments and the wait-list control. With regard to treatment recommendations, the author outlined three factors that were most frequently nominated by patients as most influential in their treatment experience. These included: (1) meeting and talking with those with similar problems in order to reduce feelings of isolation; (2) specific functional analysis of the patient's social activities and behaviors in order to reduce reluctance to look at or analyze their social fears or other problems; (3) setting specific weekly social targets and the encouragement to follow through on these targets.

Other Personality Disorders

Winston et al. (1994) examined the efficacy of psychodynamically based psychotherapies for personality disorder assessed by structured clinical interview. Excluded Axis II disorders were paranoid, schizoid, schizotypal, narcissistic, and borderline personality disorder. Eighty-one patients were randomly assigned to 40 weeks of adaptive psychotherapy, 40 weeks of dynamic therapy, or an average of 15 weeks ($sd = 7$) of a wait-list control. Adaptive psychotherapy focused on the identification of the patient's major maladaptive pattern with the goal of obtaining insight into the origins and determinants of the pattern in order to produce more adaptive relationships. Short-term dynamic psychotherapy focused on confronting defensive behavior and eliciting affect so that repressed memories and ideas would be more fully experienced in the context of the current psychotherapeutic relationship. Therapy adherence ratings were obtained via videotapes to avoid drift in techniques. Patients in the two psychotherapy treatments improved significantly on SCL-90-R, global severity index scores, and Social Adjustment Scale scores compared to the wait-list control. However, there were no significant differences between active treatments and analyses did not equalize for time in comparisons examining differences between the wait-list control (15 weeks) and the active treatments (40 weeks). In discussing therapeutic approaches, the authors indicated that both treatments focused on interpersonal behavior but that short-term dynamic treatment emphasizes affect, whereas brief adaptive treatment targets cognition.

Borderline Personality Disorder (BPD)

In a well-controlled study of BPD, Bateman and Fonagy (1999) studied the effectiveness of a psychodynamically-oriented partial hospitalization treatment compared to standard psychiatric care for 38 patients diagnosed with BPD using the Structured Clinical Interview for DSM-III-R (Spitzer, Williams, Gibbon, & First, 1990) and the Diagnostic Interview for Borderline Patients (Gunderson et al., 1981). The partial hospitalization treatment group lasted for a maximum of 18 months, included once-weekly individual therapy and thrice-weekly group therapy, and was organized around a psychodynamic focus. Interestingly, none of the psychiatric nurses administering the partial hospitalization therapy had formal psy-

chotherapy training. Adherence to treatment was assessed through verbal reports of session activities and a monitoring form that collected further information about session activities. Participants in the control group did not receive structured psychotherapy, and treatment included an average of two visits with a senior psychiatrist, inpatient admission, and a non-psychoanalytic problem-focused partial hospitalization (72% of the control condition with average length of stay 6 months). The psychodynamic-oriented partial hospital condition showed significant improvement on all measures compared to the control group, including a decrease in suicidal and self-injurious acts, reduced inpatient days, and better social and interpersonal function. The authors reported that the treatment received by those in the standard psychiatric care group "lacked coherence, was inconsistently applied, particularly at times of crisis, and was delivered by a number of uncoordinated agencies." In addition, they concluded that the essential features of an effective treatment for BPD are: "a theoretically coherent treatment approach, a relationship focus, and a consistent application over a period of time." Bateman and Fonagy (2004) refer to their manualized treatment as a mentalization-based treatment (MBT) for BPD. Mentalization involves integrating information from the actions of oneself and others on the basis of intentional mental states, such as feelings, desires, and beliefs (see Bateman & Fonagy, 2004a, 2004b, for a more in-depth description of the treatment). We incorporated other clinical comments by Bateman and Fonagy (2001) and personal communication with Peter Fonagy (2004) relevant to treatment of BPD in the section below. In a follow-up study, those in the partial-hospitalization program were provided continuing individual psychotherapy for 18 months and outcomes were compared to the control condition that continued in standard care. The significant improvement in the psychodynamically-oriented partial hospitalization group was maintained over time (Bateman & Fonagy, 2001).

WELL-ESTABLISHED TREATMENT FOR BORDERLINE PD

Using the criteria for manualized treatments established by Chambless and Hollon (1998), the cur-

Table 12.1

Summary of Randomized Controlled Trials of Dialectical Behavior Therapy for Treatment of BPD

Treatments	Inclusion criteria	Sample size	Length	Main effects	Reference
1. DBT 2. Control: Community Mental Health TAU	BPD + suicide attempt in last 8 weeks + one other in last 5 years Female	1. = 24 2. = 22;	1 year	Frequency, medical risk, suicidality of suicide attempts and intentional self-injury; treatment retention; use of emergency and in-patient treatment; anger, social, and global adjustment	Linehan et al. 1991 Linehan & Heard 1993 Linehan et al. 1994 Linehan et al. 1993
1. DBT 2. Control: Community Drug Abuse/Mental Health TAU	BPD + current drug dependence Female	1. = 12 2. = 16;	1 year	Illicit drug use, social and global adjustment	Linehan et al. 1999
1. DBT + LAAM 2. Control: Comprehensive Validation Treatment (DBT without change strategies) + 12-step facilitation and 12-step group + LAAM	BPD + current opiate dependence Female	1. = 11 2. = 12	1 year	Opiate use	Linehan, Dimeff, et al. 2002
1. DBT Oriented 2. Control: Client-Centered Therapy	BPD + referral from Emergency services for suicide attempt	1. = 12 2. = 12	1 year	Parasuicide (suicide attempts and self-injury), impulsiveness, anger, depression, global adjustment, use of inpatient treatment	Turner 2000
1. DBT 2. Control: VA Mental Health TAU	BPD Female	1. = 10 2. = 10	6 mo.	Parasuicide (suicide attempts + self-injury) frequency, suicide ideation, hopelessness, depression, anger expression	Koons et al. 2001
1. DBT 2. Control: Community Drug Abuse/Mental Health TAU	BPD Female	1. = 31 2. = 33	1 year	Frequency of self-mutilation and suicide attempts, treatment retention, self-damaging impulsivity	Verheul et al. 2003
1. DBT 2. Control: Community Treatment by Psychotherapy Experts in Suicide and BPD	BPD + parasuicide (suicide attempt or self-injury) in last 8 weeks + one other in last 5 years Female	1. = 52 2. = 49	1 year	Suicide attempts, treatment retention, emergency and inpatient treatment	Linehan, Comtois, et al. 2002

rent literature quickly reveals that treatments for only one personality disorder—borderline personality disorder (BPD) has been investigated to the extent that the treatments can be considered "well-established" or "efficacious and specific." BPD is a notoriously complex disorder that frequently co-occurs with other psychiatric disorders like major depressive disorder, anxiety disorders, alcohol and substance abuse disorders, and post-traumatic stress disorder (Linehan, 1993b; Trull & McCrae, 1994). Among the personality disorders, it is the one most frequently diagnosed in clinical settings—15% of all inpatients and 8% of all outpatients are estimated to meet full criteria for BPD (Widiger & Trull, 1993). Further, it is estimated that between 40% and 65% of individuals who commit suicide meet criteria for a personality disorder and that BPD is the personality disorder most associated with completed suicide: 8–10% of clients diagnosed with BPD commit suicide, 75% attempt suicide, and 69–80% self-mutilate (Linehan, Dimeff, et al., 2002).

Unfortunately, the number of RCTs for borderline personality disorder is small, especially when compared with the number of studies on major depression, bipolar disorder, schizophrenia, anxiety disorders, and eating disorders (Sanderson, Swenson, & Bohus, 2002). One author has argued that, given the small number of RCTs, it may be premature to generate general principles of treatment that cut across a variety of treatment models (Sanderson et al., 2002). Our discussion of principles and their attendant strategies can be drawn only from those few randomized controlled trials of treatment of reliably diagnosed patients.

The treatment with the most empirical support is dialectical behavior therapy (DBT). It is the subject of seven well-controlled RCTs for the treatment of borderline personality disorder and efficacy has been demonstrated by four independent research teams (Koons et al., 2001; Linehan, Armstrong, Suarez, Allmon, & Heard, 1991; Linehan, Schmidt, et al., 1999; Linehan, Dimeff, et al., 2002; Turner, 2000; Verheul et al., 2003). The only other randomized controlled trial for treatment of BPD is Bateman and Fonagy's (1999) study of a psychodynamic partial hospital program, but this has yet to be replicated either by the authors or in a second independent lab (see review above). We organized this section by first review-

Table 12.2
Diagnostic Criteria for Borderline Personality Disorder

1. Recurrent suicidal behavior, gestures, or threats, or self-mutilating behavior
2. Frantic efforts to avoid real or imagined abandonment*
3. Pattern of unstable and intense interpersonal relationships characterized by alternating between extremes of idealization and devaluation
4. Identity disturbance: markedly and persistently unstable self-image or sense of self
5. Impulsivity in at least two areas that are potentially self-damaging*
6. Affective instability due to marked reactivity of mood
7. Chronic feelings of emptiness
8. Inappropriate, intense anger, or difficulty controlling anger
9. Transient, stress-related paranoid ideation or severe dissociative symptoms

Note: Five (or more) of the criteria must be present.
*Do not include suicidal or self-mutilating behaviors covered in Criterion 1.

ing the diagnostic criteria associated with BPD. We then summarized the relevant RCTs for BPD using DBT (see Table 12.1). Next, we formulated treatment recommendations for BPD using principles obtained from DBT and where relevant from the work by Bateman and Fonagy (1999).

Diagnostic Criteria for Borderline PD

There are nine criteria for borderline personality disorder listed in DSM-IV (APA, 1994; see Table 12.2). An individual must meet five of the nine to receive the diagnosis. Although BPD is practically synonymous with recurrent suicide attempts, it is possible to meet criteria for BPD and *not* have a history of suicide attempts or persistent self-harm. However, the major theoretical, clinical, and/or research texts on BPD highlight suicidality as a central feature of the disorder and make its management key in the treatment (Bateman & Fonagy, 1999; Beck & Freeman, 1990; Clarkin, Yeomans, & Kernberg, 1999; Gabbard, 2000; Linehan, 1993a). Regardless of their theoretical perspective, those who study BPD agree that its overarching features are severe and pervasive affective instability, behavioral dyscontrol or impulsivity, and disturbed relations with others (Skodol et al., 2002). Clients diagnosed with BPD commonly lead lives that are truly miserable and they often create havoc for those around them. While they may form intense attachments to other people, they rarely sustain their relationships and so are subject to painful loss after painful loss. They engage in impulsive behaviors that create crises and result in multiple hospitalizations. Not infrequently, they perform below their intellectual capacities at both school and work. And they are subject to transient psychotic or dissociative states when under stress.

Object relation theorists posit that either early problems of separation-individuation or excessive aggressive drives are the main contributors to this instability; however, there is almost no empirical support for these positions (Zanarini, Gunderson, Marino, & Schwartz, 1989). Dialectical behavior therapy hypothesizes that the transaction over time between emotional vulnerability and an invalidating environment results in BPD criterion behaviors. While there is some evidence to support this theory, it is not conclusive (Linehan, 1993a; Lynch, Chapman, Rosenthal, Kuo, & Linehan, in press). Theorists from any "camp" do agree that the development of BPD *appears* to be both genetic and/or biological *and* a result of the interaction of temperament with the social environment.

Dialectical Behavior Therapy for BPD

DBT is a highly structured, multi-modal behavioral treatment. It provides an array of behavioral change strategies (problem solving, skills training, contingency management, exposure-based procedures, and cognitive modification) balanced with an array of acceptance-based procedures (validation, mindfulness, a focus on distress tolerance). DBT is based on a combined capability deficit and motivational model of BPD, which states that (1) individuals with BPD lack important interpersonal, self-regulation (including emotional regulation), and distress tolerance skills, and (2) personal and environmental factors often both block and/or inhibit the use of behavioral skills that patients do have, and at times reinforce dysfunctional behav-

iors. As a comprehensive treatment, DBT addresses five functions of comprehensive treatment. It (1) increases behavioral capabilities by teaching skills to regulate emotions, to tolerate emotional distress when change is slow or unlikely, to be more effective in interpersonal conflicts, and to control attention in order to skillfully participate in the moment; (2) improves motivation to change (by intensive behavioral analyses, application of exposure-based treatment procedures, and management of reinforcement contingencies); (3) assures that new capabilities generalize to the natural environment via a variety of strategies including *in vivo* and telephone skills coaching; (4) structures the environment, particularly the treatment network, to reinforce patient skillful behaviors: and (5) actively works to enhance therapist capabilities and motivation to treat patients effectively.

Suicidal patients with BPD enter treatment at various levels of severity. Most serious are those patients who have severe behavioral dyscontrol. The first priority with these patients is to decrease life-threatening behaviors, particularly suicidal behaviors. Once the suicidal patient has achieved adequate behavioral control, the patient's intense dysphoria and difficulties managing emotional experiencing and failure to develop a "life worth living" emerge as the central target of therapy. Treatment at this point most often will focus on reducing experiential avoidance and encouraging behavioral activation and problem solving. DBT emphasizes treating suicidal behaviors on an aggressive outpatient basis, only rarely hospitalizes, and still demonstrates lower rates of suicide attempts than the standard treatments that frequently refer to emergency services and inpatient treatment.

As mentioned, DBT is the subject of seven well-controlled trials and has been demonstrated effective by four independent research teams (see Table 12.1). The first DBT clinical trial, conducted by Linehan and colleagues (1991), evaluated a comprehensive DBT package for chronically suicidal women meeting criteria for BPD. Compared to treatment-as-usual (TAU), individuals assigned to DBT were significantly less likely to parasuicide (self-injure or attempt suicide) during the treatment year, reported fewer parasuicide episodes at each assessment point, and had less medically severe parasuicides over the year. DBT was more effective than TAU at limiting treatment dropout, lessening anger, reducing inpatient psychiatric days, and enhancing global as well as social adjustment. All patients improved over time on depression, hopelessness, and suicide ideation (Linehan et al., 1991). Treatment superiority of DBT was maintained when DBT was compared to only those TAU patients who received stable individual psychotherapy during the treatment year and when number of hours of psychotherapy and of telephone contacts was controlled (Linehan, Heard, & Armstrong, 1993). DBT superiority was largely maintained during the one-year posttreatment follow-up period. In general, results of subsequent RCTs have largely replicated the initial RCT. Suicidal behaviors were reduced significantly in all seven trials and were significantly lower in DBT than in an array of control conditions in five of the seven trials (Table 12.1). The two studies where both DBT and the control conditions did not differ in reduction of suicidal behaviors had quite low rates of suicidality at the start of treatment.

GENERAL PRINCIPLES FOR TREATMENT OF PERSONALITY DISORDERS

It is important to note that the development, evaluation, and dissemination of new mental health treatments go through at least three stages (NIDA, 1994). Research on personality disorders to date has focused on Stage I (treatment development, modification, and pilot testing) or Stage IIa (RCTs and replication studies). Once it is known that a treatment is efficacious, the next task is to improve the treatment further by making it more efficient and efficacious (Linehan, 1999). The Stage IIb phase of treatment development includes component and process-analytic studies, dismantling studies, and studies designed to analyze response predictors. However, at this time there is an absence of a programmatic line of process research examining principles of change for personality disorder treatments. In addition, as can be seen by the review above, it could be misleading to base treatment principles on treatments that failed to demonstrate between group differences, lacked

replication, and/or failed to demonstrate superiority of the experimental treatment over an active treatment control. Consequently, we focused principles on those treatments that have demonstrated treatment advantages over some type of active treatment control (Bateman & Fonagy, 1999; Koons et al., 2001; Linehan et al., 1991; Linehan, Schmidt, et al., 1999; Linehan, Dimeff, et al., 2002; Turner, 2000; Verheul et al., 2003). Principles were derived from published treatment manuals, summaries of hypothesized mechanisms in the published RCT, and/or discussions with investigators. In addition, principles were derived from general dimensions of psychotherapy that are assumed to cut across all approaches and that have been proposed by the current Task Force (Beutler & Castonguay, this volume). Regardless, the general principles that follow should be considered tentative due to the lack of therapy process research demonstrating specificity of any hypothesized treatment approach.

These general dimensions of psychotherapy that have been proposed by the current Task Force are: directive, nondirective, and self-directive procedures; interpersonal/systematic versus intrapersonal/individual procedures; thematic/insight-oriented versus symptom/skill-building procedures; intensive versus non-intensive/short-term procedures; and abreactive versus emotionally supportive procedures. We first outline how the two treatments that have demonstrated treatment advantages over some type of active treatment control, mentalization-based treatment (MBT; Bateman & Fonagy, 1999) and dialectical behavior therapy (DBT; Koons et al., 2001; Linehan et al., 1991; Linehan, Schmidt, et al., 1999; Linehan, Dimeff, et al., 2002; Turner, 2000; Verheul et al., 2003), might be categorized along these dimensions. Next we present general principles, structural principles, principles of change, and principles of motivation and collaboration based on our review of the treatment literature.

1. Directive, Nondirective, and Self-Directive Procedures

MBT: Focus is nondirective with goal of establishing self-directive attitudes and responsibility. However, at the beginning of therapy MBT is more directive, that is, the therapist may establish a crisis intervention pathway with the patient. This lessens as therapy progresses and therapists then move toward a nondirective but focused stance as they attempt to increase the capacity to mentalize (personal correspondence, Peter Fonagy, 2004).

DBT: The therapist attempts to strike a balance between empathy, support, and acceptance, on the one hand, and structured specific behavior change efforts, on the other. Directive interventions may occur throughout therapy and are especially more likely during times of crisis. Explicit skills training is emphasized with a goal of increasing a patient's repertoire and use of self-directed effective responses. The primary focus of treatment is to coach clients to intervene on their own behalf in the world rather than to intervene on behalf of the client.

2. Interpersonal/Systematic Versus Intrapersonal/Individual Procedures

MBT: Moves from an understanding of interpersonal interactions to intrapersonal procedures. Thus, there is a move from outside to inside. This changes as therapy progresses and the patient is able to tolerate more affective arousal in therapy in relation to the therapist (personal correspondence, Peter Fonagy, 2004).

DBT: Is based on the idea that interpersonal and intrapersonal realms are systemically related. Incorporates an emphasis on both the intrapersonal (e.g., emotions, cognitions, actions) and interpersonal issues (e.g., interpersonal effectiveness, working with therapeutic relationship) and the relationships between them from the start. Procedures used are a complement of interpersonal procedures, generally but not always in the context of the individual or group therapeutic relationships, and individual, intrapersonal procedures drawing from behavior therapies such as exposure-based procedures and behavioral activation procedures.

3. Thematic/Insight-Oriented Versus Symptom/Skill-Building Procedures

MBT: Focus is thematic/insight-oriented. MBT therapists do not focus on skills specifically or particular techniques to address problematic behav-

iors (personal communication, Peter Fonagy, 2004).

DBT: Focus is skill building and strengthening balanced by insight regarding the function of repeated maladaptive behavioral patterns (behavior from a DBT perspective includes all responses of the person, including cognitive functioning, physiological and emotional responses, and overt behavior). Emphasis is on teaching needed skills, enhancing willingness to utilize skills already in the repertoire, and improving generalizability of skillful responding in all relevant contexts.

4. Intensive Versus Non-Intensive/Short-Term Procedures

MBT: Intensive in nature. The published RCT utilized partial hospitalization treatment that lasted for a maximum of 18 months and included once-weekly individual therapy and thrice-weekly group therapy followed by twice a week group therapy.

DBT: Intensive in nature. Five of the six published RCTs included weekly individual therapy, weekly group skills training, and telephone coaching as needed, for up to 12 months.

5. Abreactive Versus Emotionally Supportive Procedures

MBT: Emotionally supportive as therapists attempt to identify patient affects, their interpersonal context followed by their intrapsychic meaning and consider abreaction to be iatrogenic (personal communication, Peter Fonagy, 2004).

DBT: Emotionally supportive in that therapists focus on teaching emotion regulation, tolerance of distress, and acceptance of emotional experience. Catharsis is viewed as generally iatrogenic.

General Principles

1. The therapist should strike a balance between empathy and acceptance, on the one hand, and structured specific behavior change efforts, on the other. As such, both directive and nondirective procedures are components of effective treatment of personality disorders.
2. The therapist should use a focused theo-

retically coherent approach (i.e., avoid eclecticism).

3. Treatment of BPD takes time and is intensive in nature. The therapist should plan to consistently apply treatment components over relatively long periods of time.

4. A functional ideographic analysis of specific problem behaviors should be conducted in order to formulate treatment planning.

5. Therapists treating clients diagnosed with PD should be both honest and explicit about their limits.

6. Therapists treating clients diagnosed with PD should recognize importance of both intrapersonal and interpersonal issues and the relationships between the two.

7. Procedures focused primarily on gaining insight should be used only when the client is able to tolerate affect in treatment of BPD.

8. Therapists should not assume that clients diagnosed with PD possess the necessary cognitive or emotional capacities necessary for effective living.

9. Focus in treatment for BPD patients should be present-oriented and exploration of the past should not occur until the client has solidly established behavioral and emotional control.

10. Therapists treating clients diagnosed with BPD need to be emotionally supportive.

Structural Principles

1. Therapeutic change is most likely if therapy is clearly structured such that both client and therapist specify and agree to the goals, the format, the modalities, and the treatment strategies of the therapy before it formally begins.

2. Therapeutic change is most likely if treatment is designed to be comprehensive; that is, it aims at enhancing client capabilities and behavioral skills as well as motivation, and attends specifically to generalization from the therapeutic setting to the client's ordinary life.

3. Therapeutic change is most likely if the therapist and client structure the client's everyday environment so that the client's

newly acquired, more adaptive behaviors are reinforced and his or her maladaptive behaviors extinguished.

4. Therapeutic change is most likely if the therapists treating the client in primary and auxiliary modes of therapy receive ongoing consultation and supervision.

5. Therapeutic change is most likely if treatment sessions are organized around addressing clearly prioritized treatment targets.

Principles of Change

1. Therapeutic change is most likely if treatment involves exposure to the cues setting off maladaptive emotions combined with blocking of escape behaviors and reinforcement of skillful, opposite-to-emotion responses.

2. Therapeutic change is most likely if the alteration of specific problem behaviors is done via the application of established principles of behavior change, for example, the use of contingent consequences, exposure-based procedures, and behavioral skills training.

3. Therapeutic change is most likely if case formulation and application of treatment strategies are based on individual, detailed analyses of specific factors precipitating problematic behavioral responses (cognitive, emotional, actions) as well as consequences of problematic responses that may be maintaining patterns of behavior.

4. Therapeutic change is most likely if clients are assisted in both experiential acceptance and tolerance as well as change of distressing cognitive, emotional, and behavioral patterns.

Principles of Motivation and Collaboration

1. The client's motivation for treatment is enhanced and therapeutic change is most likely if the therapist can address therapeutic impasses with nonconfrontational strategies.

2. The client's motivation for treatment is enhanced if the individual therapist is flexible in his or her limits, being more available to the client during periods of crisis.

3. The client's motivation for treatment is en-

hanced if the therapist is genuine and responsive.

4. The client's motivation for treatment is enhanced when the therapist engages in strategic self-disclosure.

5. The client's motivation for treatment is enhanced when the therapist conveys an understanding of how difficult it is for the client to change.

SUMMARY AND CONCLUSIONS

New treatments are needed either when we have no effective treatment for a particular disorder, or when the treatments we do have are not sufficiently effective and efficient. Other than for BPD, personality disorder intervention research has yet to reach a minimum level of randomized controlled trials such that conclusions can be made with regard to efficacy and specificity of interventions. Indeed, treatment research for personality disorders in general can be characterized as in its infancy compared to treatments for other disorders (e.g., depression, anxiety). Although this is changing, change is slow. This is likely due to the fact that treatment of PD is complicated, as personality disorders are chronic heterogeneous conditions that frequently co-occur with other Axis I disorders. In addition, the integrity of personality disorder diagnosis as a discrete categorical entity has been questioned. For example, there are 151 different combinations of BPD criteria that can result in a borderline diagnosis using DSM-IV approaches, and some of the individuals with borderline diagnoses will only overlap on one of nine BPD criteria (Skodol et al., 2002). In addition, whereas in biological treatments there is an enormous pharmaceutical industry to support and profit from the development of new drugs, there is no corresponding financial enterprise in the area of psychosocial treatment development (Barlow, 1994; Linehan, 1999). Thus, financial support is low compared to biological interventions, making study more difficult. Lastly, there have been no dismantling studies examining specific hypothesized mechanisms of change in the treatments that show efficacy, making a chapter focusing on the integration of therapeutic change across treatments and personality disorder diagnosis difficult to actualize. Thus, treatment principles outlined in this chapter should be considered tentative, although we are hopeful that attempts to delineate factors associated with treatment success will serve as a catalyst for additional research.

ACKNOWLEDGMENTS   The authors wish to acknowledge, with sadness and respect, the contributions Cynthia Sanderson made to this chapter before she unexpectedly died of cancer.

References

Alden, L. (1989). Short-term structured treatment for avoidant personality disorder. *Journal of Consulting and Clinical Psychology, 57,* 756–764

APA (American Psychiatric Association). (1994). *Diagnostic and statistical manual of mental disorders* (4th ed.). Washington, DC: American Psychiatric Association.

Barlow, D. H. (1994). Psychological interventions in the era of managed competition. *Clinical Psychology Science and Practice, 1,* 109–122.

Bateman, A., & Fonagy, P. (1999). Effectiveness of partial hospitalization in the treatment of borderline personality disorder: A randomized controlled trial. *American Journal of Psychiatry, 156,* 1563–1569.

Bateman, A., & Fonagy, P. (2001). Treatment of borderline personality disorder with psychoanalytically oriented partial hospitalization: An 18-month follow-up. *American Journal of Psychiatry, 158,* 36–42.

Bateman, A. W., & Fonagy, P. (2004a). Mentalization-based treatment of BPD. *Journal of Personality Disorders, 18,* 36–51.

Bateman, A. W., & Fonagy, P. (2004b). *Psychotherapy for borderline personality disorder: Mentalization based treatment.* Oxford, UK: Oxford University Press.

Beck, A. T., & Freeman, A. M. (1990). *Cognitive therapy of personality disorders.* New York: Guilford Press.

Campbell, D. T. (1957). Factors relevant to the validity of experiments in social settings. *Psychological Bulletin, 54,* 297–312.

Chambless, D. L., & Hollon, S. D. (1998). Defining empirically supported therapies. *Journal of Consulting and Clinical Psychology, 66,* 7–18.

Clarkin, J., Yeomans, F., & Kernberg, O. (1999). Psychotherapy of borderline personality. New York: John Wiley and Sons, Inc.

Crits-Christoph, P. (1998). Control groups in psychotherapy research revisited. *Prevention and Treatment, 1*, n.p.

Evans, K., Tyrer, P., Catalan, J., Schmidt, U., Davidson, K., Dent, J., Tata, P., Thornton, S., Barber, J., & Thompson, S. (1999). Manual-assisted cognitive-behaviour therapy (MACT): A randomized controlled trial of a brief intervention with bibliotherapy in the treatment of recurrent deliberate self-harm. *Psychological Medicine, 29*, 19–25.

Gabbard, G. O. (2000). Psychodynamic psychotherapy of borderline personality disorder: A contemporary approach. *Bulletin of the Menninger Clinic, 65*, 41–57.

Gunderson, J. G., Kolb, J. E., & Austin, V. (1981). The diagnostic interview for borderline patients. *American Journal of Psychiatry, 138*, 896–903.

Hardy, G. E., Barkham, M., Shapiro, D. A., Stiles, W. B., Rees, A., & Reynolds, S. (1995). Impact of Cluster C personality disorders on outcomes of contrasting brief psychotherapies for depression. *Journal of Consulting and Clinical Psychology, 63*, 997–1004.

Kernberg, O. F. (1975). *Borderline conditions and pathological narcissism*. New York: Jason Aronson.

Koons, C. R., Tweed, J. L., Lynch, T. R., Gonzalez, A. M., Morse, J. Q., Bishop, G. K., Butterfield, M., & Bastian, L. (2001). Efficacy of dialectical behavior therapy in women veterans with borderline personality disorder. *Behavior Therapy, 32*, 371–390.

Leichsenring, F., & Leibing, E. (2003). The effectiveness of psychodynamic therapy and cognitive behavior therapy in the treatment of personality disorders: A meta-analysis. *American Journal of Psychiatry, 160*, 1223–1232.

Liberman, R. P., & Eckman, T. (1981). Behavior therapy vs. insight oriented therapy for repeated suicide attempters. *Archives of General Psychiatry, 38*, 1126–1130.

Linehan, M. M. (1993a). *Cognitive behavioral treatment of borderline personality disorder*. New York: Guilford Press.

Linehan, M. M. (1993b). *Skills training manual for treating borderline personality disorder*. New York: Guilford Press.

Linehan, M. M. (1999). Development, evaluation, and dissemination of effective psychosocial treatments: Levels of disorder, stages of care, and stages of treatment research. In M. D. Glantz & C. R. Hartel (Eds.), *Drug abuse: Origins & interventions* (pp. 367–394). Washington, DC: American Psychological Association.

Linehan, M. M., Armstrong, H. E., Suarez, A., Allmon, D., & Heard, H. L. (1991). Cognitive-behavioral treatment of chronically parasuicidal borderline patients. *Archives of General Psychiatry, 48*, 1060–1064.

Linehan, M. M., Dimeff, L. A., Reynolds, S. K., Comtois, K. A., Welch, S. S., Heagerty, P., & Kivlahan, D. (2002). Dialectal behavior therapy versus comprehensive validation therapy plus 12-step for the treatment of opioid dependent women meeting criteria for borderline personality disorder. *Drug & Alcohol Dependence, 67*, 13–26.

Linehan, M. M., Heard, H. L., & Armstrong, H. E. (1993). Naturalistic follow-up of a behavioral treatment for chronically parasuicidal borderline patients. *Archives of General Psychiatry, 50*, 971–974.

Linehan, M. M., Schmidt, H., III, Dimeff, L. A., Craft, J. C., Kanter, J., & Comtois, K. A. (1999). Dialectical behavior therapy for patients with borderline personality disorder and drug dependence. *American Journal on Addictions, 8*, 279–292.

Lynch, T. R., Chapman, A. L., Rosenthal, M. Z., Kuo, J. R., & Linehan, M. M. (in press). Mechanisms of change in dialectical behavior therapy: Theoretical and empirical observations. *Journal of Clinical Psychology*.

Merson, S., Tyrer, P., Duke, P. J., & Henderson, F. (1994). Interrater reliability of ICD-10 guidelines for the diagnosis of personality disorders. *Journal of Personality Disorders, 8*, 89–95.

Millon, T., & Green, C. (1989). Interpretive guide to the Millon Clinical Multiaxial Inventory (MCMI-II). In C. S. Newmark (Ed.), *Major psychological assessment instruments* (Vol. 2, pp. 5–43). Needham Heights, MA: Allyn & Bacon.

Munroe-Blum, H., & Marziali, E. (1995). A controlled trial of short-term group treatment for borderline personality disorder. *Journal of Personality Disorders, 9*, 190–198.

National Institute on Drug Abuse. (1994). Behavioral Therapies Development Program (Program Announcement No. PA-94-078).

Perry, J. C., Banon, E., & Ianni, F. (1999). Effectiveness of psychotherapy for personality disorders.

American Journal of Psychiatry, 156, 1312–1321.

Sanderson, C., Swenson, C., & Bohus, M. (2002). A critique of the American psychiatric practice guideline for the treatment of patients with borderline personality disorder. *Journal of Personality Disorders, 16,* 122–129.

Seligman, L. (1998). *Selecting effective treatments: A comprehensive, systematic guide to treating mental disorders* (Rev. ed.). San Francisco: Jossey-Bass/Pfeiffer.

Skodol, A. E., Gunderson, J. G., Pfohl, B., Widiger, T. A., Livesley, W. J., & Siever, L. J. (2002). The borderline diagnosis I: Psychopathology, comorbidity, and personality structure. *Biological Psychiatry, 51,* 936–950.

Spitzer, R. L., Williams, J. B. W., Gibbon, M., & First, M. B. (1990). *User's guide for the structured clinical interview for DSM-III-R: SCID.* Washington, DC: American Psychiatric Association.

Springer, T. L. N., Buchtel, H. A., & Silk, K. R. (1996). A preliminary report of short-term cognitive-behavioral group therapy for inpatients with personality disorders. *Journal of Psychotherapy Practice & Research, 5,* 57–71.

Stravynski, A., Marks, I., & Yule, W. (1982). Social skills problems in neurotic outpatients: Social skills training with and without cognitive modification. *Archives of General Psychiatry, 39,* 1378–1385.

Trull, T. J., & McCrae, R. R. (1994). A five-factor perspective on personality disorder research. In P. T. Costa, Jr. & T. A. Widiger (Eds.), *Personality disorders and the five-factor model of personality* (pp. 59–71). Washington, DC: American Psychological Association.

Turner, R. M. (2000). Naturalistic evaluation of dialectical behavior therapy oriented treatment for borderline personality disorder. *Cognitive and Behavioral Practice, 7,* 413–419.

Verheul, R., van-den-Bosch, L. M. C., Koeter, M. W. J., de-Ridder, M. A. J., Stijnen, T., & van-den-Brink, W. (2003). Dialectical behaviour therapy for women with borderline personality disorder: 12-month, randomised clinical trial in The Netherlands. *British Journal of Psychiatry, 182,* 135–140.

Widiger, T. A., & Trull, T. J. (1993). Borderline and narcissistic personality disorders. In P. B. Sutker & H. E. Adams (Eds.), *Comprehensive handbook of psychopathology* (2nd ed., pp. 371–394). New York: Plenum Press.

Winston, A., Laikin, M., Pollack, J., Samstag, L. W., McCullough, L., & Muran, J. C. (1994). Short-term psychotherapy of personality disorders. *American Journal of Psychiatry, 151,* 190–194.

Woody, G. E., McLellan, T., Luborsky, L. L., & O'Brien, C. P. (1985). Sociopathy and psychotherapy outcome. *Archives of General Psychiatry, 42,* 1081–1086.

Zanarini, M. C., Gunderson, J. G., Marino, M. F., & Schwartz, E. O. (1989). Childhood experiences of borderline patients. *Comprehensive Psychiatry, 30,* 18–25.

13

Integration of Therapeutic Factors in Treating Personality Disorders

Kenneth L. Critchfield
Lorna Smith Benjamin

Personality disorders (PDs) are chronic and frequently severe conditions associated with high levels of impairment and suffering. They are relatively common, with approximately 1 in 10 people in community samples (Samuels et al., 2002; Smith, Barrett, Benjamin, & Barber, this volume) and roughly half of patients in community-based clinical settings qualifying for at least one DSM-IV Axis II diagnosis (Keown, Holloway, & Kuipers, 2002). Personality disorders have shown resistance to common treatment approaches, complicate treatment of Axis I disorders, drain resources from systems of care, and can in many cases severely challenge health care providers with their intensity, chronicity, and cost in human suffering, even involving potential lethality to self and/or others through planned and/or recklessly impulsive behaviors. This chapter seeks to summarize and integrate principles for therapeutic change in psychosocial treatment of PD and principles that are shared across disorders as identified in the Task Force reviews contained in this volume.

The review chapters in PD all allude to the fact that psychotherapy research with these disorders is still in its early stages. Research to date can be taken to support the very general assertion that at least some PDs are amenable to at least some forms of psychosocial treatment. Linehan and colleagues, who have successfully worked to develop and test a psychosocial treatment for Borderline PD called Dialectical Behavior Therapy (DBT), have made greatest progress in this research area. Across the literature, evidence exists primarily for treatment benefits for Borderline and Avoidant PDs. Other Axis II disorders have typically not been studied, but results of treatment for some "mixed" PD samples are suggestive of positive benefits. Admirable efforts have been and will continue to be made by numerous research groups. However, moderators and mediators of treatment effectiveness have not yet been sufficiently studied to allow for definitive identification of empirically supported and cross-cutting principles leading to improved outcomes for Axis II treatments. This state of affairs poses a challenge to the integrative effort undertaken in this chapter, which necessarily leans heavily on principles proposed primarily based on indirect and suggestive evidence gleaned from the relevant literature. The next section explains the approach used to summarize, parse, and integrate the relevant principles. A detailed presentation and discussion of each principle and its relevant context makes up the bulk of this chapter, concluding with a final summary section.

ORGANIZATION OF PRINCIPLES IN TABLES AND TEXT

The process used to integrate the principles in this chapter involved review and comparison of two basic sources: (1) the three personality disorder-specific chapters generated by the Task Force and contained in this volume, covering participant (Fernández-Alvarez, Clarkin, Salgueiro, & Critchfield), technique (Linehan, Davison, Lynch, & Sanderson), and relationship factors (Smith, et al.) and (2) principles identified by the Task Force as spanning across disorders based on consideration of findings in all disorders covered in this volume (i.e., dysphoric, anxious, substance use, and personality disorders). Data from these two basic sources were compared to identify whether a given principle was unique to enhancing outcome in treatment of PD, or whether it was also listed among the common principles and/or shared with another disorder.

The common principles proposed by the Task Force as applying across disorders were further identified as those that have support in the PD reviews of this volume, versus those that have not yet been studied for Axis II (see Beutler & Castonguay, and Castonguay & Beutler, this volume, for more on the strategies used by the overall Task Force to determine common principles). For principles not yet addressed in the PD literature, the Task Force guideline was to provisionally adopt them, pending future research. Thus, some of the principles reviewed in this chapter are simply generalized to PD from work with other disorders, or by default from reviews by other sources based on a sense that the findings may be salient to PD. The resulting lists of principles are presented here in separate tables based on the three broad factors used by the Task Force: (1) participant principles, (2) relationship principles, and (3) technique prin-

ciples. Within the tables, each principle is marked to indicate its status as unique to PD (u), shared with one or more other disorders (s), or generalized from work with other disorders (g).

Parsing the principles necessarily required some comparing of apples and oranges in terms of the nature and amount of support available for each principle. This is due in part to the fact that different authors chose different standards for recommending principles (itself a function of research available in the primary domain inspected by each author), and also because articulation of the common principles proposed by the Task Force involved a similar synthesis across treatment literatures. In the case of PD, most of the evidence, where present, is indirect, and empirical research directly targeting the identified principles has yet to be conducted. For example, some of the PD principles were inferred in the source chapters based on elements emphasized in the treatment manuals of approaches with empirical support (e.g., see discussion of Table 13.3, below, and Linehan et al., this volume). While these manual-based elements are believed to be active ingredients in the treatments, they have yet to be investigated using direct measurement of the principles, relevant dismantling studies, technique-outcome correlations, or other conclusive analysis of direct impacts on outcome. Similarly, the therapist-related participant principles proposed for PD (see discussion of Table 13.1, below, and Fernández-Alvarez et al., this volume) have not received any direct focus in empirical work with PD treatment, but are based instead on clinical experience coupled with a reasoned understanding of the typical course of treatment with personality disordered individuals.

Another part of the challenge in undertaking the work of this chapter involved how to treat discrepant conclusions and recommendations made by authors of the different source chapters. This issue is especially notable in the technique principles chapter, which included recommendations that touched on elements also addressed in the participant and relationship principles chapters, with each being based on a somewhat different slice of the empirical literature. The principles summarized in this chapter should thus be understood to have status as reasonable hypotheses based in part on indirect support synthesized from the empirical literature. Understanding of treatment approaches for Axis II would certainly be advanced by further study of all of these reasonable hypotheses. Part of the hope of the Task Force is that the list of principles presented here will help inform clinical practice, especially once they have been refined through focused, future research.

Specific caveats for each principle are already reviewed in the source chapters and the interested reader is referred there for detail. This chapter proceeds mainly by taking the recommendations of the source authors at face value and attempting an overall integration on that basis. A relatively low threshold was set for combining PD principles with shared principles identified by the task force if there appeared to be some evidence of overlap between them. This decision was made in part because of the primarily indirect evidence available for nearly all PD principles, as was mentioned previously. As part of the integrative process, some liberty was taken to reorganize and reword principles from their articulation in other chapters, or wed them conceptually in order to improve their coherence together. In the few instances where differing conclusions were generated in the source chapters, the source and rationale behind the recommendation is briefly noted. Also, as part of an attempt to place each principle into a context with the others, 10 general themes were identified and used to cluster principles together. The themes, nested within each Task Force factor, are as follows:

Participant Factor
1. *Problem-related* principles
2. *Patient-related* principles
3. *Therapist-related* principles

Relationship Factor
1. Principles regarding *Alliance and Joint Collaboration*
2. Principles regarding *Optimal Therapist Stance*

Technique Factor
1. Principles related to *Salience*
2. Principles related to *Transparency*
3. Principles emphasizing *Goal-oriented Structure*
4. Principles addressing an *Emphasis on Change*

(including related issues of pacing and support for change)
5. Principles involving *Support for Therapists*

The next sections present each principle in table and text, organized by Task Force factor and general theme.

DISCUSSION OF TABLE 13.1: PARTICIPANT PRINCIPLES IN PD

1. Problem-Related Principles Predictive of Outcome

The problem-related principles listed in the first part of Table 13.1 are derived from research with other disorders and are generalized by extension to PD treatment. The principles thought to be pre-

Table 13.1

Participant Principles With Suggested Links to Outcome for Personality Disorder Treatments

Problem-related
(g) Functional impairment (severity, chronicity, co-morbidity)
(g) Match between level of impairment and treatment intensity

Patient-related
(u) Willingness and ability to engage with treatment
(s) History of positive attachments or trauma/attachment style/coping style
(g) Match between client's resistance level and intervention type
(g) Expectations of success
(g) Pretreatment readiness for change (stages of change)
(g) Social class

Therapist-related
(u) Comfort with long-term, emotionally intense relationships
(u) Patience
(u) Tolerance of own feelings regarding the patient and treatment process
(u) Specialized training
(u) Open-minded, flexible, and creative in approach

Note: (u) indicates principles *unique* to PD; (s) indicates principles identified in the PD source chapters and *shared* with other disorders; (g) indicates principles tentatively *generalized* to PD from work with other disorders, but pending investigation in PD.

dictive of either decreased or enhanced outcome, and discussed in turn below are: (a) the patient's level of functional impairment, including severity, chronicity, and co-morbidity components, and (b) the match between patient level of impairment and treatment intensity.

Interestingly, PD has itself been identified as a participant factor predictive of poorer outcome in treatments of other disorders (Castonguay & Beutler, this volume). One hypothesis to explain this observation may simply be that PD is defined in part by its chronicity and is frequently associated with high levels of co-morbidity and impaired functioning. Conversely, it may also be the case that the principles themselves correlate with poor outcome in other disorders because they suggest presence of character pathology per se. Each of these principles awaits verification or refutation in PD treatment research.

Functional Impairment

Severity of impairment is presented here as a likely predictor of poorer outcome for patients diagnosed with PD. The general idea that more severe problems are more difficult to treat makes sense, especially when bolstered by observation of this link in research with other disorders. A difficult issue in the present context, however, is the question of how best to operationalize "severity" for PD patients. For example, some theorists (e.g., Kernberg, 1996; Depue & Lenzenweger, 2001) place PDs along dimensions relative to each other, suggesting that some PDs are inherently more "severe" than others. Future researchers may thus wish to explore whether the presence of features associated with certain types of PD (e.g., Antisocial PD) are worse prognostic indicators than others (e.g., Dependent PD) in addition to other more conventional indices of the degree of functional, symptomatic, and relational impairment delineated in the review by Fernández-Alvarez et al. (this volume).

An interesting aspect of the personality disorders is that a patient's perception of social support can be a function of the disruption in interpersonal functioning associated with a given Axis II disorder. For example, a patient may report feeling unsupported as part of a pattern of entitlement and/or demanding dependency in relation to current supportive others (e.g., feeling abandoned if not allowed to telephone the supportive other every hour or two, even while they are at work). Maladaptive interpersonal patterns, sustained over time, may also serve to drive supportive others away. Perceived needs for excessive social support (Dependent PD, Borderline PD) or uncommon autonomy (Antisocial PD) may thus reflect the severity of a personality disorder. Perceived social support may thus also prove to be a useful index of severity and predictor of response to treatment.

Chronicity is presented here as an aspect of global impairment that may predict poorer outcome in PD treatment. In the context of Axis II, a certain degree of chronicity and resistance to change over time is required for PD diagnosis (DSM-IV defines PD as "enduring patterns"). However, there is also a small body of research suggesting that some PDs tend to remit with age, especially those involving impulsivity, paranoia, high energy, and antisocial behavior (Coolidge, Segal, Pointer, Knaus, Yamazaki, & Silberman, 2000; Molinari, Kunik, Snow-Turek, Deleon, & Williams, 1999; Paris & Zweig-Frank, 2001). Such findings may or may not also extend to treatment responsivity, but suggest that measurement of the effects of chronicity on treatment outcome may need to take into account the patient's specific set of Axis II features along with chronological age in the attempt to measure the impact of chronicity on outcome.

Co-morbidity is another aspect of overall functional impairment that may be predictive of poorer outcome in some circumstances. Research suggests that other disorders are more difficult to treat when they co-occur with PD (Castonguay & Beutler, this volume). However, no evidence was reviewed as to whether the converse might also be true, that PD is more difficult to treat when Axis I disorders are present, or when multiple versus single Axis II disorders are present. Arguably, presence of a co-morbid Axis I disorder, especially one that can be seen by a patient as having developed as a result of an enduring personality pattern, may actually help motivate work on PD for some patients. For example, one might be less devoted to perfectionism, if he/she can see a connection between the inevitable overwhelm of striving for impossible goals and depression. Research on treatment responsiveness for varying combinations of Axis I and II diagnoses may thus be a promising area for future research. This may especially be the case for the PDs, which are well-known for dense patterns of co-morbidity on both Axes.

Match Between Level of Impairment and Treatment Intensity

The overall tendency toward longer term treatments for PD is consistent with the general idea reflected in this principle, that more severe problems require more time in treatment (dosage) or types of treatment (multiple medications, different psychotherapies, inpatient stays) in order to facilitate change. This general principle is also consistent with observations made by Fernández-Alvarez et al. (this volume), that high degrees of impairment, chronicity, and co-morbidity are more the rule than the exception in PD, as are more complex treatments. Empirically supported treatments for Axis I disorders tend to be focused on specific symptoms, and so the general outlines of this principle in PD treatments may be inferred from the preceding observations. However, theory linking personality and symptoms, supported by direct research, is needed to better articulate precisely which components might best be applied to which forms of impairment in PD. Bienvenu and Stein (2003) reached a similar conclusion in a review of the interface between personality and the anxiety disorders.

2. Patient-Related Principles Predictive of Outcome

The six patient-related principles listed in the second part of Table 13.1 have for the most part been generalized from treatments with other disorders except for the first in the list, which was unique to PD, and the second, which had overlap with research in other areas. The principles are: (a) willingness and ability to engage with treatment, (b) history of positive attachments or trauma/attachment style/coping style, (c) match between client's resistance level and intervention type, (d) expectations of success, (e) pretreatment readiness for change (stages of change), and (f) social class.

Willingness and Ability to Engage With Treatment; History of Positive Attachments or Trauma/Attachment Style/Coping Style; Match Between Client's Resistance Level and Intervention Type

In clinical work with PD, the question of whether or not a patient will engage at all can be an issue. Likely indices of the ability to do this may lie in their history of positive attachments and the degree of resolution of past traumatic experiences. Another index may be found in the patient's general tendency toward a more enmeshed, relationship-focused stance, versus one characterized by values for autonomy and achievement, identified by Blatt and colleagues (Blatt, Shahar, & Zuroff, 2002) as the anaclitic versus introjective personality styles (for more detail on the possible relationship of this theory to PD, see Fernández-Alvarez et al., this volume). Most, if not all, PD diagnoses can be seen as involving insecure attachments of one form or another, that are made manifest in current relationship difficulties (Fernández-Alvarez et al., this volume; and Smith et al., this volume). The same problems can also affect a patient's ability to engage in collaborative ways with a therapist. A tendency toward collaborative engagement and compliance (versus resistance) on the part of patients is conceptually related to the principles addressing engagement and attachment, but has only been studied in terms of outcome in the context of other disorders. More research is needed to further substantiate these principles in PD, including any possible exceptions (e.g., do low levels of resistance predict improved outcomes even for disorders characterized by overcompliance, such as Dependent PD?).

Expectations of Success

Patient expectations for success have been linked with improved outcomes in research with other disorders. While it has yet to be studied directly, this principle may also apply to PD treatment, especially to the degree that such expectations contribute to hope and mobilization for change. One potential exception to this hypothesis may be that some problems on Axis II can involve unrealistically high patient expectations for success without effort, a mistaken belief in the ability of a therapist to magically heal or unfailingly take care of him or her, or other similar beliefs that could be counterproductive if applied to the therapy itself.

PD diagnostic categories have been found to be differentiable from each other, in part, by differing attributions that patients make about themselves and others, and that may impact their expectations for therapy. For example, Beck and colleagues developed a questionnaire assessing "dysfunctional beliefs" thought to be characteristic of each PD and found good discriminant validity for the PDs they examined (Beck, Butler, Brown, Dahlsgaard, Newman, & Beck, 2001). Sample items included: Avoidant, "If people get close to me, they will discover the real me and reject me"; Dependent, "I am needy and weak"; Obsessive-Compulsive, "Flaws, defects, or mistakes are intolerable"; Narcissistic, "I don't have to be bound by the rules that apply to other people"; and Paranoid, "Other people will try to use me or manipulate me if I don't watch out." This principle thus represents another interesting and viable, but untapped, area for treatment outcome research with the Axis II disorders and may need to be taken into account in attempts to extend work with other disorders regarding patient expectations to Axis II.

Pretreatment Readiness for Change (Stages of Change)

As with expectations of success, greater readiness for change has been hypothesized to lead to improved outcomes. Future research may show the same general pattern in PD, but, as mentioned previously, this readiness may also be impacted by the potential for PD patients to desire unrealistic or problem-reinforcing forms of change that are consistent with an individual's pathology. For example, a patient with Passive-aggressive PD may believe his or her condition is the result of the faults of others (consistent with DSM criteria: complains of being misunderstood and unappreciated by others, unreasonably criticizes and scorns authority) and so desire change in other people rather than the self. As another example, a patient with Narcissistic PD may have expectations regarding change that are idealized and unrealistic (consistent with DSM criteria involving grandiosity, fantasies of success, and being special).

Social Class

Patients of lower social and economic status have been found to terminate therapy prematurely in research with other disorders (see Fernández-Alvarez et al., this volume). Personality disorder research does not clearly speak to this issue at present, but future research may find the same pattern of results in PD treatments. In addition, the pattern might be still more salient given the typical extended length of treatment for disorders on Axis II.

3. Therapist-Related Principles Predictive of Outcome

Five principles were identified in the last part of Table 13.1. All of these principles are "unique" in the sense that they were identified in the participant factor PD review chapter but not in review of other disorders. Although helpful in any treatment, they are more likely to be tested and required in successful treatment of PD, and consist of: (a) comfort with long-term, emotionally intense relationships, (b) patience, (c) tolerance of own feelings regarding the patient and treatment process, (d) open-minded, flexible, and creative, and (e) specialized training.

Comfort With Long-Term, Emotionally Intense Relationships; Patience; Tolerance of Own Feelings Regarding the Patient and Treatment Process; Open-Minded, Flexible, and Creative

These four principles were derived deductively by the authors of the participant factors chapter based on observation that treatments for Axis II are typically long, emotionally intense, progress slowly or unevenly, and involve very high stakes including life and death (Fernández-Alvarez et al., this volume). They argue that treatment with these patients has the potential to arouse intense feelings in a therapist, with better therapist coping likely being associated with improved patient outcomes. The principles listed here are all therapist attributes that might serve to positively influence/facilitate a positive therapeutic relationship. Thus, a strong connection can be seen between these principles and some of the relationship principles listed in Table 13.2 (discussed in the next major section). As such, the therapist attributes listed here can be seen as preconditions for (1) alliance building with people who have difficulties doing precisely this, and (2) creatively, but coherently implementing and sustaining a multi-faceted and long-lasting treatment for a complex set of problems. Implementation of these principles should serve to enhance a therapist's ability to relate to their patients in a positive manner that includes listening, tolerating, and accommodating, as well as an ability to provide structuring, influential, and persuasive input when necessary. Given the particular challenges of PD in the interpersonal domain, future research may show that PD has greater potential to put these therapist attributes to a strong test.

Specialized Training

Based on review of the literature addressing participant factors, Fernández-Alvarez et al. (this volume) conclude that specialized training and experience with particular types of Axis II disorder enhance outcomes. Direct research remains to be done on this issue with PD treatments, including specification of the optimal nature, length, and certification of such training. Research evidence linking training/experience with outcome in other disorders is mixed, so it is somewhat unclear the degree to which this may also be a shared factor across disorders (Fernández-Alvarez et al., this volume; see also Beutler et al., 2004).

DISCUSSION OF TABLE 13.2: RELATIONSHIP PRINCIPLES IN PD

Two major themes emerged from inspection of the relationship principles. The first theme addresses the importance of a strong alliance and collaboration between patient and therapist. The second theme, not unrelated, addresses a therapist's input to the relationship. Interestingly, no principles were reviewed that directly address the patient's input to the relationship. This is not to suggest that the patient's contribution to the relationship is unimportant, especially for Axis II disorders where a disturbed pattern of interpersonal relating is one of the hallmarks. Instead, this is likely to be a fruit-

Table 13.2

Relationship Principles With Suggested Links to Outcome for Personality Disorder Treatments

Alliance/joint collaboration
(s) Strong positive alliance (strong cohesion in group settings)
(g) Shared goals of treatment and collaboration to achieve those goals

Therapist stance
(u) Relatively high activity level (but not necessarily directive)
(s) Structures treatment and sets limits on unacceptable behavior[1]
(g) Empathy
(g) Positive regard
(g) Congruence in expression of feelings (including strategic self-disclosure) and transmission of knowledge

Note: (u) indicates principles *unique* to PD; (s) indicates principles identified in the PD source chapters and *shared* with other disorders; (g) indicates principles tentatively *generalized* to PD from work with other disorders, but pending investigation in PD.

ful, but largely untapped area for treatment research on Axis II.

1. Principles Related to the Alliance and Joint Collaboration

The alliance-related principles contain one principle that has support in empirical work with PD and is also shared with other disorders: (a) presence of a strong positive alliance. A second, related, principle is generalized from work with depression and cuts across relationship and technique factors: (b) shared goals of treatment and collaboration to achieve those goals.

Strong Positive Alliance/Strong Cohesion in Group Settings

A strong positive alliance between patient and therapist in the individual setting, and strong cohesion among members in a group setting, were both identified as important in predicting improved outcome in the review by Smith et al. (this volume). According to their review, the connection with outcome has consistent empirical support in mixed PD samples, but only mixed support from studies focusing on specific forms of PD (positive support in treatment of Antisocial PD, but less clear in treatment of Borderline PD). The precise role, process, and mechanisms linking alliance/cohesion to outcome are still under investigation across treatment settings and disorders. Thus, while the achievement of a strong positive alliance seems linked to improved outcome in PD overall, more research is needed to investigate this connection for each Axis II disorder. If the links are substantiated it will also be useful for future research to provide guidance as to how a clinician might go about enhancing or moderating the strength of the alliance with patients who have very different problems in terms of their interpersonal/relational functioning. For example, alienated personalities (e.g., Paranoid PD, Antisocial PD) may benefit from enhancement of alliance. On the other hand, those who have an unbounded notion of alliance (e.g., Histrionic PD, Borderline PD) may benefit from help in moderating it.

Consistent with findings suggesting the importance of maintaining a positive alliance, research by Safran, Muran, and colleagues has also found that attention to and resolution of alliance rupture is associated with enhanced outcome. Smith et al. (this volume) review this research and note not only the positive impact of resolution of alliance ruptures on outcome variables, but also that the study samples contained a high proportion of PD subjects. Certain therapist characteristics were associated with better ability to repair alliance ruptures and show some overlap with the therapist factor principles discussed in the previous section and listed in Table 13.1. These characteristics include a benign self-concept on the part of the therapist, perception by their patients that they are friendly, flexibility in their adherence to treatment protocols, ability to foster a sense of ease in session interactions, focus on issues of depth in therapy, and avoidance of overt expression of countertransference.

Smith et al. (this volume) also review findings regarding the technique of transference interpretation, which involves an explicit comment and interpretation of dynamics present in the therapeutic relationship (it is thus also related to a hypothesis regarding the importance of feedback in psychotherapy, an issue reviewed separately by Smith et al.). Researchers have observed that a greater frequency of transference interpretations is associated with poorer outcomes for patients having pervasive and severe problems relating with others and/or disturbances in self-concept, identity, and reality testing. This set of problems, framed as "Low Quality of Object Relations," is broadly consistent with DSM-defined PD, especially Borderline PD. These findings thus seem to suggest that transference interpretations are contraindicated for at least some Axis II disorders. However, evidence also exists in favor of the use of transference interpretation for PD in research reviewed by Smith et al. (this volume) suggesting that the accuracy of such interpretations is positively associated with outcome. In addition, some preliminary (but not conclusive due to lack of controls) positive findings have been found for a treatment for Borderline PD that uses transference interpretation as its chief technique (Clarkin et al., 2001). These apparently competing findings may suggest need for exploration of other relevant variables that could moderate the impact of transference interpretation in PD, such as accuracy (which has some positive support already), timing, or manner of delivery. In any case, this is an interesting and challenging area for future inquiry placed directly on the interface between in-session relationship dynamics (and hence alliance), and moment-by-moment application of specific technique.

Shared Goals of Treatment and Collaboration to Achieve Those Goals

This principle overlaps conceptually with a number of the more technique-specific principles listed in Table 13.3 (described in the next major section), in the sense that both sets of principles contain some reference to the importance of patient and therapist agreement on specific goals. As a relational principle, however, the emphasis here is on *collaboration* toward achieving those goals. More research is needed regarding the specific impact of collaboration in working toward shared goals on outcome in PD.

2. Therapist's Baseline Relational Stance

The five principles listed in the second part of Table 13.2 each address the therapist's relational stance. This part of the table contains one unique principle, one shared principle (also emphasized in the technique principles of the next major section), and three principles generalized from other settings. In this order, they are: (a) relatively high activity level (but not necessarily directive), (b) structures treatment and sets limits on unacceptable behavior, (c) expresses empathy, (d) shows positive regard, and (e) congruence in expression of feelings and transmission of knowledge. There are small, perhaps arbitrary, differences between what constitutes therapist participant characteristic principles and therapist relational stance principles. The distinction as it is used here is simply a function of the degree to which a therapist's capacity (i.e., "characteristic") is emphasized over the in-session expression of that capacity (i.e., "stance"). The two are clearly related, and a careful reader will certainly detect some overlap in the separate tables.

Relatively High Activity Level (but Not Necessarily Directive)

A feature that was identified through the review by Smith et al. (this volume) as being unique to effective personality disorder treatment is an emphasis on a relatively active therapist. For example, while Linehan's DBT describes optimal therapist behavior in terms involving a balance of several dialectics, what is generally endorsed is an engaged, attentive, and involved stance implied by the word "active" as it is intended here. Similarly, Transference-Focused Psychotherapy (TFP; Clarkin, Yeomans, & Kernberg, 1999) is designed as a modified psychoanalytic approach with one of the major innovations involving an increase in the therapist's activity level, especially in terms of the frequency of use of interventions related to the ongoing relationship. While a high level of therapist activity has been identified in the Smith et al. review as a common feature of promising PD treatments (specifically, treatments for Borderline PD), it has not been directly tested empirically in the form in which it is presented here, and it does not necessarily represent the optimal approach for non-Borderline PDs. Linehan et al. (this volume) note that optimal treatment consists of both directive and nondirective elements in Borderline PD. An active therapist, is thus not necessarily a directive one, but one whose emphasis is on collaborating and being flexible as needed to facilitate a patient's motivation and learning. In addition, it seems likely that the optimal level of activity will need at least some calibration relative to the needs, style, and pathology of a given patient, perhaps also in conjunction with specific goals and phase in treatment. Further research will be necessary to address these issues.

Structures Treatment and Sets Limits on Unacceptable Behavior

This principle was identified, based in large part on its presence in existing treatment manuals having some empirical support.[1] While the issue remains to be addressed directly, it is possible that structuring and limit-setting is particularly important for treatment of some Axis II disorders, such as Borderline PD, due to an increased base rate of problematic behaviors and attempts to break the treatment frame or cross the usual relational boundaries (e.g., frequent between-session phone calls, lateness to sessions, missing sessions, verbal attacks; at the extremes: stalking behavior, homicidal or suicidal threats or actions if demands not met, romantic overtures, etc.). However, since not all patients with Axis II disorders are alike, future research is needed to further explore the possibility of exceptions to this general rule. For example, structure and limit-setting may prove to be contraindicated in patients whose problems revolve around a sensitivity and reactance to control (see Smith et al., this volume). Compelling evidence for the link between high levels of reactance and poorer outcome in general patient samples has been presented by Beutler, Moleiro, and Talebi (2002), and recent work has just begun to explore this issue in PD (e.g., Seibel & Dowd, 2001).

Empathy; Positive Regard; Congruence in Expression of Feelings (Including Strategic Self-Disclosure) and Transmission of Knowledge

Expression of these three Rogerian qualities by a therapist were identified by the Task Force as principles predictive of improved outcomes across disorders, although research support has yet to be generated specifically for Axis II. Having said this, empathy, or more specifically, empathic support, has been identified as important for balancing a focus on change in the treatment of Borderline PD, and it is listed among the technique-specific principles in Table 13.3 (also see Linehan et al., this volume). In addition, nonconfrontational strategies are emphasized by Linehan et al. to resolve treatment impasses and enhance motivation for treatment, as are the closely related features of therapist flexibility, availability, genuineness, responsiveness, use of strategic self-disclosures, and communication of understanding regarding how difficult it is for the patient to change. More research is needed, but it is possible that the set of principles listed here contribute to a positive alliance and guard against potentially negative feelings and behaviors on the part of a therapist, in addition to whatever direct effects they may have on outcome. Available research suggests a possible association between negative therapist reactions and poorer in-session processes. In addition, considerable evidence exists for the efficacy of DBT, which advocates (in more specific form) these principles. Nevertheless, the impact on outcome of Rogerian qualities in PD treatments has yet to be fully and directly examined (for more detail, see Smith et al., this volume).

DISCUSSION OF TABLE 13.3: TECHNIQUE PRINCIPLES FOR PD

Technique principles are grouped in Table 13.3 according to the following broad themes: (1) salience, (2) transparency of treatment and its rationale, (3) goal-oriented structure, (4) emphasis on producing change (with sensitivity to the related issues of support and pacing), and (5) support for therapists. As explained in the technique factors review chapter (Linehan et al., this volume), the principles identified as unique to PD treatments are based primarily on work with a particular approach and population: DBT for treatment of Borderline PD. The unique principles identified there may thus be limited in their generalizability to other PDs or treatment approaches, and so where overlap seemed to be apparent with principles explored in the context of other disorders, the more

Table 13.3

Technique Principles With Suggested Links to Outcome for Personality Disorder Treatments (under the assumption that a sufficiently positive working alliance is achieved and maintained)

Salience

(u) Therapist availability / flexibility during periods of crisis

(s) Priority of focus on presenting problems and concerns

(s) Early formulation and identification of patterns (cognition, affect, and behavior) linked to problem maintenance

Transparency

(u) Therapist honesty and explicitness regarding his or her limits

(s) Discussion of the nature of the problem and rationale for treatment

(s) Facilitate knowledge and awareness of links between problems and environment, cognition, affect, and behavior

Goal-oriented structure

(s) A treatment frame established in collaboration with the patient and structured to achieve clear and explicit goals.

(s) Focused, theoretically coherent, consistent, and well-coordinated treatment

Emphasis on change (with sensitivity to related issues of pacing and support)

(u) Balance focus on change / motivation for change with empathic support

(s) Focus on increasing adaptive ways of thinking and behaving

(s) Focus on decreasing maladaptive behaviors / challenge specific "dysfunctional thoughts" and "negative core beliefs"

Support for therapists

(u) Ongoing supervision / consultation for therapists

Note: (u) indicates principles *unique* to PD; (s) indicates principles identified in the PD source chapters and *shared* with other disorders; (g) indicates principles tentatively *generalized* to PD from work with other disorders, but pending investigation in PD.

general frame was typically used to articulate the principle.

The principles listed in Table 13.3 all carry with them the caveat from the Task Force members who summarized this literature, that they are only thought to enhance outcome if carried out in the context of a good therapeutic relationship (Castonguay & Beutler, this volume). Linehan et al. (this volume) go further than this in discussion of optimal treatment of PD, offering a number of principles addressing the importance of therapist flexibility, genuineness, empathy, and so on, on a patient's motivation for treatment (these principles are discussed along with the relationship principles in Table 13.2). A good alliance is thought to be prerequisite for the effectiveness of any of the technique principles, however, it is interesting to note that many of the technique principles listed in Table 13.3 can themselves contribute to maintenance and reinforcement of a positive relationship. The possibility that technical and relationship factors are interactive and mutually dependent is not a new topic in theories of psychotherapy, but is a sophisticated methodological consideration that has yet to receive appropriate empirical attention, especially in the context of treatments for personality disorder where the patient's problems in relating may strongly influence the therapy process itself.

1. Salience

Three principles were identified that address a treatment's salience and direct, easily appreciated relevance to patient problems. There is one unique principle: (a) therapist availability/flexibility during acute crisis; and two shared principles: (b) priority of focus on presenting problems and concerns, and (c) early formulation and identification of patterns of cognition, affect, and behavior linked to problem maintenance.

Therapist Availability and Flexibility During Acute Crisis; Priority of Focus on Presenting Problems and Concerns (Over Possible Origins of Those Concerns in Past Experience)

Therapist availability and flexibility during acute crisis (e.g., suicidality) was identified by Linehan et al. (this volume) as a principle to enhance outcome. A similar general principle was identified by the Task Force, but without an emphasis on crisis management, and is articulated here as a focus on presenting problems and concerns. An underlying

theme that connects these principles is that the optimal treatment approach is one that is flexibly tailored to a patient's problems, and that also shows some clear correspondence between the patient's proximally experienced problems and the therapist's interventions.

The special emphasis on *presenting* problems and concerns is thought to be important in treatment of Borderline PD, especially early on in treatment, and may also apply to other personality disorders as well. Specifically, Linehan et al. recommend that therapists working with Borderline PD patients should only attempt to foster deeper insight about problems and their origins (as opposed to their present form and impact on life) once a patient can tolerate the affect that may be aroused by such a discussion. Similarly, they recommend emphasis on helping patients build skills to deal with present-day problems, rather than focusing on events in the past (e.g., role of early abuse or trauma experience) until a Borderline PD patient has established a stable sense of emotional and behavioral self-control. This is not to say that the past has no relevance to effective psychotherapy. Indeed, exploration of the past is often an important part of PD treatment, serving to generate sufficient motivation, awareness, and self-understanding to help patients make the choice to let go of the wishes, fears, expectations, and so on, that serve to maintain patterns in the present and then go on to learn new, more adaptive skills.

If future research in treatments for Axis II supports these propositions, a possible clinical corollary is that when there is potential for disparity between the therapist's and patient's view of "the problem," therapists should make efforts to ensure that the treatment approach "makes sense" to the patient sufficiently to allow for motivated, collaborative engagement, and also that the approach places priority on stabilizing the patient in moments of crisis and implementing pragmatic solutions to present concerns. Discussion of the origins of these concerns in past trauma or other formative early experience is used to help patients move toward more healthy choices once they have sufficient stability to use the insights rather than becoming overwhelmed by their implications.

Early Formulation and Identification (e.g., Through an Initial Assessment) of Patterns (Cognition, Affect, and Behavior) Linked to Problem Maintenance

This principle suggests that early identification of factors that contribute to and maintain a problem will serve to help improve outcome across disorders, including in PD. This should include consideration of intrapsychic, interpersonal, and environmental factors in the patient's life, as well as relations between these domains. Research and discussion of this principle outside the PD literature tends to emphasize cognition and behavior (as opposed to affect). This may be the case due to a larger number of CBT-based perspectives in the research literature, and perhaps also because most treatment research has been conducted with mood and anxiety disorders where affect is seen as the problem itself, rather than a factor maintaining the problem. Affect has been explicitly included in the present list because it is salient to PD as an area of disturbance that runs interactively and in parallel to cognition and behavior as an expression of, and contributing factor to, personality disturbance. For example, an individual with Borderline PD is likely to fear abandonment. The affect of fear arising with appraisal of an interpersonal situation drives the "frantic efforts to avoid abandonment" mentioned in the DSM. The "frantic efforts," in turn, comprise other, commonly recognized patterns of PD (e.g., attacking the "negligent" caregiver, parasuicidal behaviors, further mood instability, and so on).

Consistent with the emphasis of this section, explicit clarification of a treatment focus and sensible, comprehensive tailoring of treatment to a full formulation or other comprehensive understanding of the patient's problems is seen as a likely contributor to improved outcome. Linehan et al. strongly emphasize the importance of a comprehensive approach to PD treatment that addresses not only change in behavior (i.e., capabilities and skills) but also the patient's *motivation* for change and the generalizability of treatment to the patient's life circumstances (including making changes in the patient's everyday environment to support change). A comprehensive understanding of the individual patient through a detailed formulation is required to achieve such goals. Each of these elements fits in both with the principle of early formulation/identification of patterns, as well as the broader importance of the face-valid salience of a given treatment approach to the patient's problems.

2. Transparency of Treatment and Its Rationale

The second theme listed in Table 13.3 contains three principles related to the transparency of treatment. By transparency, what is meant is that the treatment approach used is clearly explained to, and understood by, the patient, and that the treatment can be clearly seen to flow from that explanation in addressing patient concerns. One of these principles appears to be unique to PD. The others seem to apply more generally to various disordered populations. The unique principle is: (a) therapist honesty and explicitness regarding his or her limits. The shared principles are: (b) discussion of the nature of the problem and treatment rationale, and (c) facilitate knowledge and awareness of links between the problem and environment, cognition, affect, and behavior.

The transparency principles, taken together, may be linked to outcome through providing an environment and intervention style that allows and encourages the patient to become an active collaborator in the treatment process. Clear understanding about the problem and approach to treatment can in many circumstances enable patients to internalize the approach and enhance its impact in life outside the treatment setting. Frank discussion of the treatment, its limits, and its rationale should give both patient and therapist a framework to refer to when and if problems or concerns arise about expectations, course, and goals of treatment. When therapists are clear and open about their personal boundaries and limits (i.e., those that are pertinent to the therapy), this is also consistent with the therapist-related principles discussed in the participant principles section and should also serve to enhance positive collaboration. In addition, these principles may also serve to minimize resistance based on simple misunderstanding of goals and tasks in treatment. The transparency-related principles are consistent with a friendly and open interpersonal stance expected to enhance the alliance, and are also consistent with ethical values of informed consent for treatment. Although these principles show great promise as features enhancing outcome in effective treatment for Axis II disorders, further research is needed to demonstrate this as well as to explore the precise operation and role these principles may have in improving patient outcome.

3. Presence of a Goal-Oriented Structure for Therapy

The two principles listed under the third theme in Table 13.3 emphasize the importance of explicit goals and a clear and consistent structure for successful treatment. Both principles were identified as shared with other disorders and consist of: (a) a treatment frame established in collaboration with the patient and structured to achieve clear and explicit goals, and (b) a treatment that is focused, theoretically coherent, consistently applied, and well coordinated.

While these principles are simply stated and relatively self-explanatory, they are not always easily implemented in treatment of patients with personality disorders. Simple presence of goals in the therapy is not always enough and can require invocation of the transparency-related principles discussed in the previous theme in order to be collaborative and effective. Thus, repeated and in-depth discussion of the nature, premise, and desirability of the treatment goals in light of patient concerns is strongly encouraged when treatment appears to be at an impasse, or is otherwise unfocused for extended periods (Linehan, 1993; Benjamin, 2003). Linehan et al. (this volume) further add that motivation is enhanced when such discussion of an impasse is nonconfrontational, and also that each session should be organized around clearly prioritized treatment targets. Priorities for handling multiple goals are also involved as part of establishing the optimal treatment frame early in treatment (before therapy "formally begins," as Linehan et al. frame the issue), as is the ability of both patient and therapist to discuss and revise if necessary, the goals and contract as time goes on. The process of setting and maintaining treatment boundaries has even been proposed as a central technical element in one form of therapy developed for Borderline PD (Yeomans, Selzer, & Clarkin, 1992), but has yet to become the direct focus of outcome research. These principles are in stark contrast to an approach that might endorse an "anything goes" philosophy, has an unclear focus, is not driven by a clear theoretical rationale, or is otherwise inconsistent.

4. Principles Emphasizing Change (With Sensitivity to Related Issues of Pacing and Support)

The change-related principles listed in Table 13.3 include one principle uniquely identified for treatment of Borderline PD: (a) balance focus on change and motivation for change with empathic support; and two more that have been identified as shared principles: (b) focus on increasing adaptive ways of thinking and behaving, and (c) focus on decreasing maladaptive behaviors/challenge specific "dysfunctional thoughts" and "negative core beliefs."

Balance Focus on Change and Motivation for Change With Empathic Support

Linehan et al. (this volume) offer the dialectic between acceptance and change to explain how to proceed when caught between the patient's need to engage in work on change, and the opposing need for strong, uncritical support. In DBT these two emphases are placed at the two poles of a single dialectic principle where moderation within and balance between both parts is seen as key to effective treatment. A unitary focus on change would run the risk of indirectly communicating criticism, control, and/or a lack of empathy on the part of the therapist. Such a stance runs the risk of reinforcing negative self-concepts, engendering resistance, and further entrenching the patient in his or her pathology, despite ostensible good intentions to help the patient change. Similarly, a singular focus on validating and supporting a patient, if done in a way that does not also reinforce or encourage the will to change, would run the risk of simply reinforcing problem patterns. The hypothesis described so well by Linehan, and embodied by this principle, thus suggests that it is only the careful calibration of these two elements, relative to the moment-by-moment needs of the patient as well as the shared treatment goals, that will promote positive change and improved outcomes. Linehan et al. (this volume) also note that for Borderline PD, a successful balance will typically involve both directive and nondirective technical elements, will not assume that the patient has the cognitive and emotional capacities required for successful living, and will at its core be emotionally supportive to patients while encouraging and helping them learn the cognitive, affective, behavioral, and interpersonal skills they need.

Focus on Increasing Adaptive Ways of Thinking and Behaving; Focus on Reducing Maladaptive Behaviors/Challenge Specific "Dysfunctional Thoughts" and "Negative Core Beliefs"

These two principles were both identified as principles shared with other disorders. They were also apparent in review of the PD literature by Linehan et al. (this volume), who provide additional detail about behavioral techniques found to be effective in treatment of Borderline PD (especially exposure to emotion-laden stimuli coupled with response prevention and reinforcement of opposite behaviors). Taken together the principles emphasize two complementary forms of change. In broad strokes, one involves movement toward more adaptive ways of being, and the other involves movement away from maladaptive ways of being. CBT-based research specifically articulates maladaptive patterns in terms of dysfunctional thoughts and negative core beliefs. The recommendation to "challenge" these maladaptive patterns should not be taken as encouraging an interpersonally hostile, confrontational baseline for in-session relating. While there are moments when confrontation may be necessary, adopting such a stance as a baseline position (depending on the definition of confrontation) may not be in line with other principles regarding the importance of a positive alliance, flexibility, tolerance, and balancing a focus on change with support. In addition, Linehan et al. emphasize the importance of helping the patient experience tolerance and acceptance of problems, rather than maintaining sole focus on change. Research is needed to further establish these principles in the context of Axis II treatments as well as to explore whether cognitive components are primary, or if targeting other forms of maladaptive experiencing also enhance outcome.

5. Support for Therapists

The single principle in this category of Table 13.3 was identified uniquely for treatment of Borderline PD. The principle predicts that *Ongoing supervision/consultation for therapists* (including both those having primary and auxiliary roles involved in treatment) is linked to improved outcome. Mechanisms for this link may be through therapist morale, objectivity, creative input, and related ability to work productively, especially with very demanding clients. This could very well be true for all disorders to some degree, especially when crises arise or impasse is evident. However, the need for support seems especially relevant for treatment of personality disorders given the emotional intensity, relational complexity, and potential for life-threatening behaviors associated with many of them. Ongoing supervision and/or consultation is recommended to help ground therapists in an objective perspective regarding treatment processes and goals, as well as to help prevent burn-out. As with the other technique-related principles identified as enhancing outcome in PD, research support for this comes primarily from evidence of the efficacy of DBT for Borderline PD. DBT explicitly builds support for therapists into its treatment model and we reason that it would apply to treatment of other PDs that present similar challenges (frequent crises, life and death dilemmas, attacks on the therapist, and so on). More research will be needed, however, to demonstrate conclusively that this is an "active ingredient" of therapy that might be generalized to other PDs and treatment approaches.

SUMMARY AND CONCLUSIONS

Importance of the Therapeutic Relationship

A few concepts seem to span across the principles summarized in this chapter. One recurrent theme is the importance of the therapeutic relationship. For example, many of the participant principles posed for both therapists and patients are qualities that enhance the ability of each to engage in and maintain an intense, but well-bounded, long-term relationship focused on helping the patient. The principles in the relationship factors section focus very directly on the importance of the alliance as well as other in-session therapist behaviors that can serve to enhance the connection between patient and therapist. The same theme appears again as a precondition for effectiveness of the technique-specific principles, many of which arguably serve, at least in part, to enhance the alliance by facilitating clarity and collaboration regarding specific tasks and goals of therapy.

More research is needed on the topic, and results generated so far are somewhat mixed. Nevertheless, an interesting hypothesis is that the therapeutic relationship may be particularly salient for treatment of Axis II disorders given that one of the hallmarks of this family of disorders is disturbed interpersonal functioning. As noted above, the disturbances in interpersonal functioning likely make formation of a collaborative therapeutic relationship difficult, potentially reducing outcome. At the same time, difficulties in the interpersonal domain may open up greater possibilities for productive work occurring in and through the relationship process itself, substantially improving outcomes if successfully navigated. In other words, if the patient poses an interpersonal challenge to the therapist, and both participants work out a positive resolution, the patient's interpersonal learning likely is enhanced in important ways. Consistent with this possibility, some approaches for treating PD have already incorporated technical elements that involve work with the in-session process of the relationship in treatment of Axis II disorders. While this blending of relationship and technique is typically associated with more interpersonal and psychodynamic approaches to treatment, it is also addressed in the more cognitive-behaviorally-oriented manual for Linehan's (1993) empirically validated DBT approach to treatment of Borderline PD. Linehan states:

> The relationship in DBT has a dual role. The relationship is the vehicle through which the therapist can effect the therapy; it *is* also the therapy . . . the therapist must choose an appropriate balance between these two approaches at each moment. "The relationship as therapy" facilitates both acceptance of the client as she is and development. "Therapy

through the relationship" facilitates the therapist's control of behavior the patient cannot control, as well as the patient's acquisition of skills previously unknown or insufficiently generalized. (pp. 514–515)

The importance of a good alliance in enhancing outcome, even with some mixed findings in specific disorders, is one of a very few principles proposed by the Task Force that has direct empirical support in PD populations. In addition, some promising work has begun to explore the role of alliance ruptures and resolutions in patient populations with a relatively high proportion of Axis II problems (Safran, Muran, Samstag, & Stevens, 2002; Smith et al., this volume).

A question that has not yet been addressed, but that is salient for Axis II, is the question of through what process a positive alliance can be achieved and maintained in the face of the wide variety of interpersonal patterns associated with differing Axis II diagnoses. That is, if a positive alliance enhances outcome, what empirically based recommendations can be made to guide clinicians in bringing this state about for patients who manifest different types of relational problems (e.g., some are sensitive to control, distance, closeness, affection, aggression, complex combinations of these, etc.). A few hypotheses may be found in consideration of the prototypic patterns of relating characteristic of particular PDs. Researchers may also make headway by applying overarching conceptual frameworks such as Blatt's (1992) anaclitic/introjective distinction to make predictions about differential responsiveness of the PDs to various types of intervention. In sum, future research is needed to truly begin to explore the issue of how best to manage the therapy relationship with different kinds of patients. Since PD patients typically present with co-morbid combinations of Axis II features, individualized, rather than categorical, assessment and formulation of these features will also likely be needed to help anticipate and address problems that may impact the therapeutic relationship.

The relationship factors principle of therapist empathy provides an interesting example of the issue just broached regarding the need to consider possible unique responses of individual patients or unstudied Axis II categories. For example, when used appropriately, empathic therapist behaviors have potential to enhance a patient's ability to see alternative ways of being while also letting them know that they are understood and cared about as they currently are. However, empathy also has potential to socially reinforce and thus maintain maladaptive personality patterns. Some initial empirical evidence exists suggesting that therapist expressions of empathy can have different in-session impacts, as well as be differentially linked to outcome, depending on their precise context (Karpiak & Benjamin, 2003). It can be hypothesized that some of the difference in impact may prove to be a function of timing (e.g., differential reinforcement depending on preceding comment), but is also likely to involve the particular patient's personality pathology to the degree that the patient's view of the world can filter and shape the meaning of empathic statements. For example, therapist empathy for suffering a patient reports feeling at the hands of others (i.e., warm affirmation for outrage at entitlement failures, unrealistic expectations of support, or misread attacks) would, by itself, do little to encourage a Paranoid, Borderline, or Narcissistic patient to change in any fundamental way (unless, perhaps, an alliance built on such expressions can later be used to press for deeper analysis of the situation). Thus, while a therapist baseline of empathy, congruence, and regard is certainly recommended based on indirect support from research with other disorders, future research may also need to explore the possibility that general empathy can be seen by disordered individuals as agreement with distorted perceptions, leading to an inadvertent reinforcement of problem patterns.

Importance of Therapist Flexibility in Tailoring Treatment

A second theme that repeats across the various principles involves recommendation of open-mindedness, tolerance, flexibility, and ongoing tailoring of treatment relative to the specific constellation of problems presented by the patient. The need for therapist flexibility, as it was addressed in the participant factors review chapter, is necessary as a function of the longer duration and higher degree of complexity both of Axis II pathology and treatments designed to address it. The treatment principles presented in Table 13.3 include the importance of an initial assessment of problems, and development of specific goals to address the problems. Ongoing assessment is also likely to be necessary to keep the therapy on track.

The overall suggestion here is that many of the principles in this chapter imply that an open-minded, flexible, and creative therapist may improve outcomes through a resulting ability to optimally tailor therapy tasks and goals to the patient's needs over time, while simultaneously calibrating the balance of focus on change versus support offered in the relationship. While the emphasis on openness and flexibility is less explicit in the relationship principles presented in Table 13.2, they still suggest a degree of responsiveness and attunement to patient needs that is consistent with the kind of flexibility described here. It is also interesting to note that enhancing therapist flexibility in use of principles to enhance outcome is part of the rationale used by the Task Force for pursuing empirically based principles in the first place (Beutler, 2002).

The principles related to therapist flexibility and tailoring of treatment all imply that optimal treatment for a given patient will depart in some systematic way from the optimal treatment for another patient, even one qualifying for the same broad diagnostic category. Rather than encouraging a nonspecific eclecticism, a better operationalization of what is meant here by "flexibility" might be a treatment manual that provides rules for individualizing treatment—rules that provide a wide range of specific choices for intervention based on a case formulation (or similar individualized assessment) and from which related suggestions for treatment intervention can be generated. Such an approach seeks not to "standardize" treatment in the conventional sense of the term through eliminating therapist variability, but would instead prescribe "optimal treatment variability" for each patient, based on clear principles. Of course, it would then still be important to determine through focused research whether adherence to a given principle, or set of principles, truly enhances outcome for PD.

More on Tailoring of Treatment: Further Issues Posed by the Nature and Diversity of Axis II Pathology

According to the DSM-IV, PDs consist of "an enduring pattern of inner experience and behavior that deviates markedly from the expectations of the individual's culture" and that is manifested in the areas of (two or more required) cognition, affect, interpersonal functioning, and impulse control. In practice these patterns are quite diverse, with dramatically different personality characteristics contained under the general umbrella of Axis II. Given this diversity, there likely are interactions between characteristic patterns of personality and treatment approach. Hence, there may be important, but as of yet unidentified exceptions to the principles reviewed in this chapter. For example, interventions intended to bring about change through formulation/assessment, clear goals, and so on, may be received very differently by a dependent patient (who may see them as evidence of caretaking and support) than by a passive-aggressive/negativistic one (who may read into it a form of hostile control that must be indirectly resisted). This issue is similar to the idea raised at an earlier point regarding the possible need for different relational strategies to achieve positive alliances with different Axis II patients.

In addition to the wide range of features covered by Axis II, PD is also known for high comorbidity among individual diagnostic categories as well as ongoing debates regarding the reliability and validity of the diagnoses themselves. Considerable work has been done to develop methods of assessment that reduce unreliability of diagnoses. This is important to the present discussion because if it is difficult to get reliable diagnoses, it will also be difficult to establish what treatments and treatment principles are effective with them. Part of the reason for a paucity of treatment research on Axis II may be related to difficulties the field has faced in reliably and validly specifying the boundaries of each disorder. Structured interviews have been developed relatively recently that comprehensively assess Axis II, such as the Structured Clinical Interview for DSM-IV Axis II Personality Disorders (SCID-II; First, Gibbon, Spitzer, and Williams, 1997) and the International Personality Disorders Examination (IPDE; Loranger, 1999). Still other measures have been developed for specific disorders. Current structured approaches typically reach acceptable levels of reliability (see review by Zimmerman, 1994), and are now used by most researchers in this area. Nevertheless, strong overlap among categories persists.

Co-morbidity on Axis II is a problem for research paradigms that involve focus on single disorders, on the one hand, because "pure" samples of patients with single Axis II disorders are difficult to construct, and, on the other hand, because their findings would not generalize well to real-world settings where co-morbidity is the norm. As an alternative to disorder-by-disorder research on Axis II, some have proposed studying treatment effects in terms of narrowed subsets of clinically relevant personality dimensions, targeted features, or cross-cutting behavioral markers such as high impulsivity, aggression, or suicidality (e.g., Depue & Lenzenweger, 2001; Roth & Fonagy, 1996). Still other promising approaches have been developed that use a common underlying model to tailor interventions to the patient's overall presentation or case formulation, rather than a specific Axis II category or single symptom pattern (e.g., Beck, 1996; Benjamin, 2003; Young, Klosko, & Weishaar, 2003).

Final Comments

More than a few useful principles for guiding treatment and enhancing outcome can be gleaned from the literature addressing PD and are summarized in this chapter. The literature provides a good start toward the ultimate goal of improving treatments and enhancing outcomes for patients suffering from Axis II disorders. Some promising avenues have even been explored that address the difficult and complex problem of interactions that can occur across participant, relationship, and technical domains. The work reviewed by Smith et al. (this volume) linking outcome to use of relational/transference interpretation (itself a treatment *technique* that addresses *relationship*) through the moderator of patient personality factors illustrates such work, as does research exploring the effects of therapist personal reactions (partly a function of therapist characteristics per se) on the ongoing relationship.

Good work is under way. Nevertheless, the current lack of treatment-focused research for Axis II heightens the intense need for empirically supported guiding principles for clinicians working with patients who suffer from these complex and difficult problems. The reviews in this volume have made it clear that substantial increments in research effort need to be focused on the principles reviewed here, systematically addressing each of the personality disorders as well as their more troublesome shared attributes such as high impulsivity, aggression, or suicidality. In so doing, we predict greater success for approaches that tailor make interventions according to a well-defined case formulation, rather than on categories with fuzzy boundaries.

Note

1. DBT, the approach to PD treatment that has received the most research attention, actually *proscribes* use of the term "setting limits" in favor of an emphasis on observation of the natural limits of the therapist and the therapy. That is, the limits "set" should not be artificially or capriciously imposed by the therapist or treatment model, but should instead result from the natural features of the circumstance shared by patient and therapist and that form the "reality" of the therapy situation. We tend to agree with this position and encourage the reader to keep this caveat in mind. However, use of the phrase "setting limits" has been retained in the relationship factor section to maintain consistency with discussion in the Smith et al. chapter from which this section is most directly derived.

References

Beck, A. T., Butler, A. C., Brown, G. K., Dahlsgaard, K. K., Newman, C. F., & Beck, J. S. (2001). Dysfunctional beliefs discriminate personality disorders. *Behaviour Research & Therapy*, 39(10), 1213–1225.

Beck, J. S. (1996). Cognitive therapy of personality disorders. In P. M. Salkovskis & D. M. Clark (Eds.), *Frontiers of cognitive therapy: The state of the art and beyond* (pp. 165–181). New York: Guilford.

Benjamin, L. S. (2003). *Interpersonal Reconstructive Therapy (IRT)*. New York: Guilford Press.

Beutler, L. E. (2002). It isn't the size, but the fit. *Clinical Psychology: Science and Practice*, 9(4), 434–438.

Beutler, L. E., Malik, M., Alimohamed, S., Harwood, T. M., Talebi, H., Noble, S., & Wong, E. (2004). Therapist variables. In M. J. Lambert (Ed.), *Bergin and Garfield's handbook of psychotherapy and behavior change* (5th ed., pp. 227–306). New York: John Wiley & Sons.

Beutler, L. E., Moleiro, C., & Talebi, H. (2002). Resistance in psychotherapy: What conclusions are supported by research. *Journal of Clinical Psychology/In-Session: Psychotherapy in Practice*, 58(2), 207–217.

Bienvenu, O. J., & Stein, M. B. (2003). Personality and anxiety disorders: A review. *Journal of Personality Disorders*, 17(2), 139–151.

Blatt, S. J. (1992). The differential effect of psychotherapy and psychoanalysis on anaclitic and introjective patients: The Menninger Psychotherapy Research Project Revisited. *Journal of the American Psychoanalytic Association*, 40, 691–724.

Blatt, S. J., Shahar, G., & Zuroff, D. C. (2002). Anaclitic (sociotropic) and introjective (autonomous) dimensions. In J. C. Norcross (Ed.), *A guide to psychotherapy relationships that work* (pp. 315–333). New York: Oxford University Press.

Clarkin, J. F., Foelsch, P. A., Levy, K. N., Hull, J. W., Delaney, J. C., Kernberg, O. F. (2001). The development of a psychodynamic treatment for patients with borderline personality disorder: A preliminary study of behavioral change. *Journal of Personality Disorders*, 15(6), 487–495.

Clarkin, J. F., Yeomans, F. E., & Kernberg, O. F. (1999). *Psychotherapy for borderline personality*. New York: John Wiley & Sons, Inc.

Coolidge, F. L., Segal, D. L., Pointer, J. C., Knaus, E. A., Yamazaki, T. G., & Silberman, C. S. (2000). Personality disorders in older adult inpatients with chronic mental illness. *Journal of Clinical Geropsychology*, 6(1), 62–72.

Depue, R. A., & Lenzenweger, M. F. (2001). A neurobehavioral dimensional model. In J. W. Livesley (Ed.), *Handbook of personality disorders: Theory, research, and treatment* (pp. 136–176). New York: Guilford Press.

First, M. B., Gibbon, M., Spitzer, R. L., & Williams, J. B. W. (1997). *Structured clinical interview for DSM-IV personality disorders (SCID-II)*. Washington, DC: American Psychiatric Press, Inc.

Karpiak, C. P., & Benjamin, L. S. (2004). Therapist affirmation and the process and outcome of psychotherapy: Two sequential analytic studies. *Clinical Psychology, 60*(6), 659–676.

Keown, P., Holloway, F., & Kuipers, E. (2002). The prevalence of personality disorders, psychotic disorders and affective disorders amongst the patients seen by a community mental health team in London. *Social Psychiatry & Psychiatric Epidemiology, 37*(5), 225–229.

Kernberg, O. F. (1996). A psychoanalytic theory of personality disorders. In J. F. Clarkin & M. F. Lenzenweger (Eds.), *Major theories of personality disorder* (pp. 106–137). New York: Guilford Press.

Linehan, M. M. (1993). *Cognitive-behavioral treatment of borderline personality disorder.* New York: Guilford.

Loranger, A. W. (1999). *International Personality Disorder Examination (IPDE) manual.* Odessa, FL: Psychological Assessment Resources, Inc.

Molinari, V., Kunik, M. E., Snow-Turek, A. L., Deleon, H., & Williams, W. (1999). Age-related personality differences in inpatients with personality disorder: A cross-sectional study. *Journal of Clinical Geropsychology, 5*(3), 191–202.

Paris, J., & Zweig-Frank, H. (2001). A 27-year follow-up of patients with borderline personality disorder. *Comprehensive Psychiatry, 42*(6), 482–487.

Roth, A., & Fonagy, P. (1996). Personality disorders. In A. Roth & P. Fonagy, *What works for whom?: A critical review of psychotherapy research* (pp. 197–215). New York: Guilford Press.

Safran, J. D., Muran, J. C., Samstag, L. W., & Stevens, C. (2002). Repairing alliance ruptures. In J. C. Norcross (Ed.), *Psychotherapy relationships that work: Therapist contributions and responsiveness to patients* (pp. 235–254). New York: Oxford University Press.

Samuels, J., Eaton, W. W., Bienvenu, O. J., Brown, C., Costa, P. T., & Nestadt, G. (2002). Prevalence and correlates of personality disorders in a community sample. *British Journal of Psychiatry, 180*(6), 536–542.

Seibel, C. A., & Dowd, E. T. (2001). Personality characteristics associated with psychological reactance. *Journal of Clinical Psychology, 57*(7), 963–969.

Yeomans, F. E., Selzer, M. A., & Clarkin, J. F. (1992). *Treating the borderline patient: A contract-based approach.* New York: Basic Books, Inc.

Young, J. E., Klosko, J. S., & Weishaar, M. E. (2003). *Schema therapy: A practitioner's guide.* New York: Guilford Press.

Zimmerman, M. (1994). Diagnosing personality disorders: A review of issues and research methods. *Archives of General Psychiatry, 51,* 225–245.

Part V

SUBSTANCE USE DISORDERS

14

Participant Factors in Treating Substance Use Disorders

David A. F. Haaga
Sharon M. Hall
Amie Haas

The purpose of this chapter is to identify participant characteristics that predict outcomes of psychotherapy for substance use disorders. Participant characteristics are qualities that (a) exist solely within the person (either therapist or patient) and (b) are manifest in life outside of psychotherapy sessions. We focus first on cigarette smoking, then alcohol and illicit drugs. A concluding section highlights principles that cut across type of substance used. Many of the participant characteristics highlighted by the Division 29 Task Force (Norcross, 2002), such as anaclitic and introjective dimensions, assimilation of problematic experiences, resistance, religion and spirituality, preferences, and attachment style have received little empirical attention in the study of psychotherapy for substance use disorders. As such, it is impossible to tell whether these factors relate to treatment outcome for substance abusers, and determining whether they do is a priority for future research in this area. Our review focuses on characteristics identified by the Task Force as important that have been studied in a range of substance abuse samples (e.g., expectancies, stage of change) or in specific types of samples (e.g., coping style has been a focus of treatment research relating to alcohol but not to smoking). We also consider in this chapter some additional participant factors not addressed by the Task Force (e.g., mood disorder co-morbidity, substance abuse severity) that have been extensively studied in addiction treatment samples.

SMOKING

Tobacco dependence is unique among the addictive disorders in that comprehensive meta-analyses of many aspects of the treatment of this disorder have been completed as part of the preparation of the two editions of the Practice Guidelines, a compendium of guidelines widely regarded as presenting state-of-the-art treatment in the field (Fiore 2000; Fiore, Bailey, & Cohen, 1996), as well as in the many reports of the Surgeon General on smoking and health. The most recent version of the

Guidelines, *Tobacco Use and Dependence*, published in 2000 by the Public Health Service, was formulated by a nationally recognized panel of experts, with input from clinicians and scientists around the country, and was sponsored by multiple public service agencies, all of which have the reduction of the human costs of tobacco use as a goal. These were the Agency for Healthcare Research and Quality, the Centers for Disease Control, the National Cancer Institute, the National Heart, Lung and Blood Institute, the National Institute on Drug Abuse, the Robert Wood Johnson Foundation, and the University of Wisconsin Medical School's Center for Tobacco Research and Intervention. The panel formulated clinically significant questions to be addressed in literature reviews and meta-analyses. Approximately 6,000 research articles and abstracts, including 3,000 articles reviewed as part of the first set of Guidelines (Fiore et al., 1996) were reviewed to identify appropriate studies. A careful and sophisticated set of meta-analyses were then conducted on relevant and methodologically acceptable clinical trials. The results of these meta-analyses helped shape the conclusions reached in this review.

A second source of reviews is the *Report of the Surgeon General*. The first Surgeon General's report, the landmark report clearly linking lung cancer and cigarette smoking, was first published in 1965. Since then reports have been published almost yearly, and most include reviews of the status of treatment at the time of publication. While they have not focused specifically on psychological interventions, it is often possible to glean from them the implications of the conclusions for the psychological treatment of cigarette smoking.

The treatment of cigarette smoking differs from other disorders in that the range of psychosocial interventions applied is extremely broad, ranging from single contacts, for example, brief delivery of physician advice up to 20 hours of psychotherapy provided over an 8-week period (e.g., Hall, Muñoz, & Reus, 1994). For purposes of this review, we will limit consideration to those interventions that are provided: (1) face-to-face in either an individual or group setting, and (2) involve repeated therapeutic contacts. Thus, interventions provided by telephone, mail, and over the internet will not be included, nor will interventions provided in a single brief contact. Examples of the latter are physician advice to quit smoking that is provided in a single visit.

Theoretical stance of interventions provided in smoking cessation is also broad, with the majority of them being either psychoeducational or behavioral, or cognitive behavioral. Psychodynamic interventions have yet to be evaluated in any systematic way. Psychoeducational interventions involve information about health benefits of quitting, and the provision of advice and tips about quitting and social support. Behavioral interventions usually include the content included in psychoeducational intervention, but also include detailed analyses of risky situations and discussion and rehearsal of responses. Cognitive behavioral interventions may include both psychoeducational and behavioral components, but differ from these in that clients are encouraged to explore thoughts and feelings connected with smoking and its antecedents, especially those related to affective states.

In smoking cessation research, within study comparisons of participant and therapist characteristics have been infrequent. When they are available, we focus on within study comparisons, but, when such comparisons are lacking, we draw tentative conclusions from comparisons of outcomes based on cross-study comparisons.

Therapist Characteristics

The psychological treatment of cigarette smoking differs from other areas in that providers come from a broad range of professional disciplines. Doctoral level psychologists, graduate students, physicians, nurses, and master and bachelor's level psychologist technicians have been used. The meta-analysis conducted as part of the most recent Practice Guidelines (Fiore, 2000) indicated no difference in efficacy as a function of discipline, but did suggest that involvement of multiple disciplines and providers was predictive of success.

Patient Characteristics

Demographic Characteristics

Few studies have evaluated the effect of demographic characteristics on smoking treatment outcome, with the exception of gender. Ethnicity has been rarely studied. Most psychological treatment studies have treated primarily middle-class smokers; hence, little is known about the effects of socioeconomic status on smoking treatment outcome.

Gender

The 1980 Surgeon General's Report concluded, based on 14 studies, that women were less likely to quit smoking than men. Since then, several studies have refuted that conclusion. Subsequent comprehensive reviews concluded that gender differences are inconsistent (Mermelstein & Borrelli, 1995), or impossible to determine due to the scarcity of studies reporting evaluation of such differences (Gritz, Nielsen, & Brookes, 1996; Lando & Gritz, 1996). Mermelstein and Borrelli (1995) specifically examined psychological treatments and found few treatment outcome studies that indicated gender differences. We agree with these reviewers that we cannot conclude that gender predicts differential outcome in psychological treatments of smoking. We also agree, however, that the data are sparse, and that it would be of value to the field if researchers would test for such differences and report the outcome of these tests, even if nonsignificant.

Age

Age has not been studied much as a predictor of smoking treatment outcome. The literature does contain reports of several successful intervention studies with older (over 50 years old) smokers, using both public health (e.g., Rimer et al., 1994) and psychotherapeutic (Morgan et al., 1996; Vetter & Ford, 1990) models, and, on the other end of the spectrum, adolescent smokers (Sussman, Lichtman, Ritt, & Pallonen, 1999). Cessation rates do not appear to diverge greatly from the general population, nor from each other. We found only one study of psychosocial interventions testing explicitly the effect of age on outcome. In that study, older individuals were more likely to be successful than younger ones (Barnes, Vulcano, & Greaves, 1985). Given the paucity of data, we are unable to draw conclusions about age as a predictor of outcome.

Medical Conditions

Cancer

Smoking cessation programs (mainly provision of information, advice to quit, and some phone follow-up) for postoperative cancer patients (mostly head and neck cancer) have shown little success in improving upon the high rates of cessation observed in usual care conditions (for a review, see Andersen, 2002). Interventions may need to be particularly intensive in this population to improve upon the undoubtedly motivating experience of the disease itself.

Pregnancy

A quantitative review of 36 controlled studies of smoking cessation interventions for pregnant women showed that, overall, such interventions are effective in getting more pregnant women to quit smoking than in comparison conditions (typically "usual care") (Kelley, Bond, & Abraham, 2001). In most cases, the main intervention method was provision of a self-help manual specifically for pregnant smokers. Interestingly, results were *weaker* when individual counseling was added to the self-help materials as part of multicomponent interventions. This is the opposite of what is usually found with respect to the dose/ intensity-response relation in smoking cessation counseling (Fiore, 2000). Most of the individual counseling interventions tested with pregnant smokers have been very brief (under one hour), however, and it is not known whether more extensive psychological interventions would prove useful.

Cardiac Disease

We know of no studies directly comparing patients with cardiac disease vs. healthy smokers in response to a standard set of interventions. From across-study comparisons, though, it appears that cardiac patients tend to do well in smoking cessation programs. For example, a review of controlled studies conducted among hospitalized patients found that intervention conditions exceeded control conditions in absolute quit rates by a median of 15% (46% vs. 31%). Among general admission patients, increases associated with intervention were much smaller (median of 4%, 19% vs. 15%) (France, Glasgow, & Marcus, 2001). Interventions were especially likely to be helpful if a smoking cessation specialist provided one-to-one counseling during the hospital stay, with several months of follow-up, usually by phone.

Contrasting these two cases (cardiac disease, in which psychosocial interventions seem to work especially well, and pregnancy, in which they have not, above and beyond self-help materials), we might tentatively conclude that high-medical-risk smokers will be especially receptive to individual counseling for smoking cessation only if smoking plausibly contributed to their risk status. Consistent with this conjecture, hospitalized smokers were twice as likely to agree to participate in a smoking cessation intervention if their principal diagnosis was likely tobacco-related (62%) than if not (32%) (Pelletier & Moisan, 1998).

Psychiatric Co-morbidity

Depression

The link between cigarette smoking and depressed mood is well established in population studies (Anda et al., 1990; Covey & Tam, 1990; Kandel & Davies, 1986; Perez-Stable, Marin, Marin, & Katz, 1990). There is also evidence that diagnosable depression, particularly Major Depressive Disorder (MDD), and a diagnosis of Nicotine Dependence are correlated in the general population (Breslau, Kilbey, & Andreski, 1991). Individuals with current or historical depressive disorders appear to be overrepresented among those seeking smoking treatment (Glassman et al., 1988; Hall et al., 1994). Also, smokers with a history of MDD may experience more severe mood-related symptoms when they quit smoking (Covey, Glassman, & Stetner, 1990; Ginsberg, Hall, Reus, & Muñoz, 1995). Whether a diagnosis of depression or elevated levels of poor mood are related to difficulties in quitting is controversial, with some studies finding that depressed smokers are less likely to quit smoking (Glassman et al., 1988), others not (Hall

et al., 1994), and yet others only in partial samples (Hall et al., 1998)

There have been six studies that directly address the question of whether Cognitive Behavioral Therapy (CBT) is especially effective for smokers with a history of depression. In all six studies, history of depression has been defined as a history of MDD as defined by the Diagnostic and Statistical Manual of the American Psychiatric Association (American Psychiatric Association, 1994). In three of these studies, there was a differential effect of CBT on smokers with a history of MDD (Hall et al., 1994; Hall et al., 1998; Patten, Martin, Myers, Calfas, & Williams, 1998) In a fourth (Brown et al., 2001), the effect was found in a post hoc analysis of recurrent versus single episode depression. In two of the studies (Hall et al., 1996; Smith et al., 2001) no effect was found.

There are methodological subtleties that must be considered in evaluating this literature. In the first and third of the three studies reported by Hall's group (Hall et al., 1994; Hall et al., 1998), the control condition provided less therapeutic contact than the cognitive behavioral condition, which was not the case for the second study (Hall et al., 1996), which had a time-equivalent control. That the effect was found in the first and third studies, but not in the second, suggests that therapeutic contact, rather than the content of the therapy, was responsible for the treatment effects observed. On the other hand, both Patten (Patten et al., 1998) and Brown (Brown et al., 2001) used time-equivalent controls and did see a treatment effect. The intervention reported by Smith et al. (2001) differed from the other studies, in that the manual was modified to be more appropriate to smokers in general, not just smokers with a depression history, and was abbreviated from ten 2-hour sessions to six 90-minute sessions.

Thus, the balance of the data suggests that a history of depression predicts relatively favorable outcome in cognitive behavioral therapy. Whether this is the case for other therapies is not yet clear. In general, one can safely assume that a high level of depression does not necessarily predict poor treatment outcome in psychological interventions for smoking cessation, and that CBT may be differentially effective with depressed individuals, especially those with chronic, recurrent depression.

Unanswered questions include: (1) Are patients with a history of MDD who are given CBT likely to be more successful than those without MDD? (2) What is the causative variable—is it the poor mood associated with a diagnosis of MDD or some unspecified variable associated with the disorder? (3) What is the mechanism? Studies have not shown a decrease in poor mood as a function of CBT in patients with MDD, so how it exerts its influence on outcome is unknown (Haas, Muñoz, Humfleet, Reus, & Hall, 2004).

Abuse of Other Substances

Although extremely high rates of smoking have been reported among clients in treatment for substance abuse, only a few trials of smoking cessation for individuals with these disorders are in progress. We found no published studies comparing the efficacy of the outcomes of psychological treatments as a function of drug or alcohol dependence. Humfleet, Muñoz, Sees, Reus, & Hall (1999) studied smoking treatment outcome among smokers who entered a trial in which CBT was crossed with psychoeducational treatment (Hall et al., 1998). These investigators found, that regardless of which variant of psychological treatment was offered, both alcohol use at baseline and any alcohol use during treatment predicted smoking at follow-ups. Neither use of marijuana at baseline nor during treatment predicted outcome. The lack of relationship of marijuana use to poor outcome is not consistent with other findings in the field. Gourlay, Forbes, Marriner, Pethica, & McNeil (1994) reported that marijuana use in a sample of smokers receiving NRT plus behavioral counseling predicted treatment failure.

Other Psychiatric Disorders

So far as we could find, there are no other studies that address smoking cessation in patients with concurrent psychiatric disorders as opposed to those who are not so diagnosed. We were also unable to find controlled studies of psychological interventions targeted at individuals with other psychiatric disorders. This is unfortunate, as high rates of smoking have been reported, especially in schizophrenic patients (Hughes, Hatsukami, Mitchell, & Dahlgren, 1986).

Substance Use Characteristics

Nicotine Dependence

Nicotine dependence can be measured in a variety of ways. The most common metric is simple number of cigarettes smoked, with the assumption that individuals who smoke more cigarettes are taking in more nicotine, and that level of nicotine is indicative of level of dependence. This is only considered a rough metric, however, for machine-measured nicotine dose indicated in FDA lists, and actual nicotine delivery will differ depending on smoking style. Scores on the Fagerstrom Tolerance and Nicotine Dependence (FTND; Heatherton, Kozlowski, Frecker, & Fagerstrom, 1991) scale also are used as measures of dependence, since this scale has shown considerable predictive and construct validity (Heatherton et al., 1991; Killen, Fortmann, Kraemer, Varady, & Newman, 1992; Payne, Smith, McCracken, McSherry, & Antony, 1994). Recently, however, it has been suggested that most of the power of the scale lies in a single item ("Do you smoke within 30 minutes of arising?"). Other measures of dependence have included years of regular smoking (Pomerleau, Adkins, & Pertschuk, 1978) and baseline cotinine (Hall, Herning, Jones, Benowitz, & Jacob, 1984). The major conclusion of the field has been that high levels of nicotine dependence predict poor outcome, although addition of NRT can attenuate this relationship. In psychological interventions offered without NRT, however, nicotine dependence predicts poor outcome.

Previous Quit Attempts

Some researchers have reported that a greater number of previous quit attempts is associated with relapse (Stuart & Borland, 1994), others the reverse (Scholte & Breteler, 1997). Findings on duration of previous quit attempts in relation to abstinence are also contradictory. Several studies have linked longer duration of previous quit attempts with abstinence at follow-up (Borrelli et al., 2002; Mothersill, McDowell, & Rosser, 1988; Stuart & Borland, 1994), but others show an inverse relationship between length of prior abstinence and length of current abstinence (e.g., Brandon, Zelman, & Baker, 1988). Conclusions cannot be reached due to the conflicting findings.

Lapses During Treatment

Early relapse during treatment has been shown to be a significant predictor of later relapse in both men and women (Borland, 1990; Brandon, Tiffany, Obremski, & Baker, 1990; Nides et al., 1995). However, not all relapsers necessarily return to full-time smoking. Context of a lapse may be crucial in this sense; people attempting to quit are more likely to recover from slip-ups associated with socializing and drinking (Borland, 1990).

Stage of Change

Smokers in more advanced stages of change as defined in the transtheoretical model of Prochaska and colleagues are more likely to succeed in quitting smoking (e.g., Colby et al., 1998). It is not clear whether, as predicted by the theory, stage of change moderates the effectiveness of type of intervention, with matching interventions (e.g., motivational enhancement for precontemplators, self-efficacy-related intervention for contemplators) working better than mismatched interventions. Several studies have examined this issue, but results are mixed, and in any case the interventions have generally been delivered by computer or by printed text or self-help activity suggestions, rather than in a psychotherapy interaction (e.g., Quinlan & McCaul, 2000).

Expectancies

Self-efficacy, operationalized as the extent of confidence in one's ability to achieve and maintain abstinence from smoking, is a consistent, reliable predictor of success in either self-directed attempts to quit smoking or formal cessation programs of various kinds (Ockene et al., 2000). Most studies have examined total scores on self-efficacy measures, aggregating across situations in which one might be tempted to lapse to smoking. However, consistent with social cognitive theory, self-efficacy is somewhat situation-specific, and the degree of confidence a smoker possesses in her or his most vulnerable situation may be a particularly strong predictor of lapses, with potential clinical utility

for targeting high-risk situations and thereby preventing relapse (Gwaltney et al., 2001).

ALCOHOL AND ILLICIT DRUGS

Alcohol and illicit drug abuse share a common connection to nicotine dependence in that they are substance use disorders with both psychological and physiological aspects of addiction. Yet, alcohol and drug treatment research is quite different from smoking cessation research in methodology and in current status. Alcohol and drug abuse treatment research, for instance, have not yielded a comprehensive review comparable to the Practice Guidelines for smoking cessation (Fiore, 2000; Fiore et al., 1996). However, large-scale, multi-site clinical trials such as the Drug Abuse Treatment Outcome Study (DATOS; Hubbard, Craddock, Flynn, Anderson, & Etheridge, 1997) for both alcohol and illicit drug abuse, and Project MATCH (Project MATCH Research Group, 1997) for alcohol abuse, have been completed in the past decade. Project MATCH tested Cognitive-behavioral, Motivational Enhancement, and 12-step Facilitation treatments, along with a number of patient-treatment matches, for impact on drinks per day and percentage of days abstinent (Project MATCH Research Group, 1997).

Therapist Characteristics

There are clearly differences in success rate among therapists who treat alcohol or illicit drug abuse (Najavits & Weiss, 1994), but it has proven challenging to differentiate more vs. less successful therapists on the basis of therapist characteristics identifiable outside of therapy sessions themselves. One report indicated, for instance, that therapists' personal qualities were moderately, albeit nonsignificantly, correlated with outcome, with psychologically healthier therapists (as judged by peers) achieving greater success with male drug abusers maintained on methadone (Luborsky, McLellan, Woody, O'Brien, & Auerbach, 1985). However, the therapist personal adjustment measure included such items as "very capable and skillful therapist" and "much above average in avoiding being directive and authoritarian" (Luborsky et al., 1985, p. 605). As such, the measure may have confounded extra-therapy therapist variables with therapy process variables.

Studies of purely extra-therapy therapist characteristics such as sex, race/ethnicity, and religion/spirituality, or for that matter of patient–therapist match on these dimensions, are limited in relation to alcohol and drug treatment outcomes. No replicated findings sufficient to serve as a basis of principles are evident in this area (e.g., Najavits & Weiss, 1994; Sterling, Gottheil, Weinstein, & Serota, 2001). Predictive relations that are obtained may derive from a single outlier therapist or vary across type of treatment (e.g., no therapist factors predicted success in the CBT condition in Project MATCH) (Project MATCH Research Group, 1998).

An exception to this pattern of ambiguity is therapist recovery status. Although it is often hypothesized that therapists who are themselves in recovery from substance abuse would be more effective, therapist recovery status has been shown repeatedly not to predict patient outcomes in alcohol and illicit drug abuse treatment (Culbreth, 2000; McLellan, Woody, Luborsky, & Goehl, 1988; Project MATCH Research Group, 1998).

Patient Characteristics

Demographic Characteristics

Gender

Historically, much alcohol and drug abuse treatment research was conducted in predominantly male samples (e.g., Schuckit, Smith, Anthenelli, & Irwin, 1993; Valliant & Milofsky, 1982), but in recent years study samples have been more diverse, and increased attention has been paid to evaluating gender differences in treatment outcome. One area in which gender disparity has been noted is in treatment seeking, irrespective of program completion or retention. Relative to men, women are less likely to present for substance abuse treatment (Beckman & Amaro, 1986; Nathan & Skinstad, 1987; Shober & Annis, 1996) and encounter more barriers to entering treatment (see Greenfield, 2001, for review). This is inconsistent with general psychotherapy outcome findings, which indicate that women are more likely to seek treatment than men (Garfield, 1994; Petry, Tennen, & Affleck,

2000). However, consistent with the general psychotherapy literature, women and men have comparable rates of program completion once they enter treatment (Greenspan & Kulish, 1985; Nathan & Skinstad, 1987; Sledge, Moras, Hartley, & Levine, 1990).

Recent large-scale studies on alcohol and drug treatment are mixed with regard to the effect of gender on outcome. In Project MATCH men in aftercare programs report fewer days abstinent and more drinks per day compared to their female counterparts (Project MATCH Research Group, 1997). However, this was not replicated in the outpatient arm of Project MATCH. Likewise, in the National Treatment Improvement Evaluation Study (NTIES), gender explained a relatively small amount of overall variance in outcomes (USDHHS, 1997).

Age

Substance abuse disorders can affect individuals at just about every stage of life. Consequently, several studies have evaluated the relationship between age at time of treatment and outcomes, with mixed results. Several studies found older adults to have higher rates of retention, abstinence, and employment following treatment than younger adults (Agosti, Nunes, & Ocepeck-Welikson, 1996; Hubbard et al., 1989; Joe, Simpson, & Broome, 1998; Levinson & McLachlan, 1973), whereas other studies have found no significant age differences (e.g., Janik & Dunham, 1983). Contradictory results have also been reported. In a review by Nathan and Skinstad (1987), younger adults were found to be better prospects for treatment than older clients. Similarly, using information from the DATOS study, Grella, Hser, Joshi, and Anglin (1999) found that patients under age 30 had a stronger positive relationship between treatment retention and abstinence at 1-year follow-up than did older patients.

Whereas it is thus unclear whether age predicts outcome, it clearly makes a difference in the nature of treatment. In a review of adolescent substance abuse treatment, Williams, Chang, and the Addiction Centre Adolescent Research Group (2000) examined data from 53 adolescent substance abuse treatment studies. The overwhelming majority of teens entering substance abuse treatment were between the ages of 15 and 17, male, and Caucasian. Polysubstance abuse was the norm, with alcohol and marijuana being the most commonly used substances. Rates of sustained abstinence were low for adolescents, even immediately upon discharge from treatment. However, the majority of studies in the review reported decreases in posttreatment substance use. Baseline characteristics that predicted favorable outcomes included better school attendance, lower pretreatment substance abuse, abstinence-based peer and parental social support, and higher pretreatment functioning. In this review, demographic variables (age at entry to treatment, religion, SES, and gender) were not found to be consistent predictors of outcome.

At the other end of the spectrum, older adults appear to have different clinical presentations. For example, prevalence rates for illicit drug abuse are quite low in older adult samples relative to younger substance abusers; older adults who present for services are far more likely to have problems with alcohol, benzodiazepines, and prescription pain medications (Atkinson, 2000; Gomberg, 1999). Older adults are less likely to be accurately screened for alcohol-related problems, and subsequently less likely to be referred for treatment (Gomberg, 1995; McInnes & Powell, 1994; Moos, Mertens, & Brennan, 1993). Furthermore, older adults who do enter treatment were found to have more severe problems, heavier alcohol intake, and were more likely to self-identify as alcohol dependent (Gomberg, 1995). They also are more likely to have depression as a co-occurring condition (Gomberg, 1999).

Ethnicity

There is insufficient evidence to evaluate patient ethnicity, or patient–therapist ethnic similarity, as a predictor of substance abuse treatment outcome. Several studies have suggested that Caucasian substance abusers tend to have better outcomes compared to African American, Latino, and Native Americans (McCaul, Svikis, & Moore, 2001; Query, 1985; Westhuis, Gwaltney, & Hayashi, 2001), but large-scale treatment outcome studies (e.g., NTIES) did not corroborate this finding (USDHHS, 1997).

Socioeconomic Status

Clients who are employed at the time of treatment typically have better outcomes than do unemployed clients (Elal-Lawrence, Slade, & Dewey, 1986; Emrick & Hansen, 1983; Smart, 1978). Prior reviews addressing this area in general psychotherapy studies (e.g., Petry, Tennen, & Affleck, 2000) noted that the relation between SES and outcomes may be mediated by volitional status, as lower SES clients are more likely to be mandated into treatment. This issue is particularly relevant to substance abuse treatment, given that many individuals who commit substance-related legal offenses (e.g., driving under the influence, drug possession, public intoxication) are mandated to treatment as a condition of their sentencing (see Polcin, 2001, for review).

Psychiatric Co-morbidity

Data from the Epidemiological Catchment Area Study (ECA) indicate that about one-third of persons with alcohol use disorders and one-half of persons with drug-related disorders have at least one additional co-occurring psychiatric disorder (Regier et al., 1990). Common dual diagnoses for substance abusers include depression (e.g., Flynn, Craddock, Luckey, Hubbard, & Dunteman, 1996), anxiety (e.g., Regier et al., 1990), post-traumatic stress disorder (e.g., Breslau, 2001), attention deficit disorder (e.g., Lynskey & Hall, 2001), schizophrenia (e.g., Mueser, Bellack, & Blanchard, 1992), antisocial personality disorder (e.g., Flynn et al., 1996), and borderline personality disorder (Trull, Sher, Minks-Brown, Durbin, & Burr, 2000).

Depression

As with smokers, rates of depression are higher among alcohol and drug abusers than the general population, with higher prevalence rates documented for women than men (Brady, Grice, Dustan, & Randall, 1993; Regier et al., 1990). For example, in the DATOS study 12% of participants met criteria for Major Depressive Disorder (MDD), with prevalence rates twice as high for women as for men (Flynn et al., 1996). Multiple studies have reported that treatment-seeking substance abusers with depression have worse prognoses compared to individuals who are not depressed. Co-occurring depression has been associated with lower rates of abstinence, more subsequent treatment admissions, and involvement in more intensive substance abuse treatment services (Alterman, McLellan, & Shifman, 1993; Bobo, McIlvain, & Leed-Kelly, 1998; Loosen, Dew, & Prange, 1990; Moos, Mertens, & Brennan, 1994). However, this finding has not been consistent. Some studies have found depression to be predictive of more favorable outcomes (Rounsaville, Dolinsky, Babor, & Meyer, 1987), while others have found no relationship between depression and outcomes (Charney, Paraherakis, & Gill, 2000a; Davidson & Blackburn, 1998; Sellman & Joyce, 1996). Method variations may account for the inconsistent results. In substance abuse treatment outcome research, depression has not been uniformly measured (Charney et al., 2000b). Some studies did not distinguish between primary mood disorder and substance-induced mood disorder (Rounsaville et al., 1987; Kanzler, Del Boca, & Rounsaville, 1996) or between diagnosable episodes of MDD and subclinical levels of depression (Bobo et al., 1998; Sellman & Joyce, 1996). Other studies have used all-male samples that have lower base rates of depression than female-only or mixed samples (Loosen et al., 1990; Valliant & Milofsky, 1982). In view of these diverse findings, and methods, it is not possible to draw definite conclusions about the association of depression and substance abuse treatment outcome.

Personality Disorders

Several personality disorders have been shown to co-occur with alcohol and drug problems. Of these, Antisocial Personality Disorder (ASPD) is the most prevalent and the most widely studied. Prevalence estimates from the DATOS study indicate that rate of ASPD in treatment-seeking substance abusers is remarkably higher than the general population, with 40% of the sample meeting diagnostic criteria (Flynn et al., 1996). Marked gender disparities were noted, with substance abusing men being more likely to meet criteria for ASPD than women (Flynn et al., 1996; Hesselbrock & Hesselbrock, 1999).

Substance abusers with ASPD have less favorable outcomes. For instance, in the DATOS study drug abusers with ASPD showed lower rates of program retention and completion (Broome, Simpson, & Joe, 1999). Differences in abstinence outcomes are also evident. For example, in a VA inpatient alcohol dependency treatment unit, Hunter and colleagues (2000) found that antisocial personality characteristics predicted poor long-term drinking outcomes. Comparable results were found in an alcohol treatment sample using the related construct of sociopathy. Higher levels of sociopathy predicted worse outcomes (drinks per day and percentage of days abstinent) early in the posttreatment period in Project MATCH (Project MATCH Research Group, 1997). However a significant aptitude-by-time interaction was noted, with sociopathy predicting worse outcomes in the period immediately following treatment but not later (Project MATCH Research Group, 1997). Overall, results from these studies highlight that ASPD, or personality traits consistent with ASPD, are associated with poorer outcomes; however, further research is indicated to determine if this relationship persists across the posttreatment time period or is more pronounced earlier in the recovery process.

Other Psychiatric Co-morbidity

In general, substance abusers with co-morbid psychiatric diagnoses show poorer treatment outcomes relative to those with no co-morbidity (McKay & Maisto, 1993; Moos, Brennan, & Mertens, 1994; Ouimette, Ahrens, Moos, & Finney, 1997; Rounsaville et al., 1987). Severity of co-occurring pathology is also important to consider. Prior research on psychotherapy outcomes for other disorders (e.g., depression) has repeatedly found that greater severity of psychiatric disturbance is related to poorer outcomes (Petry et al., 2000). Similarly, severity of psychiatric symptoms has been inversely related to treatment outcomes with substance abusing clients (McLellan, Luborsky, Woody, O'Brien, & Druley, 1983) as well as individuals participating in alcohol treatment (Project MATCH Research Group, 1997). In Project MATCH those with greater psychiatric severity, as measured by the composite score on the Addiction Severity Index, reported more drinks per day during aftercare, and this effect was accentuated as time passed in the follow-up period (Project MATCH Research Group, 1997).

A separate question is whether pretreatment psychiatric co-morbidity can be used to match patients with optimal treatments. An alcohol study obtained superior outcomes, through two-year follow-up, for patients scoring high on psychiatric severity or on sociopathy who received group CBT coping skills training, whereas low-sociopathy and low-severity patients fared better in a less structured interactional group treatment (Cooney, Kadden, Litt, & Getter, 1991). However, a larger prospective experiment found no difference in outcomes for alcohol dependent or alcohol abusing patients assigned to CBT vs. interactional therapy (a) based on these pretreatment matching variables or (b) randomly (Kadden, Litt, Cooney, Kabela, & Getter, 2001). Likewise, a study of psychotherapy for cocaine-dependent patients failed to yield consistent evidence of an advantage for CBT or supportive-expressive therapy, relative to drug counseling, in achieving differential benefits for patients as a function of pretreatment psychiatric severity (Crits-Christoph et al., 2001).

Coping

As with psychiatric severity, coping variables have proven useful in a prognostic sense but inconsistent as matching variables in alcohol treatment research. Independent of treatment type, patients who showed increased use of a wide range of tactics for coping with temptation to drink were more likely to sustain positive treatment outcomes (Litt, Kadden, Cooney, & Kabela, 2003). The hypothesis that coping frequency would interact with treatment type such that CBT might be especially useful for those initially deficient in the coping tactics taught in this treatment was not supported, however (Litt et al., 2003).

It may be that coping can be used to guide patient-treatment matching for substance use disorders if the focus shifts from coping *frequency* to coping *skill* (e.g., Kadden, Litt, Cooney, & Busher, 1992) or coping style. One program of research, for example, has evaluated the hypothesis that insight therapies would work best for internalizing patients, whereas symptom-focused and skill-building therapies would prove more useful for externalizing patients (Beutler, Harwood, Alimohamed, & Malik, 2002). "Internalizing" here refers to a broad dimension incorporating introversion, social restraint, self-criticism, and inhibition. "Externalizing," on the other hand, refers to extraversion, impulsivity, action-oriented, sensation-seeking coping styles. Results supportive of the hypothesized match have been obtained, but not consistently and not in the largest study of the issue (Project MATCH Research Group, 1997); for a detailed review, see Beutler et al. (2002).

Substance Use Characteristics

Severity

Severity of substance dependence itself may also be inversely related to treatment outcomes (McLellan, Luborsky, & O'Brien, 1986). Data from Project MATCH indicated that a higher level of alcohol involvement prior to treatment was related to more drinks per day during follow-up (Project MATCH Research Group, 1997). However, this finding has not been universally reported (Heather, Rollnick, & Winton, 1983). Treatment efficacy appears to be reduced for individuals reporting problems with multiple substances (e.g., alcohol and cocaine), with data suggesting that polysubstance abusers are at increased risk for relapse (Brower, Blow, Hill, & Mudd, 1994; Brown, Seraganian, & Tremblay, 1993).

Age of Onset

Although the onset of alcohol and drug problems after the age of 45 was traditionally thought to be rare, findings from community and clinical samples show that substance abuse onset can occur at any age (Atkinson, 2000). Individuals with late onset alcoholism are higher functioning at time of treatment and have better outcomes compared to individuals of the same age whose alcohol problems began earlier in life (Dupree & Schonfeld, 1998; Hesselbrock & Hesselbrock, 1999). For example, late onset alcoholism has been associated with more favorable economic status and better treatment compliance (Atkinson, Tolson, & Turner, 1990; McNeece & DiNitto, 1994). Currently there is insufficient research evaluating outcomes with regard to early versus late onset of other drug problems (e.g., cocaine, heroin).

Readiness to Change

Motivation as measured in studies inspired by the transtheoretical model has usually been operationalized as a continuous variable, as opposed to stages of change as in research on the transtheoretical model and smoking cessation. Such studies have found that increased readiness to change predicts better outcomes (e.g., Project MATCH Research Group, 1997). Efforts to match interventions to a patient's degree of readiness to change (for example, by providing motivational interviewing to those low in readiness to change), however, have yielded contradictory results—sometimes this match is confirmed (Heather, Rollnick, Bell, & Richmond, 1996), sometimes directly contradicted (Maisto et al., 2001), and sometimes neither result is consistently obtained, as in Project MATCH. All told, readiness to change is a useful predictor of outcome, but it would be premature to say that the transtheoretical model can be applied to match alcohol treatments to patient characteristics and thereby improve outcome (Sutton, 2001).

Expectancies

Several types of expectancies have been related to treatment outcome. For example, Heather, Rollnick, and Winton (1983) found a relationship between assimilation of abstinence-based beliefs and participation in harm-free drinking posttreatment. In a separate study using a harm reduction paradigm, a negative association was found between the statement "first drink, then drunk," a colloquialism associated with 12-step approaches, and engaging in problematic drinking posttreatment (Heather, Winton, & Rollnick, 1982). Clients who had never heard the phrase, or did not believe in it, were more likely to successfully return to harm-free drinking (that is, social drinking which does not result in diagnosable alcohol-related problems) than were those who strongly believed in this principle.

There is considerable evidence that alcohol outcome expectancies, defined as the perceived effects a person anticipates experiencing as a result of drinking (Brown, Goldman, Inn, & Anderson, 1980), predict treatment outcome. These expectancies may be positive (e.g., alcohol produces positive effects like tension reduction, global positive effects, or perceived sexual enhancement) or negative (e.g., drinking makes one physically ill or produces adverse consequences).

Several studies show higher positive alcohol outcome expectancies are inversely related to abstinence posttreatment. For example, in a study conducted in a male veteran population, Brown (1985) found that higher positive expectancies at intake were predictive of relapse at one-year follow-up even when controlling for confounding variables like drinking history and level of social support. Positive expectancies have also been related to treatment retention, with individuals reporting greater perceived reinforcement from alcohol being at increased risk for dropout (Ryan, Plant, & O'Malley, 1995).

Although more controversial and not as extensively studied, pretreatment negative expectancies have also been shown to predict outcomes. For example, Jones and McMahon (1994) found that negative alcohol expectancies predicted posttreatment time to first relapse, whereas no relationship was found with positive expectancies. Overall, findings from multiple studies indicate that substance-related expectancies are an essential client characteristic in alcohol treatment. However, additional work is needed to evaluate the contribution of positive versus negative expectancies in predicting abstinence rates posttreatment.

PRINCIPLES

As indicated throughout this chapter, many areas of research relating therapist and patient characteristics to psychotherapy outcome for substance use disorders have yielded conflicting or inconclusive results. In other cases, results have been nonsignificant, but in few or small studies, such that we cannot be confident that a null result really means that outcomes are equivalent. There are numerous gaps in the literature and ample opportunity for future research. This is particularly true of therapist characteristics, about which we have little dependable knowledge thus far. In this final section we distill the principles that we perceive as well supported in the work reviewed in this chapter.

Therapist Characteristics

1. Therapists with vs. without a history of substance use disorder appear to be equally effective in treating alcohol or illicit drug abuse.

Patient Characteristics

2. High-medical-risk smokers will be especially receptive to individual counseling for smoking cessation only if smoking plausibly contributed to their risk status.

3. Although the evidence is not entirely consistent, cognitive behavior therapy may be differentially effective with depressed smokers relative to comparison conditions. This prescriptive effect may apply especially to those smokers with chronic, recurrent depression.

4. Polysubstance use/abuse is a risk factor for poor outcome. For example, higher alcohol use at baseline, or any alcohol use during treatment, predicts poorer outcome in smoking cessation treatment.

5. When psychological interventions for smokers are offered in the absence of nicotine replacement therapy, nicotine dependence predicts poor outcome.

6. Smokers in more advanced stages of change as defined in the transtheoretical model are more likely to succeed in quitting smoking. Likewise, alcohol abusers reporting increased readiness to change fare better in treatment.

7. Self-efficacy for maintaining abstinence predicts success in quitting smoking.

8. Higher positive alcohol outcome expectancies are inversely related to abstinence posttreatment.

9. Clients who are employed at the time of treatment have better outcomes than do unemployed clients in substance abuse treatment.

10. Co-morbid antisocial personality disorder predicts poor outcome in substance abuse treatment.

11. In general, psychiatric co-morbidity predicts worse substance abuse treatment outcome, and the more severe the associated psychiatric symptoms, the worse the outcomes.

12. Individuals with late onset alcoholism are higher functioning at time of treatment and have better outcomes compared to individuals of the same age whose alcohol problems began at earlier in life.

References

Agosti, V., Nunes, E., & Ocepeck-Welikson, K. (1996). Patient factors related to early attrition from an outpatient cocaine research clinic. *American Journal of Drug and Alcohol Abuse, 22*, 29–39.

Alterman, A. I., McLellan, A. T., & Shifman, R. B. (1993). Do substance abuse patients with more psychopathology receive more treatment? *Journal of Nervous and Mental Disease, 181*, 576–582.

American Psychiatric Association. (1994). *Diagnostic and Statistical Manual of Mental Disorders* (4th ed.). Washington, DC: American Psychiatric Association.

Anda, R. F., Williamson, D. F., Escobedo, L. G., Mast, E. E., Giovino, G. A., & Remington, P. L. (1990). Depression and the dynamics of smoking: A national perspective. *Journal of the American Medical Association, 264*, 1541–1545.

Andersen, B. L. (2002). Biobehavioral outcomes following psychological interventions for cancer patients. *Journal of Consulting and Clinical Psychology, 70*, 590–610.

Atkinson, R. M. (2000). Substance abuse. In C. E. Coffey & J. L. Cummings (Eds.), *Textbook of geriatric neuropsychiatry* (2nd ed., pp. 367–400). Washington, DC: American Psychiatric Press, Inc.

Atkinson, R. M., Tolson, R. L., & Turner, J. A. (1990). Late versus early onset of problem drinking in older men. *Alcoholism: Clinical and Experimental Research, 14*, 574–579.

Barnes, G. E., Vulcano, B. A., & Greaves, L. (1985). Characteristics affecting smoking outcome in the cessation of smoking. *International Journal of the Addictions, 20*, 1429–1435.

Beckman, L. J., & Amaro, H. (1986). Personal and social difficulties faced by women and men entering alcoholism treatment. *Journal of Studies on Alcohol, 47*, 135–145.

Beutler, L. E., Harwood, T. M., Alimohamed, S., &

Malik, M. (2002). Functional impairment and coping style. In J. C. Norcross (Ed.), *Psychotherapy relationships that work: Therapist contributions and responsiveness to patients* (pp. 145–170). Oxford: Oxford University Press.

Bobo, J. K., McIlvain, H. E., & Leed-Kelly, A. (1998). Depression screening scores during residential drug treatment and risk of drug use after discharge. *Psychiatric Services, 49*, 693–695.

Borland, R. (1990). Slip-ups and relapse in attempts to quit smoking. *Addictive Behaviors, 15*, 235–245.

Borrelli, B., Hogan, J. W., Bock, B. C., Pinto, B., Roberts, M., & Marcus, B. H. (2002). Predictors of quitting and dropout among women in a clinic-based smoking cessation program. *Psychology of Addictive Behaviors, 16*, 22–27.

Brady, K., Grice, D. E., Dustan, L., & Randall, C. L. (1993). Gender differences in substance use disorders. *American Journal of Psychiatry, 150*, 1707–1711.

Brandon, T. H., Tiffany, S. T., Obremski, K. M., & Baker, T. (1990). Postcessation cigarette use: The process of relapse. *Addictive Behaviors, 15*, 105–114.

Brandon, T. H., Zelman, D. C., & Baker, T. (1988). Delaying smoking relapse with extended treatment. In T. Baker & D. S. Cannon (Eds.), *Assessment and Treatment of Addictive Disorders* (pp. 151–180). New York: Praeger.

Breslau, N. (2001). Outcomes of posttraumatic stress disorder. *Journal of Clinical Psychiatry, 62*, Suppl., 55–59.

Breslau, N., Kilbey, M. M., & Andreski, P. (1991). Nicotine dependence, major depression and anxiety in young adults. *Archives of General Psychiatry, 48*, 1069–1074.

Broome, K. M., Simpson, D. D., & Joe, G. W. (1999). Patient and program attributes related to treatment process indicators in DATOS. *Drug and Alcohol Dependence, 57*, 127–135.

Brower, K. J., Blow, F. C., Hill, E. M., & Mudd, S. A. (1994). Treatment outcomes of alcoholics with and without cocaine disorders. *Alcoholism: Clinical and Experimental Research, 18*, 734–739.

Brown, R. A., Kahler, C. W., Niaura, R., Abrams, D. B., Sales, S. D., Ramsey, S. E., Goldstein, M. G., Burgess, E. S., & Miller, I. W. (2001). Cognitive-behavioral treatment for depression in smoking cessation. *Journal of Consulting & Clinical Psychology, 69*, 471–480.

Brown, S. A. (1985). Reinforcement expectancies and alcoholism treatment outcome after one-year follow-up. *Journal of Studies on Alcohol, 46*, 304–308.

Brown, S. A., Goldman, M. S., Inn, A., & Anderson, L. R. (1980). Expectations of reinforcement from alcohol: Their domain and relation to drinking patterns. *Journal of Consulting and Clinical Psychology, 48*, 419–426.

Brown, T. G., Seraganian, P., & Tremblay, J. (1993). Alcohol and cocaine abusers 6 months after traditional treatment: Do they fare as well as problem drinkers? *Journal of Substance Abuse Treatment, 10*, 545–552.

Charney, D. A., Paraherakis, A. M., & Gill, K. J. (2000a). The treatment of sedative-hypnotic dependence: Evaluating clinical predictors of outcome. *Journal of Clinical Psychiatry, 61*, 190–195.

Charney, D. A., Paraherakis, A. M., & Gill, K. J. (2000b). Integrated treatment of comorbid depression and substance use disorders. *Journal of Clinical Psychiatry, 62*, 672–677.

Colby, S. M., Monti, P. M., Barnett, N. P., Rohsenow, D. J., Weissman, K., Spirito, A., Woolard, R. H., & Lewander, W. J. (1998). Brief motivational interviewing in a hospital setting for adolescent smoking: A preliminary study. *Journal of Consulting and Clinical Psychology, 66*, 574–578.

Cooney, N. L., Kadden, R. M., Litt, M. D., & Getter, H. (1991). Matching alcoholics to coping skills or interactional therapies: Two-year follow-up results. *Journal of Consulting and Clinical Psychology, 59*, 598–601.

Covey, L. S., Glassman, A. H., & Stetner, F. (1990). Depression and depressive symptoms in smoking cessation. *Comprehensive Psychiatry, 31*, 350–354.

Covey, L. S., & Tam, D. (1990). Depressive mood, the single-parent home, and adolescent cigarette smoking. *American Journal of Public Health, 80*, 1330–1333.

Crits-Christoph, P., Siqueland, L., McCalmont, E., Weiss, R. D., Gastfriend, D. R., Frank, A., Moras, K., Barber, J. P., Blaine, J., & Thase, M. E. (2001). Impact of psychosocial treatments on associated problems of cocaine-dependent patients. *Journal of Consulting and Clinical Psychology, 69*, 825–830.

Culbreth, J. R. (2000). Substance abuse counselors with and without a personal history of chemical dependency: A review of the literature. *Alcoholism Treatment Quarterly, 18*, 67–82.

Davidson, K. M., & Blackburn, I. M. (1998). Comorbid depression and drinking outcome in those with alcohol dependence. *Alcohol Alcohol, 33,* 482–487.

Dupree, L. W., & Schonfeld, L. (1998). *Older alcohol abusers: Recurring treatment issues* (NIDA Research Monograph, pp. 339–358). Proceedings of the Alcohol and Aging National Conference, Ypsilanti, MI.

Elal-Lawrence, G., Slade, P., & Dewey, M. (1986). Predictors of outcome type in treated problem drinkers. *Journal of Studies on Alcohol, 47,* 41–47.

Emrick, C., & Hansen, J. (1983). Assertions regarding effectiveness of treatment for alcoholism: Fact or fantasy? *American Psychologist, 38,* 1078–1088.

Fiore, M. C. (2000). A clinical practice guideline for treating tobacco use and dependence: A US Public Health Service report. *Journal of the American Medical Association, 283,* 3244–3254.

Fiore, M. C., Bailey, W. C., & Cohen, S. J. (1996). *Smoking cessation clinical practice guidelines no. 18.* Rockville, MD: US Department of Health and Human Services; Public Health Service, Agency for Health Care Policy and Research.

Flynn, P. M., Craddock, S. J., Luckey, J. W., Hubbard, R. L., & Dunteman, G. H. (1996). Comorbidity of antisocial personality and mood disorders among psychoactive substance-dependent treatment clients. *Journal of Personality Disorders, 10,* 56–67.

France, E. K., Glasgow, R. E., & Marcus, A. C. (2001). Smoking cessation interventions among hospitalized patients: What have we learned. *Preventive Medicine, 32,* 376–388.

Garfield, S. L. (1994). Research on client variables in psychotherapy. In S. L. Garfield & A. E. Bergin (Eds.), *Handbook of psychotherapy and behavior change* (3rd ed., pp. 72–113). New York: Wiley.

Ginsberg, D., Hall, S. M., Reus, V. I., & Muñoz, R. F. (1995). Mood and depression diagnoses in smoking cessation. *Experimental and Clinical Psychopharmacology, 3,* 389–395.

Glassman, A. H., Stetner, F., Walsh, B. T., Raizman, P. S., Fleiss, J. L., Cooper, T. B., & Covey, L. S. (1988). Heavy smokers, smoking cessation, and clonidine: Results of a double-blind, randomized trial. *Journal of the American Medical Association, 259,* 2863–2866.

Gomberg, E. S. L. (1995). Older alcoholics: Entry into treatment. In T. Beresford & E. Gomberg (Eds.), *Alcohol and aging* (pp. 169–185). New York: Oxford University Press.

Gomberg, E. S. L. (1999). Substance abuse in the elderly. In P. J. Ott, R. E. Tarter, & R. T. Ammerman (Eds.), *Sourcebook on substance abuse: Etiology, epidemiology, assessment, and treatment* (pp. 113–125). Boston, MA: Allyn and Bacon.

Gourlay, S. G., Forbes, A., Marriner, T., Pethica, D., & McNeil, J. J. (1994). Prospective study of factors predicting outcome of transdermal nicotine treatment in smoking cessation. *BMJ, 309,* 824–846.

Greenfield, S. F. (2001). Women and alcohol use disorders. *Harvard Review of Psychiatry, 10,* 76–85.

Greenspan, M., & Kulish, N. M. (1985). Factors in premature termination in long term psychotherapy. *Psychotherapy, 22,* 75–82.

Grella, C. E., Hser, Y. I., Joshi, V., & Anglin, M. D. (1999). Patient histories, retention, and outcome models for younger and older adults in DATOS. *Drug and Alcohol Dependence, 57,* 151–166.

Gritz, E. R., Nielsen, I. R., & Brookes, L. A. (1996). Smoking cessation and gender: The influence of physiological, psychological, and behavioral factors. *Journal of the American Medical Womens Association, 51,* 35–42.

Gwaltney, C. J., Shiffman, S., Norman, G. J., Paty, J. A., Kassel, J. D., Gnys, M., Hickcox, M., Waters, A., & Balabanis, M. (2001). Does smoking abstinence self-efficacy vary across situations? Identifying context-specificity within the relapse situation efficacy questionnaire. *Journal of Consulting and Clinical Psychology, 69,* 516–527.

Haas, A., Muñoz, R., Humfleet, G. L., Reus, V. I., & Hall, S. (2004). Influences of mood, depression history, and treatment modality on outcomes in smoking cessation. *Journal of Consulting and Clinical Psychology, 72,* 563–570.

Hall, S. M., Herning, R. I., Jones, R. T., Benowitz, N. L., & Jacob, P. (1984). Blood cotinine levels as indicators of smoking treatment outcome. *Clinical Pharmacology and Therapeutics, 356,* 810–814.

Hall, S. M., Muñoz, R. F., & Reus, V. I. (1994). Cognitive-behavioral intervention increases abstinence rates for depressive-history smokers. *Journal of Consulting and Clinical Psychology, 62,* 141–146.

Hall, S. M., Muñoz, R. F., Reus, V. I., Sees, K. L., Duncan, C., Humfleet, G. L., & Hartz, D. (1996). Mood management and nicotine gum in smoking treatment: A therapeutic contact and placebo controlled study. *Journal of Consulting and Clinical Psychology, 64,* 1003–1009.

Hall, S. M., Reus, V. I., Muñoz, R. F., Sees, K. L., Humfleet, G., Hartz, D. T., Frederick, S., & Triffleman, E. (1998). Nortriptyline and cognitive behavioral therapy in the treatment of cigarette smoking. *Archives of General Psychiatry, 55,* 683–690.

Heather, N., Rollnick, S., Bell, A., & Richmond, R. (1996). Effects of brief counselling among heavy drinkers identified on general hospital wards. *Drug & Alcohol Review, 15,* 29–38.

Heather, N., Rollnick, S., & Winton, M. A. (1983). A comparison of objective and subjective measures of alcohol dependence as predictors of relapse following treatment. *British Journal of Clinical Psychology, 22,* 11–17.

Heather, N., Winton, M. A., & Rollnick, S. (1982). An empirical test of "a cultural delusion of alcoholics." *Psychological Reports, 50,* 379–382.

Heatherton, T., Kozlowski, L., Frecker, R., & Fagerstrom, K. (1991). The Fagerstrom Test for Nicotine Dependence: A revision of the Fagerstrom Tolerance Questionnaire. *British Journal of Addiction, 86,* 1119–1127.

Hesselbrock, M. N., & Hesselbrock, V. M. (1999). Alcoholism in adulthood. In P. J. Ott, R. E. Tarter, & R. T. Ammerman (Eds.), *Sourcebook on substance abuse: Etiology, epidemiology, assessment, and treatment* (pp. 98–112). Boston, MA: Allyn and Bacon.

Hubbard, R. L., Craddock, S. J., Flynn, P. M., Anderson, J., & Etheridge, R. M. (1997). Overview of one-year follow-up outcomes in DATOS. *Psychology of Addictive Behaviors, 11,* 261–278.

Hubbard, R. L., Marsden, M. E., Rachal, J. V., Harwood, H. J., Cavanaugh, E. R., & Ginzburg, H. M. (1989). *Drug abuse treatment: A national study of effectiveness.* Chapel Hill, NC: University of North Carolina Press.

Hughes, J. R., Hatsukami, D. K., Mitchell, J. E., & Dahlgren, L. A. (1986). Prevalence of smoking among psychiatric outpatients. *American Journal of Psychiatry, 143,* 993–997.

Humfleet, G., Muñoz, R., Sees, K., Reus, V., & Hall, S. (1999). History of alcohol or drug problems, use of alcohol or marijuana, and success in quitting smoking. *Addictive Behaviors, 24,* 149–154.

Hunter, E. E., Powell, B. J., Penick, E. C., Nickel, E. J., Jiskow, B. I., Cantrell, P. J., & Landon, J. F. (2000). Comorbid psychiatric diagnosis and long-term drinking outcome. *Comprehensive Psychiatry, 41,* 334–338.

Janik, S. W., & Dunham, R. G. (1983). A nationwide examination of the need for specific treatment programs for the elderly. *Journal of Studies on Alcohol, 44,* 307–317.

Joe, G. W., Simpson, D. D., & Broome, K. M. (1998). Effects of readiness for drug abuse treatment on client retention and assessment of process. *Addiction, 93,* 1177–1190.

Jones, B. T., & McMahon, J. (1994). Negative alcohol expectancy predicts post-treatment abstinence survivorship: The whether, when, and why of relapse to a first drink. *Addiction, 89,* 1653–1665.

Kadden, R. M., Litt, M. D., Cooney, N. L., & Busher, D. A. (1992). Relationship between role-play measures of coping skills and alcoholism treatment outcome. *Addictive Behaviors, 17,* 425–437.

Kadden, R. M., Litt, M. D., Cooney, N. L., Kabela, E., & Getter, H. (2001). Prospective matching of alcoholic clients to cognitive-behavioral or interactional group therapy. *Journal of Studies on Alcohol, 62,* 359–369.

Kandel, D. B., & Davies, M. (1986). Adult sequelae of adolescent depressive symptoms. *Archives of General Psychiatry, 43,* 255–262.

Kanzler, H. R., Del Boca, F. K., & Rounsaville, B. J. (1996). Comorbid psychiatric diagnosis predicts three-year outcomes in alcoholics: A post-treatment natural history study. *Journal of Studies on Alcohol, 57,* 619–626.

Kelley, K., Bond, R., & Abraham, C. (2001). Effective approaches to persuading pregnant women to quit smoking: A meta-analysis of intervention evaluation studies. *British Journal of Health Psychology, 6,* 207–228.

Killen, J. D., Fortmann, S. P., Kraemer, H. C., Varady, A., & Newman, B. (1992). Who will relapse? Symptoms of nicotine dependence predict long-term relapse after smoking cessation. *Journal of Consulting and Clinical Psychology, 60,* 797–801.

Lando, A. H., & Gritz, E. R. (1996). Smoking cessation techniques. *Journal of the American Medical Women's Association, 51,* 31–34.

Levinson, T., & McLachlan, J. (1973). Factors relating to outcome in the treatment of alcohol addiction at the Donwood Institute. *Toxicomanies, 6,* 203–221.

Litt, M. D., Kadden, R. M., Cooney, N. L., & Kabela, E. (2003). Coping skills and treatment outcomes in cognitive-behavioral and interactional group therapy for alcoholism. *Journal of Consulting and Clinical Psychology, 71,* 118–128.

Loosen, P. T., Dew, B. W., & Prange, A. J. (1990). Long-term predictors of outcome in abstinent alcoholic men. *American Journal of Psychiatry, 147*, 1662–1666.

Luborsky, L., McLellan, A. T., Woody, G. E., O'Brien, C. P., & Auerbach, A. (1985). Therapist success and its determinants. *Archives of General Psychiatry, 42*, 602–611.

Lynskey, M. T., & Hall, W. (2001). Attention deficit hyperactivity disorder and substance use disorders: Is there a causal link? *Addiction, 96*, 815–822.

Maisto, S. A., Conigliaro, J., McNeil, M., Kraemer, K., Conigliaro, R. L., & Kelley, M. E. (2001). Effects of two types of brief intervention and readiness to change on alcohol use in hazardous drinkers. *Journal of Studies on Alcohol, 62*, 605–614.

McCaul, M. E., Svikis, D. S., & Moore, R. D. (2001). Predictors of outpatient treatment retention: Patient versus substance use characteristics. *Drug & Alcohol Dependence, 62*, 9–17.

McInnes, E., & Powell, J. (1994). Drug and alcohol referrals: Are elderly substance abuse diagnoses and referrals being missed? *British Medical Journal, 308*, 444–446.

McKay, J. R., & Maisto, S. A. (1993). An overview and critique of advances in the treatment of alcohol use disorders. *Drugs & Society, 8*, 1–29.

McLellan, A. T., Luborsky, L., & O'Brien, C. (1986). Alcohol and drug abuse treatment in three different populations: Is there improvement and is it predictable? *American Journal of Drug and Alcohol Abuse, 12*, 101–120.

McLellan, A. T., Luborsky, L., Woody, G. E., O'Brien, C. P., & Druley, K. A. (1983). Predicting response to alcohol and drug treatments: Role of psychiatric severity. *Archives of General Psychiatry, 40*, 620–625.

McLellan, A. T., Woody, G. E., Luborsky, L., & Goehl, L. (1988). Is the counselor an "active ingredient" in substance abuse rehabilitation? An examination of treatment success among four counselors. *Journal of Nervous and Mental Disease, 176*, 423–430.

McNeece, C. A., & DiNitto, D. (1994). *Chemical dependency: A systems approach.* Englewood Cliffs, NJ: Prentice Hall.

Mermelstein, R., & Borrelli, B. (1995). Women and smoking. In A. Stanton & S. Gallant (Eds.), *The psychology of women's health* (pp. 309–348). Washington, DC: American Psychological Association.

Moos, R. H., Brennan, P. L., & Mertens, J. R. (1994). Diagnostic subgroups and predictors of one-year readmission among late-middle-aged and older substance abuse patients. *Journal of Studies on Alcohol, 55*, 173–183.

Moos, R. H., Mertens, J. R., & Brennan, P. L. (1993). Patterns of diagnosis and treatment amount late-middle-aged and older substance abusing patients. *Journal of Studies on Alcohol, 54*, 479–487.

Moos, R. H., Mertens, J. R., & Brennan, P. L. (1994). Rates and predictors of four-year readmission among late-middle-aged and older substance abuse patients. *Journal of Studies on Alcohol, 55*, 561–570.

Morgan, G. D., Noll, E. L., Orleans, T. C., Rimer, B. K., Amfoh, K., & Bonney, G. (1996). Reaching midlife and older smokers: Tailored interventions for routine medical care. *Preventive Medicine, 25*, 346–354.

Mothersill, K. J., McDowell, I., & Rosser, W. (1988). Subject characteristics and long term postprogram smoking cessation. *Addictive Behaviors, 13*, 29–36.

Mueser, K. T., Bellack, A. S., & Blanchard, J. J. (1992). Comorbidity of schizophrenia and substance abuse: Implications for treatment. *Journal of Consulting and Clinical Psychology, 60*, 845–856.

Najavits, L. M., & Weiss, R. D. (1994). Variations in therapist effectiveness in the treatment of patients with substance use disorders: An empirical review. *Addiction, 89*, 679–688.

Nathan, P., & Skinstad, A. (1987). Outcomes for treatment for alcohol problems: Current methods, problems, and results. *Journal of Consulting and Clinical Psychology, 55*, 332–340.

Nides, M. A., Rakos, R. F., Gonzales, D., Murray, R. P., Tashkin, D. P., Bjornson-Benson, W. M., Lindgren, P., & Connett, J. E. (1995). Predictors of initial smoking cessation and relapse through the first 2 years of the Lung Health Study. *Journal of Consulting and Clinical Psychology, 63*, 60–69.

Norcross, J. C. (Ed.). (2002). *Psychotherapy relationships that work: Therapist contributions and responsiveness to patients.* New York: Oxford University Press.

Ockene, J. K., Emmons, K. M., Mermelstein, R. J., Perkins, K. A., Bonollo, D. S., Voorhees, C. C., & Hollis, J. F. (2000). Relapse and maintenance issues for smoking cessation. *Health Psychology, 19*, No. 1 (Suppl.), 17–31.

Ouimette, P. C., Ahrens, C., Moos, R. H., & Finney, J. W. (1997). Posttraumatic stress disorder in substance abuse patients: Relationship to 1-year post-treatment outcomes. *Psychology of Addictive Behaviors, 11*, 34–47.

Patten, C. A., Martin, J. E., Myers, M. G., Calfas, K. J., & Williams, C. D. (1998). Effectiveness of cognitive-behavioral therapy for smokers with histories of alcohol dependence and depression. *Journal of Studies on Alcohol, 59*, 327–335.

Payne, T., Smith, P., McCracken, L., McSherry, W. C., & Antony, M. (1994). Assess nicotine dependence: A comparison of the Fagerstrom Tolerance Questionnaire (FTQ) with the Fagerstrom Test for Nicotine Dependence (FTND) in a clinical sample. *Addictive Behaviors, 19*, 307–317.

Pelletier, J. G., & Moisan, J. T. (1998). Smoking cessation for hospitalized patients: A quasi-experimental study in Quebec. *Canadian Journal of Public Health, 89*, 264–269.

Perez-Stable, E. J., Marin, G., Marin, B. V., & Katz, M. H. (1990). Depressive symptoms and cigarette smoking among Latinos in San Francisco. *American Journal of Public Health, 80*, 1500–1502.

Petry, N. M., Tennen, H., & Affleck, G. (2000). Stalking the elusive client variable in psychotherapy research. In C. R. Snyder & R. E. Ingram (Eds.), *Handbook of psychological change: Psychotherapy processes and practices for the 21st century* (pp. 88–108). New York: John Wiley and Sons, Inc.

Polcin, D. L. (2001). Drug and alcohol offenders coerced into treatment: A review of modalities and suggestions for research on social model programs. *Substance Use and Misuse, 36*, 589–608.

Pomerleau, O., Adkins, D., & Pertschuk, M. (1978). Predictors of outcome and recidivism in smoking cessation treatment. *Addictive Behaviors, 3*, 65–70.

Project MATCH Research Group (1997). Matching alcoholism treatments to client heterogeneity: Project MATCH posttreatment drinking outcomes. *Journal of Studies on Alcohol, 58*, 7–29.

Project MATCH Research Group (1998). Therapist effects in three treatments for alcohol problems. *Psychotherapy Research, 8*, 455–474.

Query, J. N. (1985). Comparative admission and follow up-study of American Indians and Whites in a youth chemical dependency unit on the North Central Plains. *International Journal of the Addictions, 20*, 489–502.

Quinlan, K. B., & McCaul, K. D. (2000). Matched and mismatched interventions with young adult smokers: Testing a stage theory. *Health Psychology, 19*, 165–171.

Regier, D. A., Marmer, M. E., Rae, D. S., Locke, B. Z., Keith, S. J., Judd, L. L., & Goodwin, F. K. (1990). Comorbidity of mental disorders with alcohol and other drug abuse: Results from the Epidemiological Catchment Area (ECA) Study. *Journal of the American Medical Association, 264*, 2511–2518.

Rimer, B. K., Orleans, C. T., Fleisher, L., Cristinzio, S., Resch, N., Telepchak, J., & Keintz, M. K. (1994). Does tailoring matter? The impact of a tailored guide on rating and short-term smoking-related outcomes for older smokers. *Health Education Research, 9*, 69–84.

Rounsaville, B. J., Dolinsky, Z. S., Babor, T. F., & Meyer, R. E. (1987). Psychopathology as a predictor of treatment outcome in alcoholics. *Archives of General Psychiatry, 44*, 505–513.

Ryan, R. M., Plant, R. W., & O'Malley, S. (1995). Initial motivations for alcohol treatment: Relations with patient characteristics, treatment involvement, and dropout. *Addictive Behaviors, 20*, 279–297.

Scholte, R. H. J., & Breteler, M. H. M. (1997). Withdrawal symptoms and previous attempts to quit smoking: Associations with self-efficacy. *Substance Use & Misuse, 32*, 133–148.

Schuckit, M., Smith, T. L., Anthenelli, R., & Irwin, M. (1993). Clinical course of alcoholism in 636 male inpatients. *American Journal of Psychiatry, 150*, 786–792.

Sellman, J. D., & Joyce, P. R. (1996). Does depression predict relapse in the months following treatment for men with alcohol dependence? *Australian and New Zealand Journal of Psychiatry, 30*, 570–578.

Shober, R., & Annis, H. M. (1996). Barriers to help-seeking for change in drinking: A gender-focused review of the literature. *Addictive Behaviors, 21*, 81–92.

Sledge, W. H., Moras, K., Hartley, D., & Levine, M. (1990). Effect of time-limited psychotherapy on patient dropout rates. *American Journal of Psychiatry, 147*, 1341–1347.

Smart, R. (1978). Do some alcoholics do better in some types of treatment than others? *Drug and Alcohol Dependence, 3*, 65–75.

Smith, S. S., Jorenby, D. E., Fiore, M. C., Anderson, J. E., Mielke, M. M., Beach, K. E., Piasecki, T. M., & Baker, T. B. (2001). Strike while the iron is hot: Can stepped-care treatments resurrect relapsing smokers? *Journal of Consulting and Clinical Psychology, 69,* 429–439.

Sterling, R. C., Gottheil, E., Weinstein, S. P., & Serota, R. (2001). The effect of therapist/patient race- and sex-matching in individual treatment. *Addiction, 96,* 1015–1022.

Stuart, K., & Borland, R. (1994). Self-efficacy, health locus of control, and smoking cessation. *Addictive Behaviors, 19,* 1–12.

Sussman, S., Lichtman, K., Ritt, A., & Pallonen, U. (1999). Effects of thirty-four adolescent tobacco use cessation and prevention trials on regular users of tobacco products. *Substance Use & Misuse, 34,* 1469–1503.

Sutton, S. (2001). Back to the drawing board? A review of applications of the transtheoretical model to substance use. *Addiction, 96,* 175–186.

Trull, T. J., Sher, K. J., Minks-Brown, C., Durbin, J., & Burr, R. (2000). Borderline personality disorder and substance use disorders: A review and integration. *Clinical Psychology Review, 20,* 235–253.

U.S. Department of Health and Human Services. (1997). *National Treatment Improvement Evaluation Study (NTIES), Final Report.* Bethesda, MD: U.S. Department of Health and Human Services.

Valliant, G. E., & Milofsky, E. S. (1982). Natural history of male alcoholism. *American Journal of Psychiatry, 39,* 127–133.

Vetter, N. J., & Ford, D. (1990). Smoking prevention among people aged 60 and over: A randomized controlled trial. *Age and Aging, 19,* 164–168.

Westhuis, D. J., Gwaltney, L., & Hayashi, R. (2001). Outpatient cocaine abuse treatment: Predictors of success. *Journal of Drug Education, 31,* 171–183.

Williams, R. J., Chang, S. Y., & Addiction Centre Adolescent Research Group. (2000). A comprehensive and comparative review of adolescent substance abuse treatment outcome. *Clinical Psychology: Science and Practice, 7,* 138–166.

15

Relationship Factors in Treating Substance Use Disorders

Jay Lebow

John Kelly

Lynne M. Knobloch-Fedders

Rudolf Moos

INTRODUCTION

Research assessing treatments for substance use disorders has primarily focused on the impact of treatments on outcome. As in most of the substantive literatures assessing the efficacy of treatments for specific disorders, the links between process and outcome have rarely assumed a central focus. Primarily, the study of the impact of relationship factors on outcome has occurred in the context of research with heterogeneous groupings of clients who manifest a wide array of diagnoses (Norcross, 2002a). Nonetheless, our review points to a number of emerging principles concerned with the importance of relationship factors in influencing client outcomes in treatments of the substance use disorders.

In this chapter, we survey the literatures connecting several types of relationship factors and several specific domains of substance use disorders. Because of the commonalities in the role of relationship factors in substance use and eating disorders, we also include studies that have focused on eating disorders. These are literatures often reviewed without regard to one another. In the research we survey, we include studies examining treatments for alcohol, drug abuse, smoking, and eating related problems. We focus on relationship factors that assess the connection between therapist and client, the connection between family and client, and the connection between peers and client. As in the other chapters in this volume, we limit our scope to treatments of adult clients, excluding the considerable literature on adolescent substance use and eating disorders.

To identify relevant findings, we first examined studies that contributed to the formulation of empirically supported principles of treatment, as compiled in specific reviews of this area (Chambless & Hollon, 1998; Nathan & Gorman, 2002). The primary focus of these reviews was to identify treatments that were empirically associated with beneficial outcomes. In general, the studies covered in these reviews did not focus on the therapist–patient relationship, relationships with family or peers, or on within-treatment therapeutic processes. Accordingly, we extended our net beyond the studies summarized in these reviews. We thought that the quality of relationships could affect the process and outcome of treatments other than those shown to be efficacious in controlled treatment trials. Moreover, relationship factors can influence the process and outcome of nonspecific comparison or "placebo" treatment conditions. Accordingly, we broadened our search for relevant articles.

We searched the literature in PsychINFO™ and Medline™ as well as in the reference lists of relevant articles. We undertook an additional search in a database of more than 5,000 studies on the treatment of alcohol abuse/dependence, and in a further database containing 990 articles on the treatment of other drug abuse/dependence compiled as part of an ongoing effort to examine substance use disorder treatment (e.g., Moyer, Finney, & Swearingen, 2002; Moyer, Finney, Swearingen, & Vergun, 2002), and similar bodies of published research examining smoking and eating disorder. Search terms used included: alliance, therapeutic alliance, therapeutic relationship, working alliance, helping alliance, empathy, self-disclosure, rapport, positive regard, genuineness, couple, and family.

THE THERAPIST–CLIENT RELATIONSHIP

Interest in the idea that the quality of interpersonal relationships can help ameliorate mental illness emerged with the rise of moral treatment and the York Retreat almost 200 years ago (Tuke, 1813). Building on this idea, Freud (1912) thought that some mental disorders could be treated by verbal dialogue within the context of a professional relationship. More recently, Rogers (1957) asserted that the therapist's ability to be empathic, genuine, and accepting of the client was a necessary and sufficient condition for positive personal change. In the last four decades, a large body of research has demonstrated that clients of therapists who are more empathic and genuine, and who experience a supportive bond with the therapist, have better outcomes (Horvath & Symonds, 1991; Martin, Garske, & Davis, 2000; Norcross, 2002b; Truax & Carkhuff, 1967).

Broadly defined, the therapeutic alliance is the collaborative relationship between client and therapist; it reflects their emotional bond, the therapist's empathy for the client, and a shared presumption about the tasks and goals of treatment (Hatcher & Barends, 1996). Other terms, such as "working alliance" and "helping alliance," have also been used to refer to specific aspects of the therapist–client relationship. "Working alliance" focuses on the client's capacity to actively engage in treatment (Greenson, 1965), whereas "helping alliance" refers to the client's experience of the therapeutic relationship and treatment as helpful (Luborsky et al., 1996). Although these conceptual distinctions may be useful, we use the more general term "therapeutic alliance" to reflect this broad domain.

Division 29's Task Force on Empirically Supported Psychotherapy Relationships (Norcross, 2002a) reviewed two decades of empirical research that consistently demonstrates that the quality of the therapeutic alliance between therapist and client affects outcome. The magnitude of this association seems to remain constant across such variables as the type of psychotherapy, whether the outcome is assessed from the perspective of the therapist, client, or outside observer; and when in therapy the alliance is measured (Horvath & Bedi, 2002). However, despite the fact that substance use disorders are the most prevalent DSM-IV (American Psychiatric Association, 1994) Axis I diagnoses, there is a relative lack of information about treatment alliance in the substance use disorders literature. In part, this is because substance use disorders have only recently been accepted as primary or independent conditions. When these disorders are viewed as secondary to other psychopathology, therapeutic attention typically is focused on the presumed underlying problem rather than on the substance use disorder. In addition, because counselors with relatively little formal psychotherapy training often treat substance use disorders, these disorders have not been a primary focus in training programs or standard clinical practice (Miller & Brown, 1997). Most strikingly, the therapeutic alliance has rarely been investigated in the context of intervention for smoking cessation and obesity treatment, possibly because these treatments rely heavily on didactic, self-help, or group intervention formats.

As is the case with other disorders (Luborsky et al., 2002; Wampold et al., 1997), robust differences do not emerge in outcome between seemingly disparate therapeutic ideologies and practices in the substance use disorder field. However, therapists' success rates vary substantially. For example, among opiate-dependent outpatients assigned to supportive-expressive psychotherapy or cognitive-behavioral psychotherapy, variations in outcome among clients of different therapists were larger than variations in outcome between the two treatments (Luborsky, Crits-Christoph, McLellan, et al., 1986). Such findings support the search for common dimensions of different treatments.

Here we review the literature on therapist–client relationship factors in the treatment of substance use disorders, consider the determinants of these factors, examine how these factors influence the process and outcome of treatment, and formulate principles of effective treatment.

We believe that the alliance emerges from the interaction between the therapist and client, and is not due primarily to individual characteristics of either person. For example, therapists may vary widely in their empathy depending on the client with whom they are working, and clients may vary widely in their problem expression depending on the therapist with whom they are working (Moos & MacIntosh, 1970). Because of these interactional factors, the quality of the therapist–patient relationship could affect the process and outcome of treatments in ways that are not readily apparent in research that does not attend to such interactions of client and therapist.

Assessing the Therapist–Client Relationship

Studies in this area have used diverse measures of therapist empathy and helping alliance, including mainly (1) the Barrett-Lennard Relationship Inventory (BLRI; Barrett-Lennard, 1962), which measures aspects of interpersonal behavior that reflect Rogers's (1957) ideas about the conditions necessary for therapeutic change; (2) the Helping Alliance Questionnaire, which is part of the Penn Helping Alliance Scales (HAQ; Alexander & Luborsky, 1986; Luborsky et al., 1996); (3) the Working Alliance Inventory (WAI; Horvath & Greenberg, 1989); (4) the California Psychother-

apy Alliance Scale (CALPAS; Gaston & Marmar, 1994); and (5) the Vanderbilt Therapeutic Alliance Scale (VTAS; Hartley & Strupp, 1983).

The original HAQ was composed of 11 items rated on four-point scales varying from completely disagree, disagree, agree, to completely agree. It measured perceived helpfulness, or the patient's experience that the therapist is helpful (e.g., "I believe that my therapist is helping me"), and collaboration or bonding, or the patient's experience of working jointly with the therapist toward treatment goals (e.g., "I feel that I am working together with the therapist in a joint effort").

The revised HAQ-II is composed of 19 items rated on 6-point Likert scales (varying from "strongly not true" to "strongly true") that are summed to create a total alliance score. Patients and therapists complete parallel versions of the measure. Internal consistency and stability of the HAQ-II are moderate to high and there is good convergent validity with the CALPAS. Agreement between patients' and therapists' assessments of the therapeutic relationship varies from low-moderate to relatively high (Belding et al., 1997; Luborsky et al., 1996; Petry & Bickel, 1999).

The WAI is composed of 36-items rated on 7-point Likert scales (varying from never to always) that tap three dimensions reflecting the goals and tasks of therapy, and the bond between the patient and therapist. The WAI has parallel forms for the patient's and the therapist's ratings, and has well-established internal consistency, interrater reliability, and construct validity (Horvath & Greenberg, 1989; Safran & Wallner, 1991; Tracey & Kokotovic, 1989). The three WAI subscales tend to be highly correlated and, thus, the overall score is typically used to measure one general alliance dimension (Connors et al., 2000).

The CALPAS consists of 24 items grouped into four subscales that tap the patients' commitment to treatment and ability to explore problems in treatment, patient–therapist agreement on treatment procedures and goals, and therapist involvement and understanding. The CALPAS can be completed by the therapist or the patient and has high internal consistency (Gaston & Marmar, 1994; Luborsky et al., 1996; Marmar et al., 1989).

The VTAS is composed of 18 items that tap the therapist's contributions to the alliance, 14 items that assess the patient's contributions, and

12 items that focus on patient–therapist interactions or mutuality. The VTAS items are rated from interview transcripts or videotapes and interrater reliability and internal consistency of the Scale is moderate to high (Hartley & Strupp, 1983). There also is the Vanderbilt Negative Indicators Scale (VNIS), which focuses on aspects of the therapist–client relationship that could lead to negative consequences of treatment.

Other measures used to assess alliance in substance use disorder treatment include the Client Evaluation of the Counselor Form, which is composed of ten 5-point scale items on which clients rate their counselor on rapport, trust, and expertness. The items are summed to yield an overall score that reflects counselor respect (Simpson, Joe, Rowan-Szal, & Greener, 1995). There also is the Counselor Evaluation of Client Form, on which counselors rate their client on rapport, motivation, and self-confidence (Simpson et al., 1995). Finally, one study used the Client Experiences and Satisfaction Questionnaire, on which clients assess their relationship with a counselor and how well the counselor treated and understood them (Hyams, Cartwright, & Sprately, 1996).

Treatment Alliance and Treatment Engagement

Studies in this area have focused on the helping relationship established in the first assessment interview and subsequent treatment entry, as well as on the links between the treatment alliance and how long patients remain in treatment and whether or not they complete treatment.

1. When a stronger helping relationship is established at the initial intake or assessment interview, the patient is more likely to enter treatment.

Empirical evidence that clients with substance use disorders may respond positively to a counselor's respect and understanding was first obtained more than 40 years ago. In an initial study, Chafetz and his colleagues (1962) showed that treating alcoholic patients with respect and interest led to improved treatment attendance. In a follow-up study, emergency room physicians who were responsible for referring alcoholic individuals to treatment were asked to describe their experiences with these patients. Physicians who were judged to be more anxious and less angry were more successful in referring alcoholic patients for specialty treatment; that is, the patients they saw were more likely to make and keep at least one appointment for alcoholism treatment. Anxiety on the part of the physician was thought to communicate greater concern for the patient, whereas anger likely resulted in the patient experiencing rejection (Milmoe, Rosenthal, Blane et al., 1967).

When a client applies for treatment, the quality of the intake assessment interview may be especially important. In a study of alcohol treatment, Hyams et al. (1996) asked clients to use the Client Experiences and Satisfaction Questionnaire to describe the quality of the relationship a counselor established with them during an initial intake interview. Clients who felt more at ease with their counselor, and who felt that their counselor liked and understood them and was warm and friendly toward them, were more likely to subsequently engage in treatment. In contrast, clients who felt that their counselor lacked genuineness, criticized and looked down on them, or withheld information from them, were less likely to engage in treatment.

2. When a stronger alliance is established, the client is likely to remain in treatment longer and to complete the treatment episode.

In their studies of clients with drug use disorders, Simpson and colleagues noted that a stronger treatment alliance was associated with enhanced attendance in the first two months of treatment, which was associated with a stronger subsequent treatment alliance (Joe, Simpson, Greener, & Rowan-Szal, 1999). Counselors' ratings of a good alliance in the first two months of treatment, and clients' treatment attendance in the first two months, predicted the length of treatment (Simpson, Joe, Rowan-Szal, & Greener, 1997). Moreover, counselors' ratings of clients' motivation early in treatment predicted which clients remained in treatment for one year or more (Simpson, Joe, & Rowan-Szal, 1997).

In another sample of clients with substance use disorders, higher HAQ Cooperation subscale scores were associated with a greater likelihood of completing detoxification. In addition, clients who were contemplating leaving treatment scored lower on cooperation than clients who were not contemplating leaving (De Weert-Van Oene, Jorg, & Schrijvers, 1999). Among couples in conjoint alcoholism treatment, a stronger treatment alliance, as measured by the VTAS and VNIS, was associated with greater session attendance and treatment completion (Raytek, Epstein, & Hirsch, 1999).

The association between alliance and treatment retention may be stronger for clients entering a new treatment episode. In Project MATCH, WAI total scores from both the therapist and the client were positively related to the duration of treatment among outpatients, even after controlling for client and therapist characteristics, client drinking history, treatment site, and treatment modality. However, neither the client's nor the therapist's WAI total scores were associated with treatment participation among aftercare clients (Connors, DiClemente, Longabaugh, & Donovan, 1997). The treatment alliance may be less salient for patients who have just completed a prior treatment episode, as was true for the aftercare patients, than for patients who are entering a new treatment episode, as was the case for the outpatients.

The strength of the association between alliance and retention may also depend on client characteristics. In a study of opioid-dependent clients, therapists' ratings of the treatment alliance on the HAQ-II after three or more sessions was associated with treatment completion for clients with moderate to severe psychiatric problems; this relationship did not hold for those with few psychiatric symptoms. More than 75% of clients who developed a strong alliance completed treatment, whereas this was true of less than 25% of clients who developed a weak alliance (Petry & Bickel, 1999). These findings are consistent with the idea that clients who have more severe problems, are in more distress, and/or have fewer social resources, may be more dependent on the therapist and thus remain in treatment longer.

Treatment Alliance and Proximal During-treatment Outcomes

Studies in this area have considered the associations between treatment alliance, patients' mood and distress, patients' use of substances while in treatment, and the extent to which patients actively explore their problems during treatment.

3. When a stronger alliance is established, the client is more likely to explore problems in treatment. When the therapist is more confrontational, the client is more likely to show negative in-treatment behavior.

There is a relationship between the therapist's verbal behavior and the patient's immediate responses in the treatment session. Counselors who listen and offer restructuring comments are likely to elicit positive and on-task comments; in contrast, those who are more confrontational (that is, who disagree with clients and openly challenge their motivations and substance use) are more likely to elicit argumentative and negative behavior, interruptions, and off-task comments (Miller, Benefield, & Tonigan, 1993). Client–therapist cooperation, as measured by the HAQ, is positively associated with clients' work in treatment to resolve their problems (De Weert-Van Oene et al., 1999).

As part of the Drug Abuse Treatment Outcome Study (DATOS), more than 2,500 clients were studied in long-term residential treatment, outpatient drug-free treatment, or outpatient methadone treatment. In each of these three treatment modalities, clients' ratings of rapport with their counselors were positively associated with clients' reports of their confidence in and commitment to treatment (Broome, Simpson, & Joe, 1999).

4. When a stronger alliance is established, the client tends to experience less distress and more pleasant mood during treatment.

In a sample of cocaine-dependent outpatients, clients' ratings of treatment alliance at the second and fifth treatment sessions predicted lower distress one month after treatment entry and lower depression after one month and six months. Therapists' ratings of a stronger alliance at the second and fifth sessions were associated with less client distress and depression at six months. However, the connection between fifth-session treatment alliance and one-month outcome was not due to early symptomatic improvement (Barber et al., 1999).

Ojehagen, Berglund, and Hansson (1997) found a positive relationship between client–therapist alliance, as rated by independent observers from tape recordings of the third session of multimodal behavior therapy, and clients' pleasant mood, extroversion, and control after six months of treatment. This relationship did not exist for clients in psychodynamic treatment, perhaps because this treatment modality places less emphasis on clients' immediate affect. In a study of alcoholic clients, De Weert-Van Oene et al. (1999) identified a strong positive association between the helping relationship and clients' improved mood.

> 5. When the therapist establishes a stronger alliance with the patient, the patient is more likely to abstain from alcohol and drugs during treatment and show more improvement in patterns of use of other substances.

In Project MATCH, among outpatients with alcohol use disorders, WAI total scores, whether provided by the client or the therapist, predicted a higher percentage of days abstinent and fewer drinks per drinking day during treatment. In contrast, among aftercare clients, only therapists' WAI scores were associated with a higher percentage of abstinent days (Connors et al., 1997). The weaker association in the aftercare sample may reflect the fact that these clients had 90% abstinence days one month after treatment (Project MATCH Research Group, 1997).

Among clients in drug treatment, counselors' ratings of the therapeutic alliance were associated with less drug use during treatment, which, in turn, was related to better long-term treatment retention (Simpson, Joe, Rowan-Szal, & Greener, 1997). Counselors' ratings of the alliance were also associated with less cocaine use at 3-month and 6-month follow-ups, at which time many of the clients remained in treatment (Joe, Simpson, Greener, & Rowan-Szal, 1999).

Among clients in methadone maintenance, HAQ-II alliance scores after three months of treatment, as rated by the client or the therapist, were associated with lower Addiction Severity Index (ASI) drug use composite scores and a higher likelihood of drug-free urine specimens at three and six months of treatment. Clients who reported less drug use and had more drug-free urine specimens during the 30 days prior to the 3-month HAQ assessment rated the helping alliance more positively. This suggests a positive feedback loop in which a client's early treatment progress enhances the alliance, which, in turn, enhances subsequent in-treatment outcome (Belding et al., 1997). In a study of methadone detoxification, clients' CALPAS ratings of the treatment alliance were associated with reduced use of illicit opioids and less needle sharing (Tunis, Delucchi, Schwartz, Banys, & Sees, 1995).

Four observer-rated alliance measures (the Penn Helping Alliance Rating Scale, the CALPAS, the VTAS, and the WAI) were used in a randomized trial comparing cognitive-behavioral treatment and 12-step facilitation treatment for individuals with co-morbid cocaine and alcohol use disorders. Clients and therapists also used the WAI to rate the helping alliance after the third treatment session. The four observer ratings of alliance were moderately to strongly correlated, and all four were correlated with consecutive days abstinent from cocaine while in treatment. However, neither the clients' nor the therapists' perceptions of the alliance were associated with this outcome (Fenton, Nich, Frankforter, & Carroll, 2001).

In a study of cocaine-dependent patients in a controlled treatment trial, patients in a usual care or clinical management condition who developed a stronger treatment alliance by the second session of treatment, as rated by observers on the VTAS, reported more days of abstinence from drugs and had more drug-free urine screens (Carroll, Nich, & Rounsaville, 1997). In general, these findings held for all three of the VTAS subscales and for the VTAS total score. Among patients in the cognitive-behavioral arm of the trial, however, there were no associations between treatment alliance and these outcomes (Carroll et al., 1997). A positive alliance may have a stronger influence on outcomes in treatments in which the active ingredients are common factors as compared with

treatments that include more specific active ingredients, such as cognitive-behavioral therapy.

Treatment Alliance and Longer
Term Outcome

Research investigating the association between
treatment alliance and posttreatment functioning
have focused on several outcome variables, including symptom reduction, level of substance use, and
employment functioning.

6. When the therapist establishes a stronger
   alliance with the client, the client tends to
   experience better outcomes related to substance use.

Both counselor and client ratings of the therapeutic relationship have been associated with treatment outcomes among clients with drug use disorders. In two cohorts, counselors rated their
rapport with the client, as reflected in their ratings
of the client as easier to talk to, warm, caring, honest, and sincere. These ratings, which were averaged over several occasions during the first year of
treatment, were associated with a lower likelihood
of using drugs, of being illegally involved with
drugs, and of having been arrested at 12- and 18-
month follow-ups (Joe, Simpson, Dansereau, &
Rowan-Szal, 2001). In addition, clients' retrospective ratings of their respect for the counselor were
associated with better attendance in the first two
months of treatment, which predicted a longer duration of treatment, and, in turn, was associated
with better 12-month drug use and criminal activity outcomes (Simpson, Joe, Greener, & Rowan-
Szal, 2000).

Among drug-dependent patients in methadone
treatment, Luborsky and his colleagues (1985)
identified strong associations between patients'
HAQ ratings of the helping alliance after the third
treatment session and patients' 7-month treatment
outcomes. Specifically, patients who established a
stronger alliance experienced better drug use, legal, psychological, and employment outcomes.

Based on counselors' written responses about
how they would handle specific client situations,
Valle (1981) asked observers to rate counselors'
interpersonal functioning with respect to empathy,
genuineness, respect, and specificity and directness

in expressing feelings. Clients whose counselors
were higher in interpersonal functioning were less
likely to relapse, had fewer relapses, and were less
likely to use alcohol during the two years after
treatment. Conversely, Miller et al. (1993) found
that clients of therapists who were more confrontational tended to consume more alcohol at a 12-
month follow-up.

In the Project MATCH outpatient sample,
WAI scores, whether provided by the patient or
the therapist, were associated with a higher percentage of days abstinent and fewer drinks per
drinking day at the 12-month follow-up. In the
aftercare sample, only therapists' WAI scores were
associated with a higher percentage of days abstinent at the 12-month follow-up (Connors et al.,
1997). As noted earlier, the weaker findings among
the aftercare patients may reflect the fact that they
had just completed an intensive course of alcoholism treatment.

In an examination of the effectiveness of
cognitive-behavioral treatment for substance use
disorders in a community setting, treatment alliance was measured by asking the patient to complete the HAQ at the end of treatment and having
an observer complete the Bond Subscale of the
WAI on the basis of the patient–therapist relationship in the second session. Stronger treatment alliance, as judged by either of these measures, was
associated with a higher likelihood of abstinence
and fewer negative consequences of substance use
at a nine-month follow-up (Morgenstern, Blanchard, Morgan, Labouvie, & Hayaki, 2001).

Therapeutic alliance also seems to predict posttreatment outcome for bulimia nervosa. Wilson et
al. (1999) found that a greater overall treatment
alliance predicted symptom remission of women
with bulimia, although their subsequent temporal
analysis of the pattern of change suggested "it was
prior symptom change that more consistently influenced client ratings of the therapeutic alliance
than vice versa" (p. 458).

In another bulimia treatment study, which
compared motivation enhancement therapy with
cognitive behavioral therapy, clients' ratings of
agreement with the therapist on the goals and tasks
of the therapeutic alliance, as measured by the
WAI, predicted reduced binge eating and vomiting
(Treasure et al., 1999). The authors hypothesized
that clients' readiness to change influences both

the clients' ability to develop a therapeutic alliance and treatment outcome.

A few studies have failed to show a relationship between treatment alliance and posttreatment outcomes for drug and alcohol use (Barber, Luborsky, et al., 2001; Long, Midgley, & Hollin, 2000; Ojehagen et al., 1997; Raytek et al., 1999) or in the treatment of bulimia nervosa (Wilson, Fairburn, Agras, Walsh, & Kraemer, 2002). We were not able to find reasons for these discrepant findings in the study or analytic design, therapeutic alliance measure used, method of measurement (i.e., self-report vs. observer rating), or cohort demographics. Future research is needed to specify the conditions under which alliance is or is not related to longer term substance use and eating disorder outcomes.

   7. A strong treatment alliance may have an especially beneficial influence on specific subgroups of patients, such as those who have an antisocial personality or have high levels of anger.

Patients with substance use disorders who also have an Antisocial Personality Disorder may find it especially difficult to establish interpersonal relationships. Accordingly, when such patients do establish a working alliance in treatment, they may experience better outcome. This idea was supported in a study of patients who had both substance use and personality disorders and were seen for 24 weeks of treatment and evaluated at a 7-month follow-up. The patient's perception of the treatment alliance, as measured by the HAQ after the third treatment session, was associated with better 7-month drug and employment outcomes, and the therapist's perception was associated with better employment outcomes (Gerstley et al., 1989).

In the sample of outpatients drawn from Project MATCH, those who were high in anger fared better on both 1-year and 3-year outcomes after being treated with Motivational Enhancement Therapy (MET) than after either cognitive-behavioral or 12-step facilitation treatment. Among clients who were high in anger, those treated in MET had an average of 76% abstinent days, whereas their counterparts in the other two treatments averaged 66% abstinent days. Conversely, clients low in anger performed better after cognitive-behavioral or 12-step facilitation treatment than after treatment in MET (Project MATCH Research Group, 1998). These findings imply that therapist empathy and the specific therapist behaviors prevalent in MET, such as not confronting resistance directly and avoiding argumentation, may have led to enhanced treatment alliance, engagement, and positive change.

Other Relational Variables in Psychotherapy

Therapist–client relational variables other than the therapeutic alliance influence psychotherapy process and outcome. The American Psychological Association's Division of Psychotherapy's Task Force on Empirically Supported Therapy Relationships (Norcross, 2002a) identified a set of relationship variables that has been shown to have an impact, and a second set that is promising. We review these variables and some relevant findings here. These variables seem likely to be important in the treatment of patients with substance use disorders, but only a few of these variables have been sufficiently studied in this context to derive specific principles of change based on them.

The Task Force lists empathy, goal consensus and collaboration, and cohesion in group therapy as important aspects of the therapy relationship that have a clear impact on treatment. According to a recent meta-analysis, *Empathy*, or clients' and observers' perceptions that therapists understand their clients' internal experiences, accounts for 10% of the variance in treatment outcome (Bohart, Elliott, Greenberg & Watson, 2002). *Goal consensus and collaboration*, including agreement on therapeutic goals, patient cooperation, active patient involvement, homework compliance, and cooperation and affiliation between therapist and patient, also clearly enhances psychotherapy outcome (Tryon & Winograd, 2002). *Cohesion in group psychotherapy*, which is facilitated by pregroup preparation, early group structure, leader interaction, feedback, leader modeling, and participant emotional expression, is similarly associated with positive patient outcome in group therapy (Burlingame, Fuhriman & Johnson, 2002).

The Task Force points to several other relationship factors that may be associated with outcome.

Positive regard, which appears to facilitate a long-term working relationship, is associated with enhanced treatment outcome when patients' perspectives on outcome are highlighted (Farber & Lane, 2002). *Congruence or genuineness* predicted positive psychotherapy outcome in 34% (26 out of 77) of studies, while 66% (51 out of 77) produced null results (Klein, Kolden, Michels, & Chisholm-Stockard, 2002). While *feedback* has not been heavily studied, existing research has found a generally positive effect on outcome (Claiborn, Goodyear & Horner, 2002).

Research on the *repair of alliance ruptures*, although in an early stage of development, suggests that specific processes such as patient expression of negative feelings or therapists' nondefensive behavior are associated with improved alliance and treatment outcome (Safran, Muran, Samstag & Stevens, 2002). *Therapist self-disclosure* appears helpful to patients in the immediate process of psychotherapy (Hill & Knox, 2002). *Management of countertransference*, which includes such factors as self-insight, self-integration, anxiety management, empathy, and conceptualizing ability, facilitates treatment, whereas countertransference acting out hinders treatment (Gelso & Hayes, 2002). Finally, greater *quality of relational interpretations* is associated with more positive treatment outcome, especially when therapists accurately address central aspects of patients' interpersonal dynamics (Crits-Christoph & Gibbons, 2002).

In the context of substance use disorders, there is very little research on relational elements of the therapy process other than the therapeutic alliance. The major exception lies in the research concerned with the relationship variables identified by Rogers: therapist empathy, positive regard, and congruence. Several of the studies we have already considered in the context of discussing the research concerned with the therapeutic alliance also confirm the importance of these variables for process and outcome in the context of substance use disorders (e.g. Chafetz et al., 1962; Hyams et al., 1996; Miller et al., 1993; Milmoe et al., 1967; Valle, 1981). These studies suggest the following principle:

8. Therapist empathy, positive regard, and congruence have a positive impact on therapy process and on client outcomes in therapy for substance use disorders.

Despite the paucity of research to date on many of the variables identified by the Division 29 Task Force in the context of substance use disorders, we predict that the conclusions reached by the Division 29 Task Force on the importance of these variables in other psychotherapy research contexts are likely to hold for substance use disorder treatment. Yet, we also believe that it is especially important to document the impact of these variables in the context of substance use disorders. Because many clients with substance use disorders seek treatment due to external factors such as pressures from family, employers, or the judicial system, these aspects of the therapist–client relationship may have a different degree of influence on them than on other groups of more highly motivated patients.

The Broader Context of Treatment

Many clients with substance use disorders are seen in residential and group treatment; in fact, the therapeutic community is a primary modality of treatment for drug abuse (De Leon, 1997; Jones, 1953). The concept of "community as doctor" (Rapoport, 1960) asserts that relationships with treatment peers and staff members are key aspects of the healing process. A substantial body of literature demonstrates that better interpersonal relationships in residential treatment programs are associated with more favorable in-program and post-program outcome for clients with a variety of diagnoses (Moos, 1997).

9. When treatment programs create a stronger alliance with patients (that is, are involving, supportive, and expressive), patients are more likely to remain in treatment and to have better in-program outcomes.

Indices of client involvement, support, and expressiveness in residential treatment programs tap a construct that is comparable to the therapist–client alliance. With respect to in-treatment outcomes, when programs are more involving and supportive, clients tend to be more satisfied with treatment, show more self-confidence and less ag-gressive behavior, are more affiliative and self-revealing, and engage in more activity and social interaction. They are also less likely to drop out of treatment (Moos, 1997).

Among clients with alcohol use disorders, those who rated a Salvation Army treatment program as more involving and supportive were less likely to drop out (Moos, Mehren, & Moos, 1978). Accord-ing to Linn (1978), older alcoholic clients who perceived more program involvement and sup-port were less likely to leave the program prema-turely. In addition, Linn and her colleagues (1979) found that African-American clients with drug-dependence disorders who saw their program as more expressive were more likely to remain in treatment. However, these findings did not hold for younger clients or for Caucasian clients, sug-gesting that relationship quality may be especially important for clients who are members of minority groups, such as older clients and African-American clients.

The quality of the treatment alliance also seems to influence treatment engagement for women treated for eating disorders in residential programs. For example, Gallop, Kennedy, and Stern (1994) found that clients who remained in a residential treatment program perceived their therapeutic al-liance with staff to be significantly stronger than clients who left the program; in addition, clients who remained in treatment reported their thera-peutic alliance became stronger over time.

10. When treatment programs create a stronger alliance with patients (that is, are involving, supportive, and expressive), pa-tients are likely to have more positive dis-charge and post-program outcomes.

Alcohol use disorder clients' perceptions of sup-port in hospital-based programs are associated with better discharge outcomes—fewer psycho-logical symptoms, less positive expectations for substance use, more positive expectations for quit-ting, and more reliance on approach coping (Le-mke & Moos, 2002; Ouimette, Ahrens, Moos, & Finney, 1998). Perceived closeness to peers in treatment is associated with longer treatment length and reduced relapse rates (Machell, 1987). In community-based programs, clients who estab-lish more supportive relationships with other cli-ents are more likely to complete the program, to have a stable residence and be employed at dis-charge, and to instill staff members' confidence that they will recover (Moos & King, 1997).

When post-program outcomes are considered, clients with alcohol use disorders who rated their program more positively overall (including higher involvement, support, and expressiveness) con-sumed less alcohol and had fewer drinking prob-lems at a six-month follow-up (Moos, Finney, & Cronkite, 1990). Impressively, clients who ap-praised their program more positively consumed less alcohol and had fewer physical symptoms and less depression 10 years later (Finney & Moos, 1992). In another study, alcoholic clients' per-ceived treatment involvement was associated with better outcome one year after treatment (Long, Williams, Midgley, & Hollin, 2000). Although the precise mechanisms remain to be determined, cli-ents' perceptions of their treatment programs may provide important information about their inte-gration into the program; additionally, they may provide evidence about their characteristic ways of adapting to new social contexts that predict long-term functioning.

THE ROLE OF THE CLIENT'S RELATIONSHIPS WITH FAMILY AND PEERS

In the treatment of substance use disorders, the relationship between client and therapist is only one of the relationships that assume importance as factors affecting treatment process and outcome. The relationships that clients have with their fam-ilies, their relationships with peers in treatment, and the relationships of family and friends to treat-ment also exert considerable influence on client outcomes.

11. Clients who indicate they receive general social support and support for reduced substance use during the time of treatment experience better treatment outcomes.

As Westerberg (1998) notes, social support can function in two different ways—either as a posi-tive outcome factor (when the client's social network offers support for reduced substance use) or as a negative outcome factor (when the client's social network itself abuses substances or is not supportive of reduced substance use). Considerable evidence exists for the importance of social support in enhancing client outcomes for each of the substance use disorders, and research has also linked poor social support with poorer long-term outcomes (Breteler, Van Den Hurk, Schippers, & Meerkerk, 1996).

Examining the outcomes of treatments for different substance use disorders, McLellan et al. (1997) found high social support to be an important predictor of better outcome among 649 clients in opiate, cocaine, and alcohol treatments. Clients reporting more severe family problems at admission also had poorer social adjustment at follow-up.

In the context of Project MATCH, clients in alcohol treatment who received more social support, or had more abstainers or recovering alcoholics in their social networks, had better outcomes (Zywiak, Longabaugh, & Wirtz, 2002).

In another study of alcohol treatment, Booth, Russell, Soucek, and Laughlin (1992) showed that higher levels of reassurance from family and friends were associated with increased time to readmission. In the context of treatment of drug use disorders, couple factors, such as the partner's poor coping strategy for dealing with their partner's drug problem (Barber, 1995) and negative communication within the marriage (Fals-Stewart & Birchler, 1998) have also been associated with more frequent posttreatment drug use.

In the context of smoking cessation, Collins, Emont, and Zywiak (1990) found clients who reported more support and fewer hindrances from friends just after stopping smoking were less likely to return to smoking three months and six months after quitting. Similarly, Morgan, Ashenberg, and Fisher (1988) found at 2, 3, and 8 weeks following cessation from smoking, participants reported the frequencies of specific behaviors from their spouses, families, and friends were significantly related to outcome at 13-weeks post-cessation. Compared with recidivists, abstainers reported their friends exhibited more helping behaviors, and less prompting of or modeling of smoking, throughout the maintenance period. In an investigation of short- and long-term relapse rates, so-

cial support for quitting smoking was the only variable that predicted both initial and sustained quitting up to 24 months after treatment ended (Nides et al., 1995).

Hanson, Issacsson, Janzon, and Liddle (1990) found that emotional support was particularly associated with successful long-term abstinence from smoking in elderly men, while the presence of a smoking spouse increased the rate of relapse. Lichtenstein, Glasgow, and Abrams (1986), in a series of studies with three different samples, also linked greater social support to better outcomes.

12. Clients who are part of non-substance-abusing networks have better outcomes.

In Project MATCH, clients whose social networks included more abstainers or recovering alcoholics showed better outcomes (Zywiak et al., 2002). Furthermore, clients' support networks differentially influenced the efficacy of the various treatment forms: clients who reported more drinking among people in their social networks did better in 12-step Facilitation than in Motivational Enhancement Therapy.

Curry, Thompson, Sexton, and Omenn (1989) found similar patterns in smoking cessation: those who achieve long-term abstinence from smoking report a fewer number of smokers in their environments.

13. Spouse and family involvement in treatment may help engage the client in treatment; the effects are particularly pronounced when that client is not initially ready to participate in treatment.

In their review of family-based treatment methods for alcoholism, Edwards and Steinglass (1995) conclude that involving spouses and family in treatment increases the rate of client engagement in therapy, particularly for those individuals with alcohol use problems who are not ready to engage in therapy. A more recent review by O'Farrell and Fals-Stewart (2002) reaches similar conclusions.

Several studies have examined methods for helping the alcoholic's family engage the alcoholic in treatment. In a pilot study of their Community Intervention Training method, which includes coaching spouses in methods for reinforcing sobriety and in how to help the alcoholic engage in treatment, Sisson and Azrin (1986) found 86% of alcoholics engaged in treatment as compared to none in a more traditional program. In a randomized clinical trial, Miller, Meyers, and Tonigan (1999) compared three manual-guided treatment approaches aimed at helping concerned significant others engage unmotivated problem drinkers in treatment. Follow-up analyses indicated that the community reinforcement and family training approach (CRAFT) was more successful at engaging problem drinkers in treatment (64%) compared to traditional Al-Anon (13%) (which does not have a goal of engaging the problem drinker in treatment) and an alternative strategy developed at the Johnson Institute for training family in how to hold a highly confrontational meeting with the person with the substance use problem aimed at having that person engage in treatment (30%).

In another pilot study evaluating a low confrontation method called "Unilateral Family Therapy"—which only utilizes meetings with the family of the alcoholic—Thomas, Santa, Bronson, and Osterman (1987) found 61% of the alcoholics whose spouses participated in treatment either subsequently engaged in treatment or reduced their drinking. In a larger follow-up study, Thomas, Yoshioka, Ager, and Adams (1990) found that individuals whose spouses participated in Unilateral Family Therapy entered therapy more often than those whose spouses did not participate.

Examining the more dramatic "Intervention" method of the Johnson Institute described above in a pilot study, Liepman, Nirenberg, and Begin (1989) trained 24 families in strategies for confronting the alcoholic. Six of the seven families who went on to conduct the "intervention" succeeded in engaging the alcoholic in treatment. However, only 7 of the original 24 families actually went on to hold an intervention meeting with the problem drinker. A similar pattern of findings emerges for this method in the Miller et al. study (1999) reviewed above; although the "intervention" sessions were effective in engaging the substance abuser in treatment when held; few of those receiving the preparation for these meetings went on to actually hold an intervention session. Thus, on the whole the Johnson Institute method appears to only result in the engagement of a small percentage of problem drinkers in treatment.

In another clinical trial, Dakof et al. (in press) found a family-based manualized in-home drug treatment, called "Engaging Moms," resulted in greater enrollment in drug treatment than a control condition (86% vs. 46%) for women with substance use disorders.

Outside the realm of this review, but striking in their impact, are exceptional rates of engagement in therapy for adolescents with substance use disorders through methods of assertive family engagement. Szapocznik et al. (1988), Santisteban et al. (1996), Donohue et al. (1998), Waldron, Slesnick, Brody, Turner, and Peterson (2001) and Henggeler, Pickrel, Brondino, and Crouch (1996) have all reported high rates of treatment engagement and completion utilizing these methods compared to the typical rates in individual treatment for adolescents with these disorders.

14. Spouse and family involvement in treatment may help produce better outcomes.

O'Farrell and Fals-Stewart (2002) and O'Farrell and Feehan (1999), in summarizing the literature on spousal involvement in the treatment of alcohol use disorders, conclude that involvement of spouses in treatment has been associated with improved family functioning in a variety of domains, including reduced family stressors; improved marital adjustment; reduced domestic violence and verbal conflict; reduced risk of separation and divorce; improvement in important family processes related to cohesion, conflict, and caring; reduced emotional distress in spouses; and reductions in drinking and recidivism.

Several methods that have included spouse involvement have produced superior outcomes in the treatment of alcohol use disorders compared to more traditional individual treatments. The Counseling for Alcoholics Marriage Project (CALM) has developed relationship focused interventions with couples that have proved efficacious in several randomized trials (O'Farrell and Fals-Stewart, 2002). For example, in a comparison of Behavioral Marital Therapy (BMT) with individual alcoholism counseling, O'Farrell et al. (1993) found BMT produced better marital and alcohol use outcomes during and immediately after treatment than individual counseling alone. Fals-Stewart, Birchler, and O'Farrell (1996) found that married or cohabiting men with substance use disorders who participated in behavioral couples therapy in addition to individual-based treatment had fewer days of substance use and, along with their partners, reported higher levels of dyadic adjustment during and one year after treatment than men who received the individual intervention. Compared to the individually treated clients, men in the couple therapy showed significant reductions in substance use, and couples showed greater improvement in dyadic adjustment (Fals-Stewart et al., 2000).

Kelley and Fals-Stewart (2002) found Behavioral Couples Therapy (BCT) produced greater reductions in substance use and more gains in relationship adjustment than did individually based treatment or a psychoeducation control group. In yet another study, O'Farrell and Birchler (2001) found both BCT and a brief BCT were more effective in reducing substance use and increasing relationship satisfaction than individual therapy or a psychoeducational placebo control.

McCrady et al. (1986) compared treatment effects for individuals with alcohol use disorders and their spouses among three outpatient behavioral treatment conditions: minimal spouse involvement, alcohol-focused spouse involvement, or alcohol-focused spouse involvement plus behavioral marital therapy. At follow-up, all clients markedly decreased their drinking and reported increased life satisfaction. Clients receiving marital therapy were more compliant than those receiving only the alcohol-focused spouse involvement, were more likely to stay in treatment, decreased their drinking more quickly in treatment, relapsed more slowly after treatment, and maintained better marital satisfaction.

Although there now are many studies documenting the efficacy of family approaches to adolescent substance abuse (Liddle & Dakof, 1995; Rowe & Liddle, 2002), limited research exists on family involvement in the treatment of adults with drug use disorders other than those focused on alcohol. In an early study of opiate-dependent clients, Stanton and Todd (1979) found structural-strategic family therapy more effective than standard drug counseling. Galanter (1993) found a network approach for treating substance abuse that involved family and peer support was effective for 45 of 60 clients.

Some research has shown less pronounced effects for couple and family intervention, particularly with long-term follow-up. McCrady, Longabaugh, Noel, and Beattie (1987) compared treatments offered to alcohol-misusing clients seen alone, clients seen with family, and clients seen with co-workers. Family involvement proved no more effective than the individual treatment, although a trend existed for those receiving the family intervention to respond more quickly to treatment. McCrady, Paolino, Longabaugh, and Rossi (1979) found higher initial rates of abstinence in couple treatment than individual treatment for alcohol use disorder than for individual treatment, but the differences were not statistically significant and were not found at the four-year follow-up (McCrady, Moreau, Paolino, & Longabaugh, 1982).

Winters, Fals-Stewart, O'Farrell, Birchler, and Kelley (2002) randomly assigned married or cohabiting female drug-abusing clients to either a behavioral couples therapy condition or to an equally intensive individual-based treatment condition. During most of the one-year follow-up, those who received the couples therapy reported fewer days of substance use; longer periods of continuous abstinence; lower levels of alcohol, drug, and family problems; and higher relationship satisfaction compared with participants who received the individual therapy. However, in this study, as in McCrady et al. (1979), differences in relationship satisfaction and number of days of substance use dissipated over the course of the posttreatment follow-up period and were not significantly different by the end of one year.

15. The impact of family involvement in treatment may be complex, greatly affected by the interaction of client, therapy, and family variables.

Longabaugh, Wirtz, Beattie, Noel, and Stout (1995), examining treatment matching variables, recommend that the appropriate dose of relationship-enhancement treatment for alcohol use disorders should be determined based on an initial assessment of the client's relationships. They compared three treatments with different relationship-enhancement intensities: individual extended cognitive-behavioral (ECB, with no relationship-enhancement component); brief broad-spectrum (BBS, which included four sessions of partner therapy with one or more significant others); and extended relationship enhancement (ERE, which included eight sessions of partner therapy). They found that ERE was more effective in increasing abstinence for clients entering treatment with low levels of affiliative social investment or a network unsupportive of abstinence, while BBS was more effective for clients with either (a) low involvement in a social network unsupportive of abstinence or (b) high investment in a network supportive of abstinence. ECB outcomes were "neither as good as those correctly matched nor as bad as those mismatched to the different exposures of relationship enhancement" (p. 296).

The differential impact of involving family in treatment may also depend on the outcome studied. O'Farrell, Cutter, and Floyd (1985) compared two marital therapies with an individual therapy for alcohol-related problems. All three treatments reduced drinking behavior equally well. However, only the marital therapies affected marital functioning. It appears that the effects of couple intervention may uniquely target the marriage, and these effects may, in turn, lay the foundation for future "sleeper" effects on the targeted drinking behavior.

A fascinating study by Longabaugh, Beattie, Noel, Stout, and Malloy (1993) suggests that intervention pathways may be also affected by individual differences in marriage. Longabaugh et al. (1993) compared a behavioral treatment for alcohol use problems with a relationship-enhanced version including sessions with spouses. Individuals who were highly invested in their relationships and perceived a high level of support from their significant other showed great improvement, as did individuals who reported low investment in their relationships. However, those with high relationship investment and low levels of support did less well. The impact of couple intervention may be mediated by the value of the relationship to the individual.

16. Involving a supportive sponsor/peer in treatment results in better outcomes.

Interventions designed for alcohol and drug misuse, smoking cessation, and binge eating have all

demonstrated the value of involving a supportive peer or sponsor in treatment. Most prominently, in a meta-analytic review of studies of Alcoholics Anonymous (AA), having an AA sponsor was strongly related to drinking outcomes (Emrick, Tonigan, Montgomery, & Little, 1993).

Gordon and Zrull (1991) studied the social networks of 156 inpatients treated for alcohol use disorders, and found that co-workers were more active as participants in treatment than were clients' family and friends. Factors influential in recovery included active support from co-workers who did not drink regularly with the client as well as the level of perceived social support from family and friends.

Gruder et al. (1993) recruited smokers who registered for a televised smoking cessation intervention program into three treatment conditions: social support, in which participants were trained in support and relapse prevention with a non-smoking buddy; a discussion condition, in which participants and their non-smoking buddies attended separate support groups; and a no-contact control condition, in which participants viewed the television program and were given a self-help manual, but did not have contact with a non-smoking buddy. Abstinence rates were highest in the social support group compared to the discussion group, no-shows, and no-contact controls. The social support improved outcome by increasing both the level of support for quitting and program material use.

Interestingly, men and women treated for smoking cessation may respond differently to the involvement of a supportive peer. Nides et al. (1995) found that men who brought a support person along to their treatment orientation session were more likely to quit initially and resist relapse after 12 months, while bringing a support person was not related to women's initial quitting and relapse rates.

Most research has focused on the treatment involvement of a peer or sponsor chosen by the client, but Porzelius et al. (1995) created peer support within a treatment they designed for binge eating, obese binge eating treatment (OBET). In order to foster peer support within the treatment, they divided clients into small groups of two or three during weekly sessions and asked them to share experiences and problem solve together.

When they compared OBET to a standard behavioral weight loss treatment, they found women with severe binge eating lost more weight by the 12-month follow-up in OBET. Although women with moderate binge eating lost more weight initially in the standard treatment, and women who did not binge eat initially responded equally well to both treatments, neither of these groups were able to maintain their weight loss at the 12-month follow-up.

However, not all studies have found involving a peer or sponsor in treatment to have a positive effect on outcome. Crape, Latkin, Laris, and Knowlton (2002), in their study of 500 former and current injection drug users treated in Narcotics Anonymous or Alcoholics Anonymous, found that having a sponsor was not associated with any improvement in one year sustained abstinence rates compared to non-sponsored controls. However, *being* a sponsor—or being involved in religious or community organizations—was strongly associated with substantial improvements in sustained abstinence rates, even after controlling for such variables as NA/AA meeting attendance, marital status, participation in drug and alcohol treatment centers, and HIV status.

Other studies have suggested there may be interaction effects between the involvement of a 12-step self-help group sponsor and treatment type. In a study of smoking cessation treatment for participants with a history of alcohol use disorders, Patten, Martin, Calfas, Lento, and Wolter (2001) found that standard treatment was more effective for participants with an active 12-step sponsor, whereas behavioral counseling plus exercise and behavioral counseling plus nicotine gum were more effective for those without an active sponsor.

17. Peer and family involvement in programs of formal and informal care and relapse prevention may increase the likelihood of stable remission. Stabilizing and enhancing clients' community support systems can help to maintain psychosocial functioning and enhance the likelihood of stable remission.

A major problem in the treatment of substance use disorders involves the high rate of recidivism. This has led to specific efforts to prevent relapse, some of which have involved family participation. The literature examining the impact of family involvement in relapse prevention is small but encouraging.

Ossip-Klein, Van Landingham, Prue, and Rychtarik (1984) assessed the impact of a family-based incentive program for aftercare attendance after completion of an inpatient alcohol program. The family involvement program fostered better attendance in aftercare and better alcohol-related outcomes.

O'Farrell, Choquette, and Cutter (1998) found BMT for clients with alcohol use disorders was more effective when it included follow-up relapse prevention sessions than when it did not. BMT plus relapse prevention involving the family led to more days abstinent and greater use of an Antabuse contract than BMT alone, and these outcomes lasted through an 18-month follow-up. BMT plus relapse prevention also produced better wives' marital adjustment than BMT alone throughout the 30 months of follow-up. Irrespective of treatment condition, more use of BMT-targeted marital behaviors was associated with better marital and drinking outcomes throughout the 30-month follow-up period. Alcoholics with more severe marital problems had more abstinent days and maintained relatively stable levels of abstinence if they received BMT plus relapse prevention.

Not all studies have shown similar effects. Perri et al. (1987) attempted to evaluate the effectiveness of two posttreatment programs designed to help clients maintain their weight loss. They randomly assigned clients who had participated in a 20-week group weight loss treatment to behavior therapy without follow-up, behavior therapy plus a therapist-contact posttreatment program, or behavior therapy plus a peer-support posttreatment program. Although the therapist-contact condition showed significantly greater weight loss maintenance at a 7-month follow-up, by 18 months relapse rates were equivalent across conditions. In a study of alcohol treatment, McCrady, Epstein, and Hirsch (1999) found Alcohol Behavioral Marital Therapy with relapse prevention no more effective than without.

DISCUSSION

The social context of treatment may have as much or more of an impact on clients than does the type or content of treatment (Najavits & Weiss, 1994). From a review of relevant empirical studies, we have formulated some principles about how the treatment alliance and relationships with family and peers are associated with effective treatment for substance use disorders.

Broadly speaking, a good therapeutic alliance is the fundamental quality underlying effective treatment. This is a widely replicated finding in psychotherapy research with heterogeneous treatment samples, and also emerges within the more limited realm of clients with substance use disorders. Furthermore, Rogers's (1957) assertion that genuineness, warmth, and positive regard are key ingredients of effective psychosocial treatment appears to be broadly applicable to clients with substance use disorders. Similarly, clients in involving, supportive, and expressive residential treatment programs tend to develop more positive relationships with fellow residents, to report that treatment enhances their self-confidence, and to be more satisfied with and to remain longer in treatment. These clients also tend to experience better outcomes at discharge from the residential phase of treatment and better post-program alcohol- and drug-related outcomes.

A second set of findings in this review centers on family relationships and treatment outcomes. Clients with social systems supportive of treatment are more likely to enter and complete treatment and achieve better outcomes. When family members are constructively engaged in treatment, engagement and outcomes are also likely to be improved.

These findings raise the question of how to best create strong therapeutic alliances and optimize the involvement of family, which, in turn, can help lead to better outcomes. There is a need for a great deal more research on how to develop optimal treatment alliances in interventions aimed at substance use. Although there is sufficient research to establish a set of working principles for treatment of these populations, our specific principles remain in the realm of the "probably" efficacious at this point in the language of the American Psychological Association's Division 12 Task Force. Despite the clear importance of the relationship factors discussed in this chapter, these factors are rarely addressed in research on treatment outcome. Also, in combining the various literatures about different substance use disorders, we sometimes found very little relevant research concerned with a principle in the domain of a specific disorder. The problem we encountered can only be resolved by incorporating measures of relationship variables into treatment outcome research in the substance use and eating disorders.

The evidence suggests that treatment settings and counselors who are goal-directed and are moderately structured establish better therapy alliances and tend to promote positive in-treatment and posttreatment substance use outcomes. Furthermore, a good treatment alliance and a cohesive treatment setting may be necessary conditions for change, but they are not sufficient conditions. We also believe that to motivate clients to improve, therapists also need to set high expectations and specific performance goals, and to maintain a stable level of structure in treatment. Similarly, we expect that residential treatment programs that emphasize self-direction and the development of work and social skills, are relatively clear and well-organized, and create strong treatment alliances with clients, tend to engage clients in treatment, reduce clients' substance use problems and symptoms, and enhance clients' community living skills and psychosocial functioning. All of these variables require more attention in our research.

To enhance our understanding of the role of the alliance in the treatment of substance use disorders, research needs to attend to several specific issues. Among these are the role of confrontation, potential variations in the importance of the alliance in different treatment modalities, the influence of the alliance when treatment is mandated, the value of the alliance in group treatment, and the function of the alliance in relation to the match between client–therapist gender, age, race, and similarity of life experience.

One issue involves the apparent negative effects of confrontation, which literally means bringing clients "face to face" with the nature of their problems. Therapists often need to confront clients with addictive disorders by developing and reflecting discrepancies between clients' behaviors and their stated values or goals. Thus, as Miller and

Rollnick (2002) point out, confrontation often is a goal of treatment; however, it should not be a style of interaction. More information is needed to educate therapists about how they can appropriately confront their clients in a way that helps strengthen the therapeutic alliance.

Two studies of cocaine-dependent clients have noted that, in supportive-expressive therapy, individual drug counseling, and clinical management, a stronger alliance predicts treatment retention—but in cognitive treatment there is no association between the alliance and retention (Carroll, Nich, & Rounsaville, 1997) or perhaps even a negative relationship (Barber, Luborsky, et al., 2001). The highly directive version of cognitive treatment often employed to treat cocaine dependency may enable clients who develop a strong alliance to increase their self-efficacy and leave treatment more quickly. Alternatively, this modality may weaken the alliance and extend the course of treatment. In any case, more information is needed about the potential differential role of the alliance in diverse treatment modalities.

When treatment is judicially mandated, extrinsic forces that affect clients' motivation and behavior may produce an illusory alliance. For example, among boys with conduct disorders, those who had a positive working alliance at three months were more likely to improve and less likely to be recidivists in the year following placement. However, on average, boys who developed an alliance as early as the third or fourth week of treatment subsequently showed less progress (Florsheim, Shotorbani, Guest-Warnick, Barratt, & Hwang, 2000). These youth, who may have wanted to "look good" early on and thus developed a "false alliance," failed to progress as staff began to set more limits and expected higher levels of investment in treatment. Because a growing number of clients with substance use disorders are judicially mandated for treatment, we need to determine the influence of situational demands on the measurement and predictive validity of the therapeutic alliance and Rogerian interpersonal attitudes.

Although the majority of treatment for substance use disorders is conducted in a group format, we did not find any empirical studies that specifically examined the therapeutic alliance in this modality. The therapist's warmth, empathy, and genuineness, as well as interpersonal skill and ability to mediate and resolve conflict, are likely to influence group cohesion, treatment retention, and longer term outcome. However, the members' influence on each other may reduce the importance of the leader. More information is needed about the unique characteristics and impact of the alliance in group treatment contexts.

Perhaps the most profitable area for further research lies in examining matches of therapist, therapy, and client. Very little is currently known about the potential differential impact of therapist–client concordance on gender, ethnicity, age, or experiences on alliance in the treatment of substance use disorders. One fruitful area for investigation concerns whether recovering counselors establish a better treatment alliance, and, if so, whether the specific change mechanism is that "recovery status" signifies concordant life experiences between counselor and client. More broadly, studies are needed to examine the role of different aspects of counselor–client concordance in the formation of the treatment alliance. Furthermore, the existent research suggests that the matching of client, therapist, and treatment will have greatest impact when the matching is focused on more complex treatment related characteristics, such as increasing or decreasing family involvement in treatment in relation to the quality of family life, rather than in simple matching by demographic characteristics.

Further investigation is also needed to help unpack the various aspects of the relationship between client and therapist in the treatment of substance use disorders. Broad generalizations of the therapeutic alliance predominate in the existent research connecting process and outcome, while the nuances of different aspects of the therapeutic relationship articulated in the report by the Division 29 Task Force of the American Psychological Association (Norcross, 2002a) (e.g., other relational variables or the differences between tasks, goals, and bonds in the alliance) have yet to receive much attention in this substantive area.

Family and peer support of treatment appears to have special relevance for clients with substance use disorders. The impressive body of work showing the importance of social support in client outcomes naturally suggests developing better methods for achieving such support, both broadly for life functioning and specifically in relation to the treatment. Often, in these treatments, the therapy alliance emerges first with family and/or peers and only later is built with the client with the disorder. The impact of family on treatment is clear; these effects are even more pronounced in treatment studies of adolescent substance use disorders that are beyond the domain of this review of adult treatment.

We need much more research illuminating the most efficacious means for deciding when family and/or peers should be part of treatment (and when they should not) and how best to involve them. Beneficial patterns of involvement by family and friends may also vary with clients' individual personality styles.

Research must also specifically focus on the level of family involvement that is most useful at the various "stages of change" (Prochaska & Di-Clemente, 1999). Perhaps different methods for building family support and involving family and friends in treatment will prove optimal given the very different patterns for clients in the pre-contemplation stage (when problems are not identified by the client but may be by others), the contemplation stage (when problems are identified by the client but he or she is not yet ready to act), the action stage (when the client is actively seeking to alter the problem behavior), and the maintenance stage (when the problem behavior has been changed, but the change must be maintained over time).

Another issue is how much the therapist shapes the alliance and how much it is shaped by the client's characteristics at entry to treatment. In general, among clients with substance use disorders, demographic characteristics and the severity of substance use symptoms emerge as only minimally related to the strength of the alliance (Barber et al., 1999; De Weert-Van Oene et al., 1999; Simpson, Joe, Rowan-Szal, & Greener, 1995). However, several studies imply that clients who experience more distress, are strongly motivated for treatment, and regularly attend early treatment sessions, establish a stronger treatment alliance (Barber et al., 1999; Connors et al., 2000; Simpson, Joe, Rowan-Szal, & Greener, 1995). These findings highlight the need for more research into how the interaction of client and therapist characteristics shapes the development of the treatment alliance,

and how this process is affected by the therapist's level of directedness and structure and the content of treatment.

In terms of methodology, there is a need for better instrumentation to assess the quality of alliances between extended social support networks and therapists and/or treatment programs, because in the treatment of substance use disorders the therapeutic alliance often expands to include family members, friends, and co-workers. Improvement in the construct and content validity of measures designed to tap the therapeutic alliance, as well as identifying reasons for variations in measurement methods (i.e., client versus therapist self-report versus observer ratings) and the predictive validity of these different perspectives are also fruitful areas for study. In addition, newer analytic techniques, such as hierarchical linear modeling, may enable us to examine these phenomena in a more ecologically valid way (Hser, 1995). As the nature of the therapeutic process becomes more apparent, new concepts and measurement procedures may help us place the alliance in context with other common aspects of treatment, and, more broadly, with other aspects of clients' life experiences that influence the process of recovery.

To emphasize our most important suggestion for further research, relationship variables should be included as an integral part of research on the outcome of treatment for substance use and eating disorders. We hope that with such research, a subsequent review of this area will be able to confirm and expand the principles stated here, and to elaborate additional principles concerned with interactions between clients, therapists, and therapies that can inform us about how best to achieve optimal alliances and involve family in treatment.

SUMMARY

Studies that have focused on treatment for the substance use and eating disorders have primarily focused on the impact of treatments on outcomes, and only occasionally have considered the importance of relationship factors to outcome. Nonetheless, a considerable literature has identified the powerful role of the therapeutic alliance in treatment—in helping clients enter treatment, remain in treatment longer, to be confident and explore problems, to experience less distress, and to produce better outcomes. Likewise, treatment programs are more likely to engage clients more successfully and achieve better in-treatment and after-treatment outcomes when better alliances are created with clients. Relationships with family and friends also appear to have strong effects on engagement, program completion, and outcomes among individuals with substance use and eating disorders. These effects are manifested broadly in the impact of social support on outcome, and, more specifically, in the important roles family and friends can play in supporting treatment; helping to build the alliance between the client, therapist, and treatment program; and becoming involved directly in the treatment process.

ACKNOWLEDGMENTS   Preparation of this manuscript was supported by the Department of Veterans Affairs Health Services Research and Development Service research funds and by NIAAA Grant AA12718. The opinions expressed in the manuscript are those of the authors and do not necessarily represent the views of the Department of Veterans Affairs.

References

Alexander, L. B., & Luborsky, L T. (1986). The Penn Helping Alliance Scales. In L. S. P. Greenberg & W. M. Pinsof (Eds.), *The psychotherapeutic process: A research handbook* (pp. 325–366). New York: Guilford.

American Psychiatric Association. (1994). *Diagnostic and statistical manual of mental disorders* (4th ed., rev.). Washington, DC: American Psychiatric Association.

Barber, J. G. (1995). Working with resistant drug abusers. *Social Work, 40*(1), 17–23.

Barber, J. L., Crits-Christoph, P., Thase, M. E., Weiss, R., Frank, A., Onken, L., & Gallop, R. (1999). Therapeutic alliance as a predictor of outcome in treatment of cocaine dependence. *Psychotherapy Research, 9,* 54–73.

Barber, J. P., Luborsky, L., Gallop, R., Crits-Christoph, P., Frank, A., Weiss, R. D., Thase, M. E., Connolly, M. B., Gladis, M., Foltz, C., & Siqueland, L. (2001). Therapeutic alliance as a predictor of outcome and retention in the National Institute on Drug Abuse Collaborative

Cocaine Treatment Study. *Journal of Consulting & Clinical Psychology, 69,* 119–124.

Barber, J. S., Halperin, G., & Connolly, M. B. (2001). Supportive techniques: Are they found in different therapies? *Journal of Psychotherapy Practice and Research, 10,* 165–172.

Barrett-Lennard, G. T. (1962). Dimensions of the client's experience with the therapist associated with personality change. *Genetic Psychology Monographs, 76,* No. 43.

Belding, M. A., Iguchi, M. Y., Morral, A. R., & McLellan, A. T. (1997). Assessing the helping alliance and its impact in the treatment of opiate dependence. *Drug Alcohol Depend, 48,* 51–59.

Bohart, A. C., Elliott, R., Greenberg, L. S., & Watson, J. C. (2002). Empathy. In J. C. Norcross (Ed.), *Psychotherapy relationships that work: Therapist contributions and responsiveness to patients* (pp. 89–108). New York: Oxford University Press.

Booth, B. M., Russell, D. W., Soucek, S., & Laughlin, P. R. (1992). Social support and outcome of alcoholism treatment: An exploratory analysis. *American Journal of Drug & Alcohol Abuse, 18*(1), 87–101.

Breteler, M. H. M., Van Den Hurk, A. A., Schippers, G. M., & Meerkerk, G. J. (1996). Enrollment in a drug-free detention program: The prediction of successful behavior change of drug-using inmates. *Addictive Behaviors, 21*(5), 665–669.

Broome, K. M., Simpson, D. D., & Joe, G. W. (1999). Client and program attributes related to treatment process indicators in DATOS. *Drug and Alcohol Dependence, 57,* 127–135.

Burlingame, G. M., Fuhriman, A., & Johnson, J. E. (2002). Cohesion in group psychotherapy. In J. C. Norcross (Ed.), *Psychotherapy relationships that work: Therapist contributions and responsiveness to patients* (pp. 71–88). New York: Oxford University Press.

Carroll, K., Nich, C., & Rounsaville, B. (1997). Contribution of the therapeutic alliance to outcome in active versus control psychotherapies. *Journal of Consulting and Clinical Psychology, 65,* 510–514.

Chafetz, M., Blane, H., Abram, H., Golner, J., Lacy, E., McCourt, W., Clark, E., & Meyers, W. (1962). Establishing treatment relations with alcoholics. *Journal of Nervous and Mental Disease, 134,* 395–409.

Chambless, D. L., & Hollon, S. D. (1998). Defining empirically supported therapies. *Journal of Consulting and Clinical Psychology, 66*, 7–18.

Claiborn, C. D., Goodyear, R. K., & Horner, P. A. (2002). Feedback. In J. C. Norcross (Ed.), *Psychotherapy relationships that work: Therapist contributions and responsiveness to patients* (pp. 217–234). New York: Oxford University Press.

Collins, R. L., Emont, S. L., Zywiak, W. H. (1990). Social influence processes in smoking cessation: Postquitting predictors of long-term outcome. *Journal of Substance Abuse, 2*(4), 389–403.

Connors, G. C., DiClemente, C. C., Longabaugh, R., Donovan, D. M. (1997). The therapeutic alliance and its relationship to alcohol treatment participation and outcome. *Journal of Consulting and Clinical Psychology, 69*, 588–598.

Connors, G. D., Dermen, K. H., Kadden, R., Carroll, K. M., & Fronte, M. R. (2000). Predicting the therapeutic alliance in alcoholism treatment. *Journal of Studies on Alcohol, 61*, 139–156.

Crape, B. L., Latkin, C. A., Laris, A. S., Knowlton, A. R. (2002). The effects of sponsorship in a 12-step treatment of injection drug users. *Drug and Alcohol Dependence, 65*(3), 291–301.

Crits-Christoph, P., & Gibbons, M. B. C. (2002). Relational interpretations. In J. C. Norcross (Ed.), *Psychotherapy relationships that work: Therapist contributions and responsiveness to patients* (pp. 285–300). New York: Oxford University Press.

Curry, S., Thompson, B., Sexton, M., & Omenn, G. S. (1989). Psychosocial predictors of outcome in a worksite smoking cessation program. *American Journal of Preventive Medicine, 5*(1), 2–7.

Dakof, G. A., Quille, T. J., Tejeda, M. J., Alberga, L. R., Bandstra, E., & Szapocznik, J. (in press). Enrolling and retaining cocaine abusing mothers into drug abuse treatment. *Journal of Consulting and Clinical Psychology.*

De Leon, G. (Ed.). (1997). *Community as method: Therapeutic communities for special populations and special settings.* Westport, CT: Praeger.

De Weert-Van Oene, G. D., Jorg, F., & Schrijvers, G. (1999). The Helping Alliance Questionnaire: Psychometric properties in clients with substance dependence. *Substance Use & Misuse, 34*, 1549–1569.

Donohue, B., Azrin, N., Lawson, H., Friedlander, J., Teicher, G., & Rindsberg, J. (1998). Improving initial session attendance of substance abusing and conduct disordered adolescents: A controlled study. *Journal of Child and Adolescent Substance Abuse, 8*(1), 1–13.

Edwards, M., & Steinglass, P. (1995). Family therapy outcomes for alcoholism. *Journal of Marital and Family Therapy, 10*, 475–509.

Emrick, C. D., Tonigan, J. S., Montgomery, H., & Little, L. (1993). Affiliation processes in and treatment outcomes of Alcoholics Anonymous: A meta-analysis of the literature. In B. S. McCrady & W. R. Miller (Eds.), *Research on Alcoholics Anonymous: Opportunities and alternatives* (pp. 41–76). Piscataway, NJ: Rutgers University, Center of Alcohol Studies.

Fals-Stewart, W., & Birchler, G. R. (1998). Marital interactions of drug-abusing patients and their partners: Comparisons with distressed couples and relationship to drug-using behavior. *Psychology of Addictive Behaviors, 12*(1), 28–38.

Fals-Stewart, W., Birchler, G. R., & O'Farrell, T. J. (1996). Behavioral couples therapy for male substance-abusing patients: Effects on relationship adjustment and drug-using behavior. *Journal of Consulting and Clinical Psychology, 64*(5), 959–972.

Fals-Stewart, W., O'Farrell, T. J., Feehan, M., Birchler, G. R., Tiller, S., & McFarlin, S. K. (2000). Behavioral couples therapy versus individual-based treatment for male substance-abusing patients: An evaluation of significant individual change and comparison of improvement rates. *Journal of Substance Abuse Treatment, 18*, 249–254.

Farber, B. A., & Lane, J. S. (2002). Positive regard. In J. C. Norcross (Ed.), *Psychotherapy relationships that work: Therapist contributions and responsiveness to patients* (pp. 175–194). New York: Oxford University Press.

Fenton, L. C., Nich, C., Frankforter, T., & Carroll, K. (2001). Perspective is everything: The predictive validity of six working alliance instruments. *Journal of Psychotherapy Practice and Research, 10*, 262–268.

Finney, J., & Moos, R. (1992). The long-term course of treated alcoholism: II. Predictors and correlates of 10-year functioning and mortality. *Journal of Studies on Alcohol, 53*, 142–153.

Florsheim, P., Shotorbani, S., Guest-Warnick, G., Barratt, T., & Hwang, W. C. (2000). Role of the working alliance in the treatment of delinquent boys in community-based programs. *Journal of Clinical Child Psychology, 29*, 94–107.

Freud, S. (1912). The dynamics of transference. In

J. Strachey (Ed.), *The standard edition of the complete psychological works of Sigmund Freud* (pp. 99–108). London: Hogarth Press.

Galanter, M. (1993). Network therapy for substance abuse: A clinical trial. *Psychotherapy, 30*(2), 251–258.

Gallop, R., Kennedy, S. H., & Stern, D. (1994). Therapeutic alliance on an inpatient unit for eating disorders. *International Journal of Eating Disorders, 16*(4), 405–410.

Gaston, L. M., & Marmar, C. R. (1994). The California Psychotherapy Alliance Scales. In A. O. Horvath & L. S. Greenberg (Ed.), *The working alliance: Theory, research, and practice* (pp. 85–108). New York: Wiley.

Gelso, C. J., & Hayes, J. A. (2002). The management of countertransference. In J. C. Norcross (Ed.), *Psychotherapy relationships that work: Therapist contributions and responsiveness to patients* (pp. 267–284). New York: Oxford University Press.

Gerstley, L., McLellan, A. T., Alterman, A. I., Woody, G. E., Luborsky, L., & Prout, M. (1989). Ability to form an alliance with the therapist: A possible marker of prognosis for clients with antisocial personality disorder. *American Journal of Psychiatry, 146*, 508–512.

Gordon, A. J., & Zrull, M. (1991). Social networks and recovery: One year after inpatient treatment. *Journal of Substance Abuse Treatment, 8*(3), 143–152.

Greenson, R. (1965). The working alliance and the transference neurosis. *Psychoanalytic Quarterly, 34*, 155–179.

Gruder, C. L., Mermelstein, R. J., Kirkendol, S., Hedeker, D., et al. (1993). Effects of social support and relapse prevention training as adjuncts to a televised smoking-cessation intervention. *Journal of Consulting & Clinical Psychology, 61*(1), 113–120.

Hanson, B., Issacsson, S. O., Janzon, L., & Liddle, S. E. (1990). Social support and quitting smoking for good. Is there an association? Results from the population study "Men Born in 1914," Malmo, Sweden. *Addictive Behaviors, 15*, 221–233.

Hartley, S. W., & Strupp, H. H. (1983). The therapeutic alliance: Its relationship to outcome in brief psychotherapy. In J. Masling (Ed.), *Empirical studies of psychoanalytic theories* (pp. 1–37). Hillsdale, NJ: Analytic Press.

Hatcher, R. L., & Barends, A. W. (1996). Clients' view of the alliance in psychotherapy: Exploratory factor analysis of three alliance measures.

Journal of Consulting & Clinical Psychology, 64, 1326–1336.

Henggeler, S. W., Pickrel, S. G., Brondino, M. J., & Crouch, J. L. (1996). Eliminating (almost) treatment dropout of substance abusing or dependent delinquents through home-based multisystemic therapy. *American Journal of Psychiatry, 153*, 427–428.

Hill, C. E., & Knox, S. (2002). Self-disclosure. In J. C. Norcross (Ed.), *Psychotherapy relationships that work: Therapist contributions and responsiveness to patients* (pp. 255–266). New York: Oxford University Press.

Horvath, A. O., & Bedi, R. P. (2002). The alliance. In J. C. Norcross (Ed.), *Psychotherapy relationships that work: Therapist contributions and responsiveness to patients* (pp. 37–70). New York: Oxford University Press.

Horvath, A. O., & Greenberg, L. S. (1989). Development and validation of the Working Alliance Inventory. *Journal of Counseling Psychology, 36*, 223–233.

Horvath, A., & Symonds, D. (1991). Relation between working alliance and outcome in psychotherapy: A meta analysis. *Journal of Consulting and Clinical Psychology, 59*(2), 139–149.

Hser, Y. (1995). Drug treatment counselor practices and effectiveness: An examination of the literature and relevant issues in a multilevel framework. *Evaluation Review, 19*, 389–408.

Hyams, G., Cartwright, A., & Sprately, T. (1996). Engagement in alcohol treatment: The client's experience of, and satisfaction with, the assessment interview. *Addiction Research, 4*(2), 105–123.

Joe, G. W., Simpson, D. D., Dansereau, D. F., & Rowan-Szal, G. A. (2001). Relationships between counseling rapport and drug abuse treatment outcomes. *Psychiatric Services, 52*, 1223–1229.

Joe, G. W., Simpson, D. D., Greener, J. M., & Rowan-Szal, G. A. (1999). Integrative modeling of client engagement and outcomes during the first 6 months of methadone treatment. *Addictive Behavior, 24*, 649–659.

Jones, M. (1953). *The therapeutic community.* New York: Basic Books.

Kelley, M. L., & Fals-Stewart, W. (2002). Couples versus individual-based therapy for alcoholism and drug abuse: Effects on children's psychosocial functioning. *Journal of Consulting and Clinical Psychology, 70*, 417–427.

Klein, M. H., Kolden, G. G., Michels, J. L., & Chisholm-Stockard, S. (2002). In J. C. Norcross (Ed.), *Psychotherapy relationships that work: Therapist contributions and responsiveness to patients* (pp. 195–216). New York: Oxford University Press.

Lemke, S., & Moos, R. (2002). Prognoses of older clients in mixed-age alcoholism treatment programs. *Journal of Substance Abuse Treatment, 22,* 33–43.

Lichtenstein, E., Glasgow, R. E., & Abrams, D. B. (1986). Social support in smoking cessation: In search of effective interventions. *Behavior Therapy, 17*(5), 607–619.

Liddle, H. A., & Dakof, G. (1995). Family-based treatment for adolescent drug use: State of the science. In E. Rahdert & D. Czechowicz (Eds.), *Adolescent drug abuse: Clinical assessment and therapeutic interventions* (pp. 218–254) (NIDA Research Monograph No. 156, NIH Publication No. 953908). Rockville, MD: National Institute on Drug Abuse.

Liepman, M. R., Nirenberg, T. D., & Begin, A. M. (1989). Evaluation of a program designed to help family and significant others to motivate resistant alcoholics. *American Journal of Drug and Alcohol Abuse, 15,* 209–221.

Linn, M. (1978). Attrition of older alcoholics from treatment. *Addictive Diseases, 3,* 437–447.

Linn, M., Shane, R., Webb, N., & Pratt, T. (1979). Cultural factors and attrition in drug abuse treatment. *International Journal of the Addictions, 14,* 259–280.

Long, C. W., Williams, M., Midgley, M., & Hollin, C. R. (2000). Within program factors as predictors of drinking outcome following cognitive-behavioral treatment. *Addictive Behaviors, 25,* 573–578.

Longabaugh, R., Beattie, M., Noel, N., Stout, R. & Malloy, P. (1993). The effect of social investment on treatment outcome. *Journal of Studies on Alcohol, 54,* 465–478.

Longabaugh, R., Wirtz, P. W., Beattie, M. C., Noel, N., & Stout, R. (1995). Matching treatment focus to patient social investment and support: 18-month follow-up results. *Journal of Consulting and Clinical Psychology, 63*(2), 296–307.

Luborsky, L., Barber, J. P., Siqueland, L., & Johnson, S. (1996). The revised Helping Alliance questionnaire (HAq-II): Psychometric properties. *Journal of Psychotherapy Practice & Research, 5*(3), 260–271.

Luborsky, L., Crits-Christoph, P., McLellan, A. T., Woody, G., Piper, W., Liberman, B., Imber, S., & Pilkonis, P. (1986). Do therapists vary much in their success? Findings from four outcome studies. *American Journal of Orthopsychiatry, 5,* 501–512.

Luborsky, L. R., Diguer, L., Andrusyna, T. P., Berman, J. S., Levitt, J. T., Seligman, D. A., & Krause, E. D. (2002). The dodo bird verdict is alive and well—mostly. *Clinical Psychology: Science & Practice, 9,* 2–12.

Luborsky, L., McLellan, T., Woody, G., O'Brien, C., & Auerbach, A. (1985). Therapist success and its determinants. *Archives of General Psychiatry, 42,* 602–611.

Machell, D. F. (1987). Fellowship as an important factor in alcoholism residential treatment. *Journal of Alcohol and Drug Education, 32*(2), 56–58.

Marmar, C. R., Weiss, D. S., & Gaston, L. (1989). Toward the validation of the California Therapeutic Alliance Rating System. *Psychological Assessment, 1*(1), 46–52.

Martin, D., Garske, J., & Davis, K. (2000). Relation of the therapeutic alliance with outcome and other variables: A meta-analytic review. *Journal of Consulting and Clinical Psychology, 68*(3), 438–450.

McCrady, B. S., Epstein, E. E., & Hirsch, L. S. (1999). Maintaining change after conjoint behavioral alcohol treatment for men: Outcomes at six months. *Addiction, 94,* 1381–1396.

McCrady, B. S., Moreau, J., Paolino, T. J., & Longabaugh, R. (1982). Joint hospitalization and couples therapy for alcoholism: A four year follow-up. *Journal of Studies on Alcohol, 43,* 1244–1250.

McCrady, B. S., Noel, N. E., Abrams, D. B., Stout, R. L., Nelson, H. F., & Hay, W. N. (1986). Comparative effectiveness of three types of spouse involvement in outpatient behavioral alcoholism treatment. *Journal of Studies on Alcohol, 47,* 459–467.

McCrady, B. S., Paolino, T. J., Jr., Longabaugh, R., & Rossi, J. (1979). Effects of joint hospital admission and couples treatment for hospitalized alcoholics: A pilot study. *Addictive Behaviors, 4,* 155–165.

McLellan, A. T., Alterman, A. I., Metzger, D. S., Grissom, G. R., Woody, G. E., Luborsky, L., & O'Brien, C. P. (1994). Similarity of outcome predictors across opiate, cocaine, and alcohol treatments: Role of treatment services. *Journal of Consulting and Clinical Psychology, 62,* 1141–1158.

Miller, W. R., Benefield, G., & Tonigan, J. S. (1993). Enhancing motivation for change in problem drinking: A controlled comparison of two therapist styles. *Journal of Consulting and Clinical Psychology, 61,* 455–446.

Miller, W. R., & Brown, S. A. (1997). Why psychologists should treat alcohol and drug problems. *American Psychologist, 52,* 1269–1279.

Miller, W. R., Meyers, R. J., & Tonigan, J. S. (1999). Engaging the unmotivated in treatment for alcohol problems: A comparison of three strategies for intervention through family members. *Journal of Consulting and Clinical Psychology,* 67(5), 688–697.

Miller, W. R., & Rollnick, S. (2002). *Motivational interviewing: Preparing people for change.* New York: Guilford Press.

Milmoe, S., Rosenthal, R., Blane, H., Chafetz, M., & Wolf, I. (1967). The doctor's voice: Postdictor of successful referral of alcoholic clients. *Journal of Abnormal Psychology,* 72(1), 78–84.

Moos, R. (1997). *Evaluating treatment environments: The quality of psychiatric and substance abuse programs.* New Brunswick, NJ: Transaction.

Moos, R., Finney, J., & Cronkite, R. (1990). *Alcoholism treatment: Context, process, and outcome.* New York: Oxford University Press.

Moos, R., & King, M. (1997). Participation in community residential treatment and substance abuse clients' outcomes at discharge. *Journal of Substance Abuse Treatment, 14,* 71–80.

Moos, R., & MacIntosh, S. (1970). Multivariate study of the client–therapist system: A replication and extension. *Journal of Consulting and Clinical Psychology, 35,* 298–307.

Moos, R., Mehren, B., & Moos, B. (1978). Evaluation of a Salvation Army alcoholism treatment program. *Journal of Studies on Alcohol, 39,* 1267–1275.

Morgan, G. D., Ashenberg, Z. S., & Fisher, E. B. (1988). Abstinence from smoking and the social environment. *Journal of Consulting and Clinical Psychology,* 56(2), 298–301.

Morgenstern, J., Blanchard, K. A., Morgan, T. J., Labouvie, E., & Hayaki, J. (2001). Testing the effectiveness of cognitive-behavioral treatment for substance abuse in a community setting: Within treatment and posttreatment findings. *Journal of Consulting and Clinical Psychology, 69,* 1007–1017.

Moyer, A., Finney, J., & Swearingen, C. (2002). Methodological characteristics and quality of alcohol treatment outcome studies, 1970–98: An expanded evaluation. *Addiction, 97,* 253–264.

Moyer, A., Finney, J. W., Swearingen, C. E., & Vergun, P. (2002). Brief interventions for alcohol problems: A meta-analytic review of controlled investigations in treatment-seeking and non-treatment-seeking populations. *Addiction, 97,* 279–292.

Najavits, L., & Weiss, R. D. (1994). Variations in therapist effectiveness in the treatment of clients with substance use disorders: An empirical review. *Addiction, 89,* 679–688.

Nathan, P. E., & Gorman, J. M. (Eds.). (2002). *A guide to treatments that work* (2nd ed.). London: Oxford University Press.

Nides, M. A., Rakos, R. F., Gonzales, D., Murray, R. P., et al. (1995). Predictors of initial smoking cessation and relapse through the first 2 years of the Lung Health Study. *Journal of Consulting and Clinical Psychology,* 63(1), 60–69.

Norcross, J. C. (2002a). Empirically supported therapy relationships: Summary report of the Division 29 Task Force. *Psychotherapy, 38,* 345–497.

Norcross, J. C. (Ed.). (2002b). *Psychotherapy relationships that work: Therapist contributions and responsiveness to patients.* New York: Oxford University Press.

O'Farrell, T. J., & Birchler, G. (2001). Alcohol abuse. In D. H. Sprenkle (Ed.), *Effectiveness research in marital and family therapy.* Alexandria, VA: AAMFT.

O'Farrell, T. J., Choquette, K. A., Cutter, H. S. G., Brown, E. D., & McCourt, W. F. (1993). Behavioral marital therapy with and without additional couples relapse prevention sessions for alcoholics and their wives. *Journal of Studies on Alcohol, 54,* 652–666.

O'Farrell, T. J., Cutter, H. S. G., & Floyd, F. J. (1985). Evaluating behavioral marital therapy for male alcoholics: Effects on marital adjustment and communication from before and after treatment. *Behavior Therapy, 16,* 147–167.

O'Farrell, T. J., & Fals-Stewart, W. (2002). *Marital and family therapy in the treatment of alcoholism.* Paper presented at the AAMFT Research conference, Reno, NV.

O'Farrell, T. J., & Feehan, M. (1999). Alcoholism treatment and the family: Do family and individual treatments for alcoholic adults have preventive effects for children? *Journal of Studies on Alcohol, 13,* 125–128.

Ojehagen, A., Bergland, M., & Hansson, L. (1997). The relationship between helping alliance and outcome in outclient treatment of alcoholics: A comparative study of psychiatric treatment and multimodal behavioural therapy. *Alcohol and Alcoholism, 32,* 241–249.

Ossip-Klein, D. J., Vanlandingham, W., Prue, D. M., & Rychtarik, R. G. (1984). Increasing attendance at alcohol aftercare using calendar prompts and home based contracting. *Addictive Behaviors, 9*(1), 85–89.

Ouimette, P. C., Ahrens, C., Moos, R., & Finney, J. (1998). During treatment changes in substance abuse clients with posttraumatic stress disorder: Relationships to specific interventions and program environments. *Journal of Substance Abuse Treatment, 15,* 555–564.

Patten, C. A., Martin, J. E., Calfas, K. J., Lento, J., & Wolter, T. D. (2001). Behavioral treatment for smokers with a history of alcoholism: Predictors of successful outcome. *Journal of Consulting and Clinical Psychology, 69*(5), 796–801.

Perri, M. G., McAdoo, W. G., McAllister, D. A., Lauer, J. B., et al. (1987). Effects of peer support and therapist contact on long-term weight loss. *Journal of Consulting and Clinical Psychology, 55*(4), 615–617.

Petry, N., & Bickel, B. (1999). Therapeutic alliance and psychiatric severity as predictors of completion of treatment for opioid dependence. *Psychiatric Services, 50,* 219–227.

Porzelius, L. K., Houston, C., Smith, M., Arfken, C., et al. (1995). Comparison of a standard behavioral weight loss treatment and a binge eating weight loss treatment. *Behavior Therapy, 26*(1), 119–134.

Prochaska, J. O., & DiClemente, C. C. (1999). Comments, criteria and creating better models. In W. R. Miller and N. Heath (Eds.), *Treating addictive behaviors* (2nd ed.). New York: Plenum Press.

Project MATCH (1997). Matching alcoholism treatments to client heterogeneity: Project MATCH post treatment drinking outcomes. *Journal of Studies on Alcohol, 58,* 7–29.

Project MATCH (1998). Matching alcoholism treatments to client heterogeneity: Treatment main effects and matching effects on drinking during treatment. *Journal of Studies on Alcohol, 59,* 631–639.

Rapoport, R. (1960). *Community as doctor.* London, England: Tavistock.

Raytek, H. M., Epstein, E. E., & Hirsch, L. S. (1999). Therapeutic alliance and the retention of couples in conjoint alcoholism treatment. *Addictive Behaviors, 24,* 317–330.

Rogers, C. (1957). The necessary and sufficient conditions of therapeutic personality change. *Journal of Consulting and Clinical Psychology, 22,* 95–103.

Rowe, C. L., & Liddle, H. A. (2002). *Recent advances in family based treatment for drug abuse.* Paper presented at the AAMFT Research Conference, Reno, NV.

Safran, J. D., Muran, J. C., Samstag, L. W., & Stevens, C. (2002). In J. C. Norcross (Ed.), *Psychotherapy relationships that work: Therapist contributions and responsiveness to patients* (pp. 235–254). New York: Oxford University Press.

Safran, J. D., & Wallner, L. K. (1991). The relative predictive validity of two therapeutic alliance measures in cognitive therapy. *Psychological Assessment, 3*(2), 188–195.

Santisteban, D. A., Szapocznik, J., Perez-Vidal, A., Kurtines, W. M., Murray, E. J., & LaPerriere, A. (1996). Efficacy of intervention for engaging youth and families into treatment and some variables that may contribute to differential effectiveness. *Journal of Family Psychology, 10,* 35–44.

Simpson, D., Joe, G. W., Greener, J. M., & Rowan-Szal, G. A. (2000). Modeling year 1 outcomes with treatment process and post-treatment social influences. *Substance Use and Misuse, 35,* 1911–1930.

Simpson, D. D., Joe, G. W., & Rowan-Szal, G. A. (1997). Drug abuse treatment retention and process effects on follow-up outcomes. *Drug and Alcohol Dependence, 47,* 227–235.

Simpson, D., Joe, G. W., Rowan-Szal, G., & Greener, J. (1995). Client engagement and change during drug abuse treatment. *Journal of Substance Abuse, 7,* 117–134.

Simpson, D. D., Joe, G. W., Rowan-Szal, G. A., & Greener, J. M. (1997). Drug abuse treatment process components that improve retention. *Journal of Substance Abuse Treatment, 14,* 565–572.

Sisson, R. W., & Azrin, H. H. (1986). Family-member involvement to initiate and promote treatment of problem drinkers. *Journal of Behavior Therapy and Experimental Psychiatry, 17,* 15–21.

Stanton, M. D., & Todd, T. C. (1979). Structural therapy with drug addicts. In E. Kaufman & P. Kaufman (Eds.), *Family therapy of drug and alcohol abuse* (pp. 55–59). New York: Gardner Press.

Szapocznik, J., Perez-Vidal, A., Brickman, A. L., Foote, F. H., Santisteban, D., Hervis, O., & Kurtines, W. M. (1988). Engaging adolescent drug abusers and their families in treatment: A strategic structural systems approach. *Journal of*

Consulting and Clinical Psychology, 56, 552–557.

Thomas, E. J., Santa, C. A., Bronson, D., Osterman, D. (1987). Unilateral family therapy with spouses of alcoholics. *Journal of Social Service Research, 10,* 145–162.

Thomas, E. J., Yoshioka, M., Ager, R., & Adams, K. B. (1990). *Reaching the uncooperative alcohol abuser through a cooperative spouse.* Paper presented at the Fifth Congress of the International Society for Bio-Medical Research on Alcoholism, Toronto, June.

Tracey, T. J., & Kokotovic, A. M. (1989). Factor structure of the Working Alliance Inventory. *Psychological Assessment, 1*(3), 207–210.

Treasure, J. L., Katzman, M., Schmidt, U., Troop, N., Todd, G., & de Silva, P. (1999). Engagement and outcome in the treatment of bulimia nervosa: First phase of a sequential design comparing motivation enhancement therapy and cognitive behavioral therapy. *Behaviour Research and Therapy, 37*(5), 405–418.

Truax, C. B., & Carkhuff, R. R. (1967). *Toward effective counseling and psychotherapy: Training and practice.* Chicago: Aldine.

Tuke, S. (1813). *Description of the retreat* (Republished in 1996). London: Process Books.

Tunis, S. L., Delucchi, K. L., Schwartz, K., Banys, P., & Sees, K. L. (1995). The relationship of counselor and peer alliance to drug use and HIV risk behaviors in a six-month methadone detoxification program. *Addictive Behavior, 20,* 395–405.

Tryon, G. S., & Winograd, G. (2002). Goal consensus and collaboration. In J. C. Norcross (Ed.), *Psychotherapy relationships that work: Therapist contributions and responsiveness to patients* (pp. 109–125). New York: Oxford University Press.

Valle, S. K. (1981). Interpersonal functioning of alcoholism counselors and treatment outcome. *Journal of Studies on Alcohol, 42,* 783–790.

Waldron, H. B., Slesnick, N., Brody, J. L., Turner, C. W., & Peterson, T. R. (2001). Treatment outcomes for adolescent substance abuse at 4- and 7-month assessments. *Journal of Consulting and Clinical Psychology, 69*(5), 802–813.

Wampold, B. W., Moody, M., Stich, F., Benson, K., & Ahn, H. (1997). A meta-analysis of outcome studies comparing bona fide psychotherapies: Empirically, "all must have prizes." *Psychological Bulletin, 122,* 203–215.

Westerberg, V. S. (1998). What predicts success? In W. R. Miller & N. Heather (Eds.), *Treating addictive behaviors* (2nd ed.) (pp. 301–315). New York: Plenum Press.

Wilson, G. T., Fairburn, C. C., Agras, W. S., Walsh, T. B., & Kraemer, H. (2002). Cognitive-behavioral therapy for bulimia nervosa: Time course and mechanisms of change. *Journal of Consulting and Clinical Psychology, 70*(2), 267–274.

Wilson, G. T., Loeb, K. L., Walsh, B. T., Labouvie, E., Petkova, E., Liu, X., & Waternaux, C. (1999). Psychological versus pharmacological treatments of bulimia nervosa: Predictors and processes of change. *Journal of Consulting and Clinical Psychology, 67*(4), 451–459.

Winters, J., Fals-Stewart, W., O'Farrell, T. J., Birchler, G. R., Kelley, M. L. (2002). Behavioral couples therapy for female substance-abusing patients: Effects on substance use and relationship adjustment. *Journal of Consulting and Clinical Psychology, 70*(2), 344–355.

Zywiak, W. H., Longabaugh, R., & Wirtz, P. W. (2002). Decomposing the relationships between pretreatment social network characteristics and alcohol treatment outcome. *Journal of Studies on Alcohol, 63*(1), 114–121.

16

Treatment Factors in Treating Substance Use Disorders

Barbara S. McCrady

Peter E. Nathan

INTRODUCTION

Alcohol and other substance use disorders are common in adults, with lifetime prevalence among Americans of 18.2% for alcohol use disorders, and 6.1% for other substance use disorders (Grant & Dawson, 1999). Most adults with these disorders do not receive treatment—the lifetime use of any form of treatment among persons diagnosed with alcohol abuse is 12.4%, only 24% of those with alcohol dependence receive treatment (National Institutes of Health, 1998), and the majority of drinkers resolve their problems without formal treatment (Sobell, Cunningham, & Sobell, 1996). There is, however, good evidence that treatment can enhance the probability of a positive outcome (e.g., Finney, Moos, & Timko, 1999).

Although the focus of the chapter is on psychological therapies, the context in which alcohol and substance use disorders are treated bears comment. First, most psychoactive drugs have the potential to create physiological dependence, and cessation of use generally is associated with a doc-umented withdrawal syndrome that ranges from unpleasant and uncomfortable for the individual (e.g., nicotine withdrawal) to potentially life-threatening (e.g., major withdrawal syndrome from alcohol; withdrawal from long-acting sedative-hypnotics). Additionally, most psychoactive substances, used over time, cause medical disorders that also range in severity. Clinicians providing psychological treatments must provide these treatments with knowledge of the physiological substrates for these disorders. A second factor is the high co-morbidity between substance use disorders and other psychological disorders, as well as co-morbidities among substance use disorders (Grant & Dawson, 1999). Most treatment outcome studies have tested treatments in populations relatively homogeneous for a specific substance use disorder, a choice that limits the generalizability of results to ongoing clinical practice. Rigorous studies of treatments that address client populations presenting with multiple disorders are rare, and no firm conclusions can be drawn from the few studies reported. A third factor that complicates psychological treatments is the social context common to many substance abusers. Clients may be entering treatment under mandate from the judicial or social welfare system, or as a requirement of continued employment. Pending legal charges or threat of loss of custody of children may overlay treatment. Poverty and homelessness characterize certain segments of the population with substance use disorders, and social service interventions become a necessary precondition to the provision of psychological services.

A range of treatment services is available, and the selection of level of care, concomitant medical services, and pharmacological treatments become important clinical decisions that precede the delivery of any specific psychological interventions. Treatments for substance use disorders are available across a wide range of levels of care—medically supervised inpatient treatment, other forms of residential rehabilitation, intensive outpatient or standard outpatient treatment, halfway houses, or self-help groups. Although a number of efforts to match clients to level of care have been proposed (e.g., Mee-Lee, Shulman, Fishman, Gastfriend, & Griffith, 2001), research to date has not found superior outcomes for patients assigned to treatments according to patient-treatment matching criteria (e.g. McKay, Cacciola, McLellan, Alterman, & Wirtz, 1997). Similarly, although there are a number of pharmacological treatments for substance use disorders with good evidence for effectiveness (e.g., naltrexone and acamprosate for alcohol dependence; nicotine replacement therapies and buproprion for nicotine dependence; methadone for heroin dependence, reviewed in Barber & O'Brien, 1999), articulated, empirically based guidelines for the selection of psychological versus pharmacological therapies are limited.

The balance of the chapter focuses on findings from controlled research studies of specific psychological treatments for specific substance use disorders, with a primary focus on alcohol use disorders, for which the bulk of controlled clinical trials have been completed. The reader, however, must recognize both that treatments for substance use disorders cannot be viewed as existing in pure form separate from the medical, psychiatric, and social context of these clients' lives, and that only a fraction of treatment that substance abusers receive will be delivered as outpatient, psychological therapy.

Before discussing specific findings, it is important to note that there are varying approaches to defining successful outcomes of substance abuse treatment. Historically, continuous abstinence was the only standard used to judge the effectiveness of substance abuse treatment. The founding of Alcoholics Anonymous in 1935 first established and the later publication of Jellinek's *Disease concept of alcoholism* in 1960 then reinforced the view among substance abuse professionals that abstinence was the only treatment outcome that offered the recovering substance abuser the prospect of long-term enhancement in quality of life. However, this conviction was challenged by data from several broad-spectrum behavioral treatment programs for chronic alcoholics reported in the 1970s (e.g., Lovibond & Caddy, 1970; Sobell & Sobell, 1973a, 1973b). Data from these studies appeared to call into question the viability of abstinence as the sole treatment goal for alcoholics. Subsequent examinations of these findings, however, convinced most observers that they had not in fact successfully challenged the primacy of abstinence as a prime treatment goal for severely alcohol dependent individuals (e.g., Nathan & McCrady, 1987). This view was buttressed by data from Vaillant's longitudinal study of Harvard College undergraduates followed for more than four decades (Vaillant, 1995). Vaillant found that although almost all the individuals who developed alcohol problems during their lifetimes drank without problems for varying periods of time, those with more severe alcohol dependence who achieved and maintained stable sobriety did significantly better physically and emotionally than those who entered and left periods of abstinence. Data for individuals with alcohol problems, however, suggest that positive outcomes that involve moderate or occasional drinking can be achieved (e.g. Sanchez-Craig, Wilkinson, & Davila, 1995).

Given the range of severity of substance use problems, as well as the relapsing nature of substance use disorders, researchers have moved to the use of continuous measures of outcome rather than categorical outcome variables (such as abstinent versus not abstinent). The most commonly used contemporary approach assesses aggregate change in the number of drinking or drug use days as well as change in the amount consumed per drinking day, in the belief that measures of the proportion of time a person is "functioning well" provide a realistic, inclusive estimate of the impact of treatment (e.g. Project MATCH Research Group, 1997b). A complementary approach to measuring outcome is to measure changes in psychopathology and quality of life—improved life functioning—posttreatment, in the conviction that positive changes in drinking would be paralleled by improvement in quality of life (e.g., Veterans Administration Medical Centers Cooperative Study, VAMCCS; Ouimette, Finney, & Moos, 1997).

TREATMENTS WITH SUPPORT FOR EFFECTIVENESS

Sources of Data

Our identification of treatments with empirical support draws from multiple sources. In 1995, APA's Division of Clinical Psychology (Division 12) proposed a set of research criteria designed to identify "well-established treatments" and "probably efficacious treatments" (Task Force on Promotion and Dissemination of Psychological Procedures, 1995). Because the Task Force criteria for defining a treatment have been published widely, the details will not be repeated here. Briefly, the Task Force defined treatments as either "empirically-validated" or "probably efficacious." Replicated findings of controlled clinical trials, conducted by different research groups, with sufficiently large samples, formed the core of the criteria. No treatments for substance use disorders were included in the initial 1995 list developed by the Task Force. Likewise, a subsequent update by the same group (Chambliss et al., 1996) failed to include any "well-established treatments" for the substance use disorders, although it did list four "probably efficacious" treatments. In 1998, when treatments were again added to the group's list (Chambliss et al., 1998), only one treatment for substance abuse met criteria as a "well-established" treatment, "multi-component cognitive-behavior therapy with relapse prevention for smoking cessation," although several other treatments for sub-stance abuse were added to the list of "probably efficacious" treatments (Chambliss et al., 1998).

This paucity of Task Force listings of substance abuse treatments underscored the inadequacies of outcome research on psychosocial treatments for substance use disorders to that time. In attempting to explain the omission from the Division 12 Task Force listings of any "well-established" treatments for substance use disorders, McCrady (2000) applied Task Force standards to four well-accepted treatments for alcoholism, brief intervention, social skills training, community reinforcement approach, and behavioral marital therapy. She confirmed that none met Task Force criteria as "well-established" despite the widespread view in the field that they enjoyed strong empirical support.

The recent publication of findings of the VAMCCS and Project MATCH multi-site treatment outcome studies (Ouimette et al., 1997; Project MATCH Research Group, 1997a) has improved this situation. Both studies involved substantial numbers of well-characterized patients, most of whom met DSM-IV criteria for alcohol abuse or dependence. More than 1,700 patients (952 from outpatient settings, 774 in aftercare treatment after a period of inpatient treatment) participated in Project MATCH; over 3,000 patients participated in the VAMCCS. Project MATCH patients were randomly assigned to treatments following thorough multidimensional assessments; the VAMCCS employed a quasi-experimental nonrandom design that contrasted three experimental conditions that met criteria for quality and theoretical integrity. Project MATCH treatments, all of them time-limited and outpatient, included Cognitive-Behavioral Coping Skills Treatment (CBT; Kadden et al., 1992), Motivational Enhancement Therapy (MET; Miller, Zweben, DiClemente, & Rychtarik, 1992), and 12-step Facilitation (TSF; Nowinski, Baker, & Carroll, 1992). VAMCCS treatments included cognitive-behavioral, 12-step, and eclectic treatment; all were inpatient treatments. Follow-up extended through a year for VAMCCS patients and to 39 months for Project MATCH patients. The geographic diversity of the multiple sites employed in both studies increased the generalizability of their findings.

Outcome data suggest that substantial numbers of patients in the two studies improved after treatment. All Project MATCH follow-ups through the 39-month mark (Project MATCH Research Group, 1998) confirmed reductions in number of drinking days of more than 70% and in amount of alcohol consumed each drinking day of the same or greater magnitude for all three treatments. Complicating the efficacy assessment, however, was the fact that the percent of patients completely abstinent, the traditional "gold standard" for alcoholism treatment, was less than 40% at each follow-up, suggesting that although Project MATCH patients drank much less and much less often posttreatment, the majority never achieved or maintained abstinence.

Eleven outcome measures were used in the VAMCCS study (Ouimette et al., 1997). Five reflected substance use, two assessed anxiety and depression, and three tapped social variables, including arrests, employment, and living situation. Despite significant differences among patients in ethnicity, prior alcohol and drug use, and prior experience in treatment as a function of treatment condition, patients in all three treatments reduced substance use and improved in most other areas of functioning equally, both at the end of inpatient treatment and at the one-year follow-up. However, only 25–30% of patients were without a substance abuse problem, only 23–29% were in remission from their substance abuse, and only 18–25% had maintained abstinence at the one-year follow-up. Most patient-by-treatment interactions did not appear to impact on treatment response.

A third source of quality data on outcomes of substance abuse treatment comes from Finney and Moos's (2002) evaluation of effectiveness rankings of 15 psychosocial treatment models. All 15 treatments had been assessed in three or more studies designed to judge their effectiveness and were included in four earlier comprehensive reviews by Holder, Longabaugh, Miller, & Rubonis (1991), Miller et al. (1995), Finney and Monahan (1996), and Miller, Andrews, Wilbourne, & Bennett (1998). The studies on which the modalities were ranked were chosen because they were of good methodological quality. Although there is some variation in the rankings of some modalities across the reviews, most of the modalities with high effectiveness rankings could be characterized as cognitive behavioral interventions designed to enhance skills in coping with everyday life stressors. The two modalities consistently found to be most effective were social skills training and community reinforcement. Behavioral marital therapy and brief motivational counseling also appeared to be effective. Finney and Moos's (2002) review also showed, as have prior reviews (e.g., Miller et al., 1995), that many of the most widely used treatments for alcoholism—educational films, confrontational intervention, and general alcoholism counseling—appear to be ineffective. Although 12-step approaches were not included in Finney and Moos's review of treatments administered by professionals, the TSF component of Project MATCH did evaluate the efficacy of these approaches, finding them comparable to MET and CBT. From this review of multiple sources, several specific treatments for alcohol and cocaine use disorders were identified that had good empirical support for effectiveness.

Alcohol Use Disorders

Our review of the literature yielded seven major psychological treatments for alcohol use disorders with good support for effectiveness.

Motivational Enhancement Therapies (MET)

Advances in the understanding of the process of behavior change (e.g., Connors, Donovan, & DiClemente, 2001; Miller & Rollnick, 2002) emphasize the central roles for problem recognition and readiness to change, particularly with substance use disorders. A family of interventions, broadly defined as motivational in focus, has been developed and tested, primarily with heavy drinkers and persons meeting criteria for alcohol abuse. Several factors are common to these interventions, including assessment, informational feedback about the extent, severity, and consequences of the individual's current pattern of drinking, and recommendations to change. The interventions are delivered in a style that is empathic to and respectful of the individual, and often offer a menu of choices for change. Interventions typically are brief in length and may be provided in a single session. Given the brevity of the treatment, no-treatment controls often are used as the comparison. Results are consistent in demonstrating measurable decreases in drinking, as well as improvement in other psychosocial functioning indicators, such as employment or health care utilization (e.g. Fleming, Barry, Manwell, Johnson, & London, 1997).

MET models also have been used with alcohol dependent drinkers, either as an add-on to ongoing treatment, or as a distinct, brief treatment spanning two to four sessions. As an add-on, motivational enhancement appears to increase treatment retention and positive outcomes (Brown & Miller, 1993). As a stand-alone treatment, motivational enhancement has yielded outcomes similar to other, longer outpatient treatments.

Cognitive-behavioral (CBT) Coping Skills Training

Cognitive-behavioral treatments include a range of interventions. Broadly, these interventions are comprised of three major elements—identification of situations that represent high risk for drinking, development of behavioral skills to cope with high-risk situations, and development of complementary cognitive coping strategies. Behavioral skills training has included assertiveness training, broader social skills training, relaxation, other stress management techniques, and behavioral mood management training. Cognitive interventions have focused on enhancing self-efficacy for change, increasing cognitive strategies to increase thinking about potential negative consequences of drinking in high-risk situations, and enhancing positive expectancies about the outcomes of treatment. One of the complexities of reviewing research on the effectiveness of cognitive-behavioral interventions is that each treatment study has employed a different combination of cognitive-behavioral treatment elements. Despite the inconsistencies in implementation of CBT across studies, a fairly consistent literature has emerged (Carroll, 1999). When CBT has been compared to wait-list or minimal treatment controls, outcomes typically have been superior for the CBT. When compared to other active treatments, main effects differences are not typically found. Several individual studies have suggested specific patient-treatment matching effects, with CBT proving more effective for clients presenting with concomitant Antisocial Personality Disorder or other Axis I disorders (Cooney, Kadden, Litt, & Getter, 1991; Kadden, Cooney, Getter, & Litt, 1989).

Twelve-step Facilitation (TSF) Treatments

The most ubiquitous form of treatment for alcohol use disorders is treatment that draws upon the principles and steps of Alcoholics Anonymous (AA). Treatment focuses on enhancing clients' views that their drinking is a disease and that the most effective route to recovery is to use the fellowship and program of AA as a vehicle for recovery. More alcoholism treatment programs are based at least broadly on this treatment model than on any other (Nowinski, 1999). The central focus of TSF is to help the client work the first several steps of AA, thereby facilitating active engagement with AA. Twelve-step-based models often are used in inpatient or intensive outpatient treatment programs in the United States.

Despite the ubiquity of 12-step counseling, until Project MATCH the treatment approach had been subjected to virtually no randomized controlled clinical trials. Overall, Project MATCH reported no significant main effects differences among the three treatments, but TSF was significantly more effective in inducing clients to maintain continuous abstinence during follow-up (Project MATCH Research Group, 1997a). Similar results have come from a matched-groups, nonrandomized trial comparing addictions treatment units based on different treatment philosophies within the Veterans Administration system (Moos, Finney, Ouimette, & Suchinsky, 1999).

Community Reinforcement Approach (CRA)

CRA was developed and first tested in the early 1970s (Hunt & Azrin, 1973). CRA combined two major approaches to psychosocial treatment prominent at the time—contingency management procedures and community psychology. As CRA was first practiced, chronic, state hospital alcoholics were primed with access to a range of potentially desirable activities within the community, including employment, contact with their families, and social activities. After initial priming, continued access to these activities was made contingent on abstinence from alcohol, and withdrawal of the activity occurred contingent upon drinking. Later iterations of the model (e.g., Azrin, 1976) attempted to prevent relapses through contingently monitored use of disulfiram, and assignment to a community "buddy" who assisted the client with problems of daily living. CRA subsequently was developed further, retaining the focus on accessing desirable activities in association with abstinence, but decreasing the emphasis on formal behavioral contracts to make access to reinforcers contingent upon abstinence. A recent series of controlled trials with indigent alcoholics has found consistently positive results favoring CRA over traditional or comparison treatments (Meyers & Smith, 1995). No CRA studies have been reported with more socially stable or middle-class persons diagnosed with alcohol abuse or dependence.

Contingency (Behavioral) Contracting

A specific element of CRA, contingency contracting, has been evaluated independently in a series of studies. Contingency contracting establishes a behavioral contract between the client and another individual that specifies client behaviors to be rewarded through specific actions of the other individual. Client behaviors studied have included attending aftercare programs after inpatient treatment and taking disulfiram. Controlled evaluations have demonstrated better compliance with target behaviors with contingency contracting than with treatment as usual, and better drinking outcomes, at least while the contracts were in effect (reviewed in McCrady, 2000).

Behavioral Couples Therapy (BCT)

Behavioral couples therapy for alcohol use disorders combines behavioral couples therapy with alcohol-specific content. BCT includes interventions to enhance positive and pleasurable exchanges between intimate partners, boost communication and problem-solving skills, and increase partner support for sobriety (Epstein & McCrady, 2002). In one version of BCT, couples also develop behavioral contracts around the daily use of disulfiram. Controlled clinical trials have reported better drinking outcomes for BCT than

comparison treatments, and identified specific elements of the treatment, including enhancement of the couple relationship and disulfiram contracts, as active ingredients in the treatment (McCrady, Stout, Noel, Abrams, & Nelson, 1991; O'Farrell, Choquette, Cutter, Brown, & McCourt, 1993). Adding relapse prevention interventions has yielded further improvements in treatment outcome (McCrady, Epstein, & Hirsch, 1999; O'Farrell, Choquette, & Cutter, 1998).

Cue Exposure Therapy (CET)

Cue exposure therapy draws upon findings suggesting that alcoholics develop conditioned physiological responses to sight, smell, and other cues associated with alcohol. CET uses a classic extinction paradigm through repeated trials in which the alcohol dependent client is exposed to cues associated with drinking and physiological responses are monitored until there is no discernable response. Some CET studies have included imaginal or behavioral rehearsal of alternative coping responses in the presence of drinking-related cues. Several randomized clinical trials have reported results that favored CET over various comparison treatments (Drummond & Glautier, 1994; Monti et al., 2001; Rohsenow et al., 2001; Sitharthan, Sitharthan, Hough, & Kavanagh, 1997).

Cocaine Dependence

Two psychosocial treatments have demonstrable support for the treatment of cocaine dependence.

Community Reinforcement Approach With Vouchers

In a series of experiments, Higgins and his colleagues (e.g., Higgins et al., 1995; Higgins et al., 1994) have tested a treatment model that combines contemporary CRA with a strict program of reinforcement for urine samples clean for the target drug of abuse. Specifically, clients earn vouchers toward the purchase of desirable goods in the community for maintaining abstinence from the targeted drug of abuse. Schedules of reinforcement are set to provide greater rewards for greater numbers of consecutive clean urines, and counselors work closely with clients in the selection of goods that would facilitate achievement of treatment goals. Controlled trials have demonstrated consistent superiority of the CRA with vouchers over comparison treatments, and dismantling studies have demonstrated that the specific contingent relationship between clean urines and vouchers is the major active ingredient in the treatment.

Drug Counseling

Individual drug counseling varies widely from counselor to counselor. One major, multi-site study, however, the Cocaine Treatment Study (e.g., Crits-Cristoph et al., 1997), defined a specific drug counseling protocol and tested it against other standardized treatments for cocaine dependence. In their approach, individual drug counseling combined encouragement of 12-step group attendance with cognitive-behavioral elements such as identification of and avoidance of high-risk situations for use, restructuring various aspects of life functioning, and increasing healthy behaviors. Compared to supportive-expressive therapy, cognitive therapy, or group drug counseling alone, outcome data favored a combination of individual and group drug counseling in terms of drug use outcomes; but the treatments did not differ in impacting on other areas of life functioning (Crits-Christoph et al., 1999, 2001).

GENERAL CATEGORIES OF INTERVENTIONS AND PRINCIPLES OF CHANGE

The preceding descriptions have focused on specific treatments for specific substances of abuse. Treatments, however, can also be considered along a number of other dimensions; the two we consider most illuminating are discussed in this section.

The first, "General Categories of Interventions," constitutes a set of five general procedural classes on which psychosocial treatments for virtually every psychopathologic condition amenable to psychosocial treatment can be classified. They include *directive, nondirective, and self-directive procedures; interpersonal/systemic versus intrapersonal/individual procedures; thematic/insight-oriented versus symptom/skill-building procedures;* *intensive versus nonintensive/short-term procedures; and abreactive versus emotionally supportive procedures.* One aim in our discussion of this material is to determine whether a single alternative within each of the five general classes characterizes most or all of the empirically supported treatments for habit disorders. Interestingly, this is the case with only the first procedural class, *directive, nondirective, and self-directive procedures.* In the other four, some empirically supported treatments for substance abuse are characterized by one alternative, others, by the other.

The second dimension considered in this section, "Principles of Change," identifies four specific therapeutic interventions (*enhancing/maintaining motivation to change, teaching and learning of coping skills, restructuring the social environment,* and *changing conditioned responses to substances*) and two broader therapeutic effects (*changing perceptions of social norms* and *enhancing self-efficacy for meaningful behavioral change*) that underlie one or more empirically supported treatments for substance abuse. These six variables "cross-cut" the five general categories of interventions. For example, as our discussion will show, both *intensive* (Alcoholics Anonymous) and *nonintensive/short-term* (Motivational Enhancement Therapy) treatment procedures strive to *enhance motivation to change,* which many consider necessary before habit change can take place.

Together, the General Categories of Interventions and the Principles of Change more fully describe the empirically supported treatments for substance abuse than either alone.

General Categories of Interventions

Directive, Nondirective, and Self-directive Procedures

Most empirically supported treatments for substance use disorders are at least moderately directive in focus: they guide or direct clients toward specific therapy foci and, ultimately, to specific cognitive or behavioral change goals. Motivational therapies appear to be the least directive, with a commitment to helping clients select goals, an emphasis on accurate empathy, and an effort to create opportunities for client choice. Despite these nondirective elements, however, motivational therapies have a clearly defined structure that includes feedback, and an ultimate goal of helping the client accept drinking as a problem in need of a change plan.

All treatments that derive from cognitive-behavioral principles (CBT, CRA, BCT, CET) are structured and directive. Therapists set agendas for each session, sessions include active problem solving and rehearsal of new skills, and clients are directed to complete homework assignments between therapy sessions. CRA and CET are particularly directive in that they are designed to change contingent relationships between drug use and environmental consequences, thereby requiring extensive monitoring; as a result, clearly specified consequences are integral to the treatment. TSF also is a directive treatment approach. Here, too, therapists provide specific homework assignments, clients are directed to specific behaviors, particularly attendance at meetings of AA and engagement in AA program activities, and clients are encouraged to adopt specific belief systems about themselves and their drinking.

Interpersonal/Systemic Versus Intrapersonal/Individual Procedures

There are two distinct aspects to the interpersonal versus intrapersonal dimension of treatment—the degree to which treatments can be or are implemented in an individual versus larger group context, and the degree to which treatment incorporates environmental or interpersonal factors into the conceptualization and content of the treatment. Most treatments for substance use disorders with empirical support have been implemented in either an individual or group therapy context (e.g., CBT, TSF, BCT). Certain treatments, particularly MET and CET, require a graduated set of experiences in the treatment that are very specific to each individual client. These, therefore, are implemented solely in an individual therapy setting. For some treatments (BCT, behavioral contracting, CRA), involvement of significant others is integral to the treatment model.

In the broadest sense, all of the treatments focus on the interaction between an individual and his or her life environment, both interpersonal and physical. MET helps the client consider ways in which alcohol use may have impacted various areas of life functioning, including interpersonal relationships, job functioning, and health status. CBT works with clients to identify high-risk situations for use, including those that involve interpersonal situations, and helps clients develop skills to cope more effectively in interpersonal relationships. Although TSF may be delivered either individually or in a group context, it has as one of its ultimate goals that the client engages with AA, a fellowship that is fundamentally interpersonal in focus. Additionally, in helping clients work the fourth step in AA, therapists help clients engage in a deeply introspective process to identify their own shortcomings and the persons they may have harmed. Later, clients may, either with continuing therapy or solely through their involvement with AA, attempt to make amends to those they have harmed. Even CET, which focuses primarily on conditioned responses to cues associated with drinking, may include interpersonal stressors among those cues. Additionally, CET is based on the notion that the individual is functioning and responding within specific environmental contexts. Thus, each of the empirically supported treatments views drinking or other drug use as occurring in an environmental context, and through various techniques focuses on change in the individual in interaction with his or her environment.

Thematic/Insight-oriented Versus Symptom/Skill Building

Although it is possible to pose an "either/or" question about the degree to which treatments focus on insight versus building new skills, an alternative perspective, taken here, is that there is interplay between these two dimensions, with a relative emphasis on one or the other. Thus, none of the empirically supported treatments for substance use disorders posit insight as the primary mechanism of change. However, insight is integral to the treatments in a variety of ways. First, clients must recognize and accept that their substance use is a problem in need of change. Historically, many treatments for substance use disorders have incorporated the concept of "denial," and attempted to decrease it as part of treatment, with TSF treatments using this approach most. MET considers insight to be an important core element of the treatment, and the intervention is designed to help clients experience an emotional and cognitive discrepancy between their current state and their goals and aspirations as a vehicle to help them recognize the need for change. CBT may incorporate interventions to help clients identify and rehearse positive consequences for change and negative consequences of continued use, an intervention that is both insight- and skills-based.

A second important area of necessary insight is the recognition of repetitive patterns of behavior and thinking that lead to continued use of substances or relapse. In CBT, TSF, and CRA, clients learn to identify their own vulnerabilities and needs, as well as relationships between these needs and vulnerabilities and their substance use. A third area of insight follows naturally from insight into vulnerabilities—recognition and understanding of the need for active behavioral change in order to be successful. Thus, clients learn not only that there are experiences (both internal and external) connected to their drinking or drug use, but also that they must become active agents of change.

Complementing these types of insight is an explicit focus on the presenting problem, the client's substance use disorder, and an overt focus on the substance use. Thus, MET focuses on the client's experience and thinking about his or her use; CBT helps clients learn a set of behavioral coping skills to abstain or decrease drinking; TSF focuses on abstinence, involvement with AA, and explicitly working the first steps of AA, which are designed to engage the individual in the AA program of recovery; CRA focuses on skills for sobriety and the development of alternative, reinforcing experiences; behavioral contracting incorporates specific contracts for behaviors related to abstinence; CRA with vouchers provides explicit rewards for abstinence.

In contrast to treatments that view insight as necessary and sufficient to effect therapeutic change, however, the empirically supported treatments for substance use disorders promote a blend of specific types of insight and client awareness with an explicit and direct focus on the presenting substance use problem. Both elements are integral to these treatment models.

Intensive Versus Nonintensive/Short-term

Treatments may vary in intensity along a number of dimensions—frequency or length of treatment sessions, overall length of treatment, the degree to which use of multiple treatment modalities might be integral to the treatment model, and the degree to which treatment is viewed as a discrete, time-limited event. Empirically supported treatments for substance use disorders vary considerably in intensity.

At the least intensive end, MET is designed as a brief treatment, ranging from one to four sessions. Treatment is intended to stimulate motivation to change, and clients are expected to be able to implement change without further therapeutic assistance. At the most intensive end, TSF, although a time-limited treatment in itself, is based on a view of alcoholism as a chronic disease that has no cure that can be arrested only through continued abstinence and continuous involvement in an ongoing program of recovery. Thus, in the early months of recovery, members of AA are encouraged to attend AA daily, and lifelong involvement in AA is recommended. Although TSF was delivered strictly as an outpatient, once weekly treatment in Project MATCH, it is more typically delivered in an intensive outpatient treatment model, in which clients participate in several hours of group, instructional, and individual treatment, several days a week. This more intensive model for the delivery of TSF has not been evaluated in randomized clinical trials.

Between the two extremes of TSF and MET are the other empirically supported treatments for substance abuse. CRA has been delivered with varying degrees of intensity. In a program for homeless alcoholics (Smith, Meyers, & Delaney, 1998), treatment included daily skills training groups, a daily disulfiram compliance group, weekly social club events, a job club, and couples therapy where appropriate. Treatment length was variable, but averaged approximately 47 sessions during the first two months of treatment. CRA with vouchers also is a relatively intensive treatment; it is designed to span 24 weeks (Budney & Higgins, 1998). During the first 12 weeks, individual treatment sessions are scheduled twice weekly, additional telephone or in-person contacts are available, and urine samples are collected thrice weekly to test for the presence of drugs. During the second 12 weeks, individual sessions are decreased to weekly sessions and urine samples are collected twice weekly.

Cognitive behavioral treatments also have varied in length and intensity of treatment. Project MATCH provided for 12 sessions of CBT; earlier trials of the model (e.g., Kadden et al., 1989) used a six-month weekly group treatment protocol. CBT also has been used as the basis for inpatient or intensive outpatient treatment programs, combining individual and group therapy sessions. No randomized clinical trials have contrasted CBT with another treatment model at this level of treatment intensity. BCT also has been variable in intensity, from a 10-week group treatment to 15 conjoint sessions to a combination of weekly treatment followed by up to a year of intermittent continuing contacts.

Thus, empirically supported treatments for substance use disorders vary in intensity from one to four treatment sessions to multiple individual and group sessions each week. None, however, is designed to be provided over more than a six-month period, with the partial exception of TSF, which has an explicit goal of bringing about lifelong involvement in a program of recovery.

Abreactive Versus Emotionally Supportive

A fifth dimension on which to examine the empirically supported treatments is the degree to which the treatment focuses on enhancing the client's experience of emotion versus supporting clients in ways that might dampen down the emotionality of treatment. For three treatments, MET, TSF, and CET, the experience of and, at times, the intensification of emotion, are integral to the treatment. Although empathy is central to MET, the approach attempts to enhance clients' awareness of the discrepancy between their current and desired circumstances in life. Recognizing the depth of this discrepancy and recognizing the ways that alcohol might have contributed to the client's current circumstance is an emotional process that is expected to generate motivation to change. Although the hypothesized mechanisms of change and techniques used are quite different, in helping clients work the first three steps in AA, TSF also

has a substantial focus on enhancing clients' awareness of the degree to which alcohol is controlling their lives, that they have been unable to change on their own, and on developing an emotional acceptance and willingness to accept help. For many, this is a deeply emotional process. Step 4 also has an emotional focus as clients are encouraged to examine specific "character defects" such as jealousy, impulsiveness, greed, meanness, selfishness, or arrogance (Nowinski, Baker, & Carroll, 1992); are asked to describe specific instances in which these defects of character have been displayed; and are urged to consider how they have harmed others as a result. Despite the intense focus on emotion that is a part of TSF, however, some elements of the treatment have a more emotionally supportive quality. Clients are helped to recognize situations in which they have felt anger, loneliness, fatigue, or other negative emotions, and are encouraged to act to either prevent or respond to these emotions in ways that will help them to stay sober.

Other treatments, including CBT, BCT, CRA (with or without vouchers), and behavioral contracting, focus more on emotional support and helping clients develop new skills to cope with negative affect. However, even in these latter treatments, clients are encouraged to examine their emotional responses as a source of information about targets for change.

Thus, as with many of the other dimensions of therapeutic change, empirically supported treatments for substance use disorders range widely in the degree to which they focus on support versus enhanced experience of emotion. For most of the treatments, however, the complexity of emotion, and the role of emotion in the substance use and relapse process is a recognized element in the treatment, and each treatment has an explicit approach to dealing with negative emotions.

PRINCIPLES OF CHANGE

Specific Therapeutic Interventions

Therapeutic interventions to enhance or maintain motivation to change have long been considered a *sine qua non* for successful treatment for substance use disorders (Prochaska, DiClemente, & Norcross, 1992; Yahne & Miller, 1999): if the addict has not decided to change his or her substance using behavior, it is believed, treatment of any kind has little chance of success. Although the specifics of the methods differ, several of the empirically supported treatments reviewed in this chapter include motivational enhancement as a core element of the treatment. MET is clearly focused on client motivation, but other treatments are as well. Reinforcement-based therapies, such as the CRA, contingency contracting, and CRA with vouchers, enhance motivation by providing positive incentives to change through access to desired reinforcers contingent on changes in substance use or treatment-related behaviors. Similarly, much of the focus of early sessions of 12-step Facilitation Treatment is on a range of exercises, drawn largely from the first four steps, that are designed to heighten motivation to stop drinking, change the emotional context of relationships with others, and modify self-perception of strengths and weaknesses.

Concluding a brief summary of the results of contemporary research on motivation as it relates to substance abusers in treatment, Yahne and Miller (1999) made the following observations:

> One synthesis of these findings is that positive change is a natural process that the therapist does not own or originate but can facilitate. Enduring change can be triggered by a combination of an awareness that there is a problem and a belief that there is a way out, facilitated by a supportive and empathic therapeutic relationship. This can occur even in a single session, which is good news because the modal length of stay in substance abuse treatment is short. Change is usually engendered not by the therapist pushing, confronting, or directing, but by her or his listening reflectively to the client and evoking the client's own motivation for change. (Yahne & Miller, 1999, p. 239)

Teaching coping skills is a second category of intervention common to the majority of the empirically supported treatments. CBT (Kadden et al., 1992) provides the clearest example of a set of interventions designed to teach skills to enable clients to learn more successful coping skills to deal with high-risk situations for drinking. Social skills training, anger management training, relapse prevention, and assertive training are among the com-

ponents of cognitive behavioral treatment packages that have been developed by a number of behavioral psychologists through the years (e.g., Carroll, 1998; Marlatt & Gordon, 1985; Monti, Abrams, Kadden, & Cooney, 1989). Typically, these skills are taught on the assumption that they will fill intrapersonal and interpersonal voids that, in the past, have led to frustration, failure to cope, and anxiety and depression. All of these, in turn, heighten the risk for a return to alcohol or drug abuse to dampen the emotional consequences of failure.

As with enhancement of motivation, however, facilitating the acquisition of cognitive and behavioral coping skills is not unique to CBT. BCT and CRA draw upon many of the same coping skills strategies integral to CBT, and BCT also incorporates the teaching of marital communication and problem-solving skills. TSF treatment and involvement with AA also provide clients with a set of skills to cope both with drinking situations and other life challenges. AA members are taught time-structuring activities, such as AA attendance, cognitive coping strategies such as thinking about negative consequences when tempted to drink, and behavioral coping strategies, such as calling other AA members. Coping skills to manage life problems focus on introspection, prayer and meditation, making amends, and reaching out to others. Thus, a focus on the acquisition of a set of new skills to manage specific challenges associated with sobriety and broader life challenges is common to many of the empirically supported treatments.

Restructuring the alcoholics' social environments is a third element common to many of the empirically supported treatments. Community reinforcement therapy (Azrin, 1976; Azrin, Sisson, Meyers, & Godley, 1982) was designed explicitly so that behaviors contributing to sobriety were reinforced and those supporting continued abusive drinking were either punished or ignored. BCT brings a major element of the social environment, the intimate other, into the treatment, and focuses explicitly on changes in the partner's responses to drinking and sobriety, as well as changes in the interpersonal relationship. CBT includes a similar focus: to help clients identify alcohol- and drug-free behaviors and settings to replace prior alcohol- and drug-involved behaviors and settings. These alternative alcohol- and drug-free behaviors become feasible when the user acquires new coping skills that permit him or her to deal with stressors without having to return to alcohol or drug use. Alcoholics Anonymous and the other 12-step programs also restructure the substance abuser's social environment by offering the recovering abuser both a nonjudgmental, alcohol- and drug-free social environment and new friends, including a sponsor available to help around the clock. The expectation that newly recovering persons will attend "90 meetings in 90 days" buttresses this intent: involvement in an alcohol and drug-free social environment stands in striking contrast to most substance abusers' previous enmeshment in a substance-laden social environment (McCrady & Miller, 1993).

Changing conditioned responses to substances is a fourth variable with commonality across several empirically supported treatments. A variety of specific conditioning-based interventions has been attempted through the years with varying degrees of success. One of the first, aversive conditioning, paired an aversive stimulus like painful electric shock or a nausea-inducing drug with cues related to alcohol in order to induce conditioned aversion. While some success has been reported, aversive conditioning is expensive and, on occasion, dangerous (Wilson, 1978). CET (Hodgson & Rankin, 1978) is the clearest example of a classical conditioning treatment with empirical support. CET involves exposing substance abusers to alcohol- or drug-related cues to which they are prevented from responding in an effort to extinguish the craving for the substance that so often is associated with relapse. Carroll (1998) has described a related classical conditioning treatment that teaches cocaine addicts how to recognize their own unique array of conditioned craving cues, so they can then seek to avoid exposure to them and thereby extinguish the craving response.

The conceptual underpinnings of CBT are based in part on operant conditioning principles. Its basic assumption is that many alcoholics lack the inter- and intrapersonal behaviors, like anger management, assertive behavior, and social skills, to cope with the predictable stressors in their environments. As a consequence, they often experience punishment rather than reward from their efforts to cope with these stressors and may turn to alcohol to dampen the punishment experience.

Teaching them the coping skills they lack, thus enabling them to manage their lives more successfully, should be accompanied by a reduced conditioned craving for alcohol and drugs in response to negative emotions.

CBT and TSF/AA also invoke conditioning processes, for example, when they induce clients explicitly to recall the negative consequences of alcohol and drug use when confronted with drinking- or drug-related cues. In the past, these cues put them at risk to return to alcohol and/or drug use; pairing them with active recall of the negative consequences to which they have led in the past is assumed to diminish—and, ultimately, extinguish—the power of the cues to reinstate alcohol or drug use.

Therapeutic Effects

Two effects of therapy contribute to positive outcomes that occur as a result of many of the specific therapeutic interventions described in the previous sections.

Changed Perceptions of Social Norms

One of the important change mechanisms for alcohol and drug users who begin to attend 12-step meetings is the discovery that it is possible to live happy, productive lives without alcohol. This comes about when they begin to realize that many of the men and women in the group were able to reconstruct their lives on achieving stable abstinence. This discovery presumably provides impetus for newly recovering addicts to *change the social norms governing the role of alcohol or drugs in their lives* and those of their closest friends. The consequent radical readjustment of thinking that takes place—from believing that it is impossible to live without alcohol or drugs to realizing that it is both possible and desirable to do so—may well be due in part to the gradual process by which the recovering addict adopts social norms from 12-step group members concerning living a life free from substances.

Similarly, MET undertakes explicitly to change social norms by providing the abuser feedback that his or her drinking does not conform to the drinking norms of the greater society of which he or she is a part. Such feedback, as noted above, is designed to motivate the individual to change drinking, in part by changing what might be erroneous social norms concerning safe consumption levels.

Enhanced Self-efficacy for Change

CBT, MET, and 12-step approaches actively promote increases in self-efficacy for meaningful change in the substance-abusing lifestyle. CBT does so quite explicitly, by identifying and teaching new skills to enable the individual to experience more reinforcement from a substance-free social environment. MET enhances self-efficacy less directly, by providing feedback about the likely negative consequences on health and well-being were the person to continue to abuse alcohol or drugs. Accompanying that feedback are specific efforts to assure the client that he or she is fully capable of taking the steps necessary to alter the current abusive pattern. Twelve-step approaches also influence self-efficacy. For example, Morgenstern, McCrady, and their colleagues (1997) demonstrated that 12-step approaches seem to work by maintaining motivation and self-efficacy for success at achieving and maintaining abstinence, while Connors, Tonigan, and Miller (2001) reported that the positive relationship between AA participation and frequency of abstinent days found in Project MATCH treatment samples 7–12 months posttreatment was mediated by perceived self-efficacy to avoid drinking.

Factors Influencing the Effectiveness of Specific Therapeutic Interventions and Therapeutic Effects

Three major factors may exert an influence on the effectiveness of therapeutic efforts. Two of these, therapist attributes and clients attributes, are described elsewhere in this volume and the reader is referred to the chapter by Haaga, Hall, & and Haas. A third factor is the degree to which treatment addresses needs beyond those specific to the alcohol or drug use.

Comprehensive treatment services for substance abusers that address the abusers' service and medical needs as well as their substance abuse heighten the likelihood of positive outcomes. Inducing the chronic substance abuser to stop drinking or taking drugs is typically only the first step in dealing with his or her problem. Methadone maintenance treatment for heroin addiction is a good example of the value of comprehensive treatment services, in this instance, for recovering heroin addicts. Research (e.g., Cooper, 1989; Woody & McNicholas, 1996) has confirmed that when case management and counseling are added to methadone administration for heroin addicts, the risk of a return to heroin dependence is substantially reduced. Methadone alone seems insufficient to effect the profound social and emotional changes the heroin addict must make to achieve stable abstinence. McLellan and his colleagues (1993) similarly found that matching services to presenting patient problems through a comprehensive set of psychosocial services enhanced treatment outcomes for a wide variety of substance abusers.

Summary: Effective Treatment Factors for Substance Use Disorders

Integrating general psychotherapeutic strategies, specific therapeutic interventions, and therapeutic effects in treatment for substance use disorders suggests that therapists should do the following: (1) be directive and problem-focused in therapy; (2) consider the interpersonal and environmental context in which the substance use occurs; (3) provide treatment in an individual, group, or family modality, depending on the individual client and treatment interventions selected; (4) provide treatment in a time-limited fashion, but develop a long-term maintenance plan that may or may not include continued formal treatment; (5) enhance the client's awareness of the extent and severity of their substance use problem and the need to change (to enhance motivation to change as well as compliance with therapeutic tasks); (6) help the client become aware of repetitive patterns of thinking and behavior that perpetuate the alcohol or drug use and learn alternative coping skills to manage these dysfunctional thoughts and behaviors; (7) attend to the affective experiences of the client, particularly in relationship to their substance use; (8) help the client restructure his or her social environment in ways that support change, either by working with the client or by directly involving important others from the client's social network; (9) attend to the importance of conditioning in the maintenance of change by

(a) assessing specific conditioned responses related to alcohol or drug use and developing ways to change these conditioned responses, and (b) rearranging consequences of use to maximize contingent reinforcement for abstinence; (10) help the client develop new perceptions of social norms related to alcohol or drug use and to abstaining from alcohol or drug use; (11) help the client to develop a greater sense of self-efficacy for change; (12) identify other social service or medical care needs and arrange for attention to these needs.

RECOMMENDATIONS FOR FUTURE RESEARCH

Active Ingredients of Treatments

Researchers continue to search for the active ingredients of psychosocial treatments for substance use disorders, reflecting a lengthy tradition in psychotherapy research more generally. Continued research is needed into the processes by which treatments work. However, there have been a number of ongoing efforts to identify active ingredients in treatment of substance use disorders. In one of the most active such efforts, Miller and his colleagues have sought to identify the specific components of MET that contribute most strongly to enhanced motivation to change alcohol and drug use (Miller, 1983; Miller, Zweben, DiClemente, & Rychtarik, 1992). This research led first to examination of natural, predictable stages of change in addictive behavior (Miller & Tonigan, 1996; Prochaska et al., 1992) and then to the tentative conclusion that MET may facilitate the natural process of change (Yahne & Miller, 1999).

Researchers also have explored the active components of cognitive behavioral treatment for substance abuse. Carroll, one of the developers of CBT for Project MATCH, has noted that CBT, like most psychosocial treatments, "realize(s) (its) effects through a complex combination of common factors and unique factors" (p. 258). Concerning the latter, she observes that, "for cognitive behavioral coping-skills approaches, the active ingredients are thought to be skill acquisition and implementation; for cognitive therapies, the active ingredient is thought to be identification and mod-

ification of dysfunctional cognitions, and for cue exposure approaches, the active ingredient for extinction is repeated exposure to the conditioned stimulus under conditions incompatible with use" (p. 258). Unfortunately, as Carroll also observed, little systematic research to validate these beliefs or to separate the effects of common and unique factors has been reported. And when Morgenstern and Longabaugh (2000) reviewed evidence from 10 well-designed CBT treatment studies in support of the reasonable hypothesis that CBT for alcohol dependence works by enhancing cognitive and behavioral coping skills, they failed to find a relationship between measures of coping and treatment outcomes, reporting "little support for the hypothesized mechanisms of action of CBT" (p. 1475).

A lengthy history of efforts to assess the role of spirituality in outcomes of involvement in Alcoholics Anonymous also can be traced (Nowinski, 1999). Spirituality is controversial: some believe it is central to the success of AA, others believe it is an epiphenomenon. Hypothetically, the best test of the centrality of spirituality to recovery would be to compare outcomes of involvement in Alcoholics Anonymous with those of involvement in counterparts that do not emphasize the spiritual domain, such as Secular Organizations for Sobriety (SOS). Unfortunately, a direct comparison of these treatments has not yet been undertaken. However, when Horstmann, Tonigan, and Scott (2000) examined the development of two distinct forms of spiritual faith development (an early "deferring" God relationship and a later "more collaborative" God relationship) in members of two AA groups, they found that two measures of AA longevity predicted preferred spiritual coping style. And, as noted above, Morgenstern, McCrady, and their colleagues (1997) and Connors et al. (2001) independently reported that perceived self-efficacy to avoid drinking predicted positive outcomes following involvement in AA, but did not report an independent contribution of changes in spirituality to predicting outcomes.

Consistency in Measurement

The consistency of clinical assessment techniques continues to be a focal concern of clinical psychologists, including those who are called upon to assess substance users. One of the most persistent such measurement problems derives from continuing questions about the reliability of syndromal diagnosis. To this end, Garfield, a pioneering psychotherapy researcher, has pointed to the unreliability of DSM-IV diagnoses as one of several reasons to reject efforts to identify empirically supported treatments (Garfield, 1996). He does so in the conviction that psychotherapy researchers need—but have not yet been able—to assemble diagnostically homogeneous groups in order to draw valid conclusions from their studies of treatment effectiveness. Although the diagnosis of substance use disorders is one of the more reliable of the diagnostic assessments mental health professionals make (Nathan, 1998), Garfield and others who question the foundations of research on empirically supported treatments still question the feasibility of assembling diagnostically homogeneous groups of patients for psychotherapy outcome studies.

A variety of instruments and methods have been developed and used to assess quantity and frequency of alcohol use before, during, and after treatment. Because they depend on self-reports by the user or reports by family members and friends, researchers have continued to express concern about the reliability of these assessments (e.g., Litten & Allen, 1992; Maisto, Connors, & Allen, 1995), even though many reports supporting the reliability of self-reports of alcohol consumption have been published (e.g., Sobell & Sobell, 1995; Stasiewicz, Bradizza, & Connors, 1997; Wilson & Grube, 1994). The validity of self-reports of alcohol use and abuse is affected by the setting and circumstances of the assessment, substance abusers' co-morbidity and ethnicity, and the possibility of adverse consequences from reports of consumption (e.g., Cherpitel & Clark, 1995; Lapham et al., 1995). It is also the case that the validity of self-reports of drug use has generally been found to be lower than that for alcohol use, perhaps because of the serious social and legal consequences that accompany even moderate drug use (Schottenfeld, 1994). At the same time, the availability of independent sources of verification of drug use, including assays of urine and blood, has been a significant aid in determining whether individuals with a history of drug abuse are continuing to use drugs (Vereby, 1992). All these are matters researchers and clinicians who work with substance abusers must consider.

Assessment of the antecedents and consequences of alcohol and drug use and abuse commonly precedes active treatment interventions. These assessments focus on personality traits and psychological symptoms, as well as environmental and interpersonal events that both impact on and are affected by substance abuse. Although many instruments have been developed and a number have become very widely used, no single instrument or set of instruments has been established as the "gold standard" for measuring these important factors (Nathan, 1996). In like fashion, assessments of the abuser's social, interpersonal, vocational, and family history, as well as details of the nature and extent of his or her substance use and abuse history, are central to assessing use and being able accurately to reflect changes following treatment, yet a standard set of assessment instruments has yet to be accepted by the field (Donovan, 1999). Measures of attitudes and beliefs important to preparing a client for AA or other 12-step programs are especially poorly developed at this point.

Blending of Effective Treatments

The well-designed Project MATCH and VAMCCS studies established a set of treatments for alcohol dependence that appear to be substantially and comparably effective. As a consequence, it is reasonable to ask whether combining the active ingredients of these treatments would result in treatment outcomes superior to those for each by itself. That is, would combining the most robust elements of CBT, MET, and TSF lead to better results than any of these three treatments alone? Requisite to this process, of course, is determination of the most robust elements of these treatments and we have noted the complexities in doing so.

A related approach would be to construct a treatment package combining the ingredients empirical research has suggested are most effective. These elements would encompass the 12 major elements of effective treatment described earlier, such as enhancing motivation, teaching coping skills, changing the interpersonal environment, and heightening self-efficacy. One way to assemble such elements into a single treatment package would be to combine the active ingredients from the Project MATCH and VAMCCS studies with the additional factors identified above that have been shown empirically to contribute importantly to positive treatment outcomes for substance abuse.

SUMMARY AND CONCLUSIONS

Important Issues in the Treatment of Substance Use Disorders

The processes of treatment for substance use disorders differ from those for treatments for other forms of psychopathology in part because of the substantial adverse physical consequences that often accompany acute and chronic alcohol or drug abuse. As a result, the treating clinician must anticipate these consequences of substance use in the client so that, if they do occur, the client can be referred to an appropriate physician for proper diagnosis and treatment. Moreover, the substantial adverse social consequences of chronic substance abuse, including criminality and downward social and financial mobility may well require the involvement of caregivers in the community charged with the responsibility for dealing with these life problems. It is also the case that alcohol and drug abusers may be mandated by the courts to enter treatment, may be treated during or after a period of incarceration, or in lieu of incarceration. Clinicians treating clients under these conditions must consider the effects of coerced treatment on treatment outcomes.

There also are many similarities between treatments for substance use disorders and other disorders. Perhaps the greatest point of similarity is that cognitive behavioral approaches are also considered treatments of choice for the mood and anxiety disorders (Barlow, Raffa, & Cohen, 2002; Craighead, Hart, Craighead, & Ilardi, 2002; Franklin & Foa, 2002). As well, decisions clinicians must make about level of care, treatment intensity and duration, and timing and sequencing of different interventions at different phases of treatment and at different points in the lifestyle of the substance abuser are comparable to those clinicians working with clients with other conditions must also make.

The high rates of co-morbidity experienced by substance abusers represent another special problem affecting their diagnosis and treatment. Most of the data on the co-morbidity of substance abusers suggest that such common co-occurring disorders as depression, anxiety, schizophrenia, and personality disorder complicate treatment and impair outcomes (e.g., Grant, 1995; Schuckit, 1994). Persons suffering from uncomplicated substance use disorders are generally easier to treat and more likely to achieve good outcomes than substance abusers with co-morbid psychopathology, and persons addicted to multiple substances, with or without co-morbid psychopathology, are more difficult to treat than those whose dependence is on a single substance (Rosenthal & Westreich, 1999). Overall, then, the markedly increased likelihood that substance abusers will present with co-morbid disorders differentiates substance use disorders from most other DSM-IV disorders and complicates both their diagnosis and treatment.

It also is worth noting here that the psychosocial treatments for substance abuse that have garnered empirical support from the best-designed studies are virtually all treatments for alcohol dependence. One reason is alcoholism's history as a serious problem through human history. Accordingly, research on its causes, pathophysiology, and treatment has a substantially longer history than research on these issues in other substance use disorders. It is also the case, however, that dependence on substances other than alcohol almost invariably requires law-breaking. As a result, these addictions are much more often enmeshed in social issues, including criminality, thereby markedly complicating research on their treatment. It is much harder to do research on treatments for cocaine, amphetamine, and heroin addiction than on alcoholism treatments and these addictions are much more likely to reflect a range of social ills beyond the addiction process itself.

Research Design Issues in Research on Substance Use Disorders

We already have detailed the design of two recent and substantial clinical trials of alcoholism treatment, Project MATCH and the VAMCCS. Both compared three established treatments and found them comparably effective. However, despite encouraging data in both studies attesting to reduced consumption following treatment, most patients eschewed abstinence. Unfortunately, the Project MATCH and VAMCCS studies did not include a no-treatment or placebo control group that would have enabled assessment of the impact of common factors exclusive of the treatments being tested on outcomes. The nature of comparison conditions in treatment outcome studies plays a central role in what those studies tell us. At present, these studies have told us that several psychosocial treatments are associated with substantial reductions in alcohol consumption by alcohol-dependent individuals. The number of patients included in the studies and the fact that one was a randomized clinical trial while the other was a well-designed quasi-experimental study adds to their appeal. However, the fact that they did not include control conditions that would have permitted assessment of the impact of common factors on outcomes makes us ask how much of the reduction in drinking was a function of the treatments themselves, the act of seeking treatment, the natural history of alcohol use disorders, or the fact of inclusion in a large-scale study in which the investigators were strongly invested and much attention was given to patients. The fact that most patients in both studies failed to maintain abstinence also is troubling.

Although abstinence continues to be a benchmark for outcomes of treatment for substance abuse, other outcome variables have come into wider use, partly because abstinence is not always an outcome of treatment, even successful treatment. As a consequence, reduction in consumption (e.g., in drinking or drug use days/month and in amount of alcohol consumed/drinking day, as in Project MATCH) and enhancements in the quality of life (as in the VAMCCS) have become more widely employed as measures of outcome. In their favor is that they permit a finer-grained reflection of differences in treatment impact than a categorical variable such as abstinence or nonabstinence. As well, either by themselves or in conjunction with assessment of changes in drug use, assessment of improvements in quality of life provides an additional more complex window on the impact of treatment, especially given the typical fluctuating course of the substance use disorders.

Future work, then, should attempt to develop creative treatments that cross-cut currently defined treatments, study the linkages between treatment processes and treatment outcomes, and use contemporary and well-validated approaches to measurement as well as carefully conceived outcome measures.

References

Azrin, N. (1976). Improvements in the community reinforcement approach to alcoholism. *Behaviour Research and Therapy, 14,* 339–348.

Azrin, N. H., Sisson, R. W., Meyers, R., & Godley, M. (1982). Alcoholism treatment by disulfiram and community reinforcement therapy. *Journal of Behavior Therapy and Experimental Psychiatry, 13,* 105–112.

Barber, W., & O'Brien, C. (1999). Pharmacotherapies. In B. S. McCrady & E. E. Epstein (Eds.), *Addictions: A comprehensive guidebook* (pp. 347–369). New York: Oxford University Press.

Barlow, D. H., Raffa, S. D., & Cohen, E. M. (2002). Psychosocial treatments for panic disorders, phobias, and generalized anxiety disorder. In P. E. Nathan & J. M. Gorman (Eds.), *A guide to treatments that work* (2nd ed., pp. 367–386). New York: Oxford University Press.

Brown, J. M., & Miller, W. R. (1993). Impact of motivational interviewing on participation and outcome in residential alcoholism treatment. *Psychology of Addictive Behaviors, 7,* 211–218.

Budney, A. J., & Higgins, S. T. (1998). *A community reinforcement plus vouchers approach: Treating cocaine addiction.* Rockville, MD: National Institute on Drug Abuse.

Carroll, K. M. (1998). *Treating cocaine dependence: A cognitive behavioral approach.* Rockville, MD: National Institute on Drug Abuse.

Carroll, K. M. (1999). Behavioral and cognitive behavioral treatments. In B. S. McCrady & E. E. Epstein (Eds.), *Addictions: A comprehensive guidebook* (pp. 250–267). New York: Oxford University Press.

Chambliss, D. L., Baker, M. J., Baucom, D. H., Beutler, L. E., Calhoun, K. S., Crits-Christoph, P., Daiuto, A., DeRubeis, R., Detweiler, J., Haaga, D. A. F., Bennett Johnson, S., McCurry, S., Mueser, K. T., Pope, K. S., Sanderson, W. C., Shoham, V., Stickle, T., Williams, D. A., & Woody, S. R. (1998). Update on empirically validated therapies, II. *The Clinical Psychologist, 51,* 3–16.

Chambliss, D. L., Sanderson, W. C., Shoham, V.,

Bennett Johnson, S., Pope, K. S., Crits-Christoph, P., Baker, M., Johnson, B., Woody, S. R., Sue, S., Beutler, L., Williams, D. A., & McCurry, S. (1996). An update on empirically validated therapies. *The Clinical Psychologist*, *49*, 5–18.

Cherpitel, C. J., & Clark, W. B. (1995). Ethnic differences in performance of screening instruments for identifying harmful drinking and alcohol dependence in the emergency room. *Alcoholism: Clinical and Experimental Research*, *19*, 628–634.

Connors, G. J., Donovan, D. M., & DiClemente, C. C. (2001). *Substance abuse treatment and the stages of change*. New York: Guilford Press.

Connors, G. J., Tonigan, J. S., & Miller, W. R. (2001). A longitudinal model of intake symptomatology, AA participation and outcome: Retrospective study of the Project MATCH outpatient and aftercare samples. *Journal of Studies on Alcohol*, *62*, 817–825.

Cooney, N. L., Kadden, R. M., Litt, M. D., Getter, H. (1991). Matching alcoholics to coping skills or interactional therapies: Two–year follow–up results. *Journal of Consulting & Clinical Psychology*, *59*, 598–601.

Cooper, J. R. (1989). Methadone treatment and acquired immunodeficiency syndrome. *Journal of the American Medical Association*, *262*, 1664–1668.

Craighead, W. E., Hart, A. B., Craighead, L. W., & Ilardi, S. S. (2002). Psychosocial treatments for major depressive disorder. In P. E. Nathan & J. M. Gorman (Eds.), *A guide to treatments that work* (2nd ed., pp. 245–262). New York: Oxford University Press.

Crits-Christoph, P., Siqueland, L., Blaine, J., Frank, A., Luborsky, L., Onken, L. S., Muenz, L. R., Thase, M. E., Weiss, R. D., Gastfriend, D. R., Woody, G. E., Barber, J. P., Butler, S. F., Daley, D., Salloum, I., Bishop, S., Griffin, M. L., Lis, J., Mercer, D., Najavits, L. M., Moras, K., & Beck, A. T. (1997). The NIDA Collaborative Cocaine Treatment Study: Rationale and methods. *Archives of General Psychiatry*, *54*, 721–726.

Crits-Christoph, P., Siqueland, L., Blaine, J., Frank, A., Luborsky, L., Onken, L. S., Muenz, L. R., Thase, M. E., Weiss, R. D., Gastfriend, D. R., Woody, G. E., Barber, J. P., Butler, S. F., Daley, D., Salloum, I., Bishop, S., Najavits, L. M., Lis, J., Mercer, D., Griffin, M. L., Moras, K., & Beck, A. T. (1999). Psychosocial treatments for cocaine dependence: National Institute on Drug Abuse Collaborative Cocaine Treatment Study. *Archives of General Psychiatry*, *56*, 493–502.

Crits-Cristoph, P., Siqueland, L., McCalmont, E., Weiss, R. D., Gastfriend, D. R., Frank, A., Moras, K., Barber, J. P., Blaine, J., & Thase, M. (2001). Impact of psychosocial treatments on associated problems of cocaine-dependent patients. *Journal of Consulting and Clinical Psychology*, *69*, 825–830.

Donovan, D. M. (1999). Assessment strategies and measures in addictive behaviors. In B. S. McCrady & E. E. Epstein (Eds.), *Addictions: A comprehensive guidebook* (pp. 187–215). New York: Oxford University Press.

Drummond, D. C., & Glautier S. (1994). A controlled trial of cue exposure treatment in alcohol dependence. *Journal of Consulting and Clinical Psychology*, *2*, 809–817.

Epstein, E. E., & McCrady, B. S. (2002). Couple therapy in the treatment of alcohol problems. In A. Gurman & N. Jacobson (Eds.), *Clinical handbook of marital therapy* (3rd ed., pp. 597–628). New York: Guilford Press.

Finney, J. W., & Monahan, S. C. (1996). The cost effectiveness of treatment for alcoholism: A second approximation. *Journal of Studies on Alcohol*, *57*, 229–243.

Finney, J. W., & Moos, R. H. (2002). Psychosocial treatments for alcohol use disorders. In P. E. Nathan & G. M. Gorman (Eds.), *A guide to treatments that work* (2nd ed., pp. 157–168). New York: Oxford University Press.

Finney, J. W., Moos, R. H., & Timko, C. (1999). The course of treated and untreated substance use disorders: Remission and resolution, relapse and mortality. In B. S. McCrady & E. E. Epstein (Eds.), *Addictions: A comprehensive guidebook* (pp. 30–49). New York: Oxford University Press.

Fleming, M. F., Barry, K. L., Manwell, L. B., Johnson, K., & London, R. (1997). Brief physician advice for problem alcohol drinkers. A randomized controlled trial in community–based primary care practices. *JAMA*, *277*, 1039–1045.

Franklin, M. E., & Foa, E. B. (2002). Cognitive behavioral treatments for obsessive compulsive disorder. In P. E. Nathan & J. M. Gorman (Eds.), *A guide to treatments that work* (2nd ed., pp. 367–386). New York: Oxford University Press.

Garfield, S. L. (1996). Some problems associated with "validated" forms of psychotherapy. *Clin-*

ical Psychology: Science and Practice, 3, 218–229.

Grant, B. F. (1995). Comorbidity between DSM-IV drug use disorders and major depression: Results of a national survey of adults. Journal of Substance Abuse, 7, 481–497.

Grant, B. F., & Dawson, D. A. (1999). Alcohol and drug use, abuse, and dependence: Classification, prevalence, and comorbidity. In B. S. McCrady & E. E. Epstein (Eds.), Addictions: A comprehensive guidebook (pp. 9–29). New York: Oxford University Press.

Higgins, S. T., Budney, A. J., Bickel, W. K., Badger, G. J., Foerg, F. E., & Ogden, D. (1995). Outpatient behavioral treatment for cocaine dependence: One-year outcome. Experimental and Clinical Psychopharmacology, 3, 205–212.

Higgins, S. T., Budney, A. J., Bickel, W. K., Foerg, F. E., Donham, R., & Badger, G. J. (1994). Incentives improve outcome in outpatient behavioral treatment of cocaine dependence. Archives of General Psychiatry, 51, 568–576.

Hodgson, R. J., & Rankin, H. J. (1978). Modification of excessive drinking by cue exposure. Behavior Research and Therapy, 14, 305–307.

Holder, H., Longabaugh, R., Miller, W. R., & Rubonis, A. V. (1991). The cost effectiveness of treatment for alcoholism: A first approximation. Journal of Studies on Alcohol, 52, 517–540.

Horstmann, M. J., & Tonigan, J. S. (2000). Faith development in Alcoholics Anonymous (AA): A study of two AA groups. Alcoholism Treatment Quarterly, 18, 75–84.

Hunt, G. M., & Azrin, N. H. (1973). A community-reinforcement approach to alcoholism. Behaviour Research and Therapy, 11, 91–104.

Jellinek, E. M. (1960). The disease concept of alcoholism. New Haven, CT: Hillhouse Press.

Kadden, R., Carroll, K. M., Donovan, D., Cooney, N., Monti, P., Abrams, D., Litt, M., & Hester, R. (1992). Cognitive-behavioral coping skills therapy manual: A clinical research guide for therapists treating individuals with alcohol abuse and dependence. NIAAA Project MATCH Monograph, Vol. 3, DHHS Publication No. (ADM) 92–1895. Washington, DC: US Government Printing Office.

Kadden, R. M., Cooney, N. L., Getter, H., Litt, M. D. (1989). Matching alcoholics to coping skills or interactional therapies: Posttreatment results. Journal of Consulting & Clinical Psychology, 57, 698–704.

Lapham, S. C., Skipper, B. J., Owen, J. P., Kleyboecker, K., Teaf, D., Thompson, B., & Simpson, G. (1995). Alcohol abuse screening instruments: Normative test data collected from a first DWI offender screening program. Journal of Studies on Alcohol, 56, 51–59.

Litten, R. Z., & Allen, J. P. (1992). Measuring alcohol consumption: Psychosocial and biochemical methods. Totowa, NJ: Humana Press.

Lovibond, S. H., & Caddy, G. (1970). Discriminated aversive control in the moderation of alcoholics' drinking behavior. Behavior Therapy, 1, 437–444.

Maisto, S. A., Connors, G. J., & Allen, J. P. (1995). Contrasting self-report screens for alcohol problems: A review. Alcoholism: Clinical and Experimental Research, 19, 1510–1516.

Marlatt, G. A., & Gordon, J. R. (1985). Relapse prevention: Maintenance strategies in the treatment of addictive behaviors. New York: Guilford Press.

McCrady, B. S. (2000). Alcohol use disorders and the Division 12 Task Force of the American Psychological Association. Psychology of Addictive Behaviors, 14, 267–276.

McCrady, B. S., Epstein, E. E., & Hirsch, L. S. (1999). Maintaining change after conjoint behavioral alcohol treatment for men: Outcomes at six months. Addiction, 94, 1381–1396.

McCrady, B. S., & Miller, W. R. (Eds.). (1993). Research on Alcoholics Anonymous: Opportunities and alternatives. New Brunswick, NJ: Rutgers University Press.

McCrady, B. S., Stout, R., Noel, N., Abrams, D., & Nelson, H. F. (1991). Effectiveness of three types of spouse-involved behavioral alcoholism treatment. British Journal of Addiction, 86, 1415–1424.

McKay, J. R., Cacciola, J. S., McLellan, A. T., Alterman, A. I., & Wirtz, P. W. (1997). An initial evaluation of the psychosocial dimensions of the American Society of Addiction Medicine criteria for inpatient versus intensive outpatient substance abuse rehabilitation. Journal of Studies on Alcohol, 58, 239–252.

McLellan, A. T., Arndt, I. O., Metzger, D. S., Woody, G. E., & O'Brien, C. P. (1993). The effects of psychosocial services in substance abuse treatment. Journal of American Medical Association, 260, 1953–1959.

Mee-Lee, D., Shulman, G. D., Fishman, M., Gastfriend, D. R., & Griffith, J. H. (2001). ASAM PPC-2R: ASAM patient placement criteria for the treatment of substance-related disorders (2nd ed., rev.). Chevy Chase, MD: American Society of Addiction Medicine, Inc.

Meyers, R. J., & Smith, J. E. (1995). *Clinical guide to alcohol treatment: The community reinforcement approach.* New York: Guilford Press.

Miller, W. R. (1983). Motivational interviewing with problem drinkers. *Behavioural Psychotherapy, 1,* 147–172.

Miller, W. R., Andrews, N. R., Wilbourne, P., & Bennett, M. E. (1998). A wealth of alternatives: Effective treatments for alcohol problems. In W. R. Miller & N. Heather (Eds.), *Treating addictive behaviors* (2nd ed., pp. 203–216). New York: Plenum Press.

Miller, W. R., Brown, J. M., Simpson, T. L., Handmaker, N. S., Bien, T. H., Luckie, L. F., Montgomery, H. A., Hester, R. K., & Tonigan, J. S. (1995). What works? A methodological analysis of the alcohol treatment outcome literature. In R. K. Hester & W. R. Miller (Eds.), *Handbook of alcoholism treatment approaches: Effective alternatives* (pp. 12–44). Boston: Allyn & Bacon.

Miller, W. R., & Rollnick, S. (2002). *Motivational interviewing* (2nd ed.). New York: Guilford Press.

Miller, W. R., & Tonigan, J. S. (1996). Assessing drinkers' motivation for change: The Stages of Change Readiness and Treatment Eagerness Scale (SOCRATES). *Psychology of Addictive Behaviors, 10,* 81–89.

Miller, W. R., Zweben, A., DiClemente, C. C., & Rychtarik, R. G. (1992). *Motivational enhancement therapy manual: A clinical research guide for therapists treating individuals with alcohol abuse and dependence.* NIAAA Project MATCH Monograph, Vol. 2, DHHS Publication No. (ADM) 92–1894. Washington, DC: US Government Printing Office.

Monti, P. M., Abrams, D. B., Kadden, R. M., & Cooney, N. L. (1989). *Treating alcohol dependence: A coping skills training guide in the treatment of alcoholism.* New York: Guilford Press.

Monti, P. M., Rohsenow, D. J., Swift, R. M., Gulliver, S. B., Colby, S. M., Mueller, T. I., Brown, R. A., Gordon, A., Abrams, D. B., Naiura, R. S., & Asher, M. K. (2001). Naltrexone and cue exposure with coping and communication skills training for alcoholics: Treatment process and 1-year outcomes. *Alcoholism: Clinical and Experimental Research, 25,* 1634–1647.

Moos, R. H., Finney, J. W., Ouimette, P. C., & Suchinsky, R. T. (1999). A comparative evaluation of substance abuse treatment: I. Treatment orientation, amount of care, and 1-year outcomes.

Alcoholism: Clinical and Experimental Research, 23, 529–536.

Morgenstern, J., Labouvie, E., McCrady, B. S., Kahler, C. W., & Frey, R. M. (1997). Affiliation with Alcoholics Anonymous following treatment: A study of therapeutic effects and mechanisms of action. *Journal of Consulting and Clinical Psychology, 65,* 768–777.

Morgenstern, J., & Longabaugh, R. (2000). Cognitive-behavioral treatment for alcohol dependence: A review of evidence for its hypothesized mechanisms of action. *Addiction, 95,* 1475–1490.

Nathan, P. E. (1996). Assessing substance abusers. In L. L. Murphy & J. C. Impara (Eds.), *Assessment of substance abuse* (pp. xvii–xxix). Lincoln, NE: Buros Institute of Mental Measurements.

Nathan, P. E. (1998). The *DSM-IV* and its antecedents: Enhancing syndromal diagnosis. In J. W. Barron (Ed.), *Making diagnosis meaningful: Enhancing evaluation and treatment of psychological disorders* (pp. 3–27). Washington, DC: APA Books.

Nathan, P. E., & McCrady, B. S. (1987). Bases for the use of abstinence as a goal in the behavioral treatment of alcohol abusers. *Drugs & Society, 2,* 109–131.

National Institutes of Health. (1998). *Drinking in the United States.* Bethesda, MD: NIAAA.

Nowinski, J. (1999). Self-help groups for addictions. In B. S. McCrady & E. E. Epstein (Eds.), *Addictions: A comprehensive guidebook* (pp. 328–346). New York: Oxford University Press.

Nowinski, J., Baker, S., & Carroll, K. (1992). *Twelve step facilitation therapy manual: A clinical research guide for therapists treating individuals with alcohol abuse and dependence.* NIAAA Project MATCH Monograph, Vol. 1, DHHS Publication No. (ADM) 92–1893. Washington, DC: US Government Printing Office.

O'Farrell, T. J., Choquette, K. A., & Cutter, H. S. G. (1998). Couples relapse prevention sessions after behavioral marital therapy for male alcoholics: Outcomes during the three years after starting treatment. *Journal of Studies on Alcohol, 59,* 357–370.

O'Farrell, T. J., Choquette, K. A., & Cutter, H. S. G., Brown, E. D., & McCourt, W. F. (1993). Behavioral marital therapy with and without additional couples relapse prevention sessions for alcoholics and their wives. *Journal of Studies on Alcohol, 54,* 652–666.

Ouimette, P. C., Finney, J. W., & Moos, R. H. (1997). Twelve step and cognitive behavioral treatment for substance abuse: A comparison of treatment effectiveness. *Journal of Consulting and Clinical Psychology, 65,* 230–240.

Prochaska, J. O., DiClemente, C. C., & Norcross, J. C. (1992). In search of how people change: Applications to addictive behaviors. *American Psychologist, 47,* 1102–1114.

Project MATCH Research Group. (1997a). Matching alcoholism treatments to client heterogeneity: Project MATCH posttreatment drinking outcomes. *Journal of Studies on Alcohol, 58,* 7–29.

Project MATCH Research Group. (1997b). Project MATCH secondary *a priori* hypotheses. *Addiction, 92,* 1671–1698.

Project MATCH Research Group. (1998). Matching alcoholism treatments to client heterogeneity: Project MATCH three-year drinking outcomes. *Alcoholism: Clinical and Experimental Research, 22,* 1300–1311.

Rohsenow, D. J., Monti, P. M., Rubonis, A. V., Gulliver, S. B., Colby, S. M., Binkoff, J. A., & Abrams, D. (2001). Cue exposure with coping skills training and communication skills training for alcohol dependence: 6- and 12-month outcomes. *Addiction, 96,* 1161–1174.

Rosenthal, R. N., & Westreich, L. (1999). Treatment of persons with dual diagnoses of substance use disorder and other psychological problems. In B. S. McCrady & E. E. Epstein (Eds.), *Addictions: A comprehensive guidebook* (pp. 439–476). New York: Oxford University Press.

Sanchez-Craig, M., Wilkinson, A., & Davila, R. (1995). Empirically based guidelines for moderate drinking: 1-year results from three studies with problem drinkers. *American Journal of Public Health, 85,* 823–828.

Schottenfeld, R. S. (1994). Assessment of the patient. In M. Galanter & H. D. Kleber (Eds.), *The textbook of substance abuse treatment* (pp. 25–33). Washington, DC: American Psychiatric Press.

Schuckit, M. A. (1994). The relationship between alcohol problems, substance abuse, and psychiatric syndromes. In T. A. Widiger, A. J. Frances, H. A. Pincus, M. B. First, R. Ross, & W. Davis (Eds.), *DSM-IV Sourcebook* (Vol. 1, pp. 45–66). Washington, DC: American Psychiatric Association.

Sitharthan, T., Sitharthan, G., Hough, M. J., & Kavanagh, D. J. (1997). Cue exposure in moderation drinking: A comparison with cognitive-behavioral therapy. *Journal of Consulting and Clinical Psychology, 65,* 878–882.

Smith, J. E., Meyers, R. J., & Delaney, H. D. (1998). The community reinforcement approach with homeless alcohol–dependent individuals. *Journal of Consulting and Clinical Psychology, 66,* 541–548.

Sobell, L. C., Cunningham, J. A., & Sobell, M. B. (1996). Recovery from alcohol problems with and without treatment: Prevalence in two population surveys. *American Journal of Public Health, 86,* 966–972.

Sobell, L. C., & Sobell, M. B. (1995). Alcohol consumption measures. In J. P. Allen & M. Columbus (Eds.), *Assessing alcohol problems: A guide for clinicians and researchers* (pp. 55–73). Treatment Handbook Series, Number 4. Bethesda, MD: National Institute on Alcohol Abuse and Alcoholism.

Sobell, M. B., & Sobell, L. C. (1973a). Alcoholics treated by individualized behavior therapy: One year treatment outcome. *Behaviour Research and Therapy, 11,* 599–618.

Sobell, M. B., & Sobell, L. C. (1973b). Individualized behavior therapy for alcoholics. *Behavior Therapy, 4,* 49–72.

Stasiewicz, P. R., Bradizza, C. M., & Connors, G. J. (1997). Subject-collateral reports of drinking in inpatient alcoholics with comorbid mental disorders. *Alcoholism: Clinical and Experimental Research, 21,* 530–536.

Task Force on Promotion and Dissemination of Psychological Procedures. (1995). Training in and dissemination of empirically-validated psychological treatments. *Clinical Psychologist, 48,* 3–23.

Vaillant, G. E. (1995). *The natural history of alcoholism revisited.* Cambridge, MA: Harvard University Press.

Vereby, K. (1992). Diagnostic laboratory: Screening for drug abuse. In J. Lowinsohn, P. Ruiz, R. B. Millman, & J. G. Langrod (Eds.), *Substance abuse: A comprehensive textbook* (2nd ed., pp. 425–436). Baltimore, MD: Williams & Wilkins.

Wilson, D. K., & Grube, J. (1994). Role of psychosocial factors in obtaining self-reports of alcohol use in a DUI population. *Psychology of Addictive Behaviors, 8,* 139–151.

Wilson, G. T. (1978). Alcoholism and aversion therapy: Issues, ethics, and evidence. In G. A. Marlatt & P. E. Nathan (Eds.), *Behavioral approaches to alcoholism* (pp. 90–113). New Brunswick, NJ: Rutgers Center of Alcohol Studies.

Woody, G. E., & McNicholas, L. (1996). Opioid use disorders. In A. Tasman, J. Kay, & J. Lieberman (Eds.), *Psychiatry* (Vol. 1, pp. 867–880). New York: W. B. Saunders.

Yahne, C. E., & Miller, W. R. (1999). Enhancing motivation for treatment and change. In B. S. McCrady & E. E. Epstein (Eds.), *Addictions: A comprehensive guidebook* (pp. 235–249). New York: Oxford University Press.

17

Integration of Therapeutic Factors in Treating Substance Use Disorders

Barbara S. McCrady

David A. F. Haaga

Jay Lebow

Allen is 39 years old, divorced, has two children, is unemployed, has a large amount of debt, no driver's license, and rents a room. He has a 20-year history of alcohol and cocaine use, and was abstinent when he entered mandated treatment after conviction for driving while intoxicated. He had had one long period of abstinence in the past without treatment that ended when he drank with an acquaintance after a sporting event. He believes that cocaine is the only thing that gives him a sense of happiness and that alcohol helps him socialize. However, he also believes that his life is "a mess" because of his substance use. In addition to the problems with substance use, Allen reports a difficult childhood that included sexual abuse and physical neglect from his mother and the loss of his father when Allen was 12 years old. He reports a deep discomfort with intimate relationships and had no close friends when he entered treatment.

Georgia is a 60-year-old employed realtor who is divorced and has two grown children. She is married to Dave, a painter who also is divorced and has a drug dependent son who is in jail. Geor-

gia has a 30-year history of alcohol dependence, was abstinent from alcohol for 5 years through her involvement with AA, but relapsed around the time of her divorce from her first husband and has been drinking heavily for past 12 years. Her pattern of drinking is secretive—she hides bottles, and Dave can't tell when she drinks or not. She is deeply ashamed of her drinking and gets angry at Dave and at her therapist when either raises questions about her drinking. Georgia has had a number of medical problems, including diabetes, pancreatitis, and cervical cancer. She is on medication and has been told not to drink. However, Georgia also used to smoke a pack of cigarettes per day, but stopped smoking a year before entering treatment on the instructions of her physician. Georgia's parents are both deceased, and she has one sister with whom she has a poor relationship.

Allen and Georgia are typical of clients with substance use disorders, and each presents complexities to the clinician or treatment program staff responsible for helping them. Clients with substance use disorders are typically challenging, given the often chronic and relapsing nature of these disorders, the high co-morbidity with other psychological, physical, and social problems, fluctuating motivation for change, and the inadequate training in the treatment of substance use disorders received by most mental health professionals. Clinicians experience a tension between, on the one hand, the desire to provide effective treatments supported by research, and, on the other hand, the realities of busy schedules, the different "faces" of each client, and the proliferation of treatment manuals that specify a set of procedures for specific and narrow bands of clients. Clinicians resolve this tension in a variety of ways—they may provide the same familiar treatment to all clients, they may use treatment manuals that are not fully appropriate for their clients, they may refer to various treatment guidelines (such as the SAMHSA TIPS series, Substance Abuse and Mental Health Administration, 1993–2004; the American Psychiatric Association Practice Guidelines, American Psychiatric Association, 1995; or the Patient Placement Criteria published by the American Society or Addiction Medicine, Mee-Lee, Shulman, Fishman, Gastfriend, & Griffith, 2001), they may refer substance abusing clients to other practitioners, or they may "wing it." None of these alternatives is entirely satisfying, and none is optimal for providing successful treatment.

The present chapter provides an alternative for the treatment of substance use disorders by identifying empirically supported principles that underpin effective treatment systems and effective treatments and by discussing the flexible application of these empirically supported principles to individual clients. Our overall goal is to give clinicians guidance about how to deliver effective treatment for clients with substance use disorders. The chapter has three specific objectives: (1) to integrate three types of factors (therapeutic, participant, and relationship) described in the individual chapters in this section into a comprehensive description of treatment, (2) to integrate common and specific principles of changes into articulated descriptions of treatment, and (3) to identify directions for research to improve the sensitivity and specificity of treatment. Readers are referred to Chapters 16 (McCrady & Nathan, in this volume), 14 (Haaga, Hall, & Haas, in this volume), and 15 (Lebow, Kelly, Knobloch-Fedders, & Moos, in this volume) for more detailed discussions of therapeutic, participant, and relationship issues in the treatment of substance use disorders.

SOME OVERARCHING PERSPECTIVES

The body of findings emerging from research assessing treatment of substance use disorders can best be conceptualized through the lens of several overarching perspectives about these findings (Moos, 2003). First, contextual factors are important to understanding substance use disorders. Persons with these disorders "exist in a complex web of social forces" (Moos, 2003, p. 3). Treatment is only one of many forces that impacts an individual with a substance use disorder and may not be an enduring or significant long-term force unless careful attention is paid to the reshaping of the social environment as an integral part of the treatment. Life circumstances may shift in ways that impact substance use disorders (SUDs), suggesting that, "individuals who are able to establish and maintain relatively positive social contexts are likely to recover" (Moos, 2003, p. 3).

Second, the length of treatment and provision of continuity in care are significantly related to positive treatment outcome (Moos, 2003). Although there are many studies that support the effectiveness of brief interventions for mild drinking problems (Bien, Miller, & Tonigan, 1993), and randomized clinical trials of differing set lengths suggest few differences in outcome (Miller & Hester, 1986), continued attachment to treatment consistently has been associated with better outcomes, and therapeutic concern about retention and continuity of care therefore is important. Viewing substance use disorders as chronic and relapsing conditions suggests the need for a long-term perspective on the process of change, and an accompanying long-term plan to foster maintenance. Although treatment may be time-limited, a long-term maintenance plan should be integral to any treatment.

Third, the type of provider makes a difference in the outcomes of treatment for SUDs (Moos, 2003). Specifically, clients treated by addictions specialist *and mental health clinicians* typically have more success than clients treated by primary care providers. If mental health clinicians have a set of more finely honed therapeutic skills for the treatment of SUDs, they are likely to further improve treatment outcomes.

Finally, the context in which treatment is provided impacts outcome. Many clinicians see SUD clients within a larger treatment program, and attention to the organization and structure of the program may make the individual clinical work of the clinician easier and more effective. Substantial research suggests that the most effective treatment programs are clear and well organized, actively involve the clients in the program, provide a supportive and emotionally expressive environment, and emphasize self-direction, work, and social skills development.

SPECIFIC RELATIONSHIP FACTORS

Whether a clinician practices independently or within a structured substance abuse or mental health treatment system, a number of principles apply to the development of the therapeutic relationship with a person with an SUD. When thinking about relationship factors, the clinician needs to consider relationships in the broadest context, including the relationship between client and therapist, between client and the larger treatment program, between client and members of intimate and larger social network.

Most proximal to the clinician is the therapeutic alliance. When working with SUD clients, therapists should strive to develop and maintain a positive working alliance. Several elements contribute to an effective working alliance. Clinicians will be most successful if they can provide accurate empathy, respect the experience of the client in therapy, and avoid confrontational struggles. Equally important is the ability to provide goal direction for the clients along with a moderate level of structure for the therapy. Clinicians should help clients develop goals for themselves, provide moderate direction to help clients work toward their goals, and communicate a clear expectation that clients can meet their goals. The clinician needs to create structure to the therapy to help clients work toward their goals and maintain that level of structure over time. Many clients with SUDs experience chaos in many areas of their lives and the

stability and structure of the therapy may be particularly important because of the lack of structure in other aspects of their lives.

The relationship between client and treatment program also must be emphasized. To enhance retention and positive outcomes, treatment programs should be involving, supportive, and expressive. As with the individual therapy session, treatment programs should provide structure and consistency over time. Additionally, they should stress autonomy and self-direction among clients, expecting clients to take responsibility for their treatment, and to follow through on treatment requirements. A focus on development of specific skills in both the occupational and social-interpersonal realms will set the stage for clients to begin to restructure their environment outside of the treatment setting.

TREATMENT FACTORS

The common principles for the treatment of psychological disorders, described in Chapter 18, apply well to the treatment of substance use disorders. Beyond these common principles, empirical research suggests that a number of specific therapeutic elements are characteristic of effective treatments in this population.

Most prominently, therapeutic techniques should be provided within the context of a well-developed working alliance in therapy that is structured and goal-directed, as described above. These characteristics appear to be universal among all effective psychotherapy for SUD.

There is little evidence for the differential effectiveness of individual versus group therapy for treating individuals with SUDs. These decisions are probably best made in relation to client and therapist preferences and schedules. However, given the social-interpersonal nature of SUDs and the importance of the social environment to the successful resolution of these disorders, involvement of a significant other looks to be helpful in contributing to the effectiveness of treatment. Equally important is explicitly helping the client restructure his or her social environment in ways that support change; facilitating involvement with social networks supportive of abstinence, such as a specific supportive family member, sponsor, or peer; and helping the client access social environments supportive of abstinence.

A second key aspect of therapy with SUDs is a focus on client motivation. Motivation is best understood as a fluctuating state influenced by the environment as well as the client's cognitive and emotional weighing of the perceived harm from his or her substance use. A range of therapeutic techniques may be used to enhance clients' awareness of the extent and severity of their substance use problem and the need to change, such as motivational interviewing, the use of decisional balance sheets, or involvement with a self-help group, but regardless of the specific techniques used a continuing focus on client motivation seems central to successful change.

A third key component of therapy is a focus on helping the client to develop awareness of repetitive patterns of thinking and behavior that perpetuate the alcohol or drug use. Positive expectations about the positive effects of alcohol or drugs, distorted perceptions of drinking or drug use norms in their social environment, and low self-efficacy for coping with difficult situations without alcohol or drugs all are examples of patterns of thinking that may perpetuate use. Clinicians also should help clients develop a greater awareness of behavioral patterns that lead to use, such as spending time in drinking environments or with people who support and encourage use, and developing awareness of the types of experiences and events that lead to use. Helping the client develop awareness of dysfunctional patterns of thinking and behaving should be accompanied by a focus on helping the client learn alternative coping skills to manage these dysfunctional thoughts and behaviors. Cognitive-behavioral therapy provides one set of strategies for challenging dysfunctional patterns of thinking and learning new coping skills, and 12-step-oriented counseling and self-help groups also are effective in enhancing cognitive and behavioral coping skills. An indirect effect of focusing on cognitive and behavioral coping skills may be an increased level of self-efficacy for change, but therapists also can work directly to help the client develop a greater sense of self-efficacy for change. Enhanced self-efficacy may then facilitate greater use of coping skills in the natural environment.

A fourth key component of therapy is attention to the affective experience of the client. Clients may view substance use as a way to regulate or attenuate negative emotions, or as a vehicle to enhance positive experience. Additionally, affect regulation is disrupted in the early weeks of abstinence or decreased use if the client is experiencing clinical or subclinical withdrawal. Accompanying the physiological aspects of adapting to a change in drug use is the client's experience of both positive and negative emotions, which may have been blunted when using substances. Effective therapies attend to the affective experiences of the client, particularly in relationship to their substance use, help clients learn to accept a normal range of emotions, and help clients learn to manage negative emotions without use.

Finally, there is strong evidence for the role of conditioning in the development and maintenance of substance use disorders. The clinician should carefully assess for indicators of specific conditioned responses to alcohol or drugs, and develop ways to change these conditioned responses. Repeated exposure to alcohol or drug-related situations without using might both decrease the strength of conditioned responses and increase self-efficacy for success in coping with such situations without alcohol or drugs.

PARTICIPANT CHARACTERISTICS

Thousands of client characteristics have been studied to identify reliable associations between client characteristics and response to treatment (reviewed in Chapter 14, Haaga, Hall, & Haas, in this volume). Although less attention has been given to the personal characteristics of therapists, a smaller literature has examined the relationship between static therapist characteristics and outcome. Despite this extensive literature, few client or therapist characteristics are consistent predictors of response to treatment.

Three client variables appear to predict a more positive response to treatment. First, clients with positive expectancies about treatment tend to have better outcomes. Development of a working alliance with the client can enhance client expectancies, and positive client expectancies may partially mediate the relationship between a good working alliance and good treatment outcome.

Second, greater client readiness to change is associated with greater treatment success. As with client treatment expectancies, the therapist may have an important impact on client readiness to change, and as noted above, attention to maintaining and enhancing motivation is a crucial therapeutic task. One specific factor that may contribute to readiness to change is the degree to which the substance use has had direct impacts on health, both by contributing to specific medical conditions and by complicating medical conditions with other etiologies. In the treatment of smokers, those whose smoking is particularly high risk because of a medical condition are particularly responsive to therapy if the smoking contributed to their risk status. In other substance use disorders, studies have focused less on specific differences between substance users at high and low risk for medical disorders, but natural history studies suggest that those with medical conditions are more likely to change their use than those without medical conditions.

A third client factor related consistently to treatment outcome is severity of the substance use disorder. Greater severity of the substance use disorder is associated with a poorer response to treatment. Conceptually, there seems to be a contradiction between findings that greater motivation predicts better response to treatment because motivation might seem to come from more severe consequences. However, motivation is best understood as a balance between perceived positive and negative consequences of use compared to perceived positive and negative consequences of change, and individuals with the most severe problems may in fact perceive many negative consequences from their use, but not be able to envision clear and positive consequences of abstinence if they already have irreversible medical problems, or have lost their family and occupation.

INTERACTIONS AMONG PARTICIPANT CHARACTERISTICS, THERAPIST BEHAVIORS, AND THERAPEUTIC TECHNIQUES

The challenge to the clinician is to integrate the variety of empirically supported relationship factors and treatment techniques to respond to the unique presenting problems of individual clients. Here, research provides some guidance, but patient-treatment matching research methodologies are less well developed than other research methods, and research is simply absent on the complex individual matching of multiple client characteristics to multiple therapeutic interventions provided within a uniquely developed therapeutic relationship. In this section, we summarize consistent findings of relationships between client characteristics and therapeutic elements.

The approach of the therapist is particularly important when clients are ambivalent about changing or being in treatment. Therapists should titrate their level of "confrontation" to the level of the client's reactance. Therapists should avoid arguing with angry clients, or pushing them hard to accept their diagnosis or the need to change. Instead, the concept of "rolling with the resistance" (e.g., Miller & Rollnick, 2002) best characterizes a therapeutic stance to defuse and neutralize client anger and "resistance" to therapy. Recognizing the ambivalence with which many clients enter treatment, therapist behaviors and the selection of therapeutic principles and techniques should be tailored to the degree of client readiness to change. Clients who are unsure if their substance use is a problem may respond well to an intervention that helps them consider the problems caused by their use and whether they should change, whereas they may respond negatively if pushed to make active behavior changes. Conversely, clients who enter treatment ready to change may be impatient with an intense focus on motivational issues rather than simply providing the skills the client needs to change behavior.

Selection of therapeutic modality also may be determined partly by the presentation of the client. With clients who have little commitment to remain in treatment or change their substance use, therapists should involve the family or other member of the social support system in the treatment. Interventions then should focus on family support, how the family interacts with the user, limit setting, and behavioral contracts. Therapy should discourage family confrontation of the client. However, if the client's social network is one that supports and encourages substance use, therapy should focus on facilitating access to social systems supportive of abstinence, even if these social systems are completely separate from the client's family or natural social network.

A third area of client-treatment matching focuses on the presence of co-morbid disorders. About 50% of those with SUDs have another co-morbid Axis I disorder and about one-third have a co-morbid Axis II disorder. Research knowledge about the effective integration of different psychological treatments to manage multiple presenting problems is lacking. For smokers, mood management is demonstrably effective with smokers with co-morbid depression. For clients presenting with both excessive drinking and smoking, research suggests that treatment can address smoking cessation concurrent with alcohol cessation without increasing the risk for relapse to drinking. For chronically mentally ill clients with substance use disorders integrated service delivery systems that address mental health and substance use treatment needs within the same treatment setting are more effective than treatment systems that require clients to access services for their varied problems in different settings or with different providers (Rosenthal & Westreich, 1999).

A fourth area of research knowledge about patient-treatment matching focuses on the severity of the substance use disorder and intensity and length of treatment. For heavy drinkers with low alcohol dependence, less intense, briefer treatments are appropriate (Bien et al., 1993), and outcomes of intensive inpatient therapy may be worse (Rychtarik et al., 2000). Clients with severe alcohol dependence have better outcomes with more intensive initial treatment and respond more positively to treatment that focuses on 12-step counseling and involvement with 12-step groups than either cognitive-behavioral or motivational enhancement therapies (Project MATCH Research Group, 1997). For high levels of dependence on alcohol or drugs, strategies to develop a long-term maintenance plan are important (Moos, 2003).

A fifth area to consider in patient-treatment matching is the profile of problems that the client brings to treatment. Clinicians working with clients with SUDs, in addition to focusing on the presenting substance use and psychological problems, should assess for other social service and medical care needs and arrange for attention to these needs. Some research supports the greater effectiveness of treatment plans that address multiple areas of need, rather than a single focus on the presenting substance use disorder (McLellan et al., 1997).

A sixth area to consider in client-treatment matching is client sex. Research here is quite limited. However, randomized clinical trials and non-randomized comparison group studies have suggested that female-specific treatment may be more effective than generic substance abuse treatment provided in mixed male and female treatment programs. Among smokers, women, and most particularly young women, present with major concerns about weight control when stopping smoking. Treatment efforts to restructure cognitions about weight gain have shown promise in fostering and maintaining smoking cessation among women concerned about gaining weight after smoking cessation (Perkins et al., 2001).

Finally, although the overall focus of this book is on treatment of adult disorders, it is worth noting that in the treatment of adolescents with substance use disorders, it is particularly important to use approaches that involve multiple systems, including the family, peers, and others (Henggeler, Schoenwald, Borduin, Rowland, & Cunningham, 1998). Additionally, because a large proportion of adolescents with substance use disorders have other presenting co-morbid problems, addressing these co-morbid problems will improve treatment outcomes (Bukstein, 1995).

FUTURE RESEARCH DIRECTIONS/NEEDS

Controlled research has provided a set of principles that clinicians can use to treat clients with substance use disorders. However, there are many gaps in the literature, particularly in providing a nuanced treatment approach to individual clients. Six major areas of research would enhance clinical practice.

First, there is a major need for controlled studies of treatments for clients with SUDs and co-morbid disorders. The selection of appropriate empirically supported treatments for multiple problems, the timing and sequencing of provision of multiple treatments, and the complexity of delivering more than one empirically supported treatment when elements of the treatments may be contradictory are all areas for future research.

Second is the need for more research on treatments for specific demographically distinct populations. Although initial findings on female-specific treatments are promising and consistent, replication studies are needed. Research is absent on client-treatment matching for specific racial or ethnic groups, age-specific populations (such as adolescents or older adults), or homosexual clients.

Third is the need to develop more research on treatment effectiveness for "typical" substance-abusing clients who present with multiple problems and social complications. Randomized clinical trials most often screen out complicated clients with multiple disorders, as well as socially unstable clients who may be unavailable for research follow-up. Development and testing of treatment protocols for complex clients would provide useful guidance to clinicians working with these populations.

A fourth area of research that would inform practice would be studies of "master" therapists with particularly high compliance and positive outcomes. Randomized clinical trials consistently report differences in outcomes between therapists who are following the same treatment protocol. Research could examine hypothesized active relationship factors (e.g., empathy, therapist alliance), and also attempt to identify other factors such as the approach that master clinicians take to the instillation of hope, enhancing positive outcome expectancies, and flexibility in the application of standard treatment interventions.

Fifth, clinicians need to be knowledgeable about the context in which SUDs occur and the complicating problems they experience. Research is needed to consider both comprehensive care models and case management, as well as how to allocate and organize the sequencing and delivery of treatment through stepped care or other service delivery models.

Finally, evidence exists to support the effectiveness of different treatment modalities, but research is lacking that considers when to select specific treatment modalities (individual, group, family, couple), considering both client characteristics other and specific therapeutic conditions.

SUMMARY AND CONCLUSIONS

Several major principles can be drawn from the discussion above:

1. The structure and organization of the setting in which treatment is provided is important. Effective treatment programs are clear and well organized, actively involve the clients in the program, provide a supportive and emotionally expressive environment, emphasize self-direction, work, and social skills development and expect clients to take responsibility for their treatment and follow through on treatment requirements.

2. The type of provider and what the provider does in the treatment make a difference in the outcomes of treatment.
   a. Clients treated by addictions specialists or mental health clinicians have better outcomes than clients treated by primary care providers.
   b. Development of an effective therapeutic alliance is crucial. Clinicians will be most successful if they can provide accurate empathy; respect the experience of clients in therapy; and avoid confrontational struggles, while at the same time providing goal direction for the clients along with a moderate level of structure for the therapy.
   c. The approach of the therapist is particularly important when clients are ambivalent about changing or being in treatment. Therapists should titrate their level of confrontation to the level of clients' reactance. Therapists should avoid arguing with angry clients or pushing them hard to accept their diagnosis or the need to change.

3. Decisions about level of care, continuity of care, and elements of treatment all affect outcomes.
   a. Length of treatment and provision of continuity in care are significantly related to positive treatment outcome, and attention should be paid to maintaining clients in treatment.
   b. The intensity and length of treatment

should be determined partly by the severity of the substance use disorder. For heavy drinkers with low alcohol dependence, less intense, briefer treatments are appropriate and intensive inpatient therapy yields poorer outcomes. Clients with severe alcohol dependence have better outcomes with more intensive initial treatment and respond most positively to treatment that focuses on 12-step counseling and involvement with 12-step groups.

  c. Clinicians should assess the other social service and medical care needs of their clients and arrange for attention to these needs.

4. Contextual factors are important to understanding substance use disorders. Treatment may not exert an enduring impact unless careful attention is paid to the reshaping of the social environment as an integral part of the treatment.

  a. Involvement of a significant other contributes to the effectiveness of treatment.

  b. Clinicians should help clients restructure their social environments to include persons that support change and abstinence.

  c. With clients who have little commitment to remain in treatment or change their substance use, involving the family or other members of the social support system in the treatment may foster retention in treatment.

  d. In the treatment of adolescents with substance use disorders, it is particularly important to use approaches that involve multiple systems, including the family, peers, and others.

5. In general, certain client characteristics are associated with greater or lesser success.

  a. Greater client readiness to change is associated with greater treatment success.

  b. Greater severity of the substance use disorder is associated with a poorer response to treatment.

6. Several specific aspects of clients' presentation require careful attention.

  a. A focus on client motivation is crucial to successful outcome.

  b. Therapists should help clients develop awareness of repetitive patterns of thinking and behavior that perpetuate their alcohol or drug use.

  c. Therapy should attend to the affective experiences of clients.

  d. Therapy should consider the role of conditioning in the development and maintenance of substance use disorders. Clinicians should carefully assess for indicators of specific conditioned responses to alcohol or drugs and develop ways to change these conditioned responses.

  e. Clients with positive expectancies about treatment tend to have better outcomes and therapists can work to enhance positive expectancies.

7. Modifying treatment for clients with different presenting characteristics may improve outcomes.

  a. About 50% of those with SUDs have another co-morbid Axis I disorder and about one-third have a co-morbid Axis II disorder. Research knowledge about the effective integration of different psychological treatments to manage multiple presenting problems is lacking, but assessment of co-morbid disorders and use of effective treatments for additional presenting problems is appropriate.

  b. Research on differential treatments for women versus men is quite limited. However, randomized clinical trials and nonrandomized comparison group studies have suggested that female-specific treatment may be more effective than generic substance abuse treatment.

How can the findings and principles presented in this chapter assist the clinician in planning and providing treatment for Allen and Georgia? For Allen, attention to social service needs for employment, transportation, and stable housing may be important. His motivation to change appears reasonable, but the fact that he is mandated to treatment suggests the need for a focus on motivational issues. His social isolation and complex history of poor and fractured relationships suggests that the therapist will need to be particularly conscious of developing a therapeutic alliance, and that treatment will need to address means to help him develop a social network supportive of abstinence, as well as skills to deal with those in his current social network who support his continued use. Finally, a careful assessment of the possibility of co-morbid PTSD or depression and development of a treatment approach to manage these other disorders will be important.

In contrast, Georgia does not present the clinician with social service needs, but therapeutic relationship issues are likely to present continuing challenges to the clinician, who probably will need to focus very deliberately on the use of accurate empathy and communicate a nonjudgmental attitude. Her level of motivation to change is unclear, and, like Allen, a focus on motivation is likely to be important. Given that she has a stable partner, involving Dave in the treatment may enhance support for abstinence. The problems in relationships in her more extended social network, though, suggest that she may benefit from interventions to increase her support for abstinence beyond Dave. Her negative cognitions about her drinking appear to be important to address as well, and may relate to her being an older woman with a drinking problem, suggesting the importance of addressing female-specific content in her treatment.

With both Allen and Georgia, there is no empirically complete "formula" to allow the clinician to plan and deliver treatment with complete confidence, but the empirically supported principles summarized in this chapter provide a more research-informed and potentially effective approach to treatment than either the application of a treatment protocol standardized on a somewhat different clinical population, or use of idiosyncratically selected interventions.

References

American Psychiatric Association. (1995). *Practice guideline for the treatment of patients with substance use disorders: Alcohol, cocaine, opioids.* Washington, DC: American Psychiatric Association.

Bien, T. H., Miller, W. R., & Tonigan, J. S. (1993). Brief interventions for alcohol problems: A review. *Addiction, 88,* 315–336.

Bukstein, O. G. (1995). *Adolescent substance abuse: Assessment, prevention, and treatment.* New York: John Wiley & Sons.

Henggeler, S. W., Schoenwald, S. K., Borduin, C. M., Rowland, M. D., & Cunningham, P. B. (1998). *Multisystemic treatment of antisocial behavior in children and adolescents.* New York: Guilford Press.

McLellan, A. T., Grissom, G. R., Zanis, D., Randall, M., Brill, P., & O'Brien, C. P. (1997). Problem–service "matching" in addiction treatment: A prospective study in 4 programs. *Archives of General Psychiatry, 54,* 730–735.

Mee-Lee, D., Shulman, G. D., Fishman, M., Gastfriend, D. R., & Griffith, J. H. (2001). *ASAM patient placement criteria for the treatment of substance-related disorders* (2nd ed., rev.). Chevy Chase, MD: American Society of Addiction Medicine, Inc.

Miller, W. R., & Hester, R. (1986). Inpatient alcoholism treatment: Who benefits? *American Psychologist, 41,* 794–805.

Miller, W. R., & Rollnick, S. (2002). *Motivational interviewing: Preparing people to change addictive behaviors* (2nd ed.). New York: Guilford Press.

Moos, R. H. (2003). Addictive disorders in context: Principles and puzzles of effective treatment and recovery. *Psychology of Addictive Behaviors, 17,* 3–12.

Perkins, K. A., Marcus, M. D., Levine, M. D., D'Amico, D., Miller, A., Broge, M., Ashcom, J., & Shiffman, S. (2001). Cognitive-behavioral therapy to reduce weight concerns improves smoking cessation outcome in weight-concerned women. *Journal of Consulting and Clinical Psychology, 69,* 604–613.

Project MATCH Research Group (1997). Project MATCH secondary a priori hypotheses. *Addiction, 92,* 1671–1698.

Rosenthal, R. N., & Westreich, L. (1999). Treatment of persons with dual diagnoses of substance use disorder and other psychological problems. In B. S. McCrady & E. E. Epstein (Eds.), *Addictions: A comprehensive guidebook* (pp. 439–476). New York: Oxford University Press.

Rychtarik, R. G., Connors, G. J., Whitney, R. B., McGillicuddy, N. B., Fitterling, J. M., & Wirtz, P. W. (2000). Treatment settings for persons with alcoholism: Evidence for matching clients to inpatient versus outpatient care. *Journal of Consulting and Clinical Psychology, 68,* 277–289.

Substance Abuse and Mental Health Services Administration. (1993–2004). *Treatment improvement protocol series.* Rockville, MD: US Department of Health and Human Services.

Part VI

CONCLUSIONS

18

Common and Unique Principles of Therapeutic Change: What Do We Know and What Do We Need to Know?

Louis G. Castonguay

Larry E. Beutler

One of the most salient controversies in the field of psychotherapy is whether client change is primarily due to the therapist's techniques or the quality of the therapeutic relationship. As described earlier (Beutler & Castonguay, this volume), the premise of this book (as well as the Task Force it has emerged from) is that this controversy reflects, more or less implicitly, an "either/or" assumption that is conceptually flawed and empirically untenable. The complexity of the process of change requires, at least in our view, a consideration of both technical and interpersonal factors. Despite the best intention of its proponents, we also believe that by delineating separate lists of "empirically supported treatments" (EST; Chambless & Ollendick, 2001; Nathan and Gorman, 2002) and "empirically supported therapeutic relationships" (ESTR; Norcross, 2002), past APA Task Forces may have inadvertently fueled this controversy.

Of course, very few clinicians or researchers hold an extreme, all-or-none position vis-à-vis these therapeutic factors. None, we assume, would deny that without a minimum of trust and respect from his/her client, a therapist will find it difficult to effectively and successfully implement the techniques required by most treatment manuals—at least for a large number of sessions. Similarly, we would like to think that even for those who are convinced that the therapeutic relationship is healing by and of itself, there are strategies that can foster its impact. In other words, since not all kinds of relationships are likely to bring change, one needs to be aware of interventions (including modes of relating) that should be encouraged or avoided for the relationship to become a corrective experience.

Yet, as we embarked on this project, we felt that something still needed to be done for clinicians and researchers to be fully and simultaneously exposed, within a single volume, to the empirical evidence about the role that relationships and techniques, as well as client and therapist characteristics, play in the treatment of specific clinical disorders. We also felt that the time was ripe to derive from such empirical literature varis principles of change that are not tied to specific theoretical orientations and that can serve as useful heuristics for day-to-day clinical practice and future research.

A substantial number of such principles were identified in the three initial chapters of each section of this book (12 chapters in total). Four additional chapters have integrated the list of principles for each specific clinical problem. These have provided a survey of what we know in terms of the potential impact of three variable domains (i.e., relationship, techniques, and participant characteristics) in four problem areas (dysphoric disorders, anxiety disorders, personality disorders, and substance use disorders).

The goal of the present chapter is to provide yet another form of integration of therapeutic principles of change. Rather than looking across domain variables within a specific problem area, we will summarize what the empirical literature is telling us for each type of domain variable across the four problem areas covered in this book. This will allow us to identify principles that may be unique to particular disorders, and those that are likely to be common. We hasten to say that by identifying a principle as being unique to one problem area, we do not imply that it is irrelevant to the treatment of other clinical problems. Unique principles are those that have been judged to be particularly salient to one type of disorder and/or have received sufficient empirical attention to draw relevant conclusions for only one clinical problem. As such, future research may suggest that some of the principles currently viewed as "unique" actually cut across different disorders. Furthermore, by identifying some principles as being "common," we do not wish to imply that they are playing a role in the treatment of all psychological disorders. Rather, this suggests that such principles are likely to have an impact in psychological treatment for at least two of the problem areas targeted in this book.[1]

Interestingly, different sets of domain variables have raised particular challenges with regard to the delineation of common and unique principles, which could in turn lead to different contributions to the current state of knowledge about the process of change in psychotherapy. On the one hand, relationship and participant variables have been frequently studied with general clinical popula-

tions and the conclusions reached by the ESTR Task Force (Norcross, 2002) did not discriminate among disorders. This is partly based on the assumption that these variables are common to all forms of psychotherapy and should, therefore, be important in the treatment of most psychological problems. Thus, one of the challenges of this Task Force was to determine whether these conclusions are applicable to specific disorders, perhaps even revealing that some are unique to a particular one. On the other hand, most, if not all, studies conducted on technique factors have been done within the context of clinical trials, where the isolation of homogeneous and specific populations is a core feature. The challenge here is to examine whether some of the principles that were derived from the EST studies (Nathan & Gorman, 2002) cut across some disorders, and perhaps reveal themselves to be common to all of the problem areas covered in this book.

PARTICIPANT CHARACTERISTICS

Following the chapter on participant characteristics in the treatment of dysphoric disorders (Beutler, Blatt, Alamohamed, Levy, & Angtuaco, this volume), we have divided these variables into those that are "observed" versus those that are "inferred." For both categories, common and unique principles of therapeutic change have been identified. Also consistent with Beutler et al. (this volume), we have distinguished between prognosis principles (related to a client's likelihood of change irrespective of the type of treatment used) and matching principles (related to the fit of a particular treatment to specific client's characteristics).

Observed Characteristics

Common Principles

Surprisingly, despite the fact that many observable participant characteristics have been investigated, we have identified only three common principles from the current state of this empirical literature— all of them related to client's prognosis.

The first two have been retained from the treatment research on dysphoric disorders, anxiety disorders, and substance use disorders.

1. Clients with a high level of impairment are less likely to benefit from therapy than those with a better level of functioning at pretreatment.

In the treatment of anxiety disorders, the role of impairment is demonstrated by the negative correlation between outcome and numerous variables such as problem severity, problem chronicity, level of distress, interpersonal problems, and Axis I co-morbidity (see Newman, Crits-Christoph, Connolly Gibbons, & Erickson, this volume). In the review of literature on dysphoric disorders (Beutler et al., this volume), the roles of related dimensions of functioning were aggregated within one general construct, and its examination led to the same conclusion. Furthermore, the above principle of change reflects a number of more specific principles delineated for substance use disorders with regard to poly-substance abuse/use, nicotine dependence, psychiatric co-morbidity, and early onset (Haaga, Hall, & Haas, this volume).

2. Clients who have been diagnosed with a personality disorder are less likely to benefit from treatment than those who have not.

For both dysphoric and anxiety disorders, the presence of an Axis II co-morbid condition is an indicator of a worse prognosis. For substance use disorders, however, the reach of this principle may be narrower as the current state of the literature provides only evidence for Antisocial Personality Disorder as a predictor of poor outcome in the treatment of alcohol and drug abuse.

A third common principle related to an observed characteristic of the client can be drawn from the treatment of anxiety and substance use disorders.

3. Clients who face financial and/or occupational difficulties may benefit less from treatment than those who do not.

This principle is derived from the findings that lower socioeconomic status (SES) is a correlate of worse outcome in the treatment of anxiety disorders and that employment predicts good outcome in the treatment of alcohol and drug abuse. As noted by Newman et al. (this volume), however,

the findings related to SES and anxiety disorders should be considered cautiously.

Unique Principles

We have identified 13 principles of therapeutic change related to observed participant characteristics that are unique to one of the particular disorders covered in this book. All but five of these principles are derived from the treatment of dysphoric disorders. The following eight principles unique to the treatment of dysphoric disorders are taken directly from Beutler et al. (this volume). Whereas the first four of them are related to a client's prognosis, the other four reflect matching principles.

1. Age is a negative predictor of a patient's response to general psychotherapy.
2. Patients representing underserved ethnic or racial groups achieve fewer benefits from conventional psychotherapy than Anglo-American groups.
3. If patients and therapists come from the same or similar racial/ethnic backgrounds, dropout rates are positively affected and improvement is enhanced.
4. The most effective treatments are likely to be those that do not induce patient resistance.[2]
5. In dealing with the resistant patient, the therapist's use of directive therapeutic interventions should be planned to inversely correspond with the patient's manifest level of resistant traits and states.
6. Patients with high levels of initial impairment respond better when they are offered long-term, intensive treatment, than when they receive nonintensive and brief treatments, regardless of the particular model and type of treatment assigned. Patients with low impairment seem to do equally well in high and low intensive treatments.
7. Patients whose personalities are characterized by impulsivity, social gregariousness, and external blame for problems, benefit more from direct behavioral change and symptom reduction efforts, including building new skills and managing impulses, than they do from procedures that are de-

signed to facilitate insight and self-awareness.

8. Patients whose personalities are characterized by low levels of impulsivity, indecisiveness, self-inspection, and overcontrol tend to benefit more from procedures that foster self-understanding, insight, interpersonal attachments, and self-esteem than they do from procedures that aim at directly altering symptoms and building new social skills.

The majority of the principles here are considered unique to the treatment of dysphoric disorders because insufficient research has been conducted (or mixed results have been obtained) with other clinical populations. The only exceptions are for the principles related to client age and ethnicity (Principles 1 and 2), as these two variables have been investigated in the treatment of anxiety disorders and were found not to predict outcome (see Newman et al., this volume).

It should be mentioned that research has also been conducted with other disorders in relation to two of the principles above (7 and 8). These two principles focus on the moderating role played by coping styles (see Beutler et al., this volume), specifically stating that part of the outcome variance in the treatment of depression can be explained by an interaction between the client's coping style and treatment procedures. Coping, however, has also been investigated as a predictor of change. In the treatment of substance abuse, the client's ability to use coping skills to deal with the temptation to drink has been linked with outcome. In addition, dimensions of externalizing and internalizing, which are consistent with the coping style emphasized in Principles 7 and 8 above, have been investigated as predictors in the treatment of anxiety and have led to the next unique principle of change (taken from Newman et al., this volume). Addressing the client's likelihood of change without regard to the treatment use, this principle can be viewed as a "prognosis" heuristic or guideline. It should be noted, however, that the authors were cautious about drawing firm conclusions with respect to these coping skills, as the variables investigated were not originally intended to capture these constructs.

9. Psychotherapy for anxiety is less likely to be successful if the client has low internal attributions of control or high negative self-attribution. Thus, rigid externalizing or internalizing coping styles are negative prognostic indicators.

Three unique principles of change related to observed participant characteristics were derived from the treatment of substance use disorder (taken from Haaga et al., this volume). The first of them related to client prognosis, while the other two reflected matching guidelines.

10. Therapists with vs. without a history of substance use disorder appear to be equally effective in treating alcohol or illicit drug abuse.
11. High-medical-risk smokers will be especially receptive to individual counseling for smoking cessation only if smoking plausibly contributed to their risk status.
12. Although the evidence is not entirely consistent, cognitive behavior therapy may be differentially effective with depressed smokers relative to comparison conditions. This prescriptive effect may apply especially to those smokers with chronic, recurrent depression.

In addition, one unique principle (related to client prognosis) emerged from the treatment of personality disorders (see Fernández-Alvarez, Clarkin, Carmen Salgueiro, & Critchfield, this volume).

13. Therapists working with a specific personality disorder may increase their effectiveness if they receive specialized training with this population.

Inferred Characteristics   → Conclude or derived by reasoning

Common Principles

Only two common principles related to inferred characteristics of the participant characteristics were identified, and both of these were related to the client's prognosis (or likelihood of change irrespective of the treatment used). The first of these principles cut across three problem areas: dysphoric, anxiety, and personality disorders.

1. Clients who experienced significant interpersonal problems during their early development may have difficulty responding to psychotherapy.

This principle attempts to capture a number of conceptually related findings. In the treatment of anxiety disorders, the client's perception of negative parenting and attachment difficulties has been linked with worse outcome (see Newman et al., this volume). A client history of positive attachment, parental relationship, and object relations has been identified as a predictor of therapeutic change in the treatment of personality disorders (see Fernández-Alvarez et al., this volume). Attachment difficulties also seem to play a role in the treatment of dysphoric disorders, but the evidence collected so far led Beutler et al. (this volume) to tentatively draw a principle that points to its potential negative impact on the process, rather than the outcome of psychotherapy (see Beutler et al., this volume).

The second common principle was derived from the empirical literature on anxiety and substance use disorders.

2. Client's expectations are likely to play a role in treatment outcome.

In the treatment for anxiety disorders, low expectations for the success of therapy has been associated with worse outcome. Similarly, alcohol outcome expectancies (e.g., alcohol reduces tension) have been negatively associated with abstinence at the end of therapy. In contrast, clients' self-efficacy expectations (for achieving and maintaining abstinence) have also been related to successful smoking cessation (see Haaga et al., this volume). Interestingly, the current state of empirical evidence suggests that clients' expectations (with respect to the success of therapy or the role of each participant) do not appear to be associated with outcome in the treatment of depression (see Beutler et al., this volume).

Unique Principles

A total of 10 unique principles of change related to inferred participant characteristics were identified. In contrast with the unique principles related to observable characteristics, most of them were derived from the treatment of either dysphoric or personality disorders, and more than half are related to therapist variables. The following are four principles unique to the treatment of dysphoric disorders (directly taken from Beutler et al., this volume). It should be noted that the first three have only been retained as suggestive of predictive effects. They are possible contributors whose value is yet to be confirmed. Furthermore, while the first two refer to a client's prognosis, the other two reflect matching principles.

1. If psychotherapists are open, informed, and tolerant of various religious views, treatment effects are likely to be enhanced.
2. A secure attachment pattern in . . . therapist appears to facilitate the treatment process.
3. If patients have a preference for religiously oriented psychotherapy, treatment benefit is enhanced if therapists accommodate this preference.
4. Benefit may be enhanced when the interventions selected are responsive to and consistent with the patient's level of problem assimilation.

Five other unique principles, all related to client prognosis, have emerged from the treatment of personality disorders. As noted by Fernández-Alvarez et al. (this volume), these principles overlap with a number of others related to the therapeutic relationship and treatment procedures (see below). The first of these principles (which obviously relates to the quality of the therapeutic alliance) seems to reflect the emotional cost that psychotherapy especially requires for this clinical population. The other four appear to represent the counterparts of this emotionally and cognitively costly enterprise for therapists.

5. Therapy outcome is likely to be enhanced if the client is willing and able to engage in the treatment process.

6. The therapist is likely to increase his/her effectiveness if he/she demonstrates attitudes of open-mindedness, flexibility, and creativity.
7. The positive impact of therapy is likely to be increased if the therapist is comfortable with long-term, emotionally intense relationships.
8. The benefits of therapy may be enhanced if the therapist is able to tolerate his/her own negative feelings regarding the patient and the treatment process.
9. The therapist is likely to be more effective if he/she is patient.

The last unique principle of change related to inferred participant characteristics was derived from the treatment of substance use. This principle (directly taken from Haaga et al., this volume) reflects yet another dimension associated with a client's prognosis.

10. Smokers in more advanced stages of change, as defined in the transtheoretical model, are more likely to succeed in quitting smoking. Likewise, alcohol abusers reporting increased readiness to change fare better in treatment.

Summary

As specified in the guidelines of the current Task Force (see Beutler & Castonguay, this volume), the reviews of the empirical literature on participant characteristics conducted for this book were primarily based on the previous work accomplished by the Division 29 Task Force on empirically supported therapeutic relationships (Norcross, 2002). As a result of our Task Force, we have been able to derive at least one principle of change (unique to one particular problem area, or common to at least two disorders covered in this book) for each of the variables judged by the Division 29 Task Force to be "demonstrably effective" or "promising and probably effective": resistance, functional impairment, coping styles (externalizing/anaclitic versus internalizing/interjecting), stages of change, expectation, and assimilation of problematic experience.

In addition, by conducting separate reviews for four distinct disorders, the current task force has found support for a number of participant characteristics that were examined by the Division 29 Task Force, but for which insufficient research was found to enable a judgment with regard to their effectiveness. Hence, at least one principle of change was identified for the following client variables: attachment style, ethnicity, religion, and personality disorders. Furthermore, the current Task Force led to principles associated with several participant characteristics that were either not investigated by the Division 29 Task Force or not addressed in its conclusions (Norcross, 2002, pp. 441–442), such as the client's age and socioeconomic status, and the therapist's attachment style, specialized training, and numerous attitudes toward the client and therapy (open-mindedness, flexibility, creativity, patience, tolerance of negative feelings, and comfort with long-term and emotionally intense relationships).

Our reading of the reviews in this book on participant factors led to a relatively small number (five) of common principles, especially compared to the 23 unique principles that we identified. More than half of the unique principles (12) pertained to the treatment of dysphoric disorders. This, obviously, raises questions about whether or not the conclusions reached by the Division 29 Task Force are applicable to most, if not all, psychological problems. However, it should be mentioned that in line with one of the guidelines proposed in the current Task Force (see Beutler & Castonguay, this volume), the authors of the personality disorder chapter on participant characteristics have accepted by default the Division 29 Task Force's conclusions related to each of the variables for which research has yet to be conducted for this population. This involves all of the variables listed above as being "demonstratively effective" or "probably effective". Although we have decided not to do this, one might thus argue that several of the principles identified above as being unique are likely to be shared by two problem areas. In contrast, authors of the chapters on participant characteristics in anxiety and substance use disorders elected not to accept the Division 29 Task Force's conclusions unless sufficient empirical evidence supported them for their particular disorders.

THERAPEUTIC RELATIONSHIP

Adopting the categorization system used in the chapters on dysphoric and personality disorders (see Castonguay et al., this volume; Smith, Barrett, Benjamin, & Barber, this volume), the principles of change associated with relationship variables are divided into three categories: quality of the therapeutic relationship, therapist interpersonal skills, and therapist clinical skills.

3 Categories:

(i) Quality of the Therapeutic Relationship

Three variables related to the general quality of the therapeutic relationship were investigated, and each of them led to the delineation of a common principle of therapeutic change. The first of these principles cuts across all four of the problem areas covered in this book.[3]

> 1. Therapy is likely to be beneficial if a strong working alliance is established and maintained during the course of treatment.

Needless to say, such a statement is hardly surprising considering the considerable amount of research that has been devoted to the therapeutic alliance in the last two decades. It should be mentioned that with respect to the treatment of substance use disorders, this general principle reflects a number of more specific principles of therapeutic change related to the relationship between client and therapist, family and peers, and the relationship that the client develops with the therapeutic program (see Lebow, Kelly, Knobloch-Fedders, & Moos, this volume). The authors of the chapter on personality disorders have also derived a principle of change that is related to the working alliance and emphasizes the importance of the therapist's activity level, provision of structure, and limit setting (see Smith et al., this volume).

The other two common principles of change were derived from the treatment of dysphoric and anxiety disorders, with the first of them also accepted (tentatively) for the treatment of personality disorders.

> 2. Clients are likely to benefit from group therapy if a strong level of group cohesion is developed and maintained during therapy.

> 3. Therapists should attempt to facilitate a high degree of collaboration with clients during therapy.[4]

(2) Therapist Interpersonal Skills

As for the variables related to the quality of the therapeutic relationship, each of the three factors associated with client-centered interpersonal skills or attitudes led to the identification of a common principle of change. These principles were derived from the treatment of dysphoric, anxiety, and substance use disorders (with the exception of the last one related to congruence for which insufficient evidence appears to have been associated with anxiety disorders). The formulation of the following three principles was directly borrowed from the principles stated in Castonguay et al. (this volume).

> 1. Therapists should relate to their clients in an empathic way.
> 2. When adopted by therapists, an attitude of caring, warmth, and acceptance is likely to be helpful in facilitating therapeutic change.
> 3. Therapists are likely to facilitate change when adopting an attitude of congruence or authenticity.

It should be noted that the principle related to positive regard (therapist's attitude of care, warmth, and acceptance) was suggested only tentatively for the treatment of dysphoric disorders. Interestingly, it should also be mentioned that the principles about congruence and empathy/understanding have received support, at least indirectly, for the treatment of personality disorders. As described below, Linehan, Davison, Lynch, and Sanderson (this volume) have identified these variables as factors enhancing the client's motivation and collaboration.

(3) Therapist Clinical Skills

When working with the therapeutic relationship, only two (out of five) strategies used by therapists led to common principles of change. This is in contrast with the two previous clusters of relationship variables. These common principles appear to be applicable to the treatment of dysphoric and personality disorders. It should be noted, however, that the first two reflect provisional conclusions for the treatment of personality disorders, while the third one has been adopted only tentatively for the treatment of dysphoric disorders.

1. Therapists should be careful not to use relational interpretations excessively.
2. When relational interpretations are used, they are likely to facilitate improvement if they are accurate.
3. Therapists are likely to resolve alliance ruptures when addressing such ruptures in an empathic and flexible way.

It should be noticed that for the treatment of personality disorders, a broader set of factors were linked to the resolution (and avoidance) of alliance ruptures than those emphasized in the third principle, for example, therapist's benign self-concept and focus on issues of depth during treatment (see Smith et al.).

Only two unique principles of change emerged from the empirical literature on strategies designed to address or manage the therapeutic relationship. The first (stated tentatively) was derived from the treatment of dysphoric disorders and is cited here from Castonguay et al. (this volume).

1. When working with depressed clients, therapists' use of self-disclosure is likely to be helpful. This may especially be the case for reassuring and supportive self-disclosures, as opposed to challenging self-disclosures.

Indirect support for this principle has also been provided for this principle in the treatment of personality disorders, as Linehan et al. (this volume) have posited that when used strategically, self-disclosure can enhance a client's motivation and collaboration.

The second unique principle is related to the treatment of anxiety disorders.

2. Providing feedback to the client is likely to be beneficial.

Summary

The review conducted within our Task Force has led to the delineation of at least one principle of change that is related to ten of the eleven variables judged by the Division 29 Task Force's report to be either definite or promising general elements of the therapeutic relationship: [alliance, cohesion, empathy, collaboration (and goal consensus), positive regard, congruence, repair of alliance ruptures, self-disclosure, feedback, and quality of relational interpretations] (see Norcross, 2002). For the management of countertransference (an element identified by the Division 29 Task Force as "promising and probably effective"), however, no evidence was found for any of the four problem areas covered in this book. Thus, no principle (unique or common) was retained in this chapter for this variable.

Compared with participant variables, a larger proportion of the principles that were related to the therapeutic relationship cut across at least two disorders. Specifically, nine out of 11 (82%) of these principles were retained as common, in contrast with 19% (five out of 27) of the principles extracted for the participant variables. Similar to the participant variables, however, more relationship variables appear to have been investigated in the treatment of dysphoric disorders than in other problem areas.

It should also be mentioned that when insufficient research had been conducted for a relationship variable retained as effective or promising by the Division 29 Task Force, the authors of each relevant chapter accepted this conclusion by default. This, one might argue, could increase the number of factors likely to cut across different disorders.

TECHNIQUE FACTORS

In line with the guidelines proposed for the current Task Force (see Beutler & Castonguay, this volume), we have attempted to integrate the technique principles derived from the four problem areas covered in this book within five general dimensions of psychotherapy: (1) directive versus nondirective or self-directive procedures; (2) intensive versus nonintensive/short-term procedures; (3) interpersonal/systemic versus intrapersonal/individual procedures; (4) thematic/insight-oriented versus symptom/skill-building procedures; and (5) abreactive versus emotionally supportive procedures (Malik, Beutler, Gallagher-Thompson, Thompson, & Alimohamed, 2003).

To ensure that the conclusions reached encompassed a number of related principles, the first two principles that we extracted were reformulated as "therapeutic stance and general interpersonal style" and "framework of intervention," respectively.

Therapeutic Stance and General Interpersonal Style

Two common principles of change related to the therapist's working stance and style can be delineated from the previous chapters on technique factors.

1. Positive change is likely if the therapist provides a structured treatment and remains focused in the application of his/her interventions.

The need for the therapist, at least in some phases of therapy, to be directive (i.e., to guide the process of therapy) is emphasized by the authors of each of the technique chapters. This general principle reflects a number of more specific principles formulated for the treatment of personality disorders, such as the importance of using a theoretically coherent approach, specifying (and agreeing on) the therapy goals, format, modalities, and strategies before the formal beginning of the treatment, as well as organizing the sessions around prioritized targets.

The second common principle has been derived primarily from the treatment of personality and dysphoric disorders.

2. Therapists should be able to skillfully use "nondirective" interventions.

At the core of dialectic-behavior therapy (the most empirically supported treatment for personality disorders) is the therapist's ability to find a balance between the use of change-oriented (directive) and acceptance-oriented (nondirective) interventions. Nondirective techniques also have a prominent place in the early phase of process-experiential therapy, which has received empirical support for the treatment of depression. It should also be mentioned that while most empirically supported treatments for substance abuse have been described as directive, one of them (motivational therapies) emphasizes nondirective components.

In addition, six unique principles of change related to therapist stance and interpersonal style have been identified for the treatment of personality disorders (taken directly from Linehan, Davison, Lynch, & Sanderson, this volume). The first two, point to the importance of adopting a prudent, cautious, perhaps humbling (as opposed to overly optimistic) attitude when working with this difficult population. The other four principles, interestingly, describe ways to foster client engagement and collaboration in treatment. These four "principles of motivation and collaboration" explicitly address relationship variables (i.e., repair of alliance ruptures, genuineness/congruence, self-disclosure, understanding/empathy) and thus overlap with some of the principles previously formulated.

1. Therapists treating clients diagnosed with PD should be both honest and explicit about their limits.
2. Therapists should not assume that clients diagnosed with PD possess the necessary cognitive or emotional capacities necessary for effective living.
3. The client's motivation for treatment is enhanced, and therapeutic change is most likely, if the therapist can address therapeutic impasses with nonconfrontational strategies.
4. The client's motivation for treatment is enhanced if the therapist is genuine and responsive.
5. The client's motivation for treatment is enhanced when the therapist engages in strategic self-disclosure.
6. The client's motivation for treatment is enhanced when the therapist conveys an understanding of how difficult it is for the client to change.

Framework of Intervention

The framework of intervention refers to a number of structural elements (e.g., contract, setting, phases, or length) within which therapy takes place (see Castonguay, in press). Two common principles have been retained; the first is derived from the treatment of anxiety disorders, dysphoric disorders, and substance use disorders.

1. Time-limited therapy can be beneficial.

Although the actual length of treatment is varied, the majority of the empirically supported treatments for these three disorders have been conducted within the context of time-limited and relatively short-term interventions. As noted by McCrady & Nathan (this volume), however, therapists working with substance abusers should also "develop a long-term maintenance plan that may or may not include continued formal treatment" (p. 331).

The second common principle is derived primarily from the treatment of anxiety and personality disorders.

2. Therapeutic change may be facilitated by, or even require, intense therapy.

In the treatment of anxiety disorders, this principle is based on the overall, although not robust, findings suggesting that the "massed" delivery of sessions (more than once a week) leads to superior results when compared to "spaced" delivery (Woody & Ollendick, this volume). Although coming from conceptually different models, the two empirically based treatments for personality disorders involve more than one weekly therapeutic contact (Linehan, Davison, Lynch, & Sanderson, this volume). It should also be mentioned that the implementation of some empirically supported treatments for substance use (e.g., community reinforcement approach [see McCrady et al., this volume]) and dysphoric disorders (e.g., cognitive therapy [see Beck, Rush, Shaw, & Emery, 1979]) can involve more than one session per week (at least in the early part of therapy).

We were also able to identify four principles of change unique to a specific disorder. The first three were derived from the treatment of personality disorders (and were taken from Linehan et al., this volume), while the last one pertains to the treatment of substance use disorders (cited here from McCrady & Nathan, this volume). As a whole,

these principles may reflect the complexity and particularly demanding nature of treatment for these two particular problem areas.

1. Treatment of BPD takes time. . . . The therapist should plan to consistently apply treatment components over relatively long periods of time.
2. Therapeutic change is most likely if the therapists treating the client in primary and auxiliary modes of therapy receive ongoing consultation and supervision.
3. The client's motivation for treatment is enhanced if the individual therapist is flexible in his or her limits, being more available to the client during a period of crisis.
4. Identify other social service or medical care needs and arrange for attention to these needs.

Interpersonal/Systemic Versus Intrapersonal/Individual Procedures

We delineated three common principles of change related to this general dimension of psychotherapy. The first two cut across the four problem areas (at least to some extent) covered in this book.

1. A therapist may be more effective if he/she does not restrict him/herself to individual procedures: Being with others during treatment can be beneficial for some clients.

In the chapter on technique factors for substance use disorders (McCrady & Nathan, this volume), this principle is expressed both eloquently and pragmatically: Therapists should "provide treatment in an individual, group, or family modality, depending on the individual client and treatment interventions selected" (p. 331). This principle is consistent with the fact that the two empirically based treatments for personality disorders involve both individual and group therapy sessions. In the treatment of dysphoric disorders, this principle is perhaps best demonstrated by the efficacy of behavioral marital therapy and its superior impact on marital discord (a factor robustly related to depression [Joiner, 2002]), as compared to individual cognitive behavior therapy (see Follette & Greenberg, this volume; Craighead, Hart, Wilcoxon-Craighead, & Ilardi, 2002). As noted by Woody and Ollendick (this volume), however, strong support for including others in the treatment of anxiety disorders appears to be restricted to social phobia.

2. Effective therapy may require therapists to address intrapersonal aspects of the client's functioning.

When taken together, the empirically supported treatments suggest that therapists should focus on clients' cognitions, emotions, behaviors, and (in some cases) physiological responses. A number of ways to address these intrapersonal issues are captured in the principles of change included in the next two general dimensions of psychotherapy.

The third common principle of change was derived from the treatment of all the problem areas investigated, with the exception of anxiety disorders. As stated by Woody and Ollendick, even in the treatment of social phobia (where treatments are conducted in group), the intervention strategies used are intrapersonal (see below).

3. Therapy outcome is likely to be enhanced if therapy addresses interpersonal issues related to clinical problems.

This principle refers primarily to the importance of helping the client develop better interpersonal skills and change his/her everyday environment (marital, family, social), so that adaptive behaviors are reinforced and/or maladaptive behaviors are reduced. In addition, helping clients understand their relationship with others is an important aspect of psychodynamic, interpersonal, process-emotional therapies (via exploration and resolution of unfinished business) found to be effective in the treatment of dysphoric disorders. This is also the case, in the early phase of treatment, in psychodynamic therapy for personality disorders. Similarly, some empirically based treatments for substance use disorders (i.e., motivational enhancement therapies and 12-step facilitation treatments) attempt to help clients understand their impact on others.

Thematic/Insight-oriented Versus Symptom/Skill-building Procedures

We have delineated three common principles of therapeutic change related to this general dimension of psychotherapy. The first two are derived from a large number of empirically supported treatments that emphasize symptomatic change and skills acquisition. These two principles cut across all four problems areas covered in this book. The third principle reflects the support received by the thematic, or insight-oriented approach, in the treatment of dysphoric and personality disorders.

1. Therapy is likely to be beneficial if a therapist facilitates change in clients' cognitions.

This integrates a number of principles that refer to the therapist's attempt to decrease maladaptive thoughts (by raising the client's awareness toward them, challenging the evidence for them, or setting up experiments to disconfirm them) and increase adaptive cognitions. In the treatment of substance abuse disorders, for example, this principle includes therapists' efforts at raising the clients' awareness of the severity of their problems and their repetitive thought patterns that perpetuate these problems, as well as therapists' attempts to help clients learn new ways to manage dysfunctional thoughts, acquire more accurate perceptions of social norms related to substance use and abstinence, and develop self-efficacy expectations for change (see McCrady & Nathan, this volume).

2. The client is likely to benefit from therapy if the therapist helps him/her modify maladaptive behavioral, emotional, or physiological responses.

Reflecting the clinical utility of learning mechanisms (e.g., classical and operant conditioning), this general principle refers to a large number of more specific principles that emphasize the importance of eliminating maladaptive responses and/or acquiring more adaptive ones. In the treatment of substance use disorders, this involves the consideration of environmental cues (e.g., smell, sight) associated with substance use, assessment and change of conditioned responses, and the maximizing of contingent reinforcements for abstinence. With respect to the treatment of anxiety disorders, this general principle of change encompassed the reduction of fear by exposure to the feared situation, elimination of avoidance, and the development of skills to handle the feared situation. Also captured is the following principle derived for the treatment of dysphoric disorders: "Increase and diversify the patient's access to contingent positive reinforcement while decreasing reinforcement for depressive and avoidant behaviors" (Follette & Greenberg, p. 94). The same authors also argue that the challenging of the client's behavior (and cognition) with new experiences is another principle of change that reflects "the importance of evaluating and altering the social reinforcing properties of the patient's environment" (p. 94). In addition, we counted eight principles directly related to behavioral change and/or the functional analysis and modification of maladaptive responses for the treatment of personality disorders (see Linehan et al., this volume).

3. Facilitating client self-exploration can be helpful.

Based on the evidence supporting psychodynamic interpersonal and process-experiential therapies, this general principle suggests that therapeutic change can take place when clients are encouraged to arrive at a new understanding of self based on an active and mostly self-directed exploration of meaningful themes and life experiences. It should be mentioned that the related principles derived in the context of the treatment of personality disorders were stated with important caveats (i.e., treatment focus should be present-oriented and the exploration of the past, as well as insight, should not be until the client demonstrates emotional and/or behavioral control). It also seems worthwhile to mention that while insight-oriented procedures are central to none of the empirically supported treatments for substance use, the increase of client awareness about crucial issues related to their problems has been emphasized in one of the principles of change emphasizing the facilitation of cognitive change. Similarly, as cogently described in Woody and Ollendick (this volume), a client's awareness of maladaptive thoughts is an important component of cognitive therapy for anxiety disorders. However, while they recognize that insight should be investigated (as a phenomena that either precedes or follows change), these authors conclude that in the current state of empirical knowledge "effective interventions for the anxiety disorders appear to rely more on behavioral change than on insight" (p. 179).[5]

Abreactive Versus Emotionally Supportive Procedures

Related to this dimension of psychotherapy, we have identified two common principles of therapeutic change that operate, at least to some extent, in all four problem areas covered in this book.

1. Therapeutic change is likely if therapists help clients accept, tolerate, and at times, fully experience their emotions.

The extent to which the experience and expression of emotion is encouraged appears to vary in empirically supported treatments. Nevertheless, a focus on emotion seems to be indicated with all problem areas covered in this book. Therapists working with substance abusers are recommended to attend to the client's affect, and several treatment approaches encourage "the experience of and, at times, the intensification of emotion" (McCrady & Nathan, this volume, p. 328). In the treatment of personality disorder, clients are helped in accepting and tolerating their feelings. Such emotional acceptance is core to a "mindfulness" approach to psychotherapy that has begun to receive support in the treatment of dysphoric disorders. Helping clients to identify, explore, stay with, and/or deepen emotion are important interventions in psychodynamic, interpersonal, and (especially) process-experiential therapies, which have all received support for the treatment of dysphoric disorders.[6] The evocation of intense emotion (fear) is also a cardinal feature of empirically supported treatments for anxiety disorders. Interestingly, the experience of intense feelings (as a means to facilitate exposure to fear structure or deepen emotional experience) appears to be common to cognitive-behavioral therapy and process-experiential therapy, despite their different conceptual roots.[7]

2. Interventions aimed at controlling emotions can be helpful.

While none of the empirically supported treatments encourage the avoidance of emotional experience, some of them are designed to control or regulate feelings. This is the case in treatments for personality disorders (at least for borderline personality disorder), where both empirically based treatments are defined as emotionally supportive and view abreaction (or catharsis) as iatrogenic (see note 4 and Linehan et al., this volume). In the treatment of dysphoric and substance use disorders, cognitive-behavior-oriented treatments are described as methods aimed at helping clients cope with or reduce negative emotion. Although empirically supported (cognitive-behavioral) treatments for anxiety disorders primarily use emotionally evocative procedures, the evocation of emotions is viewed as a by-product of the therapist's attempts to challenge thoughts, reduce avoidance, or decrease anxiety response (Woody & Ollendick, this volume). In exposure-based treatment, for instance, the purpose "is to help the client experience the emotion in a manageable way, not to just experience intense emotion for the sake of experiencing such emotion" (p. 180).

Summary

Taken together, we have been able to identify 22 principles of change related to technique factors, 12 of them (55%) cutting across at least two problem areas. Although not as high as for the relationship variables, this ratio of common over unique principles is substantially higher than that for participant variables. At first glance this could seem surprising. Because most, if not all, controlled clinical trials are conducted with specific and homogeneous clients, one might have expected a greater percentage of technique principles unique to the four distinct problems areas investigated in this book. What our findings may reveal, however, is the prevalence of cognitive-behavioral-oriented therapy among the treatments that have been currently tested in controlled trials.

While the particular targets of interventions may vary with different disorders, these conceptually related treatments appear to share several techniques, which in turn allow for the delineation of many underlying principles of change.

In contrast with the participant and relationship variables, the list of empirically derived technique principles obtained here cannot be compared to the findings of another Task Force. Our results, however, have provided support for each pole of the five general dimensions of psychotherapy proposed by our Task Force. Across at least two disorders, there is evidence showing support for therapists to be directive (structure the process of change and be focused), use nondirective (validating) procedures, plan time-limited therapy, conduct intensive treatment, make use of nonindividual modalities, focus on interpersonal and intrapersonal issues, facilitate skills acquisition, encourage self-exploration, focus on emotional experience, and to use emotionally supportive interventions. Evidence also supports the use of long-term therapy for the treatment of personality disorders.

FUTURE DIRECTIONS

As a whole, the current Task Force has led to the identification of 61 principles of therapeutic change (albeit a number of them overlapping), 26 (43%) of them derived from the treatment of at least two problem areas. This fairly large number of clinical guidelines reflects a substantial amount of research on the process and/or outcome of psychotherapy for dysphoric, anxiety, personality, and substance disorders. There is still a long way to go, however, in adequately understanding how, as well as the conditions under which, psychotherapy works or fails to be beneficial. The following is a list of suggestions, by no way exhaustive, for future research based on some of the gaps of the current empirical literature revealed by our Task Force.

With respect to participant characteristics, our most glaring lack of empirical knowledge concerns the treatment of personality disorders. In fact, only one of the client and therapist variables retained by the Division 29 Task Force as effective or promising factors has received an acceptable level of attention for this clinical population (i.e., client's history of attachment, interpersonal relationship, or object relations). Even the principles of change about participants that have been identified as unique for the treatment of personality disorders (none of which related to variables investigated by the Division 29 Task Force) need stronger and more direct evidence (see Fernández-Alvarez et al., this volume). It would also be interesting to know whether these principles (linked to several attitudes of the therapists toward the client and therapy, their level of training, and the client's willingness and ability to engage in the process of therapy) are indeed unique or particularly salient to the treatment of personality disorders.

A number of participant variables also deserve more attention in the treatment of both anxiety and substance use disorders. Among them are the client's religiosity or spirituality, preferences, and anaclitic/introjective style; the therapist's attachment style; match between the client's level of resistance and type (more or less directive) of intervention, match between the client's level of impairment and treatment intensity, match between the client's coping style (anaclitic/introjective and/or externalized/internalized) and intervention focus, match between the client's level of assimilation and therapist interventions, and match between the client and therapist's race or ethnicity. More research is also indicated for the treatment of substance use in general with regard to client age, ethnicity, attachment style, and externalizing/internalizing coping style. Furthermore, research on coping skills, personality disorders, and social class is also needed in the treatment of smoking cessation, in particular. Although conclusions were drawn (with various degree of certainty) with respect to SES, parental and attachment issues, externalizing/internalizing style, and ethnicity in the treatment of anxiety disorders, more research appears to be warranted.

While a large number of participant variables have been investigated for the treatment of dysphoric disorders, the principles related to some of them (i.e., client's religiosity and attachment style, therapist's attachment style) have been stated tentatively and/or formulated only with respect to process (and not outcome). As such, these variables should receive more attention from researchers interested in the treatment of dysphoric dis-

orders. In addition, the potential role of the client's social class should be further investigated with this clinical population.

Furthermore, for all the problem areas covered in this book, more studies are needed on the match between a client's stage of change and focus of intervention, as well as on numerous variables related to therapist characteristics and matching therapists and clients.

As with the participant variables, researchers need to pay much more attention to the potential role of relationship variables in the treatment of personality disorders. While five relationship principles were derived for this population, three of them (related to group cohesion and relational interpretations) were adopted as being only suggestive. In fact, only issues related to the alliance (its impact and ways of repairing it) have received noticeable attention. Considering the complexity of relationship factors associated with this difficult-to-treat and heterogeneous population, much more research would be welcome (see Smith et al., this volume).

Gaps of knowledge are again shared across the treatment of anxiety and substance use disorders. More needs to be known for both problem areas about the possible benefit of therapist self-disclosure, relational interpretations, and the repair of alliance ruptures. In addition, researchers should examine the role of collaboration and group cohesion in the treatment of substance use disorders, as well as the potential impact of congruence in the treatment of anxiety disorders.

Similar to the case of participant variables, most of the relationship factors identified by the Division 29 Task Force were investigated, more or less extensively, in the treatment of dysphoric disorders. It should be mentioned, however, that the principles of change related to three of these variables (congruence, self-disclosure, and repair of alliance ruptures) were adopted only tentatively and should therefore be further investigated. More empirical attention should also be given to the management of countertransference and the provision of feedback. The limited evidence supporting the former is not specific to any of the four problem areas covered in the book. Moreover, support for the latter appears to be only applicable to the treatment of anxiety disorders, at least at this point in time.

With respect to technique factors, our Task Force has once again highlighted the paucity of research with respect to personality disorders. The technique principles related to this population were derived from only two treatments (psychodynamic and dialectic behavior therapy [DBT]), for a single type of personality disorder (borderline personality disorder, BPD). As noted by Linehan et al. (this volume) only DBT for BPD currently meets criteria for "well-established" treatment. In light of the prevalence in clinical settings and the heterogeneity of this problem area, more should be done to develop and/or test effective psychosocial interventions. In the meantime, the principles derived highlighted here should be viewed as tentative—less so, however, for DBT for BPD.

Interestingly, it would be worthwhile to determine whether some of the technique principles identified as being unique to personality disorders may actually be relevant to other problem areas (e.g., the value of ongoing supervision and of being flexible about treatment limits).

We also believe that researchers should expand the parameters of typical clinical trials across disorders covered in this book. To begin with, more energy should be spent investigating long-term therapy. Considering the fact that a substantial number of clients do not fully benefit from many of the time-limited protocols that have been tested, it seems indicated to investigate whether some clients with Axis I disorders might need the length of treatment that has been used in empirical trials for Axis II disorders. In addition, more should be done to test the efficacy of treatments that are not exclusively or primarily relying on cognitive-behavioral procedures. There is now enough supporting, or at least promising, evidence for humanistic (e.g., process-experiential), interpersonal, psychodynamic, and mindfulness-based therapies to justify substantial investment, in terms of time and funds, from our scientific community to more solidly and broadly demonstrate their therapeutic impact. More empirical attention should also be given to systemic and integrative approaches.

In line with an integrative perspective, we also believe that effective interventions should build on each other to increase their respective impact. The combination of behavioral and humanistic strategies in dialectic behavior therapy is a prefect example of this kind of integrative therapy. We suspect that a similar balance of directive (change or action-oriented) and nondirective (accepting and validating) procedures would lead to better outcome than some of the primarily directive (e.g., traditional CBT) treatments developed for dysphoric, anxiety, and substance use disorders. This is also consistent with Woody and Ollendick's (this volume) suggestion to explore the potential merit of adding interpersonal strategies to the currently supported treatments for anxiety disorders. Although preliminary, promising results have indeed been obtained by adding such interpersonal strategies (along with humanistic procedures aimed at deepening emotions) to cognitive behavioral therapy for generalized anxiety disorder (Newman, Castonguay, Borkovec, & Molnar, 2004). In addition to building on the complementary contributions of different approaches, this type of additive strategy and methodological design avoids major internal validity pitfalls associated with comparative designs that are typically used in clinical trials (see Borkovec & Castonguay, 1998).

In closing, two more general recommendations for future research should be made, or as a matter of fact, repeated. As stated at the onset of this book (see Beutler & Castonguay, this volume), it would be premature to assume, at this point in time, that the principles delineated in this Task Force are empirically supported. It seems more appropriate to refer to them as being "empirically based" (or derived), since they have inferred determinants of change from correlational analyses and/or from the inspection of supported treatment manuals. It, therefore, behooves the field to test the causal effect that these principles may have on therapeutic change via means such as mediator analyses and dismantling, additive, catalytic, or parametric designs (Behar & Borkovec, 2003).

Finally, as stated in differing ways by several authors in this book (e.g., Beutler et al., this volume; Castonguay et al., this volume; Stiles & Wolfe, this volume) each principle should be investigated within the context it takes place. Participant, relationship, and technique principles do not operate in isolation. For example, representatives of each problem area have recognized, to a greater or lesser extent, that the successful implementation of effective techniques is based on, or facilitated by, a collaborative process, well-established relationship, or empathic and genuine attitude of the therapist (Beutler, Castonguay, & Follette, this volume; Linehan et al., this volume; McCrady, Haaga, & Lebow, this volume; Woody & Ollendick, this volume). Perhaps the most difficult and exciting challenge in psychotherapy research resides in the fact that principles that are related to these three domains are in a constant flux of interaction and interdependence. While some research has begun to delineate such complex relationships, much more needs to be done before we achieve an adequate understanding of how these factors work with, against, and within one another to enhance change.

As an initial step toward this lofty goal, however, it was imperative to show that none of the three sets of therapeutic factors can be upheld as sufficient for the explanation of change. Au contraire, it was necessary to demonstrate that each of these domains plays a role in the treatment of several problem areas. This was the goal of our Task Force, and by looking at the previous and current chapters, we like to think that it was met.

ACKNOWLEDGMENTS   Preparation of this chapter was supported in part by National Institute of Mental Health Research Grant MH-58593.

Notes

1. It should be noted common factors have also been identified in two integrative chapters of this book (Beutler, Castonguay, & Follette, this volume; Critchfield & Benjamin, this volume). They have, however, been worded and organized in slightly different ways. While the current chapter derived common principles uniquely from the 12 original chapters of this book, the authors of these integrative chapters also relied on a group discussion that took place between members of our Task Force (see Beutler & Castonguay, this volume).

2. The lack of compliance with homework, which can be viewed as resistance, has been found to predict worst outcome in the treatment of anxiety disorder. As described in a note below, however, homework compliance has also been defined as a manifestation of "collaborative engagement." Because the authors representing the anxiety disorders area have integrated the findings about homework

compliance under the construct of collaboration, the principle of resistance stands as one unique to the treatment of depression. This, however, is clearly an arbitrary classification, since both constructs are overlapping.

3. With regard to anxiety disorders, the conclusions reached in this section are based on the integrative chapter written for this problem area (Newman, Stiles, Woody, & Janeck, this volume). While the authors of the chapter on relationship variables for anxiety disorders (Stiles & Wolfe, this volume) have listed several studies supporting the importance of such variables, they have elected, mainly for conceptual reasons, to adopt by default the relevant conclusions reached by the Division 29 Task Force rather than specifying which of these conclusions have received direct empirical support and which have not. However, evidence for specific relationship variables has been presented in the integrative chapter of the anxiety disorders section.

4. In the Division 29 Task Force, the variable of "collaboration" was investigated along with "goal consensus." As stated in Castonguay et al. (this volume), however, goal consensus is a component of the therapeutic alliance. The principle formulated here refers only to elements considered in the Division 29 Task Force as part of the client collaborative engagement, such as homework compliance (see Tryon & Winograd, 2002). It should also be noted that some elements assumed to reflect a client's collaboration (including, as mentioned in a note above, homework compliance) were also defined in the Division 29 Task Force as manifestations of resistance (or lack of thereof) (Beutler, Moleiro & Talebi, 2002). As such, the principle about collaboration overlaps with one of the previously formulated principles (i.e., "The most effective treatments are likely to be those that do not induce patient resistance").

5. Needless to say, the last two principles of change overlap with a previous one, that is, "Therapists should address interpersonal issues related to clinical problems." At least for the treatment of dysphoric, personality, and substance use disorders, the responses that therapists attempt to modify often involve ways of relating with others. Similarly, the exploratory interventions used in treatment supported for the same disorders focus in various degrees on interpersonal issues.

6. When applied to personality disorder, psychodynamic therapy seems to place less emphasis on the exploration or deepening of emotion. As noted in Linehan et al. (this volume), "therapists attempt to identify patients affects, their interpersonal context

followed by their intrapsychic meaning and consider abreaction to be iatrogenic" (p. 248).

7. It should be mentioned, however, that fostering emotional experience within certain circumstances and/or specific time frames may not be effective. Research has suggested that psychological debriefing conducted immediately after the experience of a traumatic event fails to prevent long-term symptoms and may even be detrimental for the recovery of some individuals (see Litz, Gray, Bryant, & Adler, 2002).

References

Beck, A. T., Rush, A. J., Shaw, B. F., & Emery, G. (1979). *Cognitive therapy for depression.* New York: Guilford.

Behar, E., & Borkovec, T. D. (2003). Between-group therapy outcome research. In J. A. Schinka & W. Velicer (Eds.), *Comprehensive handbook of psychology: Research methods* (Vol. 2, pp. 213–241). New York: Wiley.

Beutler, L. E., Moleiro, C., & Talebi, H. (2002). Customizing psychotherapy to patient resistance. In J. C. Norcross (Ed.), *Psychotherapy relationships that work: Therapists' relational contributors to effective psychotherapy* (pp. 129–143). New York: Oxford University Press.

Borkovec, T. D., & Castonguay, L. G. (1998). What is the scientific meaning of "empirically supported therapy?" *Journal of Consulting and Clinical Psychology, 66,* 136–142.

Chambless, D. L., & Ollendick, T. H. (2001). Empirically supported psychological interventions: Controversies and evidence. *Annual Review of Psychology, 52,* 685–716.

Craighead, W. E., Hart, A. B., Wilcoxon-Craighead, L. W., & Ilardi, S. S. (2002). Psychosocial treatments for major depressive disorder. In P. E. Nathan & J. M. Gorman (Eds.), *A guide to treatments that work* (pp. 245–261). London: Oxford University Press.

Joiner, T. E., Jr. (2002). Depression in its interpersonal context. In I. H. Gotlib & C. L. Hammen (Eds.), *Handbook of depression* (pp. 295–313). New York: Guilford Press.

Litz, B. T., Gray, M. J., Bryant, R. A, & Adler, A. B. (2002). Early intervention for trauma: Current status and future directions. *Clinical Psychology: Science and Practice, 9,* 112–134.

Malik, M. L., Beutler, L. E., Gallagher-Thompson, D., Thompson, L., & Alimohamed, S. (2003). Are all cognitive therapies alike? A comparison of cognitive and non-cognitive therapy process and implications for the application of empirically supported treatments (ESTs). *Journal of Consulting and Clinical Psychology, 71,* 150–158.

Nathan, P. E., & Gorman, J. M. (Eds.). (2002). *A guide to treatments that work* (2nd ed.). New York: Oxford University Press.

Newman, M. G., Castonguay, L. G., Borkovec, T. D., & Molnar, C. (2004). Integrative therapy for generalized anxiety disorder. In R. G. Heimberg, C. L. Turk, & D. S. Mennin (Eds.), *Generalized anxiety disorder: Advances in research and practice* (pp. 320–350). New York: Guilford.

Norcross, J. C. (Ed.). (2002). *Psychotherapy relationships that work.* New York: Oxford University Press.

Tryon, G. S., & Winograd, G. (2002). Goal consensus and collaboration. In J. C. Norcross (Ed.), *Psychotherapy relationships that work* (pp. 109–125). New York: Oxford University Press.

Author Index

Subject Index

Printed in the USA/Agawam, MA
February 23, 2016

631071.003